THE PARLIAMENTARY
DIARY OF
Narcissus Luttrell

THE PARLIAMENTARY
DIARY OF
Narcissus Luttrell
1691–1693

EDITED BY

HENRY HORWITZ
PROFESSOR OF HISTORY
UNIVERSITY OF IOWA

OXFORD
AT THE CLARENDON PRESS
1972

Oxford University Press, Ely House, London W. 1

GLASGOW NEW YORK TORONTO MELBOURNE WELLINGTON
CAPE TOWN IBADAN NAIROBI DAR ES SALAAM LUSAKA ADDIS ABABA
DELHI BOMBAY CALCUTTA MADRAS KARACHI LAHORE DACCA
KUALA LUMPUR SINGAPORE HONG KONG TOKYO

PRINTED IN GREAT BRITAIN
AT THE UNIVERSITY PRESS, OXFORD
BY VIVIAN RIDLER
PRINTER TO THE UNIVERSITY

CONTENTS

INTRODUCTION

As to the proceedings of the House of Commons in general, I forbear inserting them, the votes being daily printed.[1]

DESPITE Narcissus Luttrell's exclusion from *A Brief Relation* of information on parliamentary proceedings printed in the *Votes of the House of Commons*, he had a keen interest in the activities of the late seventeenth-century Commons. Indeed, although his *D.N.B.* entry fails to mention it, he twice served as an M.P. He sat first for Bossiney (Cornwall) in the second Exclusion Parliament of 1679–80. Then in 1691, after unsuccessfully contesting a seat at Newport (Cornwall) in the general election of 1690, he was returned on 30 October in a by-election for Saltash (Cornwall) to the parliament of 1690–5 (then beginning its third session).[2]

Just as a century elapsed after his death before Luttrell's contributions as an annalist were first recognized by historians, so still another century has had to pass before his labours as a parliamentary diarist have begun to be appreciated. Though the volumes containing this parliamentary diary form part of the same collection of Luttrell MSS. given to All Souls College in 1786 by his descendant Luttrell Wynne as do the volumes of *A Brief Relation*, they escaped the notice of Macaulay. Despite their inclusion in H. O. Coxe's *Catalogue of Manuscripts in the Library of All Souls College* (1842), E. S. de Beer in 1924 seems to have been the first scholar to examine them carefully,[3] and it has only been during the last decade that their systematic exploitation for political and parliamentary history has actually begun.[4]

If the neglect of Luttrell's parliamentary diary cannot be explained by problems of access, neither can it be accounted for by any of those difficulties of encipherment or illegibility sometimes encountered in

[1] *A Brief Historical Relation of State Affairs from September 1678 to April 1714* (6 vols., Oxford, 1857), ii. 113 (Oct. 1690).

[2] Although Luttrell did own some land in Cornwall, it is not known on what interests he was returned for these seats.

[3] His note comparing Luttrell's diary to Anchitell Grey's is entered in the Codrington Library's copy of Coxe's *Catalogue*.

[4] See H. Horwitz, *Revolution Politicks* (Cambridge, 1968), chap. 7; D. Rubini, *Court and Country 1688–1702* (London, 1967), chaps. 2–5; T. K. Moore and H. Horwitz, 'Who Runs the House? Aspects of Parliamentary Organization in the Later Seventeenth Century', *Journal of Modern History*, xliii. 205–27.

such materials. As extant, the diary consists of two bound volumes (each measuring 7 × 4½ in. and jointly numbered by Coxe as All Souls MS. 158), carefully written out in Luttrell's own hand and including a full index at the end of each volume. What survives, in fact, is the final form of a seventeenth-century parliamentary diary, which in turn must have been based largely on now-lost rough notes taken in the House and supplemented by copies of bills and other documents presented to the House.[1] Given the relative fullness of Luttrell's summaries of speeches and of documents read out in the House, it would seem likely that his original notes were executed in some form of shorthand, yet no holograph manuscript in shorthand is to be found among any known collection of his papers.

The question of the type of notes on which the extant volumes were based is not the only puzzle associated with the diary. Another is raised by its relative completeness for the 1691–2 and 1692–3 sessions. It opens with an entry for 6 November 1691, the day on which Luttrell records that he 'was sworn and took my place in the House of Commons'. Running then from the early days of the 1691–2 session through the 1692–3 session, it closes with an entry for 26 October 1693 when the House was prorogued to 7 November 1693—the date on which the fifth session of the parliament was opened. Luttrell's conscientiousness as a diarist to this juncture, coupled with the continuing appearance in the *Journal* of his name as a member of select committees during the remaining sessions of the parliament, suggests that he either intended or actually did keep a similar record during the latter part of his service as M.P. for Saltash.[2] Yet no trace of additional volumes has been found.

Although we may now have only segments of a larger undertaking, what remains is still very substantial. As Luttrell's own titles to these two volumes indicate, his 'Abstract[s] of the Debates Orders & Resolutions In the House of Commons, which are not printed in their Votes' was designed to supplement the printed *Votes of the House of Commons*. First published in 1680 and then resumed in October 1689, the *Votes* were an abbreviated version of the Commons Journal.[3]

[1] All Souls College MS. 152. This consists of six manuscript volumes in a clerical hand with emendations in Luttrell's hand; the first volume contains copies of documents presented to the House during these two sessions.

[2] It may also be significant that Luttrell's accounts of Commons proceedings in *A Brief Relation* become both more frequent and fuller after the end of the 1690–5 parliament.

[3] Those for the 1691–3 sessions were printed by T. Braddyll and R. Everingham.

Issued as separates for each sitting and containing the formal resolutions of the House, 'they show what business was before the House
and little besides'.[1] Luttrell aimed at recording a good deal more.
Indeed, this diary—with its 363 manuscript pages of text for the
third session and 443 pages for the fourth session—not only helps to
fill a major gap in surviving records of Commons debates but also
stands as a much more detailed account of the House's activities than
most other diaries of the later seventeenth and early eighteenth
centuries. This can be illustrated by way of comparison with
the two other extant parliamentary diaries that cover portions of
William III's reign—those of Anchitell Grey and of Sir Richard
Cocks.

On the one hand, Grey's *Debates of the House of Commons from the Year
1667 to the Year 1694* (10 vols., London, 1769) has long been in print
and is the basic source for later Stuart Commons proceedings. But
Grey was ill and absent much of the third and fourth sessions of the
1690–5 parliament, and his diary contains entries for only twenty-
eight sittings of these sessions. Luttrell, by contrast, has entries for
193 of the 194 days the House sat to do business between the day he
took his seat and the close of the 1692–3 session.[2] Moreover, some of
Grey's entries for these twenty-eight days are very fragmentary, and
sometimes they are misdated. One of his fuller entries, however, is
of the debate in Committee of the Whole on 21 November 1693 when
the conduct of the war effort was the subject of heated discussion.[3]
A detailed comparison of Grey's and Luttrell's accounts of this debate
shows that Luttrell records thirty-one separate speeches and Grey
twenty-four, of which twenty-one are common to each.[4] However,
Grey's versions of three of the five principal speeches noted by both
diarists are rather more extensive and so probably closer to verbatim,
though his account does omit entirely two speeches given reasonable

---

[1] E. S. de Beer, 'The English Newspapers from 1695 to 1702', in *William III and
Louis XIV*, ed. R. Hatton (Liverpool, 1968), p. 120.
[2] On 7 Jan. 1693 Luttrell's diary has the entry: 'I was not well, so not at the House
this day.' (The fact that Luttrell on this occasion did not enter a second-hand account
of the day's proceedings suggests that, unlike Grey's, his entries were compiled without assistance from other members.)
[3] The existence of two other manuscript accounts of this debate was an additional
reason for selecting it for detailed comparison. They are Nottingham University,
Portland MS. PwA 2389; Bodleian Carte MS. 130, ff. 339–40. Grey's entry for this
debate is at x. 264–73.
[4] Actually, Luttrell records thirty-seven separate interventions in the debate, but
in several instances he merely states that two or more members took the same stance.

prominence in Luttrell's. Even in these closing years of his diary, then, Grey at his best is still very good indeed. Yet, Luttrell's 'Abstracts' are clearly of the same standard—a standard which the other two manuscript accounts of this debate fail to approach.[1]

On the other hand, comparison with the as yet unpublished and still little-known diary of Sir Richard Cocks (member for Gloucestershire 1698–1702) is also revealing.[2] Cocks's diary begins midway in the 1698–9 session and extends to May 1702, but it is only during the spring of 1701 that Cocks's record becomes much more than the text of his own speeches and his reflections on those issues which particularly excited him. Furthermore, even in 1701–2 Cocks's entries generally consist of summaries (not always very clear ones) of the daily proceedings and only occasionally run to extensive reports of any speeches save his own. There is, however, one respect in which the yield from Cocks's diary surpasses that from Luttrell's—that of information about the diarist himself. There is a marked air of detachment about Luttrell's account which stands in sharp contrast to the strong flavour of personality conveyed by Cocks's. Then, too, not a single speech by Luttrell himself is recorded, and the only occasion on which he lets fall a note of his personal involvement in the House's proceedings comes when a servant of his was arrested in breach of his privilege as a member (7 February 1693).

But if Luttrell's 'Abstracts' fail to furnish us with information about himself or his activities, this seems a minor omission in the light of what they do provide. As Sir Keith Feiling perceived nearly half a century ago, the early 1690s were crucial years in the post-Revolution realignment of English politics—years that saw the coming together with growing frequency of what to many seemed a strange combination of 'Commonwealthmen' and 'Jacobites' in the so-called 'new country party'. To be sure, Luttrell only infrequently uses labels such as 'the Whig party', 'the Court party', or 'the friends to the Lord Nottingham' to identify contending groups in the House. But what his account does bring clearly home is how party questions such as abjuration bills and attacks on Tory ministers jostled uneasily during these sessions with Court–Country issues such as army supply, place bills, and treason trials reform. Moreover, because Luttrell was

---

[1] They are inferior to Luttrell and Grey in terms of both number of speeches and length of summaries of individual speeches.

[2] Bodleian MSS. English History b. 209–10. The diary is being edited by Miss B. Kemp of St. Hugh's College, Oxford.

very much interested in matters of procedure (as were most other parliamentary diarists of the period), his account also yields further insights into the formalization of Commons procedure after the Revolution, especially with regard to the transaction of financial business. Yet, as his diary also serves to demonstrate, the Speaker was still capable of arbitrary and evasive action, while at times the decorum of the House also left much to be desired.[1]

However, since the diary itself reveals so little about Luttrell, information about his parliamentary activity, political views, and his life 'out of doors' must be gleaned from other sources. The *Journal* reveals that he was an active committee-man in this parliament; he was three times appointed to the Committee of Privileges and Elections, nominated to over 140 select committees dealing with public matters, and designated a few times in connection with minor issues as a teller and as a manager for the Commons in inter-House conferences.[2] As for his general political position, he would seem to have been a Whig, at least if his obituary notice can be taken as a valid indicator in its remark that he was unjustly expelled by Walpole's ministry from the Middlesex commission of the peace by reason of a false allegation that he was an enemy to 'those very principles which he had all along boldly espoused while he was in parliament, and one of the warm promoters of the Exclusion bill'.[3] Then, too, some of his personal associations had a marked Whiggish tinge, especially his long friendship with Jacob Tonson and his heavy reliance on Whig newspapers and newsletters in his compilation of *A Brief Relation*. Yet he also had good friends of a rather different political persuasion, such as Francis Gwyn, and it was Gwyn who put him in touch with the young Robert Harley during the spring of 1693 when Luttrell sought to borrow Harley's manuscript of Leland's *Itinerary*.[4] In turn, when Luttrell's son Francis was seeking a commissionership of the Stamp Office in 1712, Luttrell wrote directly to Harley (by then Earl of Oxford and Lord Treasurer) to press this ultimately abortive suit and listed as 'compurgators' of Francis's 'affection to the Government

[1] Luttrell also, in his entry for 6 Mar. 1693, has an unusually full account of counsels' pleadings on the Earl of Pembroke's private bill.

[2] The Clerk does seem to have differentiated between the diarist and Captain Francis Luttrell, though it is impossible to be sure that he did so consistently. It should be added that Luttrell was not at all active in the 1679–80 parliament.

[3] *London Evening Post*, 6–8 July 1732, quoted by F. E. Ball, 'Narcissus Luttrell', *Notes & Queries*, clii. 111.

[4] *Notes & Queries*, 2nd ser., xii. 44; British Museum, Loan 29 (Portland MSS.), vol. 79, N. Luttrell to R. Harley, 24 May 1693.

and present Ministry' not only Gwyn but two other Tory stalwarts, Colonel Robert Byerley and Sir William Drake.[1]

But whatever his partisan inclinations, it is evident that Luttrell's interests were not confined to parliament or politics. Born in August 1657 in London, he was the third but eldest surviving son of Francis Luttrell of Gray's Inn, a cadet of the Luttrells of Staunton Court (Devon) and a distant connection of the Luttrells of Dunster Castle.[2] His mother Catherine named him Narcissus in honour of his maternal grandfather Narcissus Mapowder, another Devonshireman. As Luttrell, in reckoning up his estate in 1705, calculated his inheritances from his father and mother as then worth about £205 annually (apart from a bequest from his sister which in turn may have been a parental legacy), it is evident that family circumstances in his youth were at least comfortable.[3] Luttrell himself was educated at Scheen school under a Mr. Aldrich and then entered a fellow commoner of St. John's, Cambridge, in February 1674, though it is likely that his residence there was brief.[4] Even before his matriculation at Cambridge he had been admitted in August 1673 to Gray's Inn, and he was called to the bar in 1680. His subsequent election as Bencher of that Inn in 1702 and Ancient in 1706 seems to belie the notion that he never practised,[5] as does his passing comment in a letter to Robert Harley in May 1693 to the effect that he had been unable that month to finish his perusal of the borrowed Leland manuscript, 'my attendance at Westminster this term having taken up so much of my time'.[6] His service as Middlesex justice of the peace between 1693 and 1723, as well as his appointments as deputy lieutenant, commissioner of oyer and terminer, and commissioner of land-tax assessment, also suggest a greater degree of public activity than is usually attributed to him.[7]

None the less, from an early age Luttrell manifested a marked collector's bent which seems to have been the most sustained and prob-

[1] British Museum, Loan 29/150, 23 Jan. 1711[–12]. See also Historical Manuscript Commission, *Portland MSS.* v. 210.

[2] The source for the biographical details that follow is, unless otherwise noted, H. C. Maxwell Lyte, *A History of Dunster and of the Families of Mohun and Luttrell* (2 vols., London, 1909), pp. 521–4.

[3] Beinecke Library, Osborn shelves c65, Luttrell personal papers.

[4] He received an M.A. by royal mandate in 1675.

[5] The notion is Lyte's. It is also contradicted by the obituary in the *London Evening Post*.

[6] British Museum, Loan 29/79, 24 May 1693.

[7] The entries in his private diary kept during the early 1720s reveal that he remained active as a J.P. until his ouster; P. Dixon, 'Narcissus Luttrell's Private Diary' *Notes & Queries*, ccvii. 388–92 and *passim*.

ably the deepest of his many interests. It was in 1675 as a student at Gray's Inn that he began amassing the materials which would form the basis of both *A Brief Relation* and the two *Popish Plot Catalogues*.[1] Nor did his marriage in February 1682 to Sarah, daughter of Daniel Baker (a prosperous London merchant), cool his collecting zeal.[2] By 1706 he himself calculated he had laid out over £1,500 on book purchases.[3] But the money had been well spent; as even Hearne (despite his misunderstanding with Luttrell) testified, he was an 'industrious', 'curious and knowing' buyer who gradually accumulated 'great and amazing collections' of 'English History and Antiquities'.[4] However, his purchases had not outstripped his means; in 1705 he reckoned his annual income to be about £475 and his total net worth (apart from the collections) as nearly £12,500.[5] His prosperity was further signalled by his purchase for £1,200 of the third Earl of Shaftesbury's house in Chelsea in 1710. Thus, after long years of residence at a house in Holborn (part of his mother's jointure) opposite the Three Cups Tavern, Luttrell prepared to retire to a more rustic setting, though still within sight of London's smoke and within easy reach of Westminster and the City.[6] Probably his removal to Chelsea meant an even greater attention to his bibliographical and scholarly interests, shared with his son Francis, his only surviving child at his death after long illness on 27 June 1732.[7]

Despite his collecting ardour and his labours on projects such as the history of the Luttrell family, Luttrell published nothing in his lifetime. Moreover, his wish that his collections eventually be given intact to some library such as that of Gray's Inn was not wholly heeded by his descendants.[8] So it has been that a full realization of the scope and significance of his efforts as a collector and a compiler has not even yet been achieved. But, hopefully, with this edition his service to the parliamentary history of his day may now take its place among his varied contributions to our knowledge of its life and literature.

[1] *Popish Plot Catalogues*, ed. F. C. Francis (Luttrell Society, no. 15, Oxford, 1956), p. 10 n. 2.
[2] One son Francis (born Dec. 1682) survived Sarah at her death in 1722. In 1725 Luttrell married Mary, daughter of John Bearsley; she died in 1745. No children survived from the second marriage.
[3] J. Osborn, 'Reflections on Narcissus Luttrell', *Book Collector*, vi. 20.
[4] As quoted by Francis, *Popish Plot Catalogues*, pp. 9–10.
[5] Beinecke Library, Osborn shelves c65.
[6] His private diary indicates that his was not a recluse's life.
[7] Ball, 'Narcissus Luttrell', p. 111, has an account of the funeral.
[8] Osborn, 'Reflections', p. 20.

In preparing Luttrell's 'Abstracts' for the press, I have modernized spelling and punctuation throughout and have also expanded most abbreviations and contractions (including the symbols that he used for the names of the days of the week in the heading of daily entries). As far as possible, I have attempted to separate action from speech in paragraphing. The names of members speaking in the House have been printed in italics; the names of speakers in committee appear in roman. Annotations have, for the most part, been confined to a few explanatory notes, cross references to the Commons *Journal* and to other accounts of debates of these sessions in Grey and elsewhere, and the sources drawn upon to fill blanks in Luttrell's manuscript. A biographical appendix with entries for all speakers in these sessions follows the text.

I am indebted to the Warden and Fellows of All Souls College for permission to publish this edition and to the staff of the Codrington for their unfailing helpfulness while working there. I am also grateful to Professor J. M. Osborn of Yale University for allowing me to make use of his collection of Luttrell MSS. in the Beinecke Library. Nor could this edition have been completed without the award of a fellowship from the National Endowment of the Humanities enabling me to spend the 1968–9 academic year in Oxford, nor without the assistance of Mr. Lathan Windley of the University of Iowa in the reading of proofs and making of the index. Finally, I should like to express my deep appreciation to Professor B. D. Henning of Yale University, whose customary generosity has in this instance extended to the provision of very material help in the compilation of the biographical appendix and of valuable advice on the preparation of the text.

SOURCES FOR THE 1691-2 AND 1692-3 SESSIONS

WITH ABBREVIATIONS USED IN REFERENCES

THE PRINCIPAL SECONDARY SOURCES

Browning: A. Browning, *Thomas Osborne Earl of Danby and Duke of Leeds 1632–1712* (3 vols., Glasgow, 1944–51).

E. L. Ellis, 'The Whig Junto in Relation to the Development of Party Politics and Party Organization from its Inception to 1714', Oxford University, unpublished D.Phil. thesis, 1961.

K. G. Feiling, *A History of the Tory Party 1640–1714* (Oxford, 1924).

H. Horwitz, *Revolution Politicks* (Cambridge, 1968).

T. B. Macaulay, *The History of England from the Accession of James the Second* (5 vols., London, 1896).

THE PRINCIPAL PRIMARY SOURCES

Bodleian Carte MS. 130, letters of Robert Price.

B.M. Add. MSS.: British Museum Additional MS. 34096, letters of Robert Yard to Sir William Colt.

B.M. Loan: British Museum, Loan 29 (Portland MSS.), vols. 79, 185–7, Harley correspondence.

Grey: Anchitell Grey, *Debates of the House of Commons from the Year 1667 to the Year 1694* (10 vols., London, 1769).

HMC: Historical Manuscript Commission: *House of Lords MSS.*, 1690–1, 1692–3; *Portland MSS.*, Harley correspondence; *Seventh Report*, letters of Blancard to Dykevelt.

CJ, LJ: Journals of the House of Commons and the House of Lords.

Nottingham University, Portland MSS., Bentinck papers.

Ranke: L. von Ranke, *A History of England Principally in the Seventeenth Century*, (6 vols., Oxford, 1875), reports of F. Bonnet to the Elector of Brandenburg.

An Abstract

Of yᵉ Debates Orders & Resolutions
In the House of Commons, wᶜʰ are
not printed in yeir Votes

Collected by N.L. during his attendance
therein as a Member.

Beginning. fryday. 6ᵗʰ of Novemb. 1691.
& Ending. 4. Nov. 1692.

Facsimile of title-page of volume one of All Souls College MS. 158

Third Session

Friday, the 6th of November 1691

THIS day I was sworn, and took my place in the House of Commons as a member thereof.

Then *Sir Joseph Tredenham* reported the bill for establishing the new oaths in Ireland, with some amendments by the committee. And some were made in the Chair, and the bill with the amendments ordered to be engrossed. And *Mr. Harbord* had leave to bring in a clause to enlarge the time as to himself for taking the oaths in that kingdom, he having a place there, and now he was going upon the affairs of the nation as ambassador to Turkey and feared he should not be back to take them in the time required.[1]

Then the House proceeded on the Order of the Day, and resolved themselves into a Committee of the Whole House to consider of the motion for a supply to Their Majesties for carrying on the war against France. The Speaker left the Chair and Mr. Solicitor took it.[2]

Several speeches were made by Sir Thomas Littleton, Sir Robert Cotton, Mr. Dolben, etc., and at last they voted that a supply be given to Their Majesties for carrying on a vigorous war against France.

Then Mr. Neale moved that since they had voted a supply they would proceed to the sum, which he desired might be a sum not exceeding four millions.

This occasioned a great debate and many speeches.

Sir Joseph Williamson opposed it as a strange motion to vote the sum before you have computed what is necessary, and therefore moved to put the debate off till Monday.

Sir John Thompson reflected on the fleet and said he thought there was no such need of 65,000 men.[3]

---

[1] There is no mention of this clause in the *Journal*.

[2] Sir John Trevor was Speaker; Sir John Somers was Solicitor General. Other accounts of the debate on supply, adding some speakers, are at *HMC Seventh Report*, p. 206; Bodleian Carte MS. 130, f. 326.

[3] The King had requested this number of troops in his speech opening the session.

Mr. Bathurst inveighed against the largeness of the Privy Council, which he would not have consist of more than 12; that he was not for cabinet councils.

Sir Thomas Clarges moved that we might know what the state of the war was designed for next year: as to the land forces, how many, where to be employed, and how; and for our fleet, what ships and how many of each sort. Sir Peter Colleton seconded it.

Sir Edward Seymour to the same, and that the King might be addressed to for that purpose by the Privy Counsellors. He said also that there had been paid into the Exchequer within this three year 18 millions of money, and on the revenue given last year there had already £4,300,000 been paid in.

So at last the committee came to this: That it is the opinion of this committee that the House be moved that His Majesty be humbly desired that a state of the war for the year ensuing relating to the fleet be laid before this House.

Sir Thomas Littleton then moved that we might do the same in reference to the land army.

Sir Thomas Clarges opposed it, and was for adjourning at this time, thinking this enough for the present. So Sir John Thompson. Mr. Harley to the same.

Sir John Guise, Mr. Herbert, and Mr. John Howe were all for having a state and estimate of the land army for next year.

Mr. Paul Foley moved to know what alliances we were in, what quota we are obliged to furnish, so that we may see what forces are necessary, and thought this enough at this time. So Sir Thomas Clarges thought.

Sir John Lowther acquainted the House that the King was in leagues with the confederate princes; that the general part thereof was to restrain all the parties from making any peace with France till he was reduced to the state he was in by the Pyrenean treaty. And more of this the House might be acquainted with, if desired. And that as to the fleet, the Dutch are obliged to furnish ships in proportion thus—five of theirs to eight of ours.

Mr. Hampden and Sir Joseph Williamson were not for separating the land forces from the fleet; that both were very necessary and that we might make the same address for these as for the fleet.

Sir Edward Seymour said the King was not well advised to mention the particular number of land forces necessary; it was not parliamentary.

However, the committee came at last to this: That it is the opinion of this committee that the House be moved that His Majesty be humbly desired that a state of the war for the year ensuing relating to the land forces be laid before this House. And the committee ordered that the House be moved that this committee sit again on Monday next.

Then the Speaker took the Chair again. And *Mr. Solicitor* reported the resolution of the committee to the House as to the supply, to which the House agreed *nemine contradicente*. Then the *Solicitor* made the two motions as to the fleet and land forces. And the same were ordered accordingly, and that the members of the Privy Council of this House should move His Majesty therein. And they ordered that on Monday morning next at etc. this House would resolve itself into a Committee of the Whole House to consider farther of the supply to Their Majesties.

All committees revived on the motion of *Mr. Christie.*

Adjourned till tomorrow morning 9 of the clock.

Saturday, 7 November

The Order of the Day was read to inquire of the miscarriages of the fleet, and then the House resolved itself into a Committee of the Whole House. The Speaker left the Chair and Mr. Grey took it.[1]

Then the Order of the Day was read again. After which the House sitting still near half an hour and no one speaking, Admiral Russell stood up and said: the last time the state of the nation was taken into consideration,[2] such reflections were made upon the management of the fleet which he was not then able to give a particular answer to, but now if any member pleased to ask him any questions he was ready to give them an answer.

After which the House sat still for half an hour and nothing said. So it was moved by Mr. Howe that since nothing was said as to the matter of the fleet and miscarriages therein that a vote might be passed that there had been no miscarriage at all in the fleet.

Mr. Montagu moved for same reason that Mr. Grey might leave

---

[1] Parallel accounts of the debate on the fleet are at Grey, x. 162–7; *Het Archief van den Raadpensionaris Antonie Heinsius,* ed. H. J. van der Heim (The Hague, 3 vols., 1867–80), i. 35–6 (in a letter misdated by the editor); Ranke, vi. 164; Bodleian Carte MS. 130, ff. 326–7.

[2] On 3 Nov.

the Chair and that the Speaker might resume the same. Sir Robert Cotton (of Post Office) and Mr. Hampden to the same.

But some members opposing it, it came to a question whether the Chairman should leave the Chair. And the House being divided thereon, the Ayes were ordered to the right hand of the House and the Noes on the left.

Ayes Sir John Guise   147

Tellers for the

Noes Mr. Arnold   115

So the Chairman left the Chair.

Which as soon as he [had] done, Sir Thomas Clarges came in, who had made the reflections on the miscarriage of the fleet the last day.

Sir Thomas Clarges: I am sorry to see that the consideration of the state of the nation will not take you up half an hour's time. I was taken up in your service about the employment you have put me in or I should have been here sooner.[1] But since I see it is expected I should say something to the matters about the fleet, I shall.

Your fleet was ready, victualled, and manned by the 12th of April last, and no admiral was then on board. Thus they lay till about 16th of May before they got into the Downs, which cost you near £200,000. Then they had after six days a fair wind but they did not sail after they tided it through the Channel till 22 May. The 23rd of May they sailed out of Torbay, when an express was sent of a Danish vessel that came into Plymouth, who came through the French fleet some few leagues off Ushant. Notwithstanding which we were putting ourselves in lines of battle from 23rd to 29th when we were several leagues from the enemy. Thus was the time spent when the wind was fair. Then on 29th they bore away towards Ireland by Scilly Islands and not to the ocean, as if they had designed our Smyrna fleet should be taken. Then the 15th of August one Barns of Dartmouth gave intelligence that the great ships of the French were laid up. But we must keep out still at sea, which occasioned the expense of more money. Then what can be said to the running over the *Harwich*, and making to port in time of storm when we lost some of our ships? Be it knavishness or ignorance, it is all one to me.

Admiral Russell: I believe no man ever took more pains in fitting out a fleet than I did, and that was the reason you were ready so soon. There was not a week passed but I was either at the Buoy in the Nore,

---

[1] He was a Commissioner of Accounts.

Chatham, etc. There was reflections made on the fleet the last day when this was debated which I was not then prepared to answer, but now am. And if any gentleman please to ask me a question, I will give him the best answer I can. It is true I was not on board the fleet the 12th of April, and I do confess the wind was fair three days, and why I did not sail will appear by my letters and papers.

Clarges moved the Admiral might produce a journal of the transactions of the fleet. And it was seconded by *Sir Samuel Barnardiston.*

Sir William Leveson-Gower and *Sir Edward Seymour* spoke against this manner of proceedings as unusual and unparliamentary to ask a member questions in the House and the other's answering it, so fending and proving.

Sir Thomas Clarges moved to go into a Committee of the Whole House again.

Which *Sir Christopher Musgrave* opposed as unparliamentary, as also this manner of proceedings by question and answer is unusual. Let the objections be put in writing, and give a time to the other to put in his justification. *Mr. Hampden* to the same.

Sir John Thompson: What the honourable member the Admiral has done, I believe he has not done without orders from above. And I am for going up thither to search into the miscarriages.

So after a long debate it was ordered that the House will resolve itself into a Committee of the Whole House upon Tuesday next to consider of the state of the nation.

So the House adjourned till Monday 9 in the morning.

Monday, 9 November

Mr. Price moved in behalf of Sir John Morgan, a member of the House, for a breach of privilege committed on him in entering his possession. But he not being in the House then, nothing was done therein.

Jonathan Jennings esq., a new member for Richmond in Yorkshire (upon the death of his father, Sir Edmund Jennings), was introduced into the House and took the oaths at the Table and after his place in the House.

Sir Richard Onslow, a Commissioner of the Admiralty, laid before the House the estimate of the charge of the Navy for the year ensuing. And the *Lord Ranelagh* brought in the list of the land forces for the year ensuing. Which were both delivered in at the Table and read, and were referred to the Committee of the Whole House to whom the supply for carrying on the war against France is referred.

The Estimate of the Navy for the year 1692

The ordinary charge of the Navy in time of peace	100,000
Wages, wear and tear, victuals and ordnance for 30,000 men (a medium between summer and winter) at £4. 5*s*. a head per month for 13 months comes to	1,657,500
(viz., 8*s*. ordnance; wear and tear £1. 8*s*. 6*d*.; wages £1. 8*s*. 6*d*.; and victuals £1)	
Freight, victuals, etc., of 30 ketches and tenders to attend the fleet for seven months	8,400
Charge of freight, victuals, and wages for four hospital ships, seven months at £300 each *per mensem*	8,400
Building four new fourth-rate ships of 48 guns each with etc. comes to	28,864
Making one dry dock at Portsmouth and two wet ones there	15,890
The two marine regiments (viz., the pay of the officers for 13 months and the soldiers only six months when on shore)	30,000
Half pay for 50 captains, as many lieutenants, etc., when the fleet in harbour	6,000

Total   £1,855,054

Then *Sir Thomas Clarges* complained to the House of a libel reflecting on the proceedings of this House, entituled *Mercurius Reformatus: Or, The New Observator*, in giving directions in the matter of money, as a high breach of the privileges of this House.[1] So moved that author and printer might be taken into custody. *Sir Peter Colleton, Sir Charles Sedley,* and *Paul Foley* to the same.

Mr. Hampden desired the whole might be read and not a part picked out of it, which perhaps the other part of it might mollify.

To whom it was answered that it was the constant course so to do in all indictments for a libel.

So the pamphlet was censured as a breach of the privileges of this House, and the author and printer were also ordered to be taken into custody of the Serjeant at Arms to answer the same.

Sir William Whitlock moved, according to the Order of the Day, to read the bill for regulating trials in case of treason, and was seconded by *Mr. Bathurst, Lord Castleton, Sir Thomas Clarges, Sir Edward Seymour,* etc.

---

[1] The issue of this weekly in question was vol. v, no. 1, 7 Nov. 1691. Its author was James Welwood, who may have been assisted by Bishop Burnet; its printer was Richard Baldwin. See *HMC Seventh Report*, p. 206.

So the order for it was read, and after the bill was read the second time and committed to a Committee of the Whole House. And the House resolved to be in a Committee of the Whole House to consider of the said bill [upon Wednesday morning next].[1]

Then the Order of the Day was read for resolving into a Committee of the Whole House touching the supply to Their Majesties. Which they did, and the Speaker left the Chair. And the Solicitor General took it, when the Order of the Day was read again, as also the order for referring the estimates of the fleet and the army to this committee.[2]

Then Sir Thomas Clarges moved to have the estimate of the fleet read, which was accordingly. Then he spoke to it; that it was a great charge, and much more than had been in former times. In 1677 we were in a war against France, in 1664 and 1665 we were in a war against France and Holland and had 90 men-of-war at sea, and then your charge was but £108,000 *per mensem*. In this particular you have 30 tenders, but I know no service they are for unless to carry wine and victuals for the captains; the Dutch have no such thing. This amounts to a great sum, and I am for giving money as well as others, but the taxes are so great that we can hardly live under them. I move you, therefore, to appoint a particular committee to examine the estimates and to report their opinions to you, as was done in 1664 and 1677, and not to leave it to a Committee of the Whole House. For as the King expects aids and supplies from us, so I desire we may withal give him a little of our advice.

Paul Foley: The estimates now brought in do amount to above four millions. Nor is this all; when you consider the charges of the civil establishment this year, as also to discharge the anticipations that are on the revenue, you will find it amount to a far greater sum. There has been paid to this government in taxes and on the revenue since 5 November 1688 about 12 millions of money, besides the loans to the Court on some of those acts which comes to about six millions more. Now as to the particulars before you, they bring you in a charge of £4. 5*s*. per head for 30,000 men when we can have it for £4 per head. And I see no reason to maintain so many constantly in summer and winter. However, I desire we may refer it to a particular committee to inquire into it.

---

[1] *CJ*, x. 548.
[2] Parallel accounts of the debate that followed are at Grey, x. 168–70; Bodleian Carte MS. 130, ff. 327–8.

Col. Austen: As to the 30,000 men, you cannot have less. Last year in summer you had 40,000 at least, and so you must this. But 30,000 is a medium between summer and winter.

Mr. Papillon: You have but little time to prepare your fleet. It must be ready about beginning of April.

Sir John Lowther: I do think a Committee of the Whole House more proper to inquire into this matter than a private committee. For your number, it cannot be less than 30,000 men all the year round for 13 months as a medium. You will have occasion for a greater fleet than ever. The French King's fleet consisted last year of about 80 men-of-war: 12 we blocked up in Dunkirk, 16 he has now on the stocks which will be ready in spring, and a considerable squadron he had in the Mediterranean. I think it will be absolutely necessary to have as good a fleet this year as the last, if not better. And I desire you will go now upon it, since time and the suddenness of the dispatch will give a life to affairs.

Sir Christopher Musgrave: We are now on a great matter, and therefore I desire we may consider well of it. And though on one hand money must not be wanting, yet we must not lavish away our money, for the poverty of the nation calls upon us to be as good husbands as we can. We are told of great numbers of ships the French have. I am glad to see our intelligence is so good at the end of the summer, since it was so bad at the beginning. I think it is fit we have an account how many ships in particular are designed for next summer. I find in the particular here is ordnance and stores brought in as if you had spent all your powder, shot, etc., but there was little of it shot away. And I am sure there is no one will say that £4 per head a month is not sufficient.

Sir Thomas Clarges: It is very hard that we must give our money and yet must not inquire how it is to be disposed, but must lump it as we pay bills at eating-houses—without inquiring into particulars.

Sir William Leveson-Gower moved that we might go on to consider of it now particularly, and desired to husband the money as well as might be. Sir Robert Cotton (of Post Office) to the same; and the Lord Falkland.

But Sir Robert Cotton (of Chester) and Mr. Harley moved that it might be referred to a particular committee.

Sir Charles Sedley: As on one side when you cramp prerogative, you are told of making the King a Duke of Venice, so on the other side take care you make not yourselves a Parliament of Paris. I am for keeping to parliament methods, and you have been well moved to refer it to a committee. So I desire you will put that question.

So the question was put: That it is the opinion of this committee that the House be moved that a committee be appointed to inspect the estimate of the charge of Their Majesties' Navy for the year 1692, delivered into this House, and to report their opinions therein. And the Solicitor General was directed to move the House that this committee might have leave to sit again.

So he left the Chair, and the Speaker resumed the Chair. And the *Solicitor General* reported from the committee that they had directed him to move the House that a committee should be appointed, as before. And a committee was appointed and named accordingly; and to have power to send for persons, papers, and records.

Then the *Solicitor* also moved that the committee might have leave to sit again. And ordered accordingly on Thursday next that the House will resolve itself into a Committee of the Whole House to consider farther of the supplies to be granted to Their Majesties. And the House ordered that the Commissioners of the Admiralty should bring in the names of the ships, rates, guns, and men, etc.[1]

Ordered that this House will on Friday morning next resolve into a Committee of the Whole House to proceed in the consideration of the petitions about the East India trade.

Adjourned till 9 tomorrow a.m.

Tuesday, 10 November

A proviso to be added to the bill for abrogating the oaths of supremacy in Ireland was offered to the House in behalf of William Harbord esq., His Majesty's Ambassador Extraordinary to the Grand Seignior to mediate a peace between the Christians and Turks, to dispense with his taking the new oaths in that kingdom for his place of Vice-Treasurer there till two months after his arrival in that kingdom. The proviso was read thrice and ordered to stand part of the bill. So the bill was passed and ordered to be carried to the Lords by Mr. Tredenham for their concurrence.[2]

Sir Edward Seymour: There has been great taxes of late; it is hardly credible. There have been paid into the Exchequer upon the revenue

---

[1] There is no mention of this order in the *Journal*.

[2] *CJ*, x. 549 has Sir Joseph Tredenham, but *LJ*, xiv. 641 (11 Nov.) agrees with Luttrell.

and taxes with the loans about 18 millions since 5 November 1688 to this time, of which there hath been 12 millions clear to the Crown without the loans, all which will appear when you have the accounts from your commissioners appointed for taking the same. I move you, therefore, that they may be ordered to bring them in in a short time.

And it was seconded by several.

Sir Thomas Clarges: It is not possible for us to bring you an exact account of the disbursements too, for there are several officers that have not yet brought in their accounts, and some of those that have are very imperfect. We may be able in a short time to give you an account of the receipts and issues, but not of the truth of them.

Paul Foley to the same, and affirmed that the taxes and revenue of the Crown without the loans amount to 12 millions for three years past. The Court last year demanded four millions for carrying on the war and about £570,000 for building the 27 men-of-war, which you complied with and gave taxes sufficient. And which if they hold on, on the customs and other duties as they have hitherto, they will come to about £1,100,000 more than was demanded.

So after some debate, it was ordered that the said Commissioners for the Public Accounts should on Monday sevennight lay before this House a state of the incomes and issues of the public revenue from the 5th of November 1688 to Michaelmas last, with their observations thereon.

Admiral Russell: On Saturday last, I found the House expected a journal or scheme in writing of the proceedings of the fleet the last summer, which I have here prepared. So he carried up several papers to the Table and there delivered them in, viz.:

Instructions given to him by the Commissioners of the Admiralty for the management of the fleet, which were very large and an unlimited commission.

A list of the ships of the said fleet.

An extract of several letters and orders touching the proceedings of the fleet, and a journal of their proceedings accordingly.

All which were read.[1]

Then it was moved and ordered that the Lords of the Admiralty should lay before the House their several orders to Admiral Russell during this last summer's expedition. Ordered also that they lay

---

[1] For the debate that followed Russell's presentation of papers see Bodleian Carte MS. 130, f. 328; Grey, x. 170–1.

before this House a list of the ships that have been lost or damaged since the year 1688, and the captains' names that commanded the same.

And the House resolved to go into a Committee of the Whole House on Monday next to consider further of the state of the nation.

Adjourned till tomorrow 9 of the clock a.m.

Wednesday, 11 November

It was moved that some particular members might be added to the committee for repairing the highways, and ordered accordingly.

Sir Edward Seymour moved also that it might be an instruction to that committee who were to bring in that bill that they should prepare and bring in a clause to empower the Justices of Peace at the Quarter Sessions to settle the rates of wagoners and carriers, and ordered accordingly.

Col. Austen moved in behalf of the Commissioners of the Admiralty that they might have copies of Admiral Russell's papers. And [he] was told by the *Speaker* that was the privilege of any member.

A message from the Lords by Sir Miles Cook and [Mr. Keck][1] that they had passed a bill for naturalizing Sir Martin Beckman and others, to which they desire the concurrence of this House.

Then the Order of the Day was read. And the *Speaker* put the question for his leaving the Chair, and he did accordingly.

So the House resolved itself into a Committee of the Whole House and Sir Thomas Littleton was called to the Chair. So the Order of the Day was read again, and after the bill for regulating of trials in cases of high treason. So the committee went through the bill paragraph by paragraph, filling up the blanks first, and made several amendments to it, and questions were put for the several clauses so amended to stand part of the bill. And then at last (as usual), they settled the preamble, and so finished the bill and ordered it to be reported to the House.

So the Speaker resumed the Chair, and *Sir Thomas Littleton* in his place reported from the said committee the bill that they had gone through with the same and had made several amendments to it which they had directed him to report to the House. Ordered that the said report be made on Friday morning next at 10 of the clock.

Adjourned till 9 tomorrow morning.

[1] Blank in MS.; from *CJ*, x. 550.

Thursday, 12 November

After *Serj. Trenchard* had reported the case of the election of Weobley [from the Committee of Elections], he moved that the Clerk of the Crown being attending at the door with the return he might be called in. But it was opposed by *Sir Edward Seymour*, etc., as being against the Orders of the House, for that he ought not to attend the House without particular order of the House. And the *Speaker* said it was against his oath to carry the records about him. So he was ordered to attend tomorrow about it with the returns for the said borough in order to amend them.

Mr. *Freke* moved, and was seconded by *Sir Edward Hussey*, for leave to bring in a bill for the reducing of interest from six to four per cent. The House divided thereon—the Yeas went out.

	Sir Robert Cotton	
Yeas		131
	Sir Joseph Tredenham	
Tellers for the		
	Mr. Palmes	
Noes		105
	Mr. Ashe	

So leave was given to bring in a bill accordingly.

Mr. *Tredenham* moved, and was seconded by *Mr. Boscawen*, for leave given to bring in a bill for suppressing of hawkers and pedlars, and ordered accordingly.

Mr. *Clarke* moved that the petition of Richard Baldwin (the printer of *The Observator*) might be received, desiring to be brought to the Bar of the House, etc. But he having been in custody but since 10 of [the] clock last night, the reading of the petition was opposed. So to lie on the Table.

Then the Order of the Day was read for going into a Committee of the Whole House to consider of supplies to Their Majesties. So the Speaker left the Chair and the Solicitor General was called to it. Then the Order of the Day was read again.

Mr. Hampden: What methods you will proceed in I know not; I will not put you out of the ancient way. I think it is too soon to go upon raising money before you have agreed the sum, but I think it my duty to acquaint you that the double excise, which is a great part of the revenue, expires the 17th instant. This I believe you will think fit to make a part of the supply you intend His Majesty, and if so I desire you will take some public notice of it or otherwise the brewers will take advantage of the intermission of the duty and stock themselves with beer, etc., which will be a great loss in the duty. I move you, therefore, that you will either pass a vote that this shall be part of the supply you intend His Majesty, or else to desire leave of the House to bring in a bill to continue the duty of double excise for a year longer.

So after some debate, it was resolved: That it is the opinion of this committee that the House be moved that towards the supplies to be granted to Their Majesties for carrying on a war against France, the duties by way of excise upon beer, ale, and other liquors be continued for a year longer from 17 November instant, as were payable for the year last past.

Mr. Harley: You have now done a good thing. I therefore desire you will leave the Chair and report what you have done to the House.

Sir Robert Cotton (of the Post Office) moved that the estimate for the land forces might also be referred to the committee that considered of that for the fleet.

Sir Thomas Clarges opposed it, for that the committee had not yet gone through that of the fleet and by referring this it would obstruct the proceeding on that of the fleet.

So the Solicitor left the Chair and the Speaker took it. And the *Solicitor General* reported the proceedings of the committee to the House, to which they agreed and ordered the Solicitor to prepare and bring in a bill according to the said resolution. Then *he* acquainted the House that the committee had directed him to move the House that the said committee may sit again. Ordered that this House on Saturday morning next would resolve into a committee to consider further of the supply to be granted to Their Majesties.

Sir Edward Seymour moved that something might be entered in the Journal that it should not be a precedent for the time to come—*ne trahatur in exemplum*, it being a strange thing to vote such a thing to be part of a supply and you have not yet voted any sum.

Moved that Mr. Finch might have leave to attend the House of Lords in a cause there depending, and ordered accordingly.[1]

So the House adjourned till 9 tomorrow morning.

---

[1] Such orders were normally not entered in the *Journal*. See below, in the debate of 26 Jan. 1692.

Friday, 13 November

Sir Stephen Fox, a new member lately chosen for the City of Westminster (in the room of Sir William Poultney, deceased), was introduced into the House by Mr. Hampden and took the oaths, etc., at the Table.

A petition of Anthony Eyre gent. for leave to bring in a bill to sell lands on a settlement and to settle other lands instead was read, but denied on the question to refer it to a committee to examine if fitting so to do.

The engrossed bill from the Lords to take away the benefit of clergy in several cases was ordered a second reading after 11 of the clock.

Then the Order of the Day was read, and the Speaker left the Chair and Sir John Guise took it. So the Order was read again.

Then Sir Joseph Herne, according to order, presented to the House the account of the debts of the present East India Company, with a particular of their stock and other effects of the same.

Then began a debate; some for the old Company as Col. Titus, Mr. John Howe, Mr. Holt, Mr. Cary, Mr. Harcourt, Sir Robert Sawyer, Serj. Blencowe, Mr. Brewer, Major Pery, and others were for the old Company. Those for a new company and against the old were Capt. Pitt, Sir Edward Seymour, Mr. Boscawen, Mr. Hampden, Sir Charles Wyndham, Sir Robert Howard, Sir Anthony Keck, Sir Christopher Musgrave, Sir Robert Rich, Sir William Strickland.[1]

Those for the old Company were for going on and reading the accounts brought in by the Company, and that the old Company were very willing to submit to such regulations as the House should think fit. Those against it were for inquiring into the complaints against them and to examine the truth of matters of fact objected against them, and prayed there might be a new company erected for as it was now managed it was very prejudicial to this nation, so desired a new company might be established by act of parliament.

So at last it came to a resolution that the Chairman should move the House to have leave to sit again to take into consideration the complaints against the present Company, and that the several particulars intended to be insisted on against the Company might be delivered to the Governor of the Company or left for him at the East India House.

---

[1] This debate lasted over five hours; B.M. Add. MS. 17677LL, f. 260.

So then the Speaker took the Chair again, and *Sir John Guise* moved the House in the several particulars. And the House ordered that the heads of the complaints should be delivered to etc. by tomorrow morning 12 of the clock and that this House would resolve into a Committee of the Whole House on Tuesday next to hear the same.

Then the House adjourned till tomorrow morning 9 of the clock.

Saturday, 14 November

Sir William Whitlock had leave to attend the House of Lords as counsel in a cause before them.

The House divided upon the petition of Ralph Macclesfield, desiring leave to sell lands—the Yeas were ordered to go out.[1]

		Mr. Wharton	
	Yeas		50
		Mr. Onslow	
Tellers for the			
		Mr. Christie	
	Noes		77
		Mr. Grey	

So it was rejected.

Mr. Arnold brought in the petition of one David Lashley, desiring that a stop might be put to the going out of a ship that was now at Gravesend, bound for France, and laden with tin, lead, etc., to a great value.

But some members giving an account that the said ship was bound to the Straits, nothing was done in it.

Mr. Harley reported from the committee appointed to inspect the estimate of the charge of Their Majesties' Navy for the year 1692: that they had considered the same and came to several resolutions, viz.

That 30,000 men is a due medium for the fleet for the year 1692 for 13 months.

That £4 a head *per mensem* for 30,000 [men] for 13 months is sufficient and to stand part of the estimate for the year 1692, viz.: wear and tear a head *per mensem* £1. 7s. 6d. is sufficient, whereas in the estimate it is £1. 8s. 6d.; that for victuals 19s. per head a month is

---

[1] *CJ*, x. 552 has the names of the tellers for the affirmative and the negative reversed.

sufficient, and not £1 per head; that whereas the ordnance is charged in the estimate at 8s. per head, that 5s. per head now is sufficient; and that for the wages which in the estimate is said to be £1. 8s. 6d., it should continue so.

That the charge of £8,400 for 30 tenders and £8,400 for the hospital ships was included in the £1. 7s. 6d. charged for wear and tear.

That the charge of building four new fourth-rate ships should not be part of the estimate for the year ensuing.

That the making one dry dock and two wet docks at Portsmouth was necessary and should stand part of the estimate for the year 1692.

That the charge of the two marine regiments is included in the estimate of the 30,000 men.

That the £6,000 for etc. [the half-pay of officers while on shore] should not stand part of the estimate for the year 1692.

That the £100,000 for the ordinary estimate of the Navy was provided for, part in the civil list and part in the estimate of the wear and tear, so ought not to stand part of the estimate for the year 1692.

Then this report and resolutions was referred to the Committee of the Whole House who are to consider of the King's supplies. Then the House resolved itself into a Committee of the Whole House to consider of the said supplies and the Solicitor took the Chair. So the Order of the Day was read, then the order for referring the matters to this committee.

So after the whole committee considered of each particular, and put a question to agree with the [select] committee on each particular, *to which the House also agreed,*[1] viz.

That 30,000 men was a sufficient medium.

That of 5s. per head for the ordnance was urged by Sir Henry Goodricke not to be sufficient. That 22,000 barrels of powder for your fleet was but enough and 12,000 for your land forces, which makes 34,000. And there is now but 36,000 barrels in store, so that you will have but a few left. And if your fleet should come to a fight next summer, not sufficient would be left to supply that occasion. The ordnance formerly used to have an eighth part of the £4. 5s., but because a good part of the stores were returned last year, His Majesty hath allotted 8s. *per mensem* for it, and now you have even reduced that.

---

[1] My italics. Luttrell here is anticipating the full House's actions which he does report after this account of proceedings in Committee of the Whole. Thus in the following passage until Luttrell reports the Speaker's resumption of the Chair, 'the committee' is in fact the select committee and 'the House' is actually Committee of the Whole.

I thought it my duty to acquaint you herewith, and now do as you please.

So the House agreed with the committee.

As to that of the victuals, that 19s. per head settled by the committee was sufficient, and the House agreed to it.

As to that of wear and tear, the House agreed with the committee that £1. 7s. 6d. per head was sufficient, though Mr. Godolphin and Sir Richard Onslow spoke against it.

As to that of £1. 8s. 6d. per head a month for seamen's wages was sufficient, and the House agreed with the committee.

As to that of £8,400 for the 30 tenders, the House agreed with the committee that it was included in that of wear and tear, though opposed by Col. Austen and Lord Falkland.

As to that of £8,400 for four hospital ships, the House agreed with the committee that it was included in that of the wear and tear, though opposed by Sir John Lowther and the Lord Falkland.

As to that of £28,864 for building four new fourth-rate ships, it took up a long debate whether to agree with the committee or not. For not agreeing were Col. Austen, Sir Joseph Williamson, John Howe, Sir Benjamin Newland, Lord Falkland, Sir Robert Rich, Sir John Guise, Major Pery, and Mr. Montagu. And for it were Paul Foley, Sir Edward Seymour, Sir Christopher Musgrave, Sir Thomas Clarges, Mr. Bertie, and Sir John Thompson, because they said it was irregular to bring the building of four new ships into the list or estimate of the Navy for the year 1692 when it was plain that they could not be built to be serviceable in the year 1692, and then taxes were likely to be so heavy without it that the nation could not bear it.

So the question was put whether this should stand part of the estimate for the year 1692. [Committee of the Whole] House divided.

Yeas Mr. Cary 147

Tellers for the

Noes Sir Robert Cotton 174

So carried in the negative it should not; so they agreed with the committee.

As to that of £15,890 for building one dry dock and two wet docks at Portsmouth, the committee resolved they should stand part of the estimate for the year 1692 for charge of the Navy.

As to that of the £30,000 for the marine regiments, several spoke to it—Sir Richard Onslow, Col. Austen, Lord Falkland, and Sir

Richard Temple. And against it were Paul Foley, Sir Edward Seymour, Lord Ranelagh, for that they thought them to be included in
the 30,000 men. So held to agree with the committee.

As to that of £6,000 for officers etc., that was agreed not to stand
part of the estimate of the Navy this year.

As to the ordinary charge of the fleet in time of peace, viz. £100,000,
some spoke to it. To have it allowed were Sir John Lowther, Lord
Falkland, Col. Austen, Sir Richard Onslow. And others were against
it, as Sir Edward Seymour, Paul Foley, Sir Christopher Musgrave, for
that part of this was provided for in the civil list and part in that of
wear and tear; then, it was an innovation and the charge of the ordinary estimate is even in itself much less in time of war than in time of
peace. Wherefore upon the question, it was agreed it should not stand
part of the estimate of the Navy for the year 1692.

So after, the Speaker resumed the Chair and *Mr. Solicitor* reported
the said several resolutions to the House, which were all read. And
then the question was put on each resolution to agree with the committee, in all which the House agreed with the committee. And then
he acquainted them that the committee had directed him to move the
House that the committee might sit again. So the House resolved on
Wednesday morning next to resolve into a Committee of the Whole
House to consider further of the supplies to be granted to Their
Majesties for carrying on a vigorous war against France.

So the House adjourned till 9 on Monday morning.

Monday, 16 November

Mr. John White, being chosen knight for Nottinghamshire (in the
room of Mr. Sacheverell, deceased), came in this day to the House,
and was ushered up to the Table by Mr. Thornagh and took the
oaths, and after sat in the House.

It was moved to add some instructions to the bill for the speedy
recovery of small tithes on its reading a second time and being committed that a clause might be added for settling the tithe of *sylva
cadua*[1] and that great tithes under the value of 40s. might have the
like remedy as is by this act appointed for small tithes. So the bill was
committed on the debate of the House and a committee named to
meet at 4 this afternoon.

---

[1] *Silva cedua*—coppice wood.

The defaulters were called over this day. Some were excused. Those that were not were ordered to be sent for in custody by the Serjeant at Arms attending this House (and were about 12 of them).

A List of the Ships lost since 1688

Coronation	2nd rate	Capt. Skelton	cast away 3 September 1691
Victory	2nd rate		cast away 27 February 1690/1
Ann	3rd rate	Capt. Tyrrel	burnt 6 July 1690
Breda	3rd rate	Capt. Tennant	blown up at Kinsale
Dreadnought	3rd rate		foundered 16 October 1690
Henrietta	3rd rate	Capt. Newel	cast away at Plymouth
Harwich	3rd rate	Capt. Robinson	cast away there
Exeter	3rd rate	Capt. Mees	burnt there 1691
Pendennis	3rd rate	Capt. Churchill	cast away
Centurion	4th rate	Capt. Beaumont	cast away at Plymouth
St. David	4th rate	Capt. Graydon	sunk and weighed up and made a hulk
Mary Rose	4th rate	Capt. [blank]	taken by the French 1691
Portsmouth	4th rate	Capt. St. Loe	taken by French and after burnt by them
Sedgemore	4th rate	Capt. Lloyd	cast away
Constant Warwick	5th rate	Capt. [blank]	taken by French 1691
Dartmouth	5th rate	Capt. [blank]	cast away on coast of Scotland

Lively prize, retaken by the French
Charles & Henry (a fireship), cast away
Alexander, burnt
Hopewell, burnt
Emanuel
John of Dublin
Sampson, sunk
Firedrake, taken
Dragoon Sloop, cast away
Drake, cast on a survey
[blank], cast away
Dunbarton, cast on a survey
Deptford ketch, cast away at Virginia
Kingfisher ketch, taken by the French
Talbot, taken
Two hulks, sunk

Damaged

Vanguard, 2nd rate

Northumberland ⎫
Royal Oak   ⎪
Elizabeth   ⎪
Hope   ⎬ all 3rd rates and damaged at Plymouth   September 1691
Eagle   ⎪
Stirling Castle ⎭

Mr. Comptroller Wharton moved that now these papers had been read they might be referred to the committee to whom the state of the nation was referred.

Sir Thomas Clarges: You have here but a sad account of our shipping. And therefore moved that an account might be brought in by the Admiralty what inquiries, examinations, and proceedings thereon have been either by the Commissioners of the Admiralty or in a court martial touching ships cast away, ships taken, and ships run aground.

And it was ordered accordingly.

Mr. Brydges having by order of the House named the Earl of Danby to be the captain that had seen the papers taken in the French boat—some of which was a true copy of General Ginkel's letter to Sir Ralph Delaval and another entitled 'a copy of a letter of the Lord Nottingham to Sir Ralph Delaval'. But being a member of the House of Lords, this House could not come at him to inquire into the matter, which occasioned a debate in the House. Some were for naming some members as a committee to repair to his Lordship, desiring his information in the matter. Others, as *Sir Thomas Clarges, Mr. Hampden, Sir Edward Seymour*, etc., thought the most regular way was to have a conference with the Lords to acquaint them therewith and to desire them to inquire into the matter and communicate the same to this House.

So after some debate, the question was put for a committee to be appointed to repair to the Lord Danby to desire his information therein. The House divided—the Yeas went out.

		Sir Jonathan Jennings	
	Yeas		66
		[Mr. Henry Herbert][1]	
Tellers for the			
		Col. Granville	
	Noes		186
		Sir Thomas Trawell	

[1] Blank in MS.; from *CJ*, x. 554.

So that then a conference was resolved on, and the Lord Colchester was ordered to go to the Lords and desire a conference with their Lordships upon an information made to this House of matters relating to the safety of the government.

Sir Edward Hussey moved, *Sir Charles Sedley, Mr. Arnold,* and *Sir Francis Blake* to the same, that an address be made to His Majesty that the examinations and confessions of the Lord Preston and Mr. Crone may be laid before this House, and that such members of this House as are of His Majesty's Privy Council may present the same.

And it was ordered accordingly.

So the House adjourned till 9 tomorrow morning.

Tuesday, 17 November

A petition of one John Keble for selling certain lands etc. and settling lands of better value in their stead was read, and prayed to refer it to a committee to examine the matter and to report their opinions to the House. But it was denied, so nothing done thereon.

A committee was named to whom the bill for preventing false and double returns was referred and are to meet at 4 this afternoon in the Speaker's Chamber.

The Serjeant at Arms attending this House informed the House that he had inquired to find out Sir Ralph Delaval, but that he was not yet come to town. So ordered he should send a messenger to him at Portsmouth to attend this House.

The Lord Colchester went up with a message to the Lords to desire a conference, and several of the members of the House went up with him. And being returned, *he* reported at the Bar that the Lords do agree to a present conference in the Painted Chamber.

So the House named their managers and appointed the heads or subject-matter thereof and gave it in writing. They accordingly went up. And being returned, *Mr. Montagu* at the Bar reported that they had according to the order of this House attended the conference and acquainted the Lords with what they had in command from this House.

Then the Order of the Day was read for the House resolving into a Committee of the Whole House to take into consideration the complaints against the East India Company. So the Speaker left the Chair and Sir John Guise took it. So the Order of the Day was read again. Then Capt. Pitt, a member of the House and a prosecutor of the East

India Company, delivered into the committee the heads of complaint against the Company, consisting of 16 articles. And the Company's answer thereto was delivered into the House in writing by the Governor of the Company. Both which were read.

Then the witnesses against the Company were called in to prove the several articles. But as to the first, they had no witnesses but referred to the Journal of a former parliament—which was long debated whether it should be read, but at last on the question resolved it should. So after, they examined divers witnesses to prove the several articles of oppressions and miscarriages committed by the present East India Company, and finished the same.

Then Sir John Guise left the Chair and the Speaker resumed the same. And *Sir John Guise* reported from the said committee that they had examined the matter of the complaints against the East India Company and had gone through the several heads thereof and that the committee had directed him to move the House for leave to sit again. So the House resolved that on Friday next they would resolve into a Committee of the Whole House to consider further of the petition against the East India Company.

All committees were ordered to be adjourned.

So the House adjourned till 9 tomorrow morning.

Wednesday, 18 November

Sir William Whitlock moved to have the engrossed bill for regulating of trials in cases of treason to be read the third time. Seconded by *Mr. Bertie, Sir [Ralph]*[1] *Dutton, Sir Edward Seymour*, etc.

Sir John Lowther and *Sir Robert Cotton* (of the Post Office) moved that the House would resolve into a Committee of the Whole House and take into consideration the supply for Their Majesties, for that the House had sat near a month and hardly done anything in it when the King's occasions call so much for it. In former sessions this House sat *de die in diem* upon the same, but now it is a hard matter for the King's business to get one day.

But upon the question it was carried for the bill to be read a third time, and it was accordingly.[2]

---

[1] 'Richard' in MS.
[2] Grey, x. 171–5 has a somewhat fuller account of the debate on the trial of treason bill that follows.

Sir John Lowther: This is a bill which alters the law in diverse particulars. It orders a criminal to have a copy of his indictment 10 days before he pleads. This will render trials for treason at the assizes wholly impracticable, for there are no assizes hardly that hold 10 days, so that the party cannot be tried but must lie in prison till the next assizes. Then if there be the least fault or slip in a letter of the indictment, by having a copy the party shall take exceptions and put off his trial for that time till he can be anew indicted. The law as it now stands makes it difficult enough to convict a man, but now this gives more liberty and will encourage men to be the bolder in committing treason. The enemies of this government appear publicly and barefaced, persons come from France daily with intelligence and carry it back again, and you can do nothing to them. Therefore, I am against the bill.

Mr. Hutchinson, Sir Charles Sedley, Mr. Finch spoke for the bill—the latter very largely and handsomely.

Mr. Clarke spoke against several particulars of it, as also *Sir George Treby*.

But upon the question, the bill was passed and ordered to be carried to the Lords by Sir William Whitlock for their concurrence. And he went up with it accordingly, attended with several members of the House.

Then the Order of the Day was read. So the Speaker left the Chair and Mr. Solicitor took it. And the Order of the Day was read again when the House had resolved into a Committee of the Whole House.

Mr. Hampden moved that the committee might, as they did last year, pass a vote that the estimate as it now stands settled by the House is reasonable and that a sum not exceeding £1,575,890 be given to Their Majesties for the charge of the Navy for the year 1692.

Mr. Henry Herbert and Mr. Papillon moved that a sum not exceeding £1,600,000 be given for the service of the fleet.

Sir John Thompson and Sir John Lowther opposed it as irregular, for that the committee could not vote another sum of money than what the House had agreed in the estimate.

Whereon the committee came to this resolution: That it is the opinion of this committee that a sum not exceeding £1,575,890 for the charge of the Navy for the year 1692 (including the ordnance and the charge of building one dry dock and two wet docks at Portsmouth) be given to Their Majesties as part of the supply for carrying on a vigorous war against France.

Sir John Lowther: I am glad to see the House of Commons of opinion that a speedy supply is necessary for the King's occasions. I move you, therefore, that the estimate of the land forces for the year 1692 may be referred to the Committee of the Whole House we are now in. Mr. Hampden, Sir William [Leveson-]Gower, and Sir Charles Sedley to the same.

Mr. Paul Foley moved that it might be considered of first what land forces you think necessary and how they are to be employed and where. And then that you would after (as you did that of the fleet) refer it to a private committee. And Sir Christopher Musgrave to the same.

Mr. Bathurst: I desire we may know what sums of money have been sent to the Duke of Savoy, to the Dutch, and to the beggarly princes of Germany.

Sir John Guise: I think no man ought to say such a thing in this House.

Sir Edward Seymour: I wish they were richer than they are. It would be for our benefit and theirs, and I am sure we should pay less.

Sir Thomas Clarges: I think it is fit you should give the King your advice as well as your money. I think we ought to have some light into the alliances, and what men are designed for England, what for Ireland. And I know of no need there is for more till we have an account given thereon. This was the method in 1677 and I desire it may be so now.

Sir Robert Sawyer to the same. For that this was a different matter from that of the fleet, for therein all agreed to have as good a fleet at sea as we can; not so for land forces.

Sir Thomas Littleton was for referring it to a private committee.

Mr. Foley against it, for he thought it too great a thing for a private committee. So Mr. Bertie and Mr. Harley.

But at last the question was put whether it should be referred to a private committee, and carried in the negative. So it was referred to a Committee of the Whole House.

Sir John Thompson and Mr. Bertie moved for an address to be made to His Majesty to have some account how the forces were to be distributed. Sir Charles Sedley, Sir Christopher Musgrave, and Sir Thomas Clarges to the same.

Sir Henry Goodricke acquainted them that His Majesty had commanded him to let this House know he was willing to give them all reasonable satisfaction. That His Majesty was resolved to draw all his foreign forces out of all his three kingdoms. That he would keep no more forces in England and Ireland than was absolutely necessary for the defence of the same. That he intended to employ the rest beyond sea, either by making a descent into France or otherwise to annoy the common enemy. That the terms of the treaty between the confederates were to assist one another *totis viribus*. And that His Majesty had renewed the treaty with the King of Denmark for his forces to be employed in any other place out of his own three kingdoms.

So after some time, the Solicitor left the Chair and the Speaker resumed the same. And *Mr. Solicitor* reported the resolution of the committee as to the £1,575,890, to which the House agreed *nemine contradicente*. Then the *Solicitor* moved that the committee might have leave to sit again. Resolved that this House will tomorrow morning resolve itself into a Committee of the Whole House to consider of the supply in relation to the land forces.

Resolved that this House will on Saturday next resolve itself into a Committee of the Whole House to consider further of the state of the nation.

Ordered that all committees be revived.

Adjourned till 9 tomorrow morning.

Thursday, 19 November

Sir Robert Henley, being chosen Knight of the Shire for Hampshire (in the room of Col. Norton, deceased), came into the House this day and took the oaths to Their Majesties at the Table.

The Lords at a conference delivered the managers several papers and a packet sealed up. Which being returned, *Mr. Hampden* reported the conference and delivered in the papers at the Table where some of them were read, as the Lord Danby's information in the House of Lords touching these matters (which mentioned his having seen two papers—a letter from General Ginkel to Sir Ralph Delaval and another entitled 'a copy of the Lord Nottingham's letter to Sir Ralph Delaval') which was read, and a letter from Sir Ralph Delaval to the Lord Nottingham touching these papers (dated 16 November 1691). Then the packet sealed up was opened by the Speaker, containing 18 papers in number, with a parchment cover, most of which were in French. The Speaker looked them over and marked them, but the letter of the Lord Nottingham to Sir Ralph Delaval was not amongst them.[1]

[1] Grey, x. 175 has a brief account of the discussion that followed.

So the perusal, examination, and translation of them was referred to a committee, and they are to report their opinions to the House. So a committee was named to meet at 4 this afternoon, and were empowered to send for persons, papers, and records.

Sir Francis Blake and *Sir Edward Hussey* moved to know if the members of the Privy Council had attended His Majesty with the address about the papers of examination and confession of the Lord Preston and Mr. Crone.

Sir John Lowther acquainted the House that they were to attend His Majesty this afternoon, and he did not doubt but His Majesty would signify his pleasure in that matter.

The *Lord Ranelagh* delivered in a list of the forces His Majesty designed for the service of the year 1692 and how they were to be disposed. Which was read and is as follows:

In England

Four regiments of Horse, two of 300 and two of 213 each, in all		1,026
One regiment of Dragoons, of		480
Twelve regiments of Foot, each of 780, in all		9,360
One independent company, of		50
	In all	10,916

In Ireland

One regiment of Horse, of		300
Two regiments of Dragoons, each of 480, in all		960
Fifteen regiments of Foot, each 780, in all		11,700
	Total	12,960

In Scotland

One troop of Scotch Guards, of		118
One regiment of Dragoons, of		360
Two regiments of Foot, each 780		1,560
	Total	2,038

West Indies

One regiment of Foot, of		780
Three independent companies, each 60, in all		180
	In all	960

So there are thus employed:

Of Horse		1,444
Of Dragoons		1,800
Of Foot		23,630
	Total of all	26,874

Besides a body of men to be transported beyond sea to annoy the
common enemy, consisting of   38,050
   Of which are Horse   [6,630]
   Dragoons   [1,640]
   Foot   [29,780][1]
So the total of all the forces—Horse, Foot, and Dragoons—for the
service of the year 1692 are   64,924 men

Which list was read and referred to the consideration of the Committee of the Whole House.

Then the Order of the Day for resolving into a Committee of the Whole House to consider of the supplies was read. The Speaker left the Chair and the Solicitor General took it. And the Order of the Day was read again.[2]

Sir John Lowther: You have before you a matter of very great importance, not only the concern of this nation but of all Europe. It is that of assisting your confederates against the common enemy, the French. We have now a King which I will venture to say is the best general in the world; you have strong alliances against this common enemy; and yet you see he is able to cope with them all. So that it is now come to that, that we must either reduce him to a lower condition or we are lost. If there should happen to be any misunderstanding between the confederates or a peace should ensue, if he that is now able to deal with the confederates thus united, what will he not do when the confederacy is broke and he has but a single prince to deal with? There is, then, no way left but to attack him vigorously, and that in his own country with a force sufficient. The only way is to land an army upon him; hereby he must either come out at sea to fight you or suffer his country to be wasted by a powerful army. Then his own subjects will be apt to rise against him, being overwhelmed with so many oppressions and taxes. I remember former parliaments have been very desirous of a war with France, even at a time when there was just reasons to fear the government was not so inclined. But now you have a King of your own to lead your forces, to head a victorious army—a King that is entirely in your interests and one whom you may confide in will prosecute this war heartily. My motion, therefore, is that you will come up to the number of men His Majesty has thought necessary.

[1] Blank in MS.; from *CJ*, x. 557.
[2] Grey, x. 175–80 has a parallel account of the debate on supply. See also *HMC Seventh Report*, pp. 207–8.

Sir Christopher Musgrave spoke to order. You have not yet read the paper delivered in by the Lord Ranelagh, which was referred to the committee.

So the Lord Ranelagh's paper was read.

Mr. Cary: I take this to be the critical moment of our happiness or misery, and that now we have an opportunity to save ourselves by a hearty prosecution of the war. France cannot be overrun but by a torrent of forces. I shall move you, therefore, to pass a vote that it is the opinion of this committee that an army of 65,000 men is necessary for the defence of these kingdoms and carrying on a vigorous war against France. Sir Thomas Mompesson seconded it.

Paul Foley: You have now before you a great matter. It is urged by some that it is necessary to have an army of 65,000 men, but I desire such to consider how they will raise money to pay them. The revenue is already so clogged that little will arise thence; the nation is already two millions in debt. I must declare for my part I do not see any necessity for so many men, and therefore I do desire we may not agree to the list brought in unto us.

Sir John Guise: I do not wonder the member that spoke last understands not what belongs to an army; he has not been used to those things. But now suppose we do as that gentleman would have us—not agree to the list brought in. Here is the confederacy broke—which is the consequence thereof—and we have nothing to do but to defend ourselves at sea. The proportion now as to your fleet with the Dutch is you are to be two-thirds and the Dutch one, and both of us joined together are but now strong enough for the French. But if the French should overrun Holland and force the Dutch to join their fleet with his, what would become of you then? You have voted a war with France, that you would give His Majesty supplies for carrying on the same vigorously; you have entered into alliances for that end; and it will be a fine thing to have it appear that for the carrying on the war vigorously this year you thought fit to disband above 30,000 men.

Sir John Thompson: You are not now regular. Therefore, I move you that you will go on by particulars—head by head, as it stands in the list delivered in. As to the army designed to be kept in Ireland, it was told us the revenue of that kingdom should maintain them. I think it is fit for to keep up what intended for that kingdom. But as to those designed (as pretended) for a descent, I look upon it only as a colour. I declare I am against a standing army. I am very jealous of

it, and therefore I pray we may go head by head to see what is necessary and what not. Sir Christopher Musgrave to the same.

Sir John Lowther: It is not intended the army in Ireland should be
paid by this kingdom. The revenue there will be applied to it as far
as it will go.

Sir Thomas Clarges: Here are many fair pretences laid before you.
But on the whole matter, though we came the last into the alliance, yet
we shall pay for all. I think our coming into it was of more advantage
to the confederates than it was to us. The only way for you to oppose
France is to strengthen yourselves by sea. Since the last summer all
Ireland is now reduced, and yet here is an abatement but of 5,000 men
of what you had the year before. But I think your main care ought to
be that of your fleet. And therefore since we are now upon the land
forces, I desire we may consider the list brought in head by head.

Sir Robert Howard: As to the objections against coming up to the
number of forces thought necessary, it is said you are not able; if that
be so, your debate is at an end, but I hope we are able. It is said it is to
prevent slavery, but I declare myself not to be for that on any score,
and in our case there is no danger. We have a magnanimous and a
courageous prince, and from such there is no fear of slavery; that
rather proceeds from effeminate princes. So that on the whole matter
I am for the general question, and the rather I would not limit how
many should be kept in one kingdom and how many in another but
leave it to His Majesty, for I think we may have fewer in this kingdom
and more abroad.

Mr. Jeffreys moved that the House would proceed upon the particulars head by head.

Sir Thomas Clarges: I would have gentlemen consider how so great
an army shall be maintained abroad. The money for keeping them
will amount to near half the money in the kingdom. Therefore, I
desire you will go head by head that we may save what we can.

Mr. Hampden: His Majesty is a great captain, and since he thinks
65,000 men necessary, I that am but a private man cannot but think
there is weight in it. Let any gentleman but consider the consequences if we must submit to France. Do you think he will let you
be at home here, and be merry? No, certainly. It is true I cannot but
say the charge is great and very considerable, but yet if the French
should invade you I believe there is hardly any would think much of
a greater charge to oppose them. I think, therefore, you have been
well moved to put the question in general.

Sir Robert Cotton (of Post Office): Do but consider how ready the Dutch and other confederates were to assist you in a time of need, how they lent their armies and fleets to deliver you when your laws, your religion, and all were in danger. And shall we be so ungrateful to leave them when they have most need of our help? I desire, therefore, we may pass a vote that such a number in the whole is sufficient for carrying on the war.

Sir Robert Sawyer was for going head by head.

Sir George Treby: We have not this many years had a prince so heartily in our interests as His present Majesty is, and one who is for a hearty prosecution of the war. And therefore I desire we may come up to what His Majesty thinks necessary, and therefore pray put the general question.

Sir Charles Sedley was for going head by head.

Sir Christopher Musgrave: You must go head by head or you will conclude yourselves if it should pass in the negative. But suppose it should pass, you hereby oblige yourselves to keep that exact number in England and Ireland and Scotland, which is fit to be considered.

Sir John Guise was for going upon the general, and not head by head.

Sir Richard Temple for the same, for that it was necessary to have what force we can. For if we have no more than last year, we shall at the end of the next year be at the same pass we are now.

Sir Henry Capel: I am for the lump, and for this reason. What the event of the war next year may be, I know not. But if the French should attack Ireland or other part of the King's dominions, who would be so bold to advise His Majesty to withdraw any of his forces from the other parts of his kingdom, thereby to lessen what the Commons have thought fit to establish for the defence of those kingdoms?

Mr. Bertie: I am for going head by head. Sir Edward Hussey and Sir John Mainwaring to the same.

Sir Thomas Clarges: I think the naming a number of men to us is the same as naming the sum, for if we must provide so many men we must take care to pay them. This is only what the Parliament of Paris do. They have a sum named to them and they raise it, but I desire we may not come to that. We are called together to advise, but this sort of proceeding by naming a sum takes away our liberty.

Sir William Leveson-Gower: I am for putting the question generally by the lump, and that because I think His Majesty's judgement better

than my own, so I submit to him. Mr. Dolben and Sir Thomas Littleton were for the general question.

Col. Granville and Mr. Harley were for going upon the heads
particularly. Sir John Knight, Sir William Strickland, Mr. Palmes to
the same.

But Mr. Montagu, Sir Robert Rich, and Sir Joseph Williamson
were for putting the question in general.

So at last the question was put, and it was resolved that an army
of 64,924 men is necessary for the service of the year 1692 for securing
the peace of this kingdom and the carrying on a vigorous war against
France. It was also ordered that the Solicitor General should report
this resolution to the House and should also move the House by direction from the committee that the committee may sit again.

So the Solicitor left the Chair and Mr. Speaker resumed the Chair.
And the *Solicitor* reported the said resolution to the House, unto
which they agreed, and moved that the committee might sit again.
So resolved that the House would resolve itself on Monday next into
a Committee of the Whole House to consider further of the supply in
relation to the land forces.

Ordered that all committees be adjourned.

So the House adjourned till 9 tomorrow morning.

Friday, 20 November

Ordered that Mr. Finch and the Solicitor General have leave to
attend a cause depending in the House of Lords.

Sir Robert Clayton moved that the petition of Richard Baldwin, the
printer, might be read.

Sir Edward Seymour: I desire that when he is brought up you would
inquire of him the author of that pamphlet and the supervisor thereof,
for they are the persons that have made so bold with the proceedings
of this House.

Ordered that he be brought to the Bar of this House tomorrow and
that his petition be then read.

Then the Order of the Day was read, according to which the
Speaker left the Chair and Sir John Guise was called on as Chairman,
and the House resolved into a Committee of the Whole House to
consider of the trade to the East Indies.

So the Order of the Day was read again. Then the witnesses on the
behalf of the old East India Company were called in; and their solicitor

managed their defence, and examined their witnesses to the heads of complaint against them, and proceeded on the four first heads.

And after a considerable time spent therein, the Speaker resumed the Chair. And *Sir John Guise* reported from the said committee that the East India Company had made some progress in their defence to the heads of complaint against them and that the committee had directed him to move the House that they might have leave to sit again. And it was ordered accordingly on Tuesday next.

Ordered that all committees be adjourned.

So the House adjourned till tomorrow morning 9 of the clock.

Saturday, 21 November

A petition from the town of Taunton against Scotch pedlars was presented to the House, and ordered to be read when the bill for suppressing hawkers and pedlars was read a second time.

Sir Samuel Dashwood presented two clauses to the House to be added to the bill for the excise, which he carried up to the Table, and the same were read. One was for the allowing any private person leave to brew his own drink, though he hath not brewed for a year past, without incurring the penalty of £100, provided he pay the excise for the same. The second clause was to regulate the abuses in distilling of spirits and low wines.

Sir Edward Seymour, Sir Christopher Musgrave, and *Sir Robert Sawyer* strongly opposed the first clause, for that it was only a sly pretence to make way for a general home excise. For under colour hereof, they might search all private houses to see if they brewed their own drink to make them pay excise.

However, the clause was read once, and the question being put to read it a second time, it was carried in the negative.

Richard Baldwin, the printer, when he was at the Bar, being asked who was the author of *The Observator*, he acquainted the House one Dr. James Welwood was. Then he was ordered to withdraw from the Bar; and being called in again he received a reprimand from the *Speaker* on his knees and was ordered to be discharged, paying his fees.

The bill for transferring the collection of the duty of aulnage to the Custom House and giving the Crown a recompense for the same was read a second time.

But *Sir Joseph Tredenham* and *Sir Christopher Musgrave* opposed it as a very irregular thing, it being a bill imposing a duty on the subject and it was brought in with the blanks or sums filled up, which was very unparliamentary.

But it being a public bill and of great use, it was ordered to lie on the Table and that a new bill should be brought in.

Adjourned till Monday 9 of the clock in the morning.

Monday, 23 November

Mr. Walpole, a member of this House who was sent for in custody of the Serjeant at Arms for not attending the service of this House, having surrendered himself to the Serjeant at Arms attending this House, was ordered to be discharged, paying his fees.

Sir Ralph Delaval attending at the door of the House, he was called in after the Speaker had been directed what questions to ask him. And he gave answers to them to the following effect.[1]

The papers were taken in a French advice boat by Capt. Gillam and he sent them unto me, and those which I received I sent them all to the Lord Nottingham. They were loose in a parchment cover, not sealed up. Being in French I understood them not, but my captain who looked on them said they imported little more than the agreement or treaty between Mr. D'Usson (the French General) and the English General. After I had them, the weather proving bad, I had no opportunity to send them away. But when I came to Spithead, I sent notice thereof to the Lords of the Admiralty, and after I sent them up to the Lord Nottingham sealed with two seals of my crest. I never sealed them till I sent them to the Lord Nottingham.

So then he was ordered to withdraw. Then some members desired the Speaker to ask him some other questions. So he was called in again and gave the following account.

The packet was sent me by Capt. Gillam two days before either he or the French captain came aboard me, and when they came the Lord Danby with several others was aboard me. The Lord Danby asked him several questions, who answered: he came from Brest, that he was sent to find out Château Rénault with the French fleet (whose station was 15 leagues west-south-west of Scilly), and that he fell into our hands thinking our fleet to be theirs, being in the same station.—Capt. Gillam told me he sent me all the papers he took and I sent them all to the Lord Nottingham. There was no copy of any

[1] Grey, x. 180–3 has a parallel account of Delaval's interrogation and the subsequent debate.

instructions the Lord Nottingham sent to me nor the copy of any letter of his to me.—These papers were taken the 25th of October, and on the report thereof the Lord Nottingham sent me a letter to send them up to him, which I did.—I have not now the Lord Nottingham's letter with me, but will bring it when this House shall command.—I had no orders to go to Ireland.—I kept the papers in my closet in my cabin, my servant kept the key.

Then he was ordered to withdraw, and some other questions were directed to be asked him.

So he was called in and answered to them as follows. The Lord Danby read the papers in French, in which language they were writ, and after he read them in English and told me they imported only the Treaty of Limerick.—I remember the Lord Nottingham was named in one letter once or twice which occasioned, I suppose, the Lord Danby's mistake, for I saw no letter of the Lord Nottingham unto me amongst them.—The French captain told me that Château Rénault was at sea and had with him upwards of 20 sail of men-of-war and several store ships for the supply of Limerick.—As to the instructions I had the last time I went to sea, they were to be in the same station the French were—15 leagues west-south-west of Scilly. That I was to send one ship to Kinsale to give the merchant ships there notice to come out and join me and was to detach a squadron to conduct them to Spithead. But I had no orders to fight or to seek out the French, but was to continue in my station.—I had not one letter from the Lord Nottingham since I went last to sea.—There was not one paper (as I remember) in English amongst them.—The weather was very bad for 10 days together, so that I was forced to lie under a main sail to preserve my squadron.

Then he was ordered to withdraw, and to fetch the Lord Nottingham's letter to him and his last sailing orders and instructions touching the same.

A message from the Lords by Sir Miles Cook and Sir John Franklin that they desired to have the papers returned which were delivered at the last conference, they having present occasion for them.

Speaker acquainted the House that this was an unparliamentary message, for all matters and papers of inquiry belong to this House. It is your business, and the papers ought to have been sent to you.

Sir Thomas Clarges: I desire the messengers may be called in and acquainted that this House would send an answer by messengers of their own.

So they were called in and acquainted therewith.

Sir Thomas Clarges: We are strangely unhappy in the management of our naval affairs. When our ships meet with the enemy's, they are not to fight without orders. This seems to me very strange, for if matters be thus managed our naval war will signify very little. I desire the Lords of the Admiralty will let us know something hereof, whether when a French fleet were waiting for a fleet of 150 sail of our merchant ships he had no orders to fight them.

So Sir Ralph Delaval returned and came into the House and produced the Lord Nottingham's letter and his sailing orders. The Lord Nottingham's letter dated 14 November to Sir Ralph Delaval was read, desiring him to send up the copies of such papers he took in the French boat. And he said he did accordingly send them up by Capt. Ward. Then the several orders and instructions to Sir Ralph Delaval by Admiral Russell and by the Lords of the Admiralty were read, dated some 12 September 1691, others of 16 September, others of 6 October, and others of 12 November. Which after were redelivered to Sir Ralph again. So he withdrew, not appearing faulty in the matter.

The letter of the Lord Nottingham to Sir Ralph Delaval was referred to the committee who were to peruse and translate the several papers.

Sir Thomas Clarges: I thought one standing order in all our sea affairs to all captains had been to annoy or destroy the enemy wherever they met them, but I find it is otherwise, which I am sorry to see.

Then the members of the House called to the Order of the Day, which was that for bringing in the public accounts.

Sir Thomas Clarges: Ever since you made the order for bringing them in, we have spent two hours every morning and three hours in the afternoon to prepare them for you, which we have done, and they want only transcribing, so that they will be ready for you in three or four days.

Adjourned till 9 tomorrow morning.

Tuesday, 24 November

Notice being taken in the House that the members came very late to the House so that it was near 11 every morning before the Speaker took the Chair, *Sir Edward Seymour* moved that the House would order

†

that everyone who was not at prayers should pay 1*s.* to the use of the poor. But the House made no order in it.

The papers the House received from the Lords were delivered in by *Col. Granville*. And being they were received sealed from the Lords, the Speaker was ordered to seal them and Col. Granville was ordered to carry them up to the Lords by way of message, as in this case the properer way than to return them by way of a conference.

Then the House, according to their order, resolved into a Committee of the Whole House. The Speaker left the Chair and Sir John Guise took it. So the East India Company were called in and proceeded in their defence to the heads of complaint brought in against them, beginning at the fifth where they left off last, and concluded the whole.

So after a great while Mr. Speaker resumed the Chair, and *Sir John Guise* reported from the said committee that they had made some further progress touching the East India trade and that the committee had directed him to move the House that they might have leave to sit again, which was ordered accordingly on Friday next.

Then *Sir Joseph Herne* (Governor of the East India Company) delivered in the several accounts of the debts and of the stock of the East India Company. The titles whereof were read and the consideration thereof was referred to the said Committee of the Whole House.

So the House adjourned till 9 tomorrow morning.

Wednesday, 25 November

The *Speaker* took notice of a packet of seditious papers which he had sent him, which he believed came from Mr. Stafford in Bedlam. It was recommended to Sir William Turner, Governor thereof, to take care that he should by no means have pen, ink, or paper, to prevent his writing such scandalous papers.

Sir Thomas Roberts, having been chosen Knight of the Shire for the county of Kent (in the room of Sir [Vere Fane],[1] now Earl of Westmorland), he was introduced into the House, and took the oaths at the Table, and subscribed the declaration.

Then the Order of the Day was read, and the House accordingly resolved itself into a Committee of the Whole House to consider farther of the supplies to Their Majesties. And the Solicitor General was called to the Chair, and then the Order of the Day was read again.[2]

[1] Henry Vane in MS.
[2] Grey, x. 184–6 has a partial account of the debate that follows.

Sir John Lowther: You have already voted the number of men. I desire next you will take into consideration the other particulars, as the artillery, general officers, garrisons, hospitals, transport ships, and other contingencies, and go upon them head by head.

Mr. Hampden thought it necessary to consider what the pay of the soldiers should be and to compute that charge.

Then the papers delivered in by the Lord Ranelagh touching the land forces were read.

Paul Foley: I think it proper since you have voted the number of men to consider how to pay them. And in order to it that you will ease this kingdom as much as you can, and therefore I would begin with the head of the forces designed for Ireland. The last sessions we were told the money arising by the forfeiture of Irish estates should go towards the charge of the war. I desire further that the revenue of that kingdom may be applied towards payment of the forces designed there and that you will consider of some way to raise a tax on that kingdom besides to carry on the war. I move you, therefore, to pass this vote: that it is the opinion of this committee that the forces allotted for the service of Ireland shall be borne by that kingdom.

Sir Thomas Clarges: I think we are not yet ripe for that question. I think we ought to consider of the estimates. I observe the regiments now are not as formerly; the companies now are not above 40 or 50, and many officers, whereas anciently they were 100 in a company and fewer officers. It is fit, therefore, to consider how many a company shall consist of, to have particulars of the estimates brought in. For I find in the accounts brought before us as Commissioners you are charged to have 38,000 men in Ireland. The charges whereof as brought in amount to a vast sum, occasioned by the smallness of the regiments and the great numbers of officers. The establishment in Ireland formerly in King Charles II's time was less than now—but 1s. 6d. a day for a horseman, 1s. 2d. for a dragooner, and 6d. a foot soldier.

Mr. Hampden moved that the House might be moved that an address be presented to His Majesty that the pay of the land forces in Ireland might be reduced to what it was in King Charles II's time.

Sir Thomas Clarges: I am not for addressing to His Majesty but for passing this vote; that the pay of the officers and soldiers to be employed in Ireland for the year 1692 be in like manner and proportion as in the reign of King Charles II.

Which resolution was passed accordingly.

Sir Thomas Clarges: You have voted an army of 64,924 men for the year 1692. I desire to know whether the officers are reckoned therein.

Lord Ranelagh: The estimate and particulars I delivered in was that the 64,924 men was so many private sentinels only, not including the officers therein.

Sir Thomas Clarges: You see how necessary it was to have this matter explained. If this be your meaning, your army—instead of 64,924 men—with officers and all will come to near 80,000. Sure it was never thought by any that we should have an army without officers, and therefore I desire you will pass a vote that the 12,960 men designed for Ireland includes officers and men. Sir John Thompson to the same.

Sir Christopher Musgrave: This is a very strange motion, for no one thought that an army could be without officers, and you have voted an army of so many men as necessary for the year 1692 which certainly included officers. And you cannot, if you would, in this committee enlarge the number of men (which this will if officers be not included), but you must go to the House for that, they having voted but so many men.

Sir John Lowther was against that, for that it was plainly the intention—as appears by the particular brought in—that it did not include officers but intended only so many private sentries.

Col. Sackville: When you voted the number of men, it was not intended to have an army without officers. Then for your regiments, I would not have less than 1,200 men in a regiment of foot and 100 in a company. This was the way formerly. But I am for advancing the pay of officers, without which you will never prevent false musters.

Mr. Gwyn, Sir Robert Howard, and Sir Robert Cotton all: That it could not be thought that the House intended otherwise than to include the officers in the army.

Sir Henry Goodricke: That it was intended only of so many private men is very plain by the list brought in by the Lord Ranelagh. It was done so in 1672, 1677, and formerly. The number you are contesting for is not great; you have but three commission officers.

Lord Ranelagh: The matter in dispute is about 11,000 men. In every company there are 11 officers of all sorts—the captain, lieutenant, ensign, three sergeants, three corporals, and two drummers—and in every troop there is nine officers. The whole is about 11,000 officers, which your army will be lessened if you include the officers in the number you have resolved on.

Sir Robert Howard: I never understood there was more than three commission officers in a company. I am not for making your companies above 60 men, and 50 in a troop. I think that enough.

Paul Foley: Last year you voted about 69,000 land forces, but as they managed it with officers besides, they have brought in accounts of many more.

Sir Robert Rich: I think an army of 65,000 men a great army and am for the question. I desire we may not divide at this time. Mr. John Howe to the same.

But Sir John Guise was not for including the officers in the 65,000 men.

So it was at last resolved: That it is the opinion of this committee that the 12,960 men which His Majesty has been pleased to signify are intended to be continued in Ireland for the year 1692 do consist of officers and soldiers making up that number.

Paul Foley: Now you have passed this vote, I desire we may pass this farther; that the charge of the forces for Ireland should be laid upon that kingdom. Sir William Cowper to the same.

Sir John Lowther: Before you pass this, I desire you will consider if that kingdom is able to bear it. For if not, the consequence must be that the soldiers will quarter on the country.

Hampden to the same. For will you lay a load on that kingdom before you know what the revenue thereof amounts to? Which as yet is very little, the kingdom being not settled.

Sir Thomas Clarges desired that the House might be moved to appoint a committee to inquire into what the revenue of Ireland will amount to. Mr. Bertie to the same.

Sir Richard Temple thought it too soon to pass such a vote, but that the House might be moved to appoint a committee to state the charge of the men allotted for Ireland. Sir Robert Sawyer to the same.

Sir Thomas Clarges: I believe the revenue of Ireland will not this year amount to above £200,000. But there are besides several forfeited estates in that kingdom of persons outlawed, in number about 3,000. Perhaps some of these by the Articles in that kingdom may be lessened, but there will be that left which is very considerable. Some persons think it may amount to £300,000; I believe more. But on the whole I desire we may proceed regularly in this matter.

So it was ordered that the House be moved to appoint a committee to consider what the charge of the army in Ireland will be for the year

1692 and how far that kingdom can contribute towards the support of that charge.

Sir Edward Seymour: The revenue of Ireland formerly was farmed at £240,000 per annum in King Charles II's time. This two or three years past it hath yielded very little, but now it will increase considerably; the excise and customs will now be very great.

Sir Thomas Clarges: The revenue thereof formerly was £320,000. The revenue next year will be considerable for that people now will be flocking over, which will increase the excise and customs much greater than the two or three last years.

Sir Christopher Musgrave moved that the Lord Ranelagh might be appointed to bring in an estimate of the charge of the land forces including of officers, except of such as are in Ireland.

So ordered: That the House be moved that an estimate of the charge of the number of the land forces which His Majesty has been pleased to signify he thinks necessary to be continued in England, Scotland, and the West Indies, and to be transported beyond sea for the service of the year 1692 (including the officers) may be laid before the House. That the House be moved that an estimate of the charge of the general officers, with the number of them and their pay, and the charge of the hospitals and train of artillery and garrisons for the service of the year 1692 may be laid before the House. That the House be moved that an estimate of the charge of the hire of the transport ships and other charges of transportation for the service of the year 1692 may be laid before the House. That he [the Chairman] move the House that this committee may sit again.

Lord Ranelagh acquainted the committee that he had prepared estimates of four of them already, which he was ready to present to the House. But for that of hospitals and contingencies, they are uncertain and cannot but be guessed at and here they are very moderate —the first depending on what sick there are, the other on various accidents.

So then the Speaker resumed the Chair and *Mr. Solicitor* reported the two resolutions of the committee, to which the House agreed. *He* also made the several motions, which the House ordered accordingly, and named a committee as to that about the revenue of Ireland. Ordered that the Lord Ranelagh, the officers of the Ordnance, and the Commissioners of the Navy do respectively lay the said estimates before this House. Ordered that the House will resolve itself into a Committee of the Whole House on Saturday morning next to consider farther of the supplies to be granted to Their Majesties for the carrying on a vigorous war against France.

So the House adjourned till Friday morning 8 of the clock.

Thursday, 26 November

The House did not meet this day, it being the day appointed for a Thanksgiving for the reducing of Ireland. But the Speaker went by himself, and the several members as they pleased, to St. Margaret's Church, Westminster, where Dr. Jane (Dean of Gloucester) preached before the House.

Friday, 27 November

Upon the report from the committee about transport ships, there was reported to be due to the persons concerned about £309,369.

The *Lord Colchester*, *Major Pery*, and *Mr. Norris* moved that the same might be referred to the Committee of the Whole House to whom the consideration of supplies for Their Majesties was referred.

But opposed by several old members, because this House could give no aids or supplies unless the King demanded them.

So after a long debate it was ordered that the report should lie on the Table. And the sense of the House was that the persons concerned might apply to His Majesty or the Privy Council, that the matter might come regularly before the House.

The petition from the clothiers of Gloucester was to the effect that they might trade with the Armenians and desiring they might not be barred from carrying cloth out of this kingdom. The other petition was from three widows concerned in the joint stock of the East India Company. Both which were referred to the Committee of the Whole House.

Then the House, according to the Order of the Day (which was read), resolved itself into a Committee of the Whole House to consider of the East India Company. So the Speaker left the Chair and Sir John Guise was called to the Table. Then the Order of the Day was read again. Then the two petitions, lately referred, were read. Then the accounts brought in by the Company of their stock and of their debts both in England and India were read.

Mr. Papillon spoke against the old Company very fully, both as to their miscarriages and to their inability to carry on the trade, and took several exceptions to their accounts—as that they had on the balance of their debts in England but £38,000 clear stock, as they bring in. It is true in India they have, as they say, above £800,000 clear, but it is a great way to disprove them; they put what value they please on the same. They have accounted for nothing of the charges of the war with the Great Mogul nor made any deductions for the returns they are to make of what they have plundered from his people. So that on the whole matter, I move you to establish a new company. Mr. Methuen to the same.

Sir John Thompson: I desire before we destroy the old Company, we may regulate abuses and establish rules for a new one.

Sir Thomas Littleton: I think this trade has been managed neither for the interest of the kingdom nor the Company itself. But what are you now doing? Will you punish men for crimes which have been pardoned by the late General Pardon? Besides, there are but a small number of men that have sinned, and will you punish many that are innocent for that? There are many widows and orphans concerned. But I think the most proper way, whether for the old or a new Company, is to establish certain rules and regulations of the same. There is one will go a great way to prevent the mischiefs, by avoiding plurality of voices on having many shares. This will prevent private contracts. It may be fit also to establish a member shall not have above such a sum in the Company.

Sir Henry Johnson and Sir Robert Clayton strongly against the old Company.

Sir Edward Seymour: I am for a new company to make this trade, which is become so large, to be as national as possible, which this present Company is not. Nor are they able to carry on the trade. For if they were, what makes them license ships to carry on so beneficial a trade? I shall move you, therefore, that we may address to His Majesty that he will be pleased to dissolve this Company according to the power reserved in the charter and that he will permit this House to regulate a new company.

Mr. Howe moved for leave to bring in a bill to regulate the old Company.

Mr. Methuen seconded Sir Edward Seymour's motion.

Mr. Neale moved to go on to regulate a company, whether old or new, and then to propose it to those that will give the most for it and apply it to the public service. It may raise £200,000 or £300,000.

Sir Richard Temple: I am for regulating the old Company, for they are able and sufficient to carry on the trade. Their stock is very great in India, which has lain a considerable time dead on their hands, but they have carried out great quantities of the manufactures of the nation.

Mr. Godolphin desired leave to bring in a bill to regulate the old Company.

Mr. Heneage Finch argued very largely against the old Company being not able to carry on the trade. They have in their accounts brought in nothing for the charge of the war, what prizes they have taken, and what they are to return again. So that they are incapable to manage the trade and it is impossible to regulate them for the good of the kingdom. I am, therefore, for making the address, as you have been moved, to dissolve the Company, and they have no injury for that the King may if he please dissolve them at any time giving them three years' time to fetch off their effects. And it appears their credit and reputation in those parts is very small. The Company, or at least the majority of them, is in the hands of 20 persons.

Sir Robert Howard: I am for a new company as large as may be; I would not exclude even the members of the old Company. And to prevent all clamour and injury to those concerned in the old Company, I am for dissolving the old Company and establishing a new one presently: that ships be fitted out and sent with all expedition, that all persons shall be admitted to be subscribers, that some persons on both sides shall be appointed on oath to value the effects of the old Company, and that whatever they have clear after all their debts are paid they shall be admitted to come into the new company with the same (though at three years' end) and have the same advantages as the new adventurers in the new company that went in at first. Hereby if they have any real stock, they will have the advantage of it; if only an imaginary one, they have cozened the nation long enough.

Sir Richard Temple: As to the objection of permission ships, that makes not against them, for it was in time of war and to trade to such places as the Company never did. I think the best way is to proceed to regulations first.

Sir Christopher Musgrave: I am for a new company, and there is no injury to them if the old Company be dissolved, for the Crown hath power at any time to dissolve them and give them three years' time to draw off their effects. The trade is now become a national concern and much greater than formerly, therefore fit to be lodged in more hands than now it is. Therefore, I am for the address to His Majesty that he would be pleased to dissolve the present Company.

Sir Robert Henley, Sir Edward Seymour, and Mr. Hutchinson against the old Company.

Sir Thomas Clarges: I am not for destroying the present Company and the rather for that whenever this business comes on, I see so many foreigners in the Lobby. It has been told you that this Company brought home four ships, the customs of which came to £50,000, and they tell you they are now sending out six ships more.

Mr. Holt and Sir George Hutchins were for the old Company.

So at last the question was put that this committee will in the next place proceed to the regulations of an East India Company by a joint stock. The [Committee of the Whole] House divided—Yeas to the right hand of the House and the Noes to the left.

Yeas Col. Granville 159

Tellers for the

Noes Col. Cornewall 128

So the Chairman was ordered to report to the House that the committee had made some progress on the petitions relating to the East India trade and to move to have leave to sit again.

So the Speaker resumed the Chair and *Sir John Guise* reported and moved as directed. Ordered that this committee shall sit again on Wednesday next.

So the House adjourned till tomorrow morning 8 of the clock.

Saturday, 28 November

Bill for regulating hackney coaches was carried on the question not to be now read.

Then *Sir Thomas Littleton*, according to order, presented to the House an estimate of the charge of the war in the Office of the Ordnance for land service for the year 1692. As also the *Lord Ranelagh* presented a list of the general officers and their pay, and an abstract of the establishment of Their Majesties' garrisons. Both which were read and referred to the Committee of the Whole House who are to consider of the supplies to be granted to Their Majesties.[1]

[1] Grey, x. 187 (misdated 27 Nov.) has a partial account of the debate that follows. See also *HMC Seventh Report*, p. 209.

Sir Thomas Clarges: In the lists presented you, particularly that of the garrisons, there is a charge of gunners and other persons in garrison. I hope the House when they voted 64,924 men intended they should serve all occasions, and not to have others added to them. Therefore, I desire to know whether there be any soldiers computed there, as also whether there be any general officer allotted for the service of Ireland for then he will come in under the establishment for Ireland.

Sir John Lowther: I cannot hear this without declaring myself freely. You have voted 64,924 men in which number no officers were included, and now you are going to strike off 11,000 men, which the officers come to, besides gunners and others in garrison here. You have already made a vote in reference to Ireland which I will not speak against, but if you do the same for the other places I will say England is undone. For my own part, I can share the common fate as well as others, but let gentlemen consider: here is not more money asked of you, for the pay of the officers is included in the particular sums brought in. I desire, therefore, we may strike off the residue of the forces in setting aside so many officers.

Sir Christopher Musgrave against that proposal.

Sir Henry Goodricke: I cannot but wonder at this debate. However, I think fit to acquaint you that the King himself has taken notice of your *Votes*. He pulled them out of his pocket in Council. And he has empowered us to say that he was resolved to make a descent in France, and withal that if you did strike off the number as proposed (and is done in Ireland by including the officers) you would spoil all His Majesty's designs and break all his measures and he can never go on further.

Mr. Cary to the same, and that the officers might not be included.

Sir John Thompson that they might.

Sir Robert Howard: I am for good husbandry as much as any but would not have our good husbandry ruin us. We had better give a little more rather than not do our work. I am not, therefore, for striking off so many men as the officers amount to, near 8,000 men.

Mr. Bathurst on the other side.

Sir Thomas Clarges: As to that of doing nothing in our fleet, I am informed it is impossible to be otherwise. If our fleet will lie still in the night and sail only in the day, which was the course of ours, it is indeed not possible to meet our enemies. But our merchantmen who sail in the night fell in with them. The last year you voted about

69,000 men, not including officers, and as they contrived it you paid for above 75,000 men, though as appears by the public accounts you had not 50,000 men. Then the manner of the debates now is irregular; it is not usual to hear the King's name used herein so as to influence our debates, which ought to be free, and therefore I desire we may go into a committee.

Sir Joseph Williamson for excluding the officers out of the number.

Paul Foley: I never saw such things done in a House as has been done this day. To say if we do not comply we shall break the King's measures, this is wholly irregular.

Mr. Francis Robartes: I desire this matter may be referred to a committee. And since His Majesty has been more plain to us, I desire we may alter our minds and come up to what he thinks fit.

Sir John Guise: The question now is come to this—whether we shall be irregular (as some pretend) or else be unsafe. I believe no one will be against going on what is for our safety, and therefore I desire we may not strike off 6,000 or 7,000 men.

Lord Ranelagh: The number in dispute is 7,386 men, officers—the sum and charge whereof amounts to but £89,875, besides in which is above £5,000 for the officers' servants.

Sir Thomas Clarges: The method of bringing in this is very extraordinary, and therefore I am against it. This is a way to ask money when the King does not. As to the officers, it is pretended but such a number, which cannot be known now, for I hope we may bring our companies to be 100 effective men; they have been so formerly.

Mr. Bale: I am for complying with the number desired.

Sir Joseph Tredenham and *Mr. Comptroller Wharton* to the same, for that the eyes of all Europe are upon you and the fate not only of this kingdom but all Christendom depend thereon.

Sir Edward Seymour: I look on it that messages brought from the King after this manner are wholly irregular and strike at all freedom of speech—this as to your method. But now to the matter; I think you have either given too few men or too many. If no descent be intended, you have given too many; if it is, you have given too few. Therefore, I would not stand out for so few men. Since we have gone so far, I am not for sticking at these numbers but desire the question may be put for having so many men exclusive of officers. *Sir Henry Capel* and *Mr. Hampden* to the same.

Sir Christopher Musgrave against it and *Sir John Thompson* too, for that we must show the King we are not able to bear these loads.

I think our King has too much fire and spirit, that we cannot come up to it.

So the question was put that it be an instruction to the Committee of the Whole House etc. that the number of the land forces which His Majesty has been pleased to signify he thinks necessary to be continued in England, Scotland, the West Indies, and to be transported beyond sea for the service of the year 1692 do consist of private soldiers (not including officers) making up that number. The House divided—the Yeas went forth.[1]

		Sir John Guise	
	Yeas		176
		Mr. Cary	
Tellers for the			
		Sir John Thompson	
	Noes		151
		Mr. Travers	

So carried in the affirmative.

Then *Sir John Lowther* moved that the Speaker might leave the Chair and that the House might resolve into a Committee of the Whole House.

So the *Speaker* put the question whether he should leave the Chair. And a debate arising, *he* ordered the Noes to go out. Which being disputed and a debate likely to arise, *he* that first moved it quitted his motion; so the House did not divide.

Resolved that this House would take into consideration on Thursday next the state of the nation. And the supplies for Their Majesties to be considered on Monday next.

So the House adjourned till Monday morning 8 of the clock.

Monday, 30 November

The several amendments made by the Lords to the bill for the Irish oaths were read. To the first, the House agreed.

To the second, that for allowing Popish lawyers a licence to practise on their taking the oath of allegiance only, *Sir Thomas Clarges* and *Sir Joseph Tredenham* were for agreeing to the clause.[2]

---

[1] This division is not recorded in the *Journal*.
[2] Grey, x. 188–90 has a parallel account of the debate on the Irish bill.

Mr. Levinge, Sir Richard Reynell, and *Mr. Hampden* against it, for that now the government began to be settled, and here you will go and unsettle it again.

Mr. Hampden: I think we ought to have a conference with the Lords to have the Articles of Limerick before us.

Sir Thomas Clarges: I am for this bill with this clause, and the rather for that I am informed some are for throwing out the bill which I am not. For this bill is to obtain what you never had in that kingdom since the Reformation—an English Protestant parliament—and then this is only for such as are now in being.

Mr. Montagu: I am against this clause until we know on what grounds the Lords went. If there be anything about the Articles of Limerick, I desire we may see them. I am informed the Lords had them before them, and if you have a conference they will acquaint you therewith.

Mr. Howe: I am for the clause and that because I would not break the public faith.

Solicitor General: I am against your agreeing with the Lords till we know on what terms the Lords did it. *Mr. Bathurst* to the same.

Paul Foley: I am for agreeing with the clause, and the rather because there is no more in the bill. I expected all the Articles of Limerick to be confirmed therein but this act gives them no more privilege than they had in King Charles II's time.

Sir Robert Sawyer, Mr. Greenfield, and *Thomas Wyndham* against the clause.

So at last the question was put for agreeing with the Lords in this amendment but carried clearly in the negative.

Then another clause was tendered, empowering two justices to tender the oaths to any person. And a clause was offered by *Sir Peter Colleton, Mr. Bowyer, Mr. Clarke,* etc., to excuse the Quakers from taking the oaths on making and subscribing the same. And the said clause was read thrice and agreed to. So the whole clause was passed and to stand part of the bill.

Then the clause added by the Lords to empower the King to dispense with this law was read and disagreed unto by the House.

Then the House agreed to have a conference with the Lords upon the said bill and named a committee to draw up reasons to be offered at the conference, and the committee were to meet tomorrow morning at 8 of the clock.

Mr. Price Devereux, a new member chosen for the town of Montgomery in Wales (in the room of Col. Herbert, deceased), came into the House, took the oaths at the Table and the declaration, and so sat in the House.

Then the Order of the Day was read. So the House resolved into a Committee of the Whole House to consider of supplies to be granted to Their Majesties, the Speaker leaving the Chair and the Solicitor was called to take his place at the Table as Chairman.

Mr. Howe: We are now in a committee in order to vote a sum of money to supply the charges of the war for the next year. I desire, therefore, we may come up to what is necessary for the service, and that because I would have nothing to stick at our door.

Mr. Hampden: I desire we may go upon the other particulars brought in for the land forces, and that head by head.

Then the estimate brought in of the general officers was read.

Mr. Dutton Colt and Sir John Lowther moved to agree to the whole list as brought in without alteration.

Mr. Harley: I desire this paper may be referred to a particular committee to examine, as the estimates of the fleet were.

Sir Robert Cotton: I am for continuing the general officers as they were the last year.

Paul Foley: Your land army has cost you these three last years as much again as your fleet. The war in general hath been very great and chargeable, occasioned by your great allowances to general officers—the establishments that are now being much advanced, and by comparing them with former you will find they are come to an exorbitant height. The House of Commons in 1677 thought it worth their while to settle an establishment. If you will do so now, money may be saved, in order to which whether you will do it in this committee or refer it to a private committee I leave it to you. Sir John Thompson to the same.

Lord Ranelagh: The charge is not now so high as heretofore. The late Duke of Schomberg had £10 a day which was continued afterwards to General Ginkel, but this is now taken away and nothing charged in the present estimate for him. There are two generals—one of horse, the other of foot—both which have but £6 a day apiece, which no one can think too much considering the great charge they are at and the figure they make.

Sir Thomas Clarges: I was in good hopes when the Crown came to us for aids they would have left us to consider what our troops and companies should consist of, what the pay of generals and other officers should be. The charge brought in is very great, and I doubt not £150,000 may be saved by good management. I, therefore, desire it may be referred to a private committee.

Sir John Lowther: I wish the advice of saving your money had been given at first. All persons seem to applaud the behaviour of your officers, and will you now cast this reflection upon them as to bring in a new discipline amongst them? And I am afraid of the consequences thereof.

Sir Robert Cotton (of Chester): I am for considering the condition of the nation and to see in what condition you are—whether able to bear such a charge. And therefore I desire it may be referred to a select committee.

Henry Herbert and Mr. Charles Montagu were for agreeing to the list of general officers.

Sir Peter Colleton: I am for carrying on a vigorous war against France but at this rate we shall never be able to carry it on. I am for saving your money and therefore to refer it to a committee.

Sir John Guise: I desire we may pass a vote to agree with these estimates.

Sir Christopher Musgrave: I must say the pay now to the army in England is much advanced to what formerly. A colonel is now come to 40s. a day. But now it is objected against regulating the pay of the army because we did it not formerly. Then we were fond of it, but now it is because we are not able to bear it. But if gentlemen intend to agree with all the particulars as brought in, it is best then to lump it; but if not, to refer it to a private committee.

Sir Thomas Clarges: I am for referring these matters to a particular committee that we may compare the present establishment with those heretofore.

Col. Austen: I desire we may proceed to consider the same in this Committee of the Whole House. It may be done here as well.

Sir John Lowther: I will be clear in this matter. I am not for altering your establishment this year but continue it as now brought in.

Mr. Palmes: I am for inspecting into matters, though it is true some gentlemen will take away our liberty of advising and considering of these things, and therefore I am for a private committee.

Sir Charles Sedley: I am for going on as we may hold and not for precipitating matters—not to ride at the same rate for 100 miles as a citizen does if he were going but to Islington. This is like to be a long war so that you must be as saving as you can. The French carry it on with much less charge than we do. I desire, therefore, we may refer it to a private committee to save what may be.

Sir Thomas Littleton: I am against delaying this matter any longer. You have lost several days already, and therefore I desire we may now consider of the estimates.

Sir Robert Sawyer for referring them to a particular committee.

Mr. Hampden: I see no person offers anything against the general officers, either that they are too many or that their pay is too great, that would have been proper to refer to a committee. And we might have here debated it and it would have been determined in less time than this now, and therefore I desire we may proceed on it now.

Sir William Strickland: I desire the establishment and all the estimates may be referred to a particular committee.

Goodwin Wharton: Though we are not all generals, yet we are sent hither to advise of matters. The King's name ought not to be used in this House to influence our debates, which ought to be free, and therefore I desire all may be referred to a particular committee.

Sir Henry Goodricke: I am for dispatching the head of general officers now, but the other heads perhaps may be proper for a private committee.

Col. Granville was for referring all the estimates to a private committee.

Mr. Comptroller Wharton to the same, and the rather for that it is most methodical.

So the committee resolved that the House be moved to appoint a committee to consider of the list of the land forces as to all except those appointed for Ireland, as also the list of the general officers and the estimate of the Ordnance and the abstract of the establishment of the garrisons, and to report their opinions therein to the House. He [the Chairman] was also directed to move the House to sit again.

So the Speaker resumed the Chair and the *Solicitor* in his place made those two motions. On the first, a committee was named accordingly to whom the estimates were referred, and to meet at 4 this afternoon. And for the second, the House resolved to sit again tomorrow morning upon the supplies.

The *Speaker* acquainted the House that he had received two letters from one William Fuller, a prisoner in the King's Bench, intimating he had great discoveries to make to this House in relation to the plot wherein Crone was concerned and in matters that relate to the safety of the King and his government. And it was ordered to be considered of when the state of the nation comes on upon Thursday next.

So the House adjourned till 8 tomorrow morning.

Tuesday, 1 December

The engrossed bill from the Lords to enable the executors and trustees of Sir Thomas Putt to lease divers lands passed the House, and Mr. Christie was ordered to carry it up to the Lords.

The *Chairman* of the Committee of Elections [Sir John Trenchard] reported the case of the election of the borough of Chippenham in Wiltshire and the resolution of the committee thereon, viz.: That Sir Basil Firebrace is duly elected a burgess to serve in this present parliament for the borough of Chippenham. And the question being put that the House do agree with the committee in the said resolution, the House divided—the Noes went out.

		Sir Robert Davers	
	Yeas		147
		Mr. Gwyn	
Tellers for the			
		Mr. Papillon	
	Noes		151
		Sir Walter Yonge	

So carried in the negative.

Then the question was put that Sir Humphrey Edwin is duly elected a burgess to serve in this present parliament for the borough of Chippenham, and it passed in the negative.

Then resolved that the said election is a void election. So ordered that the Speaker issue his warrant to the Clerk of the Crown to make out a new writ for the election of a burgess in the said borough in the room of Mr. Kent, deceased.

The *Chairman* also reported the case of Aldeburgh election and that the committee had resolved William Johnson esq. to be duly chosen a burgess for that borough. And the question being put to agree with the committee in the said resolution, it passed in the affirmative.

Goodwin Wharton, Sir Richard Onslow, and *Sir William Strickland* moved about the election of Chippenham that since bribery had been proved on both sides, the House would pass a vote to incapacitate both parties to be elected a burgess to serve in this present parliament—but it was let fall.

Mr. Paul Foley presented to the House from the Commissioners for taking the Public Accounts a book of the state of the incomes and issues of the public revenue from 5 November 1688 to Michaelmas 1691 with their observations thereon. Which he delivered in at the Table, where the same were read.[1]

Sir John Thompson: You have a matter here before you of great concern. The King himself is wholly ignorant of these matters, and therefore I think we ought to address to the King to acquaint him therewith. The way is to pass an act to appoint these gentlemen to be Commissioners again for the next year, with some further powers.

Sir Charles Sedley to the same, that the King might be acquainted with these matters. He keeps at Kensington and the courtiers keep him there as in a box.

Sir Edward Seymour: I think these gentlemen have discharged their parts very well and are the only persons that deserve their salary in your accounts. You see what great sums have been given to idle persons who sleep at home whilst we are not able to bear this war longer. I desire we may consider of these matters. I cannot at present speak to particulars, but let the book lie on the Table and be pleased to appoint a day to examine into the same on Thursday next and that you will order all your members to attend the service of the House on pain of incurring the displeasure of the same. *Lord Castleton, Sir Edward Hussey, Mr. Palmes*, and *Sir Richard Onslow* to the same.

So the House ordered to take into consideration the said state and observations on Thursday morning next and nothing to intervene. Ordered, no member do take the said book out of the House.

Leave was given to Mr. Finch to attend a cause in the House of Lords.

Several motions were made to add divers particular persons to several committees.

Ordered that the House on Friday next will resolve into a Committee of the [Whole] House to consider of ways to raise supplies for Their Majesties.

Adjourned till 8 tomorrow morning.

---

[1] The report is printed in *HMC House of Lords MSS.*, 1690–1, pp. 356–401, 404–8.

Wednesday, 2 December

The petition of William Hallyday about the East India Company was against the same, that they might not suffer the Armenians to trade to India in their permission ships, being very prejudicial to the trade of the woollen manufacture.

The Order of the Day being read, the House resolved itself into a Committee of the Whole House to consider about the East India Company and Sir John Guise was called to the Chair.

Sir Edward Seymour then presented the House with several heads, for a regulation of a company trading to the East Indies to be established by act of parliament.

And to the first head, it was much debated whether they should limit the stock to consist of such a sum and not exceeding such a sum.

Sir Samuel Barnardiston: I think it is necessary to establish a stock whether you fix the old or a new Company. You can't have less than £1,500,000—one-third part to be in India, another in England, and the other trading to and from India.

Mr. Methuen and Sir Robert Sawyer, Sir Robert Clayton and Mr. Papillon desired to have such a stock. But Mr. John Howe, Mr. Neale and Serj. Blencowe, Mr. Montagu and Sir Thomas Clarges against it. And it held a long debate. Some were for the stock to be unlimited. Others against employing so great a stock for that it would destroy the other trade of the nation as the Turkey, Hamburg, etc. It would also be a mischievous trade, it bringing in so great a quantity of silks which would ruin all our woollen manufacture. It is a trade pernicious to the nation; it is a trade that carries out much of the bullion and brings back little that is useful except a few spices, as pepper, etc., and some saltpetre, but the generality of the trade is silks, etc., which minister to the luxury of the nation and take away wearing your woollen manufactures. So on the whole, most agreed it had been better the trade had never been found out. But since it was, we must carry it on to prevent other nations from engrossing the same. So at last the question was put and resolved:

1. That it is the opinion of this committee that a sum not less than £1,500,000 and not exceeding £2,000,000 is a fund necessary to carry on the East India trade in a joint stock.

2. That no one person shall have any share in a joint stock for the East India trade exceeding £5,000, either in his own name or the name of any others for him.

3. That no one person shall have above one vote in a company trading to the East Indies and that each person that hath £500 in it shall have one vote.

4. That the company trading to the East Indies shall be obliged to export every year in their trade of goods being of the growth and manufacture of this nation to the value of £100,000 at least.

5. That no private contract shall be made but all goods sold at public sales by inch of candle, except saltpetre to the Crown.

6. That the East India Company be obliged to sell the King saltpetre double refined not exceeding four or five per cent refraction— 500 ton at £30 per ton.

7. That no lots shall be put up at one time of above £500.

8. That the East India trade shall be managed by a governor, deputy governor, and 24 committees[1] to be chosen annually by a general court of the members.

9. That no person shall be governor or deputy governor in the company who hath less share in the stock than £2,000 or a committeeman that hath less than £1,000.

10. That no person shall be governor or deputy governor of the company above two years in seven.

11. That the election of governor, deputy governor, and committees of the company be made every year.

Then the Speaker resumed the Chair and *Sir John Guise* reported that the committee had made some farther progress in the matter about the East India trade and had directed him to move to sit again. Resolved that the House would resolve itself into a Committee of the Whole House on Monday next to consider of the same.

Divers members upon motion were added to several committees.

Sir Francis Blake and *Sir Charles Sedley* acquainted the House that they had received letters from one William Fuller (a prisoner in the King's Bench) that he had matters of great importance relating to the safety of the King and this government to acquaint this House with, desiring he might be brought before them to that purpose.

Ordered that he be brought to the Bar of the House on Saturday next by the Marshal of the King's Bench.

Adjourned till 8 tomorrow morning.

---

[1] i.e. committee-men.

Thursday, 3 December

The bill for relief of the orphans was read the first time, but exceptions were taken to it by several members. Some moved to throw it out, as *Sir Edward Seymour, Mr. Methuen, Sir Christopher Musgrave, Mr. Dutton Colt,* and *Sir Joseph Tredenham,* for that it is a bill that lays a tax upon all the neighbouring counties—imposing a duty of 1*d.* a quarter upon corn, a tax upon every chaldron of coals coming to the port of London, the farm of hackney coaches—to the paying the interest of the orphans' money, and that for ever. Then, it came in irregularly for that it ought to have come from a Committee of the Whole House, being laying a tax on the King's subjects.

Sir George Treby, Sir Thomas Clarges, Sir Robert Cotton (of Chester), and *Sir Robert Clayton* desired that they would not throw it out, but let it lie on the Table to be amended as they saw occasion.

So ordered to lie on the Table.

Sir Thomas Clarges desired in behalf of the Commissioners of the Accounts that they might have the direction of the House, the Lords having sent to them (who are all members of this House) to have the said accounts brought before them.

The House would make no order in it. But the sense of the House was that the Commissioners might send their secretary to attend them with it since the act of parliament had given them a power to demand it. (But I think that was not so regular.)

Then the Order of the Day for taking into consideration of the public accounts was read.[1]

Sir John Thompson: The accounts are very amazing to me. We have the best of kings but he is in hands that do not understand their business. We were told the last sessions we did not understand some matters but by the accounts brought in I think it is plain the Lords of the Treasury do not understand their business. Therefore, I think they are not fit for the place. There are great sums for secret service of which you have no account brought in. I shall move you, therefore, that everyone may clear himself, and I will begin with myself: I do declare I never had any place or pension nor ever will.

Sir John Lowther: I will close with that gentleman's motion and I hope the King in a little time will give me leave to retire. But I do not wonder that a gentleman should be so warm who I heard not long

---

[1] For parallel accounts of the debate on the report of the Commission see Grey, x. 191–200; Bodleian Carte MS. 130, f. 330.

CORRIGENDA

page 59, line 3 and footnote 1: *for* Perrera, *read* Pereira
page 68, line 22: *for* Dunsmore, *read* Dunmore
page 70, lines 31 and 33: *for* Dunbarton, *read* Dumbarton
page 495, line 21: *for* 1699, *read* 1689
page 499, line 4: *for* 1071, *read* 1701
page 501, lines 13 and 14: *for* Ordance, *read* Ordnance

since accused at your Bar for drinking King James's health. But now as to your accounts, I must tell you there are several mistakes therein. Some material things are omitted, as the account of Perrera the Jew,[1] those of the Navy. And on the whole matter, I am very willing that gentleman should come in my place.

Sir John Thompson: I have observed, touch a sore place and it will wince.[2] I do as before declare I never did nor ever will receive any pension. I wish that gentleman would say the same.

Sir Thomas Clarges: I did expect after what that honourable gentleman had said that spoke last but one we should have been called to the Bar as delinquents. We took all possible care in our inquiry and have discharged the trust to the best of our judgements. As for our discretions, which that gentleman questions, no man can have more than God has given him, and if we have not so much as that gentleman we cannot help it. I desire we may go regularly on the book and read the observations head by head, and then any gentleman may say what he has to them.

Sir Robert Rich: I should have been glad if that honourable gentleman who spoke last but two would, amongst his other weighty affairs, [have] spent some time with us and informed us how we should have proceeded and let us have known our duty and we would have followed it. But I think that gentleman hath not done well with us. He has in effect said we throw dust in the eyes of the House, which without doors is to call us little less than knaves, but only he hath put it in softer words.

Mr. Hampden stood up in a heat and called to the orders of the House, matters growing high between Rich and Sir John Lowther.

Mr. John Howe and *Mr. Bertie* desired matters might be compromised and that no further notice should be taken of what said in the House, and the sense of the House was so accordingly.

Mr. Done: Mr. Harbord had £180,000 for provisions for the army and has not brought in an account of above £4,000 or £5,000 laid out.

Sir Christopher Musgrave: I desire to know what is the reason the Commissioners had not the accounts brought into them sooner.

Sir Thomas Clarges: We did send out above 300 precepts requiring the several accountants to bring in the same, the last of which were returnable in June last, but we could not get them. We have done our parts but some of them we could not get at all, several of them are very imperfect, some of them contain divers volumes and were

---

[1] Perrera was a victualler.   [2] 'winch' in MS.

brought in but since your order so not possible for us to look over them. So that you have our accounts as perfect as we can make them in the time required of us.

Sir Christopher Musgrave: I cannot but take notice of our unhappiness and the misery we lie under. Here are some accounts not brought in in two or three years.

Sir Thomas Clarges, Sir Robert Rich, Sir Samuel Barnardiston, Sir Peter Colleton informed the House that most of the accounts of the House-hold, the Navy, Treasury, and the duplicates of the aids you gave are not yet brought in—some of which have not been brought in these 20 years. That there was very ill management in the accounts so that it is impossible to give you a clear account.

Then the House proceeded to read the Commissioners' observations and came to several resolutions upon divers of them.

Upon the fifth [that several officials with great salaries now make the King pay the charge of passing their patents and accounts at great cost]:

Paul Foley: We made not this observation without great reason, and if you please to have a list of such persons who, having great salaries, have made the King pay the charge of their patents and of passing their accounts—nay, even have made him pay the taxes charged on them for their salaries—we will give you account thereof.

Sir Thomas Clarges: No fees ought to be taken but such as are from time immemorial or have been established by act of parliament. We have seen great fees and such as are fit for your consideration.

So ordered that the Commissioners of Accounts lay before this House a list of such persons.

Upon the sixth [that recently those with great salaries have had them increased without good reasons and their bills of expenses have had easy allowance]:

Paul Foley: The Receiver General of the Customs particularly has of late got his salary increased £300 per annum. It was but £1,000 per annum formerly; now it is made £1,300, and he has incident bills of charges of £300 or £400 per quarter easily allowed.

Ordered that the said Commissioners lay before this House the particulars of this sixth head.

Upon the seventh [sinecures]:

Paul Foley: The salary to the Auditors of the Fee Farm Rents is still continued though that revenue is quite gone—as particular, Mr. Shales hath £200 per annum paid to him though the reason thereof is gone.

Ordered to have the particulars upon this seventh head.

Upon the eighth [receivers lending the King's own balances to him at interest]: Ordered the Commissioners do give a list of such persons who have lent the King his own money and made him pay interest for the same.

Upon the ninth [that it has been impossible to secure a full account of government payments to M.P.s, especially out of secret service funds]:

Paul Foley: We were told we should have no account of that money for secret service.

Sir Charles Sedley: I think we ought to have an account of this, and I see no reason against it.

Sir William Strickland: I am for every man in this House laying his hand on his heart and declare as I do that he hath had no part of this money. And therefore I desire we may vote such persons betrayers of their country and enemies to the King and kingdom.

Mr. Bertie, Mr. Goodwin Wharton, Sir Robert Sawyer, and *Lord Castleton* much to the same, and said if there be any such men among us I pray God bless King William and Queen Mary.

Mr. Comptroller Wharton and *Sir Robert Rich* informed the House that they had discourse with Mr. Jephson[1] when living, and that he had upon some occasions declared there were not above four persons in this House had received those moneys for secret service and that what they had was not for their own use but to dispose of to some persons employed to make discoveries for Their Majesties' service which it was absolutely necessary to conceal.

So this matter fell, having occasioned warm debates.

Upon the eleventh [excessive and illegal fees]: Ordered the Commissioners bring in a list of such persons who exact great fees without any legal precedent.

Adjourned till tomorrow morning 8 of the clock.

Friday, 4 December

The House, according to order, resolved into a Committee of the Whole House to consider of ways to raise the supplies, and a land tax was proposed. Then a great debate was whether it should be by a pound rate or by a monthly assessment. The members that served

---

[1] Late Secretary to the Treasury.

for the associated counties[1] laboured hard to have it by a pound rate of 3*s.* in the pound, which they urged to be the more equal tax. And for the monthly assessment, they were not able to bear it, particularly the counties of Norfolk and Suffolk—the members for which informed the House they paid 7*s.* and 8*s.* in the pound to that tax, which was very unequal. But the majority of the House, especially the western and northern members, being for a land tax by a monthly assessment, it was carried for the same. So the same tax of £1,651,702. 18*s.* was voted for this year as was the last, to commence from 25th of December 1691.

So the Speaker resumed the Chair and the *Solicitor General* reported the same to the House, to which they agreed. Resolved this House will resolve into a committee tomorrow to consider of further ways to raise supplies for Their Majesties. Ordered that a bill be prepared and brought in according to the said resolutions, and a committee was named to prepare and bring in the same.

Sir Charles Wyndham acquainted the House that he had received a letter from Edward Batten which contained matters of importance, which he delivered in at the Table.

And being read, it was dated 23 November 1691 and reflected upon the Lords of the Admiralty. But it being looked on as a frivolous matter, nothing was done thereon.

Adjourned till 8 tomorrow morning.

Saturday, 5 December

Sir Thomas Clarges reported from the conference with the Lords that they had attended the Lords and their Lordships had agreed to the bill with an amendment allowing the lawyers in that kingdom to practice their profession. That they had also delivered reasons for their disagreement in that particular and had delivered them the Articles for the surrender of Limerick.

So the Articles were read, after some debate whether [they] could be read in the House, being not read at the conference.[2]

Sir Thomas Clarges: The clause as sent down by the Lords is larger than the Article for the surrender of Limerick, and therefore I am against your agreeing therewith and that you would consider very

---

[1] The counties of the Civil War Eastern Association?
[2] Grey, x. 200–2 has a parallel account of the debate that follows.

well before you confirm it by act of parliament. *Sir John Lowther, Sir Richard Reynell*, and *Mr. Levinge* to the same.

Sir Thomas Clarges: I desire two or three members that managed the conference may withdraw and compare the clause in the bill and the Articles together to see if they agree and report the same to the House. *Sir Richard Temple* to the same.

But it was opposed by *Sir Christopher Musgrave* and *Mr. Hampden*, being the most regular way was to examine it here in the House and not refer it to a committee.

So after some debate it was moved by *Montagu, Sir Richard Temple*, and *Sir Thomas Clarges* to adjourn the debate that the House might consider further of it.

So it was adjourned till Monday next.

Col. Austen informed the House that the Lords had sent to the Commissioners of the Accounts for the accounts. And they being members of this House desired their direction whether they should send to them a copy of their observations, too.

Sir Christopher Musgrave: I am against your Commissioners giving the Lords a copy of their observations. The accounts they are obliged to give them by the act of parliament, but their observations are no part of the account but made by a particular order of this House.

So the general sense of the House was not to let them have the observations, but they would not make any order therein.

Then the Order of the Day for going into a Committee of the Whole House upon the excise bill was read and the Speaker left the Chair, the Solicitor to it. So they proceeded on the bill, first postponing the preamble, and were going on. But the Solicitor having not his papers about the rates of the beer, ale, etc., the Speaker resumed the Chair. And they resolved to sit again on Monday next in a Committee of the Whole House to go on with the said bill.

So the House adjourned till 8 [o'clock][1] on Monday morning.

Monday, 7 December

Leave given to Serj. Tremaine, Mr. Finch, and the Solicitor General to attend a cause in the House of Lords.

Then the Order of the Day for going into a Committee of the Whole House upon the excise bill was read. So the Speaker left the

---

[1] In MS. 'a clock'. Not hereafter noted.

Chair and Mr. Solicitor was called to be Chairman. So they postponed the preamble, then began on the first clause, filling up the blanks in each clause. So to the rest and made several amendments therein and finished the bill.

Then Sir Thomas Clarges offered a clause to excuse both the Universities from paying any excise for the future.

It was read once. And a question being put to read it again, the committee divided—Yeas on the right hand and Noes on the left.

Yeas 109
Noes 88

So it was read a second time. And another question was put, if it should stand part of the bill. The committee divided.

Yeas 117
Noes 106

So it was passed and ordered to stand part of the bill.

Then another clause was tendered, enjoining that the brewer should not raise the price of his drink nor lessen the measure above what in 1690. But on the question it was rejected.

Then another clause was tendered, to exclude excise men or those concerned therein to intermeddle with elections of members to parliament from and after the 2nd of February next under the penalty of £100, which was ordered accordingly.

Then the preamble of the bill was agreed to. So the Solicitor was ordered to report the committee had gone through the said bill.

Then the Speaker resumed the Chair and the *Solicitor* acquainted the House they had finished the bill and had made several amendments and that he was ready to report the same. Ordered to be reported tomorrow morning.

Adjourned till 8 tomorrow morning.

Tuesday, 8 December

Sir Thomas Clarges acquainted the House with the variance between the amendments made by the Lords to the bill about the oaths in Ireland and the Articles about Limerick and then moved that some amendments might be made to the Lords' amendments and offered a new clause for enrolling the names of all persons who are to take the benefit of those Articles.

So after some debate, the managers of the former conference were ordered to prepare some amendments to the Lords' amendments and also reasons to be offered at a conference with the Lords upon the same.

Mr. Serj. Trenchard, Chairman, reported from the Committee of Elections etc. the case touching the election for the borough of Ludlow in Shropshire with the resolutions of the committee thereon:

1. That Silius Titus esq. is duly elected a burgess to serve in this present parliament for the said borough. And the question being put, the House divided—the Noes went out.

<table>
<tr><td></td><td>Col. Granville</td><td></td></tr>
<tr><td>Yeas</td><td></td><td>191</td></tr>
<tr><td></td><td>Mr. Palmes</td><td></td></tr>
<tr><td>Tellers for the</td><td></td><td></td></tr>
<tr><td></td><td>Mr. Bickerstaffe</td><td></td></tr>
<tr><td>Noes</td><td></td><td>145</td></tr>
<tr><td></td><td>Mr. Kynaston</td><td></td></tr>
</table>

2. That Francis Lloyd esq. is duly elected a burgess to serve in this parliament, etc., to which the House agreed.

Then the *Chairman* reported the case of the election of the borough of Tavistock in Devon: That Sir Francis Drake is duly elected a burgess to serve in this present parliament for the said borough—to which the House agreed.

Then the *Chairman* reported the case touching the double return and election for the borough of Dunwich in the county of Suffolk and the resolutions of the committee thereon:

1. That the right of election for that borough is not in the freemen of the said borough, commonly called outsitters, as well as in the freemen inhabiting in the said borough. The House divided—the Noes went out.

<table>
<tr><td></td><td>Sir Thomas Darcy</td><td></td></tr>
<tr><td>Yeas</td><td></td><td>237</td></tr>
<tr><td></td><td>Mr. Bickerstaffe</td><td></td></tr>
<tr><td>Tellers for the</td><td></td><td></td></tr>
<tr><td></td><td>Sir Robert Rich</td><td></td></tr>
<tr><td>Noes</td><td></td><td>119</td></tr>
<tr><td></td><td>Col. Granville</td><td></td></tr>
</table>

2. That the right of election for that borough is only in the freemen inhabiting within the said borough.

3. That John Bence esq. is duly elected a burgess to serve in the present parliament for the said borough.

To all which the House agreed.

The *Solicitor General* reported the bill for the double excise with the amendments. But the proviso for excusing the two Universities from paying any excise admitted a debate. And objected against it that it was brought in irregularly, being brought into the committee at first and not referred to them from the House, for it not only excuses the Universities from this present double excise but from all former excise established by preceding acts of parliament, all which this would repeal. But said on the other side that it was only declaratory what and how far the former laws extended, and it was the excise men [who] stretched the laws to extend to the Universities and thereby make them public alehouses when they were but in a manner private families and could not be thought retailers of ale and beer.

So the question being put upon this clause whether to stand part of this bill, the House divided—Yeas went out (because to repeal former laws).

	Sir Robert Cotton (of the Post Office)	
Yeas		94
	Mr. Charles Montagu	
Tellers for the		
	Sir Walter Yonge	
Noes		121
	Mr. Freke	

So this clause was thrown out and the bill was ordered to be engrossed with the other amendments.

Sir Ralph Dutton presented the House a paper, being an abstract of depositions concerning a trade carried on between the island of Jersey and the French. And it was suggested that the witness to prove the same had been threatened and menaced.

He was ordered to be called in.

Then some of the Privy Council informed the House that they did believe a trade had been carried on as was suggested and that His Majesty had granted a commission empowering several persons to inquire thereof and of other matters in that island.

So the witness came into the House. And being asked by the *Speaker* who menaced himself, he gave an account of no such thing. So the matter was let fall.

Adjourned till 8 tomorrow morning.

Wednesday, 9 December

The Attorney General and Mr. Finch, being members of this House, had leave of the House to attend a cause in the House of Lords.

The bill for the sale of lands of one Mr. Roberts in Leicestershire was read the first time and ordered a second reading.[1]

Mr. Bence, a new member for the borough of Dunwich, came into the House up to the Table, and took the oaths and test there and subscribed his name, and sat in the House.

Then the House went to consider of the state of the nation. And being informed the Marshal of the King's Bench attended with William Fuller, the said William Fuller was called in to the Bar and asked what information he had to give to the House. He then desired to be examined by a private committee, which the House was against. Then he took out some papers, being a narrative of what he had to acquaint the House with, which he read, and was in general to the effect following.[2]

That he was employed in carrying intelligence to and from England into France. That he carried several letters to the late King James and Queen Mary in which the Earl of Aylesbury was said to be a friend to them and the French King and that 30,000 men would rise when an opportunity offered. That there was one letter from the Lord Feversham, another from the Earl of Lichfield desiring the French might land here in June or July next, another from the Earl of Huntingdon, another from the Lord Preston, another from the Lord Peterborough, another from the Lord Castlemaine, another from the Lord Arran out of Scotland that 10,000 men in those parts would do more good than 30,000 in the south. There was another from the Lord Montgomery. The Lord Salisbury also sent bills for £4,000 for that service to Father Emmanuel, who was a person much trusted by the French King and had spies in the Council and in the Secretary's office whereby he had intelligence when there were any warrants out against him.

The late Queen Mary named the Lord Godolphin to me that I should apply to if I was taken and that he was a friend to King James and gave intelligence of transactions in the Council. That there were 23,000 men already listed for King James and to assist the French.

He desired the protection of the House for himself and two persons

---

[1] The reading of this bill is not recorded in the *Journal*.

[2] For parallel accounts of Fuller's testimony and the subsequent debate see Grey, x. 202–6; Bodleian Carte MS. 130, f. 333.

more who would confirm much that he had said—nay, that would produce some of the original papers under those persons' hands.

Then Fuller was ordered to withdraw.

Mr. Chadwick: The gentleman has named my father,[1] the Archbishop of Canterbury, very often. I do believe this fellow may know somewhat of a plot but not so much as he pretends. He came several times to my father, desiring to be brought to the Lord Portland to discover matters. But whenever you came to fix a time or place for him to come to, he always shuffled and could never be brought to anything. I believe you will find him a shuffling fellow.

Sir John Guise: I believe you will find him a great rascal for I have that character of him from one Morisco. He has personated several persons beyond sea and cheated divers of great sums of money.

Then Fuller was called in to know what further he had to acquaint the House with. Then he acquainted the House that there was an address signed by several lords and gentlemen in February 1690/1 unto the King of France in behalf of King James to restore him and that they would be ready to assist him. It was signed by the Archbishop of Canterbury (the late one), Duke of Beaufort, Duke of Northumberland, Marquess of Halifax, Earls of Mulgrave, Clarendon, Aylesbury, Winchilsea, Lichfield, Lords Weymouth, Dartmouth, Castlemaine, Arran, Dunsmore, Clifford, Middleton, Preston, Bishops of Durham and Ely, Sir Edward Hales, William Penn, Rowland Tempest, Sir John Fenwick, Sir James Smith.

So ordered again to withdraw.

Sir Charles Sedley moved that the House would send and secure all his papers to prevent any tricks. And some others to the same purpose, but after some debate it went off.

Then he was called in and asked some questions, to which he gave the following account.

That he had some money from this government for his services. He had £100 from the Lord Nottingham when he went for Ireland, £100 from the Lord Shrewsbury formerly when he went for France, but never any from the Lord Sidney. He declared he laid out £1,500 in the service of this government in France, Flanders, and Ireland. He said he was page to the late Queen Mary in France. That he had from her at his coming into that kingdom and at his leaving the same 400 pistoles which, with the debts he was now in prison for, would amount to £1,500.

---

[1] Chadwick was Archbishop Tillotson's son-in-law.

So he withdrew and was afterward called in. And said that those two gentlemen he would bring over had original papers to produce under the hands of some of the King's Privy Council. So he withdrew again.

Sir Francis Blake moved that this House would address to the King to give this man some allowance.

Sir John Lowther: Whatever this man's credit is now, it appears it was not so inconsiderable when the Secretaries of State employed him to go to and from France. There are many great persons named in his information. It concerns you to have this matter cleared for their reputation, the government being concerned herein. And you can do no less than hear him since he offers so fair as to bring in others to confirm his testimony.

Sir Edward Hussey and *Sir John Morton* moved to address to the King to allow him something for his support and to enable him to fetch over those gentlemen he speaks of.

Sir Thomas Clarges: I am against putting a question for an address to His Majesty for a supply for him, here being some Privy Counsellors here in the Court and they may take notice of it without its appearing on your books.

Mr. Hampden acquainted the House that he thought it not fitting to address to the King for such a matter as this. So small a sum should not be wanting.

So the sense of the House was intimated to be that he might have some allowance for his maintenance and bringing over those other persons. And that they should have the protection of the House.

Then arose a debate how those he should bring in should be examined, whether by this House first. But it was let fall, being too nice a thing to preclude the King from examining them.

Then debated whether this House should order the seizing of his papers. Some would have the Serjeant attending the House to send a servant to do it. Others that some members of the House might go and secure them and seal them up. But after a long debate, it was let fall.

Then it was moved and seconded to adjourn. And the question being put, it was carried in the negative.

Then the House went upon the consideration of the state of the nation. And the packet wherein were the Lord Preston's and Mr. Crone's confessions and examinations were opened. And the same were read at the Table by the Clerk.[1]

---

[1] This and the following interrogations of Preston and Crone are printed in full at *HMC Finch*, iii. 314–20, 329–45.

The first paper of the Lord Preston was sworn 13 June 1691 before some lords of the Privy Council and was to the following effect.

Mr. Lawton came to me and told me that King James was willing to receive me as Secretary to him in France. This I had heard from my brother Col. Grahme before. After I determined to leave England, but before I inquired of the posture of affairs here in order to promote King James's service. That thereon I discoursed with the Lord Clarendon touching the heads of a declaration, which was taken and were in the Lord Clarendon's own hand, and of this the Bishop of Ely well knew.—The account that was taken about the English fleet I had from the Lord Clarendon.—I saw the Lord Weymouth and Sir Edward Seymour at my house, but had no great discourse with them because my wife was there, but I expected Sir Edward there again. The Lord Dartmouth was there also another time and gave me that account of the English Channel and the particulars about the fleet.— I saw the Marquess of Halifax another time, and he was with me in order to settle some matter about my debts. I acquainted him with the declaration intended but he thought it not proper and would not be concerned in it.—I sent to the Archbishop of Canterbury by the Bishop of Ely before I went for France, and he presented his service to King James and to assure him that they would do all they could for his service to promote his interest and that this was not only his own sense but his brethren's. I had frequent converse with the Lord Clarendon and William Penn. And in the conference between the Whigs and Tories, the Lords Shrewsbury and Macclesfield with others were concerned.—Crone came over from France and brought divers letters—one from Queen Mary with bills for £6,000 for carrying on the service—and brought blank commissions for the land and sea service. The Lord Dartmouth and Captain David Floyd were for the sea, and Sir John Fenwick, Col. Orby, and Sir Theophilus Oglethorpe were for the land.—A servant of the Lord Dunbarton came to tell me that 6,000 men should be sent to Scotland round Ireland but that many horse could not be expected. The Lord Dunbarton was intended to command them.

Second examination of the Lord Preston, *jurat.* 13 June 1691 before several lords of the Privy Council.

I received a letter from the Earl of Annandale to meet him and others at York. At Boroughbridge Sir James Montgomery and we discoursed, and they were dissatisfied with the reception they had from King William.—That many disaffected were in the west part of Scotland who would join with the French if they might have the liberty of their religion.—Sir John Cochrane dined with me often but I had no discourse with him about a rising intended in Scotland.—I met one Nevile in the habit of a divine, and he told me there was a design carried on in Scotland for King James; that several commissions were sent thither, one for the Lord Annandale to be high commissioner at a parliament to be called in King James's name; that 60,000 louis d'ors would be sent to that kingdom; that Major Wildman was a well-wisher to King James and that Ferguson had a pardon from King James.

Mr. Crone's first paper, *jurat.* 3 May 1691 before the Lord Notting-ham, and was to the like effect.

When I was going to Ireland, one Capt. Donniland told me that I might do King James a greater service than by my sword in Ireland.—I had discourse with Mr. Penn, and he told me there was a lord I was to go to at Col. Grahme's by Bagshot by the token of an agate head of a cane. I went accordingly, and there was the Lord Clarendon, where Col. Grahme began King James's health. His lordship gave me assurances of his truth and acquainted me how matters stood in England and Scotland.—I came from Bagshot 12 October 1690 and had frequent conferences with Penn about matters.—There was one Mrs. Clifford, a notable agent for King James.—The instructions I had from the Lord Clarendon consisted of several heads: the countries had their bellies full of taxes, that the gentlemen in the west country were ready, that King James had never such a time to come for Eng-land as when King William with his army were employed about Ire-land. As to the navy office[rs], they were ready to mutiny for the arrears; that the taxes were so great that the country could not bear it; that King William had sent a great sum of money and plate to pay debts in Holland; that the nobility of England were weary with his proud carriage, making them to wait two or three hours at his closet door while he was alone with Bentinck; that there were 20,000 tinners in Cornwall that would be ready to join the French if King James did but come with them and the French fleet set up the English colours; that if King James was not yet ready to come that he would take care to settle a correspondence here; that the French fleet might easily secure St. George's Channel and prevent supplying of Ireland.—Mr. Penn gave me the like instructions, but pressed much for money for the service in England, and also for men and arms and some money for Scotland.

Crone's second paper of 5 May 1691, *jurat*. 20 June 1691 before the Lord Nottingham.

Col. Grahme brought to King James in Ireland the same instructions as I carried, whereon the Lord Seaforth and others were ordered to prepare to go beforehand for that King James intended suddenly to land in England. And when I was in Ireland and [I] had frequent conferences with the Lord Tyrconnel about settling a correspondence with England.—I went also with instructions from King James to his friends in Scotland, whom he was sorry to disappoint but that he had no ships, but was promised some from France and 5,000 men with which and some others he intended to land in England. Several Irish regiments were nominated for this service. And King James advised his friends to bring in as many horses as they could and that they should endeavour to bring over the Governors of Portsmouth and Plymouth by promising them money.—I had also notes or letters from King James to the Lord Clarendon, the Countess of Dorchester, and Col. Grahme, with directions to apply to one Mr. Archer in Bristol to employ a ship to carry passengers and packets to and from Ireland for the service of King James.—I accordingly took shipping and came for England with instructions, and delivered the notes from King James to the several persons. That to the Earl of Clarendon I delivered at Mrs. Clifford's, who received it with great transport of joy and uplifted hands and remained speechless for a time.

Crone's third paper of 7 May 1691, *jurat*. 25 June after, before Lord Nottingham.

I had frequent conferences with the Lord Clarendon, Col. Grahme, and Mr. Penn, and received from them two or three sheets of paper with instructions; it was writ by one Mr. Leighton as secretary. Where was a discourse happened relating to King James in Ireland— whether he should stay and fight King William in Ireland or give him the go-by and land here in England. And it was advised as best for King James to come for England with 20,000 men and declare for a parliament.—I had letters from Lord Clarendon, Countess of Dorchester, Col. Grahme, [and] Mr. Penn to carry to King James, which I made up in washballs when the stuff was soft, which I bought in the Strand, and I believe Fuller saw them.—King James was advised to give out a general pardon.—When I went for France, there was one Mr. Hayes in the smack. So I went and carried the letters, papers, and memorials to King James.—A place in Wales was pitched on for

King James to land in, as most convenient for persons to come in from the north and the west.

Crone's fourth paper of 7 May 1691, *jurat.* [20] June 1691 before Lord Nottingham.

My dispatches from the late Queen Mary when I returned to England was that their friends should not expect them so soon, for that the French king would not venture his fleet without a safe port to harbour in and when he did they should come and transport King James and his army. That as for money, it was very scarce; what she had she had laid out in arms. That Mr. Fuller had promised to furnish £6,000 for King James's service. That the French king would not believe King James's interest was so great. I brought over several commissions both for land and sea service. The Lord Dartmouth and David Lloyd were to command at sea, and Sir John Fenwick, Sir Theophilus Oglethorpe, Col. Sackville, and Col. Arp at land. And we had orders to use our endeavours to tempt all sea officers from the usurper, the Prince of Orange, and that they which brought away their ship should have the value of it and be retained in present service.—One Mr. Fuller brought a letter to the late Queen from the Governor of Sheerness.—The late Queen ordered £3,000 of the money Mr. Fuller was to provide to be paid to Mr. Penn and the other £3,000 to be paid to me.—I went for England with Mr. Fuller and what he swore about me at my trial was true.—I went when I arrived to Mr. Penn's and delivered the letters and commissions. The Lord Clarendon took the latter away with him.—The Lord Clarendon, Col. Grahme, and others came to my chamber one day and named several lords who were to give assurances to King James of their affection for his service. They named two bishops, the Duke of Newcastle, and the Lord of Worcester or the Duke of Beaufort.—Mr. Fuller came to me when here in town and pretended to pay me the money in the City, and there he trepanned me so I was taken.

So the papers were sealed up by the Speaker according to order.

So adjourned till 8 tomorrow morning.

Thursday, 10 December

Leave was granted to the Solicitor General to attend a cause in the House of Peers.

Mr. Papillon and Mr. Mayne had leave to attend a committee of the House of Peers about the bill for preserving two ships lading of bay salt, they being victuallers of the Navy.

Sir Samuel Barnardiston, being a Commissioner for taking the Public Accounts, moved the House for their direction, the Lords having sent to them to desire they would let them have a copy of their observations upon the same. Some were against it; but others were for it, and the rather for that it being designed to continue the Commissioners another year, the Lords if denied might obstruct the said bill. But the House would make no order in it, but generally seemed to be of opinion they might give a copy of them if they pleased. So left them to do as they thought fit, their observations being taken as Commissioners and not as members of this House.

Then the Order of the Day was read for the House to resolve into a Committee of the Whole House touching the East India Company. The Speaker left the Chair.[1]

Sir John Guise was Chairman. And after some time spent, they made several regulations. Then at last they cried out to the Chairman to leave the Chair, others no. So thereon the committee divided —the Yeas on the right hand, the Noes on the left.

Yeas Col. Granville   120

Tellers for the

Noes Mr. Onslow   85

So the Speaker resumed the Chair. And *Sir John Guise* reported the committee had made some farther progress and desired time to sit again. Ordered to sit again tomorrow after the bill of treasons.

Adjourned till 8 tomorrow morning.

Friday, 11 December

Sir Richard Reynell was ordered to carry up to the Lords the bill for naturalizing Sir Martin Beckman and others.

Then the Order of the Day for the House to consider of the Lords' amendments to the bill for regulating trials in cases of treason came on and was read.[2] And several of the amendments were agreed to by the House. But there being one that levelled impeachments by this House with indictments, giving the party the same advantages thereon, it took up a long debate. Those that spoke for agreeing to

---

[1] For an account of the debate that followed see Bodleian Carte MS. 130, ff. 333–4.
[2] Grey, x. 206–15 has a fuller account of the debate that follows.

it were *Mr. Finch, Sir Charles Sedley, John Howe, Col. Granville, Sir Richard Temple, Sir Edward Seymour, Dr. Barbone, Sir Christopher Musgrave, Sir Thomas Clarges, Mr. Bertie,* and the *Lord Castleton.* But it was strongly opposed by *Mr. Hampden, Mr. Clarke, Serj. Blencowe, Sir Thomas Littleton, Sir Henry Capel, Sir Robert Howard, Solicitor General Sir John Somers, Goodwin Wharton, Sir George Treby* (the Attorney General), *Mr. Montagu, Sir Robert Rich, Mr. Arnold,* etc.

But after a long debate, some amendments were proposed to the clause and part of it to be left out. So the question was put for agreeing with the Lords with this amendment to their amendments. House divided—the Yeas go forth.

		Mr. Gwyn	
	Yeas		208
		Mr. Fenwick	
Tellers for the			
		Dutton Colt	
	Noes		153
		Mr. Clarke	

Then another amendment made by the Lords to the said bill was long debated—which was a new clause that upon the trial of any peer the whole House of Peers should be summoned. *Sir Edward Hussey, Sir John Guise, Sir John Thompson, Sir Thomas Littleton, Sir John Somers, Mr. Hutchinson, Mr. Arnold, Sir Francis Drake, Sir Joseph Williamson,* and others spoke against it. *John Howe, Col. Granville, Mr. Bertie, Sir Richard Temple, Mr. Finch,* and others for it.

So at last the question was put for agreeing with the Lords in this amendment and carried in the negative. So a committee was appointed to prepare reasons to be offered at a conference with the Lords upon the said amendments.

Upon motion, divers particular members were added to several committees.

So House adjourned till 8 tomorrow morning.

Saturday, 12 December

Sir Thomas Clarges informed the House that the roof of the house they sit in was decayed and become dangerous, and therefore moved that the King's Surveyor might be ordered by the House to view the same and report his opinion therein on Tuesday next.

And it was ordered accordingly. (And of this there are some precedents where the House have done the like without addressing to the King, as in King James I his time, etc.)

The bill for settling £100 per annum on the Bishop of Ely out of Hatton Garden etc., was on motion recommitted, there being some mistakes in the bill.[1]

The bill to prevent false and double returns of members to parliament was read the third time.

Sir Joseph Tredenham, Sir Christopher Musgrave, Paul Foley, and others spoke against it. *Sir John Darell, John Howe, Serj. Blencowe, Sir Charles Sedley*, and others for it.

So after some debate, the question was put for passing the bill. The House divided—Yeas went out.

		Sir Walter Yonge	
	Yeas		95
		Mr. Clarke	
Tellers for the			
		Sir Joseph Tredenham	
	Noes		169
		Mr. Dolben	

So the bill was rejected.

Sir Edward Seymour and *Sir Joseph Tredenham* moved that, lest this should encourage officers to make false returns, this House would—as formerly in Queen Elizabeth's and King James I his time—punish all persons offending therein with imprisonment, by fine, etc., as heretofore done.

So a committee was appointed to inspect the Journals of the House for that purpose and report their opinions therein, and they to sit *de die in diem*.

Then the House, according to the Order of the Day, went upon the further consideration of the public accounts and the observations thereon and proceeded in the consideration of the 14th, 15th, 16th, and 17th observations.

On the 15th, relating to the patent for the Royal Oak lottery:

It was objected against it that the King's power of *non obstante* to any statute was now taken away, so could not grant the same with dispensation to the several statutes of gaming; then it was a pernicious thing and destructive of youth and so not fit to be encouraged. But

---

[1] The recommittal of this bill is not recorded in the *Journal*.

answered there was no *nonobstante* in the patent but it stood of itself upon the validity of the grant; then there was £4,000 per annum reserved upon this grant, which never was upon any former.

So no order or vote was passed thereon.

On the 16th, that pensions and allowances to persons dismissed of their offices hath much increased the civil list:

And *Mr. Paul Foley* instanced in some particulars; as salaries are paid to some of the underofficers about the hearth money and some of the victuallers, the Lord Warrington hath a pension and also the Lord Montagu for such places which are disposed of to others.

Sir John Lowther: The two first are only some few collectors which are kept in to collect the arrears of those duties.

The House hereon ordered the particulars to be brought in of pensions and salaries to persons discharged of their offices.

On the 17th, relating to Mr. Tempest (a member of this House) and the Bishop of Winchester being in arrear to the Crown upon collecting some of the revenues of the Crown:[1]

Sir John Lowther informed the House that the Bishop of Winchester had received great losses, but was preparing to pay the same.

Then for *Mr. Tempest*, he stood up in his place and informed the House that he had received a great misfortune by the running away of one employed under him but however desired about 10 days to look out his papers and make up his accounts.

Then arose a long debate upon a motion that no member of this House who is a public receiver of the King's revenue should have the privilege of the House as to his receivership, but this went off.

Then a debate began upon a motion that no member of this House should be a receiver of any public money, which held some time but it went off.

Then a debate happened upon a motion of *Admiral Russell* that all persons having any places from the Crown the profits whereof were above £500 per annum, the same should go to carry on the charge of the war. *Sir Richard Onslow, Sir Robert Rich, Sir John Lowther, Sir Robert Cotton, Mr. Howe, Sir Stephen Fox* to the same.

So at last it was resolved, *nemine contradicente*: That the salaries, fees, and perquisites of all offices under the Crown shall be applied to the use of the war except £500 to be allowed to such respective officers—except the salaries to the Speaker of the House of Commons, the Lords Commissioners of the Great Seal, the judges, foreign

---

[1] Grey, x. 215–17 has an account of the debate that follows.

ministers, and to the commission officers serving in the fleet and army—for the said offices.

So ordered to go upon the accounts again on Friday morning next.

So adjourned till 8 of the clock on Monday morning.[1]

Monday, 14 December

Sir Joseph Tredenham was ordered to carry up the bill for settling £100 per annum on the Bishop of Ely etc., to the Lords.

Sir John Darell was also ordered to carry up to the Lords the bill for better tithing of hemp and flax.

The engrossed bill for the double excise for one year was read a third time. Then *Sir Francis Blake* offered a rider obliging every gauger to leave a note at each house of such liquors as he shall gage within one day after he shall take the same, under the penalty of etc. Which clause was read twice and ordered to stand part of the bill. So the bill was passed and ordered to be carried up to the Lords by Mr. Solicitor for their concurrence.

Mr. Arnold gave information to the House that he had an account of one Capt. Gilport[2] who would inform this House of divers merchants and others that carried on a trade to France for lead, etc., but that he was taken by one Davis, a Messenger, and kept at the Guard House till he would deliver up his letters and papers touching the same and that the Messengers would let no one come near him and had refused to bring him up on a Habeas Corpus.

But the House looked upon it as a trivial matter if true, but did not believe it, some members giving a very slender account of it. Then, it was no matter of privilege and the party if injured has a remedy on the Habeas Corpus against the Messenger.

However, the question was put to send for this person to give an account to the House. House divided—the Yeas went forth.

	Sir Robert Cotton	
Yeas		36
	Sir Charles Wyndham	
Tellers for the		
	Sir Robert Davers	
Noes		177
	Mr. Fenwick	

[1] The House finally adjourned 'near 5'; B.M. Loan 29/79, Robert Harley to Sir Edward Harley, 12 Dec.   [2] *CJ*, x. 584 has 'Capt. Tilford'.

Then *Sir John Guise* reported from the committee the resolutions that had been agreed on touching the estimates relating to the land forces in England, Scotland, the West Indies, and to be transported beyond sea.

Sir Thomas Clarges took exception to the said report for that it had not the reasons inserted upon which they came to those resolutions.

But it appeared to be otherwise on reading the report. So they were referred to the Committee of the Whole House that are to consider of the supplies.

Adjourned till 8 tomorrow morning.

Tuesday, 15 December

Upon the conference had with the Lords relating to the papers taken in a French vessel and the report thereof to this House by Col. Granville, nothing being done thereon for some time, *Mr. Hampden* moved that the conference might not go off so but that as the Lord Nottingham had been reflected on in the transaction of this affair, so he might have justice done him. And the least this House can do is as the Lords have done to pass a vote that you are satisfied there was no letter of his Lordship's found in the said packet.

Sir Edward Seymour to the same, and desired this House would agree with the Lords therein.

Sir John Guise moved to adjourn the debate.

Col. Titus moved that since by the reasons sent from the Lords for their coming to that resolution it appears the Lord Kiveton[1] had mistaken and owned the same in the House of Peers, some notice might be taken of that in the resolution of this House.

But *Sir Henry Goodricke* and *Mr. Dolben* desired it might be left out and not cast a reflection on the Lord Kiveton to say he was mistaken when it is not very material to the vindication of the Lord Nottingham.

So after some debate it was left out, and the question put and resolved: That this House doth agree with the Lords that there was not a copy of a letter from the Lord Nottingham to Sir Ralph Delaval taken on board the said French vessel.

Sir John Guise reported from the committee to whom the estimates about the army and other charges in the kingdom of Ireland were referred that they had considered the same and made several

---

[1] Styled by courtesy the Earl of Danby.

resolutions thereon, which he delivered in at the Table, where the same were read and referred to the consideration of the Committee of the Whole House who are to consider further of the supplies to be granted to Their Majesties for carrying on a war against France.

Then the House read the Order of the Day and resolved itself accordingly into a Committee of the Whole House to consider further of the supplies to be granted to Their Majesties. And the Speaker left the Chair and the Solicitor General was Chairman.

So the committee proceeded on the report from the [select] committee touching the estimates that relate to the army in England, Scotland, etc. And they were all read by the Clerk together, then after again singly.

To the first about the numbers of officers and soldiers in a regiment:

Sir Christopher Musgrave opposed the said resolution of the committee and moved that the foot companies might be each advanced to 80 men, whereas now you have not above 50 men in the company. But by enlarging your companies, you will have the same number of men as you have resolved and yet you will save £100,000 by the reducing the number of the officers—for as your companies will be larger, you will have the fewer companies and consequently not so many officers. The Danish regiments of foot have about 1,000 men in each. The Dutch are more than yours. Our English Guards here have 80 men in a company. And why one captain should not be as well able to command 80 men as another captain I see not. Paul Foley to the same.

Col. Godfrey: The manner of fighting is now much altered to what it was. The French, the enemy we have to deal with, fights after another manner. His companies now consist of fewer men but his officers are trebled; they have two captains and two lieutenants to each company. And you would find it more for your service if you would increase your officers rather than lessen them. I will not deny your men are brave, but without officers to lead them on you will, I am afraid, not have the success you expect.

Mr. Neale and Sir Ralph Dutton to the same, and desired we might increase our officers.

Sir Robert Cotton (of Chester) opposed that.

Lord Ranelagh: If you make this reduction as desired, what will you do with so many officers as will be supernumerary? Will you disband them presently after they have done you so good service? There

are no new forces going to be raised whereby to employ those officers
—only new recruits making to supply the regiments in being of which
there are officers complete. There is not in the whole army as I know
of one Catholic a subject of His Majesty. Upon the matter I am no
soldier, but it is the opinion of one of the best soldiers in the world,
our King, that there rather ought to be more officers. However, I
would not at this time discourage so many gentlemen who have
served you well by turning them out—the number of which is considerable, amounting to 700 or 800 officers.

Sir Thomas Clarges: I have in my hand an establishment of the
forces that is now making in France, where it appears they are making
their companies 107 effective men in each. Therefore, I am against
agreeing with your committee.

Sir Robert Howard, John Howe, and Col. Erle were for agreeing
with the committee.

So the question put for agreeing with the committee in this resolution and carried in the affirmative.

To the second about the additional pay to the two regiments:

Sir Christopher Musgrave and Mr. Hutchinson spoke against it.

Col. Cornewall and Lord Fitzharding spoke for it as reasonable,
because these two regiments live generally here in town at a dearer
expense than those regiments quartered in the countries. Then these
two regiments are always attendant on the King's person whereby
they are obliged to go finer and keep a better equipage than others
and so are at greater expense.

So on the question the House agreed to this second resolution.

Then the third and fourth resolutions of the private committee
were read and agreed to by the Committee of the Whole House.

To the fifth about the pay of the Dutch forces:

Col. Cornewall spoke against agreeing with the committee herein,
for that since these Dutch troops are to return to Flanders and Holland and are to be joined with their own countrymen he desired they
might not have English pay but be allowed no more than others of
their countrymen had, for it was very mischievous to have different
pay to soldiers of the same nation in one and the same army. A Dutch
trooper here has 2*s*. 6*d*. a man but in their own country they have but
1*s*. 3*d*., which is a great difference. And when soldiers return to their
own country (though in the pay of another prince), they never have
so much as strangers that go into the country should for the natives
can live cheaper in their own country than foreigners.

Lord Ranelagh: These are part of those troops that came over hither to your deliverance and the King did promise them English pay when they came hither. And auxiliary troops are always favoured in their pay.

Sir Christopher Musgrave: I think it is not fit for some troops of one nation to have one pay and others of the same nation to have another.

Sir John Lowther was for agreeing with the committee. Sir Robert Rich, Lord Falkland, Sir Robert Cotton (of Post Office) for it. Sir Richard Temple, Sir Stephen Fox, Sir Thomas Littleton, and Sir Joseph Williamson also, which last also hinted the rather for that he heard some offers of considerable advantage were offered to the Dutch for a peace and there had been some unseasonable reflections made on the Dutch this day which had been better spared.

But Col. Granville, Mr. Bertie, etc. were against it and proposed an amendment to the question.

Which being put, was disagreed to. Then that question itself was put in reference to the Dutch forces and was agreed to.

Then the sixth and seventh resolutions relating to the Dutch forces were read and put and agreed to.

Then the Solicitor was ordered to report to the House that the committee had sat and made some further progress and desired leave to sit again.

So the Speaker resumed the Chair and the *Solicitor* reported accordingly and moved to have leave to sit again. Ordered that this House will go into a Committee of the Whole House to consider further of the supplies tomorrow morning after the bill for regulating musters of the army.

A report was delivered to the Speaker from Sir Christopher Wren, the King's Surveyor, touching the roof of the House. That upon the like order he had viewed it eight years since and put in timber and other necessaries as was then thought fit. That he had viewed it now again and did not find any of the timber shrunk or decayed to give any cause of fear. But the ceiling being of plaster of Paris and a way not now used, it was not so well understood. And therefore in a recess of parliament, he thought it fit to be altered and a new ceiling made and, in the meantime, that some of the records kept over the ceiling should be removed.

So adjourned till 8 tomorrow morning.

Wednesday, 16 December

The bill for registering servants that go to the plantations was read the third time.

Sir Christopher Musgrave and *Sir Robert Henley* spoke against it. This bill pretends to prevent kidnapping, but if this pass into a law it will establish kidnapping by a law. It is a pretence only to establish an office for Mr. Thompson.

Mr. Palmes, *Mr. Waller*, and *Mr. Thompson* spoke for it.

But the question being put for the passing the bill, the House divided—the Yeas went out.

	Mr. Colt	
Yeas		29
	Sir Thomas Barnardiston	
Tellers for the		
	Sir Edward Hussey	
Noes		90
	Sir Robert Henley	

So the bill was rejected.

Sir Robert Davers, *Sir John Guise*, *Major Pery*, and *Mr. Colt* moved the House for leave to bring in a bill for encouraging privateers against France and for better security of the trade of this nation.

Sir Ralph Dutton spoke against the bill.

Sir Thomas Clarges was for the bill, but desired the House would go into a Committee of the Whole House to consider thereof. That a great duty might be laid on all French goods to prevent a collusion of the act of prohibition of French goods; otherwise, this would open the trade again with France. That what goods should be so taken by privateers should be publicly sold by inch of candle and that the King should have one-third part thereof to his use. That the book of rates might be reviewed in order to lay a greater duty on French goods, whereby you may raise £100,000 for the King and will in some measure prevent the carrying on a trade with France.

Mr. Papillon and *Sir Samuel Barnardiston* moved for such a bill, being very useful to advance our trade, prevent the taking of our merchant ships, and in a great measure save our charge of keeping a winter guard.

So ordered such a bill to be brought in upon the debate of the House, and a committee of five or six persons were named to bring it in.

Then the bill for the land tax was read a second time and committed to a Committee of the Whole House.

Mr. Hampden moved for the expediting business this act might have a clause of reference to the last land tax empowering the commissioners thereon to be likewise here with like powers and authorities as in that act is mentioned.

But this was opposed by *Sir Christopher Musgrave* and others as not proper to have such bills of reference to other acts. Then there are several of the commissioners in the first act that are dead since and others that would not act, which are not fit to be put in.

Then *Sir Thomas Vernon* moved that the Inns of Court might be taxed to this act and commissioners appointed for that purpose. So *Major Pery, Sir Samuel Dashwood*, and *Sir John Knight* to the same.

But it was let fall and nothing done therein.

So ordered that the members of this House do on Saturday morning prepare and present to the House the names of commissioners for the several counties, cities, and boroughs (as usual) to be inserted in the said bill, when the House will go into a Committee of the Whole House upon the said bill.

Committee for the sale of Mr. Robert's [land] bill was revived and to sit this afternoon.

So House adjourned till 8 tomorrow morning.

Thursday, 17 December

Then the Order of the Day was read, and the Speaker left the Chair and the House resolved itself into a Committee of the Whole House to consider of the East India Company. Sir John Guise was Chairman and acquainted the committee with what they had formerly done and how far they were gone.

Sir Edward Seymour moved for another regulation—that the power of peace and war was a royal prerogative and not to be entrusted in their hands. Mr. Hampden and Mr. Finch to the same.

But this regulation was upon debate waived, being thought necessary to support this trade which could not be carried on without it.

Thus having finished the regulations, a debate was whether the question should be for a bill to be brought in to establish the old Company or erect a new one according to these regulations or to report the regulations to the House to have their opinion therein, if agree to them or not.

So the question was put and carried for reporting the regulations to the House.

So the Speaker resumed the Chair and *Sir John Guise* at the Bar reported the said regulations, which he delivered in at the Table, and the same were read.

To the first, that for the quota of stock:

It was objected against as being too much to be employed in one trade and will ruin the other trade of the nation. Then it is not safe for the government, for this company having so great a stock will have credit to take up what money they please, which may be prejudicial to the government. Then this trade will in a little time ruin your woollen manufacture, which has never thriven since this trade was so great.

So after a long debate, an amendment was proposed to the question by leaving out the word '£1,500,000' in the regulation. On which the question was first put if it should stand part of the question. House divided—Noes went out.

	Yeas	Sir Samuel Barnardiston	147
		Foot Onslow	
Tellers for the			
	Noes	Sir Robert Cotton	111
		Mr. Hopkins	

So to the first regulation the House agreed, for that the trade was now so great that it could not be well carried on to the advantage of the nation with a less stock.

So the second regulation, for none to have above £5,000 stock, was put and agreed to by the House.

So the third, for none to have but one vote and every person for £500 to have one.

As to the fourth, of what the company shall export every year of the manufacture of the nation, it was long debated. The committee thought fit to restrain them to export yearly the value of £100,000 in the goods and manufacture of the nation.

But some spoke against that as being too little for so vast a trade and it appears how mischievous this trade is when they carry out no more of our manufacture. Others opposed the altering it and said £100,000 was more than they could export to profit.

So the question was put whether '£100,000' should stand in the question, and carried in the negative. Then the word '£200,000' was proposed to stand instead thereof and carried. And after the whole question was put and agreed to.

To the sixth, of the company's furnishing the King with saltpetre, it was agreed.

So the seventh was put and agreed to, for the value of the lots at a sale.

So the eighth, as to the governor and deputy governor, and agreed.

And the ninth [qualifications for holding office in the company].

The 10th about the dividends to be in money, the 11th that the stock shall be left sufficient, the 12th the stock to be valued every five years, the 13th that no ships shall go to the Indies but such as are of a company, 14th as to what bylaws shall be binding to the company, and the 15th that the company shall not continue above 21 years, were all severally put and agreed to by the House.

Sir Edward Seymour spoke very largely and fully against the old Company and showed how unfit they were to manage the trade to the Indies. That they made a war to support their sinking credit, which was grown so low that no persons would trust them in India for any money except their factors were security for it, so that they had not credit sufficient to carry on the trade. You see, therefore, how necessary it is for you to do something in it or the trade will be lost. If the parliament rise without doing anything in it, then the old Company continue and they will commit the same extravagances as formerly. I think at present it will not be fitting to go upon an act of parliament, for that is still delaying the matter because the Company will give all the opposition they can to the same in the House of Lords as they have here. I think, therefore, the best way to put an end to this matter and to preserve the trade itself is to make an address to His Majesty to dissolve this present Company according to the power in the charter and that he would be pleased to establish a new company according to the regulations agreed upon by this House.

Sir Richard Temple: I think this is very irregular and a strange motion, the committee having come to no such resolution nor any report made to you of the evidence gave at the Bar in this case so that you can form any such resolution.

Mr. Methuen seconded the motion of Sir Edward Seymour.

Sir Joseph Williamson took notice of arguments drawn by the gentlemen that were against the old Company from the evidence given at the committee which was never reported to the House by the Chairman, which was very irregular. *Mr. Hopkins* to the same.

Mr. Finch spoke at large against the old Company and showed the impossibility of their being able to comply with the regulations of this House and so concluded with the motion of Sir Edward Seymour.

The *Lord Falkland* and *Sir Richard Temple* spoke both for the old Company and thought the most regular way was for the House to resolve into a Committee of the Whole House again to proceed further upon the evidence that the committee may come to some resolution.

So the question was put for this House to resolve itself into a Committee of the Whole House tomorrow morning at 10 of the clock to consider further of the petitions about the East India trade. House divided—Yeas went out.

		Mr. Gwyn	
	Yeas		124
		Col. Granville	
Tellers for the			
		Sir Robert Cotton (of Chester)	
	Noes		117
		Mr. Clarke	

So carried in the affirmative.

The further proceedings and examination touching the public accounts was put off till Monday next.[1]

Adjourned till 8 tomorrow morning.

Friday, 18 December

Order of the Day was read for the House to go into a Committee of the Whole House touching the East India trade. So the Speaker left the Chair; Sir John Guise was Chairman.

Sir Joseph Herne moved that the committee would proceed to inquire into the accounts brought into the House, for therein it would appear that they had stock sufficient to carry on the trade.

But the House generally seemed to be against it, for that it was an endless business and would spend too much time and was thought only for delay.

---

[1] There is no mention of this in the *Journal*.

Sir Joseph Herne, after the aforesaid matter had been debated, proposed in behalf of the old Company (whose Governor he was) that the Company would be obliged to give good security that the accounts as presented to the House were true. And if it should prove otherwise, they would be bound to make it up to that value and be answerable for interest of what they wanted to make it up.

This debate lasted long. Those that spoke against the old Company were Sir Christopher Musgrave, Mr. Heneage Finch, Mr. Methuen, Sir Henry Ashurst, Mr. Papillon, Mr. Hampden, Mr. Onslow, Sir Robert Howard, Sir Robert Clayton, Sir Robert Rich, Col. Austen, Mr. Boscawen, Mr. Pollexfen, Lord Ranelagh, Sir Francis Drake, and Mr. Hutchinson. Those that spoke for it were Sir Richard Temple, Sir Thomas Clarges, Major Pery, Sir Joseph Herne, Mr. Neale, Lord Falkland, Sir John Morton, Serj. Blencowe, Sir Thomas Littleton, Sir Robert Sawyer, Sir John Lowther, Sir Joseph Williamson, Mr. Ettrick, Lord Colchester, etc.

Upon the debate they came to some resolutions:

1. That all persons having above £5,000 stock in the said Company should be obliged to sell it at £100 for every £100.

2. That they shall give security such as this House shall approve of that their stock be £744,000, all debts paid.

3. That (security being first given) an address be made to His Majesty to incorporate the present East India Company by charter according to the regulations agreed on by the House, that the same may pass into an act of parliament.

So the Speaker resumed the Chair and *Sir John Guise* reported the same, which were read and agreed unto by the House. Ordered that the committee of the East India Company attend this House on Wednesday next to give security according to the said resolution.

Adjourned till 8 tomorrow morning.

Saturday, 19 December

Mr. John Smith, a new member for the borough of Beeralston in Devonshire, came into the House and took the oaths at the Table and after his seat in the House.

The Order of the Day was read for the House to resolve into a committee to consider of the land tax. And the members for the several counties, cities, and boroughs delivered into the Clerk the commissioners' names for executing the said act. Then it was ordered as an instruction to the committee to prepare a clause for appropriating £1,000,000 for the service of the Navy and Ordnance relating to the same.

Then the House went into a committee and the Speaker left the Chair; Sir John Somers, Solicitor, was Chairman. So the whole act was read over. Then the preamble was postponed as also the commissioners' names—the lists of all being not yet perfect. Then they proceeded to fill up the blanks for each county to pay, as was in the preceding act. Then the committee proceeded on the other clauses paragraph by paragraph, first filling up the blanks in each and then made some amendments as they went along, till they had finished the clauses as brought in in the bill. Then they began to read the several lists of the commissioners' names alphabetically and proceeded therein as far as the letter 'E'. So the Solicitor was ordered to report to the House that the committee had made some progress on the said bill and that the committee desired leave to sit again.

So the Speaker resumed the Chair and the *Solicitor* reported accordingly and moved from the committee to have leave to sit again, and ordered accordingly on Monday next. Ordered that the committee do prepare also a borrowing clause upon the said bill.

Adjourned till 8 on Monday morning.

Monday, 21 December

The House, according to order, proceeded [in Committee of the Whole] on the bill for the land tax and proceeded in the lists of the several commissioners to be inserted in that act till they had finished the same. Then a clause for appropriating £1,000,000 for the service of the Navy and Ordnance was brought in and read, and agreed to with amendments. As also another clause to enable His Majesty to borrow on the credit of the said act, which was agreed to. Then another clause to excuse marsh lands in Essex, Kent, etc., that had been drowned and no profits made of it, as also another clause was offered to excuse one part of a parish in Surrey for lands that were purchased in the same and made part of Richmond Park to pay the taxes thereof—both which clauses were rejected. Then another clause was offered to empower mortgagers to deduct the taxes out of the interest money they pay, but this was also rejected on the question. So the Solicitor was ordered to report to the House that the committee had finished the said bill and to desire leave to sit again.

So the Speaker resumed the Chair and the *Solicitor* reported that the committee had finished the bill and made several amendments and prepared an appropriating clause as also a borrowing clause, according to order, to be added to the said bill, which they had directed him to report to the House. Ordered that the said report be made tomorrow morning. And the House resolved to go into a committee tomorrow (after the said report) to consider further of the supplies to be granted to Their Majesties, etc.

Adjourned till tomorrow morning 8 of the clock.

Tuesday, 22 December

Mr. Norris and Capt. Reynolds had leave to go into the country for a short time.[1]

Ordered that leave should not be asked for any member of this House to go into the country but between the hours of 11 and 2 in the afternoon.[2]

Mr. Harris had the leave of the House to waive his privilege in a certain suit.

Mr. Solicitor General, according to order, reported the bill for the land tax from the committee with the several amendments, which he delivered in at the Table—where the same were read, with the commissioners' names, and all agreed to and the bill ordered to be engrossed.

Adjourned till 8 tomorrow morning.

Wednesday, 23 December

Col. Sackville moved, and he had leave accordingly, to bring in a bill to regulate the abuses committed by carts and wagons in running over people as also to prevent the stealing of rogues in the time of a fire.[3]

Then the Order of the Day was called for. And the House being informed that the committee of the East India Company attended the House, they were called in—as Sir Thomas Cook, Sir William

---

[1] According to *CJ*, x. 594, 595, leave for Reynolds was denied on the 22nd but given on the 23rd.

[2] This order is recorded in *CJ*, x. 589 (15 Dec.).

[3] There is no mention of this in the *Journal*.

Langhorn, Sir Thomas Rawlinson, and others. And at the Bar, Sir Thomas Cook delivered in writings—proposals from the General Court of the Adventurers of the East India Company signed by their Secretary —concerning security to be given. Which was read and they were ordered to withdraw.

So being withdrawn, the order of the House for their giving security was read as also their proposals delivered in. Which was to the effect that they would give security that their stock was really worth as much as alleged by them in their accounts delivered in (viz., £1,300,000) and that three ways—either by the Company's common seal, or by every particular member to secure his own stock, or by so many of the principal members of the Company as this House shall think fit and proposing that a clause should be for every particular member to assign his stock to those persons who are security for it.

Sir Charles Sedley thought this security they proposed not pursuant to the order of the House. *Sir Christopher Musgrave* and *Sir Thomas Clarges* to the same.

Some members were for calling them in again.

Mr. Hampden was against it, for that it appears their design is only to delay and gain time. And therefore I am for coming directly to a vote, for which you have sufficient matter before you.

Mr. Howe: I desire we may know what their security offered is, for certainly those which are security for £1,300,000 are much better but for £744,000.

Mr. Finch: I think the Company have not done well by this House but look on their answer as unsatisfactory and indecent and not pursuant in the least to your vote. Then as to the security proposed. First, for their common seal, it is little worth to say their stock shall secure their stock. Then for the second, for each proprietor to secure his own stock, but that cannot well be, there being divers infants and others concerned that are not capable of giving security. And then for the last, for some persons to give security and they to have the stocks of the other adventurers assigned to them, this is to put a trick upon the House, for you have voted no member shall have above £5,000 stock and yet by this last way you are going to put the trade into 20 men's hands to carry it on. I move you, therefore, to pass a vote that this proposal of theirs is unsatisfactory.

Sir John Lowther to the same, and to give them till tomorrow to produce security according to your vote or else that you would come to other resolutions.

Col. Austen moved to vote the Company's proposals unsatisfactory, and *Mr. Finch* seconded it.

Sir Richard Temple spoke for the Company.

Sir Robert Howard against it.

Sir Samuel Dashwood and *Sir Joseph Herne* thought the security proposed very good. But if not, desired to know what security the House would have. *Sir Thomas Littleton* to that effect, and *Sir Robert Sawyer* for the Company.

But *Sir Robert Clayton* and *Sir Robert Rich* were against it.

Sir Thomas Clarges was for it and thought here was a good ground to work on to make a sufficient security. *Sir Joseph Williamson* spoke for the Company.

So after some debate, the question was put that the proposals of security from the committee of the East India Company are pursuant to the resolutions of this House, and carried in the negative *nemine contradicente*.

Then it was debated whether the committee of the East India Company should be called in again, and upon a question resolved they should. So they were and the *Speaker* asked them several questions according as he was ordered.

Sir Thomas Cook['s] answer: He did not doubt but they that were willing to give security for a greater sum would do it for a less, and that they did propose about 20 members of the committee and about 40 of the adventurers at large that would give security. Then as to the regulations proposed, we must submit that to such as shall be agreed on and pass into an act of parliament, but hope there will be some mitigation. For I should be very loath to part with all my stock but £5,000 at such a rate but should be glad to make the best of my shares.

So the House ordered them to withdraw again. Then a debate arose about the persons that were to be the security. So the members of the committee were called in again and asked by the *Speaker* if they could give a list of such persons as they intended for security.

Sir Thomas Cook answered he could not but desired time to prepare it, for he had not yet acquainted the several members that were to be security that it was under the regulations agreed on.

So they withdrew again.

Sir John Lowther: I desire you will give them no more time than till tomorrow to give in the names of their security, for I find they intend only delay. *Mr. Finch* and *Lord Cornbury* to the same.

So after some debate, ordered that the committee of the East India Company do upon Tuesday morning next bring to this House the persons they shall propose to be security.

Adjourned till 8 tomorrow morning.

Thursday, 24 December

Sir Walter Clarges reported from the committee the bill for supplying the defects in a former act about St. Ann's parish, Westminster; that they had made several amendments to the bill, which he read and after delivered the same in at the Table, where the same were read by the Clerk.

Then *Dr. Barbone* presented a petition to the House from several inhabitants of that parish against the bill, it being to lay a tax of £1,700 on that parish towards building and finishing that church when £500 would do it.

The petition was read but nothing done thereon. So the amendments were severally put and agreed to and the bill ordered to be engrossed.

After the House had read the bill for the land tax, *Mr. Goodwin Wharton* tendered a rider (engrossed in parchment) to be added to the bill, purporting that the Treasurer of the Navy and of the Ordnance should pay bills in course.

But this was opposed by *Mr. Hampden* and *Sir [Robert][1] Rich*: That this clause would extend to pay the debts contracted in King Charles II's and King James II's time.

But on a second reading, it appeared to be limited to the service of Their present Majesties. So the clause was read thrice and agreed to and ordered to stand part of the bill.

Then another rider was offered by *Mr. Brockman*, to limit and regulate the fees of the Exchequer officers, which was read and passed and ordered to stand part of the bill.

So the whole bill was put and passed with the title, and the Solicitor ordered to carry it up to the Lords.

A message by the Black Rod [came] for the Commons to attend the King in the House of Lords. And accordingly the Speaker with the House went up, and the King was pleased to give the royal assent to four public bills and to seven private bills. So the Commons returned

---

[1] 'Peter' in MS.

to their house and the *Speaker* reported to the House the same accordingly.

House adjourned till Tuesday morning next at 9 of the clock.

Tuesday, 29 December

The committee to whom the bill for erecting a court of conscience in Westminster was committed was revived.

Sir Basil Firebrace, being chosen again for the borough of Chippenham in Wiltshire, came this day into the House and took the oaths at the Table.

Sir John Guise presented a petition against the Speaker and Sir George Hutchins as Lords Commissioners of the Great Seal in relation to Mr. [Edward Stephens],[1] a Justice of Peace of Middlesex, complaining against them for discouraging the said justice in the punishment of those that expose things to sale on the Lord's Day. *Mr. Arnold* seconded it and desired it might be read.

The *Speaker* and *Serj. Hutchins* informed the House that this gentleman and some others had set up an informing office in Lincoln's Inn and had levied moneys more or less on divers poor people under colour of the law made for better observation of the Sabbath. Whereas if they had been guilty of the fact, the law warrants no such thing but a forfeiture of the goods exposed to sale.

Sir Richard Temple, Mr. Done, and *Sir Joseph Tredenham* spoke against the petition.

So the question was put for a committee to inquire into it and it was rejected.

The bill to encourage privateers was read the first time.

Sir John Fagg, Sir John Darell, and the *Solicitor General* spoke against the bill as a thing that would let in the carrying on a trade with France.

However, ordered to be read a second time.

Mr. Bennett, a new member chosen for Newton in Lancashire (in the room of Sir John Chicheley, deceased), came into the House and took the oaths at the Table.

A petition from the Lord De La Warr was read, according to order, against Sir John Cutler (a member who was now in the House), praying leave to execute a decree in Chancery against him—he having in

---

[1] Blank in MS.; from *CJ*, x. 597.

a suit of Chancery waived his privilege, but when he found the decree of the court would be against him he then insisted on the privilege of this House.

Sir Christopher Musgrave and *Sir Robert Sawyer* spoke for the petitioner.

Sir Joseph Tredenham for your member, it being a great matter and concerns the privileges of this House.

Mr. Boscawen moved to refer this matter to a committee to inquire into the matter and search precedents in the case.

Mr. Hampden moved to let the matter fall and to give no answer to it as the most advisable way.

Sir Thomas Littleton moved that the member might be obliged to waive the privilege of this House as being for the honour of this House not to protect anyone from doing right and justice.

Sir Christopher Musgrave: Your member having once waived the privilege of this House, I desire he may not now resume it in a cause that appears to be just and honest—this being only a suit in Chancery to compel him to take in his money upon a mortgage of the petitioner's estate.

Solicitor: This is a great matter you are upon and which ought to be duly considered and to make one false step herein is very dangerous, and therefore I desire you will appoint a committee to inquire into it.

Mr. Smith: I have heard, indeed, that a member could not waive his privilege because it was the privilege of the whole House and so to do was penal to him, but never heard that a man who had once waived it should ever be admitted to resume it again.

Mr. Montagu: I think since your member hath broken the privileges of this House in waiving his privilege you ought to punish him for it. But certainly, you will never admit him to resume it when it appears so just and reasonable not to do it.

Sir Robert Rich: If you will not admit your member to resume his privilege, I think you ought to allow him the liberty to appeal from the decree unto the House of Lords or else your member will have a harder case than any other. You will not let him stand on his privilege nor will let him appeal, which any other subject may do.

So at last it was resolved: That Sir John Cutler, having formerly waived his privilege without the leave of this House, ought not to resume the same.

Mr. Montagu, being returned with the other managers from the conference with the Lords, he reported that the Lords had agreed to all the amendments made by this House to the said bill of treasons except that last in reference to the lords, providing that on the trial of a peer the whole House of Peers should be summoned, on which they insist and delivered reasons for the same—which he carried up to the Table, and the same were received and laid on the Table. Afterwards, the House read over the Lords' reasons and ordered to take them into consideration on Thursday next.

The committee of the East India Company were called in, and Sir Thomas Cook (one of them) delivered in a paper of the names of such persons as were willing to be security with the sums of how much—some of which are as follow:

	£		£
Sir Joseph Herne	30,000	Sir William Langhorn	40,000
Sir Thomas Cook	100,000	Sir Humphrey Edwin	30,000
Sir Benjamin Bathurst	20,000	Col. Pery	30,000
Mr. [George] Boone	5,000	Sir Jeremy Sambrook	20,000
Idem [Thomas Boone].	5,000	Mr[s]. Howland	10,000
Sir Samuel Dashwood	15,000	Sir John Chardin	10,000
Sir Josiah Child	100,000	Sir [Samuel] Etherege	10,000
Josiah Child	20,000	Mr. Goodall	8,000

So many others making in the whole above £800,000.[1]

Adjourned till 8 tomorrow morning.

Wednesday, 30 December

The bill for discouraging the exportation of bullion, etc. was read the second time and committed to a Committee of the Whole House.

Some (especially the merchants) spoke against this bill, who said it would not do the service expected for that the lowering the weight of the money would not help it for that money would take its value as the standard was in foreign parts. And though great sums had been melted down, yet making the money lighter would not remedy it, because as much as you take off from the coined money so much more would bullion advance per ounce, for it is foreign exchange that governs it.

Col. Sackville presented a petition from Edward Tilford, mariner, offering to discover several persons that carried on a trade with France for lead, etc. [It] was read and laid on the Table.

[1] *CJ*, x. 602 has the complete list.

Order of the Day was read for going into a Committee of the Whole House to consider of the supplies, etc. The Speaker left the Chair and the Solicitor was Chairman, and he acquainted the committee how far they had proceeded in the estimates. Then they went on next to the head of the two generals and their pay.

Mr. Foley and Sir Christopher Musgrave objected against it for that when these gentlemen came over hither they had each but £3 a day and when we are less able it must be doubled.

Lord Ranelagh: This is but a small matter for gentlemen who have served you well; one of them lost his father in your service. And though they had not so much when they first came over, it is far different now. They command many more now than at that time, and therefore fit their pay should be greater.

So the question was put that the pay for the general officers is reasonable and fit to be continued for the year 1692. Committee divided—Yeas to the right, Noes to the left.

		Yeas	Dutton Colt	129
Tellers for the				
		Noes	Col. Granville	104

Carried in the affirmative.

Then Sir Thomas Clarges and Col. Granville spoke against employing so many foreigners among the general officers, there being few English among them, which would be a great discouragement to the English.

Mr. Hampden: I think it is for your interest to have foreigners rather than natives, for thereby your own men will not be bred soldiers and so prevent the fear of a standing army, which I am against.

Then the question was put that the pay to the rest of the general officers is reasonable, and agreed accordingly. Then it was agreed that the charge of the garrisons should stand upon the civil list and be paid out of the revenue. So the several questions upon the Ordnance were put and agreed to. Then the committee came to the estimate for the transport ships. Some of them were agreed to, others not—as that 45s. per tun for beer should be reduced to 39s., that 5s. a stall for transporting each horse be reduced to 2s. 6d. apiece. So the committee agreed to the rest of the resolutions in reference to the land forces to be continued in England, Scotland, etc., and to be sent beyond sea.

Then the committee proceeded on the estimate for the forces designed for Ireland.

Sir Thomas Clarges offered an establishment he had prepared for the forces designed to be kept in that kingdom which he said would save a considerable sum of money.

But it was opposed to be received because this committee ought to go first on the resolutions of the private committee which ought first to be determined. So after some debate, the establishment of the Paymaster of the Forces (Mr. Fox) in that kingdom, which the private committee received and went according to, was read first. And after the establishment which the private committee rejected of Sir Thomas Clarges was read, which was the same as in King Charles II's time, *anno* 1682.

And the question was put to go according to the establishment of the Paymaster. Committee divided.

Yeas   Sir Thomas Littleton   61

Tellers for the

Noes   Col. Cornewall   92

So the establishment of Sir Thomas Clarges was gone on and the committee proceeded head by head. Some of them were agreed to, others not, and others were not finished.

So the Chairman was ordered to leave the Chair and to report the committee had sat and made some progress and desired time to sit again. Speaker resumed the Chair and *Solicitor General* reported and moved accordingly. And the House ordered to be in a committee again tomorrow upon the supplies after the report of the conference about the bill of treasons.

Adjourned till 8 tomorrow morning.

Thursday, 31 December

A message from the Lords that they had agreed to the bill for the land tax with some amendments, which the House read and agreed to. And the bill was sent up to the Lords by Mr. Solicitor to acquaint them that this House had agreed to the said amendments.

Sir Thomas Samwell was denied leave to go into the country.

Then the Order of the Day was read for taking into consideration the report of the conference touching the amendments to the bill of treasons.[1] And it was moved that the paper given at the conference containing the Lords' reasons for their disagreement might be read.

---

[1] Grey, x. 219–24 has a parallel account of the debate that follows.

But opposed as irregular. However, it was upon the question ordered to be read. Then the clause added by the Lords was read, and after the paper containing the Lords' reasons etc. was read.

Sir William Whitlock moved to agree to the Lords' clause, and seconded by *Sir Richard Temple.*

Sir John Guise opposed it.

Sir Robert Sawyer: I am for the bill and do think the Lords' reasons very satisfactory and fully to have answered your reason. *Sir Charles Sedley, Mr. Bathurst*, and *Mr. John Howe* were for this clause of the Lords.

Serj. Blencowe and *Mr. Dolben* were against the clause.

Mr. Finch spoke largely for the clause and the usefulness of the bill.

But in the midst thereof the Black Rod came (Sir Thomas Duppa) commanding the attendance of this House upon His Majesty in the House of Peers, which they did accordingly. And His Majesty passed two bills—the land tax and a private bill—and after made a speech to both Houses.[1]

Then *Mr. Finch* continued his speech in behalf of the bill and the clause about the Lords; that he did not see one clause in the bill that weakened the government and the clause is only to prevent a great hardship to the lords in their trials for treason.

Sir George Treby: I am against this bill for I think it tends to alter the frame and constitution of the government and may be a temptation to the lords to plot and conspire against the government. Then for the timing of this, I think it is not now so seasonable to pass this law since the government is assaulted on all sides, and if this act pass [it] will make an impunity for offenders.

Mr. Bertie and *Col. Granville* were both for the bill and clause.

Mr. Montagu: I am against agreeing with the Lords, for that though this House disagree with the Lords now yet the bill is not lost. As for our disagreement, I doubt not but we have better reasons to maintain the same, and therefore I desire we may offer them at a free conference. And I will observe this upon your bill—that in times of trouble you will not make treasons more unpunishable than in a time of peace. In the 15th E. III c. 2 a law was passed for the trial of peers in parliament, but the same year in October after that law was repealed, being found pernicious and of evil consequence. So upon the whole matter I take notice the Lords have been always grasping at this privilege.

[1] *CJ*, x. 604 records the summons to the Lords before the beginning of the debate on the Lords' amendment.

They have power over your estates by their pretended judicial power, over your tongues by their *Scandalum Magnatum*, and now you will give them farther all you can possibly and instead of a monarchy set up an aristocracy.

Sir Richard Temple spoke for the clause.

Sir John Darell, Mr. Clarke, and *Sir Thomas Littleton* were against it, for that now this is a great time of danger. And though the bill were to be desired in some times and be a good bill, yet not at this time.

Mr. Smith: I am against this clause. There is one thing in it not hitherto taken notice of. And that is if it pass as now drawn, the bishops themselves are admitted judges in capital cases. As for my part, the Lords have already advantages enough and I think this not a time to give them more.

So the question was put to insist upon disagreeing with the Lords in the clause. House divided—Noes went out.

		Sir William Whitlock	
	Noes		126[1]
		Mr. Bertie	
Tellers for the			
		Sir Robert Cotton (of Chester)	
	Yeas		186
		Mr. Montagu	

Speaker informed the House the next thing was a free conference, but whether the Lords or you are to desire it I am in doubt.

Sir Christopher Musgrave: I think it is our part to desire a free conference upon the subject-matter of the last conference for how can the Lords desire it when they know not what you have done?

So the question was put and carried for a free conference with the Lords on the subject-matter of the last free conference.

Mr. Montagu was ordered to go up and desire it, and the managers of [the] last conference had intimation to consider of reasons to be offered at the free conference.

Adjourned till 8 tomorrow morning.

Friday, 1 January 1691/2

Mr. Christie was ordered to carry up the bill for the better recovery of small tithes and to desire the concurrence of the Lords.

[1] 120 in *CJ*, x. 604.

Then the Order of the Day for the House going into a Committee
of the Whole House to consider of supplies, etc., was read and the
Speaker left the Chair. Solicitor General, Chairman, acquainted the
committee how far they had gone upon the estimates, and then they
proceeded on that for Ireland.

As to that that £18,000 be allowed for the civil list in Ireland for the
year 1692:

Mr. Fox informed the House that the charge of the civil list was
more formerly—about £23,000—and now there is more need it is but
£18,000.

Sir Christopher Musgrave: In the civil list then there was £5,000
reckoned for interest of money then owing, which we take to be now
paid and so the charge remains but £18,000.

So this question was put and agreed to.

To that that the customs inward and outward and the imported
excise of Ireland for the year 1692 may amount to £80,000 neat
money:

Mr. Culliford: I cannot agree to this, for that these duties never
made by a medium of three years but £125,000, of which £20,000
went to the several officers for collecting it. And the country is now
so ruined it will come far short. I have letters from some in that
country that they rid 30 miles together in some parts of the kingdom
and saw neither man, woman or child, bird or beast. And at the
highest computation, I do not believe the duty will amount to £65,000
neat. Sir John Lowther and Mr. Levinge to the same.

Mr. Paul Foley: What is now said here was said at the private committee and yet they thought fit to bring it up to £80,000, for there
will be more goods imported into that kingdom from foreign parts
than hath been of late years to stock and furnish the same. Sir Christopher Musgrave and Mr. Harley to the same.

So the question was put and agreed to.

To the third, that the inland excise and ale and wine licences in
Ireland for the year 1692 may amount to £50,000 neat money:

Mr. Culliford: This branch in the best times never made above
£75,000 or £76,000 and it costs the King yearly a great sum collecting. It cannot, I am sure, make above £40,000 now clear—the army
being now drawing off and the country is much depopulated and
in a wretched condition and there is great want of people, many
being destroyed by the war. Sir Robert Cotton (of Chester) to the
same.

Paul Foley: The inland excise itself came to that sum. Then here is the ale licences which yielded £9,000 and wine licences came to about £3,000, for which two last nothing is reckoned.

So the question was put and agreed to.

To the fourth, that the quit rents and Crown rents of Ireland for the year 1692 may amount to £33,000 neat money:

Mr. Culliford: Formerly the quit rents of Ireland were £65,000 per annum, but for this year you cannot at most receive above half a year and it will make for that time £30,000—land being so wasted and the stock thereof destroyed that it is worth little. And if you depend on this to supply the forces there, you will be deceived.

However, this question was put and agreed to.

To the fifth, that the casual revenue and the rents of the forfeited lands in Ireland for the year 1692 may amount to £10,000 neat money:

Mr. Culliford: That which is called the casual revenue is the first-fruits, tenths, sheriffs' fines, etc., which amount to about £4,000 per annum. Then for the forfeited estates, I did think once they might amount to £30,000 per annum, but since the reducing of Limerick most of the forfeited estates are restored to the owners by the capitulation so that I believe now they will not come to £6,000.

The question was put and resolved that the casual revenue may amount to £3,000. But for the forfeited estates, it was thought a great concern.

Mr. Colt: I had a letter from one Mr. Riggs and Mr. Rogers, two eminent merchants at present in Bristol who belong to Cork in Ireland and know that country very well, who seem to offer to advance in 18 months on the forfeited estates in Ireland and that of King James there the sum of £1,500,000.

Whereon this matter of the forfeited estates was postponed till the House came to consider of the ways and means to raise the money.

To the sixth, that the hearth money in Ireland for the year 1692 may amount to £17,000.

Mr. Culliford: This duty in the best of times never amounted to above £33,000 neat. And now a third part of the houses of the kingdom are destroyed, many of them are untenanted and the country depopulated in many places, and the charge is great in collecting this duty, so that it will not amount to above £10,000 neat.

Sir Peter Colleton, Sir Christopher Musgrave, Sir John Darell, and Mr. Arnold were for agreeing with the resolution of the committee because this revenue did chiefly arise from the towns where little mischief has been done.

So the question was put and agreed to.

Then there were several questions and resolutions thereon by the committee put and agreed to, which being contracted were to this effect: that the whole revenue of Ireland for the year 1692 may amount to £190,000, whereof £18,000 should be applied to bear the charge of the civil list; that £165,000, the residue of the revenue, should be applied to the payment of the army there; that there remains for England to pay towards the charge of Ireland £24,640. 18s. 8d.

So the heads being over, the Solicitor left the Chair and the Speaker took his Chair. The *Solicitor* reported that the committee had finished their resolutions, which he was commanded to report and which he was ready to make. And it was appointed to be made tomorrow morning.

Mr. Smith, *Mr. Arnold*, and *Sir Peter Colleton* moved for a committee to be appointed to receive proposals for raising moneys on the forfeited estates in Ireland. And ordered accordingly.

The *Speaker* acquainted the House he had received two letters from Mr. William Fuller—the first of them dated the 15th of December 1691 and another of this day—both of them desiring that six members of this House might confer with and advise him how to manage matters for the better bringing over the two persons he spoke of. The members of this House he desired to acquaint with these matters were Sir John Lowther, Sir Francis Blake, Sir Thomas Taylor, Mr. Arnold, Mr. Papillon, etc.

The letters were read, and therein he writes they were men of quality and estates, that they are men that will not desire their pardons till they have merited them and are above desiring any reward for their pains.

Speaker informed the House that Mr. Fuller had a blank passport from the Lord Sidney as he desired, and if you order me to give him a protection I will.

Mr. Arnold: The only thing he desires is your protection.

Sir Christopher Musgrave and *Sir Joseph Williamson* opposed that matter as a strange motion for he has all that he did desire and more than usual to have a blank pass.

Sir Henry Capel and *Mr. Bertie* moved that he might be brought to the Bar and tell his own story what it is he would have and wherefore.

Then it was proposed as a question that Mr. Fuller should have the protection of this House in going to and coming from the same.

Mr. Finch opposed this, for that he was already in the protection of the law safe enough, being in the custody of the Marshal of the King's Bench, and I hope you do not intend to take him out of his custody. The protection of this House he has of course, having been examined here.

Then it was moved that Mr. Fuller might have this House's protection for his two friends. But opposed as a strange motion and a thing never seen to trust him with the honour of this House for they knew not who. So moved that he might attend this House on Monday next to see what it is he does desire. Ordered accordingly.

Then the report of Sir Christopher Wren relating to the roof of the ceiling was read, showing the dangerous condition of the same. And it was ordered neither to be printed nor entered on the Journal.[1]

Major Vincent informed the House that he had viewed the roof and top of the same; that he found it in great danger and that the main beams were started out of the walls, which were also very rotten.

So a committee was appointed, consisting of six or eight members, who were to view the same with workmen and give their opinions thereon to the House.

Adjourned till 8 tomorrow morning.

Saturday, 2 January

Sir John Darell moved to appoint a committee to inspect the book of rates to see what was the duty set upon the manufactures and goods of the nation when exported, for as at present they are very high which prevents the carrying them out to the great prejudice of the country and the King gets nothing thereby—as particularly upon beef, bread, and biscuit, and several other things great duties are, so no encouragement to export them. *Mr. Colt* to the same.

So a committee was appointed accordingly.

Mr. Arnold moved to read the bill for relief of poor prisoners. Which the *Speaker* opposing, *Arnold* told him that he must not now think he was in Chancery but in the House of Commons to whom he was but a servant and that each member had a liberty of speech in the House.

[1] But see *CJ*, x. 605, where it is entered.

To the bill for preventing escapes, instructions were added by the House for the committee to consider of to whom the bill was referred as

1. moved by *Mr. Harcourt* that care might be taken to prevent the sponging houses of bailiffs, etc.;
2. moved by *Sir George Hutchins* that a man should not be obliged to come up hither to give bail before a judge but that he may do it before the commissioners appointed for taking affidavits in the country;
3. moved by *him* also that declarations may be delivered to persons in the custody of the sheriff as well as if in the prisons here in town.

Leave being asked for Mr. Burrard to go into the country, [it] was denied.

The *Solicitor General* reported from the Committee of the Whole House the several resolutions as to the land army, which were read and several of them agreed to. But as to those about the transport ships, they—coming to altogether about £106,000—were disagreed unto, for that in the estimates delivered in at first but £100,000 was demanded for the charge of the transport ships. So a general question was put and resolved that the charge of the transport ships be but £100,000 according to the estimate first delivered in.

Lord Ranelagh informed the House that the committee had taken no consideration of the charge of hospital ships nor other contingencies, and therefore desired the House would consider it.

Speaker: You cannot do it here, but it must come from a Committee of the Whole House.

Then the House proceeded upon the resolutions of Ireland relating to the two regiments of dragoons being put into one and the 15 regiments of foot being reduced to eight, which occasioned a great debate.

Sir John Lowther moved to disagree with the committee therein for that this would disband a great many officers and thereby disoblige them; that it would quite alter the frame and discipline of the regiments as now they are; and then that kingdom is not in such safety as imagined that it is necessary to lose so many at this time. *Sir Henry Capel, Sir Robert Cotton, Sir Robert Howard, Sir Stephen Fox, Sir John Guise,* and *Mr. Bathurst* to the same.

But it was opposed by *Sir Thomas Clarges* and *Paul Foley* for that the reason urged because we should not disband so many officers is no further an argument than it is against disbanding the army at any time. It was agreed by the House that the forces there should be according to the establishment in King Charles II's time, which this is as now agreed by the committee. And for the reason that it is not good to lessen them at this time for fear of the French, I think there is no great fear of that for they have not got so much there before as to venture again.

Sir Henry Goodricke: There is this further reason for disagreeing with the committee that the forts and garrisons are in so bad a condition that if 3,000 or 4,000 men did but land there, with the assistance of the Irish they might take the strongest fort there.

Sir Stephen Fox: I hope this House will not make this alteration at this time when the army there are so much in arrear, at least £400,000, that it is not safe so to do.

So at last the question was put to agree with the committee upon the resolution relating to the dragoons. The House divided—the Noes went out.

	Sir Robert Cotton	
	Yeas	100
	Sir Robert Henley	
Tellers for the		
	Sir Jonathan Jennings	
	Noes	176
	Mr. Cary	

So the House disagreed with the committee as to the resolution about the dragoons.

Then the question was put for agreeing with the committee for reducing the regiments of foot from 15 to eight. The House divided —the Noes went out.

	Mr. Price	
	Yeas	93
	Col. Pery	
Tellers for the		
	Col. Cornewall	
	Noes	150
	Mr. Dolben	

So the House disagreed with the committee.

Then the question was put for agreeing with the committee in their computation of the whole charge of the forces for Ireland. The House divided—Noes went out.

                              Sir Charles Wyndham
                    Yeas   88
                              Col. Granville
          Tellers for the
                              Sir John Guise
                    Noes   145
                              Mr. Smith

So disagreed with the committee.

Then the other resolutions of the committee relating to Ireland were read and agreed to.

Then they came to that of the total that was to be applied to the army out of the revenue there.

And the putting it was opposed by *Sir Thomas Clarges* and *Sir Christopher Musgrave*: That it could not be put for that the committee had disagreed to the total that was to be applied to the army and will you now vote that so much of the revenue of Ireland shall be applied to the army? So that you must go to the Committee of the Whole House again to compute the charge of the dragoons and foot as now settled before you can apply the revenue to them, and this is regular.

So after some debate it was recommitted to the Committee of the Whole House to consider further of the charge of the dragoons and foot soldiers to be in Ireland.

Capt. Bubb had leave to attend the House of Lords as a witness in a cause depending there.

So adjourned till 8 o'clock on Monday morning.

Monday, 4 January

The bill for recovering of small debts and relieving poor creditors in Westminster was ordered to be carried up to the Lords by Sir Walter Clarges.[1]

Mr. Solicitor and Serj. Tremaine had leave to attend a cause in the House of Lords.

Then the House, according to order, went into a Committee of the Whole House to consider farther of the supplies and the matter recommitted to them touching the charge of the dragoons and the foot for Ireland. And after some debate they resolved

[1] Sir Thomas Clarges in *CJ*, x. 609.

1. that the dragoons allotted for the service of Ireland for the year 1692 do consist of two regiments, 480 men in each including officers;
2. that the foot designed for Ireland do consist of 15 regiments of 780 men in each including officers;
3. that the charge of the two regiments of dragoons to be continued in Ireland be £31,015. 12s.;
4. that the charge of the foot there be £169,066. 16s.

Then the Lord Ranelagh informed the House that they had omitted the consideration of one particular—that of hospitals and other contingencies. That the charge of the hospitals in Ireland for last year amounted to above £10,000. Now there was in that kingdom two hospitals—a fixed one and a marching one. The establishment of the fixed one came to about £4,000 per annum and the marching one about £6,000. Now the matter is what you will think fit for the service of Flanders, nothing being desired for the forces in Ireland. The total of the hospitals in Ireland last year was £10,750. 16s., but now the army this year in Flanders will not be so great as was in Ireland, and therefore I shall propose the sum of £8,000 for the next year for the service of hospitals in Flanders.

So the question was put that the charge of the hospitals for the year 1692 should be £6,000—being a question proposed by Col. Granville and seconded, and being the lesser sum was first put by the rules of the House. Committee divided—Yeas on the right and Noes on the left.

	Yeas	Mr. Brownlow	50
Tellers for the			
	Noes	Sir John Morton	186

So carried in the negative. Then the question was put that the charge of the hospitals for the year 1692 should be £8,000 and carried in the affirmative.

Lord Ranelagh: Your next head to consider of is that of contingencies. And they are things of several heads such as wagons for bread, maintaining of prisoners, intelligence, rewarding of persons that signalize themselves in your service and for such as lose their limbs in your service. And for these ends and other casualties I shall propose a moderate sum—£30,000 for the next year.

So resolved that the charge of contingencies for the year 1692 be £30,000.

So the Solicitor was ordered to report to the House [the] several resolutions and to move to have leave to sit again. Then the Speaker resumed the Chair. And the *Solicitor* reported the said resolutions which he delivered in at the Table, where the same were read by the Clerk and after severally read and agreed to. And then *he* moved to have leave for the committee to sit again, and the House resolved itself into a Committee of the Whole House immediately to consider of the supplies.

The Speaker left the Chair and the Solicitor was Chairman. And after some time the committee came to this resolution: That it is the opinion of this committee that a sum not exceeding £1,935,787. 16s. 3d. (together with the sum of £165,000 to be answered out of the revenue of Ireland) be the sum for the land forces for the service of the year 1692 in order to the carrying on a vigorous war against France. The Solicitor was ordered to report this resolution and to ask leave to sit again.

So the Speaker resumed the Chair. And the *Solicitor* reported the said resolution to which the House agreed and resolved to go into a committee again tomorrow to consider of the ways and means for raising the supplies.

Sir Robert Cotton (of Cheshire) moved that the thanks of this House might be given to General Ginkel for the great service he has done this King and kingdom in reducing of Ireland. And was seconded by *Sir William Strickland.*

Sir Christopher Musgrave: I am not very fond of this way of this House giving thanks. But if you do, I hope you will do the like for the English officers and soldiers who behaved themselves very bravely.

Col. Granville: I do not speak against the service done by Monsieur Ginkel in Ireland, but I am afraid it is made use of to another end. There is a report that this gentleman is to be Master of the Ordnance and I am not willing to be made a colour to advance him to that place and I am against putting the forts and garrisons into a foreigner's hands.

Mr. Hampden: I am sorry to see such jealousies and suspicions in this House; I do not like it. But if you put it for the General to have thanks, put it also for the other officers.

Sir William Strickland: This way of thanking is not a new thing. It was formerly done to Duke Schomberg, to Mr. Walker, and to Lord Torrington who was beaten by the French at that very time and he did what the English fleet never did—run from the French.

So resolved that the thanks of this House be given to General Ginkel and the officers that served in Ireland for the great service they have done His Majesty and this kingdom in reducing of Ireland.

Then it was moved that some members might be appointed to attend the General and acquaint him with the resolution of the House and to desire him to communicate it to the rest of the officers. Others moved that the General might be admitted into the House and have the thanks of the House given him by the Speaker, he having a chair for him within the Bar. But the House chose the former way and appointed a committee of seven members of the House to attend the General and acquaint him with the thanks of this House and desire him to communicate the same to the officers that served in Ireland.

The managers that managed the last conference were ordered to think of reasons to be offered at the free conference with the Lords tomorrow.

Then Mr. Fuller (the evidence) according to order was called in. And he desired that he might acquaint six or seven members of the House with what he had further to say and to have their advice and direction about sending for those two persons he would bring over, who could not only give an account of former designs but also of what were at present carrying on. I have a blank pass from the Lord Sidney for one person to go out of England but not for any to come into England. And before I had that I sent for one over, and since I hear from the two persons that they will come over. They are men of some quality and will not expose themselves without the protection of this House, for there are great men deeply concerned in this plot. So that all I desire is that they may have the protection of this House and that they may not be brought over in the packetboat.

So Fuller was ordered to withdraw.[1]

Sir Francis Blake and *Sir William Strickland* moved that an address might be made to His Majesty to give his protection to the two persons that were to come over. *Mr. Hutchinson, Sir Walter Yonge,* and *Mr. Clarke* to the same.

Ordered that such an application be made to His Majesty by the members of the Privy Council that are of this House to grant Mr. Fuller a blank pass for two persons for safe coming from beyond sea or any other place hither to give their evidence and for their safe protection while here and their safe return if desired.

Sir Christopher Musgrave opposed this House's giving a protection

---

[1] Grey, x. 225–6 has a parallel account of the brief debate that follows.

as being a matter altogether new. And what will it signify, for perhaps this House may be up before they can come over and then what will it signify?

So Fuller was called in again and acquainted with the resolution of this House. Then Fuller moved that he might have a habeas corpus for himself to attend His Majesty and to acquaint him with this matter. But this not a proper court for that.

Adjourned till 8 tomorrow morning.

Tuesday, 5 January

The bill for better regulation and encouragement of the Company of Fishermen of the River of Thames and providing seamen for Their Majesties' fleet and preventing frauds in stealing of customs was read the first time.

Several members spoke against it, as *Mr. Montagu, Sir John Parsons, Solicitor General*, and *Mr. Chadwick*: That it was an attempt to set up the greatest monopoly that could be, that of fish; that it encroaches upon the privileges of the Lord Mayor of London as Conservator of the River Thames; that it entrenches on the Vice-Admiralty of Kent because it incorporates only the fishermen of the River of Thames, exclusive of others. It tends to the Company's exacting on all inhabitants of London and destroys the fishermen of Kent.

Serj. Trenchard and *Mr. Arnold* spoke for it.

So the question was put for reading it a second time and it passed in the negative.

The time for the free conference being come, the same managers were appointed to manage the free conference with the Lords as managed the last conference, and their names were read over and some more added. So they went up. And being returned, *Mr. Montagu* reported from the conference at the Bar: That the managers had attended the same and that he began to open the conference. Then the Lord Mulgrave began on the part of the Lords, and after the Lord Stamford and others argued. Then some of the Commons replied. That the Lords Rochester, Nottingham, Monmouth, and several others spoke in it. That the debate had been very long on both sides, and therefore he desired some time to confer with the managers and would collect the debate as well as they could and report the same to the House as soon as possible.

Adjourned till 8 tomorrow morning.

Wednesday, 6 January

The House went into a Committee of the Whole House to consider of the ways and means for raising the supplies for Their Majesties. The Speaker left the Chair and the Solicitor General was Chairman.

Mr. Neale proposed as one head for raising of money for carrying on the war an imposition upon all salt—all foreign salt to pay 2*s*. 6*d*. a bushel at the Custom House and 1*s*. a bushel upon home salt to be paid at the salt pans. This will raise at least £200,000, for I compute in England there are about eight millions of people, who may one with another consume about half a bushel of salt. This will raise a great sum and not be felt.

Sir Robert Sawyer: I think you are not ripe for that yet. You ought first to compute what the total charge amounts to, what you have given may come to, and what more is yet to raise.

Col. Sackville seconded Mr. Neale's motion.

Sir Christopher Musgrave seconded Sawyer's motion as the most regular way.

Sir John Lowther: The land tax will not amount to above £1,500,000 neat money besides the charges of collecting and for the interest of the loans thereon. Then for the excise, till July next there are three ninepences to be deducted, and after but two. And for each ninepence deducted comes to about £156,000, so that this whole duty will not come to £350,000. The customs computed at a medium for three years past may come to about £372,065 per annum, but deducting the debt already charged thereon of £153,823 it will not amount to above £218,000 clear. Post Office is computed at £60,000 per annum; small branches about £26,000 per annum; casual revenue about £14,000 or £20,000. Then for the charges of the civil list, they are computed at about £600,000 per annum. Besides which you have charged on the revenue the ordinary of the Ordnance about £60,000; garrisons, forts, etc., £31,000; ordinary of the Navy about £92,000. So it appears the revenue of the Crown will not bear the charge of the civil list by above £100,000.

Sir Christopher Musgrave: I think your proper method is to compute what the land tax will amount to neat money and then go head by head upon the rest. Besides, the land tax is computed at £100,000 neat money less than the sum given; I would gladly see how that comes to pass.

Sir Stephen Fox: There is deducted for the land tax collecting near

£50,000 and the interest of the loans is about the like sum. Therefore, I believe that tax may be computed at about £1,550,000 or £1,560,000 neat money and no more.

Paul Foley: Part of the land tax is to be applied to the use of the army, so that the money taken up for that end on that act the interest whereof will be paid out of the money arising by the 12*d.* reserved in your bill to prevent false musters. Therefore, you may compute the land tax at more.

Sir Stephen Fox: That is very true, but the 12*d.* will not come in till the clearings of the army which may not be in 12 months after.

Sir Richard Onslow: The charges of the fleet this year will be very great. It will be £600,000 at least before they can go to sea.

Resolved that the land tax this year may amount to £1,570,000 neat money.

Paul Foley: As to the double excise estimated to be worth but £350,000, it yielded the last year from 17 November 1690 to Michaelmas 1691 about £412,000, so that I think the excise may be fairly computed at £400,000.

Sir John Lowther: I think it is impossible for the excise to amount to above £370,000.

Sir Samuel Dashwood: I do really believe the excise this year will not amount to what it did the last year—nay, not £370,000.

Mr. Foley: I wonder at what is here affirmed. There was upon the double excise paid into the Exchequer the last year at least £600,000, and they do not use to pay in more than the duty amounts to, out of which—deducting for the ninepence that falls off—it may really yield £400,000 clear.

Mr. Godolphin: Every sixpence upon a barrel by way of excise comes to yearly £100,000, which being deducted out of the double excise there will remain about £400,000. And for the charges of collecting the duty, that is paid out of the old excise.

Second, resolved that the duty of double excise may for the year 1692 amount to £400,000 neat money.

Then the House went to consider what the revenue might bear.

Sir John Lowther: The revenue of the Crown is so far unable to be charged anything towards carrying on the war that there is £130,000 wanting thereof to bear the charge of the civil list by reason of several debts thereon already.

Sir Charles Sedley moved that the House would consider of offices under the Crown. Some persons have two or three offices, others have great salaries, and then there are divers unnecessary officers which are fit to be regulated, and thereby you may raise a good sum of money.

Mr. Godolphin: The customs consist of three parts—the old customs, those upon tobacco and sugars, and that on East India goods. There is so much already charged on them that nothing can be got thereout.

Paul Foley: The revenue for the last year came to in all £2,294,862, which included the double excise. This must be deducted thereout, as also the debt contracted by the Crown taking up a million on the credit of the revenue, a good part of which remains still due; so also the impositions on tobacco and sugars and the charges of collecting these duties, all which must be deducted. Which being done, I cannot value the revenue at less than £800,000, so that I think it may well bear the charge of the government and £200,000 over towards carrying on the war.

Sir John Lowther: I desire we may go to particulars and not lump it thus.

Sir Christopher Musgrave: As we must not lump it in the revenue, so I desire we may not in that of the civil list but may have the particulars thereof laid before the House.

Sir Stephen Fox: The charge of the civil list is about £600,000 without including that of the garrisons, the ordinary charge of the Navy, and the ordinary of the Ordnance, which you have now thrown upon the revenue, so that the whole charge of the civil list comes to about £800,000.

Mr. Palmes and Mr. Smith moved that the particulars of the civil list and a state of the revenue might be brought in and laid before the House.

And it was upon a question resolved accordingly.

Then the Speaker resumed the Chair and the *Solicitor* reported that the committee had sat and made some progress in the matter referred to them and had directed him to move that a particular state of the revenue and a computation of the civil list might be laid before the House, which was ordered accordingly. Then *he* moved for leave for the committee to sit again, and the House ordered again tomorrow to go upon the supplies after the bill against mutineers and deserters is reported.

Sir John Lowther acquainted the House that His Majesty had been attended with the address in reference to Mr. Fuller and that His

Majesty had been graciously pleased to say a pass should be granted
as was desired.

So adjourned till 8 tomorrow morning.

Thursday, 7 January

All the members that serve for the county of Somerset were added
to the committee to whom the Lord Waldegrave's bill was committed.[1]

A message from the Lords that they desired a present free conference in the Painted Chamber upon the subject-matter of the last free
conference. The messengers being withdrawn, the *Speaker* informed
the House that though the Lords had the power to appoint the time
of conferences, yet if the House thought fit they may put it off or else
in time the Lords will command this House when they please.

Mr. Hampden: That is very true, but then at the same time this
House hath sent up messengers of their own to acquaint them with
the reasons of your disagreement to such conference.

Sir Christopher Musgrave: I never saw such a precedent yet that
where the Lords have sent for a present free conference on the subject-
matter of the last that you have ever denied it. This would break all
good correspondence between the two Houses, and no one can deny
but that the Lords have the privilege to appoint time and place.

Sir John Guise: I think you have a very good reason to put off the
free conference now, for you have ordered the managers to report the
last free conference to you and when that report is made you may
debate it if you have the bill before you, otherwise not.

Sir Robert Sawyer: You do not know but the Lords desire this conference to agree with you and return the bill to you, and will you not
then have one?

The *Speaker* then spoke to and debated as to the privileges of this
House. But *Sir Christopher Musgrave* and *Sir Thomas Clarges* took him
down to the orders of the House for that he ought not to debate any
matter whatsoever. But *he* insisted on it that in matter of privilege he
might.

Mr. Finch: It is true if there be any dispute what is the order of the
House it is the duty of the Chair to set the House right in that matter
but not to debate concerning any order of the House. Now to the
matter itself, what reason can you offer for disagreeing to a present

---

[1] There is no entry of this in the *Journal*.

free conference that will be for the honour of this House? And then it is the direct way to destroy the good correspondence between the two Houses.

Solicitor General: I am against this present free conference because I do not find there have been any.

Speaker, having looked over the Journals, informed the House that he found several precedents of conferences from one House to the other in 1690, but then there is a clause in each conference desired of either House—'if it may seem convenient'. Then there is one of a present free conference but that is qualified with this—'so soon as it may stand with the conveniency of this House'—and you have returned an answer by their messengers that you will return an answer by messengers of your own. I do not say you can refuse such conference, but you are not obliged to grant it if it be inconvenient to you.

After some debate, the question was put for agreeing to a present free conference with the Lords. The House divided—the Yeas went out.

		Mr. Gwyn	
	Yeas		110
		Mr. Bertie	
Tellers for the			
		Sir John Guise	
	Noes		139
		Mr. Cary	

Sir Thomas Littleton and *Sir Robert Rich* moved that the messengers might be called in and acquainted that this House would return an answer by messengers of their own with all convenient speed to their Lordships.

So the messengers were called in and acquainted therewith accordingly.

So House adjourned till 8 tomorrow morning.

Friday, 8 January

Mr. Bere presented a petition to the House from the clothiers in and about Tiverton in Devonshire praying them to take some care that the woollen manufacture be not set up in Ireland, there being many workmen concerned therein going thithre. It was referred to a committee appointed to consider of others of the like nature.

Mr. *Whitley* presented to the House a petition of one Mr. Dodsworth desiring that some application might be made to the King for some allowance for the great charges he had been at in prosecuting his information against the papists in Lancashire for intending to make an insurrection there. [It] was received and read and ordered to lie on the Table.

A bill for the lessening the interest of money was read the second time.

Several spoke against it as *Sir Christopher Musgrave, Sir George Hutchins, Sir Samuel Barnardiston, Sir John Knight, Sir Henry Gough, Sir Robert Sawyer, Mr. Clarke, Sir John Brownlow, Sir William Strickland, Sir Peter Colleton*, and *Mr. Smith* for that it was a dangerous experiment to be tried at this time. It was taking away a sixth part of the monied man's estate. That it would ruin daughters and younger children. That money was a commodity and would rise or fall in interest according to the plenty or scarcity of money and was not to be restrained.

Several spoke for it as *Sir Robert Henley, Mr. Brockman, Lord Castleton, Sir Edward Hussey, Sir John Lowther* (of Lowther), *Sir Charles Sedley, Mr. Howe, Mr. Papillon, Mr. Bowyer, Mr. Hampden*, and *Sir Thomas Littleton* and urged that the passing this law would be very advantageous to the kingdom. It would raise the value of land and the rents thereof, and make the poor farmer better able to live, and bring money to a nearer proportion with land, which bore all the charges of the government. It would mightily encourage trade for though plenty of money, it is true, will make interest low, yet it is trade makes plenty of money and the lowness of interest will increase trade, for it is observed that in Spain and Ireland where interest is high, at 10 per cent, yet they have little money, trade being not great, but in Holland where interest is low there is a great trade.

So at last the question was put for committing the bill. The House divided—Yeas go forth.

		Mr. Bickerstaffe	
	Yeas		169
		Sir Robert Henley	
Tellers for the			
		Sir Samuel Barnardiston	
	Noes		153
		Col. Granville	

So the bill was committed and a committee named.

Lord Colchester having been up at the House of Lords with their answer—that this House doth agree to a free conference desired by their Lordships—he acquainted this House that the Lords had appointed the same to be tomorrow at 12 o'clock in the Painted Chamber, to which this House agreed.

Mr. Robartes presented a petition from Sir John Molesworth, Sheriff of Cornwall, on the behalf of himself and other the inhabitants of that county, as also letters patent granted by King Charles I at Oxford in the 17th year of his reign to the men of Cornwall of a free trade to all parts of the world.

The petition and charter were received and read. And the same relating to the trade to the East Indies, *Mr. Boscawen* prayed they might be taken into further consideration when the House came to settle the East India trade.

Then the House went upon the consideration of the answer and proposals given in by the committee of the East India Company.

Mr. Methuen moved, and was seconded by *Sir Thomas Littleton*, that the House would be pleased to vote the security offered by the Company to be sufficient.

But this was long debated. Those for a new company were for calling in the members of the old Company and acquainting them with the regulations made by this House that the security expected was a recognizance to answer so much stock as they propose to be a security for.

So the members were called in and acquainted with the same. And being asked some questions, Sir Thomas Cook in the name of the rest answered that they were willing to submit to the regulations made by this House and to such others as they should think fit and would give the security desired.

Resolved that this House doth approve of the security proposed by the East India Company.

Sir John Lowther moved, and *Mr. Finch* to the same, that an humble address be made to His Majesty to dissolve the present East India Company, for that there was no end to be put to this matter otherwise—it having taken up so much of your time already and would more.

So after a long debate, a question was stated: that leave be given to bring in a bill to establish an East India Company according to the regulations agreed upon by this House. But those that were for the old Company took exceptions to the word 'an' in the question and would have the word 'the' inserted. And after some debate, the question was put whether the word 'an' should stand part of the question. The House divided—the Yeas went forth.

Mr. Smith

Yeas   115

[Sir Francis Drake][1]

Tellers for the

Sir Robert Davers

Noes   85

Mr. Harcourt

So the whole question was put and carried clearly.

Adjourned till tomorrow morning 8 of the clock.

Saturday, 9 January

Dr. Barbone reported from the committee appointed to take a view of the House of Commons and the roof thereof that they found the timber very rotten and the walls much decayed, that the building was dangerous and not in a condition to be repaired. Upon which it was resolved that an humble address should be made to His Majesty by such members of this House as are of the Privy Council that a convenient place may be provided for the Commons in Parliament to sit, the condition of this present House being very ruinous and dangerous.

Then the House proceeded to consider of the amendments made by the Lords to the bill for better discovery and punishment of deer stealers. And the same were read, to some of which the House agreed. But the Lords having added a clause to impose a penalty of £10 on anyone that should pull down a pale or wall of a park in the night-time, this was opposed by several members because the Lords have no power to impose a penalty, for it is levying money on the subject which the Lords have no power to do. For this very reason, the bill about employing of seamen was lost the last sessions. So proposed that the penalty should be left out and to enforce the clause that the party offending therein should be committed to prison for three months without bail, which was ordered accordingly. And the Lords' clause agreed to with these amendments and Sir Robert Henley was ordered to carry it up to the Lords.[2]

---

[1] Blank in MS.; from *CJ*, x. 617.

[2] For an account of a debate, not mentioned by Luttrell, on the bill for continuing the Commission of Accounts see B.M. Loan 29/79, Robert Harley to Sir Edward Harley, 9 Jan.

Several members on particular motions were added to divers committees.

The managers went up to the free conference with the Lords. And being returned, *Mr. Montagu* reported that they had attended the conference and the Lords had returned the bill with some reasons. But withal it being now late, he desired some little time and he would prepare himself to report both the free conferences together. So ordered that they be both made and taken into consideration on Tuesday morning next.

Adjourned till Monday morning 8 of the clock.

Monday, 11 January

Henry Mordaunt esq. (brother to the Earl of Monmouth) was introduced into the House, being chosen a member for Brackley in Northamptonshire (in the room of Sir William Egerton, deceased), and took the oaths at the Table.

Then the Order of the Day was read for going into a Committee of the Whole House upon the supplies.

Mr. Grey presented a petition of several merchants and others that serve the Navy with stores, setting forth they had supplied the Navy with great stores and that the tallies assigned them for their money on the excise for four years was so far behind and after so much that it was little worth—the fund proving not sufficient for the sum the King was enabled to borrow thereon. *Capt. Pitt* also presented another from divers artificers and tradesmen that had served the Ordnance to the same effect.

They were both read and referred to the Committee of the Whole House.

Then the papers of the state of the revenue and that of the civil list were read and referred to the consideration of the Committee of the Whole House.

Then the House resolved itself into a Committee of the Whole House, the Speaker leaving the Chair, and Mr. Solicitor was Chairman. The papers of the revenue and the civil list were read again.

Mr. Paul Foley: I observe in this paper of the revenue there are divers particulars undervalued, as that of the customs; it is computed at but £372,065. 13s. It yielded in 1689 above £500,000, so in 1691, but in 1690 it yielded but little above £300,000; the reason of that was because of the stop or embargo upon trade at that time. But the

fairest computation is to take it from Michaelmas 1690 to Michaelmas 1691, and it produced in the gross receipt £558,654 and deducting all charges it [produced] £419,939 neat money.

Sir John Lowther: I think the best computation of this revenue is
as in like cases—by a medium of three years—and not to take one
year by itself, for that will be very unequal. For this year, you had
a great Smyrna fleet came home, which is not to be expected the like
in two or three years. Then you had some ships from the East Indies,
the customs whereof came to near £50,000. Then you had a great
West India fleet. All which have raised this year's customs considerably.

Mr. Harley moved that the customs might be computed at
£419,939 for this next year.

After a long debate pro and con about what the customs would
amount to, it was proposed to compromise the matter that they might
be taken at £400,000. But yet it was after put and resolved that the
customs for the year 1692 beginning this first of January might
amount to £419,939 clear money.

Then a debate arose on the debts and other moneys to be deducted
out of the customs and after it was resolved that what money remains
due of the £500,000 taken up on the customs and the interest thereof
that is due thereon on 1 January 1691/2 be deducted out of the
£419,939; resolved that the sum of £8,817. 8s. 6d. be deducted out
of the £419,939; resolved that £2,000 be deducted thereout for the
Queen.

Mr. Foley: Now as to the excise, there will be for a year about
£521,000, which is reckoning but 2s. 6d. to the barrel—which is only
what now remains clear, the other parts of it being appropriated. The
whole excise at 6s. 6d. a barrel comes to above £1,352,000, but there
remains now only 2s. 6d. a barrel clear, which according to that proportion comes to £521,000.

Sir Samuel Dashwood: What is now said is very true, but then the
£521,000 is the gross sum out of which must be paid £95,000 for
charges of collecting the whole excise.

Mr. Paul Foley: The excise that is collected in the country is
returned neat money up here and they deduct the charges of collecting it there out of the money they receive there so that there ought
only the charges of collecting the duty here in town to be deducted
out of it, which is but £24,000.

But this admitting of debate, it was postponed.

Then resolved that £65,000 and £2,000 be deducted out of the £521,000. The head of the duty of low wines was postponed, the committee not being fully instructed in it. Resolved that letter money may for the year 1692 amount to £51,000 neat money. Resolved that the casualties and small branches may amount to £60,000.

So then the Solicitor was ordered to leave the Chair and to acquaint the House that the Committee of the Whole House had met and made some further progress in the matter referred to them and had directed him to move for the committee to have leave to sit again. All which the *Solicitor* did when the Speaker resumed the Chair, and the House resolved to sit again tomorrow thereon.

Adjourned till 8 tomorrow morning.

Tuesday, 12 January

The House went into a Committee of the Whole House, according to the order, to consider of the supplies; Mr. Solicitor, Chairman.

Sir John Lowther: You yesterday postponed several particulars about the excise. Now the excise in all parts did make but £1,313,700 from 17 November 1690 to 17 November 1691 and we reckoned it in our particular £15,000 more whereby we overcharged the King so much.

Sir Thomas Clarges and Mr. Paul Foley: The only question now before you is whether £95,000 shall be deducted for collecting the old excise, which is the total charge of collecting that in London and the country too, or but £24,000 for collecting only that in town. For that in the country being returned up clear or neat money, out of which the charges of collecting is deducted, there remains only the charge of what here in town to be deducted.

This was denied by Sir John Lowther and took up a long debate pro and con.

At last Mr. Smith and Mr. Foley, to put an end to the debate, proposed that £200,000 may be raised upon the revenue for carrying on the war this next year.

Sir Thomas Clarges to the same, but took exceptions to the civil list now brought in—that it was the highest that ever was. And I hope in a short time those gentlemen concerned in the King's revenue will take care to regulate expenses of His present Majesty as was in King Charles II's time.

Resolved that out of the revenue for the year 1692 the sum of £200,000 be applied to the carrying on the war.

Mr. Neale then proposed as one of the means to raise money that an excise of 12*d.* a bushel be laid on all home salt and 2*s.* 6*d.* a bushel on foreign salt. I compute there are in this kingdom about six millions of people that eat salt and that each head, one with another, may eat half a bushel of salt, which by computation may raise about £150,000. And I value it at but £100,000; if it comes to more you will have the advantage of it.

Mr. Howe opposed it for that it would be a heavy tax upon the poor farmer.

Paul Foley: You are now upon the ways of raising money. I have heard of a great debt owing by the Crown to the bankers, and the law seems to allow of the same. I am informed they will advance you £1,000,000 of money at five per cent if they may have their money now owing to them secured by a good fund to pay a perpetual interest. I am informed also that the East India Company—whichsoever you establish by act of parliament—will for the same advance £200,000 for carrying on the war.

Mr. Hampden: As to the proposal relating to the bankers, I think it the easiest and readiest way of raising money at this time and therefore it is advisable for you to consider of it and hear what proposals they will offer to you.

Sir Thomas Clarges: I think no one will question the justice or honesty of the debt to the bankers, the seizing of whose money was a most wicked thing and the keeping it from them now is I think as bad. But now as to the proposition before you, there are some difficulties in it but I think it is fit to be considered of, and therefore I move you would appoint a committee to consider of the same and to receive such proposals as shall be made touching the same.

Sir Charles Sedley: I am against this proposal for I would not ever have this House give so great a countenance to our kings' taking up money without parliament. And as you pay this debt, so you may many others. And this is a bill contrived to encourage future kings to do the like.

Sir Joseph Tredenham: I think this proposal is honourable, just, and convenient for us—to pay a debt that is a crying debt upon the nation, and very convenient since it helps us to such a sum of money who want it now at this time so much.

Sir Christopher Musgrave was for the proposal but not to allow them all their interest and principal.

Mr. Hampden: If you approve of this proposal, there is no great difficulty but to provide a fund sufficient for the payment of a perpetual interest.

Mr. Smith: I am against this proposal for I would by no means encourage alienations by the Crown of their revenue; it was that which ruined the Crown of Spain. And the bankers in this matter are those that exacted upon the necessities of the Crown and therefore I would not countenance them.

Mr. Jeffreys: I am against allowing this debt, but I doubt not if you will settle a perpetual fund there will be money enough brought in.

Sir Edward Hussey against this proposal because he would have the revenues of the Crown as sacred as those of the Church.

Henry Herbert was for the proposal.

Mr. Palmes: I think the business of this committee is to consider how to raise moneys for carrying on the war and not how to pay old debts of the Crown. This project has been proposed before in this House but would not go down, and therefore I hope now it will take the same fate.

Sir Robert Sawyer: I am against this that is proposed because I believe nothing will come of it and I look upon it only as a shoeing horn to draw on something else, for the generality of the persons concerned in this matter are so poor they are not able to advance the sum proposed.

Mr. Smith: If this project go on, I believe the only persons that will be benefited hereby are the bankers and such as have bought the first assignments from them at half the value or less, there being— I believe—few of the first creditors left. And there is this hindrance that if some of those concerned will not come into your proposals, what will you do then?

Mr. Harley, Mr. Ettrick, and Sir Samuel Barnardiston were all for a committee to be appointed to hear proposals and to report the same to the House.

Sir John Lowther: I am for this matter for the reasons alleged. There is this farther; the bankers are ready for a judgement upon their patent against the King in the Exchequer, and if it be for them there will be so much of the hereditary excise struck off from the Crown which this House must supply some other way or else the service will be neglected.

Sir Walter Yonge and Mr. Arnold were against this proposal, that a public bank might be established for taking up of money.

Mr. Finch: I am for a committee to state and propose this matter to you. And I think no one can deny the legality of the debt, for the doubt in Westminster Hall was not as to the right of the parties, that being never denied, but the question was which was the proper way to attain the same. The judges in the court below seem to be of opinion they are in a proper way by their petition of right, and if they have judgement there accordingly, as any money comes into the Exchequer upon the excise they may lay their hands upon it.

Sir Robert Henley and Sir Thomas Littleton were against it.

Sir John Trevor: I am against referring this to a committee for either you must take this debt as a stated debt or else ravel into it. I know of my own certain knowledge that money frequently went amongst some persons to state that debt as now it is and I am sure it was an arrant cheat on the Crown, and therefore I am for rejecting this proposal.

Sir John Lowther and Mr. Hampden were against rejecting this proposal, it being the most plausible and speedy way of raising money as much as you want. Sir Christopher Musgrave to the same.

Col. Austen: I am against this matter going to a private committee but would rather have it let fall. And let the Lords of the Treasury receive the proposals and if likely to turn to any account we shall hear of it again. Mr. Methuen and Lord Eland to the same.

Sir Robert Cotton (of the Post Office) was for committing it.

Mr. Hampden and Sir Christopher Musgrave opposed its going to the Lords of the Treasury as being unparliamentary, but it ought to go to a committee. So Sir Joseph Williamson.

Mr. Montagu: I think it will be most for your service and the benefit of the public to pass a vote in general terms for settling of a fund for payment of a perpetual interest.

So the question was put and resolved that the House be moved to appoint a committee to receive proposals for a fund of perpetual interest in order to the raising a sum of money for carrying on the war against France.

So Solicitor left the Chair and Speaker resumed his Chair. And the *Solicitor* reported that the committee had made a further progress in the matter to them referred, and then *he* made the motion for a committee to be appointed. And a committee was appointed accordingly

of eight or 10 members, and any five to make a quorum and to sit
de die in diem.

Adjourned till tomorrow morning 8 of the clock.

Wednesday, 13 January

Mr. Fenwick was ordered to carry up Mr. Shelton's bill to the Lords.

Mr. Powlett had leave to go into the country.

Mr. Montagu, according to order, reported the two free conferences
with the Lords and desired to make use of his papers. He began with
the first conference.

That the Commons began that conference and offered their reasons
for insisting on disagreeing to the Lords' clause marked 'A'. That this
clause alters the nature of the trial in the case of peers and lets in the
spiritual lords to the same advantages as the temporal lords have,
whereby the constitution of the Lord High Steward's Court is quite
altered. That this method of trial (as now) is very ancient, there being
a precedent of it in 1 H. IV, not but that it was ancienter. Then this
clause brings in an impunity for treason by rendering it not punishable, which may prove very destructive to this government and the
constitution thereof.

The lords that spoke at that conference were the Duke of Bolton,
Marquess of Halifax, Earl of Mulgrave, Pembroke, Stamford, Nottingham, Monmouth, etc. That the time to provide for the good of the
people was in good kings' time. That this is the proper work of a
parliament. That times of trouble may come by an oppressive king
and then such a law will be wanting, and the Commons at such a time
will be glad to have the assistance of the peers, who will not then
perhaps be so forwards to help them if this clause pass not. That this
manner of trial by a High Steward as now used—only by a select
number of the Lords—was not ancienter than Henry VIII's time.
Then that the book of H. IV is no authority for it appears by
Rot[ularum] Parl[iamentum] 2 H. IV that he was beheaded by the
rabble. Then the course is not altered by appointing more judges
than it is by making three judges in the King's Bench when they are
four judges. Sheriffs are made by the King before the trial of a commoner but a Lord High Steward is made by the King after the crime
[is] committed and may be chosen out of the prisoner's enemies. Nay,
if a great man fear an impeachment of the Commons, he may get
himself to be tried before a Lord High Steward in an interval of parlia-

ment and so avoid the impeachment by getting himself acquitted and for which he cannot be tried again. That the noblemen tried out of parliament are generally friends to the Commons, and therefore why should the Commons press so hard upon the lords who cannot in probability have a fair trial? For that if the Court have a mind to take off any lord, it may easily be done by summoning 13 lords (the usual number) who may be enemies of the lord to be tried, for he hath no benefit of challenge and seven of them are sufficient to condemn any lord.

The Commons reply that they wondered to hear it said that this trial was no ancienter than H. VIII. But the statute 15 E. III c. 2 is a proof to the contrary, for that appoints the lords to be tried by the whole House of Peers. But that was repealed in less than a year after, being found very mischievous. This way of trial by a Lord High Steward is the *judicium paribus* mentioned in Magna Carta c. [39]. And though it is pretended seven lords are enough to find a peer guilty, it is otherwise for there ought to be 12 that give such verdict. So Lord Dacre's case, 24 H. VIII ([Sir Francis] Moore, [*Cases Collect and*] *Rep*[*ort*], f. [86]), where it is laid down for law that no one can be convicted for his life but by verdict of 24, 12 of the grand jury and as many of the other. It cannot be presumed the Lords will so far misbehave themselves as to convict one of their honourable body unjustly. And as to that of a great man getting himself to be acquitted to avoid an impeachment, it cannot well be. And though perhaps it should happen, the parliament notwithstanding might lay their hands upon him.

Second conference: The Lords are pleased to say they have not power to amend their own clause, but the Commons may; and if they think fit to limit the number of them or to impose a penalty on such of the lords as do not appear or to make what other alteration this House shall think fit, their Lordships are willing to consent to anything that is reasonable and to that end have returned you the bill to do as you shall think fitting and consent to the inserting the word 'temporal' or exclude the bishops as you will.[1]

Mr. Waller: Since the Lords are willing to have this clause amended to pass this into a law, I will offer you some amendments to it—to insert the word 'temporal'. Then as [to] the limiting the number of peers at a trial for a peer, it is said to be law that 12 must agree to find a peer guilty; therefore I would oblige that 23 of necessity must be

[1] Grey, x. 237–40 has a parallel account of the debate that follows.

present under the penalty of £1,000, and no one shall be condemned without 12 at the least find the party guilty.

Mr. Clarke: I am against these amendments, for it is not parliamentary for the Lords to prescribe rules to this House.

Sir William Whitlock seconded Mr. Waller's motion, this being only to set some bounds to a Lord High Steward that he shall not summon less than 23—it being now in his power to summon what peers he will or the whole House if he please.

Mr. Hutchinson: Though this method of trial of a lord have some inconveniences, yet I am sure a commoner is under greater. We have had judges and sheriffs who have actually hanged men without cause, yet the Lords to their immortal honour in a late reign acquitted the Lord Delamere though the Court then would have gladly had him found guilty. For my part, I think this not a time to give the Lords this privilege; they have sufficient already. But if they will give us something in amends, as quit their judicial power in cases of appeal from decrees in courts of equity, I will be for the clause thus amended. Otherwise I am against it.

Sir Charles Sedley, Sir Henry Gough, and *Mr. Bickerstaffe* were for the amendments and desired the House would proceed to the same.

Mr. Bathurst was for it, and he observed thar the case cited 1 H. IV was when the parliament was sitting, and the first trial of a lord by a High Steward was that of the Duke of Bucks in H. VIII's time.

Sir John Guise opposed the amendments for that it was unparliamentary for the Lords to propose amendments for you.

Sir Thomas Clarges: I would have all men have an equal and a fair trial, and therefore I am for this clause. This clause will make the peers honest and not be influenced by the Court but on all occasions they will be ready to stand up in defence of the English liberties. And I know a time when the honest part of the Lords kept a correspondence with some members of this House and were very serviceable in procuring several good laws—as that to prevent papists from sitting in either House, the act of habeas corpus, and several others. The law now in question is such another, and therefore I desire we may put the amendments in the order proposed.

Sir Henry Capel: It is true what that worthy member said last; several lords then did in the late reign make a stand. But the case now is different. Popery was then bringing in, we had a King then not in the interests of his people, but now you have and there is no danger in the least of popery. But I will take notice of one thing done at the beginning of this revolution. It was carried in the House of Lords but by four or five against the regency in favour of Their Majesties, so that there is no great reason to pass this law for them especially when this clause will be so great a weakening to the government.

Sir John Lowther: The true interest of England is to preserve the government in all its parts in an equal balance and not to set one part above the other. It is agreed by most that this is a good government and that so good a law as this must be got in such a time and that there is no fear now of the mischiefs in the former reign. I agree [with] this; and therefore if there had been a provision that nothing in this act should extend to this reign but take effect in the next I would have come up to it then. But as it is now I cannot. It is pretended this will make the Lords ready to appear at any time in defence of the English liberties. I think otherwise, for when they find themselves in some safety they will the easier admit the encroachments of the government. So on the whole matter, I think your proper question is to adhere.

Mr. Bertie, Sir Robert Sawyer, Sir Christopher Musgrave, and *Mr. John Howe* were for the clause and desired the amendments might be put in order as proposed.

So the several amendments were put and agreed to in order as they came on in the clause.

Sir Edward Hussey offered a clause to the bill that impeachments should hold from parliament to parliament and no pardon be allowed against it.

But *Sir Christopher Musgrave* opposed this as irregular.

So it was laid aside.

Then the question was put for the clause 'A' thus amended to stand part of the bill and agreed to. So ordered that a free conference be desired with the Lords upon the subject-matter of the last free conference. Ordered that Mr. Montagu do tomorrow morning go up to the Lords and desire the said free conference.

Adjourned till 8 tomorrow morning.

Thursday, 14 January

Mr. Christie was ordered to carry up the bill for the sale of Mr. Smith's land unto the Lords and acquaint them this House had agreed to the same without any amendments.

Sir Joseph Tredenham was ordered to carry up the bill to enable the Lord Waldegrave's trustees to make leases unto the Lords and to acquaint them that this House had agreed to the said bill with amendments to which they desire their concurrence.

Mr. Carter was ordered to carry up to the Lords the bill for sale of Sir Thomas Burton's land and to acquaint them this House hath agreed to the same without any amendments.

Mr. Colt, upon the message from the Lords with several private bills, spoke against the multiplicity of them which the Lords sent down for cutting off entails and unsettling of settlements as if this House had nothing else to do.

Mr. Hampden to the same as a strange thing that our *Votes* must be filled with nothing but private bills, and therefore I desire no private bills may be read till after 11. *Mr. Clarke* to the same.

Several members were added to divers committees.

Mr. Montagu reported from the conference that the managers had been at the same and had delivered the bill with the clause and amendments thereto to the Lords. And the Lords were pleased to say to this effect: That it could not be expected they should give an answer to it presently, but they would communicate it to their House and that we might expect an answer in a short time.

So adjourned till 8 tomorrow morning.

Friday, 15 January

Mr. Biddulph moved that since there was a day approaching which by act of parliament was appointed to be kept (to wit, the 30th of this month) as a day of humiliation for the martyrdom of King Charles I, he desired that the Dean of St. Paul's might preach before this House. Which was seconded by *Capt. Dyott*.

Ordered that the Dean of Paul's be desired to preach before this House at St. Margaret's, Westminster, upon the 30th of January instant and that Capt. Dyott, Mr. Biddulph, and Mr. Arnold do acquaint him therewith.

The interest bill was reported with amendments and agreed to. And upon the question for engrossing it, it was opposed by *Sir Christopher Musgrave, Mr. Pollexfen, Mr. Bathurst, Col. Sackville*, and *Mr. Clarke*.

But *Sir Edward Hussey* and *Sir John Darell* were for it.

But on the question it was ordered to be engrossed.

To the bill against mutineers and deserters, *Mr. Ramsden* offered a rider in behalf of the town of Hull that they might not be hindered from quartering any part of the garrison in the town if they would.

This was opposed by *Sir Thomas Clarges, Mr. Smith,* etc.

And on the question to be read the second time, it was carried in the negative.

So the bill was passed and the Attorney General ordered to carry it to the Lords for their concurrence.

Then the Order of the Day was read and the House accordingly went into a Committee of the Whole House upon the supplies for Their Majesties. Then the petition of the merchants and others that had furnished the Navy with stores, etc., as also the petition of divers artificers and tradesmen relating to the Ordnance, setting forth that they had provided those offices [with][1] stores and other necessaries on the credit of the excise granted for four years, but that security falling short they prayed that fund might be strengthened by some further security.

Sir John Lowther: The contents of those petitions are true, for that duty of excise for four years upon a fair computation it comes to at least £300,000 less than you made it a fund of credit for, and therefore I will propose a way to make that good and no new burden. If you will continue the same excise for one year and half longer than the four years, it will do what is desired.

Paul Foley thought the continuing it a year longer would do the work.

Mr. Boscawen: There is great complaint by the merchants for want of convoys and by the Admiralty that that sort of ships—fourth and fifth rates—are more wanted than any, and therefore I desire we may continue it for two years and then there will be one half year to be applied to the building ships for convoys.

But Sir Thomas Clarges opposed this latter part as irregular in this committee now.

So it was resolved that the House should be moved to give leave to bring in a bill for continuing the said additional duties of excise granted by the act in the second year of Their Majesties' reign for four years until the 17th of May 1697 for the uses in the said act mentioned.

So the Speaker resumed the Chair, and the said resolution was reported by the *Solicitor* and agreed to by the House. And *he* moved

<hr>

[1] 'were' in MS.

also for leave for the committee to sit again and resolved accordingly on Monday next to go into a Committee of the Whole House to consider of the supplies.

Adjourned till 8 tomorrow morning.

Saturday, 16 January

Sir John Darell was ordered to carry up to the Lords the bill for the encouragement of the breeding and feeding of cattle for their concurrence.

Mr. Christopher Stokes, a new member chosen for Whitchurch in Hampshire (in the room of Mr. Wallop, deceased), was brought into the House and took the oaths, etc. at the Table and after his place in the House.

Mr. Onslow reported from the committee the bill for suppressing of hawkers and pedlars with several amendments, some of which were agreed to and others disagreed.

The question was proposed for the engrossing of it.

Mr. Hampden: I am against this bill. It has been travelling in several parliaments but never could be effected. This bill if you pass it will do great mischief and restrain many men's trades whereby many people will be undone.

Sir Christopher Musgrave: This bill has travelled this House this 20 years but never arrived to the forwardness it is now. I think this a most dangerous and destructive bill. It will hinder the consumption of your commodities, ruin many families, and deprive yourselves of many conveniences. Your wares and goods are now brought home to your doors. But if this bill pass, you must all send to market towns by your servants to fetch from thence what you want. You must pay their price, your servants hereby will be forced to neglect their masters' service and learn debauchery in the towns, and therefore I am against this bill.

Sir Robert Henley, Sir Charles Sedley, and *Mr. Neale* were against this bill for that it would set up trades in corporations and make them exact more of you. It would restrain trade and tend to establishing monopolies.

Sir Ralph Carr and *Mr. Solicitor General* were for this bill, for these pedlars are a sort of people the nation is never the better for. They are a vagrant, wandering people, beneficial to none but themselves. Whereas it satisfies that this bill is for the interest of the nation because it is solicited by all the corporations of England, of whom we ought to take care.

Sir Robert Sawyer: I am against this bill for as it is now drawn it will undo the corporations for none of the inhabitants of one corporation can sell their goods in any place but the open market of their own town and are restrained from selling in other towns. Then as we are to mind the interest of corporations so we must that of the counties in general, which is to promote trade everywhere as much as is possible.

Col. Sackville: I am against the bill because it is against the liberty of the subject to carry on trade. It is to establish a monopoly. It is for the advantage of some few tradesmen in corporations to have this bill pass but against the interest of the generality of the people.

Henry Herbert was for this bill.

Mr. Papillon: I wonder at this debate, for by this bill you are going to establish a sort of people that are vagrants and foreigners and therefore I desire this bill may lie on the Table.

Mr. Bathurst offered a proviso to be annexed to the bill and desired leave to bring it up.

But it was opposed because irregular to bring in provisos after a debate against the engrossing of the bill; it ought to have come before, after the amendments agreed.

Sir Joseph Tredenham was against the bill.

Mr. Boscawen: I am for this bill because it restrains a pernicious sort of people who carry about your treasonable libels, scandalous letters and papers, drive on a trade with France—a people that pay no taxes, for whom the government is never the better nor do they contribute towards bearing the charge thereof. But I confess I do not like this bill as now drawn and therefore desire it may lie on the Table that a new one may be brought in instead thereof. *Sir John Tremaine* to the same.

Sir Thomas Vernon was for the bill.

But *Jeffreys* was against it.

Papillon, *Sir Joseph Williamson*, and *Mr. Sandford* moved that the House would adjourn the debate. So *Sir Thomas Littleton*.

But *Mr. Hampden* opposed that question as irregular to put now after the matter had been debated so long and the House were ripe for the question of engrossing it.

Mr. Smith: I am for a bill of this nature, but I think there is too much in this and therefore I desire it may lie on the Table and a new one be brought in.

Sir Christopher Musgrave: That method is a new practice, and if so there is no end of business it will run round. Then some I hear pro-pose the previous question but that is irregular. The proper question is to adjourn the debate, and so a new bill may be brought in.

Speaker informed the House that by adjourning the debate it would not do to bring in another bill, for any member might call for and resume the debate at any time.

Solicitor General: I think the proper way is to let this bill lie on the Table and so a new one may be brought in, as was done in the poor prisoners bill in the Convention Parliament.

Hampden: I cannot deny but bills have been laid on the Table but that is when the general sense of the House is so by a tacit consent. But the properest question is for engrossing it. And as to the previous question, it is strange for you to put that whether a regular question (as that of engrossing is) shall be now put.

Speaker: That is the most regular question that is debated. And if the House go from one thing to another, the latter becomes the proper question. Now as to the previous question, I cannot deny it if insisted on in the House; [it is] otherwise in a committee.

So after a long debate, the main question was stated and the pre-vious question was put—whether that question shall be now put—and carried in the negative. So it lies on the Table.

Mr. Smith moved for leave to bring in a bill or bills to vest the for-feited estates in England and Ireland in Their Majesties to be applied to the uses of the war, and ordered accordingly and a committee was appointed to prepare and bring in the same.

Adjourned till 8 of the clock on Monday morning.

Monday, 18 January

The petition of Charles Lehardy related to a trade carried on by several merchants with France.

Mr. Smith was ordered to carry up to the Lords the bill for the sale of Mr. Moore's lands and to acquaint them this House had agreed to the same without any amendments.

Col. Goldwell presented a petition of several persons inhabiting in and about the Tower of London setting forth that great quantities of gunpowder were kept in storehouses and warehouses near the Tower so that if any of them should happen to take fire it might endanger the Tower.

Leave was given to bring in a bill to prevent the same.

Bill for the relief of poor prisoners ordered to be read tomorrow morning.

Several members were added to the committee who are to bring in a bill for settling the militia.

Sir John Leveson-Gower, being newly chosen a member for Newcastle under Lyme in Staffordshire (in the room of his father, deceased), was introduced into the House and took the oaths at the Table.

Mr. Hampden acquainted the House with His Majesty's answer to the address for the King to provide a convenient place for the Commons in Parliament to sit in to this effect: That there could not be a place convenient presently provided, but he would order his Surveyor and Comptroller to attend some members of this House to view the same and see in what condition the roof was that care might be taken thereof. And the House appointed the same members of their House that had viewed the same before.

Paul Foley reported from the committee to whom it was referred to receive proposals for raising a sum of money upon a fund of perpetual interest: That some persons had attended the committee accordingly who were concerned in the bankers' debt who complained that they had not timely notice to consider of such a matter, but in the short time allowed them they had spoke with several persons and they were willing to lose all their interest and would advance a sum equal to their principal—both which principals should be secured for the payment of a perpetual interest at the rate of six per cent. That there were persons who had about £80,000 there that would come into this and gave in their several names and that they did not doubt if longer notice had been given to write into the countries many more would have come in, perhaps to have raised £1,000,000.

And this report was referred to the Committee of the Whole House who are to consider of the supplies.

So the Order of the Day for the House to go into a Committee of the Whole House about the supplies was read and the Speaker left the Chair; the Solicitor was Chairman.[1]

Mr. Neale: Since the bankers stand out and trust to have their judgement in Westminster Hall, I move you that a clause may be brought in and added to the bill for taking the public accounts to empower those commissioners to examine and state the said debt to

---

[1] Grey, x. 226–7 has a partial account of the debate that follows, misdated as of 11 Jan.

the bankers and to see how it stands. For I am of opinion that debt is not half so much as is pretended.

Mr. Hampden: I think it is fit for you to do something in this matter so that if you intend to pay this debt that it may be inquired into. For if it be recovered against the Crown, it will lie on the nation to bear it which you must take care to supply if that branch of the excise charged therewith be lopped off; otherwise, the government must want a considerable part of the revenue that is to bear the public charge of carrying on the war. And therefore I think it convenient to have a bill to stop any further proceedings in the courts below.

Sir Robert Sawyer: This motion is very irregular because nothing is now before this Committee of the Whole House nor is any bill for taking the public accounts now under your consideration. Then the motion is as strange for a bill here to stop proceedings in the courts below in a course of justice, for shall a man have a right to a matter—be it against the Crown or not—and will you foreclose him of it? This, I am sure, is contrary to all reason and justice. But it is true I have been told by one of the Barons of the Exchequer before whom this cause depends that it has been hinted to them that care should be taken they should not come to a judgement.

Sir Robert Henley: I second the gentleman's motion that spoke last but one.

Sir Christopher Musgrave: I am wholly against this as irregular and therefore I desire we may go on the ways and means to raise money pursuant to the order you sit by.

Mr. Neale: You have taxed most things in this kingdom but money. If you will tax that, you may raise £200,000 at least. And to this, I propose two per cent on all money out at interest and in stock and none else. And there may be ways found to bring it in without bringing in question the persons' names who owe it.

Sir Charles Sedley: I think you are very well moved as to the matter but I would not go so high as two per cent; I think one per cent is enough.

Mr. Brockman moved that since the gentlemen who have the honour to serve His Majesty in places made so generous an offer we might not quit the same but that the House would embrace it as one of the ways to raise money. Sir Ralph Carr, Mr. Bathurst, Mr. Serj. Montagu, Sir William Strickland, and Sir Charles Sedley to the same.

Admiral Russell: I was the person that moved this at first and I am no ways altered in my opinion. But put the question as soon as you will and I will give my vote for it.

Sir John Morton: The proper way is to move the House for leave to bring in a bill to that purpose.

Sir Robert Cotton (of the Post Office): This sum will not be very considerable. But if the country gentlemen please, I will propose that which will raise a considerable sum—that is, that all gentlemen having an estate of above £500 per annum shall contribute the same above that sum to the carrying on the war by making the same a fund for taking up money whenever the government shall want it.

Sir John Morton: As to that gentleman's motion, the country gentlemen are not wanting. And if our estates and rents came in as well as their pensions and places we would double it.

Sir Stephen Fox: The revenue is already loaded sufficiently. You have now towards this year's war charged it with £200,000. And the Crown is also in arrear to the officers under it three quarters, so that if you trust to that nothing will be done and the King's service will be totally disappointed. And I am afraid little of the arrears will be paid. And if the revenue were clear, I would not only give all my pension but a great part of my estate.

Sir Edward Seymour: I am not very fond of this matter because I think it will raise but little and then it will lie very hard on some persons. I shall, therefore, propose you another way and that is a poll bill. And though some may be offended at it, yet when you have so much money to be raised it cannot be without grieving some persons. But I think a quarterly poll will be the least oppressive and will do your work—that is, all persons under the degree of a gentleman to pay 1s. a quarter and all of that quality and above to pay 20s. a quarter. This, by modest computation, will raise you £1,000,000 at least. There need no money be taken up upon it; it comes in quarterly. And I think this as little oppressive as any, for I am satisfied of our necessities and the poverty of the country gentlemen by your bill passed for reducing the interest of money. And therefore if you approve hereof, you may put it.

But the question was put and resolved: That the salaries, fees, and perquisites of all offices under the Crown (except £500 per annum to be allowed to such respective officers) except the salaries to the Speaker, Commissioners of the Great Seal, judges, foreign ministers, and officers serving in the fleet and army for the said offices and also all pensions granted by the Crown (except pensions payable to the

Queen Dowager and the Princess Anne of Denmark and such other pensions as shall be excepted by this House) be applied to the carrying on the war against France.

Col. Goldwell: I think there is no tax more equal than an excise and that upon some commodities. And this may be collected without the officers coming into your houses—as 1*d.* per pound on candles to be received at the tallow chandlers, 1*d.* per pound on soap to be received at the soap boilers, 1*s.* per bushel on home salt to be paid at the salt pans, and 2*s.* 6*d.* a bushel on foreign salt to be paid at the Customhouse. This, I believe, will raise you £300,000 or £400,000.

Mr. Neale: I am against that motion for it is a downright excise.

Mr. Hampden: I am for that proposal of a quarterly poll. It will advance a great sum if it will raise £1,000,000. It will save you a great deal in interest and come in quarterly to supply your occasions.

Mr. Smith: I am against this proposal and think it is the unequallest tax that can be. But I will propose it a way to make it more equal: that all the poor shall pay a double poll, viz. 6*d.* per quarter; a gentleman, 15*s.* a quarter; an esquire, 50*s.* a quarter; and a baronet more; so proportionably.

Sir Christopher Musgrave: I am of opinion that a poll is the unequallest tax of all. But if you will have it, I desire we may take care to ease the poor and I shall submit to it. But if you lay 1*s.* a quarter on the poor, they will not be able to pay it.

Sir John Guise: I am for this but think you should consider the poor, and therefore I would excuse all the children of such poor but not their servants.

Col. Austen: If you will reach all men and raise money by an equal tax, I know no better way than that of an excise on some commodities. This tax now proposed confirms me in it. And I find we shall try other ways till they are so oppressive that we must come to an excise at last as the equallest—that which will reach all men and no man farther than he pleases himself.

Mr. Machell: I am for laying a further duty upon wines. And because there are arts used to bring in French wines, I desire we may lay £4 a tun above all other duties upon red wines. This will raise a good sum. Your French wines after the beginning of your prohibition act were sold at 2*d.* a quart there. They are now rose to 6*d.* a quart by reason they have found ways to bring them in here under other names. But by laying this duty on all manner of red wines you will come at them.

Sir John Lowther: I thought a poll an unequal sort of a tax at any time, but I shall submit to it. It is proposed to you that this poll will raise a million of money, but that cannot be for there are divers things omitted in this poll which were charged in former polls—as money, offices, servants' wages, practice, the titles of esquires, knights, baronets, etc., are reduced to less than before. And the highest of your polls came to about £300,000, and therefore I am of opinion this poll will not come to above £900,000.

Resolved that towards the supplies to be granted to Their Majesties for carrying on the war against France a tax by a quarterly poll for one year be granted to Their Majesties.

Then the Solicitor was ordered to report these two resolutions to the House and to move to have leave to sit again.

So the Speaker resumed the Chair and the *Solicitor* reported accordingly, to which the House agreed. And then *he* moved to have leave for the committee to sit again and the House appointed tomorrow to resolve into a committee to consider of the supplies.

Adjourned till 8 tomorrow morning.

Tuesday, 19 January

Serj. Trenchard was ordered to carry up the bill of accounts to the Lords for their concurrence.

The House, according to order, went into a Committee of the Whole House upon the supplies. Mr. Solicitor was Chairman.

Mr. Neale: You are now to go upon the heads of the poll bill, and in order to it I propose that all who have trades and hang out signs shall pay 20*s.* as gentlemen. This I believe will raise £100,000.

Sir Edward Seymour: You ought to proceed in some method and that is first by naming what persons shall pay in this act and ascertaining the sum, and thus you will dispatch your business.

Then it was proposed that every person and persons should pay 1*s.* a quarter for their poll.

Mr. Arnold and Sir Christopher Musgrave spoke against it and proposed the paying of but 6*d.* a quarter.

Sir John Lowther: 1*s.* a quarter is very hard for our northern counties where there is a sort of tenure called border service, of the nature of inheritance, who pay to your land taxes too.

Mr. Arnold: You are now going for the sake perhaps of 100,000 shillings to disoblige and lose the hearts of 100,000 people.

Sir Edward Seymour: Those that will be your enemies for 2*s.* are not in my opinion worth preserving to be your friends.

Sir John Guise: I doubt you can raise no taxes but what will be oppressive to some people, but it cannot be helped if you will support this government.

Sir John Lowther: If the House be at leisure to hear a proposal, I think there is that which may be better than this of a poll bill and that is raising a fund for a perpetual interest. I have heard the reasons for the same and it has convinced me. It is this: that there should be a fund for a perpetual interest at five per cent and this settled on trustees; that their bills of credit or paper be current and all obliged to take them; and that from the very time such bills are given he shall have interest at five per cent without paying any taxes and without any further charge. I believe this will be for the advantage of the public, and is not like brass or leather money but like to a mortgage and as good—which may be assigned over. A man may part with it easier than the land, both for the revenue it brings in and for the advantage in parting with it. It is more beneficial to the merchant, trader, grazier, etc. I would also have the Crown obliged to take it in taxes or other payments, and it will be no prejudice to any for I may transfer it over. It is objected by some that this will not pay daughters' portions or debts. Why not, if it be transferable and gain credit? It is that which will establish it, like goldsmiths' notes which are as good as so much ready money. This proposal has also this advantage; while ready money lies dead by a man and yields nothing, these bills will yield five per cent and avoid paying great interest to the bankers. Thus the whole tax is raised at once, paying about £60,000 per annum for interest and that one of the ninepences on the excise will do.

Mr. Neale: I think this a very good project and the more it is considered I believe the better it will be liked.

Mr. Hampden: I think this proposal a very dishonourable reflection on the English nation that can be and very impracticable. It will be prejudicial to trade in putting a stop to the same and will have such mischiefs attending it as can't be imagined.

Sir Ralph Carr: I am for this proposal, and take it in a little time after its erection when it hath gained credit and it will be as good as the bank in Holland.

Sir John Knight: This is not in the least like that of Holland. There if you do not like your note, you may have it in ready money what you have occasion for, but in this there is no ready money.

Henry Herbert: This matter has put off the other business. Therefore, I desire we may go on the consideration of the poll bill.

Mr. Goldwell: Since money is so scarce, I know no reason why papers should not supply the want thereof if it will carry on our business.

Mr. Finch: I think this new project will in the end prove a cheat upon the people. Then this matter broke in irregularly upon the proper business, the poll bill, which you had under consideration. I am for the paying 1s. a quarter per head and no man to pay above 20s. But then for the poor, those that are not able to pay I would excuse them and lay it upon the men of estates in those parishes.

Sir Robert Sawyer: I believe there may be eight millions of people in this kingdom. Perhaps three millions of these may be excused paying to this poll and that about five millions may pay, which will raise about one million of money. But I would have you consider that you go not too high for that may go near to raise a rebellion in the kingdom. So Mr. Smith, Boscawen, Sir [Ralph][1] Dutton.

Sir Robert Henley to the same and thought 6d. a quarter enough.

So the question was put upon the least sum first (as it ought by the rules of the House)—that all and every person and persons pay the sum of 6d. a quarter for one year—and carried in the negative. Then the question was put and resolved that all and every person and persons should pay the sum of 1s. a quarter for one year.

Mr. Hoby and Mr. Bowyer moved that since you had thought fit to raise this head four times as much as before, so every other person might pay four times as much as he did before to any other poll.

But it would not go.

Then proposed to make some exceptions to this head—that all such as receive alms of the parish and their children under 16 and all children of day labourers and servants in husbandry under 16 to be excused—and ordered accordingly. Then proposed that all poor housekeepers or householders who by reason of their poverty are exempted from church and poor [rates] should be excused, but opposed by some [as] being too general for it would excuse servants and journeymen who have great wages and live well. So then the question was put to excuse the children only of such poor housekeepers that are under 16. Then resolved also that the children of such who are not worth £50 and have above four children or more [be excused].

[1] 'Richard' in MS.

Sir Edward Seymour moved that all servants that have above statute wages should pay 4s. in the pound out of so much of the wages as are above the statute, for they are come to so great a height there is no bearing it.

Mr. Hoby, Sir Ralph Dutton, Mr. Freke, and Sir Walter Yonge desired that all persons might pay four times as much as they did upon former polls.

Mr. Smith: I am that gentlemen should pay according to their titles but would have some restrictions to it, for I would not lay it on others and excuse ourselves. And therefore I am for paying four times as much, for without it I cannot answer it to myself.

Sir Walter Yonge: I am against this for it will be very hard on gentlemen and others who pay for their lands. And therefore I will make a proposal to tax every person so much a quarter for every horse and every foot arms he finds to the militia.

Mr. Finch: To make the paying to the militia the measure of the tax I doubt will not answer your end. The laying it on titles is very unequal because many have quality and no estate. But I think paying 20s. a quarter is the least unequal. But as to that of the militia for your measure, the Lord Lieutenant and most of the officers of the militia and deputy lieutenants pay little or nothing. So that I think the equallest way is to rate all so none will escape. And if there be any who are not able, the respective parishes should pay for them.

Mr. Papillon moved that he that keeps two horses should pay so much, he that keeps four to pay so much, and he that keeps six so much.

Mr. Smith and Sir Christopher Musgrave moved that every gentleman keeping a coach and two horses in the country should pay £5, if in town £10; every coach and four horses to pay in country £10, and in the town £20; and every coach and six horses in the country to pay £20, and in the town £30.

Sir Edward Seymour: This that is now proposed is a way to hinder gentlemen from living in any degree suitable to their quality. But this I look on only as a jocular motion and not a thing really intended.

Mr. Montagu: I am for making no distinction between all of the degree of a gentleman and under the degree of a peer.

Resolved that every person of the degree of a gentleman or so reputed and worth £300 or more and every person who is above that quality and under the degree of a peer shall pay 20s. a quarter for one year.

Mr. Machell moved, and Mr. Neale to the same, and it was put and resolved: That every tradesman, shopkeeper, and artificer having an estate of the clear value of £300 or upwards do pay the sum of 10*s*. quarterly. (Hinted at, not intended to reach farmers.)

So the Solicitor was ordered to report the committee had made some further progress and to move to have leave to sit again.

Then the Speaker resumed the Chair and the *Solicitor* reported accordingly, and the committee was ordered to sit tomorrow again upon the supplies.

So adjourned till 8 tomorrow morning.

Wednesday, 20 January

Sir Robert Davers was ordered to carry up the aulnage bill to the Lords for their concurrence.

Sir Edward Acton had leave of the House to go into the country upon extraordinary business.[1]

The House, according to order, resolved itself into a Committee of the Whole House upon the supplies. The Speaker left the Chair, and the Solicitor took the Chair of the committee and after acquainted the committee what progress the committee had made at their last meeting.

Sir Walter Yonge: I desire that the proposal made about the militia may be the rule for persons that are gentlemen to pay, viz., after the rate of 20*s*. a quarter for a whole horse besides what before.

Sir Christopher Musgrave: I think this should be your question— that every man that is charged or chargeable to the finding a horse for the militia shall pay £1. 10*s*. a quarter, so proportionably for every horse over and above the 20*s*. a quarter. And I would not have the very officers themselves excused for I think some difference ought to be between ourselves and others.

Sir Ralph Carr thought this too high.

Sir Henry Capel: I am for this motion, and the rather for that it includes the peers.

Mr. Boscawen: This is only a tax upon the gentlemen and commoners, for the lords will be hereby excused for they will appoint commissioners of their own to rate them.

Mr. Montagu: I think this the most improper way of taxing of all

---

[1] This is not entered in the *Journal*.

others. Your bill is for a poll, and you are now going to rate land again when it lies already under so great a burden. Therefore I shall propose that all under the degree of a peer and above that of a gentleman shall pay 30s. a quarter besides, and this will raise a great sum.

Sir John Guise: I am for the same thing.

Sir Robert Cotton (of Post Office): I think you should have no distinction but that of a gentleman and under, for he that is above will feel it in his estate and the intent of this bill is to reach those that have not paid sufficiently to the public charges. As to that of the militia, I think it is very hard and is a second land tax, and then the militia are like to be much out this summer and therefore it will be very oppressive.

Sir Charles Sedley opposed that of the militia.

Sir Edward Seymour: I am against your taxing according to the militia for that this is but another land tax in masquerade. Then this will not reach the lords, or at the best but few of them, for they are Lords Lieutenant of counties and there none of them find any horse to the militia, and if you consider how many counties there are you will see how many you excuse. Then the militia itself in many counties is very grievous, and will you now go and make it worse?

Sir Christopher Musgrave: I am for bearing a little more than the common people and therefore I am for this of the militia, being the likeliest way to reach the men of estates. If you charge titles, it must come out of the land for no man can pay it out of his title.

Sir Edward Hussey: I am against this of the militia, for what you have done already will raise the sum itself you want and therefore no need of more.

Paul Foley: It is objected that if you do not this of the militia gentlemen of estates will pay no more than other inferior persons. I think this not material for they that have estates will pay for them to your land tax. Then this act will raise your money desired without the militia, as may in some measure be gathered by a computation in the case of chimney money heretofore. There are about 663,000 families in England which computed at seven persons to each family will at 4s. a head come to about £800,000. And if there be but 100,000 gentlemen at £4 a head [that] comes to about £400,000—in all, £1,200,000. And what you tax the lords and other matters will no doubt advance the whole sum intended.

Sir Christopher Musgrave: All the calculations made of what this poll will amount to are very uncertain and I am afraid this poll will not raise so great a sum as is imagined. For if so, how comes it your former polls never made above £300,000?

Mr. Godolphin: The methods proposed are all liable to great exceptions and therefore I desire—instead of taxing qualities or lands—that to make up the tax for those who are unable to pay in any parish such other inhabitants as are able may pay for them and be rated according to their expenses in the parish.

Mr. Chadwick proposed that every gentleman of £500 per annum should be obliged to pay 30s. a quarter, besides other matters.

Sir Richard Temple: I am for this of the militia as the most equal.

Mr. Goldwell: I would have the tax of all who are not able to pay it that the sum be advanced by an equal land tax.

Sir Robert Henley and Mr. Palmes against this.

Mr. Harley: I think this the equallest sort of tax that can be.

So the question put and resolved that every person having an estate that is charged or chargeable to the finding of horse to the militia do for every horse pay 20s. a quarter for one year over and above what already charged in this act.

Sir William Strickland moved that all men who were disaffected to this government, both papists and nonjurors, might pay double. And seconded.

So the question was put and resolved that all and every person refusing to take the oaths to Their Majesties do pay double the sums charged by the respective heads.

Mr. Colt moved that all persons that found foot arms to the militia might be charged for every foot soldier 4s. a quarter.

Sir John Guise and Sir Christopher Musgrave opposed it, for this would be very hard and oppress the middling people who bore the chief charge of the war.

Sir Francis Drake and Sir Robert Henley moved to lay a tax upon all persons keeping coaches and who do not contribute to horse might pay £5 for two horses, £10 for four horses, and £20 for six horses. Sir Charles Sedley, Mr. Boscawen, Serj. Tremaine, and Mr. Colt to the same.

So question put and resolved that every person not contributing to the finding a horse to the militia and keeping a coach and horses do pay 20s. a quarter for one year over and above what he is chargeable with on the aforesaid heads, except such as keep hackney and stage coaches.

So the Solicitor was ordered to report the committee had made some further progress in the matter to them referred and had directed him to move the House to have leave to sit again.

So the Speaker resumed the Chair and the *Solicitor* reported and moved accordingly. And the House resolved to go into a committee again tomorrow upon the supplies.

Some particular members were upon motion added to divers committees.

So adjourned till 8 tomorrow morning.

Thursday, 21 January

The bill for preventing the buying and selling of offices was ordered to be read a second time in a full House.

Mr. Christie was ordered to carry to the Lords the bill for enfranchising copyhold lands, with amendments.

To the bill for disabling brewers to be maltsters, after the House had agreed to the amendments from the committee, *Mr. Arnold* offered a clause to disable brewers from being Justices of Peace in the same county where they were brewers.

It received some opposition, but, however, amendments were made to the clause and then it was upon the question ordered to stand part of the bill.

So the whole bill was ordered to be engrossed.

The House agreed to the free conference with the Lords and the messengers were called in again and acquainted therewith.

Sir John Guise was ordered to carry up to the Lords the bill for raising the militia for their concurrence.

Mr. Fenwick was ordered to carry up to the Lords the engrossed bill for relief of creditors against fraudulent devices for their concurrence.

The bill for encouraging the making saltpetre was read a second time.

Mr. Brewer: I am against this bill, it being to establish a monopoly for the sole making of saltpetre to some persons when it appears others can make it. And why any should be excluded from making it when there is so great occasion for the thing I understand not.

Sir Thomas Littleton: It is very true saltpetre was made many years in England, but never in any quantity to make it serviceable to the public. But the persons to whom your act is granted are obliged thereby to furnish the Crown with 500 tons in the space of three years.

Sir Christopher Musgrave: The trade of stockjobbing is now become the sole business of many persons, which has ruined great numbers of tradesmen and others. And to encourage this trade there have several very ill patents passed which are even scandalous to the government, and therefore I am not fond of these things. I look upon this as such—only a project to make money of your act of parliament, by dividing it into so many shares. Therefore I am for the pretenders trying this some time, and then when the public is like to reap a benefit by it let them then come for your act of parliament.

So the bill was committed and a committee appointed accordingly.

Time of the conference being come, the managers' names were read over and they went to the same. And being returned, *Mr. Montagu* reported that the Lords had agreed to some of your amendments and disagreed to others. They have agreed to your amendment to the clause by inserting the word 'temporal'. To that where 'no less than 36 peers' shall be summoned they have disagreed, as also to that of imposing a penalty on such lords as shall [be] absent upon such summons, for that this respects only the number of the lords that shall appear and their Lordships think the whole House of Peers ought to appear. And then this penalty is ineffectual for it is not appropriated. And upon the whole matter, the Lords did insist upon their clause.

Sir John Guise moved to put the consideration of the report of the free conference off for a fortnight, and was seconded by *Sir Charles Raleigh*.

But *Sir Christopher Musgrave*, *Sir Edward Seymour*, and others opposed it and desired it might be taken into consideration on Saturday next, for it was a matter of great concern and it was not usual to defer so long the consideration of the reports from conferences.

So appointed for Saturday next.

Then the House, according to order, went into a Committee of the Whole House upon the matter of supplies. Speaker left the Chair and the Solicitor took the Chair of the committee.

Sir Edward Seymour proposed that every hackney coach should be charged to pay £5 for a licence to drive for one year.

Some also proposed to insert stage coaches.

So the question put and resolved that every person or persons keeping a hackney or stage coach do for every such coach and coaches pay the sum of 25s. a quarter.

Sir Christopher Musgrave moved that the peers might be charged
—that every duke should pay £12. 10s. a quarter—and this would
make the bill go easier.

Mr. Neale and Sir Robert Sawyer, etc. proposed that every one of
the degree of a baron or above should pay £10 a quarter. And this is
but proportionable for you make no difference between a plain gentleman and a baronet of a great estate. Therefore I think it is best to go
as it is.

So question put and resolved that every peer of this realm, spiritual
or temporal, should pay the sum of £10 quarterly.

So the Solicitor was ordered to report that the committee had come
to several resolutions which they had directed him to report to the
House.

So the Speaker resumed the Chair and the *Solicitor* acquainted the
House that the committee had come to several resolutions which he
was ready to report to the House. Ordered that the report be made
tomorrow morning.

So adjourned till 8 tomorrow morning.

Friday, 22 January

The House divided upon the question for a second reading of the
engrossed bill from the Lords to enable the Bishop of London to sell
the manor of Bushley—the Yeas went out.

		Sir Jonathan Jennings	
	Yeas		33
		[Sir John Darell][1]	
Tellers for the			
		Sir Francis Drake	
	Noes		30
		Mr. Waller	

So ordered a second reading.

The bill for establishing an East India Company was read the first
time, and being moved to have a second reading it was opposed by
*Sir Robert Sawyer, Sir Thomas Littleton, Sir William Wogan, Sir Thomas
Clarges, Mr. Howe, Sir George Hutchins, Sir Richard Temple, Sir Henry
Goodricke,* and *Sir Joseph Williamson,* for that this bill came in irregu-
larly—a committee of three bringing it in, who met at an unknown

[1] Blank in MS.; from *CJ*, x. 636.

place without giving notice to the others of the committee. Then this bill absolutely dissolves the old Company and vests their stock in the new company.

Sir Christopher Musgrave and others answered that this bill was brought in according to order, being any three of the committee had power to bring in such a bill and the bill itself is pursuant to the order and regulations of the House.

So the question was put for reading this bill a second time. House divided—Yeas went out.

		Sir Francis Drake	
	Yeas		171
Tellers for the		Mr. Travers	
		Sir John Guise	
	Noes		116
		Mr. Gwyn	

So resolved that the bill should be read a second time.

Serj. Trenchard (Chairman of the Committee of Elections) reported from the committee the case of the election for the borough of Chippenham in Wiltshire at large and the resolutions of the committee thereof, and delivered in the same at the Table, where the Clerk read the same. And the three resolutions of the committee thereon were severally put.

To the first, that of bribery, it was long debated. And at last, the question being put for agreeing with the committee that [Sir Basil] Firebrace, etc., were guilty of bribery, etc., the House divided—the Noes went forth.

		Mr. Bickerstaffe	
	Noes		91[1]
Tellers for the		Mr. Tancred	
		Mr. Colt	
	Yeas		175
		Mr. Onslow	

Then the second and third resolutions were read and agreed on, and the Clerk of the Crown was ordered to attend the House tomorrow to amend the return.

Col. Granville and others moved that though the House had voted

---

[1] 92 in *CJ*, x. 638.

Sir Basil Firebrace guilty of bribery, yet that they would not order the vote to be printed, because the gentleman being a citizen this vote would much reflect upon him and blast his reputation.

But it was opposed by *Lord Powlett, Col. Austen, Mr. Hutchinson, Sir Henry Capel*, and others.

And it appearing to be the general sense of the House that it should be printed, no question was put for it.

So adjourned till 8 tomorrow morning.

Saturday, 23 January

Major-General Tollemache, having carried the election for Chippenham, was brought into the House and took the oaths at the Table and after his place in the House.

Mr. Waller was ordered to carry up to the Lords the engrossed bill for preventing of malicious informations and more easy reversal of outlawries in the Court of King's Bench for their concurrence.

Engrossed bill for reducing of interest was read the last time.

Several spoke against the bill as the *Solicitor General, Sir Christopher Musgrave, Mr. Jeffreys, Mr. Finch, Sir John Knight, Mr. Lloyd, Sir Peter Colleton*, etc. and urged it to be a hard law to take away a fifth part of those men's estates whose concerns lie in money. That this bill would have little effect, being great sums were now to be had at five per cent, some at four per cent. That this would be prejudicial to such men who had small sums of money. Then the time of this bill is unseasonable, for interest is now in Holland at five per cent and it will not be very proper to lower it now when money is so scarce. Then this will discourage people to bring money into this kingdom. And as to the pretence that it will advance the price of land, I do not think so for what you advance in your land you will lose in the interest of the money. Then this will render it difficult for a merchant to take up money on personal security to carry on his trade. And to allege that where interest is low there is plenty of money, it is taking the effect for the cause for it is plenty of money that lowers the interest of money and it is trade that makes plenty of money.

Others urged for the bill as *Sir Joseph Tredenham, Mr. Papillon, Sir Richard Temple, Sir Charles Sedley, Mr. Holt, Sir Robert Henley*, etc. and said this bill would mightily encourage trade, which was become now so dead and little profitable. That since more profit was to be made by money at interest than could be cleared by trade, few persons would employ their money in trade. Then said it will discourage persons to bring their money in here to let it at interest. I like it not, for such do more hurt and carry out of the nation both interest and principal. Then low interest will benefit trade and much advance the same, for where that is low you may be better able to trade with your neighbours and they cannot then undersell you.

So at last the question was put for passing the bill. The House divided—Yeas go forth.

		Sir Edward Hussey	
	Yeas		150
		Mr. Methuen	
Tellers for the			
		Sir Robert Davers	
	Noes		101
		Mr. Goldwell	

Then the title of the bill was passed and Sir Edward Hussey ordered to carry it to the Lords for their concurrence.

Solicitor reported the several heads or resolutions of the poll bill, which were severally put. And some exception was taken to the eleventh head, that of a lord of parliament paying £10 a quarter. It was proposed to lessen it and reduce it to £5 a quarter each because it would be hard on some lords to pay it, and then many of them did not pay the last poll nor will this. However, the resolutions were all agreed to. So a bill was ordered to be brought in pursuant to the said resolutions, and referred to the Attorney and Solicitor General.

Col. Pery offered to the House a petition from the former licensed hackney coachmen against laying £5 per annum upon them.

But this was opposed as irregular because before the bill is brought in, and then it was never known a petition was offered against a money bill. So rejected.

Sir Christopher Musgrave moved that all attorneys, solicitors, clerks in Chancery, proctors, etc., should be charged as gentlemen, and ordered accordingly.

Ordered that all clergymen, teachers, and preachers in any congregation having a benefice or contribution of £80 per annum or upwards should be charged as gentlemen.

Mr. Neale moved that all money out on interest might be charged in the bill, but not ordered.

So adjourned till 8 on Monday morning.

Monday, 25 January

Engrossed bill for securing the portions, debts, and legacies of the Earl of Salisbury ordered to be carried to the Lords and that their concurrence be desired to the amendments.

Serj. Trenchard reported the bill for repair of Dover harbour from the Committee of the Whole House with amendments—some of which were agreed to, others not. The House divided on one—Yeas went out.[1]

		Mr. Gwyn	
	Yeas		78
		Mr. Methuen	
Tellers for the			
		Mr. Bickerstaffe	
	Noes		98
		Mr. Fuller	

Several clauses were offered in behalf of divers ports as Yarmouth, Lyme, but upon the question were rejected.

Several also spoke against the bill: That it was to lay a tax upon all the shipping of England that came to the port of London though they came not by Dover, so not likely to have any benefit by that harbour.

So the question was put for engrossing it. House divided—Yeas went out.

		Sir Thomas Hussey[2]	
	Yeas		107
		Mr. Chadwick	
Tellers for the			
		Sir Walter Yonge	
	Noes		136
		Mr. Fuller[3]	

So the bill stood rejected.

Then the House, according to the Order of the Day, proceeded to take into consideration the report from the free conference touching the amendments to the clause marked 'A' added by the Lords to the bill for regulating trials in cases of treason.

---

[1] *CJ*, x. 640 has the total for the Yeas as 97 and for the Noes as 78.
[2] Sir Edward Hussey in *CJ*, x. 641.
[3] Mr. England in *CJ*, x. 641.

Sir Henry Gough moved that the House would disagree to the Lords' amendments to the clause and that they would adhere to the bill itself.

Sir Edward Seymour: The method of your proceedings stands thus. This House passed the bill for regulating trials in cases of treason and sent it to the Lords. They sent it down to you again with amendments, to some of which you agreed and to others not, and they added this clause which you disagreed to and offered your reasons at a conference. The Lords at another conference offer reasons and insist upon the clause. You after make amendments to this clause, to some of which they agreed, to others not, which with reasons they offer at another free conference. And thus it stands. Now I take your proper question to be to agree to the clause without your amendments to it, which I desire we may not but disagree to such clause. *Sir Richard Temple* to the same.

Mr. Hampden: I take your proper question to be to adhere to your amendments.

Speaker informed the House that on this clause both Houses have insisted. Then there was a free conference, whereon this House made some amendments to the clause, which you delivered at a free conference. And after the Lords at another free conference agree to some of this House's amendments and to others not. And now the matter is what question to put. I am ready to put what you shall order.

Sir Edward Seymour: The matter is only whether you will agree to this clause without your amendments, but I observe by no question yet have you admitted the clause without your amendments or that to be made part of your bill otherwise than with your amendments. But if you insist on the clause with your amendments and the Lords insist on it without them, the bill is lost.

Mr. Hampden: I think what you agree to and the Lords too without putting it to be part of the bill stands part of it without a question.

Sir Henry Capel: I think your proper question is adhering or not.

Sir Edward Seymour: It is true you did agree to the amendment made by the Lords to the bill in adding the clause 'A' but it was conditionally—that they agreed to your amendments made thereto, which if they do not you did not agree to their clause. Therefore, the question is to insist on that amendment of yours to the clause.

Paul Foley: I do not think you can put any question on the clause, but the most proper is upon the amendments and not the clause.

Sir Christopher Musgrave: I take it you are now as you were when the amendments first came down. You agreed to the clause with some amendments, which if they agree not to then the question is to agree to the clause or not. *Mr. Finch* to the same.

Sir Richard Temple: The whole clause is but one entire amendment which you agree to with limitations—which the Lords not agreeing to, the whole clause stands still for you to agree with or not.

Sir Thomas Clarges: Neither House have always kept strictly to the same method in conferences. This clause I take to be one entire amendment and so I think the proper question is to agree or not to the clause.

Attorney General: You ought to read the amendments one by one and put the question on them.

Speaker: The proper question is to agree or disagree to those amendments you made. The Lords have disagreed to them, so you must either insist or not thereon.

Mr. Hampden: The Lords do insist upon the clause in those points wherein they disagree with you. I do agree you may recede from your amendments. But the question is to 'insist' upon the amendments or else to 'adhere' to them, which latter I think is most regular—'insisting' being but a new word.

Mr. Montagu: You cannot come to any question until you dispose of the amendments. You have agreed to the clause with amendments, and will you now disagree to the clause you agreed to before? You ought, therefore, to put the question for insisting upon the amendments. *Sir Joseph Williamson* to the same.

So the question was stated to insist upon the amendments sent to the Lords to the clause marked 'A'. But then the previous question was demanded and seconded and after insisted upon, so ought to be put. So it was whether that question be now put. The House divided —Noes went out.

		Col. Granville	
	Noes		125
		Mr. Gwyn	
Tellers for the			
		Sir John Guise	
	Yeas		120
		Mr. Clarke	

Carried in the negative that the question should be put.

Then the question was stated that this House doth adhere to their disagreeing with the Lords as to the clause marked 'A'. And a debate arose thereon by the Court Party who opposed that question and after moved to adjourn the debate, which was seconded and so must be put. Question put that the debate be adjourned. House divided—the Yeas went out.

		Sir Jonathan Jennings	
	Yeas		106
		Mr. Cary	
Tellers for the			
		Sir Robert Davers	
	Noes		127
		Mr. Goldwell	

Then the question was put that this House doth adhere to their disagreeing with the Lords to the clause marked 'A'. Then it was moved to have a free conference with the Lords to acquaint them with this resolution, and resolved accordingly to have a free conference. Ordered that Mr. Montagu do tomorrow morning go to the Lords to desire a free conference upon the clause marked 'A' added by their Lordships to the bill entitled 'for regulating of trials in cases of treason'.

So adjourned till 8 tomorrow morning.

Tuesday, 26 January

Some members upon motion were added to several committees to whom matters were referred.

Moved for Serj. Tremaine to have leave to attend a cause in the House of Lords between etc. But opposed because it countenanced their judicial power. But answered, these motions were never entered on the Journal.

Engrossed bill for sale of the estate of John Crips read the third time and passed, and Mr. Brewer ordered to carry it to the Lords for their concurrence.

Mr. Godolphin moved for leave to bring in a bill to explain a clause in the act of new impositions on East India goods, declaring those goods should pay 20 per cent as the intention of the House was when that act passed.

But opposed by *Sir Edward Seymour* and *Sir Thomas Clarges* as a strange motion, for how could any man say what the intention of the House was but by their public resolutions? Then that this being a matter of money could not be done but in a Committee of the Whole House.

So it was laid aside.

Engrossed bill for repair of the highways was read the third time.

Mr. Bowyer presented a rider to take away *certiorari*'s in such cases.

And it was received and read thrice and after upon the question ordered to be made part of the bill.

Sir John Fagg and *Mr. Machell* opposed the bill, being very destructive to their country.

But, however, the bill was put, passed, and Mr. Bowyer ordered to carry it up to the Lords for their concurrence.

Moved for the protection of the House to be granted to Sir William Halford, a gentleman who had a private bill sent down to this House from the Lords which had not been yet read here.

But opposed by *Sir Christopher Musgrave* as a strange motion, for this House were not possessed of his bill till reading so ought not to have the privilege of this House in attending his bill.

So laid aside.

The bill for establishing an East India Company was read a second time and committed to a Committee of the Whole House.

Sir Thomas Littleton moved that it might be an instruction to the committee to alter this bill as they shall think fit, according to the regulations agreed upon by this House. *Sir Thomas Clarges* to the same.

Mr. Heneage Finch opened the bill and the reasonableness of it and concluded that the members of the Company that proposed to give security might come here tomorrow and give the same. *Mr. Methuen* to the same; so *Sir Edward Seymour*.

Sir Christopher Musgrave desired they might come here and give security pursuant to their undertaking to make good their stock £744,000.

But this was opposed by several for that the security they offered was in case the present Company was confirmed, not in case they were destroyed.

The *Marquess of Winchester* presented a petition of several mariners and seamen against the East India Company, that they might have their share of the prizes taken from the Mogul pursuant to the agreement of the Company. And the consideration thereof was referred to the Committee of the Whole House.

Sir Edward Seymour: The Company must come and give their security or else you cannot go on with the bill until their stock be adjusted to £744,000. *Col. Austen* to the same.

Ordered that the persons proposed to this House by the committee of the East India Company on the 29th of December last do attend this House tomorrow to give security according to their proposals.

Sir Thomas Littleton moved to revive the committee about the salt-petre bill for that at their last meeting they had adjourned themselves for a week longer, which is not regular to adjourn for so long. It is next door to throwing out the bill. And if this be allowed, any committee—though it cannot directly throw out a bill—may in effect throw it out by delaying and putting it off from time to time and do nothing in it.

Answered that the House is judge of the time of adjournment by such a committee, whether reasonable or not. And if the House think it unreasonable, they may revive that committee and appoint a time when they shall sit.

But this matter fell without further debate, so the committee stood adjourned.

So adjourned till 8 tomorrow morning.

Wednesday, 27 January

All committees were revived.[1]

Mr. Harcourt was ordered to carry up Mr. Molineux's private bill unto the Lords for their concurrence.

Then the managers' names for the free conference were read over and they were ordered to carry up the resolution of the House. But *Mr. Montagu* did desire the House would be pleased to excuse him and that some of the gentlemen who were so zealous for the clause might manage the same, for he doubted he should not be so well able to maintain the resolution of the House which was against his own opinion. But he was ordered to do it, being the duty of every member to maintain and defend the resolutions of the House though his own opinion was otherwise.

So the managers went up to the conference. And being returned, *Mr. Montagu* reported that they had been at the conference and had

[1] Cf. *CJ*, x. 643 (26 and 27 Jan.).

communicated the resolution of the House to their Lordships and had left the bill with them. And they were pleased to tell us they would report the same to their House.

Then the committee of the East India Company were called in and acquainted with the resolution of the House. Sir Thomas Cook answered for them that they were ready to give the security proposed according to the terms agreed on the 18th of December last.

So then they were ordered to withdraw, and the House debated a long while about the security, etc.

Sir Robert Rich tendered a clause in nature of the condition of a recognizance to be given by the security, which he brought up and delivered in at the Table.

After a further debate, the committee were called in again and asked if they would give security for £744,000 on such other terms as this House should think fit. Sir Thomas Cook answered they were ready to give security for that sum according to the resolutions of this House on 18th of December last. But for any new terms, he was but one man and could not give an answer without calling a General Court to consider thereof.

Then they were ordered to withdraw again. And after a little time, they were called in and acquainted that there was a bill brought into this House which had had some progress, and it was to establish an East India Company and that the adventurers in the former Company might have a stock in this new company of £744,000 if they would give security that their present stock is worth so much, all their debts being paid. Sir Thomas Cook: This is a new proposal to us, and to which I cannot give an answer without consulting the General Court.

So they withdrew again and were after called in again and were ordered to deliver in their answer positively against Tuesday next when the House will be in a committee of the Whole House upon the East India bill.

Sir Richard Temple moved, and urged by others, that the East India Company might be ordered to have a copy of that bill and of what the Speaker spoke to the committee of the Company.

But opposed for that it was irregular to have a copy of his speech, being it was no resolution of the House. But hinted that the Governor being a member of the House, he might take a copy of what he thought fit.

So adjourned till 8 tomorrow morning.

Thursday, 28 January

The bill for vesting the forfeited estates in Ireland in Their Majesties to be applied to the uses of the war was read and committed to a Committee of the Whole House.

Sir Thomas Clarges moved that it might be an instruction to the committee that some persons might be named in the act to take the claims of such as pretend to be within the several articles there, as also that care might be taken of such persons as were killed in the war either to attaint them by name or inquisition, etc.

Hampden: It is not so regular for you to give an instruction to a Committee of the Whole House, but you may order some members to prepare some clause to that purpose. I remember also the last sessions there was a part allotted to the King out of the forfeited estates to dispose of to such as had served him well in Ireland; I think it was about £30,000 per annum. I hope you see no cause to lessen it now and therefore I desire there may be care taken as to that.

Mr. Smith: I second the motion of the gentleman that moved last but one and that a commission may be appointed to examine the claims of the several pretenders and to report the same to the Commons in Parliament. And as to the motion for a share to the King, I am not against it but it cannot be limited to such a sum till known what the forfeited estates will amount to. They are much lessened to what they were by the Articles of Limerick and if you reserve such a certain part of them I doubt you will make but little more. Care will be taken to advance that part, but after I doubt the rest will come short, and therefore I am rather for allowing the King a third or fourth part as you shall think fit. But I desire we may take care to provide a court of claims or else (if it be true, as I hear, they are setting up in Ireland something like it among themselves) little will be made of those forfeitures. And I hear money is stirring there, so that it is fit for your consideration.

Sir Robert Cotton (of the Post Office) seconded the motion of Mr. Hampden for the King to have £30,000 per annum.

Sir Thomas Clarges: The clergy in Ireland are very poor which is the reason that popery increases there. The living for the Protestant clergy being not sufficient to keep them, being generally so small, that they live not on the place. And therefore to encourage them for the future, I desire that the forfeited tithes, impropriations, and appropriations there may be applied towards increasing the livings of the Protestant clergy.

Speaker informed the House that if they would take care of the Protestant religion there, care should be taken that the churches should be built up. For you may go many miles and see no churches, but the clergy belonging to them live here in London and Dublin and have their tithes paid them where they are and leave the management of their flocks to a popish priest.

Resolved that the said committee do prepare and bring in a clause that the forfeited impropriations in Ireland be settled for the benefit of the Church there.

Capt. Bickerstaffe offered a petition to the House of one Mr. Tilson, relating to an office he had in Ireland in the name of a Papist there which by the Irish [oaths] act would be forfeited, praying a saving of his right. But upon the question, [it] was refused to be brought up to the Table.

Leave was given for the Committee of the Whole House to bring in a clause to be added to the poll bill in behalf of the Quakers from paying double though they do not take the oaths, upon signing a declaration to that effect.[1]

Sir John Lowther: I desire that the committee may consider what this poll bill may amount to. You have voted the sums for carrying on the war this next year of which remains yet unraised £1,341,677. 16s. 3d. It is computed the poll bill will raise that sum which I am afraid it will not do, for your former poll bills the highest never amounted to £300,000 so that I do not believe this poll will amount to £1,000,000. Though it is true you have added some things to this poll, but you have taken away several others that were in the former, so will not amount to four times as much as the former. I desire, therefore, we may come to some computation to see what more is wanting.

Sir Edward Seymour: It is too soon yet to compute that until the bill is passed for perhaps some things are now in the bill which you may think fit in the committee to leave out or perhaps you may add some other things. Your proper time, therefore, to compute it is after the bill is passed. And for what that honourable gentleman says that the whole bill will not amount to £1,000,000, I desire him to consider but one head. I would fain know if he does not believe there are 200,000 gentlemen in England; if so, at £4 a head that part of the bill

---

[1] Not entered in the *Journal*.

without any other will raise £800,000. I believe the bill will come to more than the £1,341,677.

Sir Robert Sawyer: I desire it may be an instruction to the committee that the commissioners for putting this act in execution may be appointed by the King out of the land tax.

Sir Christopher Musgrave: I believe this poll will come to the money proposed, if not more. However, whether or no is not now proper for you to consider; when the bill comes to be engrossed, then is the time. Then for what was moved last, I am against the King's naming commissioners. I know no reason to distrust the country gentlemen. And as we have voted such a sum, so there is no intention in the House but to make it up.

Mr. Hampden moved that there might be a clause that it was the intention of the House this bill should amount to £1,341,677 and that what it wanted they would make it up.

Mr. Hutchinson moved to have a clause to apply all salaries, fees, and perquisites of offices above £500 a year might for so much as they exceed £500 a year be applied towards carrying on the war. *Sir William Strickland* to the same.

Sidney Godolphin moved to have a clause that whatever this bill fell short of the sum intended this House will at the next sessions make it good.

Sir Christopher Musgrave: I am against this last motion for that it will tend to destroy your bill and make people careless in executing it and not much matter how much it raise. Then I think there is no necessity of this House for there is no reason to suspect this House will be backward to comply with anything the King desires.

Then the House proceeded to take into consideration the amendments made by the Lords to the bill of accounts appointing commissioners to examine, take, and state the same, which were read over by the Clerk. The first was that wherein the Lords added four other commissioners to those of the Commons—viz., Sir Cyril Wych, Sir Philip Meadows, John Hampden, and Alexander Davenant, esqs.

Sir Richard Temple: I am against your agreeing with the Lords in this amendment. They are daily growing upon you. They offered at this thing in King Charles II's time but it was denied. It will behoove you to be very careful, for the Lords are endeavouring to be meddling with your money and in time they will put their hands in your pockets. For this is a matter of money for they do not intend, I suppose, these gentlemen shall serve for nothing. *Mr. Hutchinson* to the same.

Sir Henry Capel: I am against the Lords' amendment, for to what end should they have an account of the moneys given and issued? It is a considerable thing and therefore I am for putting it off for two or three days to search precedents.

Sir Edward Seymour: There are not many instances of matters of this kind: the first was that of the Palatinate war in King James I's time, there was another in 19 of King Charles II and then your last act under this government, in all which the commissioners were named by this House. Then the Lords have no power in the matter of money either in giving it or having an account thereof. The Lords are very tender of their privileges; so I would have you be of yours, especially in and about money which is the great thing this House has to recommend itself to the Crown. And therefore though the Lords are endeavouring to grow upon you, yet I would not have you part with anything of yours to them and I hope there may a time come when you will inquire into their pretended judicial power.

Sir Thomas Clarges: The Lords have nothing to do in the matter of money and so are all the precedents which I have looked over. In the case of the Palatinate war in 21 Jac. 1 c. 34, the Commons named commissioners and treasurers to take and receive the moneys then given and to pay it out and they were to give an account thereof to the Commons in Parliament. In 1667, 19 Car. II c. 8, an act passed for appointing commissioners to take the accounts of moneys received; [they] were nominated by the Commons only. In 1679, 31 Car. II c. 1, an act passed for disbanding the army wherein the Commons appointed four members of their own House to disband the same. Thus it is very clear the Lords have no foundation of right to name commissioners but it is only in the Commons. And though it is pretended they name but four, that is not material, for as they name four so they may many more. Therefore on the whole matter I am for disagreeing to the Lords' amendments.

So the question was put for agreeing with the Lords in their amendments and carried clearly in the negative. And a committee was appointed to draw up reasons to be offered at a conference for disagreeing to the Lords' amendments and they were ordered to meet tomorrow morning at 9 and to sit, though the House be then sitting.

So adjourned till 8 tomorrow morning.

Friday, 29 January

Sir Robert Henley had leave to use his discretion in waiving his privilege in reference to a trial at bar in the Court of King's Bench.

Some members were added to the committee that were to prepare and draw up reasons to be offered to the Lords at a conference touching the bill of accounts.[1]

Sir William Wogan was ordered to carry up to the Lords the engrossed bill for taking away [benefit of] clergy from some offenders etc., and to desire their concurrence to the said amendments.

House went into a Committee of the Whole House to consider of ways to satisfy the debts due to the orphans of London and Mr. Harcourt was Chairman of the committee.

Sir William Turner presented the House with an account of what was due to the orphans of London only, and not to any other, which amounted to

Principal money	£531,082. 15s. 0d.
Interest thereof till Michaelmas last	£183,072. 03s. 8d.
Total	£714,154. 18s. 8d.

Sir Edward Seymour: I am of opinion that this debt, which comes to a great sum of money, be paid by the City itself. And in this I will go as far as any but not to lay it upon others that were not concerned in the matter but let such as had the advantage of it pay the debt. And I do not think the City are so very desirous to do this matter but only to take the clamour from themselves and put it upon you that it may lie at your door.

Sir Robert Clayton, Col. Pery, Sir Thomas Vernon, Sir William Turner, Sir Samuel Dashwood, and the Attorney General spoke in behalf of the orphans and proposed that the City were very willing to contribute what they were able to the paying the orphans and therefore proposed that a certain fund for ever might be settled to pay a perpetual interest after the rate of four per cent, and in order to it the City revenues should be all charged with the payment of £8,000 per annum constantly for carrying on the same.

Sir Joseph Tredenham: You ought to inquire in what condition the City of London are to pay their debts, what this debt is and how due, and then is the time proper to consider how to pay it.

---

[1] Not entered in the *Journal.*

Sir Charles Sedley spoke against the orphans.

Then the question was put and carried that the lands, markets, waterbailage, King's Beam, Outroper's office, and other revenues of the City of London be charged with the payment of £8,000 per annum towards the raising of a fund for the payment of a perpetual interest to the orphans of London.

Sir Samuel Dashwood moved then for a further fund there might 2*d.* a chaldron be laid on all coals that come to the port of London.

Sir Edward Seymour: I am against this proposal for that this was to raise a tax upon a great part of the people of England which this committee cannot do except it come recommended from the King. Then this is a private matter and not to raise money for the public so that the proceedings of this committee are wholly irregular.

Mr. Bathurst to the same, and he desired that as the City had committed great faults in incurring this debt so I would have them pay for it in their private capacities.

Sir Christopher Musgrave: I am against this of coals because it will oppress the poor. And therefore I will propose a way to do this matter, and that is by laying 12*d.* a year on every chimney within the City of London to be paid by the respective inhabitants. Sir William Turner and several others to the same.

Sir Thomas Littleton: I can by no means consent to the matter that is now proposed because this would open a way to bring in the whole duty of chimney money again upon us, which was so oppressive a tax. For as you give it now unto the City, I hope you would not deny it to the Crown if they request it the next sessions. But I think the duty upon coals much less oppressive.

Sir John Darell: I like neither of these ways, that upon coals or the chimney money; they are both grievous. And therefore I will propose another. There are divers companies in the City who have great rents and revenues and little to do with them. They are persons within the City and who have helped towards this debt, and therefore I am for laying 5*s.* in the pound upon their lands.

Sir Charles Sedley moved for that of chimney money.

But after some time the question was put upon coals: resolved that 2*d.* a chaldron or a ton be laid upon all coals imported to the port of London, to be collected at the Meetage Office.

Sir Edward Seymour: I conceive all that you are now doing is very irregular, for by the rules of this House you can give no public aids but for the service of the public and that too when the King demands it in parliament. But this case I take to be a private matter, and as you take care to pay the debts of this city so you may of any other place and there will be no end. I think the way proposed of chimney money will be very oppressive and may be a door to let in chimney money all over the kingdom, and this of coals is a tax for ever.

Then it was moved and resolved accordingly that all freemen of London shall pay the duty of prisage and butlerage upon wines of 4s. a **tun** (as foreigners do) towards raising a fund for a perpetual interest for paying the orphans of London. Then it was moved and accordingly ordered that for a further fund every person that is bound an apprentice should pay 2s. 6d. and every freeman to pay 5s. Then it was further moved and ordered that every person that now is, hath been or shall be, or fine for Alderman or Sheriff of London do pay £20, every Common Councilman £10, and every liveryman £5.

Sir Edward Seymour moved that all the moneys arising by the sale of all offices and employments within the City of London should be also applied towards the raising a farther fund of perpetual interest.

But this was opposed for that it would ruin the grandeur of the City, it taking away all the profits and perquisites of the Chair. So not put.

Sir Robert Sawyer moved that all persons that keep taverns might pay £5 for a licence from the Lord Mayor within the City to sell wine. But it was not put.

Then moved for the Chairman to leave the Chair and that he might report to the House that the committee had [made][1] some further progress and desired leave to sit again.

So the Speaker resumed the Chair and *Mr. Harcourt* reported accordingly, and the committee were ordered to sit again on Wednesday next.

Mr. Herbert reported the reasons to be offered at a conference with the Lords upon the bill of accounts. And the same were read at the Table by the Clerk and agreed to and on a question ordered to be offered at a conference. Resolved that a conference be desired with the Lords upon the subject-matter of the amendments made by the Lords to the said bill and Mr. Herbert was ordered to go to the Lords and desire the same.

The petition of the clothiers of Worcester was presented by *Mr. Solicitor General*, and the purport of it was to pray that the East India Company might be obliged to export yearly such a quantity of our

[1] 'more' in MS.

woollen manufactures. And the same was referred to the committee to whom the bill about the East India Company is referred.

So adjourned till 8 on Monday morning.

Monday, 1 February

The Lord William Powlett was ordered to carry up the bill for naturalizing the Marquess of Monpouillon to the Lords and desire their concurrence.

Sir Jonathan Jenning was ordered to carry to the Lords the bill for naturalizing Mainhardt Duke of Leinster and desire their concurrence to the said amendments.

Mr. Henry Herbert reported that he had, according to order, been to desire a conference with the Lords upon the amendments made by them to the bill for taking the public accounts. That the Lords had agreed to the same and appointed it to be presently in the Painted Chamber. Then the persons' names that drew up the reasons were read over and they were appointed managers of the said conference and went to it accordingly. And being returned, *Mr. Herbert* reported that they had attended the conference with their reasons and had delivered the same to their Lordships why they could not agree to the said amendments.

Sir Robert Henley reported from the committee the examinations and informations relating to the proposals and disposals of Irish estates, which he delivered in. But notice being taken by some members that the name of a member of this House was often mentioned therein about matters that seemed to reflect on him and the committee had proceeded to examine into the same without leave of the House, which was wholly irregular, for no private committee can by the rules of the House examine any matter or accusation that reflects upon a member without particular order of the House. But whenever they find the same, they ought to proceed no further but come back to the House and acquaint them to this or the like effect: that a member of this House was mentioned to be concerned in the matters directed by this House to be inquired into and therefore the committee proceeded no further till they had the directions of the House. So the House in this matter ordered that the matter should be re-examined by the committee (though the member himself was at the committee when it was examined) and the committee had power to inquire into the matter to them referred notwithstanding any members of this House may be concerned therein. And the member himself might be present at the committee if he pleased and when it comes to be reported the House will give some short time to make his defence or put in his answer thereto in writing.

Then the Order of the Day was read for going into a Committee of the Whole House on the bills for forfeiting the estates in England and Ireland.

Sir Joseph Tredenham then presented a petition from the Lord Abercorn relating to the Irish bill.

Mr. Smith, Sir Edward Seymour, and *Mr. Arnold* spoke against receiving this petition for this was the proper work of a court of claims to settle, and then if you take the method of receiving petitions there will be no end.

Sir Thomas Clarges spoke on behalf of it.

But no question was put upon it but it was left on the Table.

Then the Speaker left the Chair and Mr. Palmes was called to the Chair of the committee. So the committee proceeded on the bill for forfeiting the estates in England, and made several amendments to it and finished the same. Then they proceeded upon the bill for Ireland and made some progress which he was ordered to report and to move to have leave to sit again.

So the Speaker resumed the Chair and *Mr. Palmes* reported that the committee had met and had finished the English bill which he was ready to report when the House should order, and that they had also made some progress in the bill about Ireland, and moved for leave to sit again which the House ordered should be tomorrow morning.

Several members were upon motion ordered to be added to divers committees.

So adjourned till 8 tomorrow morning.

Tuesday, 2 February

Mr. Waller complained on the behalf of a member, Mr. Backwell, for a breach of privilege committed by one Roberts and Johnston in arresting a menial servant of John Backwell esq., a member of this House, and prayed that they might be sent for in custody for this breach of privilege.

Mr. Smith opposed it, desiring it might be referred to a committee to examine and to report their opinions to the House, and not to punish a man for a crime before you have examined whether it be true or no.

However, the *member* being in the House and affirming it was true, they were ordered to be sent for in custody of the Serjeant at Arms.

Capt. Bickerstaffe presented a petition from the officers, innkeepers, and soldiers touching the arrears due to the army in 1677 and 1679, which took up some debate. And the consideration thereof was referred to a committee to examine into and report it to the House.

The bill to prevent the keeping of gunpowder about the Tower of London was reported with amendments. Some were agreed to and others disagreed unto. Then a clause was offered and it was read twice and then the question was put whether it should be made part of the bill. House divided—Yeas went out.

Sir Gilbert Clarke

Yeas   73

Mr. Francis Gwyn

Tellers for the

Sir John Morton

Noes   67

Mr. Cary

So carried to stand part of the bill. Then the question was put for the engrossing the bill with the amendments and carried in the negative.

Then the House, according to order, went into a Committee of the Whole House upon the bill for vesting the forfeited estates in Ireland in Their Majesties. And Mr. Palmes took the Chair and opened to the House how far they proceeded in the bill the last time. So they proceeded on it to the other part of the bill and made divers amendments to several of the clauses. And the committee divided on a clause for forfeiting the remainders on estates tail for treason committed by the tenant in tail: whether it should stand in the bill—Yeas on the right hand, Noes on the left.

Yeas Mr. Montagu   75

Tellers for the

Noes Mr. Godolphin   84

So the clause was thrown out.

The committee went through the other clauses.

Then Sir Thomas Clarges offered a clause to save those Protestants that were not in actual arms on 1 September 1689. This was long debated, but at last upon the question it was ordered to be made part of the [bill].

So the committee finished this bill and the Chairman was ordered to acquaint the House that they had finished the bill and that he was ready to report it when the House ordered. And after, the Speaker resumed the Chair and *Mr. Palmes* reported accordingly, and the report of the bill was ordered to be made on Thursday.

So adjourned till 8 tomorrow morning.

Wednesday, 3 February

Sir John Darell presented to the House a petition from the merchants, planters, and traders to the sugar plantations in the West Indies on behalf of the refiners of sugars here. And it was received and read and referred to the same committee that the petition of the refiners of sugars here in England was referred.

Then the Order of the Day was read and the Speaker left the Chair and the House resolved itself into a Committee of the Whole House to consider of the bill for a quarterly poll. The Solicitor was called to the Chair. Then they proceeded on the same and began with the clauses in order and made several amendments, alterations, and additions therein. Some new clauses were added and others rectified. Then a debate was about teachers and preachers in separate congregations.

The Lord Norris to have them taxed 20*s.* a quarter whatever their congregation or contribution is worth for that it would be hard upon beneficed clergymen to pay to this tax for £60 per annum and who pay first-fruits, tenths, taxes, and other public charges. Others spoke to this effect as Sir Edward Seymour, Sir John Knight, Sir Christopher Musgrave, Mr. Shakerley, etc.

Mr. Boscawen, Mr. Hampden, and Sir Henry Ashurst opposed it and moved to excuse them for that this was putting a mark upon these people and would rather widen the differences between us.

However, it was put and carried in the affirmative to charge them.

So the committee almost dispatched the bill and ordered the Solicitor to report the committee had made a considerable progress and desired leave to sit again. So the Speaker resumed the Chair and the *Solicitor* moved accordingly, and the House appointed Friday next to go into a Committee of the Whole House again upon this bill.

Adjourned till 8 tomorrow morning.

Thursday, 4 February

Mr. Palmes reported from the committee the bill for vesting the forfeited estates in England in Their Majesties with the amendments, which were agreed to.

The *Lord Colchester* offered a clause on the behalf of the Lord Dover which was received, read twice, and made part of the bill.

Mr. Comptroller Wharton offered a clause on behalf of the Earl of Torrington.

But it was opposed by *Sir William Strickland*, *Sir Edward Seymour*, *Mr. Smith*, etc. for that this clause as drawn confirmed his grant and it was intended he should only have a saving clause from anything in this act.

So the former clause was withdrawn and *Mr. Herbert* offered a clause of saving only, which was made part of the bill.

Capt. Thomas Howard offered a clause in behalf of George Lord Howard and it was received, read twice, and made part of the bill. So was another clause on behalf of the Earl of Monmouth which was tendered by the *Marquess of Winchester*. *Mr. Ettrick* presented another on behalf of Mr. Preston, a member of this House, and received and passed. *Mr. Harley* presented another, on behalf of some charities, which was received, read, and passed.

So the bill with these amendments was ordered to be engrossed.

The committee of the East India Company attended and were called into the House and Sir Thomas Cook delivered in at the Bar their answer in writing. So they withdrew again and the consideration thereof was referred till Saturday next.

All committees adjourned but that of the Irish.[1]

So adjourned till 8 tomorrow morning.

Friday, 5 February

Some members upon motion were added to the committee to whom the Irish affairs are referred.

Then the managers' names for the conference were read over and some more were added thereto. So they went to the conference. And being returned, *Sir Joseph Tredenham* reported the conference, and that the Lord Rochester managed the same, and that their Lordships had

---

[1] Cf. *CJ*, x. 651, 653.

not agreed to the reasons offered by this House but did insist on all their amendments. And he delivered the same in at the Table. Then they proceeded to take the same into consideration.

Sir Richard Temple and *Sir Edward Seymour* moved that this House would insist for this is no new business, the Lords having been long nibbling at money matters. Now to justify this there can be but precedents and reason. The precedents are against them and there is hardly any reason for it, for to what purpose should they have an account of the public moneys when, if they fall short, the Lords have no power to make it up, for they will not pretend to give money? Then they cannot desire it to punish offenders because they are to be the judges, and will not then take on them the part of accusers and prosecutors, too. But if this be admitted of, the Lords will then come to give money as well as you.

Sir Christopher Musgrave and *Mr. Charles Montagu* to the same and that the House would insist upon disagreeing with the Lords' amendments.

Mr. Bathurst moved that the House would withdraw their disagreement to the Lords' amendments to the bill.

Then the question was **put** and resolved that this House doth insist upon their disagreeing with the Lords in the amendments to the said bill. Resolved that a free conference be desired with the Lords on the subject-matter of the last conference and Sir Joseph Tredenham ordered to go up and desire the same. And the managers were appointed by the House to meet at 4 this afternoon to prepare reasons to offer at the same.

Then the House proceeded to go upon the report about the bill for the Irish forfeitures. But the House being very thin, the Serjeant at Arms was ordered to take the Mace and repair to the respective courts in Westminster Hall and the Court of Requests and to command the immediate attendance of the members upon the service of the House. Which being done and he returned and the Mace on the Table, the House went upon the said report from the committee of the bill for the vesting the forfeited estates in Ireland in Their Majesties. And several of them were agreed unto. Then there was a clause for forfeiting the remainders on estates tail which was brought in in the bill but left out by the committee, which now admitted of a great debate.

Some moved to disagree with the committee in leaving it out as *Mr. Boscawen, Sir Charles Sedley, Mr. Hampden, Charles Montagu,*

Mr. Bowyer, Serj. Blencowe, Sir William Strickland, and others, and urged that the inserting of the clause was for the advantage of the public, the security of the Protestant religion there, and would for ever prevent a rebellion again in that kingdom. And that if this clause were left out, the bill would signify but little. That this is no unjust thing, for if tenant in tail commit treason his estate is forfeited as long as tenant in tail hath issue. The King hath a base fee in the estate but after issue extinct it goes to him in remainder, yet notwithstanding that is so tenant in tail may cut off any remainder by a recovery. So no such great prejudice to vest these estates in the Crown—no more than for tenant in tail to dispose of this estate and cut off the remainders—and to throw out this clause would not benefit the remainderman, for who will buy a remainder that hath nothing until after issue extinct? And though this clause is left out in the English bill for that the Irish are inclined to rebellion naturally, the English not.

There were others moved to agree with the committee as *Sir Robert Sawyer, Sir Richard Temple, Sir Joseph Tredenham, Sir William Wogan, Mr. Price, Mr. John Howe,* etc. urging it to be a very hard thing to punish men for a crime who are in no fault and perhaps at that time were innocent.

But after a long debate, the question was put for agreeing with the committee. But the House divided—Noes went forth.

	Mr. Bickerstaffe	
Yeas		91
	Mr. Pigott	
Tellers for the		
	Mr. Charles Montagu	
Noes		118
	Mr. Colt	

So the House disagreed with the committee and the clause stood part of the bill.

Then there was a debate on another clause to save all the judgements, securities, etc. that Protestants have on popish estates.

Hampden and some others spoke against it for that many papists had made sham securities and encumbrances to Protestants to cover their estates.

But *Sir John Lowther, Sir Thomas Clarges,* and *Sir Christopher Musgrave* spoke for it as a most reasonable thing that a man should not be barred of any right he had by encumbrance or otherwise on the papists' estates.

Then the Court drove it on and pressed much to have this clause recommitted, but it was opposed. However, the question was put for recommitting it and carried in the negative. Then the question was put for agreeing to the clause and carried in the affirmative.

So the further consideration of this report was adjourned till Monday next.

So the House adjourned till 8 tomorrow morning.

Saturday, 6 February

Sir Thomas Mackworth had leave to go into the country for some time upon extraordinary business.

Mr. Robartes presented to the House a petition from Sir John Cutler, a member of the House, praying leave that he might resume his privilege in the case between him and the Lord De La Warr or else that he might be at liberty to take such course therein as he shall be advised. The same was read and ordered to lie on the Table.

Mr. Onslow was ordered to carry up to the Lords the bill for better ordering and collecting the duty upon low wines, etc., for their concurrence.

Then the House proceeded to take into consideration the business of the East India Company and read their answer given into the House lately in writing, wherein they refused to give security according to the terms demanded by the House unless they might be established and confirmed in that trade by the bill that lay before the House.

Sir Edward Seymour spoke largely against the old Company and that they had not dealt fairly with the House. I think, therefore, you have nothing left but to consider of some way how to preserve the trade. The sessions now draws towards an end so that you will not have time to finish a bill for it and therefore I am for addressing to the King to dissolve the present Company according to the powers reserved in his charter and to establish a new one for the benefit of trade, according to such regulations as he shall think fit.

Mr. Neale seconded that motion, for though I always was for the old Company, yet now seeing their designs and intended delay I am for such an address.

Mr. John Howe spoke in behalf of the old Company and desired that the House would keep their words with them and pass an act to confirm the old Company.

Mr. Hutchinson was for the address.

Mr. Bathurst was against it and for going into a committee upon that bill.

Mr. Methuen was for the address but was for passing a vote first: that the House, upon the examination of this matter and the proofs given, were satisfied that the Company had not managed the trade for the good of the nation.

Sir Richard Temple: I am for going into a Committee of the Whole House to proceed upon the bill according to the Order of the Day, for you have already approved of the sufficiency of the security they have offered you for £744,000. Hereby you will keep your word with the Company. You will preserve the trade to this nation which otherwise will be inevitably lost to the Dutch, and the French are now putting in for it, too.

Sir Thomas Littleton: I am against the address for a new company for that will be only changing of hands—taking it out of the old and putting it into new—and therefore I am for going on with your bill for regulating the present Company.

Sir John Guise then proposed the question that an humble address should be made to His Majesty to dissolve the present East India Company, according to the power reserved in their charter, and to incorporate a new one according to such regulations as His Majesty in his royal wisdom shall think fit.

Sir Edward Seymour: The debate is very regular and it arises properly on the answer of the Company. And though it is objected that a new company is liable to the same objections as the old one was, perhaps it may be true but the King in his royal wisdom may prevent this by settling them according to your regulations.

Then a debate arose whether to go on with the address or with the bill.

Those for the old Company were for going on with the bill, such as *Sir Charles Sedley*, for he would not leave it to Whitehall to determine it.

John Smith thought the address would not do the business, for the King's charter cannot compel them to pay their debts nor hinder interlopers. Therefore, go on with the bill as brought in. And I am not for the old Company for I think they have forfeited all pretence to your favour.

Sir Robert Sawyer for going on with the bill.

Those against the old Company were for going on with the address such as *Sir William Strickland, Sir Robert Cotton* (of Chester), and *Sir John Lowther* (of Lowther) for that he saw no prospect of passing the bill this sessions. And though it should go in this House it could not in the Lords' House, so that if a prorogation come all is lost and you must begin again. So that I am for the address, and what you find wanting in the new charter may be remedied by a bill at your next meeting. This is for the honour of the nation and is the only way now left. *Sir Robert Henley* was for the address and so was *Dutton Colt.*

Lord Ranelagh: I am not for the address, but moved for an amendment to the question that no person that hath sold out himself in the old Company shall be concerned any way in the new. *Mr. Montagu* seconded the same.

Mr. Papillon: I am against dissolving the old Company for many mischiefs may happen thereby; their debts may be left unpaid, they may sell their forts to the enemy, etc. Nor am I for setting up a new company. But I think it best to address to the King to terminate the stock of the old Company, but not to dissolve them but to lay open their books for new subscriptions. And this I think the only way to preserve the trade.

Then it was proposed to divide the question—to make the first for dissolving the present Company without addressing for a new one. But this was opposed by all that were really against the old Company, for they would have a new one established on the dissolution of the old one. And no words ought to be left out of a question after it is stated without putting a question whether such words shall stand part of the question, though *Seymour, Musgrave*, and *Hampden* thought it might be put into two questions without putting a question for it.

Mr. Hampden: I am for the address and for the whole question as the quicker way, and this House may the next sessions pass the charter into a law.

Mr. Heneage Finch: I am against the latter words from the difficulty that may arise in the erecting a new company. But I am for dissolving the old Company by way of address but am for leaving it to the King to constitute a new one according as His Majesty shall think fit.

Then an amendment was proposed to the question if 'incorporate' should stand in the question and carried in the negative and the word 'constitute' brought in the room thereof. Then it was proposed to leave out these words in the question, 'according to such regulations'.

And the question was put whether they should stand in the question. The House divided—Yeas went out.

Sir Thomas Littleton
Yeas 85
[Mr.] Thompson
Tellers for the
Mr. Goldwell
Noes 103
Mr. Cary

So the words were left out and these words—'in such manner'—were upon the question inserted.

So then the main question at large as before, with these alterations, was put and clearly carried.

Sir Edward Seymour then moved that the Privy Council might attend His Majesty to know his pleasure when he would be attended with the address.

And it was ordered that the address should be made by the Speaker attended with the whole House.

Sir Edward Abney presented a petition from the Earls of Scarsdale and Huntingdon against Bernard Granville, a member of the House, praying that he—having once waived his privilege in a suit—might not have liberty to insist on it again. But Mr. Granville not being in the House, the petition was received but not read.

Sir Joseph Tredenham, being returned from the Lords, reported that their Lordships had agreed to a free conference on the subject-matter of the last and had appointed Monday morning next at 12 of the clock in the Painted Chamber.

So adjourned till 8 on Monday morning.

Monday, 8 February

The time for the free conference being come, the managers' names were read over. So they went up to the same in the Painted Chamber. And the Lords being come, Sir Joseph Tredenham opened the same, Mr. Charles Montagu proceeded therein, then Sir Richard Temple went on. Then on the Lords' part the Earl of Rochester began and urged some precedents. Then Sir Robert Sawyer replied thereto. Then the Earl of Nottingham answered. Then Sir Christopher Musgrave spoke on the Commons' side. Sir Robert Sawyer and Sir

Richard Temple and the Earls of Rochester and Nottingham urged some things further and explained some things they had before insisted on. Earl of Devon then spoke and insisted on the Lords having the naming commissioners to take the public accounts.

So the conference being ended, the managers returned. And *Sir Joseph Tredenham* reported that they had attended the said free conference according to the order of the House and had offered their reasons and acquainted the Lords that this House did insist on the disagreement to their amendments.

George Booth esq., newly elected a member for the borough of Malmesbury in Wiltshire (in the room of Sir James Long, deceased), was introduced into the House and took the oaths accordingly.

So the House adjourned till 8 tomorrow morning.

Tuesday, 9 February

The House went upon the Lords' amendments to the tithe bill. And upon one clause added by the Lords to make the Justices of the Peace to execute the sentences of the spiritual courts, the House divided— those for agreeing with the clause went out.[1]

		Sir Robert Cotton	
	Yeas		66
		Granado Pigott	
Tellers for the			
		Sir Robert Cotton (Chester)	
	Noes		86
		Mr. Clarke	

So disagreed with this, as also several others.

So several persons were appointed as managers to prepare and draw up reasons to be offered at a conference with the Lords for disagreeing with their amendments. Ordered that a conference be had and that Mr. [name missing] do go up and desire the same.

The House, according to order, proceeded in the farther consideration of the report of the amendments to the Irish bill of forfeitures.

Mr. Pelham offered a clause in favour of the Lord Sidney, which was received, read twice, and ordered to be made part of the bill.

Mr. Hampden moved that a clause might be added to give His

---

[1] *CJ*, x. 658 has the figures in this division as 84–56.

Majesty power to dispose of £30,000 per annum of the forfeitures as he should see fit. *Sir Robert Cotton* (of the Post Office) to the same.

Mr. John Smith and *Mr. Harley* moved that the King might have power to dispose of a third or fourth part of the forfeitures and not be so much per annum, for it is not known what they may amount to, whether to the value of £30,000 or no. *Col. Granville* to the same purpose.

Then after some debate the question was put upon the proviso to fill up the blank with £30,000 and carried in the negative. Then it was filled up on the question with one-third part of the value of the whole.

Sir John Somers offered a clause in favour of Mr. Poultney for his place of Clerk of the Council, and received, read, and agreed to.

Mr. Brydges presented a clause in behalf of the Duke of Ormonde, which was received, read, and agreed to.

Sir Joseph Tredenham presented a clause in favour of the Lord Abercorn, which was also received.

Sir John Trenchard presented a clause in favour of Mr. Fitzmorris, son to the Lord Kerry, and it was received.

Mr. Bickerstaffe presented a clause to save the Usher of the Court of Chancery there, and it was received.

Mr. Levinge presented a clause in favour of the Protestant creditors of Col. Brown, and it was received.

Mr. Clarke moved that no one should have the benefit of this act as a Protestant without taking the oaths and subscribing the declaration, and received.

And the bill with the amendments was ordered to be engrossed. Adjourned till tomorrow morning 8 of the clock.

Wednesday, 10 February

Sir Francis Masham presented to the House a petition from the old Victuallers of the Navy relating to an arrear due to them for serving the Navy.

But it was opposed referring [it] to the Committee of the Whole House for they had no power to pay it. Then those commissioners had not yet stated their accounts. Wherefore it was ordered to lie on the Table.

Then the House, according to the Order of the Day, went into a Committee of the Whole House upon the poll bill and filled up the blanks and passed several of the clauses.

Then the hour of going to the free conference being come, the Solicitor left the Chair and the Speaker resumed it.

And the managers' names were read over and they went to the conference with the Lords. Where being come, the Lord Rochester managed the same for the Lords and acquainted the Commons that the Lords had desired this conference to return the bill and to acquaint them that they had reported the reasons offered by the Commons at the last conference and that their Lordships had a due consideration of them. And upon the whole, he was ordered to acquaint them that their Lordships saw no reason to depart from their amendments but did adhere to the same. Sir Edward Seymour then spoke very largely to the unusualness of adhering upon the first free conference as taking away all intercourse between the two Houses. That it was the undoubted right of the Commons to give or dispose of money, and so declared in 9 H. IV, and that this was breaking in upon that. That if the necessary supplies desired should be denied the next winter till the Commons saw how the money already given was disposed of, it will lie at the doors of those that obstruct this bill. Lord Rochester said he was very sorry that learned gentleman had not offered his reasons at the last conference. It might have gone a great way with their Lordships. But now he had no order to reply to it but had only in command to acquaint the Commons that their Lordships adhered. Sir Edward Seymour: I did reserve myself till I heard what it was that stuck with your Lordships that I might offer my reasons then at a second free conference and did not expect this unusual method of adhering upon the first free conference.

So the managers returned and *Sir Edward Seymour* at the Bar reported the conference: That they had been there to attend the same and that the Lords did adhere to their amendments and had returned the bill, which he delivered in at the Table.

Sir Richard Temple said it was unparliamentary to adhere at the first free conference.

Solicitor Somers then moved that a committee might be appointed to search and examine the Journals and precedents touching the method of conferences and free conferences between the two Houses, and to report the same to the House. And it was ordered accordingly and a committee was appointed.

Then the House, according to order, went into a Committee of the Whole House—Speaker leaving the Chair and Solicitor General was Chairman—and proceeded upon the poll bill. Several clauses were offered to be added thereto, as the clause for taking the oaths, and received to stand part of the bill.

The clause in behalf of the Quakers by Mr. Hutchinson was received and made part of the bill.

Sir John Lowther offered a clause to the committee to give credit on this act for £1,341,000, which is the sum this act is computed to raise.

But this was opposed by Mr. Bertie and Mr. Harley as irregular, the committee having no power to receive such a clause except empowered by the House.

Sir Christopher Musgrave and Sir Edward Seymour to the same, as irregular and altogether new.

So the clause was by consent withdrawn.

Col. Cornewall offered a clause of appropriation of such a part of it to the land forces, but this clause was also withdrawn for the same reason as the last.

Sir William Strickland offered a clause to charge offices, fees, and perquisites if above such a value. But this was also withdrawn upon the same reason.

So the bill was finished and then they passed the preamble and so was ordered to report it to the House.

So then the Solicitor left the Chair and the Speaker resumed it. And the *Solicitor* reported the committee had gone through the bill and made several amendments which they had directed him to report to the House. Ordered that it be reported on Monday morning next.

So the time being come to attend the King in the Banqueting House, the House adjourned till tomorrow morning as usual and then went up in a body with their Speaker, and he presented to His Majesty the resolution of the House touching the East India Company. And His Majesty was pleased to tell them it was a matter of very great importance and therefore could not expect a present answer, but he would consider of it and in a short time give a positive answer.

Adjourned till 8 tomorrow morning.

Thursday, 11 February

Speaker reported that the House had attended His Majesty with the address about the East India Company as also His Majesty's answer thereto.

An engrossed bill from the Lords for relief of the orphans of London was read the first time and ordered a second reading. The bill confirmed only the several orders of the Common Council empowering them to charge their lands with £8,000 per annum towards payment of the interest of the orphans' debts.

But this bill was spoke against for that the Lords herein do touch the privilege of the Commons in giving money. But answered, this is no more than is done in the case of any private bill for the sale of land and then it confirms only what the City have already done.

Then the House, according to order, went into a Committee of the Whole House upon the orphans' debts. Several ways were proposed to raise money to pay them. One was by laying a duty of 6d. more upon every chaldron of coals. But it was opposed as unreasonable for that the charge would fall on the poor and on those who had no ways been concerned in the City as well as on those that had.

Then proposed to lay a tax upon hackney coaches. And after some debate, resolved that the benefit arising by licensing 600 hackney coaches at the yearly rent of £5 a coach be applied to the satisfaction of the debts of the orphans of the City of London.

Sir Robert Clayton then moved that the duty of waterbailage might be another head. So resolved that the duty of waterbailage and weighing at the King's Beam be applied to the orphans of London.

And Mr. Bowyer, the Chairman, was ordered to report these resolutions to the House.

So adjourned till 8 tomorrow morning.

Friday, 12 February

Sir Samuel Barnardiston reported Sir William Halford's bill. But it was recommitted to consider of a petition relating thereto which was not yet taken into consideration.

Mr. Waller was ordered to carry up to the Lords for their concurrence the bill to prevent clandestine mortgages.

The bill for subjecting copyhold estates to the payment of debts and for better recovery of fines was read the first time.

Sir Christopher Musgrave opposed this bill as a very pernicious bill that would destroy all the copyholds in England and ruin the lords and tenants.

So upon the question it was denied a second reading.

Lord William Powlett was ordered to carry up to the Lords for their concurrence the bill for building good and defensible ships.

The engrossed bill for vesting the forfeited estates in England in Their Majesties was read the last time.

Comptroller Wharton offered an engrossed clause on behalf of Mr. Bruno Talbot, which was received, read thrice, and ordered to stand part of the bill.

Mr. Vaughan offered a clause on behalf of Adam Colclough, and received, read thrice, and made part of the bill.

Sir Francis Blake offered a clause on behalf of Thomas Vanton esq., which was received etc., and made part of the bill.

So the bill was passed with the title and Mr. Palmes was ordered to carry it up to the Lords for their concurrence.

The engrossed bill for vesting the forfeited estates in Ireland in Their Majesties was read the last time.

Mr. Smith tendered a petition from the Speaker to tender a clause to preserve a debt upon the Lord Clancarty's estate. It was read, with the bond for the debt, and granted. And a clause engrossed tendered, received, read thrice, and made part of the bill.

Dutton Colt presented an engrossed clause on the behalf of Col. Henry Luttrell which was received and read once. And upon the question for second reading, House divided—Yeas went out: Yeas 25, Noes 109.[1] So it was rejected.

Mr. Bertie presented a clause in favour of Mr. Wray, which was received, read thrice, and made part of the bill.

Col. Cornewall presented a clause that the third part of the estates forfeited reserved to Their Majesties' share shall be given to such officers and soldiers as served in person in Ireland.

Mr. Boscawen, Sir John Lowther, and *Sir John Guise* spoke against it, and several for it.

So upon the question to make it part of the bill, the House divided —Yeas went out.

		Col. Granville	
	Yeas		86
		Mr. Bertie	
Tellers for the			
		Lord Falkland	
	Noes		57
		Mr. Travers	

Mr. Hutchinson then tendered a clause in behalf of the Quakers in that kingdom. The House divided—Yeas went out.

[1] For tellers in this division see *CJ*, x. 663.

Mr. Arnold

Yeas   63

Dr. Barbone

Tellers for the

Col. Goldwell

Noes   66

Major Pery

So rejected.

Major Vincent tendered a clause in behalf of the Bishop of Cloyne, but it was rejected on the question.

Sir Joseph Tredenham tendered a clause in favour of Sir Robert Southwell; [it] was received, read, and made part of the bill.

A clause or two more was tendered. And then the bill at last was passed, then the title, and Mr. Palmes was ordered to carry it to the Lords for their concurrence.

Adjourned till 8 tomorrow morning.

Saturday, 13 February

The House proceeded to the consideration of the amendments to the bill of naturalization of the Marquess of Monpouillon, which were read and agreed to—being only the addition of some other persons to be naturalized. And certificates of their having taken the Sacrament according to the Church of England were produced and witnesses examined to the same. So the bill was passed and Mr. Gwyn was ordered to carry it up to the Lords.

The engrossed bill for sale of the lands of Keble was reported by *Col. Goldwell* without amendments, but a mistake being in naming of the lands therein it was recommitted.[1]

Engrossed bill of the Bishop of London was read the last time and passed, and Mr. Travers ordered to carry it to the Lords to desire their concurrence to the said amendments.

Engrossed bill of the Lord Stanhope, son to the Lord Chesterfield, read the last time and passed, and Mr. Gwyn ordered to carry it to the Lords for their concurrence to the amendments, etc.

The House took into consideration the Lords' amendments to the bill for repairing the highways, which was read and agreed to by the House, and Mr. Clarke ordered to carry it to the Lords to acquaint them therewith.

---

[1] There is no entry of this in the *Journal*.

The House took into consideration also the Lords' amendments to the bill for settlement of the poor and agreed to the same. And Mr. Hutchinson was ordered to carry it to the Lords to acquaint them therewith.

Upon the report of *Sir Robert Clayton* from the committee to consider of the case of the French Protestants and of ways to relieve and supply them, it was moved that the House would go into a Committee of the Whole House to consider of ways to raise money to do something for them. But it was opposed as irregular for the House can't give money but upon request from the Crown. So it was left as the sense of the House that they should apply to the King to recommend their case to the House.

Sir Joseph Tredenham reported the two last free conferences about the bill of accounts, which he read at the Bar and then delivered the same in at the Table.

Mr. Hampden: You must not stick here but come to some question —either to adhere or to desire a new conference. I hear the Lords have adhered. It is very soon and have come quick upon your heels. I think you have appointed a committee to search precedents. If so, it is fit to stay to see what they do.

Sir Christopher Musgrave: Of late the practice has been to adhere and then the House that does so is bound up thereby. But formerly they have departed from it; it is not usual to adhere so soon as done in this case. But now they have adhered, it is fit for you to consider what to do. I think for my part the giving of money the inherent right of the Commons and so great a privilege not to be parted with, though this be a very good bill. And therefore I see no other way but to adhere likewise. *Sir Joseph Tredenham* to the same.

So the question was put and resolved that this House doth adhere to their disagreeing to the amendments made by their Lordships to the bill of accounts etc., and doth adhere to the said bill as sent up by this House.

Mr. Arnold moved that since the Lords were encroaching upon the privileges of this House that we might remonstrate the same to the King and that it might be known where the fault lay.

Mr. Bowyer, according to order, reported from the committee the several resolutions of the committee relating to the orphans of London which he read and delivered the same in at the Table, where they were read.

Sir Edward Seymour opposed the report for that this House could not give any money for the payment of any person's debts whatsoever by raising a tax upon the subject.

Mr. Boscawen: The matter before you is no such strange thing. You have granted a toll or money to repair a bridge, amend highways, to build churches, etc.

Sir Edward Seymour: The committee have not gone regularly on. They are empowered only to consider of ways and ought to have taken an account in what condition they are and how able to pay themselves. And as to those precedents, that of highways it is in effect to the King for they are his ways; and for building churches, that is for the public benefit. But here this case is of private concern, and as you pay the debts of one corporation why should you not those of another?

Sir George Treby: This is a matter of public nature and is a great act of charity.

Sir Christopher Musgrave: You are here going to lay a charge on the people and that for ever, wherein I think the committee have exceeded their power. The tax you are going to lay is upon many persons and countries who are not at all concerned with the City. And why more should be done for the corporation of London than for any other corporation, I know not. They are all in some measure serviceable to the public.

Sir Charles Sedley and *Sir John Guise* against the report.

So the several resolutions were read over: viz. to charge the lands of the City with £8,000 per annum for ever; to lay 2*d.* per ton or chaldron upon coals; to appropriate the 4*s.* per tun upon prisage of wines; that every apprentice shall pay 2*s.* 6*d.* when bound and every freeman 5*s.* when made free; that every Sheriff or Alderman that is or hath fined for them should pay £20, every Common Councilman £10, and every liveryman £5; that the duties of waterbailage and weighing at the King's Beam be applied that way, too. To all which resolutions being severally put, the House agreed. As to that of the waterbailage, the House divided on it—the Yeas went out.

		Mr. Herbert	
	Yeas		67
		Mr. Harcourt	
Tellers for the			
		Sir John Knight	
	Noes		43
		Mr. Culliford	

But as to that about £5 per annum for licensing 600 hackney coaches, the House was against it so disagreed with the committee therein.

Mr. Harcourt moved and had leave to bring in a bill pursuant to the said resolutions.

Sir Edward Seymour: Since you have granted a perpetuity to the City of London, it cannot be denied by you if the Crown should request any such thing. But what I shall move you now is that the same persons who formerly cheated the orphans may not do it again. I desire the moneys arising hereby may be put into commissioners' hands to be appointed for that end and that there be a clause that no orphan shall for the future be forced to bring their money into the Chamber of London; then that no persons who have bought from the orphans shall have any further benefit hereby than to such sum they really paid; then that none have advantage hereof but only such who were forced to bring in their money; and a yearly account to be made of the moneys arising hereby.

And a bill was ordered to be brought in on the debate of the House and it was referred to eight or nine persons to prepare a bill accordingly.

Adjourned till 8 on Monday morning.

Monday, 15 February

Engrossed bill for sale of Vincent Grantham's land read the last time and Mr. Clarke ordered to carry it to the Lords and to acquaint them this House had agreed to the same without amendments.

Mr. Price ordered to carry up Mr. Vaughan's bill to the Lords and to acquaint them this House had agreed to it without any amendments.

Mr. Solicitor General, according to order, reported the poll bill with amendments and read the same at the Bar and then delivered it in at the Table, where they were read again and after the question put upon each of them and agreed unto by the House.

Mr. Boscawen presented a clause in paper to tax the several Inns of Court, Serjeants' Inns, and Inns of Chancery. And the same was read twice and agreed to.

Col. Granville presented another clause to revive the bill of accounts and to enlarge the time for the former commissioners (leaving out two of them) to take and state the said accounts.[1]

---

[1] For another report on the debate that follows see Ranke, vi. 178.

Sir Edward Seymour urged strongly against this clause, for in the beginning of the sessions you were for carrying on a vigorous war against France but now at the close you are in a fair way to carry on a vigorous war between the two Houses. This is a method to undermine the constitutions of this government and therefore not now to be practised. You passed a bill this sessions for taking the public accounts of the kingdom and the Lords were against it, but now you are going to do the same thing by way of proviso in an irregular way. Here is no way for the Lords or the King to give their free assent to it for they must give their assent to the whole bill and cannot to one part without the other. This matter (though I was for the bill) I think not fit to do for it alters the methods of your constitution and is of so dangerous a consequence that though I am for an account yet I am not for it this way. I would fain see any precedent where a bill has been lost between the two Houses a clause has in the same sessions tacked that matter to another bill. *Sir Henry Capel* to the same.

So the clause was read twice.

Sir Joseph Tredenham: I am against this clause for that it is altogether irregular. For if the Lords should oppose it and this House stick to it, then the bill is lost. And what will be the consequences thereof? Either the bill is lost or you must comply with the Lords in their amendments to your money bill.

Mr. Hampden, Mr. Montagu, Sir Stephen Fox, Col. Austen, Sir Robert Cotton (of Post Office), *Sir Thomas Littleton, Sir John Somers, Serj. Trenchard, Mr. Bowyer, Sir George Treby, Sir Robert Rich,* and *Lord Falkland* all spoke against it.

But the *Lord Castleton, Mr. Bathurst, Mr. Bertie, Col. Cornewall, Sir Charles Sedley, Sir Christopher Musgrave, Mr. Smith, Mr. Waller, Sir John Knight, Mr. Goodwin Wharton, Mr. Herbert,* and *Mr. Goldwell* all spoke for it.

Mr. Smith: I am for this clause and do not think this clause enough but would appoint commissioners also to issue out the money.

Sir Thomas Littleton: I am for addressing to the King to grant such a commission under his broad seal to the same persons with like powers as you have in your bill of accounts, and this I think a better way than this strange method of tacking bills after it hath been lost between the two Houses in the same sessions. And I would have those gentlemen consider who are so zealously for the clause whether they are able to maintain it.

Sir Christopher Musgrave: It is objected by some gentlemen that if a bill be brought in in one sessions and thrown out, it is not usual to bring in another of like nature. But this thing hath been done, as on 22 November 39 Eliz. a bill for setting the poor to work was thrown out and the 10th of March after the same sessions the same bill was brought in again. So in February 1666 a bill about logwood was rejected and in a few days the same bill was brought in again. And this very sessions the bill about hawkers and pedlars you rejected, and yet this day you read the same bill with another title brought in since. But then it is objected you here take away the negative voice from the King—no more now than in King Charles II's time when a clause against quartering of soldiers was tacked to a money bill. It is also said the King desires an account may be taken of the moneys given; if so, it is no doubt but the Lords will pass it. And this clause will tend much to satisfy the country whom you have loaded so much, and therefore I think it is for the service of the King to pass it. And this clause is not foreign at all to the bill but very proper.

Sir Edward Seymour: As to those precedents urged by the gentleman that spoke last, they do not relate to any proceeding between the two Houses, so come not up to this case, but only to your own House wherein you may do as you please.

Sir John Knight: There are other precedents of tacking bills: as to a poll bill in King Charles II's time you tacked a clause to prohibit French commodities; to a bill for £1,300,000 in 25th of Car. II you tacked a clause for drawbacks of transporting corn beyond sea.

The question at last was put for reading this clause a second time. The House divided—Yeas went out.

		Col. Granville	
	Yeas		145
		Mr. Herbert	
Tellers for the			
		Sir John Guise	
	Noes		104
		Mr. Cary	

So it was read a second time and ordered to be made part of the bill.

Col. Cornewall presented to the House an appropriating clause for part of the money on this bill to be applied for the Army, which was received. But on the question to have it read, the House divided—Yeas went out.

Col. Cornewall

Yeas   101

Mr. Fagg

Tellers for the

Mr. Cary

Noes   66

Mr. Goldwell

But upon motion, the reading of the clause was put off till tomorrow.

Then the *Speaker* informed the House he had received a letter from Mr. Fuller, which he had not yet opened. So he opened it and it was read, and it was to desire the protection of the House on 22nd of this month to perform what he had undertaken and that he might have the protection of the House in the meantime. But nothing was done therein.

So adjourned till 8 tomorrow morning.

Tuesday, 16 February

Mr. Clarke was ordered to carry up to the Lords the engrossed bill of Elizabeth Curtis to desire their concurrence to the amendments to the same.

An engrossed bill from the Lords of Thomas Kinersley was read the third time. And a petition of one Bryan Janson, etc., creditors of the said Kinersley, was presented to the House against the said bill.

Mr. Hampden and *Sir Edward Seymour* spoke mightily against private bills, the number and multitude of them, which held some debate.

So at last the question was put for passing the bill. The House divided—Yeas went out.

Mr. Cary

Yeas   60

Mr. Arnold

Tellers for the

Sir Thomas Samwell

Noes   86

Mr. Travers

So the bill was rejected.

Engrossed bill for navigating English ships with foreign seamen to and from the West Indies, etc., was read the third time and passed and the title, too, and Sir Samuel Barnardiston ordered to carry it to the Lords for their concurrence.

Then the House, according to order, went upon the appropriating clause of £875,000 of the money arising by the poll bill unto the Navy.[1]

Col. Cornewall (who presented it) saying that since the House had agreed to continue the Commissioners of Accounts for one year longer, he thought there was no great need of this clause. So he withdrew it by consent.

Sir John Lowther presented a clause that since it was uncertain what this poll would amount to and since the House did compute it would raise £1,341,700, that whatever it should be found to fall short of that sum upon the return of the duplicates for the two first quarters the King might be enabled from that time until the 1st of January next to take up and borrow thereon as much money as should, with what raised thereby, make up the whole sum of £1,341,700 at seven per cent to be paid out of the money the parliament should give at their next meeting or be secured by the revenue.

The clause was read twice and the blanks were filled up.

Several spoke against the clause as *Col. Cornewall, Mr. Bertie, Mr. Bathurst*, etc. for that this laid an obligation on this parliament at another sessions or else on a new parliament to pay the debts of a former whereas the succeeding parliament is not bound by any of the resolves or promises of a preceding.

But the clause was put and passed.

Sir Robert Rich offered a clause that the Navy might not be obliged to pay in course but have impress money to supply extraordinary occasions.

But this was opposed because it was the direct way to ruin the credit of the Navy by destroying the payments in course. Then it is irregular to repeal in one act what you but lately passed in another act in the same sessions; besides it is unparliamentary. And if this should pass persons would not know which to observe for they are acts of the same sessions—all in law intended of one day.

The clause, however, was read twice. And upon the question to be made part of the bill, it was rejected.

Mr. Pigott tendered a clause that all persons who keep setting dogs, a fowling-piece, etc., and have not paid as gentlemen shall pay 20*s.* a quarter.

---

[1] On the day before, Luttrell describes this as an appropriating clause to the Army; the *Journal* does not help since it describes it only as an appropriating clause.

It was read once, and on the question for a second reading the House divided—Yeas went out.

	Sir Samuel Barnardiston[1]	
	Yeas	91
	Sir Robert Clayton	
Tellers for the		
	Mr. Hopkins	
	Noes	81
	Mr. Freke[2]	

But the House being informed that this clause was offered yesterday in the House and refused—it being against the rules of parliament to receive it after [in] the same sessions when once rejected—it was laid aside as irregular.

Adjourned till 8 tomorrow morning.

Wednesday, 17 February

Mr. Biddulph was ordered to carry up to the Lords the Earl of Suffolk's bill and to acquaint them that this House had agreed to the same and that without any amendments, and also to put them in mind of the bill for reducing of interest.

Mr. Arnold presented a petition from one Mr. Dodsworth desiring some consideration of his circumstances for discovering the design that was carrying on by the Papists in Lancashire. Received and ordered to lie on the Table.

Upon the report from the Irish committee by *Sir Robert Henley* for receiving proposals for raising money on the Irish estates that are forfeited, *Mr. Culliford* (a member of the House) took notice that his name was mentioned therein. He said he was wholly innocent of the matter therein laid to his charge. He desired he might have a copy thereof and he doubted not to give a satisfactory answer to every particular.

So he was ordered a copy and to give in his answer on Monday next.

Mr. Hampden acquainted the House from His Majesty that His Majesty had received a petition from the poor French Protestants which His Majesty recommended to this House to take into their

---

[1] *CJ*, x. 672 has Sir Thomas Barnardiston.
[2] *CJ*, x. 672 has Col. Granville.

consideration to enable him to do something for them. So he delivered in at the Table their petition and case with His Majesty's declaration of 25 April 1689, which were received and read.

Mr. Arnold, Sir John Darell, Mr. Colt, and *Mr. Boscawen* moved that this being a matter of money the House might go into a Committee of the Whole House to consider of this message from the King.

And it was resolved to go into such a committee accordingly to-morrow.

The engrossed bill for ascertaining the commissions and salaries of the judges was read the third time.

Mr. Travers presented a rider to it to this effect: that no fees should be taken by the judges or other officers at sessions, assizes, etc. but the ancient legal fees, and tables should be made of the same and set up in each respective office.

This clause was read twice and an amendment made therein and the blank filled up. And then the clause was read the third time and made part of the bill. Then the bill was put and passed and the title also. And Sir Walter Yonge was ordered to carry it up to the Lords for their concurrence.

Adjourned till 8 tomorrow morning.

Thursday, 18 February

Sir Robert Cotton (of Chester) was ordered to carry up to the Lords Mr. Pelham's engrossed bill with amendments and to acquaint them this House had agreed to the same with amendments to which they desire the concurrence of their Lordships.

A motion being made for reading the engrossed bill from the Lords for relief of the orphans and the question being put, the House divided—Yeas went out.

		Sir Joseph Tredenham	
	Yeas		41
		Sir John Banks	
Tellers for the			
		Sir Matthew Andrews	
	Noes		70
		Mr. Bowyer	

So carried in the negative.

The poll bill being engrossed was read the third time and some literal amendments made in the Chair.

Mr. Machell offered an engrossed clause requiring all tradesmen to take the oaths, but it was rejected.

So the bill was put and passed, with the title, and Mr. Solicitor ordered to carry it to the Lords for their concurrence.

Mr. Bertie moved that this bill might lie on the Table till Monday next and that a message should be sent to the Lords to put them in mind of the bills about the forfeited estates in England and Ireland so that they might be first passed. *Lord Castleton* to the same.

Sir John Lowther opposed this for that it might anger the Lords and perhaps obstruct the passing those bills. Let it be considered how great necessity there is for passing this bill by the great advance of the season of the year, the forwardness your enemies are in, and the necessity there is of the King's being at the head of your armies. I desire, therefore, Mr. Solicitor may carry up the bill and put their Lordships in mind of those bills. *Sir Robert Cotton* (of the Post Office) to the same effect.

Sir Thomas Clarges: It is very regular and usual for this House to lay their hands upon money bills and not hastily to send them up till some good bills the House hath before them be first ready; thus was done to get the bill passed for disabling papists to sit in either House of Parliament. And the reason is this House hath nothing to get a good bill passed but their money, which when they have once parted with they have no great power. Therefore I desire it may stay till Monday, and there is no great prejudice for the sum cannot be altered nor the time. *Sir Charles Sedley* to the same.

Sir Edward Seymour: It is very regular for either House to put the other House in mind of any good bill if they hear nothing about it. But I think the bills you now offer at are not of that great benefit. You have clogged them with so many clauses and provisos and by that time the Lords have added what they think fit I believe your bills of forfeitures will signify very little. For my part I think union at this time is of absolute necessity against the common enemy and therefore I would not show any distrust or jealousy at the end of a sessions, but as you have given the money so let the King have it in season since his necessities press for it. Therefore I desire you will send it up.

Sir Joseph Williamson and *Mr. Hampden* were for sending it up.

Mr. Bathurst against carrying it up. So *Mr. Smith*, and that very strongly and reflected severely on the Court in making opposition to these bills of forfeitures. And that though thereby he had no prospect of their passing this sessions, yet he hoped if ever this parliament met again they would lay their hands on the forfeited lands and apply them to carrying on the war—though grants may be made thereof to particular persons—and that before they give any money the next sessions.

Sir John Guise was for carrying up the bill.

Sir John Knight was for letting it lie on the Table till Monday.

So the question was put for this bill lying upon the Table till Monday and carried in the negative. So the Solicitor went up with it immediately and was ordered also to put the Lords in mind of the two bills for vesting the forfeited estates in England and Ireland in Their Majesties.

Adjourned till 8 tomorrow morning.

Friday, 19 February

Mr. Clarke was ordered to carry up to the Lords the Lord Villiers' engrossed bill and to acquaint them this House had agreed to the same with an amendment and desired their concurrence thereto.

Col. Titus presented Mrs. Hammond's petition against the bills for confirming the charter of the University of Cambridge, which was received and read.

Several members spoke against that bill as *Mr. Clarke, Sir John Darell, Mr. Arnold, Sir Edward Seymour*. But *Sir Robert Sawyer, Sir Thomas Clarges, Mr. Bickerstaffe, Mr. Christie*, and *Mr. Finch* spoke for it.

But upon the question, she was ordered to be heard by her counsel at the Bar of the House on Monday next against the said bill, and the King's Counsel also to be heard against it at the same time.

The engrossed bill from the Lords to prevent corresponding with Their Majesties' enemies was read the second time.

Sir Thomas Clarges: I desire this bill may be committed to a Committee of the Whole House. I think it is a very odd bill to establish new treasons at this time. There are many treasons committed at sea, but this bill appoints no manner of trial thereof and I think they cannot now be well tried by 35 H. VIII c. 15. Then there is a clause for imprisonment during pleasure; there is the habeas corpus act taken off at one step. Then I think it is necessary to ascertain the manner of trials for treason in all cases and that by remedying the mischiefs in former reigns—that the accused may have a copy of his indictment and of the panel of his jury, that the witnesses for him may be sworn, and that the overt act may be specified in the indictment. *Mr. Bathurst* to the same.

Sir Thomas Vernon took notice that the commencement of this act was very quick—too soon for merchants in foreign parts who cannot have timely notice of it. And our merchants from Aleppo, Turkey, etc., are forced to bring their goods in French vessels to Leghorn or else they can't trade.

Sir John Lowther spoke very largely for this bill for the necessity hereof since treason is now committed openly. Then the usefulness of it is great and very fitting in this juncture since France is too well acquainted with our concerns and it is high time to prevent it.

It was moved to commit this on the debate of the House. But opposed by *Hampden*, etc., for that this is but a temporary law and yet you are going to add to it things to make it perpetual. Then this is to tack a clause to it that hath been rejected already this sessions in the other treason bill.

Sir Thomas Clarges, Paul Foley, Sir John Darell, Col. Granville moved to have it committed on the debate of the House.

Col. Granville moved to have a clause added to make it treason to correspond with King James, as well as with France. But answered, that is provided for in corresponding with His Majesty's enemies.

So the question was put for committing this bill to a Committee of the Whole House and resolved accordingly. But the question of committing it on the debate of the House being not insisted on, it was not put.

Then a motion was made to take [up] the report from the committee about the saltpetre. But it being moved also to adjourn and which was first seconded, this question was first put (as it ought, being after 1 of the clock). The House divided—Noes went out.

		Sir Samuel Barnardiston	
	Yeas		80
		Sir Gervase Elwes	
Tellers for the			
		Sir Thomas Littleton	
	Noes		70
		Mr. Arnold	

Carried in the affirmative.

So the House immediately adjourned till 8 tomorrow morning.

Saturday, 20 February

Major Vincent was ordered to carry up to the Lords the engrossed bill of Philip Hildeyard esq. and to acquaint them this House hath agreed to it without any amendments.

The engrossed bill about St. Paul's Shadwell waterworks was read the third time.

It was opposed by *Sir John Darell, Mr. Arnold*, and *Sir Robert Henley* for that it seemed to give a countenance to the Council Board to hear matters of property between party and party.

However, it was passed and Sir Matthew Andrews ordered to carry it to the Lords and acquaint them this House had agreed to the same with some amendments to which they desire the concurrence of their Lordships.

Engrossed bill from the Lords of George Vernon read the last time and passed and Sir Richard Onslow ordered to carry it up to the Lords and acquaint them this House had agreed to the same without any amendments.

Sir Samuel Barnardiston was ordered to carry up to the Lords the engrossed bill of Sir William Halford and acquaint them this House had agreed to the same with some amendments to which they desire their concurrence.

But as Sir Samuel was going up with it, *Sir Edward Seymour, Mr. Hampden*, and *Mr. Montagu* took notice of it and that there was in the bill several blanks, which ought not nor any interlineations or blots because the records ought to be fair and clear nor ought bills to come from the other House so. And in this case the House sent their Clerk to recall the messenger, Sir Samuel, which being done he returned. And the House debated the same and ordered a conference to be desired with the Lords about the bill and to communicate to them the amendments made by this House and to acquaint them of the mischiefs may happen by sending down bills either with blanks, blots, or interlineations of several hands. But in this case, the *Speaker*—to prevent delay—said for the future he would take care to remedy the same; this bill was admitted and ordered to be sent up without a conference.

The *Speaker* communicated to the House a letter of 19th of the instant February from Mr. Fuller, desiring to be brought to the Bar of the House, saying his witnesses were now ready and that he was prepared to make out what he had said. And he was accordingly ordered to be brought up by the Marshal of the King's Bench on

Monday next and the persons mentioned by him were then ordered
to attend and to have the protection of the House.

Mr. Clarke was ordered to go to the Lords to desire a conference with
their Lordships touching the amendments made to the bill of tithes.

A motion was made for reading the engrossed bill [from the Lords]
for relief of the orphans. Several spoke [to] it (especially all the Whigs),
and the question being put for reading it now a second time, the
House divided—Yeas went out.

	Sir Richard Hart	
Yeas		68
	Mr. Cary	
Tellers for the		
	Sir Walter Yonge	
Noes		116
	Mr. Clarke	

So passed in the negative.

The House, according to order, resolved into a Committee of the
Whole House to consider of the engrossed bill from the Lords against
corresponding with Their Majesties' enemies and the Speaker left the
Chair. And some cried Mr. Boscawen to the Chair, others Mr. Montagu, others Serj. Trenchard. On which the *Speaker* retook the Chair,
and put the question for Serj. Trenchard to the Chair, which was
carried. So the Speaker left the Chair and Serj. Trenchard was Chairman. Then the order of the House was read; then the bill at large by
the Clerk; then the Chairman read the preamble, which they postponed; then he read the first clause, so the others till they had gone
through the bill and made several amendments to it.

Mr. Bertie tendered a clause to limit the time for prosecution of
the offender to be within six months after the fact.

But it was opposed by Sir John Guise, Sir John Somers, and Mr.
Montagu, and upon the question it was rejected.

Col. Cornewall tendered a clause that no one should be prosecuted
on this act without two witnesses, but the law being so already it was
laid aside.

Then the preamble was read and passed and he was ordered to
report it.

So the Speaker resumed the Chair and *Serj. Trenchard* reported
the bill with the amendments, unto which the House agreed. And
upon a motion from the Court party, but 74 members being then
in the House, the bill was read the third time and passed and Serj.

Trenchard was ordered to carry it up to the Lords and desire their concurrence to the said amendments.

Adjourned till 8 on Monday morning.

Monday, 22 February

Mr. Harcourt was ordered to carry up to the Lords Mr. Newton's bill and to acquaint them that this House had agreed to the same without any amendments.

Mr. Travers was ordered to carry up to the Lords Sir Edwin Sadler's bill and to acquaint them that this House had agreed to the same without any amendments.

Engrossed bill from the Lords for taking the solemn answers of Quakers was read the second time.

Mr. Hutchinson, Mr. Clarke, Sir John Morton, Mr. Boscawen, Sir Robert Henley, Sir John Bolles, Mr. Machell, and *Mr. Arnold* spoke for the bill and said they were a useful people and would secure so many persons to the government. That this was tantamount, an oath only laying the hand on the book. Here was the solemn calling God to bear witness and besides hath the same punishment annexed for the breach thereof as in the case of perjury. And therefore they desired it might be committed.

But this was opposed by *Col. Granville, Mr. Shakerley, Sir John Lowther, Sir Charles Sedley,* etc. for that they are a people not well affected to this government; that they are generally a sort of poor people and no interest and will not fight (if occasion) in defence of the nation; that they were friends to King James and were for taking off the penal laws and test under him; and above all, this would be a shelter for papists and enemies to the government. And therefore they were against committing it.

So the question was put that the bill be committed. The House divided—Yeas went out.

		Sir Samuel Barnardiston	
	Yeas		73
		Mr. Machell	
Tellers for the			
		Sir Thomas Vernon	
	Noes		103
		Mr. Shakerley	

So carried in the negative.

Then the question was put for rejecting the bill and it was carried in the affirmative.

The Marshal of the King's Bench was then called in. And he gave an account that according to the House's order, he was with Mr. Fuller to bring him up to the House this morning but that he found him in his bed and, as he said, very ill—that he had a great vomiting and looseness and could not come. He was first taken ill on Friday last. I would have sent for a physician but he said he would send himself, but I saw none that came. So the Marshal withdrew.

Mr. Arnold informed the House that he went over yesterday to Mr. Fuller and saw him. That he was in a bad condition and he said he believed he was poisoned and should not live.

Mr. Hutchinson, Sir Robert Cotton (of Cheshire), and *Mr. Arnold* moved that some members might be immediately sent to see in what condition he was and to take his examination and information on oath. So those three gentlemen, with Sir Francis Blake, Mr. Bowyer, and Mr. Chase, were ordered immediately to repair to him to take his information on oath and to secure his papers. So they withdrew to go. And the Serjeant attending this House was ordered to send his man to Dr. Fielding to desire him to repair forthwith to Mr. Fuller and see in what condition he was. And the gentlemen that went were ordered to examine Mr. Fuller about the witnesses he pretended he had and where they live and are to be found. But Mr. Arnold went not with the other five gentlemen but went about the two witnesses Mr. Fuller had informed him of where they would be. And Sir Matthew Andrews went in Mr. Arnold's room with the others.

The bill for enabling Their Majesties to make leases of the duchy lands of Cornwall was read the last time and Mr. Boscawen was ordered to carry it to the Lords for their concurrence.

The bill for borrowing money on the credit of the excise act for building ships was read the second time. Then moved to fill up the blanks at the Table, but opposed as irregular. Then moved to go into a Committee of the Whole House upon it immediately, but opposed also as irregular especially being in the matter of money. So ordered to go into a Committee of the Whole House tomorrow and a clause was ordered to give credit upon the act for building of the three ships.

Then, according to order, the House went upon the bill for confirming the charters of the University of Cambridge. And Mr. Darnel and Mr. Cowper of counsel for Mrs. Hammond and Mr. Ward of counsel for the University for the bill were called in and spoke for and against the bill. So they withdrew.

Then *Mr. Paul Foley* and *Sir John Darell* took some exceptions to the bill.

Mr. Montagu offered a clause that the fellows of colleges (if they think fit) should not be obliged to go into orders above such a number. [It] was read twice, the blanks filled up, and question being put for reading it the third time and carried in the negative.

Sir Robert Sawyer offered a clause for saving of the King's first-fruits and tenths. [It] was read twice and an amendment made, and read the third time and ordered to be made part of the bill.

Sir Robert Henley offered a clause in behalf of Sir John Bolles about Sidney College to save his right, and [it] was read thrice and made part of the bill.

Paul Foley spoke very much against the bill for that it confirms all the statutes of the University and the several colleges but none of them are recited nor does it appear what they are. Then this repeals all the laws made since these statutes, if contrary to them.

Sir John Darell spoke against the bill also, and *Mr. Hampden*, *Mr. Brewer*, *Sir Edward Seymour*, and *Sir George Treby*. But *Sir Robert Sawyer*, *Mr. Finch*, *Sir Richard Temple*, *Sir Robert Cotton* (of the Post Office) spoke for it.

So after a long debate, the bill was read the third time and the question was put for passing of the bill. The House divided—Yeas went out.

	Mr. Montagu	
Yeas		69
	Mr. Bickerstaffe	
Tellers for the		
	Sir Walter Yonge	
Noes		119
	Mr. Bennett	

So it passed in the negative.

Engrossed bill for weighing and packing of butter read the last time and passed, with the title, and Col. Goldwell ordered to carry it to the Lords for their concurrence. Col. Goldwell was ordered also to carry up to the Lords the Duke of Grafton's engrossed bill and to acquaint them this House had agreed to the same without any amendments.

Then a motion was made for adjournment. The House divided—
Noes went out.

Sir Jonathan Jennings
Yeas   51
Mr. Montagu
Tellers for the
Mr. Clarke
Noes   56
Col. Goldwell

Moved to read the hawkers and pedlars bill, but on the question
it was carried in the negative.

House adjourned till 8 tomorrow morning.

Tuesday, 23 February

Col. Goldwell was ordered to carry up Mr. Keble's bill to the Lords
and to acquaint them this House had agreed to the same with an
amendment to which they desire the concurrence of their Lordships.

Mr. Bowyer, according to order, reported from the committee that
had attended Mr. Fuller. That they had done it accordingly. That
they found him very ill of a vomiting and looseness which he had
ever since Friday last. That he did [? discharge] blood both ways, and
that the Dr. and Mr. Chase[1] did both agree he was in a dangerous
condition. That they had examined him on his oath and that his
information was here sealed up, as also his papers which he had sent
to a friend's for fear he should miscarry. That he had named his witnesses to them, and [said] that all he had given in on oath was really
true, as he was a dying man, which he believed he was.

And then *Mr. Bowyer* delivered in the papers and informations
which were sealed up by the several members of the committee, and
laid them on the Table.

Mr. Hutchinson and *Sir Robert Cotton* opposed the reading of them,
believing it to be more for your service, and for the witnesses they
are willing to come, but he would willingly come with them between
this and Thursday. Otherwise, they shall come without him on
Thursday without fail.

Sir John Morton moved to have them read.

So the packet was opened and they were read.

---

[1] Chase, one of the committee, was an apothecary.

His examination taken on oath, 22 February 1691/2. That since Friday he had above 100 vomits and stools, and believes if his sickness was occasioned by any it was by one Weaver's wife, who was suspected to be a papist, whence he hath his diet. That one Mrs. Clifford, Sir John Fenwick, Sir Theophilus Oglethorpe, and the Countess of Dorchester came one day to the end of the alley where he lay, whom he believed to be concerned in it. That for his two witnesses, they were one Mr. James Hayes and Col. Thomas Delaval, the latter of whom was a Privy Councillor to King James in Ireland, and lodged at one Mr. Richardson's (an apothecary) on the left hand going into Bloomsbury Square out of Holborn—the corner house. And they had sent him word they would be ready to attend the House of Commons with him.

So Mr. Hutchinson, Sir Matthew Andrews, and Mr. Arnold were ordered (being attended with some messengers) to go immediately to that place and bring them with them.

First paper of Fuller's. Gave an account of the names of those persons who signed the address to the French King for restoring King James. [They] were the late Archbishop of Canterbury; Dukes of Beaufort, Northumberland, and Newcastle; Marquess of Halifax; Earls of Clarendon, Salisbury, Huntingdon, Aylesbury, Winchilsea, Feversham, Scarsdale, Lichfield, and Mulgrave; the Lords Widdrington, Arran, Dunmore, Castlemaine, Clifford, Griffin, Montgomery, and Dartmouth; Sir John Gage, Sir Theophilus Oglethorpe, Sir John Fenwick, Sir Adam Blair, Sir Edward Hales, Will Penn, Bernard Howard, David Lloyd, James Smith, and Rowland Tempest.

Second paper of his had nothing material.

Third paper, *jurat*. That he had letters by Mr. Hayes: one from the Lord Aylesbury pressing the landing of the French and that here were 30,000 ready to join them; another from the Lord Feversham to Queen Mary to the like effect; another from the Lord Lichfield, another from the Lord Huntingdon, another from the Lord Preston, all expressing their great zeal for and fidelity to King James and assuring how ready they would be to join the French when they land here. There were others from the Lords Peterborough, Salisbury, and Castlemaine, Lord[s] Arran and Dunmore. That the Lord Montgomery had already advanced £17,000 for their service, and Father Emmanuel had £4,000 for it and was much trusted in the matter and was the maker of King James's declaration. That this man had friends in the Council and in the Secretary's office and knew what was done there. I brought also out of France letters from the late Queen to the Lord[s] Feversham and Montgomery. That the Lord Godolphin was their friend, to whom he was to apply if he should be taken. That he brought commissions for Sir John Fenwick, Sir Theophilus Oglethorpe, and Sir Adam Blair. That 20,000 men were listed in England for King James.

Fourth paper, *jurat*. Queen Mary assured him of the fidelity of Crawford to her but desired to have it under his hand. A Romish father, Ennis, showed him a letter which he said came from Col. Crawford, assuring them of his fidelity and that the governor of Upnor Castle was true to them also. And they delivered me a letter for him in a key, which I carried to King William first and after to Mr. Crawford, but he would not receive it but had me clapped up. But the next day he told me he had notice of my coming.

Then several letters and papers of Mr. Fuller were read: a letter from Father Sabran to him that if he could get over he would take care and provide for him; an abstract of the rebellion intended— 23,000 men were ready, 200 horse were to seize the King at Kensington, W. Penn and his party were to contribute £20,000, E. N.[1] their friend.

Then an account was read of what he had expended in this affair, about £1,236, of which he had received £100, £110, £100, £150, £50, £50: total received, £560; remains due to him, £776.

Sir Matthew Andrews reported that he, with the other gentlemen, had been at the place where Mr. Fuller's two witnesses were said to lodge. But they could hear of no such persons there nor did they ever lodge there.

Mr. Arnold acquainted the House that he had been abused in this matter and did therefore recommend it to the House to do what they thought fit, assuring them that what he did was for the service of the kingdom. But by a paper he met with at Fuller's, he believed we were all abused, finding one which reflected highly on this House.

Mr. Montagu and *Sir Robert Cotton* (of Chester) moved that Fuller might be ordered peremptorily to produce his two witnesses by such a day or else that he might be proceeded against as a cheat. So he was ordered peremptorily to produce them against tomorrow morning 10 of the clock.

The House took into consideration the amendments made by the Lords to the bill for punishing mutineers and deserters—some of

[1] Earl of Nottingham?

which were agreed to and others not, as there being one wherein an officer is to forfeit £50 for misbehaviour. This House in the bill applied it to the poor of such parish where the offence was committed; the Lords apply the forfeiture to Chelsea College.

Sir Christopher Musgrave and *Sir Edward Seymour* opposed this, for if it should pass you will make a precedent for the Lords in time to dispose of your money. It is true they have one precedent of 2*s.* 6*d.* in the case of a churchwarden, which they much value themselves upon. And if you give them this, they will in time get purse and strings, too.

So the House disagreed with the Lords in this amendment, as they did also in two more for the same reason. So also in clause 'A' empowering officers to press carts—the House disagreed therein, too. So a committee was appointed to prepare reasons to be offered at a conference with the Lords on disagreeing to their amendments.

Adjourned till 8 tomorrow morning.

Wednesday, 24 February

Sir Edward Seymour: Since our days are numbered and we have not much time left for any matters, I desire before we part we may do an act of justice. And as we were willing to receive any information that was pretended for the good of King and kingdom, so I desire when we find knaves out we may put a mark upon them and therefore I shall move you in reference to this Fuller. The time you appointed for his bringing his witnesses is passed and therefore I think you can do no less than declare him an impostor and to recommend it [to] the King's Counsel to prosecute him as such.

Sir John Lowther and *Sir John Morton* to the same; it was an act of justice due to so many noble persons whom he has slandered. *Sir Robert Cotton* (of Cheshire), *Sir Charles Sedley*, *Mr. Howe*, *Sir Robert Sawyer*, *Sir John Guise*, and *Mr. Colt* to the same.

So resolved, *nemine contradicente*, that this House doth declare that William Fuller is a notorious impostor, a cheat, and a false accuser, having scandalized Their Majesties and the government and abused this House and falsely accused several persons of honour and quality, and that His Majesty be humbly desired by such members of this House as are of the Privy Council to command his Attorney General to prosecute him accordingly.

The House being informed that the Marshal of the King's Bench was without at the door attending, he was called in and asked several questions by the *Speaker*. And his answer in substance was that Fuller was a prisoner in execution for £100 debt and he was ordered to keep him safely. And he said Fuller told him his witnesses could not be ready today, but Delaval—he said—was with him yesterday, though I cannot find by my servants that anyone came to him at all yesterday. He still continues ill of a fever and the doctor says his distemper is very odd. He says Mr. Hayes will not attend the House, being not willing to be a common evidence.[1]

Then the House, according to order, went into a Committee of the Whole House about the French Protestants. The Speaker left the Chair and Sir Robert Clayton was made Chairman.

Mr. Howe was against doing anything at this time. We had a more crying debt of our own people to take care of and that is the transport ships—a just and honest debt. But if you will address to the King for a brief for the French Protestants, with all my heart.

Sir Charles Sedley moved to lay 12*d.* in the pound on all places at Court, which will be some relief to them for the present and what the gentlemen that have those places, I hope, will not think much of.

Lord Ranelagh moved that an address might be made to the King that he would be graciously pleased to supply them as well as he was able and that this House would supply him for it at the next meeting.

Sir Edward Seymour: I am for the first part of this motion but am not for pawning the House nor laying a nest egg the last day of a sessions. Therefore I cannot come up to the latter part of it—to break into our constitutions.

Sir Christopher Musgrave: For my part I am against both parts of it, for it is in a manner engaging this House the last day of a sessions to give money at their next meeting. Therefore I desire you may leave the Chair for the present.

So the Speaker resumed the Chair. And the Black Rod came with a message from His Majesty to command the House to attend him immediately in the House of Peers. And accordingly the Speaker, with the House, went up to attend His Majesty. And being returned, *he* reported His Majesty had been pleased to give the royal assent to several public and private bills, viz.:

1. The act for raising money by a quarterly poll.
2. The act to raise the militia for one year, viz. 1692.
3. The act for better ordering and collecting low wines, etc.

---

[1] There is no entry of the Marshal's attendance in the *Journal*.

4. The act against corresponding with Their Majesties' enemies.
5. The act for more effectual punishment of deer stealers.
6. The act for repair of the highways.
7. The act to encourage the breeding and feeding of cattle.
8. The act for relief of creditors against fraudulent devices.
9. The act about settlement of the poor.
10. The act to take away clergy from some offenders.

(And to the act about the judges, the King denied by saying '*Le Roy et La Reine s'aviseront*'.)

And to these private bills:

1. An act for sale of Nicholas Martin's estate.
2. An act to vest Drax's estate in Thomas Shatterden.
3. An act for Sir Dudley Cullum to raise moneys.
4. An act for the sale of Maurice Shelton's estate.
5. An act to enable trustees to sell Edward Smith esq. his estate.
6. An act to enable Sir Thomas Burton to sell land to pay debts.
7. The like for William Davile.
8. An act to enable the Earl of Winchilsea to make a jointure.
9. An act to enable the trustees of Richard Campion to perform his will.
10. An act to enable the Lord Waldegrave's trustees to make leases.
11. An act to enable Francis Moore to sell lands and purchase others.
12. An act to enfranchise copyhold lands in Hertfordshire.
13. An act to secure the portions, debts, and legacies of the Earl of Salisbury.
14. An act for the sale of John Crips' estate.
15. An act to vest lands of William Molineux in trustees to raise money.
16. An act to naturalize Mainhardt, Duke of Leinster, and others.
17. An act to enable the Lord Stanhope to make a jointure.
18. An act to enable Henry Halstead to lease his prebend.
19. An act to enable Bishop of London to sell lands and to purchase others.
20. An act to sell lands of William Vaughan, etc., to pay debts.
21. An act to enable Vincent Grantham to lease lands to pay debts.
22. An act to naturalize Marquess of Monpouillon and others.
23. An act to enable trustees of late Earl of Suffolk to sell lands.
24. An act for speedy payment of the debts of Elizabeth Curtis, deceased.

25. An act of Lord Villiers' to vest lands etc. in trustees to be sold and buying of others.
26. An act to secure £5,000 out of Charles Pelham's estate for his daughter.
27. An act to settle lands in trustees for payment of Philip Hildeyard's debts.
28. An act for better assuring four acres in Ebisham to George Vernon.
29. An act to incorporate the proprietors of Shadwell works.
30. An act for sale of Sir William Halford's estate for payment of debts.
31. An act to vest the lands of Barbara Newton and John Newton.
32. An act for the sale of lands of Sir Edwin Sadler to pay debts.
33. An act to vest lands of Duke of Grafton in trustees to be sold.
34. An act to enable John Keble to sell lands and to settle others.

After which His Majesty made a speech to the effect following: He thanked them for the demonstration they had given him of their affections and of their zeal for the government, and particularly the House of Commons for the great supplies they had given him in prosecution of the war, assuring them he would take care the money should be disposed of to the satisfaction of the whole nation; that he intended speedily to go beyond sea and therefore thought it necessary to put an end to this meeting, the season of the year being very far advanced. And then the Lord Chief Baron of the Exchequer declared to both Houses it was His Majesty's pleasure that both Houses should adjourn themselves to the 12th day of April next.

So the Commons returned to their House, and both Houses accordingly adjourned themselves to the 12th of April next. So the House adjourned till the 12th of April next accordingly.

Friday, 12 April

So the House met according to former adjournment—such members as were in town—and after some time the Speaker took the Chair.

And a motion was made for a new writ for Scarborough in the room of Mr. Thompson, deceased, as also another for the City of Carlisle in the room of Capt. Bubb, deceased. And the Speaker was ordered to issue his warrant to the Clerk of the Crown to make writs out accordingly, which was done forthwith.

After some time the Black Rod came with this message: Mr. Speaker, the Lords Commissioners appointed by Their Majesties' commission desire the attendance of this honourable House immediately in the House of Peers to hear the said commission read.

So the Speaker went up, attended with the House, where the commission was read in Latin. And then the Earl of Pembroke, Lord Privy Seal, spoke: By virtue of Their Majesties' commission to us directed, we do prorogue this parliament to the 24th of May next, and this parliament is prorogued to the 24th of May next accordingly.

From 12 April 1692 to 24 May 1692.

Tuesday, 24 May

This day the parliament met pursuant to their last prorogation, and such members as were in town met in the House and the Speaker took the Chair. And the Black Rod came for the House to attend in the House of Peers. Where being come, the King's commission was read for further proroguing the parliament to the 14th of June next ensuing, to which time they were prorogued by the Lords commissioned for that purpose.

From 24 May 1692 to 14 June 1692.

Tuesday, 14 June

This day the parliament met again pursuant to the last prorogation and were by commission, as formerly, prorogued to the 11th of July next.

From 14 June 1692 to 11 July 1692.

Monday, 11 July

This day the parliament met pursuant to former prorogation. But the Speakers of neither House were present; that of the House of Lords was in the northern circuit, the other was not well, so that for the Speaker of the Commons they had none. And after they were by commission, as before, prorogued to the 22nd of August next.

From 11 July to 22 August 1692.

Monday, 22 August

This day the parliament met again pursuant to their last prorogation and were by commission prorogued further to the 26th of September next.

From 22 August to 26 September 1692.

Monday, 26 September

This day both Houses of Parliament met in their own houses pursuant to the last prorogation. The Commons met in the new house made for them since the sessions last winter. But their Speaker was not in the House. So about 12 the Usher of the Black Rod came as usual, making his bows to the Chair. And instead of addressing himself to the Speaker, [he] did it to the gentlemen of the House: Gentlemen, the Lords authorized by Their Majesties' commission desire the immediate attendance of this honourable House in the House of Peers to hear the said commission read. So the members went up, where the Clerk read the commission. And after the Duke of Norfolk (as chief in commission) by virtue thereof prorogued the parliament to Friday, the 4th day of November next.

From 26 September 1692 to 4 November 1692.

An Abstract

Of ye Debates Orders & Resolutions
In ye House of Commons, wch are
not printed in yeir Votes.

Collected by N.S. during his attendance
therein as a Member.

Beginning. fryDay. 4th of Novemb. 1692
& ending S. 7th of Novemb. 1693.

Facsimile of title-page of volume two of All Souls College MS. 158

Session the fourth

Friday, 4 November 1692

The members of the House of Commons met this day in their new house and about 10 they went to prayers—the Common Prayer. Some time after, the Black Rod came (just before which the Speaker took the Chair) to command the House to attend His Majesty in the House of Peers immediately.

So the Speaker with the House went up, where His Majesty made a speech to both Houses. And being returned, the *Speaker* reports the same and that to prevent mistakes he had obtained a copy of the said speech, which he read in the Chair (to which I refer). After which the *Speaker* informed the House that it was usual to open a sessions with a short bill. So the bill to prevent butchers from selling live cattle was read the first time and ordered a second reading.

Then the House appointed their several Grand Committees: that for religion, to sit every Tuesday in the afternoon in the House; that for grievances, to sit every Thursday; that for trade, to sit every Saturday; that for courts of justice, to sit every Friday in the afternoon in the House. Then the Committee of Elections was appointed and a committee named to meet every Monday, Wednesday, and Friday in the Speaker's Chamber at 3 in the afternoon and all that come are to have voices; and they are to take into consideration all matters touching elections and privileges and to proceed on double returns first; and they are to report their proceedings to the House; and all persons that will question returns are to do it in 14 days; and the committee have power to send for persons, papers, and records; and all members chosen for two or more places are to make their election in three weeks for which place they will serve, if there be no question on the return for that place.

Three new members chosen upon vacancies since last sessions came into the House and took the oaths at the Table and after their places in the House: viz., William Lowther esq. for Carlisle (in the room of Capt. Bubb, deceased); [Robert][1] Balch esq. for Bridgwater (in the

[1] Blank in MS.

room of Mr. Bull, deceased); and John Hungerford esq. for Scarborough in Yorkshire (in the room of Mr. Thompson, deceased). Then several motions were made to supply the vacancies of members in the House, and ordered that the Speaker issue his warrant to the Clerk of the Crown to make out a new writ for the electing a new member for the borough of Plympton in Devon, in the room of Sir George Treby (Chief Justice of the Common Pleas), on the motion of *Mr. Hampden*; for Saltash in Cornwall, in the room of Sir John Carew (deceased), on the motion of *Col. Granville*; for Tewkesbury in Gloucestershire, in the room of Sir Henry Capel (called up to the House of Peers), on the motion of *Sir John Guise*; for the county of Radnor, in the room of Richard Williams (deceased), on the motion of *Sir Rowland Gwynne*; for Launceston, in the room of William Harbord (deceased), on the motion of *Bernard Granville esq.*; for Cambridge University, in the room of Sir Robert Sawyer (deceased), on the motion of *Sir Robert Cotton*; for Grampound in Cornwall, in the room of Walter Vincent esq. (deceased), on the motion of *Major Vincent*; for Morpeth in Northumberland, in the room of the Lord Morpeth (now Earl of Carlisle), on the motion of *Sir Robert Eden*; for Colchester in Essex, in the room of Edward Cary esq. (deceased), on the motion of *Sir Francis Masham*.

Mr. Gwyn presented a petition to the House from Mr. John Gardner, merchant, complaining of an undue election for the borough of Bridgwater in Somersetshire, and it was referred to the Committee of Elections and Privileges.

Mr. Neale moved that since the House had been pleased in former sessions to order their votes to be printed they would do so now; and was seconded by *Col. Mildmay* therein. And the question was put and ordered that they be printed, being first perused by Mr. Speaker.

Sir Edward Seymour moved that since the House was so thin they would be pleased to appoint a day for calling over the House and that all that were not present might be sent for in custody of the Serjeant at Arms. Ordered that the House should be called over on Monday sevennight and that such as do not then attend the House should be sent for.

Sir Thomas Clarges: I am sorry to see so thin a House when we are like to have affairs of such weight come before it. If you please to adjourn for some little time I believe you will have many more, and therefore I move to adjourn till Thursday next. *Mr. Brockman* seconded the same.

Sir John Guise: I desire you will not adjourn for so long a time. I think Monday is long enough when you have so much to do, and therefore I desire you to put the question for adjournment till Monday.

But the first being the regular question, it was put and carried clearly to adjourn till Thursday next.

So the House adjourned till Thursday next.

Thursday, 10 November

The House met about 10 and went to prayers. And after some time, the Speaker took the Chair and for half an hour there was a great silence. But at last Mr. *Neale* moved that upon Friday last this House had a most gracious speech from His Majesty, which he desired might be now read and that the House would take it into consideration.

So the *Speaker* stood up in the Chair and read the speech.

Sir Robert Cotton (of Post Office): There is so great sincerity and hearty expressions in His Majesty's gracious speech that this House can do no less than thank His Majesty for the same.

Mr. Neale: I stand not up to second that motion only but to thank him effectually by passing a vote you will supply him according to his occasions.

Sir John Darell: I think the speech is a very good speech, but what was moved last is a little too fast. I think you have a Committee for inspecting the Public Accounts from whom it is fit for you to have a state of matters, and then you will be better able to judge what is necessary.

Mr. Bickerstaffe seconded the motion to give His Majesty thanks for his most gracious speech to both Houses of Parliament.

Mr. Robartes: I am not only for your giving of thanks for His Majesty's speech but that in your address you congratulate the King on his safe return to his kingdoms and that you will stand by him in carrying on a vigorous war against France. *Sir Richard Temple* seconded the same.

Sir Thomas Clarges: I am for any congratulation you shall think fit but I am against the latter part; it is engaging this House beforehand in the matter of money, which I like not. I desire we may see first how matters are and then we will give our advice and assistance as we are able. And in order to this I desire we may address to His Majesty that he will be pleased to order the leagues and alliances he has with any foreign princes [? to be laid before the House], for this nation is in a very bad condition and great sums of money have gone out of it already, which impoverishes you mightily. I am for preserving order and method and going upon your address of thanks, leaving out the latter part of your question. *Paul Foley* to the same.

Sir John Lowther: There is no man more tender in cases of money than I am. The method you are now in I think is very regular and is not in the least engaging this House to give money when required. *Lord Cornbury* to the same, very handsomely.

Mr. Harley was for leaving out the last part of the question.

Sir Edward Seymour: I am against engaging this House underhand in a matter of money, and therefore I am for these words to stand because I do not think they any ways tie you up to such a thing but import only what no man I believe will deny—to assist this government. But now since it has been moved I think it absolutely necessary to have those words in the question, for if it come once to be known that this House once made a question of assisting His Majesty what fine work your enemies will make with it.

So the question was put and resolved *nemine contradicente* to thank His Majesty for his speech, to congratulate him on his return to his people, and to assure him this House would be ready to advise and assist him against all his enemies. So a committee was appointed and named to prepare such an address, and they were ordered to meet at 4 this afternoon in the Speaker's Chamber.

Lord Ranelagh moved that the same committee might have an instruction to prepare another address to the Queen to thank her for her prudent administration of the government in the King's absence. So the question was put and passed *nemine contradicente* for it accordingly.

Goodwin Wharton moved that the Commissioners of Accounts might prepare a state of the same and bring [it] to the House on Saturday next; and seconded by the *Lord Castleton*.

Sir Thomas Clarges: I hope the House will not put more upon us than we can do. We have taken some care about it and are preparing them to present unto you, and they will be ready on Tuesday next. *Mr. Paul Foley* to the same.

So ordered an account of the incomes and issues of the public moneys to be presented to the House on Tuesday next.

Sir Thomas Clarges: I think it is absolutely necessary for this House to see how this nation stands with foreign princes, and therefore I desire an application may be made to His Majesty to send to this House the alliances made with Holland in April and August 1689. And if there be any other alliances fit for us to advise in that we may see them to know on what grounds we stand with the confederates, and then we can tell how to advise the King.

Sir John Thompson: You have been very well moved as to the alliances, which I think absolutely fit for you to know for I am afraid there is much money goes out of this nation that way. There is a gentleman lately come from Holland that was ambassador there, the Lord Dursley; he can give you an account thereof—he has a book wherein you will see how your money has gone, if you can tell how to get at it.

Hampden moved that the House would appoint a day to take His Majesty's gracious speech into consideration and that it might be on Tuesday next. *Sir Robert Cotton* seconded the same.

Mr. Bertie: If we shall carry on a vigorous war against France and we must advise thereon what is necessary, it is fit to see the treaties with other princes. It is what the King seems to hint at in his speech and what will enable you to go on with the supplies the better.

So resolved on an address to His Majesty by the members of the House that are of the Privy Council that the alliances made with the Dutch in April and August 1689, and the alliances therein mentioned, and all other alliances with any other princes or states of Europe be laid before the House. Resolved the House would take the King's speech into consideration on Tuesday morning next at 10 of the clock.

Sir Thomas Clarges: It hath been always the method of parliaments to go upon redressing of grievances before they went upon supplies. I desire, therefore, that on Saturday next the House would resolve itself into a Committee of the Whole House to take the state of the nation into consideration. *Sir Peter Colleton* to the same.

So it was put and ordered accordingly.

Sir William Honeywood: You had a very good sermon preached before the House at St. Margaret's Church on the 5th instant by your chaplain, Dr. Maningham. I desire, therefore, you will please to give him the thanks of this House and to desire him to print the same. *Sir Charles Raleigh* seconded the same.

And it was ordered accordingly, and that Sir William Honeywood and Sir Charles Raleigh do acquaint him therewith.

So adjourned till 9 tomorrow morning.

Friday, 11 November

Sir William Whitlock: You had a very good bill which passed this House the last sessions but was lost in the House of Peers. It was the bill for regulating trials in cases of treason. I desire leave to bring in such a bill.

Sir Thomas Clarges seconded the same, and that the member that moved it might bring in the same copy of the bill which depended the last sessions and which the Clerk hath in his custody, and that he may present it now to you.

Speaker opposed this and said it was not regular to bring in such a bill without leave.

Sir Thomas Clarges: It is not at all against the rules of the House to present a bill to the House without asking leave, except in the case of a money bill, for this asking of leave is but a new way and an innovation in the House. Then the House is no stranger to this bill, for this very bill was passed in this very House of Commons the last sessions. *Sir Joseph Tredenham* to the same.

So the question was put and passed, and Sir William Whitlock brought up the bill to the Table and it was received.

Sir Thomas Clarges moved that it might be read.

So the bill was read the first time and ordered a second reading.

Sir Peter Colleton: Since you are to go into a Committee of the Whole House tomorrow upon the state of the nation, to make matters more easy and that you may have some fruit of it I desire the Admiral that commanded your fleet will attend in his place tomorrow to give some account of matters relating thereto. *Sir Thomas Clarges* to the same.

Admiral Russell: I shall be ready to answer any question that shall be asked me.

Sir Thomas Clarges: There are two general questions that are very material: why the victory was prosecuted no farther and why your merchants' ships are no better protected and the trade preserved? I desire we may have some account of these matters since your sessions is not like to be long. *Sir John Knatchbull* to the same.

Sir John Darell was against putting the Admiral to give an account of these matters.

Col. Granville thought it most proper to apply to the Lords of the Admiralty, who are fittest to give you an account; and if there have been miscarriages let it lie at their door.

Col. Titus to the same and said that if there had been miscarriages he hoped the House would not be against hearing them.

Sir Thomas Clarges: I desire to add this further. You gave the last sessions a great deal of money for a descent upon France but it ended in a descent at Ostend. There was a council of war on board about the descent; I hear some were for it and some against it, with their reasons on both sides. I hope these papers are in the hands of your Admiralty and I desire they may be brought also.

Charles Montagu: I am against your making an order upon that worthy gentleman, your member, who commanded your fleet last summer; he hears what the inclination of the House is and no doubt will comply therewith. This House, I think, should be far from casting any reflections upon your Admiral but should rather give him thanks for that great service he did you in destroying so many and such great ships of the French, your enemy—the greatest victory that was ever obtained at sea.

But it being pressed much for an order for the Admiral to give an account of the last summer's expedition at sea, it was moved by *Goodwin Wharton* that to prevent all reflections upon your Admiral he desired he might have the thanks of this House for his great courage and conduct of your fleet the last summer. *Sir Robert Henley, Sir Peter Colleton*, and *Lord Castleton* to the same.

Col. Granville: I am very well satisfied the more you inquire into this matter the better you will be satisfied with the conduct of your Admiral, and therefore I am for giving him thanks. But you will find some above who are the occasion of all, who give orders in matters they understand not to control others that do.

So resolved that the thanks of this House be given to Admiral Russell for his great courage and conduct in the victory obtained at sea last summer.

So the *Speaker* (seeing the member in his place) he—in the name of the House—in a short speech addressed himself to him and gave him the thanks of the House; which the *Admiral* returned in a short speech.

So then an order was made that the Commissioners of the Admiralty and the honourable member that commanded the fleet should give an account tomorrow of the last summer's expedition.

The addresses to the King and the Queen were twice read and then agreed to by the House.

Mr. Solicitor General, Sir Thomas Trevor, being chosen a member for Plympton (in the room of Sir George Treby, Lord Chief Justice), came into the House, and was sworn and took his place accordingly.

Sir William Honeywood presented a petition from the Companies of Weavers in London and Canterbury which he brought up to the Table and it was read—praying a temporary suspension during the war of the act prohibiting the importation of Italian and Sicilian thrown silks and that they might for that time be brought in overland. So the petition was referred to a committee to consider of and to report their opinions to the House, and a committee was named and to meet at 4 in the Speaker's Chamber.

Mr. Clarke moved for leave to bring in a bill to prevent false and double returns of members to serve in Parliament, and ordered accordingly.

So the House adjourned till 9 tomorrow morning.

Saturday, 12 November

Lord Falkland presented the House (according to order) with an account from the Admiralty of the last summer's expedition of the fleet as to what relates to them, as full as can be in so short a time, with several papers of letters, orders, and instructions, and the results of councils of war touching the same which he delivered in at the Table.

Sir Peter Colleton moved that they might be read.

So the general paper or diary to which the others refer was read, as also the particular papers to justify the same—a list of which follow:

14 April 1692—the Admiralty's orders to Admiral Carter.

22 April 1692—their orders to Admiral Russell.

22 April 1692—Lord Nottingham's letter to the Admiralty to send Delaval towards the coast of France.

24 April 1692—orders from the Admiralty to Mr. Russell, pursuant to a letter from the Queen.

3 May 1692—orders from the Admiralty to Admiral Russel with instructions touching the grand fleet and a full power to do and act as he thought fit, with a list of the ships he was to take with him (viz, six first-rate ships, 10 second-rates, etc.).

5 May 1692—orders from the Admiralty to Russell to sail westward to join Carter and Delaval.

5 May 1692—orders to Delaval from the Admiralty to cruise between the Isle of Wight and Cape La Hogue.

Goodwin Wharton: You have read the papers but I think there is nothing material in them. Therefore I must desire to ask some questions for farther satisfaction: (1) Why after the fight the French ships were not better pursued when many of their ships were disabled, had few cables or anchors? It cannot be pretended for want of pilots because we were in sight of the enemy. Then it can't be said to be for want of water because the ships they pursued were as big as their own.

Admiral Russell: I have prepared a short journal of what happened after the fight and the stations of the fleet. But I will rectify some mistakes I took notice of in the debate yesterday. There was nothing done in the fleet without a council of war nor any council of war in which there was one of a different opinion; and councils of war consist only of flag officers and not any private captains thereat.

Lord Falkland delivered in several papers of the results of divers councils of war, which were read in the following order:

9 May 1692—a council of war by flag officers on board the *Britannia*, relating to Delaval.

15 May 1692—another by flag officers, English and Dutch.

12 June 1692—another held on board the *Neptune* by the captains commanding the ships before St. Malo.

8 July 1692—another held on board the *Berwick* touching the ships at St. Malo: where held not possible to burn them, it being very hazardous to get in—nay, morally impossible without pilots and then because of the many rocks—and though there be pilots, if the French have taken up the landmarks they will not undertake to carry them in.

14 July 1692—another held in Torbay on board the *Britannia* by flag officers wherein was agreed the stations for our fleet to keep the French ships in St. Malo.

25 July 1692—another council of war by flag officers upon a letter from the Lord Nottingham of 17th July relating to the forces.

28 July 1692—another between the flag officers and the Duke of Leinster (Lieutenant General) and the field officers about the French ships at St. Malo: that it was not practicable to burn them till the town were reduced by the land forces, and the land forces could do nothing without the men of war; that as to the attempt upon Brest and Rochefort, the season was too far spent and those places so far round that it was not safe to venture; and for St. Malo, it was very dangerous by reason of the rocks.

30 July 1692—another by the flag officers and the field officers with the General: unanimous that they see no reason to alter their resolutions on 28th past, but that if the Queen will send her positive orders for attempting it they will endeavour.[1]

[1] Grey, x. 244–8 has a parallel account of the debate that follows.

Sir Thomas Clarges: I know not who had the management of our descent. But I would very willingly be satisfied why it was made so late and not got ready by the time of our victory at sea—viz., about 19th of May.

John Smith: I find by these papers here are two things before you—the miscarriages of the fleet and not improving the victory, the other relating to the descent. So if you please, go upon that of the fleet first.

Mr. Russell then delivered in his papers giving an account of the victory at sea and of the care and diligence used to destroy the enemy's fleet, and therein seemed a little to reflect on Sir John Ashby, as if he had not fully done his duty in the pursuit of the French after the fight. Then for the other question, why the fleet stayed so long in port after the fight, he gave in a short diary how the [log][1] stood every day and affirmed that from 27th of May to the 13th of June (which was the day the fleet sailed again) there was not 12 hours fair weather and a wind, too.

Sir Robert Howard: I desire we may first inquire why the French fleet were not pursued, and that must be required from those that were not in the fight—Sir John Ashby and Admiral Almonde. But as to your own Admiral, I cannot say but he behaved himself bravely and fought the Admiral of France hand to hand.

Then Mr. Russell's letter to Sir John Ashby and to Admiral Almonde with orders to pursue the French through the Race of Alderney was read.

Paul Foley: How true it is I can't tell, but there is a relation printed in France of the fight with Tourville wherein they lay a blame on Sir John Ashby and do in effect say that if he had done his duty their fleet must be ruined.

Sir William Strickland and *Sir Charles Sedley* moved that Sir John Ashby might be sent for to give an account of his proceedings.

Sir Edward Seymour: I have often seen the House upon this subject and as seldom any fruits come of it. Unless you will punish some, you confirm them in their miscarriages. There are now three things before you: why the French were not pursued after your victory at sea; why so many of your merchant ships are taken; and then about the descent. You are come to a point—that about Sir John Ashby—and therefore I desire he may be sent to attend you.

Sir Thomas Clarges: I know not one thing we have done to pull down the French by sea but this one—your victory at sea. There are some

[1] 'long' in MS.

things I would desire to be satisfied in now: why your fleet lay still after 13 June unto August when the ships got away from St. Malo; then we had a project upon the French at Newfoundland—we sent some ships thither to destroy the French there but we sent them not hence till the middle of July, when all the world know the French come away thence the beginning of August; then I desire to know who had the ordering of the descent and why it was so late; then I observe in the councils of war held the flag officers say they could do nothing without the land forces and the general officers of your forces say they could do nothing without the men-of-war, and both agree that the season of the year was too late to do anything.

Mr. Russell: Give me leave to rectify some mistakes of that worthy member that spoke last. As to the design upon Newfoundland, the Lords of the Admiralty knew nothing of it; it was by particular order from the Queen to me and accordingly I sent three fourth-rate ships upon that design. He that commanded them was unexceptionable both for courage and conduct and you had some fruits thereof, though not so much as wished, by destroying some of their ships there. And for your fleet after the fight, they kept such stations as were thought most proper to prevent the French ships at St. Malo from getting home.

Mr. Robartes: I desire you will put the question about Sir John Ashby.

Then the *Speaker* proposed to the House whether the Lords of the Admiralty should send for him (being he was under their care) or whether the House would send for him?

Sir Christopher Musgrave: It is proper for the House to do it and not to order particular men to do it.

Ordered that Sir John Ashby do attend this House with all speed.

But then a dispute arose how this order should be signified to him —whether by a letter from the Speaker or by the Serjeant attending this House.

Sir Christopher Musgrave and *Sir Edward Seymour* and others were for the latter as the best, most usual, and customary; and it was no disparagement to be sent for to attend this House, being he comes not here as a criminal but only for the information of the House, and this House hath none but the Serjeant to summon persons to attend them.

Mr. Russell: As to some matters desired—why the descent was made no sooner—I cannot tell; I was at sea and this matter was transacted at land. And why it was no better prosecuted, the councils of war give you an account that it was the lateness of the season. As to the design upon St. Malo, besides the lateness of the year the sea thereabout is very dangerous. Then for Brest and Rochefort, they were thought too far about to expose the fleet so late in the year.

John Smith: As to the descent, your Admiral has given you as good an account of it as he could. But the chief thing is how came it to be made so late, when it appears your forces were ready some time before your provisions and transport ships were.

Mr. Bertie moved that the Commissioners of the Transport Ships and the officers of the Victualling Office might give an account of their proceedings.

Sir Christopher Musgrave moved that we might know who had the descent under their direction and order, and how it came that it was so late and no sooner put in execution. *Sir Peter Colleton* and *Mr. Jeffreys* to the same.

Ordered that the Commissioners for the Transport Ships do attend this House on Monday next and bring their papers with them relating to the descent.

Sir Henry Goodricke acquainted the House he would prepare the papers relating to the descent in the Office of the Ordnance and present [them] to the House in some few days. So did *Mr. Papillon* the like for the Victualling Office.

So left as the sense of the House they should.

Sir Joseph Tredenham: You have taken some care of two of the matters, and for the third I desire the Lords of the Admiralty may give an account how it comes to pass so many of your merchant ships have been taken.

Sir Robert Rich: If the House please, we will lay before you the papers to show what care we have taken for preserving the trade of this nation.

So ordered that the Commissioners of the Admiralty might give an account of what cruisers and other men-of-war have been ordered for security of your merchants this last summer.[1]

So House adjourned till 9 on Monday morning.

Monday, 14 November

Mr. Blofield had leave to bring in a bill for transferring the collection of the duty of aulnage to the Customhouse and giving a recompense to the Crown for the same.

---

[1] No such order is entered in the *Journal*.

The House was called over, beginning with the counties according to the alphabet, and those that made default were noted down in a paper. Then the defaulters were called over again a second time and the absence of several excused.

Mr. Palmes, Mr. Clarke, Col. Titus, and Mr. Smith took notice that several members were abroad upon other services, as in Ireland and in foreign service as ambassadors, and that as one or so were sent abroad so more might, so the service of the House would not be attended as it ought—those several boroughs, etc. that sent them hither had not their true representatives. And therefore they moved either to give them a day to appear or else to appoint a committee to search precedents to see what the House have done in cases where members have been employed in foreign service beyond the seas or where members have been otherwise absent from the service of the House in case of sickness or other disability. *Sir Edward Seymour* to the same.

So a committee was appointed accordingly and to report the same to the House, and the committee to meet *de die in diem*.

His Majesty's answer to the address for dissolving the present East India Company gave an account of His Majesty's proceedings thereon: that they had refused to submit to the regulations His Majesty proposed; that His Majesty had consulted with his judges touching the power reserved in their charter, who were of opinion that he could not dissolve the same without three years' notice; and therefore he thought it not advisable to dissolve them, believing that if they were dissolved they would not mind preserving the trade for the three years who were not like [? to receive] the benefit thereof. So he referred them to the bringing in a bill for the same.

So the House resolved to take the matter relating to the East India Company into consideration on Wednesday morning next.

Sir Thomas Clarges complained of a breach of privilege on Christopher Musgrave esq., a member of this House, committed by the council of the City of Carlisle for disfranchising him and turning him out of his freedom of that corporation—which is a sort of freehold of which a man cannot be deprived without just cause.

The order of disfranchisement was read, with the names of the town council, and the town clerk was called in and examined touching the same. And being withdrawn, resolved that the disfranchising C. M., a member of this House, by etc. is a breach of the privilege of this House.

Sir John Lowther moved against passing so severe a censure on them before the House had heard the matter.

Harley moved to declare it a breach of privilege. *Mr. Harcourt* strongly to the same.

Sir Edward Seymour: You can do no less than declare it a breach of privilege; you did the like in disfranchising a member of this House for the city of Canterbury.

Sir Henry Goodricke: I have heard something of this matter, and if I be truly informed, there was a breach of the peace, in which case privilege does not hold.

Paul Foley: Though there was a breach of the peace, there is a proper remedy for it—by indictment, etc.—not by turning a man out of his freehold as this of disfranchising a member is.

So it was voted a breach of the privilege of this House, *nemine contradicente*. So after some debate, though the whole town council were guilty of this breach of privilege, yet the *member* on whom it was committed desiring that but some of the most notorious might be sent for in custody to answer the same, it was ordered that AB, CD, EF, etc., to the number of six, be sent for in custody of the Serjeant at Arms attending this House for such their breach of privilege.[1]

Ordered that the defaulters of the House for whom no excuse has been made be called over on Wednesday sevennight next, and that such of them as do not then appear be sent for in custody of the Serjeant at Arms attending this House.

So adjourned till 3 in the afternoon.

3 *post meridiem*

The House met and went up with their Speaker at the head on foot to Whitehall to attend Their Majesties with their addresses and then adjourned till 9 tomorrow morning. The Speaker presented the address to His Majesty in the Banqueting House, who sat in a Chair of State, and that to the Queen in the Withdrawing Room, she standing by her Chair of State.

---

[1] For the names of these councillors see *CJ*, x. 700.

Tuesday, 15 November

The *Speaker* reported that he had presented the addresses of the House to Their Majesties, and that they received the same very graciously, and reported their answers.

Mr. Bickerstaffe complained of a breach of privilege committed on Sir John Bland in suing him in the Court of Exchequer by AB, CD, and EF as their attorney.[1] Which the *member* affirming in his place and that he had not sued them at law, they were ordered to be taken into custody of the Serjeant at Arms to answer the said breach of privilege. Though it was contested by several members to have this matter referred to the Committee of Privileges first to examine the same— being more for the honour and justice of the House to hear the parties before you condemn them for it, being sometimes you have after examination found there was no great cause of complaint and you have ordered the parties to be discharged without fees.

Marquess of Winchester complained also of a breach of privilege committed by JD, WL, and JS in arresting one SR, a menial servant of Sir John Guise.[1] Which *he* also affirming in his place that he was his menial servant, eat at his table and lay in his house, the said JD, etc. were ordered to be taken into custody for the said breach of privilege.

Sir Edward Seymour and *Mr. Hampden* moved to go upon the business of the day and that the House would read His Majesty's speech and go upon the same as a matter absolutely necessary.

Sir Thomas Clarges: I think it is proper first to have the alliances laid before the House to see what we are obliged to and we shall be better able to know how to advise His Majesty, who desires very graciously your advice as well as your assistance. *Mr. Bathurst* to the same.

Sir John Lowther was for going on the speech first, for the alliances would be presented time enough.

Lord Eland: I think it proper to go upon the accounts and to have the alliances before you and not to go into a committee of the House to give money only, for when that is done farewell to accounts and alliances, too. *Mr. Smith* and *Sir Christopher Musgrave* to the same.

Sir Robert Cotton (of the Post Office) was for going on the King's speech, for that which is desired is only in general for a motion touching a supply, nothing as to the *quantum* or going into a committee.

Mr. Montagu to the same for that the methods of the House in matters of money is only that a motion being made for a supply, the

[1] See *CJ*, x. 700.

House will appoint a day then to take it into consideration in a Committee of the Whole House.

Col. Granville was for going on the alliances and the accounts.

Sir Joseph Tredenham was for going on the King's speech.

Sir Robert Rich: I am for going upon His Majesty's speech to give life to your government which subsists now only on credit—the clause you annexed to the poll bill for His Majesty to take up money which is what the government now subsists by, the poll bill itself falling much short, it is said £740,000.

Lord Falkland thought it proper to go upon the speech first, and when you come to a committee about supplies you may refer the alliances and the accounts to the same committee.

Sir John Guise and *Sir Richard Temple* were for going on the speech.

Mr. Palmes and *Goodwin Wharton* were for the accounts.

Sir William Strickland: If we are to give our advice your best way will be to go upon the accounts and the alliances. But if we must only just give money and nothing else, then go upon the speech.

Col. Titus and *Sir Peter Colleton* moved to read the several Orders of the Day to see which first in order, which was done.

Sir Robert Howard desired the House would receive the book of accounts.

So *Mr. Foley* presented the House with the book of the accounts of the incomes and issues of the public moneys, and delivered it in at the Table.

Col. Granville moved to have it read. And it was read accordingly.

Sir Edward Seymour then desired that the book might be ordered to lie on the Table that any member might have resort to it as there was occasion. So ordered accordingly.

Sir Christopher Musgrave: Since I doubt not it was the design of this House to have some fruit of this Commission of Accounts by your appointing them to be taken, I desire this House will resolve itself into a Committee of the Whole House upon Thursday next to take the same into consideration.

Lord Ranelagh and *Sir Edward Seymour* both opposed it as too soon for so many gentlemen who are concerned in the book of accounts to look over the same, and therefore desired it might be put off till Monday.

So it was accordingly put off till Monday.

Sir Peter Colleton: The next order in course on your book, now you have dispatched that of the accounts is that of the alliances, of which I hope we shall now have some account.

Sir Edward Seymour: As to that of the alliances, they are many and long; and as soon as they can be transcribed and translated (which I am informed they are doing, some being in French and others in Latin) they will be laid before you, which I suppose may be tomorrow.

Lord Ranelagh: Now you have dispatched the several orders about the accounts and the alliances I desire you will proceed on the other order, which is to take into consideration the King's speech.

Then the Order of the Day was read and after His Majesty's speech was read.

Sir Scrope Howe: There is no man but is sensible of the early preparations of the French, and therefore that we may be as early I humbly move you for a supply for His Majesty for carrying on the war against France. *Sir Thomas Hesilrige* seconded the same.

Sidney Godolphin: You having a motion made for a supply, your next step is to go into a Committee of the Whole House to consider of the said motion, which I desire may be tomorrow.

Sir Thomas Clarges and *John Smith* opposed the same and desired that the House would first look into the alliances and your state of the accounts to see how matters stand, whereby you will be better able to know how to advise the King, which is what he desires as well as your assistance. And since His Majesty has been so very gracious in his speech to ask our advice, which is more than your kings of late have been used to do, I desire we may with all duty give him the best we can.

Sir Edward Seymour: As I believe there are hardly any in this House against giving their assistance to His Majesty, so I would not have us unseasonably defer it, for to delay in this case is next door to denying it, and therefore I am for the House to resolve itself into a Committee of the Whole House upon Thursday next to take the said motion into consideration.

Paul Foley: I am not for putting this off. But I think it is fit for you first to have a day to consider what advice you will give the King which I move may be on Thursday next, and then on Friday next, if you please, you may go upon your assistance.

Sir Christopher Musgrave: I think that a little too soon for it is absolutely necessary for you to have the alliances and the accounts before you first, and therefore I think Tuesday next is soon enough for the supply.

Sir John Lowther seconded the motion of Mr. Foley and that the matter of a supply might be deferred no longer. *Sir Robert Cotton* to the same.

Goodwin Wharton: The motion you are now debating is in plain English giving of money. The day first moved and seconded was Tuesday, and therefore must be first put.

But a dispute arose which was the question ought to be first put.

The *Speaker* said by the rules of the House the least sum and the longest day in matters of charge upon the people ought to be first put. But this he thought no charge on the people but only a dispute about taking a matter into consideration.

Sir Thomas Clarges: If anything be a charge upon the people I think this is—being plainly giving of money—and therefore the longest day ought to be first put.

Sir Robert Howard and *Sir Richard Temple* were for Friday and that the business of the alliances and the accounts refers only to that of the *quantum*, but now at the committee on Friday you will only vote a supply in general to His Majesty for the carrying on the war, which I hope no one will be against.

Col. Granville: I desire you will put the question for Tuesday.

Sir Edward Seymour: If a question be on proceeding upon a bill between two days, the proper question is the first day because business ought to be dispatched, and if carried against the first it is of course to be upon the longer day. So the question now under debate ought to be on the soonest day.

John Smith: I think it is absolutely necessary for this House to give their advice for I think matters are so out of order in this government that unless we give our advice and that very freely we can never hold together one year longer.

Lord Castleton spoke to the same and reflected on the many persons in places in the House, very boldly.

Sir Stephen Fox: I observe it is the opinion of some gentlemen that there is no present need of money and that things go on as well as if you gave money. I do assure you it is no such thing, for the Exchequer was never barer than now and we have nothing to live on but the clause of credit given by this House upon the poll act and the act for the double excise, which now expires the 17th of this month. So that all things are at a stand till you set them going.

Mr. Papillon: I must acquaint you that the time for victualling your fleet is now come, and I can assure you without money there can be no provisions got, so it will be impossible for your fleet to be out early.

Lord Colchester: I cannot deny but there is great need of money and that the nation is in a bad condition. But I hope we are not so bad

that two or three days will ruin us, and therefore I desire the question
may be put for Tuesday to go into a Committee of the Whole House
to consider of the motion for a supply for carrying on a vigorous war
against France.

So it was, and resolved *nemine contradicente.*

So adjourned till tomorrow morning 9 of the clock.

Wednesday, 16 November

Col. Titus complained of a breach of privilege in arresting one RC,
a menial servant to Mr. Lloyd (a member of the House), by HW
and DP.[1] Mr. *Lloyd* then stood up and affirmed him to be his menial
servant that received his rents and lay in his house.

Moved then that they might be sent for in custody of the Serjeant
at Arms for the said breach of privilege.

Sir Edward Seymour opposed it and desired it might be referred to
the Committee of Privileges to examine, who examined all these
matters formerly, but now of late you are come to execution *per
saltum.*

Sir Joseph Tredenham to the same and that it was not for the honour
of the House nor becoming their justice to condemn men unheard.

Mr. Hampden. It was never yet made a question when a member in
his place stood up and affirmed the party to be his menial servant,
but you have always sent for them in custody.

So ordered in this case.

Sir William Turner presented a petition from divers merchants and
owners of ships—setting forth the great losses they had sustained to
the number of at least 1,500 ships and three millions of money taken
by the French for want of convoys, etc. It was read.

Sir John Knight, Sir Thomas Vernon, Sir Robert Howard moved to refer
it to a particular committee to examine.

Sir Edward Seymour: This matter, I am afraid, for the greatest part
is too true and is worth your inquiry, as also how it comes to pass that
so many merchant ships have been taken. I believe it will be found
as much their fault as for want of convoys. And though so many have
been lost, I can assure you the customs are much higher now than in
times of peace heretofore.

So the petition was referred to a particular committee who are to

[1] See *CJ*, x. 701.

report the matter to the House, and they have power to send for persons, papers, etc.

The Commissioners for Transportation were called in, and after they had delivered in their papers were asked some questions by the *Speaker*. To which Mr. Ellis (one of them) answered: That there were in the river 114 transport ships for the service of the descent, and that if the ships ordered to Bideford had been ready those in the river would have been by the time we expected. But though they had, we could not sail till the wellboats were ready, which was not till the 28th of July.

The committee to whom the papers about the descent were referred were ordered to sit *de die in diem*, and to send for persons, papers, and records, and the Commissioners of Transportation were ordered to attend them.

The original treaties and alliances between the several confederates being delivered into the House, they appeared to be some in French and others in Latin—languages not so commonly understood by all the members perhaps or at least not by your Clerk, or [not][1] so easily in reading them over to the House. It was debated some time what to do with them.[2] Some gentlemen were for returning them to the Secretary's Office to let them translate them. Others were for a public [notary] to translate them. But these were thought improper because they seemed to reflect on the House, and the latter would make them too public. So that at last they thought it most proper to do as was done in the case of Coleman's letters. So they were referred to a committee of the House to translate them and to prepare abstracts thereof, and the committee was ordered to meet as soon as the House was up that they might deliver out the treaties to particular members of the committee to translate as soon as possible.

So adjourned till 9 of the clock tomorrow morning.

Thursday, 17 November

Isaac Rebow, being newly chosen for the town of Colchester in the county of Essex (in the room of Mr. Cary, deceased), came into the House and was sworn and took his seat accordingly.

Upon the petition from the City of London touching the orphans, *Mr. Harcourt* moved that the House would go into a Committee

---

[1] 'no' in MS.   [2] Two hours; B.M. Add. MS. 34096, f. 216, 18 Nov.

of the Whole House to consider of ways and means to satisfy the debt due to the orphans. *Col. Pery* seconded the same.

But the *Speaker* and *Sir Christopher Musgrave* opposed it as very irregular to go into a committee to consider of ways and means before you have resolved of the thing itself, but that the proper motion was to move to have the House go into a committee to consider of the said petition.

And ordered accordingly to be on Thursday next.

Sir John Darell moved to bring in a bill to encourage the exportation of our own manufactures, which is a matter will raise the value of your land. If you take off the duty on these English commodities at the exportation, there will more be transported and of these the countries will have the advantage, and it is but a small loss to the Crown in their customs in a year—about £1,500 per annum. The duty I would have taken off on these several commodities are mutton, veal, oats, grafts, raw hides, English soap, tallow, and biscuit flour.

Sir Edward Seymour: I am against this matter for that your own service now requires these things should not be sent beyond sea, for that your consumption at this time is very great in this nation (greater almost than the product thereof) whereby these things already bear a great price, so that if they be sent beyond sea you will want them here for your own occasions. Therefore I desire you will very well consider of this motion before you do anything in it.

Then the Order of the Day was read about the East India Company; and the message from His Majesty in answer to the address of this House, as also the judges' opinion upon the clause reserved to the Crown in their charter, with the regulation proposed to the Company by the committee of Council and their answer to each head (refusing to submit to any of them), were all read.

Mr. Neale and *Sir Charles Sedley* moved that since the Company had refused all regulations, this House would vote to have a new company.

Sir Robert Howard spoke very largely against the Company and of the great abuses committed by them, the sad condition this trade was in by the mismanagement thereof, the insolency of their answers to His Majesty, and concluded that since the King recommends it to you to take care of this so beneficial a trade I move you for leave to bring in a bill to erect a new company.

Col. Pery: I am against that motion for I do not think the Company in so bad a condition as some gentlemen represent it. Since the last sessions they have sent out five ships, on board of which there was above £200,000; there was a sixth which had to near the value of £80,000 on board which the government thought fit to put a stop to it.

Sir Joseph Herne to the same and that these ships lately sent out were on the Company's own account and not permission ships.

Mr. Bathurst was for a bill to establish a new company.

Sir Edward Seymour: This trade is a fifth part of the trade of the whole nation and therefore may well deserve your consideration to preserve the same from being lost, which I assure you is very much endangered, and to make it more beneficial to the nation. I do think it very necessary for you to that end to have a bill but I think it consistent with your justice to hear the Company to it before you quite destroy them, for though you examined matters last sessions very thoroughly yet you cannot regularly take notice now what you did then.

Sir Thomas Clarges: I think it necessary to have a bill to supply some defects in the Company's charter. But I cannot be of opinion that the Company are unable to carry on the trade, and therefore I think you ought in justice to hear them before you bring in such a bill.

Col. Titus: If the Company have not trifled with you enough already and spent sufficient time the last sessions, then pray hear them again. But if they did, I am for bringing in a bill pursuant to the regulations offered by His Majesty.

Sir Samuel Barnardiston and *Mr. Hutchinson* were for bringing in a bill.

John Howe: I am against bringing in a bill before you hear the Company for the House now can not regularly take notice of what done in a former sessions. *Sir Thomas Littleton* and *Sir Richard Temple* to the same.

Sir John Guise was for a bill and not against hearing the Company if they desire it. *Sir Robert Rich* to the same.

Mr. Dolben was for hearing the Company.

Sir Christopher Musgrave: I do not think you are ripe for a bill until you have agreed of the heads of which such bill shall consist, and therefore I think the right way is to go into a Committee of the Whole House to consider of the regulations now laid before you by the King.

Mr. Robartes was for a bill.

Sir Samuel Dashwood: I am a member of the East India Company, and as a member of this House I demand the right to be heard against the said bill before my right be precluded.

John Smith: I am for hearing the Company and I think it is consistent with your justice so to do. But you have not yet agreed what you will hear them to, and therefore it is proper for you to consider of regulations in the first place and then you may hear them thereto. *Sir Joseph Tredenham* to the same.

Paul Foley: The proper time to hear them is when the bill is brought in, when it comes to be read a second time, or at the commitment of it.

So at last the question was put and resolved *nemine contradicente* that a bill be brought in for the regulating, preserving, and establishing the East India trade to this kingdom.

Mr. Attorney General[1] acquainted the House that pursuant to their order he had prosecuted Fuller and that his trial was to be the next week. He desired the House would give leave to Mr. Arnold, Mr. Hutchinson, Sir Robert Cotton, Sir Matthew Andrews, Mr. Bowyer, etc., members of the House, and their Clerk to attend the Court of King's Bench to give evidence against him.

And it was ordered accordingly.

Friday, 18 November

Bill to prevent butchers selling live cattle was read the second time.

Mr. Bowyer and *Mr. Greenfield* objected against it that it altered the old way of trials by a jury and put it to a conviction before a justice of peace, which was severe.

So committed on the debate of the House.

Mr. Hawtrey presented the petition about the convex lights. And it was referred to a committee, or any five of them, to prepare and bring in a bill.

Sir Francis Winnington, chosen a member for the borough of Tewkesbury in Gloucestershire (in the room of Sir Henry Capel, made a lord), came into the House and was sworn and took his place accordingly.

The bill for transferring the collection of the duty of [aulnage] to the Customhouse and giving a recompense to the Crown for the same was read the second time. And a debate arose whether it should be committed to a private committee or to a Committee of the Whole House because it raised money on the subject. But answered it made

[1] Sir John Somers.

no new imposition on the people but only the duties that are now collected. However, the question was put to refer it to a Committee of the Whole House, but carried in the negative. So the House as of course proceeded to name a private committee.

The Serjeant attending this House was sent with his mace to the several courts in Westminster Hall to require the immediate attendance of all the members of the House that are of the long robe. And he being returned, then the bill for regulating trials in cases of treason was read the second time.[1]

Sir William Whitlock moved, and *Sir Thomas Clarges*, that this bill might be committed.

Sir John Lowther: I am as much concerned as any man to preserve myself and my family, but however I cannot be for this bill. That which has been a security to our ancestors for 300 years past may be so to us now, especially when we have so good a government as this now is wherein this law is needless. And if a bad one come I am sure this law will signify little and be no protection to the innocent. But now if this law pass at this time it will weaken this government and be a benefit only to the enemies of this government, who are bold enough already without such a law to back them, and therefore I am against committing this bill.

Attorney General Somers: Though I am against this bill and several clauses of it, yet I am also against it because it is by no means well timed. But there is that besides which I think this House will never admit of—to cramp yourselves in the matter of impeachments which, with your money, are the two only things that make this House considerable. Then on the observation I have made in history, in great revolutions it has been the chief care of that government how to support and preserve the same, and not to weaken it as this does by rendering treason more difficult to be punished than before. And there is no danger from this government by a too severe prosecution for treason for the fault thereof is it is too gentle, and therefore I am against this bill.

Sir Christopher Musgrave: I think this a very good bill and therefore am for it. But if any gentleman has any just exception to any part of it, if you please to commit it the proper time to amend it is at the committee.

Solicitor General Sir Thomas Trevor: Some gentlemen, I observe, in their arguments for this bill have objected that there have been

---

[1] Grey, x. 249–52 has a parallel account of the debate that follows.

misconstruction of laws in the case of treason in former reigns. I do agree it. Yet by making a new law this mischief will not be remedied, but you ought to have punished some and made them examples for so doing, for otherwise as there were men found that abused former laws so there will be such as will venture to misconstrue this present act you are about. But then to the bill itself, it is at this time a protection to the guilty by making treason more difficult to be punished and gives encouragement to the enemies of your government to undermine the same, who are the only persons will reap advantage by this bill. Then if this do pass into a law, what will it signify under an ill government? Then it is said by some gentlemen that this bill passed this House the last sessions; perhaps so, but I think the reasons urged against it then were strong and there has that happened this last summer that makes them much stronger. You were very near an invasion by the French and I am afraid you had too many enemies here at home that were ready to join with them, and therefore I am against this bill.

Robert Harley: I cannot but take notice though some gentlemen are now against this bill, yet they complained much of the misconstruction that was made in the last reign in cases of trials in treason. It is what you took notice of when you presented the crown to Their Majesties and made it one of the heads of grievances against the late King. But now some of those gentlemen that were so zealous then are against it now and say it is not timely. For my part I think it the proper time to get good laws in a good reign, and therefore I am for this bill now. *Bathurst* for the bill.

Sir Charles Sedley: I am for this government, and yet I am for this bill and do not think one inconsistent with the other. Some exceptions have been taken to the bill; therefore I desire it may be committed.

Lord Coningsby: I am against this whole bill at this time for I think it will only be a benefit to the enemies of this government—those that will not own it—and give them an advantage to bring back a government which, I am sure, will make traitors of all of us.

Paul Foley: I am for preserving this government but I am also for protecting the innocent, and therefore I am for this bill.

Sir Thomas Littleton: I was against this law last sessions, and see nothing to alter my opinion but rather to confirm me in the same. And I think this bill will very much weaken your government and help the sooner to ruin it, and therefore I am against the bill.

Mr. Bertie was for committing the bill.

So the question was put for committing the bill. The House divided
—Yeas went out.

	Sir Gilbert Clarke	
Yeas		170
	Capt. Bickerstaffe	
Tellers for the		
	Mr. Montagu	
Noes		152
	Sir Thomas Littleton	

So upon the question it was carried the bill should be committed.

Sir Christopher Musgrave moved that since it was a bill of a general concern, it might be committed to a Committee of the Whole House. *Sir John Guise* to the same.

So on the question it was resolved to be committed to a Committee of the Whole House, which was to sit on Thursday next.

Lord Cornbury presented to the House a letter from one whom they had ordered into custody for a breach of privilege in arresting one Samuel Rich, a servant to Sir John Guise. But bringing up the letter to the Table was opposed, because not parliamentary to read letters in the House. So his Lordship opened the purport of the letter.

Sir Thomas Clarges and *Sir Robert Henley* gave a very sad account of this Samuel Rich: of his lewdness and debauchery, adulteries and fornications; and that he was a clergyman, having a rectorship of £500 per annum, so could not be the member's menial servant, because his living requires his residence there.

Then it was debated whether a chaplain having a benefice with cure of souls could be a menial servant to a member to enjoy privilege.

Sir Christopher Musgrave: If a member keep a chaplain in his house and he lies therein and pays him wages, this is a menial servant to have the benefit of privilege. But the case before you it appears he has a living with cure of souls on which he ought to reside, so cannot be a menial servant; and a gentleman only is not qualified to keep such a chaplain.

Sir Thomas Clarges and *Mr. Smith* moved to have the order for the commitment of them to be discharged.

So they were all ordered to be discharged without paying any fees.

Several particular members were upon motion added to divers committees.

Adjourned till tomorrow morning 9 of the clock.

Saturday, 19 November

The Lord Hyde (son to the Earl of Rochester) and one Mr. Hill being lately chosen members, the first for Launceston (in the room of William Harbord esq.) and the latter for Saltash (in the room of Sir John Carew, deceased), both in the county of Cornwall, came into the House this day, and took the oaths at the Table and signed the test, and after took their places in the House.

The bill for the importation of fine Italian thrown silk overland was read the first time.

Mr. Onslow and *Sir Thomas Vernon* opposed reading it a second time for that it would tend very much to the destruction of the woollen manufacture. For by this means they would not only bring in this sort of silk but all others; and amongst the rest the silk which is brought from Turkey hither in exchange for your woollen manufacture, which will much impoverish that trade. Then this will take away the employment of many of your poor here, the silk throwsters, and this will throw that trade into the Dutch's hand.

Then said for this bill that it is a good bill; that it does not bring in any of your Turkey raw silk but only your fine Italian silk which was to make alamodes and other silks which you formerly had from France and for which a great deal of money was sent out thither, but now we were arrived to great perfection in making those silks which would preserve the money here; then that they could not make these silks without this fine Italian silk, and the more is used of the fine silk the more is of that which comes from Turkey, which is a coarser silk and mixes well with this fine silk.

So upon the question this bill was ordered a second reading.

The report made by *Col. Granville* from the committee to whom the petition of the merchants of London touching their losses at sea was referred reflected much on the Lords of the Admiralty, as if they had been very careless in the appointing cruisers at the chops of the Channel and some towards the north to secure our merchants' ships.

The House being informed Sir John Ashby was at the door, *Sir John Darell* moved that the Speaker would ask him some questions when he came in: to give some account of the transactions of the fleet after the victory and particularly that squadron under his command; and how he executed the orders he had given by the Admiralty to him; and to give his narrative of the whole matter. *Mr. Hampden* to the same.

So Sir John Ashby was called in to the Bar and the *Speaker* asked him the several questions, to which he answered to the following effect:

Our squadron had very little share in the fight, the wind being against us that we could not come up to them, but about 6 I had a brush with the enemy which lasted till near 9. This was the 19th of May, the day of the fight. The next day was thick and rainy, but about 12 it cleared up and I saw 24 of their ships in the Race. 16 of them were by the strength of the tide drove from their anchors, which he thought were those burnt at Cherbourg.

That he saw a sail of 15 which he pursued till he had lost the chase of them; and after consulting with the pilot what he believed were become of them, he said that he believed they had taken the opportunity of that tide and got into St. Malo, on which I told him we must pursue them. The pilot said he would not undertake it to carry in our ships—it being very dangerous and hazardous to the ships—for it being a rough sea and full of rocks, there was no going in if they had taken away the marks, and he would not undertake it though he were hanged for it.

That he had with him 13 English men-of-war on board of which he had but one pilot. The Dutch squadron under Almonde was also with me, but they went thereon to find out the Admiral to give him an account of matters.

Sir John Ashby was ordered then to withdraw. And several members desired some other questions might be asked him. *Col. Granville, Goodwin Wharton*, and *Mr. Clarke* proposed some, and the Clerk noted them in a paper.

Sir John Ashby was called in again and the *Speaker* put the several questions to him, and he answered to the following effect:

When the signal was made for chasing, we all cut and the ships that were lightest came up with me. And I believe none of them had any more pilots on board, for the pilots were distributed chiefly among the great ships.

We did pursue the enemy about the Gascates, and I anchored between Guernsey and the Gascates. Admiral Almonde I did look upon to be under my command, but he bore away without any order from me, though I believe if I had been in his place I should have done as he did; I cannot blame him.

As for calling a council of war, I could not. The tide was so very strong that but two captains could get on board me, and they two were both of opinion it was not advisable to attempt anything upon

St. Malo lest we hazarded the King's ships. One of them was very well acquainted with the port of St. Malo but he would not undertake to carry in a vessel of 60 tons, for the weather was but bad, the entrance into the port very dangerous because of the rocks, so that there was no going in if the enemy had taken down their marks, and the pilot I had would not undertake to carry us in. So that I returned with my squadron after I had done all I could and joined the Admiral in Hogue Bay and gave him an account of matters.

So he withdrew.

Mr. Henry Herbert moved that since Sir John Ashby had given a very good account of the matter required, the sending for him up carrying some reflection on him, he desired the House would make some public declaration of their being satisfied with the account he had given and that he might be acquainted therewith.

Sir John Darell to the same and that the House would further vote him thanks for the good services he had done.

But opposed by *Goodwin Wharton* and *Sir Christopher Musgrave*, for though he was a very brave and stout man, yet they thought it was not becoming the wisdom of the House to give thanks to men for doing their duty.

So that was let fall. But he was called in again and the *Speaker*, by direction, acquainted him that the House was satisfied with the account he had given and was dismissed from further attendance.

Adjourned till Monday morning 10 of the clock.

Monday, 21 November

Order of the Day read for the House to go into a Committee of the Whole House to consider of that part of His Majesty's speech whereby he desires the advice of this House. So the House resolved itself into a Committee of the Whole House and the Speaker left the Chair; Sir Francis Winnington was Chairman. Then the Order of the Day was read again.[1]

Mr. Dolben: I desire for the method of your proceedings that since you are in a Committee of the Whole House to consider of that part of the King's speech which relates to advice that the speech itself may be read over.

[1] For parallel accounts of the debate that followed see Grey, x. 264–74; Nottingham University, Portland MS., PwA 2389; Bodleian Carte MS. 130, ff. 339–40. This debate, with a House 'about 400', lasted over five hours; B.M. Loan 29/186, f. 213.

So His Majesty's speech was read over.

Sir Thomas Clarges: We are now in a Committee of the Whole House to consider of what advice to give the King. The first step, I think, is to know in what state or condition we are now in. We have now been three years in a war against France and unsuccessful therein in a great measure. As this kingdom is an island, our chief security is by sea. But I know not whether by ill management, ignorance, or by unfaithfulness, the first year you set out a fleet, but the French drove you here upon your own coasts. The next year you had a greater, but nothing done. Then the enemy were not to be found. And though this year you had a victory, what fruit thereof when even the conquered now cover your seas so that there is no trading almost for your merchants? I believe since that victory the French have taken not less than 300 ships.

Then for your army at land, I think we have undone our allies. We ought to have applied ourselves to sea and attacked them there—to have burned his ships if possible so to have weakened him there, whereby we should have done ourselves the best service, and not to have gone into Flanders to attack him where he is strongest. Then for the army there, what have they done? Your countrymen, it is true, behaved themselves very bravely and laid a good foundation for an entire victory if they had been seconded as they ought.

Then for your government here at land in the absence of the King, I must say the government here has been very loose; no act done here by the Queen but must first be sent beyond sea to have directions from foreign councils.

Thus I have plainly opened some matters to you. I hope some gentlemen will touch upon a particular head to go upon.

Col. Sackville: As to the war in Flanders, it is a most pernicious war to this nation. The French have so many strong garrisons, there are so many rivers and passes, that [it] is almost impossible to do anything with the French there to our advantage. And though we could perhaps gain a town or two there, what benefit is it to us? It will but put us to a greater expense and not compensate the charge or loss of our men.

Then for your fleet, it is true you had a victory at sea whereby I do believe the French will not dare to meet you at sea to fight. Yet he hath ships enough to transport an army hither and hath 20,000 men lie ready to put on board to invade you, for I doubt not he hath the same design upon you as he had the last year, and therefore I think in the first place you ought to consider of your own safety and the security of the nation.

Mr. Bathurst: I am for an address to His Majesty to take care of the sea and let your confederates take care of the land for I think we get nothing by them. As for our King, though he has the title of Stadtholder in Holland, yet when he goes with the army he has always some of the High and Mighty Deputies with him without whom he can do but little. I am afraid we have some Deputies on board the fleet, too. My advice is for to address to the King to stay at home with us.

Mr. Mordaunt: I will take the freedom to acquaint you with some things that my country I serve for think worthy of your advice and consideration—that our King may stay at home and not expose himself so much. Though I for my part reap the benefit thereof, who have the honour to serve His Majesty in the army, by the warm influence of his presence amongst us, yet for the nation's good I should be contented to be deprived thereof. Then they could wish our army abroad were commanded by our own countrymen; that our Privy Council was wholly free from foreigners; that His Majesty would be pleased to take the advice of his great council here, and in your absence the Privy Council, and not of a cabal of four or five. Then for your allies, that we either take better or mend these we have, and not to pay some for coming late into the field and make them that come sooner do something. I am for giving such advice as may be for the interest of old England and not to have a commonwealth *in commendam*.

Goodwin Wharton: The matter of the King's going beyond sea is a tender part and I would not meddle with it, for I am afraid if it be once made a doubt the confederates will be apt to break, which I would not willingly have, being I think it is a great security to you. There is one thing, I confess, I do not like—the putting foreigners over your men. You see the mischievous consequences of it the last year in Flanders where, for want of your men being seconded, you lost the prospect of a great victory. Then for the sea affairs, I will not reflect on the management of those gentlemen that have the care thereof but I may venture to say matters have not been as they ought. Therefore if you please to, make it one head of your advice that His Majesty would be pleased to put in some seamen amongst them that understand those affairs better.

Then for the affairs of your civil government and first for your Secretary of State, I think to have but one is too much for one man only. Then he that is in that station ought to have courage and resolution and to be of a free and generous temper—the first to enable him to go through his business without fear and the other to be liberal in rewarding men for intelligence and services done. Then we have a thing called a Cabinet Council, which is not for your service because therein you cannot know who they are that give ill advice, and therefore if we must have it I desire they may be obliged to set their hands to the advice they give so we shall know who to blame for this and they may answer for it. There are many other things out of order; your militia in the country and in London, too, want to be regulated. I am not for making parties and factions and would have only two—who are for this government and who against it. There is also another thing worthy your care to do something in—the unhappy falling out between the Queen and the Princess. Therefore if you think fit to, send three or four members to wait on the Queen and the Princess to see how that matter stands and to put some end thereto, if possible.

Mr. Robert Harley: That we may have some fruit of this day's debate, I desire for method sake you will first go upon the consideration of the fleet, which is your chief care. You had a great victory at sea this summer but your enemies reap the benefit thereof by their trade, of which you may soon be masters if you will make yourselves entire masters at sea.

Mr. Waller (of Bucks.) was for addressing to the King to put the Admiralty into such hands as are able, both for skill and fidelity, for that place.

Goodwin Wharton: I am absolutely against the last word 'fidelity' in the question for I think there is not the least pretence to question the same. But I think it necessary to have some seamen among them, and therefore I am for the question. Upon this head of the sea there are two matters worthy your consideration—one, to impoverish France by reducing the two northern Crowns to prohibit a trade with France, for at this time they carry on an open trade therewith and furnish them with naval stores without which they could not subsist. And though it will be objected that you will hereby oblige them to break with you, perhaps Denmark may but then Sweden will join with you. The other thing is I would let privateers go abroad and give them the prizes they take to encourage them. And if these two things were done you would quickly find the benefit.

Sir Charles Sedley was for the address about the Admiralty.

Mr. Smith: It is certainly the interest of this nation to unite at this time for our common preservation and to proceed in matters fairly without any consideration of friendship. As to those gentlemen who have the management of your fleet, I doubt not of their fidelity and industry; but if they had as much skill too, as long as they have not power within themselves but must receive their orders from above from others, I expect no better success. There is the true reason of the miscarriage of the descent.

But then for the taking so many merchant ships, the reason thereof is for want of cruisers at the mouth of your Channel to guard your merchants. Then great embargoes and for a long time have been laid on them that they could not get out in a considerable time. Then for those cruisers you have, when they came in to clean they have lain long in port without orders to careen; and when they have, have lain long after it. But on the whole matter, I close with the question proposed.

Sir John Knight: I think the mismanagement of all your affairs and miscarriage of the same proceeds from your secret cabal. I do not think you are yet ripe for the question about the Admiralty.

Mr. Dolben: I will not oppose your question, but wish when we change we may change for the better.

Sir Richard Onslow spoke in justification of the Commissioners of the Admiralty.

Col. Granville spoke very largely against them, and assured the House that he had not any enmity to the persons entrusted therewith but they were very wise and honest gentlemen, faithful to this government. But he thought this burden too great for their experience and did believe the government thought so too by reserving a power to send what orders they thought fit, and therefore I think your question is very necessary.

Lord Falkland: I wish your change of the Admiralty may procure a remedy for your distemper. I am afraid not but that the true cause of these mischiefs complained of proceeds from the want of cruisers and convoys, of which sort of ships there is great want. I told you so the last year that your service would suffer for want of them when you denied the building of four, and now you have not so many by reason of the great squadrons going to the Straits and to the West Indies. Then his Lordship reflected on the merchants' petition and the report from the committee thereon, took notice of some omissions therein and reflected on the same, and concluded he doubted not but the Chairman [Col. Granville] had made a report according to his ability.

So there was some contest between Col. Granville and the Lord Falkland about it, on which Sir Thomas Clarges called to the orders of the House—that when a matter is reported from a committee and the House hath approved of it, it is not very usual to have the Chairman or committee to be arraigned as that noble lord hath. But now to the matter. Your losses, I doubt not, are very great in merchant ships. I would not have them made more particular; I think it is not for the interest of the nation. Then I am sure the want of seamen cannot be pretended. We are obliged by our treaty with Holland to furnish 50 men-of-war in all, 15 frigates, and 10 fireships, on board of which are to be 17,000 men; and in the estimate for your Navy you allowed for 30,000 seamen round the whole year, so that there is 13,000 remaining to be employed in trade.

Sir Edward Seymour: If this House once come to make a doubt of their alliances, I am afraid you will do yourselves most disservice for they will be beforehand with you; they can have a peace and you cannot. I am, indeed, of the opinion your safety lies chiefly in your fleet, but if you have a great fleet to go only from Spithead westward and so come back that will not do; something further must be attempted. Then to the power of the Commissioners of the Admiralty, it is as large as any ever were; the government in all times did exercise a power to lay embargoes and order matters as to the grand fleet. But then for convoys, you want ships of that kind; you have not sufficient for your grand fleet and to carry on trade, too, which if you will do you must have more ships and that cannot be without money. Now as to your question, I am not for it. I think you ought to examine matters a little better before you so severely reflect on gentlemen who, though perhaps they had not the experience requisite at first, yet now I believe they have it at your costs, and therefore I think they may be serviceable.

Sir Thomas Clarges: I do not think we ought to change hands in the Admiralty only but in all other places. And for your Admiral himself, I think it is too great a trust to be lodged in one man's hands but he ought to have some joined with him.

Col. Austen: I will not confess myself so ignorant as some think me. You have been told you have not ships enough for your service, and it is true. Then for the complaint as to the merchants, I observe it is only proved by insurers and hence arises the losses in a great measure.

The merchants get leave to go, pretending to be bound to such a port where a convoy is going; and when they have got such orders, away they go to other ports and that without a convoy, only for the sake of the first market. Then they insure their ships and so venture home without convoys. If the ship be lost, they have their loss of the insurer, so the merchant has no prejudice but the kingdom. But if the ship come home safe, the merchant gains mightily by having his commodity the first market, and hence arises your great losses by this method of insurance.

Sir Robert Cotton and Capt. Pitt spoke as to the truth of the report from the committee; and the latter said that he believed 1,200 of the 1,500 ships that were taken were taken within the Soundings, in the chops of the Channel, for want of stationary ships to guard them. That as to the number of them taken belonging to the several ports of this kingdom, they would by far exceed the number of 1,500—nay, that he believed there were more taken than were left in the kingdom. Then he desired to know that since the winter was come on so far, how it comes to pass there is no winter guard at sea? And though it is said it is no sign of the decrease of the trade of this nation because the customs are as high as usual, yet it arises not from thence but because of the great duties now on commodities, but if you abstract all the new duties from the old you will find a difference.

Paul Foley: I have seen many of your orders relating to the descent, and all come from one man and no more sign it. This, I think, is too much for one, for if the French can corrupt him it is in this man's power to render your fleet ineffectual, and therefore I am for changing hands to see what success then you shall have.

Lord Castleton moved for to put the question.

Sir Christopher Musgrave was for the question and took notice of the irregularity in arraigning a committee.

Sir Robert Cotton (of Post Office): I think it very hard to make a vote against these gentlemen, who are men of credit, and that without hearing them. I am informed by intelligent merchants that the loss is not so great as represented to this House, and therefore I am against the question.

Sir John Lowther: I should not trouble you at this time but that I think there is something in the question which will not be for your service and which is fit for you to consider—that way of insurance in the City. A merchant when he has freighted a ship, he goes and insures the same; if it comes home safe he makes 40 per cent, if not he has his own by insurance so minds not much what becomes of the ship. Then as to your question, I am against the latter part of it; you will take it out of the hands of the Crown to interpose any ways in matters of the fleet, which has ever been the custom in this nation.

Mr. Finch: When I am to pass a judgement upon men I must have something to found my judgement on which I see not in this case, and therefore I am against your question.

Col. Churchill: As to the management of matters in the fleet, it has been somewhat strange. Men have been preferred to commands in it no ways fit for it—such as have not been seamen but bred a brewer's clerk, particularly one Capt. Warren. There is another condemned for cowardice in betraying one of your men-of-war to the enemy without fighting in the West Indies—one Capt. Bumsted.

Sir Robert Rich answered and gave an account of Capt. Warren, and that he did believe the wound lay not in the Admiralty but that as long as captains take convoy money you will find your service no better employed.

Col. Churchill: I hope as you made some examples for taking convoy money, so you will put the question and do your Admiralty justice.

Attorney General, Lord Coningsby, Solicitor General, Admiral Russell, Sir Stephen Fox, and Sir Orlando Gee were all against the question proposed.

However at last the question was put and resolved: That it is the opinion of this committee that, pursuant to His Majesty's speech, His Majesty be humbly advised to constitute a Commission of Admiralty of such persons as have known experience in maritime affairs and that all orders to the fleet may pass through the said Commissioners so constituted.

Sir Francis Winnington was then ordered to report the Committee of the Whole House had sat and made some progress and had directed him to move the House to have leave to sit again. So the Speaker resumed the Chair and *he* reported accordingly, and the House resolved to sit again on Wednesday next, and nothing to intervene.

So the House adjourned till tomorrow morning 10 of the clock.

Tuesday, 22 November

The bill for granting to the partners concerned in the convex lights a longer term was read the second time.

Sir William Wogan opposed the committing of it for that this bill was to confirm a monopoly, and it has been found so in Chancery in the contest between the patentees and the tin men on which the latter had for their interest £4,000. Then the patent itself is void in law, being not granted to the first inventor.

Then the Order of the Day was read for going into a Committee of the Whole House to consider of the motion for a supply. So the Speaker left the Chair and the Attorney General took the Chair of the committee, and the order was read again.

Marquess of Winchester: You are now in a Committee of the Whole House to consider of a motion you had made in the House for a supply for His Majesty and, if you please, I move you to vote a supply for His Majesty for carrying on the war. Sir Scrope Howe seconded the same.

Lord Cornbury: I am for this question but would go a little further —that the House be moved that His Majesty will be pleased to lay before the House a state of the war for the Army and Navy for the next year.

But this was opposed by some who thought it irregular and that it was a distinct matter.

Then a debate arose about the words of the question and a question was put whether the word 'vigorous' should stand part of the question, and carried it should. Then the whole question was put and resolved: That it is the opinion of this committee that a supply be granted to Their Majesties for carrying on a vigorous war against France.

Mr. Pelham and Col. Beaumont moved that the House should be moved that His Majesty be humbly desired to lay before the House a state of the war for the year 1693 in relation to the Navy and the land forces. Which was ordered accordingly, though it was irregular before see[ing] whether the House agree to the vote for a supply.

So the Chairman was ordered to report to the House the said resolution and to move for leave to sit again. So *he* reported the said resolution to the House, to which they agreed *nemine contradicente*. Then *he* moved that His Majesty might be humbly addressed to lay before the House a state of the war for the next year, and ordered accordingly by the members of the Privy Council. So *he* moved for leave for the committee to sit again; so resolved that on Friday morning next at etc. this House will resolve itself into a Committee of the Whole House to consider further of the supply to be granted to Their Majesties for carrying on a vigorous war against France.

Then the translations and abstracts of the several alliances was read:

1. That between the Emperor and the States General of 12 May 1689 into which we came 8 September 1689.
2. That between the Emperor and the King and the King of Spain of 31 December 1689.
3. That between England, the States General, and the Duke of Savoy, 20 October 1690, with a secret article for the restoration of the Vaudois.
4. That between England and Holland of 29 April 1689 for joining their fleets.
5. That between England and Holland of 24 August 1689 of a league offensive and defensive by sea and land with all their force.
6. That between England and Denmark, 3 November 1690, with a secret article to assist each other, with such a number of forces, in case of invasion.
7. That between England and the Elector of Brandenburg of 16 May 1690 with a secret article to assist each other, with such a number of men and ships.
8. That between England, Holland, and the Duke of Hanover of 29 June 1692 wherein agreement is made with him to furnish 7,940 men—horse, foot, and dragoons.

Then the abstracts of the several leagues were read. And it was remarked upon them that they were offensive and defensive, *totis viribus*.

Sir Thomas Clarges took notice herein that Holland and the Emperor were the principals in the war; that Spain was to be drawn in by the Emperor as we were by the Dutch; that though we were drawn in by them, yet we were higher charged in proportion than they. In the fleet we are to find five parts in eight parts and they but three; then in the subsistence to Savoy we are to find 20,000 crowns a month and the Dutch but 10,000—a great inequality when heretofore, in former leagues, we were always equal.

Some members on motion were added to several particular committees.

Moved for Mr. Finch to have leave to attend a cause in the House of Lords. But opposed for that it countenanced the Lords' usurped jurisdiction in the matter of appeals. So refused.

So adjourned till tomorrow morning 9 of the clock.

Wednesday, 23 November

Sir Thomas Clarges presented the petition of one Abel Atwood and Ann, his wife, praying leave to bring in a bill for sale of lands etc. for payment of debts.

But *Sir Edward Seymour* opposed it as an unjust thing, for by doing it you will give an encouragement to all extravagant persons who run out their estates and then come here to you to sell their estates thereby to disinherit their heirs, who are infants, or no need to come to you —they themselves may do it without a bill.

So upon the question for reading the petition, it was carried in the negative.

Then the Order of the Day was read and the House went into a Committee of the Whole House upon that part of His Majesty's speech which relates to advice: Sir Francis Winnington Chairman. So the Order of the Day was read again.[1]

Mr. Mordaunt: I have been told by some that the last time you were in a committee upon this subject I was too hot and that I said more than was fit for a young man to say. A lord told me so. But I am sorry I was not plainer. I think he has been too long here already; and if elder men will not, younger men must see to rectify abuses. The last time you met you made a considerable progress, but if you stop there you had as good do nothing. But I hope you will not let those gentlemen be the only sufferers. If ignorance was their only fault, that is not any fault of their own.

Then for the administration of affairs here by the Queen in the King's absence, I wish she had dispatched more herself without sending abroad for orders. Then I think it is too much for one man to manage all matters of state; all orders come from him alone, even to the licensing of books. Then to the army, where I believe I shall not long continue, and therefore I shall speak of some of our grievances. You were yesterday talking of land admirals, I am sure we had in the army sea generals. Then there are great arrears to the army; at most the soldiers never received more than subsistence money and the officers but half-pay, and this was not constantly paid. But I hear it is pretended by some that the army exacted great sums of money of the people in Ireland. I know of no such thing and I wish the gentlemen that came lately out of those parts will make it out.

[1] For parallel accounts of the debate that followed see Grey, x. 252–63 (misdated 21 Nov.); Nottingham University, Portland MS., PwA 2385.

Lord Coningsby: There was great misdemeanours committed by the army in Ireland but the government there was not able to suppress them. The power then was in the general of the army and not in the civil power.

Sir Peter Colleton: I think it is not consistent with the interest of this kingdom for to have foreign officers over an English army when we have so many brave, courageous men amongst us. The Englishman can have no interest but the good of his own country; what foreigners may have I cannot tell. There are few persons but have heard of the action last summer at Steinkirk and how your men were served. I fear it may be of fatal consequence, and therefore I think it a head worthy of your advice that our English armies may be commanded by natives of our own.

Goodwin Wharton to the same, that the world may see the English are able to officer their own armies.

Lord Falkland: I am very sensible of the merit of the English soldiers and also of their courage, and doubt not the King is so also. And therefore I would not have this come from us but from himself, who I doubt not will take care therein, and therefore I desire you to suspend this for the present.

Sir Robert Cotton (of Cheshire) was for the general officers to be English.

Sir Edward Seymour: I would not have this House run hastily upon any advice to be given to the Crown; it will come better with more deliberation. Now as to the army I will venture to say this (because I know it): [the] army was never better paid; the common soldiers have their subsistence money duly paid them, viz. 6*d.* a day; there is a day out of the off-reckonings goes for the clothes and other necessaries; but it is true the officers have but half-pay.

Then as to the complaints about the soldiers, I fear it is not without some reason in Ireland. There are commissioners appointed to inspect these matters—what there is due from the army to the country and what arrears are due to the army. I do believe the army is indebted to the country, the cause of which, I am afraid, arises hence: the officers have not their full pay so are apt to detain the soldiers' subsistence money to supply themselves, whereby they must live upon the country.

Then for foreign general officers, it is fit for you to consider very well of it before you advise the removing them, for a man is not born a general but attains it by time and long experience. And if you remove the present, I am afraid you will find a want to supply them. They are not many and are such persons as assisted in bringing about the present happy revolution.

Then the Chairman stated the question.

Sir John Lowther: I do agree this nation is in much better condition as to martial affairs than two years since, which is owing in a great measure to this happy revolution, and I doubt not but in a little time we may have general officers of our own. But we have lost four since this government: two died by sickness, Douglas and Kirk; and two were killed the last summer, Mackay and Lanier. So that there is not that plenty of Englishmen fit for that service. But if you make the question that for the future no foreigner shall be put in, I will be for it. But I think it very hard to turn out them that are in who have done you good service.

Sir Charles Sedley was for restraining them for the future.

Lord Ranelagh: There is no man desires more the preferring of Englishmen than I do but yet I cannot be for turning out the present general officers. The number of them is very small; besides divers of them are English and others of them are naturalized, except two. They were concerned in bringing about this revolution; they ventured their life very freely for your service in Ireland; and now to turn them out is a little ungrateful. Then I would not have you yet meddle in it till you see whom His Majesty will put in for the year ensuing; perhaps most of them, if not all, may be English.

Sir Thomas Clarges: I am well assured we have natives sufficient of these kingdoms that are experienced in affairs of war; nay, that if they were in other kingdoms would have been marshals before now. You have several of them; and for my part I would not open my mouth for them but that I desire as the King hath the purses, so he may have the hearts of his people. And I do it seriously for the service of this government to hinder jealousies among his soldiers who are not very willing to serve under foreign officers and prevent alienating the affections of His Majesty's people, and therefore think it necessary our army be commanded by English officers.

Sir Robert Howard: I am afraid the question you have before you will not answer His Majesty's service, and therefore I am against it.

Lord Colchester: I will do justice to all persons and give you some account of the action at Steinkirk, on which gentlemen have made their reflections and which I find sticks much with them. I think the chief occasion of our miscarriage there was the King's being wrongly informed in the ground; it was enclosed ground whereby our horse and foot were intermixed, which ought not to have been. The attack on the left, where I was, was composed of troops of the Dutch, English, and Brandenburgs, who behaved themselves very well. Monsieur Ouwerkirk exposed himself to the greatest hazards and your men beat the French from hedge to hedge for some time till we were over-powered by numbers and forced to give way. But we made good our retreat in the face of the enemy who dared not to attack us.

Lord Castleton: There were many reports about that action at Steinkirk, more than were true, particularly a discourse said to be between Count Solms and myself which was all a story. But, however, I am of opinion if you had all English officers then, you would have had a better account thereof, and therefore I am for the question.

Col. Erle gave an account of the action at Steinkirk (much as the Lord Colchester) and spoke as to the courage of the English, which he thought very great, but therefore I do not think them presently fit for generals. For my part, I have served this four years in the army as a private colonel but do assure you cannot pretend to any great skill in such matters, and therefore before you put the question I desire gentlemen will think a little where they will supply the places of those you turn out. Lord Coningsby to the same.

Mr. Bertie: I am for letting this alone till we see what His Majesty himself will do as to the general officers.

Col. Godfrey: There has been much complaint of the action at Steinkirk, perhaps not without some reason. But this I will say: if your men had been supported you might have had a better account, but if you had not succeeded you had hazarded all your army and Flanders, too. I was on the right in the attack but was only passive. Your men behaved themselves bravely and were merely overpowered by numbers, and I think in such circumstances the prudentest part was to make a safe retreat, which we did. The chief reason of our miscarriage was the King was misinformed in the ground; it was enclosures and not capable to form a line. I must declare I saw no miscarriage in any officers but all served you bravely. Therefore I am against the question for the time present, but if you please that for the future none but English be preferred, I am for it.

Col. Cornewall: I am sorry to see that your English officers are so fond of foreigners; I doubt not but they will make their hearts ache before they have done. There is Lieutenant-General Tollemache who has served as long as any of the general officers you have now in pay. But as to a general of horse, I think you cannot supply his place. But for foot, I am sure you have many as fit as Count Solms, for he was made a general officer but just on this revolution and General Tollemache deserves it better and has served longer and done as bravely as any ever did. Count Solms is a proud, haughty man, and not at all grateful to your men nor treats your officers with any civility. I am told General Tollemache sent an aide-de-camp to Count Solms for orders to sustain our men, but he would not admit it.

Lord Colchester: I think there is not a braver man in the world than General Tollemache nor one who has done you so signal service, fitter to command your men and not in the least inferior to Count Solms.

Col. Godfrey spoke also in praise of Tollemache; and that one Ross told me he was sent by Lieutenant-General Tollemache to Count Solms, that with 10 battalions he would rescue our men, but Ross said of Count Solms, 'damn him, he would not go near him'.

Goodwin Wharton: I have spoke with several officers, and they all speak with some indignation of Count Solms. And since it is said the King intends to send a list of general officers, I think now is the properest time to advise about it, and therefore pray put the question.

Mr. Waller and the Lord Norris were for such general officers only as were naturalized.

Mr. Smith: It is the endeavour of the enemies of this government to corrupt the people with the thoughts of governing with a standing army and that we have so many foreigners brought hither to govern us. I think it necessary for you to give some satisfaction in this particular and to pass a vote that no foreign officers shall for the future command your army. I am not for us to turn out generals or put in others.

Sir John Guise: I desire you will word the question, 'that for the future', etc. And as to Count Solms, against whom some gentlemen have objected, I believe he will not command your army again because I am well informed he is gone to command in Germany.

Col. Cornewall: I know Count Solms very well and do not believe him near so good an officer as represented. He is no old officer neither nor had any high command in the army till this revolution when His present Majesty preferred him. I do really think Lieutenant-General Tollemache a better soldier and one who has done you extraordinary service and is well beloved by the soldiers, which the other is not, and therefore I am for an address to His Majesty to lay Count Solms aside.

Sir Christopher Musgrave: Some gentlemen have spoke against the question in general and said it is unseasonable. I think not, for now is the time, if ever, before the King does settle the general officers, for afterward you will be cramped and told the King is a great soldier, knows better who is fit to command than we do. Therefore I desire you will proceed in it now. Then for the words proposed to be added to the question 'for the future'; this, I think, is approving of all that are now in and to continue them, and then I think there is no need of your address. As for Lieutenant-General Tollemache, whom I take leave to name, I think he deserves as well as any in the world, but I do not think it decent in the House to name one to His Majesty. But I am in general for an address to His Majesty that the general of the foot may be an Englishman.

Sir Edward Seymour: The King desires your advice, but he requires it not only from the House of Commons but from the Parliament, and therefore I am for giving such advice as we may justify and not for us to advise one thing and the Lords may the quite contrary.

Sir Edward Hussey: I hope such doctrine shall not pass here; that would lay aside all advice. As there are lords to advise and consult with, so I hope there will always be commoners in this House who will be faithful to this nation, though I see some men by preferment have their mouths gagged up against the interest of the people. Yet I am for this question that no foreign officers be preferred to any vacancy for the future and that an address be made to His Majesty to lay aside Count Solms.

Mr. Bertie: I see no reason for us to sit still to see what the Lords will do. His Majesty desires your advice, and as one part of it I desire you will put the question.

Mr. Hampden called in a heat to the orders of the House and spoke against making reflections on any persons in the House. It is wholly irregular and not to be suffered. Then to the question you are upon, I think it not for your service, and therefore I am for laying aside the whole debate.

Lord Norris proposed the inserting in the question these words— 'or such as shall be naturalized'.

Mr. Harley proposed at the end of the question to add 'that the general of the foot may be an Englishman'.

Mr. Foley: There are many mischiefs which arise from the general officers of an army being foreigners. It often occasions a great discontent through the army and tends to prolong and spin out a war. For my part, I am for Englishmen who are men of estates; they will be for the interest of this nation because they have a stake in the hedge, and will be therefore willing to put an end to this war and make not a trade of war. Then when you have foreign officers, the orders are sent down frequently to other inferior officers in a language they do not generally understand—either Dutch or French.

Lord Castleton: Orders were sent to me in French, which I profess neither I nor any of my officers understood.

Sir Thomas Littleton: I am for the question that for the future no vacancies be filled up with general officers but of such persons as are natives of Their Majesty's dominions.

Mr. Montagu: I desire that you will state a question and keep us to that, or else we shall never come to an end of the debate.

Col. Granville: Your regular question is the first, and if any desire to add the words 'for the future' thereto, they must be brought in by a question and such amendment must be first put. Mr. Goodwin Wharton and Sir Christopher Musgrave to the same.

Mr. Clarke, Mr. Herbert, and Sir Walter Yonge and Sir Robert Rich were for inserting the words 'for the future' in the question.

So the amendment proposed was put to the question and carried to be inserted in the question.

Then it was moved to make another amendment—to add at the end of the question 'that the English foot might be commanded by a native of Their Majesties' dominions'.

This took up some debate, and was opposed by Sir John Lowther and Mr. Montagu, who moved to insert the words 'as often as vacancies shall happen' before the other amendment, being first in order in the question and therefore ought to be first put or by adding the amendment at last you will exclude the other.

The question was put for the amendment about the general of the English foot and carried. Then the amendment 'as often as vacancies shall happen' was put and carried.

So the whole question was put and **carried:** That it is the opinion of this committee that the House be moved that His Majesty be humbly advised that for the future, as often as vacancies shall happen, no persons be appointed general officers of the English army but such as are natives of Their Majesties' dominions and that the general of the English foot be a native of Their Majesties' dominions.

So the Chairman was ordered to report the committee had made some further progress and desired leave to sit again. So the Speaker resumed the Chair and [*Sir Francis Winnington*] reported accordingly and made a motion for the committee to sit again. Resolved that the House would go into a Committee of the Whole House on Saturday morning next to consider further of His Majesty's speech desiring the advice of this House, and nothing to intervene.

So adjourned till 10 tomorrow morning.

Thursday, 24 November

Mr. Clarke presented the petition of Blackwell Hall factors against the bill for encouraging the woollen manufactory.

Mr. Nicholas presented the bill against hawkers and pedlars, entitled 'for preventing the decay of trade in cities, corporations, and market towns'.

Sir John Darell presented the petition of Mr. Vernatti against the bill for convex lights.

Sir John Morton presented the petition of the Horners Company against the said bill.

Sir John Mainwaring presented another from the Tallow Chandlers Company against the said bill.

Mr. Smith presented the petition of the merchants and others against the East India Company.

Then the House, according to order, resolved itself into a Committee of the Whole House to consider of heads for a bill to preserve, regulate, and establish the East India trade. Mr. Smith took the Chair of the committee. Then the Order of the Day was read, with several other orders and petitions and other matters referred to this committee.

Sir Robert Howard moved to proceed head by head in order to frame a bill for a new East India company.

Sir Peter Colleton was against the old and against the new company and a joint stock as pernicious to trade, but was for a regulated company—being most for the interest of the nation.

Sir Samuel Dashwood: The body of the General Court of Adventurers of the old East India Company are willing to submit to any regulations the House or this committee shall think fit to make, though it is true the private committees are against it.

Sir John Lowther was for closing with that motion, and desired pursuant thereto the House would go upon the King's regulations and frame a bill, and this will shorten your work.

Sir Samuel Barnardiston: I am well assured this trade cannot be carried on but in a joint stock. I was formerly of this Company and remember in Oliver's time the trade was open, which had near endangered the loss of the trade, and so they were forced to get a charter for a joint stock to preserve it.

Mr. Finch: I think the first foundation you are to make is for the carrying on this trade and that by a joint stock.

Resolved that the East India trade be carried on by a joint stock.

It was proposed to add the words at the end of the question 'exclusive of all others'. But it was opposed by those that were for a new company. And after some debate the question was put to add them, but carried in the negative.

Then the *quantum* of the stock was proposed and resolved that a sum not less than £1,500,000 and not exceeding £2,000,000 be the fund for carrying on the trade to the East Indies.

Then the time for the continuance of this trade was proposed. Resolved that the joint stock of a company to trade to the East Indies be for 21 years and no longer.

Then the persons who should have this trade were proposed and resolved that the joint stock of a company to trade to the East Indies be made by new subscriptions.

Then the sum that persons should subscribe was moved and resolved that no one person shall subscribe less than £100 or above £10,000 in a joint stock of a company trading to the East Indies, and the persons so subscribing shall pay in a third part of the sum subscribed at the time of the said subscription.

So he was ordered to leave the Chair and to ask leave to sit again and [to report] that the committee had made some further progress. So the Speaker resumed the Chair, and *Mr. Smith* reported the Committee of the Whole House had sat and made some further progress and then he moved for a further day to sit again. Resolved the House would go into a Committee of the Whole House again on Tuesday next to consider of heads for a bill for preserving and establishing the East India trade.

Some gentlemen on motions were added to several particular committees.

Adjourned till 9 tomorrow morning.

Friday, 25 November

The estimate of the charge of the Navy for the year 1693, presented by the *Lord Falkland,* was read. The list of the land forces for the service of the year 1693, presented by the *Lord Ranelagh,* was also read.[1]

Mr. Harley: You have now read the estimates, and I desire they may be referred to a Committee of the Whole House and not to go roundabout as done the last sessions to a private committee.

Sir Thomas Clarges: The estimates you have now read come to a very great sum of money; I wish the nation be able to pay it. I observe in that of your army there are forces for Ireland and for abroad, whereby I find poor England must bear all. I am for their lying on the Table for two or three days for gentlemen to look over them, unless we must vote all in a lump.

Sir John Lowther: I am for referring them to the Committee of the Whole House to consider thereof, who are to sit this day.

Sir Christopher Musgrave: I cannot agree with the gentleman that moved last, for that it is impossible for gentlemen to debate so many particulars without some time to consider of them.

Lord Eland and *Col. Cornewall* were for putting them off.

Mr. Montagu and *Lord Coningsby* were for referring them to the Committee of the Whole House immediately.

Sir Stephen Fox assured the House that the Exchequer at this time was very low; that there was not enough in it to continue the weekly payments; that they had already taken up on the clause of credit in the poll act about £500,000 and can get no more unless this House do give some life thereto—there remaining yet about £180,000 to be taken up thereon.

Sir Edward Seymour: I would not delay this matter too long, for to delay is next door to denying. But because we may be unanimous, I desire the estimates may lie on the Table till Tuesday next.

Resolved to go into a Committee of the Whole House on Tuesday next to consider of the supplies to be granted to Their Majesties, and the said estimates were referred to the same committee.

Adjourned till tomorrow morning 9 of the clock.

---

[1] Grey, x. 279–81 has a parallel account of the debate that follows.

Saturday, 26 November

Mr. Waller presented the petition in behalf of the Quakers.

Sir Thomas Clarges complained of a breach of privilege committed upon Sir Carbery Price, a member of this House, in bringing an information of intrusion against him in the Court of Exchequer touching certain lead mines of his, pretending them to be royal mines. This gentleman, having had two trials already touching the same and verdicts for him both times, and now they are bringing it about again, so there is no end. And though it be in the King's case, yet I desire this gentleman may have the privilege of the House. *Sir Edward Seymour* to the same, and said it was abominable.

Resolved that Sir Carbery Price have the privilege of this House against the said information.

Col. Churchill complained of the Lords of the Admiralty who had summoned him before their Board to give an account of what he had said in the House relating to the cowardice of some persons that Board had preferred to the command of ships, which he thought a breach of the privilege of the House and would not give any answer thereto till he knew the pleasure of the House.[1]

Col. Austen, Sir John Lowther, Sir Robert Rich acquainted the House that it was only upon the account of a person condemned for cowardice in betraying a ship in the West Indies unto the French. The King had been pleased to refer it to the consideration of the Admiralty Board to see if the man be a fit object for the King's mercy.

Mr. Hampden and several others spoke against its being a breach of privilege.

Paul Foley: I think this is a very great breach of privilege; to require an account of what said or done in the House is certainly so and then to threaten your member by tendering an oath is insufferable. I desire, therefore, as usual you will take the member's information and state the fact on your paper, and then you ought to hear the gentlemen concerned to it in their places, and then they are to withdraw. *Sir Christopher Musgrave* to the same.

Many persons spoke on the behalf of the Commissioners of the Admiralty, who denied the fact as stated and that they did not require an account of what said in the House, but that he being a captain of a ship was under their jurisdiction and the words he had said publicly abroad in other places of which they spoke to him about.

[1] Grey, x. 281–5 has a somewhat fuller account of the debate on Churchill's case.

Sir Christopher Musgrave: I think you ought to do something in this matter; and therefore, if you please, in general to pass a declaratory vote to this effect—that it is the undoubted privilege of the House that no member be questioned for anything said in the House.

But this was thought by several to be unnecessary because it is the known, undoubted right of the House. So the matter was let fall.

House went into a Committee of the Whole House upon that part of His Majesty's speech relating to advice; Sir Francis Winnington to the Chair.[1]

Mr. Foley: You have two great matters before you—the consideration of the fleet and the army. At the first beginning of this war, you had a powerful enemy to deal with—the King of France—who was then ready to swallow up Europe, till Holland, foreseeing the common ruin, began to make confederacies against him, and hence arose their coming hither to assist you that by a joint uniting all your forces you might be able to oppose him. But what fruit have you had of this? You have prohibited all trade and commerce with France but even at this time several of your allies openly trade with him. Then to your success by land, he has taken several towns from the confederates and they not one from him. You had a victory at sea last summer, but what advantage have we reaped thereby? England bears almost the charge of the war and others reap the benefit of it. Then you are talking here of a descent upon France and they are really designing one upon you, which is more than ever the French dared to talk of heretofore. Now the reason hereof may be our great divisions at home and the management of our affairs here that encourage them to it. We have enemies here amongst us who will for money betray our concerns to the French. Then for the management of matters, how near was our Smyrna fleet falling into the hands of the French? What destruction among your men-of-war had you at Plymouth by keeping your great men of war at sea after we had notice our enemies had laid up theirs? Then the beginning of this last summer, how near were you to an invasion? What good intelligence have we when he can draw together so many men and transport ships and yet we hear nothing of it? They that manage things thus, I am afraid, at last will betray you, either by treachery or want of intelligence. Then for your army, they have committed great irregularities, been quartered upon several gentlemen—nay, in diverse places have taken free quarter. Then

[1] For parallel accounts of the debate that follows see Grey, x. 274–9 (misdated 23 Nov.); Nottingham University, Portland MS., PwA 2387.

there is another thing—the setting guards upon persons after they have been discharged by due course of law. That which I shall then move you is that it is the opinion of this committee that in regard many of the great affairs of the government have been for the time past unsuccessfully managed by those who have had the direction thereof under Their Majesties, the House be moved humbly to advise Their Majesties to prevent the like mischiefs for the future by employing men of known ability and integrity. Lord Castleton to the same.

So the question was put and resolved *nemine contradicente.*

Sir William Strickland moved that His Majesty be humbly advised that all matters of state may be resolved on and determined in the Privy Council and that the management of state affairs by a Cabinet Council is dangerous and destructive to the government. Edmund Waller seconded the same.

Sir Richard Temple opposed it for that there is no government but has a secret council for some matters. You complain of your councils being betrayed, but do you think by having them discovered to more persons they will be the more concealed?

Sir John Lowther to the same very zealously, for that a Cabinet Council or a committee of Council is what this nation never was without for the management of the more important affairs.

Edmund Waller: I find many gentlemen do not relish this question but are for naming of persons. I hope there are some Englishmen in this House who are not afraid to do it and to prefer an impeachment against any person, if occasion. But perhaps we are not come to a head proper for that purpose, though in general I think many of our miscarriages come from the want of intelligence by the Secretary.

Goodwin Wharton, Sir Thomas Clarges, and others spoke to this.

Paul Foley: Since as long as there is a Cabinet Council we cannot tell who to accuse for ill advice, I desire that all persons who give any advice in matters of government may set their hands to it by way of assent to or dissent from it. Sir Edward Hussey to the same.

But these motions fell. So the Chairman was ordered to report further progress and to desire leave to sit again and to leave the Chair, all which he did upon several questions. Speaker resumed the Chair. *Sir Francis Winnington* reported accordingly and moved to sit again, and ordered again on Wednesday next.

Mr. Palmes reported from the committee about the descent the proceedings touching the same.

It was moved by some to recommit the said report to the same committee to consider of it further, to report their opinions thereon, and to come to some resolution, for now they had only reported matter of fact.

But it was opposed by *Sir Edward Seymour, Sir Christopher Musgrave,* etc. for that the House was not as yet possessed of the report because they have not read it. But if the Chairman, when [he] reported it, had at the beginning desired an enlargement of their order so as to report their opinions, it might have been referred to that committee. But when the whole is reported, no exception can be taken to any part of it till the House become possessed of it by reading it at the Table, after which any member may take exception to it or then the House may refer it back to the same committee.

Ordered that the said report be read on Monday morning next.

House adjourned till Monday morning 9 of the clock.

Monday, 28 November

Sir Walter Yonge presented the petition from the gentlemen, clothiers and others in the West, touching the woollen manufacture.

Sir Joseph Tredenham, Sir Edward Seymour, etc. promoted the bringing in a list of the fees of the several courts of justice, etc.

It was moved also that the spiritual courts and register might do the same. But the first was thought sufficient at present lest the matter should be clogged too much.

Order of the Day read for going into a Committee of the Whole House about the bill for regulating trials in cases of treason. The House being very thin of the gentlemen of the long robe, the Serjeant went with the Mace to the several courts of justice in Westminster Hall, requiring the immediate attendance of the members. And he being returned, the House resolved into a committee upon the said bill; Mr. Harcourt to the Chair as Chairman. Then the order of the House was read. Then the Clerk read the bill over, which contained these several heads: that each person indicted, etc., shall have a copy of the indictment before he pleads, so many days; shall make his defence by counsel; the party's witnesses to be on oath; judges shall assign him counsel; none to be convicted of treason but on oath of two lawful witnesses to the same treason; none to be prosecuted for treason unless the indictment be prosecuted within [blank] years after the fact; to have a copy of the panel of the jury so many days before trial; to have like process to bring in his witnesses as the King hath; no overt act to be given in evidence but what laid in the indictment; this act not to extend to impeachments.

Then the Chairman read over the preamble, and on the question it was postponed. Then he read over the first clause and after the committee proceeded to fill up the blanks therein—the first being the time when the act shall commence.[1]

Some proposed to fill it up to commence after the expiration of the war as Goodwin Wharton, Sir William Strickland, Sir Charles Sedley, Sir Henry Goodricke, Solicitor General Sir Thomas Trevor, Sir Robert Cotton, Sir John Lowther, Mr. Comptroller Thomas Wharton, Mr. Smith, Serj. Trenchard, Sir John Guise, and others spoke to it: for that there were many enemies now plotting against this government and when we are in a war abroad it is not safe to have such a law pass now to enable them to carry on their designs the better and make them more unpunishable. It is difficult enough already upon the government to punish such offenders and will you now pass a law at this time to render them wholly unpunishable? And there is no fear of constructive treasons in this reign when the lenity of this government is perhaps its only fault.

Others again proposed the blank to be filled up with the 10th of January next as Sir William Whitlock, Mr. Bathurst, Sir Thomas Clarges, Mr. Harley, Mr. Finch, Sir Christopher Musgrave, Mr. Bertie, Mr. Price, Col. Granville, Sir Francis Winnington, and others, who spoke to the excellency of this bill, how necessary for the security of the subject, how careful several good princes have been to settle treasons to ascertain the same and not leave them to be construed as some men please.

Others proposed to fill it up with the 25th of March 1693 or 1694, hoping by that time the government might be settled, as Sir Edward Hussey, etc.

So after a long debate, it was proposed to fill up the blank with these words: 'after the determination of this present war with France'. Committee divided—Yeas to the right hand and the Noes to the left.

Yeas Lord Falkland   175

Tellers for the

Noes Mr. Gwyn   140

---

[1] For details of some of the speeches in this debate see Grey, x. 285–90.

So the committee proceeded through the remainder of the bill, filling up the blanks and made some alterations and finished the whole bill. And the Chairman was ordered to report it. So he left the Chair on the question.

Speaker resumed the Chair. *Mr. Harcourt* reported from the said committee that they had gone through the bill and made several amendments, which they had directed him to report to the House. So ordered that the said report be made on Thursday morning next.

So adjourned till tomorrow morning 9 of the clock.

Tuesday, 29 November

Sir Edward Seymour informed the House that in the estimates delivered in of the charge of the war for the year 1693 one particular was twice charged, that of the ordnance. There is a distinct estimate of it and then it is computed in the other estimate—the ordnance for land service is demanded in the estimate for the army and the ordnance for the sea service is computed in that of the fleet.

So the House went into a Committee of the Whole House to consider of the supply to be granted to Their Majesties; Mr. Attorney General Somers to the Chair. The estimate of the Navy was read.

Sir Thomas Clarges: I am desirous for my part and I doubt not but all gentlemen will go as far in this of the Navy as they are able, for here is our main security. The whole estimates brought in do amount to about £5,000,000—a prodigious sum. I wish there be so much wealth in the nation. However, we must take this matter in consideration and in order proceed to that of the fleet first, and therein I desire we may go head by head. Then first to that of the ordinary charge of the Navy; this ought not to be charged here but ought to be transferred to the civil list and stand thereon and paid thereout, and thus was done the last year and so I desire it may now.

Sir Christopher Musgrave: This is borne by the government in times of peace and paid out of the revenue. The act of tunnage and poundage provides for it and the last year you threw it on the civil list, and so I desire it may be now and that you will read the resolutions of the committee hereon the last year.

So those resolutions were read, whereon resolved that the ordinary charge of the Navy be not part of the supply to be granted to Their Majesties for the service of the year 1693.

Then the second head—the number of men the last year—was read, which came to 30,000 men, the medium of the whole year computed at 13 months to the year. But for this year here is 3,010 men more than last, which is occasioned by a considerable squadron going to the West Indies and you will have in the summer above 40,000 men at sea.

Sir Thomas Clarges took notice that by the marine treaty with Holland we are to furnish 50 ships men-of-war on board of which are to be but 17,000 men, and here you provide for near double that number so that sure there is no want of cruisers and convoys.

Lord Falkland informed the House how these men were disposed of: about 26,646 men on board the main fleet consisting of six first-rates, 10 second-rates, 28 third-rates, four fourth-rates, four fifth-rates, 18 fireships, and one bomb vessel; about 9,000 men on board cruisers and convoys; above 3,000 on board the Straits fleet consisting of five third-rates, six fourth-rates, etc.; 3,010 men on board the fleet to the West Indies consisting of two third-rates, eight fourth-rates, etc.; and 375 men on board two fifth-rates and two sixth-rates for New York and Virginia. In all, above 42,000 men.

Sir John Lowther and Sir Edward Seymour informed the House that it is true by the treaty produced we are to find but 17,000 men, but by agreement after (more being thought necessary for the common safety) we advanced, and the Dutch their proportion.

Paul Foley: I find the Navy is a growing charge. It still increases on you every year, but I see no reason for it to increase now when you beat your enemy the last year, so that I think if you have as good a fleet as you had the last year it is sufficient.

Sir Joseph Williamson: Since our defence between the Dutch and us is mutual, I hope they bear their proportion with us, and as we increase so that they do the like. I desire to know what advance they have made. You have a great fleet going to the Straits; I hope the Dutch find their proportion, as also in that to the West Indies, or else I would know what satisfaction or amends they make us for it. For if not, we pay their reckonings.

Admiral Russell: As you have increased your main fleet, so have the Dutch according to their proportion. And though they furnish but 36 men of war, no more than they were obliged by the treaty, yet the quality of their ships being greater they are at the charge of one-third more of men than before, and to the Straits they send a number of ships in proportion to yours.

Lord Coningsby: I am not for letting in an exasperated, abdicated King, and therefore I think we are engaged deeper in the war and are more concerned therein than they are.

Sir Christopher Musgrave: I expect no more mercy if he comes back than that gentleman, yet I see no reason to increase your charge or to bear more than your just proportion.

Sir Edward Seymour: Though it is true in your estimate the last year you had but a medium of 30,000 men, yet you really had a medium of 33,000.

Sir Henry Goodricke: You are now setting out a great fleet to the West Indies to protect your own trade in those parts, which is very great. You cannot expect the Dutch will preserve it, who have but a small share there. You have had very good success in your attempts there and have almost rooted out the French from most of the islands there but Martinique, of which I hope you will also have a good account in some short time. There is a complaint also that your trade is interrupted. There will be care taken of that by keeping a squadron on the Irish coast to guard the same.

Mr. Papillon informed the House that the last year there was victuals provided for 33,000 in the fleet.

Sir Robert Rich acquainted the House that the Dutch did send an equal number of ships into the Mediterranean with us.

Sir John Lowther: The reason of the increase of the seamen is not because the grand fleet is enlarged but the better to preserve our trade and secure the merchant ships, for I hope as good a fleet as we had the last year may serve.

Col. Granville: If you increase your squadron in the Mediterranean, your main fleet need not be so large, for the French must increase theirs in those parts, so decrease their main fleet.

So the question was stated, and by the rules a dispute being between two sums, the question ought to be first put on the lesser by the rules of the House. So it was that 30,000 men for 13 months is a medium necessary for the service of the Navy for the year 1693, and carried in the negative. Then the other sum was inserted, viz. 33,010 men, in the same question, put and carried in the affirmative.

Resolved that the charges of the wages, victuals, wear and tear, and ordnance stores for 33,010 men serving in the fleet be computed at £4. 5s. per man per month for the service of the year 1693. (This was last year but £4 a head last year. But in regard victuals were dearer and ordnance stores, too, the House allowed £4. 5s. a head.)

That the charge of the tenders to the fleet and of the hospital ships to attend the same is included in the £4. 5s. a head. (Thus done the last year; said they were included in the wear and tear.)

Resolved that the sum of £23,406 for the charge of making, completing, and finishing Their Majesties' naval yard at Hamoaze near Plymouth (with dwelling-houses for the officers, storehouses, workhouses, etc., enclosing the said yard with a wall) be part of the estimate of the charge of the Navy for the year 1693.

To the question about the marine regiments, they were by consent struck off as being included within the 33,010 men, as was done the last year.

To the question about building four bomb vessels and eight new fourth-rate ships, Sir Thomas Clarges opposed these because it came in irregular, for it is demanding more money of the people which ought to be asked by the King himself and not come in in this manner, and ought not to be part of the estimate for the year 1693. Then at best it is a new thing to ask aids in parliament for building of ships; it was never done till the latter end of King Charles II's time when he had supply for building 30 men-of-war. And there is great reason for it, because the wear and tear of any new ship will in two years' time build the same ship anew. You allow out of the £4. 5s. a head £1. 8s. 6d. a head for every man in a ship for the wear and tear of that ship; and I have examined the books of the Admiralty Office and can not find that ever the wear and tear of a ship ever exceeded 19s., that was expended generally but 17s. a head, so that the overplus ought to go to build those lesser ships. Paul Foley to the same.

Charles Montagu: This is no such new matter as suggested. You did the like in 1689 and allowed them to be part of the estimate.

Sir Edward Seymour: That was a very irregular thing; it was by a motion of a particular member to give money to build ships. But this comes in properly in the estimate which His Majesty has commanded to be laid before you so that it is a demand from the King himself.

Mr. Palmes: I am afraid of making these precedents. The old way of asking a supply was not by way of estimate but by the King in a speech to the Commons.

Sir Christopher Musgrave: I do believe gentlemen would not so freely have come to the £4. 5s. a head but only in hopes to strike off some of these things.

So the question put that the sum of £10,908 for the building four bomb vessels be part of the estimate for the Navy for the year 1693. Committee divided—Yeas on the right hand and Noes on the left.

Yeas Sir Thomas Littleton 112

Tellers for the

Noes Col. Cornewall   93

Then the question was put upon the marine regiments, and by consent left out of the estimate.

Then the question about building eight new fourth-rate ships was proposed.

Lord Falkland: This head is as necessary as any in the estimate, and for want of which you suffered much this summer. You were informed the last winter how much your service would be endangered for want of the same, but you would not admit of it then; I hope you will now. And to obviate an objection made the last winter that they would not be ready against that summer, I can assure you now they are upon the stocks and will be ready against the next summer.

Sir Edward Seymour: What you gave the last year to the fleet was applied to that end, for if otherwise and any of it had been misapplied the gentlemen entrusted to take the accounts would have given you notice of it. But then to the accounts themselves, there is nothing in them considerable, but what any clerk in the office would have done as well.

Clarges and Musgrave spoke against it and urged the reasons on the bomb vessels, etc.

The Lords of the Admiralty did assure the House that these ships could not be built without the supply demanded. And if not done now the public would be very much prejudiced by it; and if you give not money to finish them, as they are upon the stocks so they will continue.

Question stated that the sum of £68,400 for the building eight new ships of the fourth rate of 48 guns each and furnishing them with rigging and eight months' boatswains' and carpenters' sea stores be part of the estimate of the charge of the Navy for the service of the year 1693. Committee divided hereon—Yeas on the right hand, Noes on the left.

Yeas Henry Herbert   104

Tellers for the

Noes Sir Walter Yonge   80

So carried in the affirmative.

Then the Attorney, according to order, left the Chair. Speaker resumed the Chair. *Mr. Attorney* reported that the committee had taken the estimate of the Navy into consideration and had come to several resolutions which they had directed him to report. Ordered it be made on Thursday morning next at 9 of the clock. *He* moved also for the committee to sit again. Resolved the House would go into a committee again to consider farther of the supply upon Thursday morning next.[1]

So adjourned till tomorrow morning 9 of the clock.

Wednesday, 30 November

Mr. Christie presented the petition of the feltmakers.

Mr. Jeffreys presented a petition of Daniel Price and Henry Williams, in custody of the Serjeant at Arms for a breach of privilege committed in arresting the menial servant of Mr. Francis Lloyd, praying to be heard touching the same as the House should think fit.

It was received, read, and referred to the Committee of Elections and Privileges, and to report the matter with their opinions touching the same to the House. And it was ordered to be heard by the said committee on Monday next in the afternoon.

Several members were added to the committee to whom the consideration of the book of rates was referred, and directions were given to that committee to take care not to raise money but only to consider what commodities were fit to be raised and what to be brought down, and to report the same.

Order of the Day read and the House went into a Committee of the Whole House upon the matter of advice to His Majesty. Speaker left the Chair; Sir Francis Winnington Chairman to the committee. So Order of the Day read again. Then the several papers about the descent were read.[2]

Mr. Bathurst: By the papers you have read, you see the mismanagement of the descent; and though the officers themselves thought it impracticable, yet you see some men above press it on. It cost you near £400,000 and was made the great discourse of last sessions to draw you in and pick your pockets. But if you will come to manage matters with any success, you must let trade be carried on as much

[1] There was a division on this final motion: *CJ*, x. 728.
[2] Public Record Office, State Papers 8/12, no. 146, has a parallel account of the debate that follows.

as you can, and that in fleets; that no convoy money be taken; that the Dutch maintain the grand fleet; and that we go with 30,000 foot and 10,000 horse and dragoons to attempt a landing in France and 20 men-of-war to guard them.

Mr. Mordaunt: Some persons have made various reflections on what I said the last time. However, I can say that some cannot: His Majesty has my advice freely; it costs him nothing and it shall always be the same. We are now upon advice, but it is my opinion give what advice you will, if the same men have the management of affairs you will have but little effect of your advice or your supplies. You did yesterday give very liberally to the fleet—nay, advanced your estimate considerably to what before—so that if you do so every year your victory at sea will cost you dear. Now as to the matters before you, I think there are three things to be considered: (1) the dangers we have been exposed to and by what means we came so exposed; (2) why the victory at sea was no better pursued and improved; (3) why the descent was no better prosecuted and so little done in it.

Mr. Clarke: As to the heads before you, I think they are very proper. To the first, that happened to you for want of intelligence. To the second, it was because orders were not pursued. Then to the third about the descent, you have the papers before you and the miscarriages therein appear to arise by the great delays. Then he reflected on several parts of the papers, that there were great mistakes in some of the orders. Then he observed that the transport ships from Bideford came not to Portsmouth till the 8th of July and those from the river not till the 18th; that the foot embarked not till the 23rd of July, the horse not till the 25th; and then they sailed, which was too late in the year to expect any fruit thereof. So that I doubt not you will be of opinion that the councils that managed the descent are an occasion of great charge.

Lord Castleton: If we are in such danger of a descent as is talked of, the things for our consideration are to see in what case our militia are, what stores, and how our maritime towns are provided. I hear talk some things of Scotland, too.

Sir Charles Sedley: I think it proper since there is such talk of a descent that you give His Majesty advice to prevent it, and that I take to be by keeping a sufficient body of men here.

Mr. Jeffreys: If you will know whence your maladministration comes, you must go to the council that manage matters.

Sir John Knight: All your false steps in these matters come from those, I believe, that advised this descent, which was gone upon without considering beforehand of matters. Your transport ships from Ireland with the stores were ordered to come to Minehead—a port not capable to receive them. They came without convoy trusting to an insurance and the King made the insurer, and if they had miscarried what had become of you? I think, therefore, you can do no less than address to His Majesty to remove all the Cabinet Council from him who appear to have the management of these matters.

Mr. Jeffreys: I am against that motion and also making a descent upon France, and therefore I am for advising His Majesty not to make a descent upon France, but take care to provide your fleet and that will best secure you.

Sir Edward Seymour: Since there has been these reflections on the management of the descent, I think it becomes me to say something of it since I am concerned in a station where this was managed. Some gentlemen have been pleased to make us either fools or knaves. This matter was agreed on before I came into that station but not without the best advice; your Admiral at sea, your General at land, and some very knowing persons were consulted with in this affair. As to the report from your committee about this matter, I must say it is very partial. There are several orders and letters not taken notice of therein and others—very material ones—I find were not before the committee, and therefore I desire that the committee may have the whole matter before them and this may be referred to them. This matter is now under examination in the House of Lords and they have all the papers laid before them, which I desire you will have before you come to any resolution therein. And when you have examined them, I believe you will find the fault lies in another place.

Mr. Palmes: I cannot but take notice how that gentleman who spoke last has taken occasion to harangue your committee. I think it is not for the honour of the House to have committees so used when they have done all they can for your service. I was in the Chair of this committee and do assure you I have no letters or papers in my hands or which were before the committee but they are reported, unless where there be several to the same effect. And though some gentlemen now by their places and offices are taken off, yet in former parliaments the greatest men have not thought themselves too good to attend committees for the service of the House.

Admiral Russell: Though that worthy member who spoke last but one is pleased to charge me with not laying before the House all the orders and letters I had, I do assure you I do not know of one that is not.

Mr. Smith: I am sorry to see we have spent so much that after all when your committee has gone through the matter they have not had all the papers before them, though I cannot but take notice not one word was said before of it. I must observe to you there is a coolness in people's minds to this government which arises, I think, because they believe you have not a rightful king but only *de facto*, and that if King James comes back they may return to their allegiance to him. Hence arises your mischief and this, I think, ought to be your first head of advice.

Mr. Comptroller Wharton: I think we are a miserable people but the merriest that I ever saw of undone men. The gentleman that spoke last has touched upon the true cause of your grievance; it lies deeper than you are aware of. Your chief men that manage matters are such as submit to this King upon wrong principles—because he has the governing power—but will be as ready to join another when he prevails. They are such as came not into your government till it was late, and I think it no policy to take men into a government because they were violent against it. I will not at present name these persons, but I would address to His Majesty against them in general (for he knows them best) and that he would be pleased to receive such men only under him who are of known integrity and will come up both to the principles and His Majesty's right to this government.

Sir Henry Goodricke: I confess there appears to be a coldness in Their Majesties' service; I cannot deny it. But that which calls me up is something let fall by that honourable gentleman that spoke last which seems to point at some persons who, I can assure you, are most firm to this government and very zealous in the service of it. And if you please to consult the minutes of the Council book, you will see who are most diligent in attending the service of the government there.

Mr. Comptroller: The mischiefs to you do not proceed from some gentlemen's not attending but from some men who ought not to be there at all.

Sir Charles Sedley: I doubt not some gentlemen were willing to come into this government to get money by it, but I desire you will address to His Majesty to employ such men as are of his principles.

Goodwin Wharton: We have had some rambling discourses hinting at some persons but nothing particular. There is a stitched pamphlet lately come out entitled *The Preten[ces] of a French Invasion Examin'd*,[1] licensed by a Secretary of State—the only one I may say now. In it are principles laid down inconsistent with this government, and therefore I think such men are not fit to be trusted therewith. I have, therefore, prepared a question that you will address to His Majesty to remove from his councils those men who have declared by their principles that they are not for this government.

Sir John Guise: As to the report before you, you have in the like cases of great mismanagement of affairs required an account of matters from your ministers of state, as was done by the Duke of Buckingham; and if you please, you may go some such way now.

Sir Walter Yonge: Since you cannot know men's hearts, I think new oaths will signify very little. At first all matters went on very successfully, but since some men have come into employ all things have gone backwards, matters have been very dilatory, and your intelligence has done little service. Therefore I am for the address that the King will be pleased to employ only such men as are for his interest against that of the late King and such as think this government to be *de jure* as well as *de facto*.

Sir John Lowther (of Lowther): No man can be false to his own interest, and therefore I am satisfied the King would not employ such men about him that he thought false to him and therefore I think it very odd to address to him to turn out such under him that he thought false to him. You have a Prince now on the throne that is in the interests of this nation—one firm to the Protestant religion and averse to the French. But the fault of this government is it has not the power it had formerly. Refusing to take the oaths was heretofore a *praemunire*; now it is barely paying 40*s*. Then if there be but one witness against a man for a fact which would be treason if there were two, but therefore he shall come off. These, with many other weaknesses in this government, are fit for you to remedy that it may exert its due power and authority and that there may be a distinction between men that are for this government and others that are not.

Mr. Comptroller: I am not for coming to particulars in this matter but in general to advise His Majesty to employ such men as are for his interest and true to the principles on which this government is founded.

Mr. Norris: If there be any men that are against this government I believe the King (if he knew it) would remove them, and therefore till we come to particulars I can say nothing to it.

[1] [William Lloyd], London, 1692.

Mr. Arnold: I will take liberty to name one and that is the Lord Nottingham, who has beat two Secretaries into one, who has prohibited the licensing some books writ in defence of this government, and has discouraged some witnesses in matters carrying on against this government.

Sir Edward Hussey: I have seen many gentlemen turned out who were very zealous for this government and others put in who are not so now. I would, therefore, move for an address to remove all them that protested against the bill of recognition.

Sir Richard Temple: I am of opinion your mischiefs proceed from some men getting into places and endeavouring to promote men of their own faction; hence it is come our divisions. And therefore I think the best way is to advise His Majesty to remove such men as are for promoting factions and particular interests and do not endeavour the public service.

Peregrine Bertie junior: It is agreed by most that there is a coldness to this government, if not treachery. I doubt not there are several men in this King's councils that are not true to him, though I cannot name them. But such a general address I think not for your service, and therefore I am for searching into particulars.

Mr. Smith: The weakness of your government I cannot deny; that there are some men false to it I believe; and if there be men in office that have a principle of another King's right I would address against such persons.

Mr. Lloyd: There were some persons about me in the country whom I had good cause to suspect to be no friends to this government upon which I thought it my duty to tender them the oaths. Soon after which, I received a summons to attend the Council where some persons here hinted at were very busy in asking me questions about the matter, but at last I was dismissed but had no sort of encouragement given me for doing my duty or check to my adversaries for complaining.

So at last the question was stated: That it is the opinion of this committee that His Majesty be humbly advised for the necessary support of his government to employ in his councils and management of his affairs such persons only whose principles oblige them to stand by him and his right against the late King James and all other pretenders whatsoever.

Admiral Russell: I am well assured there are some men in the council that think this government not a rightful one and there are others cold in the service of it in prospect if King James comes back they may make better terms with him.

Sir Robert Howard: What can any man think of things when we see it maintained in print that we are slaves, that this King from the title of 'deliverer' is made a 'conqueror', and this by licence of public authority? It is time to look about you, and therefore I desire you will put the question.

So the question was put and resolved *nemine contradicente*.

So the Speaker resumed the Chair and *Sir Francis Winnington*, according to order, reported the committee had made a further progress in the matter of advice and had directed him to move for leave to sit again. Resolved the House would go into a committee again upon it on Saturday next.

A motion was made by the friends to the Lord Nottingham that all the papers and letters relating to the descent might be laid before this House. But it was opposed by his enemies, the Whigs; so carried in the negative.

So adjourned till tomorrow morning 9 of the clock.

Thursday, 1 December

Mr. George Nicholas, a new member lately chosen for the town of Morpeth in Northumberland (in the room of the Lord Morpeth, now Earl of Carlisle), came to the House and took the oaths at the Table and subscribed his name to the declaration as required and after took his seat in the House.

A committee was appointed to inspect the laws proper to be revived or continued, upon the motion of *Mr. Attorney General*.

Sir John Guise presented the petition from the clothiers of Gloucestershire, praying that the Hamburg Company might be established.

But hereon arose a debate. And said this was to put the woollen manufacture into a few hands, whereas now it is free for all persons to buy our commodity and to export it, and so more was exported than otherwise would. But it was answered that [?it is not] true this was a present profit to the nation, rather to some parts of it only as Devonshire, etc. Then said this open trade is managed at present by foreigners chiefly, who will in time get the trade from this nation, at least set their own price upon the commodity. Then wool is rather fallen in its price since this free trade. For these reasons it was prayed that this petition might be referred to the same committee to whom the bill for the free exportation of the woollen manufacture stands committed.

So the question was put for referring the petition to a committee and resolved accordingly. Then the question was put to refer it to that committee to whom that bill was referred. House divided—Yeas go out.[1]

		Sir John Guise	
	Yeas		99
		Sir Thomas Littleton	
Tellers for the			
		Mr. Clarke	
	Noes		139
		Mr. Waller	

So a particular committee was named, and they were ordered to meet at 4 this afternoon in the Speaker's Chamber and they are to consider of the petition and report their opinions therein to the House.

Attorney General reported from the Committee of the Whole House the resolutions of the committee in relation to the Navy, which he read over in his place at the Bar and after delivered them in at the Table, where they were all read over by the Clerk and after severally put.

To the first, that the charge of the ordinary estimate for the Navy be paid out of the civil list, the House agreed.

To the second, that 33,010 men for 13 months is a medium necessary for the Navy for the year 1693, the House agreed.

Mr. Harley and *Sir Thomas Clarges* moved that the Lords of the Admiralty might present the House with a list of the ships on which so great a number of men was to be employed.

To the third, that the charge of wages, victuals, wear and tear, and ordnance stores for 33,010 men be computed at £4. 5s. a man per month for the Navy for the year 1693, to which the House agreed.

To the fourth, that the charge of tenders was included in the wear and tear, the House agreed.

To the fifth, that the charge of the hospital ships to attend the fleet was also included therein, to which the House agreed.

To the sixth, for allowing £23,406 for the charge of making and finishing the naval yard at Hamoaze near Plymouth, with dwelling-houses for officers, storehouses, and workhouses, etc., and enclosing it with a wall:

---

[1] *CJ*, x. 729 has the two sets of tellers on this division reversed.

Sir Christopher Musgrave was against agreeing with the committee for that this came not in regularly. It ought to have been demanded by the Crown, as all supplies must to this House, and not to leave it in the power of particular men to ask what they please. I cannot say but the thing is necessary enough. However, it comes in irregularly, and we must preserve our methods in giving supplies. *Sir Thomas Clarges* and *Mr. Bathurst* to the same; also the *Lord Castleton* and *Sir John Knight* against it.

Sir Edward Seymour: I am as much for preserving your methods in giving of money as any man but I think this comes in very regularly. You made application to His Majesty for the estimates of the charge of the war for the Navy and Army to be laid before you, and accordingly you have them presented you. That of the Navy is now before you in which is this head now under debate, which comes to you very properly—I may say from the King himself. Therefore that can be no exception. And for the usefulness of it, I think that will not be denied by any nor the great necessity there is for it. *Sir John Lowther* was also for it.

So at last it was agreed to by the House.

To the seventh, for allowing £10,908 for the building four bomb vessels:

Sir Thomas Littleton acquainted the House that in this estimate here was a charge brought in for building ships and vessels by the Admiralty, but they have never consulted with the officers of the Ordnance about the charge of guns and other stores for them. The very gunning of the bomb vessels will come to each vessel at least £3,000.

However, the House agreed thereto.

To the eighth, that the two marine regiments were included in the 33,010 men, the House agreed.

To the ninth, for allowing £68,400 for the building eight new fourth-rates of 48 guns each and furnishing them with rigging and eight months' boatswains' and carpenters' sea stores:

Sir Christopher Musgrave, Sir Thomas Clarges, Mr. Harley, Mr. Foley, Sir John Knight, Col. Granville, and others opposed it for that this was higher this year than in proportion they demanded for four the last year—viz. but £28,864 for four, and now they demand above double for eight this year. Then this also came in irregularly. Then it hath not been usual for the Crown to demand supplies of the Commons for building ships—never done till about the 29th of King Charles II's time for building the 30 ships of war—but it always used to be done out of the wear and tear of a ship which in two years' time would raise enough to build a ship of the same bigness. And this wear and tear of a ship is to discharge all the charge of a ship; it comprehends all things but wages, victuals, and ordnance.

Answered by the *Lord Falkland* and others: To that of the increase of the charge, it is very true there is more this year and that is because the charge is greater and building dearer. However, there is no more than is really contracted for now brought in; the former year was but upon computation. Then as to the wear and tear, it is not so great as is represented and it is to charge at least 30 several particulars which usually comes to (as will appear by the books) 29*s*.; the others are pleased to say, not to above 20*s*.

But at last it was agreed to by the House.

Mr. Harcourt reported from the Committee of the Whole House the bill for regulating trials in cases of treason with several amendments, all which with their coherences he read over at the Bar and then laid them on the Table, where they were all read over by the Clerk, and after read again severally and severally put. Some were agreed to; others took up great debate.

To that of the time for the commencement of this bill, it was made to be after the [end][1] of the war. By those for the bill, moved to disagree with the committee and to give it a certain time—either from the 25 of April 1695, 1696, etc.—so that it might have a certain day for its commencement, which was very uncertain and words never seen in an act of parliament. It is an indefinite and indeterminate [thing];[2] there have been bills to determine at an uncertain time but never to commence so. Answered, if it began before the war was ended, it would tend to encourage the enemies of this government.

So question was put to agree with the committee in this amendment. House divided—Noes went out.

		Charles Montagu	
	Yeas		145
		Col. Goldwell	
Tellers for the			
		Col. Granville	
	Noes		120[3]
		Col. Cornewall	

[1] 'commencement' in MS.   [2] 'king' in MS.
[3] *CJ*, x. 730 has the minority as 125.

Others of the amendments were not agreed to and some amendments were made in the Chair.

Mr. Smith tendered a clause to be added to this bill—that if any person shall publish, affirm, or declare that Their Majesties are not rightful King and Queen of this realm or that they are usurpers or that others have a greater right, they shall incur the pains and penalties of high treason.

Sir Christopher Musgrave and *Col. Goldwell* opposed this clause because it was irregularly brought in, being not proper in a bill to regulate trials in cases of treason to insert a clause to make new treasons which has no dependence or relation to the bill. Then this is made but a temporary clause but the bill is perpetual; and though the matter might be desirable enough, yet it is most fit for a bill by itself.

Answered, it is very usual in perpetual laws to put in temporary clauses.

However, the clause was read a first time and a second upon the question.

Mr. Harcourt objected against the clause because it came in very irregularly, being to repeal a law (the statute of 25 E. III) by making words to be treason, which could not be brought into the House without leave first had. This clause, besides, is very penal and may have very mischievous consequences. For my part, I am at all times against making words to be treason; many times they are spoken out of heat and very apt to be mistaken and misconstrued. Words have seldom been made treason but in troublesome and difficult times and often prove snares to honest men, and therefore I am against this clause.

Sir Edward Seymour: The proviso offered I agree with in the matter, and it is fit for you to do something in it if you will support this government. But I think this is not brought in so regularly, for I believe it was never seen that new treasons have been enacted in provisos in a bill. Then the manner of it seems to reflect on Their Majesties, as if this would not pass without tacking. But the House seeming to agree in the thing, I think you may make a bill of it by itself.

Others were for adjourning the debate of the clause—some to have the clause withdrawn; others that the bill, with the clause, might lie on the Table and leave to be given to bring in a bill for the preservation of Their Majesties and their government.

So resolved *nemine contradicente* that leave be given to bring in a bill for the better preservation of Their Majesties' persons and government. And it was referred to Mr. Attorney and Mr. Solicitor General to prepare and bring in a bill accordingly.

Ordered that all committees be adjourned.

So the House adjourned till 9 tomorrow morning.

Friday, 2 December

Mr. Clarke presented to the House the petition of the clothiers of Wiltshire and Somersetshire.

So the House, according to order, went into a Committee of the Whole House upon the matter of supplies. Speaker left the Chair. Mr. Attorney was Chairman, and the order was read.

Col. Goldwell: You have the last time finished the estimate of the fleet and agreed upon the several heads, all which comes to £1,926,516. 10s., which I move you to vote as part of the supply to be given to Their Majesties for carrying on the war against France. Mr. Robartes to the same.

So the question was put and resolved: That a sum not exceeding £1,926,516. 10s. for the charge of the Navy for the year 1693 (including the charge of the ordnance and the finishing Their Majesties' naval yard at Hamoaze near Plymouth and the building four bomb vessels and eight new ships of the fourth rate) be granted to Their Majesties as part of the supply for carrying on a vigorous war against France.

Sir Christopher Musgrave: Since you are come to this resolution and voted the sum for the fleet, your next regular step is to leave the Chair and report it to the House and desire leave to sit again, for there can be no fruit of this resolution till the House have agreed to it. Lord Castleton seconded it.

Lord Coningsby: Though I would not lose the fruit of what you have done, yet I would not lose a day. And since you are now in a committee, I desire you will proceed on the estimates for the Army and report them all together.

Sir Edward Seymour: I do not see any reason why you should leave the Chair to lose any time especially if you saw what I did last night— of some intelligence from France of their vast preparations by sea and land and their great forwardness. Their fleet for the next year consists of 60 sail of men-of-war from 100 to 60 guns and 30 sail more from 60 to 50 guns and none under. Then for his land forces, all his recruits are ordered to be ready by the 1st of January. This I thought fit to acquaint you with that you may consider whether you have any time to spare, whereon not only your well-being but even your very being depends. Then the Treasury at this time is very low; there is hardly money to pay the army their weekly subsistence money. These things I lay before you, and do as you shall please I have done my duty.

But, however, it was ordered that he report this resolution and desire leave to sit again, and so he left the Chair on the question.

Speaker resumed the Chair. *Mr. Attorney* reported the said resolution, which was read once and after on the question read the second time. And then the question put to agree with the committee in the said resolution and carried in the affirmative with two negatives—Sir Christopher Musgrave and Sir John Knight. And *Mr. Attorney* also moved for leave for the committee to sit again.

Sir Christopher Musgrave: When the House was in a committee there was an account given by an honourable member of the great preparations of the French King and of the forwardness of the same which I think calls upon us to take timely care to secure ourselves, and therefore I desire we may resolve ourselves in a committee to consider of ways and means for raising the sum you have voted for the fleet that we may be as early out with it as our enemies.

Sir John Lowther (of Lowther): Though I am not against that question in the general, yet I am not for going on that now. This is but half the work we are to provide for; there are also land forces which are also very necessary, which I desire may go along with your fleet. It is now desired to go into a committee to provide for the fleet first. It is true that is to be preferred, but withal if you should apply the whole sum to the fleet which you are pressed to go into a committee to raise, it could not all be employed if all were laid on the Table. So that there is at present necessary for the fleet only sufficient to set it out and the residue would be useless, and therefore I would have the fleet and the Army go on together.

Sir Stephen Fox: As your fleet is your best safety, so it is fit to consider what you will do with the Army. They have hitherto been constantly paid till within a week or a fortnight—to the soldiers subsistence, and half-pay to the officers. But money now falls short, and if you cannot pay them you must consider to disband them, else an unsatisfied army will be a dangerous thing. Therefore, I think you had best consider of the Army and the Navy together.

Charles Montagu: Here are two motions before you: one to go into a Committee of the Whole House to raise the supply for the fleet, the other to take into consideration the estimate of your Army. The latter I think the most proper at this time that you may have all your work before you and see what your whole charge amounts to.

Mr. Palmes was for going into a committee on the ways and means to provide for the fleet.

Attorney General Somers: I am against a standing army as much as any in this House, but yet as long as an army is necessary for your service I am for using them well, and therefore I am not for passing them over without some consideration but would take the estimate thereof into your thoughts.

Lord Eland: I am for providing for the fleet first as being our security, for if the fleet be out we need not matter the French forces, and therefore I am for providing first for ourselves in the fleet before we provide for others in an army.

Sir Henry Goodricke: The army now before you have served you very well and helped to reduce Ireland and been very instrumental in your preservation and are well affected to this government, and therefore I would not put them under such a discouragement.

Sir Thomas Clarges: I am for providing for the fleet first; the security of this nation lies therein.

Sir Henry Goodricke: I think it equally necessary for you to have your army provided for as for your fleet and to support your alliances, without which you will find yourselves in an ill condition.

Sir Edward Hussey and *Sir John Parsons* were for providing for the fleet.

Mr. Hampden and *Sir John Lowther* opposed putting the question for applying the sum to the fleet and desired the House to consider of the clause of credit given on the poll act which fell short, and there was already £500,000 taken up on that act to supply the defect of the same and desired the House would proceed first to make good their credit.

Sir Edward Seymour to the same and opposed that of the fleet, for if this money were given for the fleet the money borrowed on the clause of credit on the quarterly poll would first take place and then the sum given towards the fleet will fall short of the sum you intend for the fleet. And therefore if you please to, let the committee consider first of ways and means to satisfy the deficiency of the poll bill.

Mr. Smith thought it best for the House first to dispatch all the estimates.

Lord Coningsby: You have three things before you—the support of your credit, the providing for your fleet and for your army—all which must be supported or you are ruined, and therefore before you put the question about the fleet, I desire that the previous question may be put.

Mr. Harley: As to the clause of credit, the money is to be paid out of any of the next aids and so you may apply it to any of the aids given this sessions.

Sir Robert Howard: I am against your going on in this separate way, which you never yet took. Heretofore you proceeded in all your estimates together, for they must all be supported—your Navy, Army, and alliances. And therefore I am for putting the question to go into a committee to consider of ways and means for raising supplies generally.

Sir Henry Ashurst and *Col. Austen* were for going upon considering the clause of credit.

So the clause of credit in the act for the quarterly poll was read, which appeared to be supplied out of any of the next aids given by parliament. Some were for putting the question about the fleet; others were for proceeding on the other estimate; and some were for going on the clause of credit and that the committee might consider of ways to satisfy the same.

Sir Christopher Musgrave: You are moved for the committee to consider of ways and means to satisfy your credit, but that is irregular until the committee have agreed and voted the sum or come to some resolution thereon. You cannot do it; it was never seen before. And therefore your only question that is regular is that about the fleet, which you have on your paper, and therefore I desire it may be put.

Mr. Comptroller Wharton was for putting the previous question.

So the *Chair* stated the main question for going into a committee to consider of ways and means for raising the sum of £1,926,516. 10*s*. for the service of the Navy for the year 1693. And then *he* put the previous question—that that question be now put—and it was carried in the negative. Ordered to go into a Committee of the Whole House tomorrow to consider further of the supplies to be granted to Their Majesties for carrying on the war against France, and they are in the first place to consider of supplying the defect upon the poll bill.

Dutton Colt and *Sir Christopher Musgrave* complained of matters in reference to the army in Ireland—the clamour whereof for their arrears is very great, pretending they are 26 months' pay behind.

So ordered that the accounts of the army in Ireland since the 1st of

April last be forthwith laid before the Commissioners for taking the Public Accounts.

So adjourned till 9 tomorrow morning.

Saturday, 3 December

John Buller esq., being newly chosen a member for Grampound (in the room of Capt. Vincent), came into the House and was sworn at the Table and after took his place in the House.

The bill to prevent the exportation of coney wool and hare's wool was read for the first time.

Sir Christopher Musgrave and *Sir John Darell* spoke against it because it limits the price of our own commodity.

But answered, it does not. It is true it prohibits the exportation of this wool when it is above 7*s.* the pound, which is a mighty rate and what it never bore before. But now here being a great manufacture of hats set up here (as at Wandsor, Putney) which will take up all your wool, whereby you are able to supply the markets abroad with this commodity which France did before. But now by sending it abroad the price is much increased by reason this wool is carried to Portugal and so to France who give this great price for it—being they cannot be without it as not being otherwise able to make these hats without our wool, which is finer than theirs. Then it is not so beneficial for the King's customs, because this wool exported pays to the King but 4*d.* in the pound but a pound of wool which being manufactured here will make three hats which pays 6*d.* to the King when exported; besides, it employs so many poor persons to manufacture it. And if the wool should happen by the tricks of the hatters to come under 7*s.* per pound, it may then be exported.

The question was put for the second reading. House divided—Yeas went out.

		Col. Pery	
	Noes		119
		Mr. Bennett[1]	
Tellers for the			
		Sir Thomas Roberts	
	Yeas		56
		Mr. Arnold	

So carried in the negative.

[1] Sir Levinius Bennett in *CJ*, x. 731.

Lord Falkland presented the House with a list of the ships to be employed at sea for the year 1693—consisting of six first-rates, 10 second-rates, 35 third-rates, 40 fourth-rates, 31 fifth-rates, 18 sixth rates, 10 yachts, seven ketches, 23 fireships, five hospital ships, two bomb vessels; in all, 187 ships of all sorts.

House went into a Committee of the Whole House upon the supplies; Mr. Attorney to the Chair.[1] And the committee proceeded first to consider of the defect of the poll bill.

Sir Edward Seymour and Mr. Hampden informed the House it would fall short about £800,000.

Paul Foley: The quarterly poll was made a fund for £1,341,700, but as it has been managed I do believe it will, and you may compute it to, fall short about £750,000.

Sir John Guise: I am for a review of the poll and that the King may put in persons to execute it. Then you may perhaps get £300,000 or £400,000 of persons who have as yet paid nothing towards it.

Sir Charles Sedley: I believe one reason of the poll bill's falling short was that the lords, I hear, paid nothing towards it.

Sir Stephen Fox desired that the sum might be £781,000 for so much (with interest and charges of collecting it) would it, according to the best computation, fall short.

Question stated and resolved: That it is the opinion of this committee that for making good the sum of £1,341,700 intended to be raised by the quarterly poll a sum not exceeding the sum of £750,000 be granted to Their Majesties.

Sir Thomas Clarges and Col. Cornewall desired that the Chairman would leave the Chair and report what done and desire leave to sit again. Young Peregrine Bertie to the same.

But others against it and were for going on the estimate of the Army as Sir John Guise, Sir Thomas Littleton, Mr. Smith, Thomas Freke.

So it was waived and they went upon the estimate of the land forces, which was read.

Mr. Harley moved that since a noble lord had acquainted the House with a message from His Majesty that he intended to keep 20,000 men in England for the defence of this nation, he desired that question might be first put.[2]

---

[1] The following debate on supply lasted over seven hours and did not end till 9 p.m.; B.M. Loan 29/186, f. 223; B.M. Add. MS. 34096, ff. 230–1.

[2] Lord Ranelagh had earlier brought this message; *CJ*, x. 732.

Sir Thomas Clarges: His Majesty is a valiant prince, but yet I would not have him be governed by Dutch advice and manage us accordingly. If the States General are to order what force we shall send abroad we shall be loaded sufficiently, but it is against our interest for they and we are on different foundations. What we are obliged to furnish our treaties will tell us, and if we come up to them it is sufficient. But first I am for taking care of ourselves, and therefore I desire the question upon the 20,000 men may be put.

Sir John Lowther (of Lowther): There never was a greater power than that of France now since the days of Charlemagne the Great nor a greater alliance and confederacy formed against him than now, and I would not do anything to break it. We are under this union, and therefore I would give no jealousy to any of our allies, for if when we are united we are not able to master him, what shall we do when we are left alone? As to the war in Flanders I do think we can do nothing in it; it is running our heads against a wall. He must be attacked in another place and that I am for and not for so great an army in Flanders. But first I am for taking care of ourselves and to provide for our own safety, but before I think it ought to be agreed in general what forces you will have.

Sir Christopher Musgrave: You have now read the estimate over and it consists of several particulars of different natures, and therefore I desire you will consider them head by head.

Sir Edward Seymour: I desire gentlemen to consider if they think they can support themselves when they are left alone. Some gentlemen are pleased to call this a defensive war, but I am sure if you help not to support it it will prove an offensive one upon you. The seat of the war is now in another kingdom, but if you break the alliance you may chance to bring it into your own. And though the confederates have not performed their part so strictly as they ought, yet you must have been at a greater charge if you stood alone if you will support yourselves, for your all lies at stake—your being and well-being, too.

Sir Thomas Clarges: Why we should be at a greater charge than our treaties oblige us to I see no reason for. I know it is a received opinion with the Dutch and the Germans that England is an inexhaustible fountain, but if you go on at the rate you have I am afraid you will quickly be drawn dry. The security of this nation with our interest lies in having a good fleet at sea and, if we can, to destroy that of our enemies, and not to send armies abroad which will drain the nation both of our people and our money, too.

Sir Henry Goodricke: The King tells you in his speech that the same fleet and army are necessary, and he is a great judge of these things.

Paul Foley: It was urged to you the last year to encourage you to come up to the number of men desired that it was for but one year and by pushing on the war vigorously you might the sooner put an end to it. But for my part I see no likelihood of an end, and therefore I am for managing it so that we may be able to hold it on. And therefore in order to that I am for going upon the particulars and not to lump it, and then I would know what use the army desired is for.

Sir Edward Seymour: Let gentlemen consider that if we withdraw our forces from Flanders whether the confederates will be able to carry it on without us. Are they able to raise more men to supply the want of ours? If not and we withdraw ours, they will withdraw their assistance by sea and then consider whether you can stand alone. I believe not, at least not to carry on your trade also. Then the Dutch —who will be at liberty, either by peace with France or at least to remain neuters—will follow their trade and beat you soon out of it and get all into their own hands. Let gentlemen seriously consider with themselves if it is not better to bear some small inconveniences now than to have King James come back with a French power— whether the hardships now are comparable to the mischiefs that will then follow? This is your case and fit to be considered of.

Col. Granville: I am for going upon that head His Majesty hath sent you a message about concerning the 20,000 men to be left here in England. Secure ourselves first and then you may consider of your allies.

Sir Robert Howard was for voting the whole number of men as brought in in the estimate. Lord Cornbury to the same.

Sir Christopher Musgrave: The estimate brought in consists of several heads of different natures, therefore fit for you to consider of particularly. In order to that, the first step is to secure ourselves, which if you had done the last year you would not have had a French descent here. Keep a good fleet at sea and you need not fear King James's return.

Col. Austen: I think the whole number of men in the estimate is necessary, and therefore I am for it.

Lord Coningsby: I think the question properly before you is whether you will have so many men for the defence of England.

Lord Ranelagh: I find several gentlemen run upon a great mistake and think that the last year this kingdom was left without any body of men to defend the same. There were not all last summer less at any time than 15,000 men here in England—viz., 2,600 horse, about 1,000 dragoons, and the rest foot to make up 15,700 men.

Sir Richard Temple: I am for the whole number because I had rather we should fight for Flanders than for England.

Mr. Harley: Some gentlemen are for putting the whole number and lump it, and so shut out all debate and consideration thereon. But I am for going on head by head as you did last year, and therefore would begin with what necessary for England's safety and after for your allies.

Lord Falkland and the Lord Ranelagh were for putting the question that 54,562 men be the number of land forces for the service of the year 1693. Sir Charles Sedley, Sir Robert Rich, and Sir Robert Cotton (of the Post Office) all to the same.

Sir Thomas Clarges: If you will go and weaken yourselves by your great voluntary supplies to the allies, more than you are obliged by any treaty, you will not be able to defend yourselves if anything should happen. The confederates are defending their own country; let us not put ourselves out of a condition to do the like to ours. It is said they can make a peace, we cannot. I do not believe that but am of the contrary opinion.

Mr. Bertie: I desire the first question may be put upon the 20,000 men, being according to His Majesty's message.

Lord Colchester: I am for the whole number, for if you come not up to them I verily believe all Flanders will be lost the next year.

Col. Granville: If no gentlemen in this House will own the advising of this list now brought in or consulting with about this estimate, I am afraid foreign councils reign too much amongst us, which I am very sorry to see. I think we are now about a matter of great concern and I think it is very late in the day to go upon it, and therefore I would put it off to another time. But if not, I am sorry to see that so late in the day we can go upon nothing but multiplying of troops and multiplying of treasons.

Then candles, upon the question, were called for in.

Col. Godfrey and Mr. Smith, with Dr. Barbone, Mr. Montagu, Lord Colchester, Sir Robert Cotton (of the Post Office), were for the whole number of 54,000 men.

But Sir Peter Colleton, Lord Digby, Col. Cornewall, Henry Boyle were against it and for putting the question of the 20,000 first.

Goodwin Wharton: I am for the whole number that Flanders may not be lost. Since you could hardly oppose the French the last year, it is not likely you should be better able to do it by lessening your forces when he is raising more—I am told several thousand. Consider with yourself; if he swallows Flanders Holland must follow, and if France be once master of Holland pray think what will become of you. Will your fleet alone be able to deal with that of France and Holland, too, for that will be the consequence.

Sir Robert Cotton (of Chester): I am against putting the question for the whole for that here is one particular for Scotland, which being an independent kingdom having a revenue of their own they ought to maintain their own troops.

Solicitor Trevor: I cannot give my consent clearly to this question for the 20,000 men in England until I know what the whole is. If the whole number of 54,000 men be first agreed on, then I think 20,000 necessary for England, but otherwise I cannot tell whether 20,000 be a proportion.

Sir John Trevor (the Speaker) and Lord Marquess of Winchester were for the whole number.

Charles Montagu: Since I find the question of 20,000 men is insisted on to be first put as being first moved, I propose an amendment to it by way of addition—'and that the number of 34,000 men be maintained for the service of the year 1693'. Sir Robert Howard, Lord Falkland, and Sir Robert Rich were for the addition.

Mr. Harley and Sir Christopher Musgrave opposed it and said this question cannot be put for this is in effect giving money. You vote £1,000,000 in the first part of your question and are now by way of addition voting another £1,000,000, which was never seen. This is by a trick to hook in the whole general question.

Col. Granville against it for he believed it was never seen where the addition to a question was more than the question itself, as it is here.

This addition to the question was long debated. Those gentlemen who were for the question of the 20,000 were against the addition.

Mr. Comptroller Wharton: I am against this addition to the question because of the dangerous consequence of such a precedent—to a small sum to tack a greater, as this is no more. But I desire the first question of the 20,000 men may be put, and then I doubt not but gentlemen will see the necessity of coming up to the remainder of the forces.

So the question of the addition being retracted, the question was put and resolved *nemine contradicente*: That 20,000 men, part of the land forces mentioned in the list to be delivered into the House, are necessary to be continued in England for the year 1693 for the security of this kingdom.

Then it was proposed to put the remaining question about the residue of the forces—34,562 men.

Sir Christopher Musgrave: I am against that question for we are not obliged by any treaty to send so many men to our allies. But what is our quota I am for fully coming up to that, but no more. But then it is said a descent is intended. I think the best service we can do ourselves is to put a small body of men on board our fleet and to try to burn their ships, and for this the forces proposed in the question are too many. But if it be designed to make a conquest in France they are too few, and if you could get a province or two therein what would it signify when you will not be long able to keep it? Then if these men are designed to send to Flanders, your treasure out of this kingdom will be much exhausted and hardly ever return to you again.

Col. Titus: It is a strange opinion that when our enemies are stronger and we are hardly able to deal with them already that we shall go to weaken ourselves more.

Several speeches were made against the 34,000 men to be sent beyond sea, especially by them who were for the 20,000 in England. And urged that 20,000 more might be for other services and that the remaining 14,000 men (of the 34,000) which were Dutch troops might be sent home and paid by them, because they want their own troops now and are forced to maintain so many foreign troops in their room and that though we must have 34,000 men in Flanders the Dutch had not above 18,000 in the field all last summer.

Lord Colchester informed the House that to his certain knowledge the Dutch had in the field 30,000 men last summer.

So after a long debate it was resolved: That 34,562 men, other part of the land forces according to the list delivered into the House, are necessary for the service of the year 1693 to be employed abroad.

Then it was moved to report these two resolutions to the House about the forces. But it was opposed because irregular to report the resolutions on part of an estimate before the whole was gone through. So that was let fall. But then the Attorney was ordered to report the resolution of the committee for making good what the poll bill fell short and to desire leave to sit again.

So the Speaker resumed the Chair and the *Attorney* reported the said resolution accordingly, to which the House agreed *nemine contradicente*. Then the *Attorney* moved for leave to sit again, and the House ordered upon Tuesday morning next to go into a committee to consider farther of the supply to be granted to Their Majesties, etc.

All committees adjourned.

So adjourned till Monday morning 9 of the clock.

Monday, 5 December

Sir Robert Cotton moved that Col. Shakerley might have leave to waive his privilege in a suit against him. But the House would not meddle with it but let him do as he would.

Sir Christopher Musgrave for leave to bring in a bill to take away the custom within the province of York by which a woman shall have her share of her husband's personal estate, though he hath made a settlement on her before and even contrary to a man's own will yet she shall have her part.

Mr. Waller (of York) opposed it.

But, however, the House thought it reasonable and gave leave accordingly.

The bill for making perjury and subornation of perjury felony in capital cases was read the first time.

Mr. Hutchinson opposed its having a second reading for that it would discourage witnesses in criminal cases.

Mr. Greenfield thought it would do well to extend it only in the case of high treason.

However, ordered a second reading.

Mr. Clarke reported from the committee the Quakers' petition, with their opinion thereon that leave be desired to bring in a bill according to the prayer of the same—viz. to take their solemn asseverations in courts of justice and to make the same perjury as in cases where the person is sworn.

Mr. Hutchinson, *Mr. Arnold*, and *Mr. Clarke* spoke in their behalf for that it was often very mischievous to many people. Sometimes a witness to a deed is a Quaker; sometimes one who was none when a witness turns Quaker afterward and for want of this man's oath the party is without remedy to prove his deed.

But *Mr. Greenfield*, *Sir Joseph Tredenham*, *Col. Goldwell*, *Sir Christopher Musgrave*, etc. spoke against them and knew no reason why their word should go further than others or they should have more privilege than other subjects, who have not deserved such encouragement from this government and it might be of very dangerous consequence.

So the question was put to give leave to bring in a bill according to the petition and carried in the negative.

Sir John Lowther presented a petition from the persons in custody of the Serjeant at Arms that were brought from Carlisle for a breach of privilege committed against Christopher Musgrave esq., a member of this House, on behalf of themselves and others acknowledging their offence and begging pardon of the House for the same. [It] was read.

But it was said against them they had not made their application to the member and begged his pardon.

Sir Edward Seymour: As to that matter, it is not material. The privilege is the House's, and if the House be satisfied you may discharge them; and the end of punishing is but to assert your privilege.

But then said they had not restored the member to his freedom as they ought, so the contempt continued.

And the member not being in his place, they were ordered to be brought to the Bar of this House on Wednesday morning next.

Then the House, according to order, went into a committee upon the matter of advice to His Majesty; Sir Francis Winnington to the Chair.

Capt. Pitt: As the last time you made a good step to remove foreign officers, so I am now for removing foreigners out of your councils. Therefore I am for an address to His Majesty that foreigners may not be dictators of affairs here in England.

Sir Charles Sedley: I think there is no great need to trouble ourselves about that. If there be but one in the council that is a foreigner, he can do no great hurt as long as the majority is against him.

Paul Foley: You have had a report relating to the descent which I think very considerable and very fit to do something therein. I think it is thereon very apparent that things were not well managed about that matter, and therefore I shall propose a question to you—that it is the opinion of this committee that there hath been an apparent miscarriage in the management of the affairs relating to the descent the last summer. Mr. Smith, Sir Charles Sedley, and Mr. Bathurst to the same.

So the question was put and resolved accordingly.

Sir Walter Yonge: The next thing naturally for you to come to is where to fix this fault, which appears to me to be in not giving timely orders necessary about the same. Mr. Clarke to the same.

So the question was stated and resolved: That it is the opinion of this committee that one cause of the miscarriage of the descent was for want of giving timely and necessary orders by such persons to whom that matter was committed.

But Mr. Paul Foley proposed to add to the question the persons who were to give those orders, who were the council that had the management thereof.

Sir John Lowther: I must own I have the honour to be of Their Majesties' Privy Council and to be one of the committee of Council who had this matter under their care, but by reason of sickness and some necessary affairs I was very little present the last summer. But, however, I think in the matter proposed we are running too fast—to proceed to censure persons of honour and worth upon a report *ex parte*—and therefore I shall desire you will have the papers before you and fully inform yourselves in the matter, and that soon as you will. Sir Robert Cotton and Sir Joseph Tredenham to the same.

Sir Edward Seymour: I must say, as I have done formerly, that the committee who made this report had not all the papers before them. There are several letters and orders precedent to those they have taken notice of which you have not now before you, and therefore that you may judge aright I would have all things before you and then what judgement you make will carry the more weight. But I believe what is done is rather designed against persons than to rectify things. However, if you will go on to judge persons without hearing, yet assure yourself they will be heard in another place. And as to what has been hinted at of the Lord Nottingham and the reflections upon him, I will say never any person has taken more care and industry to serve this government than he has. And therefore I think the properest way is to examine the matter thoroughly before you pass your censure, and after let it fall where the fault is.

Sir Christopher Musgrave: I, for my part, can make but little as yet of this report, and therefore think you are not yet ripe for a judgement but ought first to have all the papers before you. Without it I cannot give my opinion, for I am not altogether for going on common fame to accuse men without some good proof of the matter.

Several others spoke pro and con. But at last the question was put as above and resolved accordingly upon a division of the committee—the Yeas on the right hand and the Noes on the left.

	Yeas	Goodwin Wharton	156
Tellers for the			
	Noes	Francis Robartes	155

So the Chairman was ordered to report the committee had made some further progress and to desire leave to sit again. So he left the Chair on the question.

The Speaker resumed the Chair. *Sir Francis Winnington* reported accordingly, and the committee was ordered to sit again on Thursday next about the advice.

All committees were revived.

So adjourned till 9 tomorrow morning.

Tuesday, 6 December

Mr. Waller (of York) presented a petition from some persons in custody for a breach of privilege committed against Sir John Bland, begging pardon of the House and acknowledging their offence. [It] was read.

And the member, *Sir John Bland*, being in the House, he stood up in his place and acquainted the House he was satisfied and if the House pleased he was willing they should be discharged. And they were ordered to be brought to the Bar tomorrow morning to be discharged.

Upon the question for engrossing the bill for convex lights arose a debate.

Sir John Darell: I am against this bill because I look on it as pernicious to the interest of England. It hinders the consumption of your tallow, which is the concern of all landed men, and you have prohibited it from being exported, which has reduced it from 5*d.* per pound to 2½*d.* per pound. And what now will this bring it to?

Sir Edward Seymour and *Sir Thomas Clarges* spoke for it.

Sir Thomas Vernon presented a petition to the House from the Lord Mayor, Aldermen, and Common Council of the City of London, praying leave to be heard by their counsel touching some matters relating to the said bill.

Several persons spoke against the said petition as coming in very irregularly and late in time, this bill having lain before the committee above a fortnight, in all which time they might have presented their petition and been heard against the bill. But now when the bill has been gone through at the committee and several amendments made to it and they agreed to by the House and now when the question for engrossing it is next, to present this petition is a sort of artifice to obstruct the proceedings of this House and very unparliamentary, and therefore desired it might be rejected.

But, however, the Whig interest prevailed for the City [and] got the bill referred back to the said committee to consider of the said petition and to report their opinions therein.

Then the House, according to order, went into a committee to consider farther of the supply to Their Majesties; Mr. Attorney to the Chair. So after the Order of the Day was read he acquainted the committee how far they proceeded the last time.

Paul Foley and Sir Thomas Clarges desired the committee would compute what the pay of those men they voted the last time would come to that they might see if they could bear any more. That here was a list of general officers for whom the pay was very high, exceeding all former establishments. Then here were several officers amongst them that had plurality of offices and the pay is allowed to them for each office though one person has them—as several of the officers have regiments, too. Then here is a sum to foreign princes, which is very strange; the parliaments of England used to give supply to their own princes but never to strangers.

However, after some debate the House proceeded on the list of the general officers, which was read.

Sir Christopher Musgrave took exceptions to the great pay that was allowed them which was grown very extravagant, and hoped the committee would consider and retrench them in this time of hardship as well as the country gentleman was forced to retrench—it being not fit they should live at so great a height when others have hardly wherewith to supply their real necessities.

Lord Ranelagh: The pay of these officers is no higher this year than it was the last year and the year before.

Sir Edward Seymour was for going upon the general officers as they were in order, head by head.

So the head of the General of the Horse and the General of the Foot was read, and it was proposed to be the same as it was the last year.

Paul Foley proposed to allow the General of the Horse £4 a day.

Sir Thomas Clarges was against entering any sum on our books of pay to the general officers because it might be dangerous, and therefore proposed in general to vote £20,000 for general officers and let His Majesty dispose thereof as he please.

But, however, it was at last resolved: That the pay for the General of the Foot and General of the Horse for the service of the year 1693 be £6 *per diem* each; That the pay of five lieutenant generals be £4 a day each; That the pay for five major generals be £2 a day each; That the pay for 10 brigadiers be £1. 10s. a day each; That the pay for two adjutant generals be £1 a day each; That the pay of the Quarter-master General be £1 a day, and his two assistants each 10s. a day; That the pay for the Paymaster General be £1 a day; That the pay for the Commissary General and his deputies be £7. 9s. 4d. a day.

Then for the Secretary of War, proposed his pay to be £3 per day. But opposed because his pay formerly never was above £1 a day, and though the army now be greater so are his advantages without increasing his pay. So proposed to reduce it to what formerly, viz. 20s. a day. Committee divided thereon.

		Yeas	Col. Cornewall	147
Tellers for the				
		Noes	Charles Montagu	128

So the pay of the Secretary at War was reduced to 20s. a day.

[Resolved]: That the pay for the Judge Advocate and his deputies be £1. 12s. 6d. a day; That the pay for the Physician General and for the Surgeon General be each 10s. a day; That the pay for the Apothecary General be 10s. a day; That the pay for the Provost Marshal be 8s. a day, and for 24 men 3s. a day each.

Then it was proposed to consider the pay of the Danish general officers. And first of the Lieutenant General (the Prince of Württemberg), it was moved for £4 a day. But this was opposed because they come into our service by a treaty according to which they are to have but Dutch pay when in Holland and not English pay unless when in Their Majesties' dominions. But it was urged for him that he was a brave man and had done very good service. Said, this was a good reason to vote him a reward but not to raise the establishment contrary to our capitulation. Therefore because the House did not know what the Dutch pay of general officers was they postponed this head that they might inquire into it.

Then the House proceeded in the consideration of the train of ordnance for the land service, which is the same as was last year though it was said the office is above £300,000 in debt and that there was no consideration of the descent the last year (which was ordered after the end of the last sessions) so that the money you gave was for the Flanders train, besides which there was a train for the descent which alone cost £123,000 besides the officers who belonged to it who had their pay.

Sir Henry Goodricke informed the House that it was the custom of the Office of Ordnance whenever they issue out ammunition or any stores out of the magazines to bespeak new and fill them up again. I suppose no one will think it fitting to leave your stores empty; but it you do, less than £210,773. 4s. 5d. (which is the sum demanded) will do.

Sir Thomas Clarges: I am not for lumping so great a sum nor is there such need for it as is pretended, for all your arms and trains are ready in a great measure. The last year you were forced to buy them all new, which you need not now; a small charge will fit them up for your service this year, so I am sure you may save something. For my part I cannot but take notice that foreigners must have the chief commands even in your most necessary concerns, wherein it is not safe to trust foreigners nor any policy to let them have the knowledge of. The chief officer of your train is one Col. Goer, a Dutchman and suspected a papist, too; there are several gunners, engineers, and matrosses which are foreigners too, which I think not for our security when we have Englishmen enough, than which there are no better men in the world.

Sir Christopher Musgrave desired that the House would take notice that if this estimate was allowed the charge of the train for the descent was paid.

So resolved: That the sum of £210,773. 4s. 5d. be allowed for the charge of the Ordnance for the land service for the year 1693.

So it being late, it was moved for the Chairman to leave the Chair, to report some further progress, and to desire leave to sit again—all which were resolved on the question. That for leaving the Chair was put last. So Mr. Attorney left the Chair.

Speaker resumed the Chair and *Mr. Attorney* reported that the committee had sat and made some progress and desired leave to sit again, which was resolved on Friday next.

Some members were added to several committees.[1]

Adjourned till 9 tomorrow morning.

Wednesday, 7 December

The bill for the importation of fine thrown silk overland was read a second time.

It was opposed being committed by *Foot Onslow, Sir Thomas Vernon, Sir Samuel Dashwood, Sir John Darell*, and others as a matter that would

[1] No such order is entered in the *Journal*.

be very prejudicial to the woollen manufacture, ruin your Turkey trade, and destroy the throwing of silk here in this nation.

However, it was committed on the debate of the House.

Ordered that the persons of the City of Carlisle who were taken into custody for a breach of privilege committed on Mr. Christopher Musgrave should be discharged, paying their fees. They being at the Bar on their knees received a reprimand from *Mr. Speaker* and were told they were discharged but for the present until they restored the said Mr. Musgrave to his freedom, which they were wished to do forthwith.

Ordered that the committee to whom the petition of the clothiers of Gloucestershire was referred should have power to send for persons, papers, and records.

Order of the Day read and the House went into a Committee of the Whole House to consider of heads for a bill to preserve and establish the East India trade. Mr. Smith took the Chair of the committee.

Sir Edward Seymour moved that since it was well known that the mischiefs of the late Company were occasioned by plurality of voices, therefore that every £500 to £2,000 should have one vote, £4,000 to have two votes, so for £10,000 to have five votes.

So after some debate upon each of the heads, the committee came to these following resolutions. Resolved: That every person having £500 stock in the said company have one vote; That no one should have but one vote; That no one shall be elected to be governor but he that hath £5,000 in the said stock; That none shall be deputy governor or a committee-man in the said company that hath less than £1,000; That the company be obliged to export £150,000[1] of the manufactures of this nation; That no ship shall trade by permission or licence on any private account; That no sale shall be on any private contract but for the company at public sales by inch of candle, unless for saltpetre for the use of the Crown; That every year the company shall be obliged to furnish the Crown with 500 ton of saltpetre at £35 per ton, the refraction whereof shall not exceed five per cent; No foreigner to have any interest in the said stock or shall be employed abroad in the said company; That no contract for transferring any stock shall be good in law unless it be executed in one week or that the party have so much stock in the company in his own name; That no lot by candle at one time shall exceed £500, except in jewels;

---

[1] In error for £100,000; see *CJ*, x. 740.

That all dividends shall be made in money and the original stock to be left entire.

So according to order, Mr. Smith left the Chair. Mr. Speaker resumed the Chair and *Mr. Smith*, according to order, reported from the committee that they had gone through the matter to them referred and had come to several resolutions which he was ready to report. Ordered to be reported on Saturday next.

Committees adjourned.

So adjourned till 9 tomorrow morning.

Thursday, 8 December

The two bills for furnishing Their Majesties' Navy with seamen were read and referred to one committee to make a good bill out of them, and all the members that serve for the Cinque Ports or any of the seaports to be of that committee and to have power to send for persons, papers, and records.

Sir Ralph Carr presented the petition from the merchants of London against the bill for exportation of the woollen manufactures, which was read and ordered to lie on the Table till that bill is read a second time.

The bill to prevent the exportation of gold and silver was read the first time.

Sir John Darell: This bill is to prevent the exportation of your money, which is a beneficial trade to your merchants for they get three per cent by exporting it. I wish this may prevent it; therefore I desire it may have a second reading.

Then the Order of the Day was read and the House went into a Committee of the Whole House to consider of His Majesty's speech wherein he desires the advice of this House. Sir Francis Winnington took the Chair.

Sir Richard Temple: There is one thing His Majesty takes notice of in his speech to you which is worthy your consideration. You are now like to have an army abroad, which of necessity must occasion great payments there. Therefore I think it fit to consider how to keep your money at home by supplying your army with stores, ammunition, provisions, clothes, etc. from hence, so less of your money need be exported.

John Jeffreys: I think the best expedient to keep your money here is as the Dutch are obliged by treaty with you to provide a certain number of ships, you may provide them yourselves and they may pay the land forces in Flanders, and that will answer the end.

Sir John Darell: I think the first proposal is very good for that the more of your own commodities you export beyond sea, you raise the value here of what is left. Then the exportation of your money is very pernicious unless it bring in such commodities that being carried out will bring in more money.

Sir Thomas Clarges: I think it may be practicable to buy all our clothes, our bread, etc. here. But the King is obliged to pay so much money to foreign troops. How we can come at that I can't tell. It were better for us that the capitulation was to give such a proportion of the manufactures of our own nation.

Sir Christopher Musgrave: It is no doubt but great payments of your money abroad is very prejudicial to you and will occasion a scarcity at home unless you can find some way to have it brought in again. Now the way to prevent this is to lessen your exportation of the money as much as you can and increase that of your manufacture. I would have all soldiers in your pay, natives or foreigners, have their bread made of English corn, that all their clothes be bought here, that all the accoutrements and equipage of your officers be provided here, and this will in some measure help you.

Sir Thomas Clarges: Though this be a considerable thing you are upon, yet I desire it may keep cold till tomorrow because I think you are not now ripe for it, being it relates to some heads in your estimate which you have not yet agreed on.

Mr. Arnold to the same for that these matters are but tithing mint and cumin. I shall, therefore, propose a thing that may be of weight and that is to move the House from the committee that a conference may be desired with the Lords to consider of the state of the nation and the posture of our affairs.

Mr. Bickerstaffe: I desire the House may be moved to appoint a committee to consider of proposals and the method to furnish your army abroad.

Col. Cornewall and Sir John Guise informed the House that things were cheaper in Holland than here and that is the reason you give your soldiers less pay there than here.

After some time a question was stated and resolved: That it is the opinion of this committee that the House be moved to appoint a committee to consider of ways how the army abroad may be supplied with provisions, clothes, and other necessaries from hence to prevent the exportation of the coin of this kingdom.

Mr. Godolphin moved that the House would make some application to His Majesty to renew the treaty with the Duke of Hanover or such others as he pleases.

But it was rejected as an irregular motion being in effect but giving of money.

So it being moved for Sir Francis Winnington to leave the Chair, he put the question presently and declared it for leaving the Chair without any report being ordered to be made or leave to be desired to sit again, which was very irregular and could not now be done. So Sir Francis Winnington left the Chair.

The Speaker resumed it. No report could be made from the committee. Therefore *Sir Ralph Dutton* and *Sir John Morton* took notice of the irregularity, and that since the committee for the advice was fallen desired it might be revived and sit again. So ordered on Monday next.

All committees revived.

Adjourned till 9 tomorrow morning.

Friday, 9 December

Sir Joseph Tredenham brought in the naturalization bill.

Mr. Arnold presented the Poulterers' petition, which was praying they might be inserted in the hawkers and pedlars bill.

Mr. Gwyn presented a petition from Mr. Popham, a member of the House, desiring leave to bring in a bill to enable him to make a jointure on his wife and make provision for younger children, etc. But it was opposed as irregular, being in the case of a member; he ought not to petition the House but ought to move the House for it. So *Mr. Gwyn* turned the petition into a motion to the House, and it was ordered accordingly.

Some members were added to the committee to inspect the laws now expiring, and they are to meet this day at 4 in the afternoon.

Then the Order of the Day was read and the House resolved itself into a Committee of the Whole House to consider of the supply to Their Majesties. Mr. Attorney General took the Chair of the committee, and he acquainted them how far they went last time and that they left off at the head of the transport ships.

Mr. Harley: The sum demanded in your estimate for this service is £200,000, which is double what it was the year before. But if it must be so, I desire if any be left thereon it may be applied to pay the arrears due for them the year before.

Sir Edward Seymour: It is true this head is double what it was before and the reason is the service is much greater than it was. And what is proposed to you I think very fitting—that after this year's service is supplied the residue may be applied to payments of debts upon this service.

So question stated and resolved: That the sum of £200,000 be allowed for the transport service for the year 1693; and if the whole sum be not employed in that year's service, the remainder to be applied towards discharging the debts now owing for the transport service.

The next head is His Majesty's proportion of the subsidies to be paid to the Dukes of Savoy and Hanover, viz. £150,000.

Sir Thomas Clarges: After we had voted 34,562 men for foreign parts, I was in good hopes we should have heard of no more. But this is a new thing never, I believe, seen in any estimate before—for the Commons of England to give money to foreign princes. Then besides, I observe poor England must bear the load; in the treaty of Savoy we are to pay 20,000 crowns and the Dutch but 10,000, and in all the wars that the Dutch and we were together engaged in they bore a proportion equal to us, but here it is more though it be their concern more than ours. But besides, here is a random sum of £150,000 brought in which is more than it comes to: we pay 20,000 crowns to Savoy and 15,000 dollars to Hanover which—at 5*s.* a dollar and 5*s.* a crown—comes to at most £105,000.

Lord Ranelagh: The King pays as much to Hanover as he does to Savoy—20,000 crowns to Savoy and 20,000 dollars to Hanover—and the Dutch 10,000 apiece to each. Now the King's share comes to £5,000 for each a month—viz. £10,000 a month for both—which comes to for the whole year £120,000. But then the King is obliged to find two-third parts of the bread and forage for the Hanover troops, for which the odd £30,000 is reckoned. And this treaty is to expire at April next, but it is so advantageous to this government that it is about renewing.

Sir Thomas Clarges: I cannot but take notice that though we were drawn into this war by the Dutch—they being the principals—yet we must bear a greater share of the burden. These things, I am afraid, are occasioned by having one of the Dutch [E]states[1] in your council.

---

[1] Probably a reference to Bentinck, now Earl of Portland.

Sir Edward Seymour: I do agree giving money to foreign princes is not very usual in our parliaments, but consider this is to our friends who have done us good service. And I must tell you if you had not got them just as you did, they would have been employed against you—I mean the Hanover troops. Then for those of Savoy, you have great reason to encourage them, having done you great service, and it is the only way you can attack France. Whether your allies can bear more I will not determine, but I am well assured the Dutch pay more now to this war than they did in the war against England and France, too.

Sir Thomas Clarges: If a King of England will make war out of his own purse, God forbid we should meddle in it. But if a King of England will make war by our advice, I desire we may look a little into matters, and alliances to carry on the same may be made also with our advice. I am afraid if we of ourselves had not made such large offers our allies would have come up to their proportion. And in looking over the accounts, though we were not principals in the war but drawn in by the Dutch, I find great payments to the forces of the Emperor, Elector of Bavaria, and others, who are more concerned in the war than we.

Sir Christopher Musgrave: As to the head you are upon, I believe we shall not save much money in it. But I would not have us give a countenance to these alliances wherein our proportion is greater than that of the Dutch.

Paul Foley: To the end that no such thing may appear; if you please to, vote it in general and take in the two other particulars in the gross and vote £200,000 in all for hospitals and other contingencies. It will do and answer the end.

So after some debate, it was put and resolved: That it is the opinion of this committee that the sum of £200,000 be allowed for hospitals, contingencies, and other extraordinary charges of the war for the year 1693.

Lord Ranelagh informed the House as to the pay of the Danish general officers: the Lieutenant General, English pay £4 a day, Dutch pay about £2. 19s.; a Major General, English 40s. a day, Dutch about £1. 12s.; a Brigadier, English £1. 10s. a day, Dutch £1. 5s. So that with what you have saved already in your Secretary of War, you may save about £1,600 per annum. So that upon the whole if you please to vote £30,000 for general officers, I think you do very well.

But it was moved by some that since the Prince of Württemberg

(the Danish General) had behaved himself so bravely that we ought
to give him as much as the other or else to give him a bounty.

Sir Thomas Clarges, Sir Edward Seymour, and others opposed that,
being irregular for this House to meddle with rewards, being that is
the proper act of the Crown.

Then proposed to lump the head of general officers as before. But
that could not be because the committee had gone through some of
the heads of the general officers already and passed them.

Hampden proposed to compute what the heads of general officers
you have passed already comes to, and then you may add for the
residue to make it up in the whole £30,000.

Sir Thomas Clarges: You have nothing to do but to compute the
charge of the general officers already passed and to add the pay of
these three Danish officers according to the Dutch establishment.

But, however, the worth of the men prevailed to have it computed
according to English pay. So the question was stated and resolved
accordingly: That the pay for the general officers of the Danes for the
year 1693 be the sum of £2,737. 10s.

Then the Chairman acquainted the committee that they had
nothing to do but to compute the charge of the 54,562 men—horse,
foot, and dragoons. So it was computed and the question stated and
resolved: That the pay for the horse, foot, and dragoons according to
the list delivered into the House for the year 1693 be the sum of
£1,448,732. 6s. 7d.

So the Chairman was ordered to report these resolutions and to desire leave to sit again (to compute the gross sum), and left the Chair.

Mr. Speaker resumed the Chair and *Mr. Attorney General* reported
from the said committee that they had agreed upon several resolutions which they had directed him to report. Ordered that the report
be made tomorrow and nothing to intervene.

Several members were added to divers committees.[1]

So adjourned till 10 tomorrow morning.

Saturday, 10 December

Mr. Smith presented the petition of Mr. Bayntun and others.

Sir [John Franklin][2] and Sir John Hoskins, Masters in Chancery,
brought the message from the Lords.

[1] No such order is entered in the *Journal*.
[2] In MS. 'William Frankland'. Not hereafter noted.

Mr. Attorney General, according to order, reported from the Committee of the Whole House the several resolutions they had agreed upon touching the land forces and the general officers. Some of them were opposed, as that for the pay of the Generals of the Horse and Foot.

Sir Thomas Clarges spoke against it that it should not be so high, being a great pay and an extravagant establishment. Therefore desired it might be one entire sum for the general officers and not to appear on our books.

Sir Edward Seymour thought it was very strange for the House to do what they were ashamed of.

Then to the resolution about the pay for 54,562 men:

Sir Christopher Musgrave took exception to this and thought it very hard upon us to pay for forces to guard Scotland, who are an independent kingdom and ought to bear their own burden.

But, however, all the resolutions were severally put and agreed to as resolved by the committee.

Then the *Attorney General* moved for leave for the committee to sit again.

Mr. Montagu moved that the House would go into a Committee of the Whole House presently for that it was only to cast up the several sums and agree upon the total, which would not be half an hour's work.

So the Speaker left the Chair; Mr. Attorney General took the Chair of the committee. So the Chairman cast up the several sums and added them again, whereupon a state was stated and resolved: That it is the opinion of this committee that a sum not exceeding £2,090,563. 19*s.* 6*d.* be granted to Their Majesties for the charge of the land forces for the service of the year 1693, including the extraordinary charge of the Office of Ordnance relating to the land service, and the charge of the transports, hospitals, contingencies, and other extraordinary charges of the war. Then the Attorney General was ordered to report this resolution and to leave the Chair.

Speaker resumed the Chair and *Mr. Attorney* reported the resolution, to which the House agreed and resolved to go into a committee on Tuesday next to consider of ways and means for raising the supply to be granted to Their Majesties.

(A madman came into the House, up to the very Table with his hat on, and bid the Speaker come out of the Chair. But he was put out, and if he had not been a madman would have been taken into custody of the Serjeant at Arms.)

Mr. Goodwin Wharton and *Sir Peter Colleton* spoke against agreeing with the Committee [of Elections] in their resolution touching the election of Bridgwater for Mr. Balch. However, it was put and clearly carried on his behalf to agree with the committee.

Mr. Smith reported from the committee the several resolutions touching the trade to the East Indies which he read in his place at the Bar and delivered them in at the Table, where they were all read over and afterwards read over severally and put.

That for a joint stock—agreed to.

The joint stock not less than £1,500,000 and not more than £2,000,000—agreed to.

The stock to continue for 21 years—agreed to.

The stock to be raised by new subscriptions:

Mr. Neale: I am against this head. I am for your regulations but think this trade may be better carried on than by new subscriptions, as thus: I would have 40 persons chosen by this House to manage the trade and to be accountable to parliament; and they to be empowered to take up money at interest, the profit to go to paying the interest and after the money borrowed; and for a fund for the money a tax to be of £70,000 *per mensem* for one month, which will pay five per cent for £1,400,000; and when the principal and interest is paid, then the profit to be divided amongst the contributors to the £70,000 land tax. This is what I collect at present, but if you please to postpone this head for a day or two I will offer you something further to it.

However, the resolution of the committee was agreed to.

None to subscribe less than £100 nor more than £10,000, and to pay one-third down—agreed to.

That £500 stock should have a vote—agreed to.

No person to have above one vote—agreed to.

The governor not to have less stock than £5,000—agreed to.

Deputy governor or committee-man not less than £1,000—agreed to.

Company to export £100,000 of our own manufactures—agreed to.

No private contract to be made but all at public sales, except saltpetre to the King—agreed to.

To furnish the King yearly 500 ton of saltpetre at £35 *per centum* (112 pounds to the *centum*) and at five per cent refraction—agreed to.

No foreigner to have any stock therein—agreed to.

That no contract be good unless executed within a week or party transferring have so much stock in his own name—agreed to.

No lot to be above £500 value, except in case of jewels—agreed to.

And dividends to be in money leaving the original stock entire—agreed to.

After which it was ordered that a bill be brought in pursuant to the said resolutions, and it was referred to Mr. Smith.

Mr. Solicitor General, according to order, presented the House with a bill for better preservation of Their Majesties' persons and government. And it was received, read the first time, and ordered a second reading on Wednesday next at 11 of the clock. (The bill consisted of several parts: making words against this government the first time a *praemunire*, the second time high treason; and to express the same by writing, printing, etc., to be high treason; enjoins all persons taking the former oaths to take a new oath in nature of an abjuration of King James; and persons refusing the first time imprisonment and forfeiture of etc., and the second time a *praemunire*.)

Several members added to divers committees.

Sir William Turner was ordered to take care of the madman that came into the House and to put him into Bedlam.

So adjourned till 9 on Monday morning.

Monday, 12 December

Mr. Smith presented the petition of Sir George Brown, etc. for a private bill.

Mr. Smith also presented a petition from several clerks in the Crown Office relating to the bill depending in the House, praying leave to be heard by their counsel against it. It was ordered to lie on the Table till that bill be read a second time.

Mr. John Howe moved that a committee might be appointed to inspect the privileges of this House to make our fellow subjects easier in their prosecutions against any member of this House, for if something is not done in reference to this matter this House will become the greatest grievance of the kingdom. *Mr. John Smith* and *Sir John Morton* to the same.

Sir Thomas Clarges: This is a very good motion and worthy your consideration. I remember in the Long Parliament before the Restoration there was the like thing wherein, as I remember, they ordered no member should have any privilege but for his own person, and if any man had a cause of action against a member he went to a judge who sent a summons to the member, and if he did not appear to such action process went out against his estate. Therefore I think you are well moved to appoint a committee.

Sir John Lowther: I like the thing that is moved very well but think it more proper to appoint a committee to search into the privileges of this House and to report their opinions therein to you. For now since prorogations and adjournments are so short and sittings so long, it is all privilege time and there is no coming at their right for any person against a member.

So a committee was appointed to consider how the privileges of the members of this House in relation to suits in equity may be regulated and limited, and to report their opinions therein to the House. Ordered that they sit *de die in diem* and have power to send for persons, papers, and records.

The House, according to order, went into a Committee of the Whole House upon the advice to His Majesty. Speaker left the Chair; Sir Francis Winnington took the Chair of the committee.

Mr. Hutchinson moved that the House might be moved to address to His Majesty that the Lord Nottingham and the Cabinet Council might give an account why there was not timely orders and necessary sent for the descent.

Sir Charles Sedley thought it proper to address to His Majesty that all the papers about it may be laid before the House.

Admiral Russell and Sir Robert Howard desired this matter might be postponed for that in a short time all the papers about it will be laid before the House.

So it was let fall.

Then the matter about supplying the army abroad with necessaries from hence came under debate. And after some debate it was resolved: That it is the opinion of this committee that the House be moved to appoint a committee to consider how the army abroad in Their Majesties' pay may be supplied with bread, clothes, and other provisions of the growth of this kingdom to prevent the exportation of the coin thereof. And he was ordered to make the motion to the House and to leave the Chair, which he did.

And the Speaker resumed the Chair. *Sir Francis Winnington* reported the Committee of the Whole House had sat and made some further progress and commanded him to make a motion to the House, which *he* did as above. And a committee was accordingly appointed, to sit *de die in diem. He* moved also for another day to sit, and ordered again on Friday next.

So adjourned till 9 tomorrow morning.

Tuesday, 13 December

The committee to whom the bill about the woollen manufacture stands referred had power to send for persons, papers, and records.

Sir Miles Cook and Sir Robert Legard brought the message from the Lords.

The bill for free and impartial proceedings in parliament disabled any member of the Commons' House from and after his election to accept of any place or office from Their Majesties, their heirs and successors, after the [blank] day of etc., and that if he does his election in this House shall be void.[1]

Then the House went into a Committee of the Whole House to consider of the ways and means for raising the supply to be granted to Their Majesties; Mr. Attorney General to the Chair.

Mr. Goldwell spoke very well and largely of the justice of equal taxing and how fitting it was that all persons should pay their share and not some to pay so much over others, as in their counties of Norfolk and Suffolk where they paid 6*s.*, 7*s.*, 8*s.*, and 10*s.* in the pound to the last land tax and other counties not above 2*s.* or 3*s.* and some not so much, and therefore he desired there might be a land tax by way of a pound rate of 4*s.* in the pound. Mr. Hoby to the same.

Mr. Bathurst was against the tax by way of a pound rate for that it was an uncertain tax and the King will be deceived, and so you will have an arrear to pay next sessions as you had in the quarterly poll.

Sir Charles Sedley to the same and that the King might name commissioners.

Sir Christopher Musgrave was for a monthly assessment to raise the sum of £2,000,000.

Col. Austen was for a land tax by a pound rate.

So Mr. Smith, and inveighed much against a general excise as the most destructive tax to this government, for it is uncertain what it will raise, not practicable in a year or two, and though you give it but for a year yet when it is once up you may [find] a parliament of officers to continue it.

---

[1] It was at this juncture that the place bill was first read.

Sir John Kay was for the monthly assessment.

Sir Thomas Clarges: I am for a monthly assessment because it is certain. I am not for unequal taxes and wish some way might be found to remedy the inequality. I am for £2,000,000 to be raised by a land tax by a monthly assessment, which I would give for 15 months at £137,000 *per mensem*, which will come to two millions and 60-odd thousand pounds.

Mr. Boscawen and the Lord Falkland were for a pound rate. So Sir Thomas Littleton, Sir John Guise, and Sir Robert Howard for that it was the equallest way of taxing by a pound rate.

Mr. Bickerstaffe was for the monthly assessment, and Sir Henry Ashurst.

Lord Norris, Mr. Harley were for the pound rate of 4s. in the pound, for though some counties might not come up to the height as they ought, yet there was this justice that no man would be oppressed by paying more, whereas the other is apparently unjust by rating some so much more than others.

Sir Thomas Clarges and Sir John Morton were against a pound rate for that it multiplies oaths, and the consequence of it will be the King must appoint commissioners.

Mr. Charles Montagu: I am for the 4s. tax for that it will raise you more money, as particularly here in Middlesex. That county pays to the monthly assessment but £6,000 a month, but to the 3s. in the pound tax they paid £175,000 in the whole.

Mr. Greenfield and Sir Ralph Carr were for the monthly assessment.

Sir Robert Cotton (of Cambridgeshire) for the pound rate.

Mr. Clarke: As to the method of going by the poor's rate which some propose to rectify unequal taxing, that is a very unequal sort of tax itself. It is not the interest of a particular place we are to consider but the interest of England in general, and therefore I am for a monthly assessment.

Sir Robert Davers was for the pound rate.

So Sir Richard Temple, and wondered this House should make the manner of taxing in troublesome times to be the same now.

There was a long debate about it. The north-country gentlemen as Yorkshire, Northumberland, Durham, Cumberland, Westmorland, Lancashire, Derbyshire, etc., [and] those gentlemen who have estates here in houses in Middlesex, etc., were for the tax by way of a monthly assessment. But Norfolk, Suffolk, Essex, Wilts., Bucks., Bedford,

Kent, Surrey, etc. were for that of a pound rate because on this they paid less than to a monthly assessment.

So at last the question was stated and put: That it is the opinion of this committee that towards the supply to be granted to Their Majesties there be a pound rate of 4*s.* in the pound for one year charged upon all lands, tenements, and hereditaments according to the true yearly value thereof. Committee divided—Yeas on the right hand and Noes on the left.

	Yeas	Mr. Goldwell	226
Tellers for the			
	Noes	Mr. Bickerstaffe	148

So carried in the affirmative.

Mr. Attorney was ordered to report this resolution and to desire leave to sit again when he left the Chair.

Speaker resumed the Chair. *Mr. Attorney* reported the said resolution, to which the House agreed. Then *he* moved to sit again, and ordered on Thursday next.

So adjourned till 8 tomorrow morning.

Wednesday, 14 December

Mr. Ettrick presented Mr. Walcott's petition.

Mr. Shakerley and *Mr. Gwyn* moved for the bill of royal mines.

Sir John Guise reported from the committee to whom the consideration of the book of rates was referred: That they found it a matter of great concern, worthy the examination of this House; that the field was very large, but that they had only considered of the trade of France, which was now more immediately concerned, and that they found the duties on all French commodities very low; and therefore they had thought to raise them in several particulars as to which they had come to several resolutions, which were received and read.

Sir Christopher Musgrave opposed the putting them because it was in a manner raising of money upon the subject, being laying impositions on merchandises, which could not be done but in a Committee of the Whole House, and therefore desired this report might be referred to the Committee of the Whole House who are to consider of the ways and means for raising the supplies for Their Majesties.

And it was ordered so accordingly.

Sir Robert Clayton presented a petition from several merchants trading to Portugal, praying that the duty set upon Portugal wines (which was very high) might be lessened. And he urged for it that these wines are brought in in return for our cloth, lead, etc. to the value of £200,000 yearly and there is now so great a duty upon them —almost equal to the French—so that unless you lower these and raise the French, the French wines will still have the preference. They can afford them cheaper, which is against your interest, for the French wines are bought with ready money but these Portugal wines are returned for your own manufacture. And I am told if you lessen the duty on these wines, the Portugal Envoy here will engage his master shall take off a duty that is laid upon your cloth in that kingdom which hath been upon it these 10 years—which if taken off you would export £100,000 worth more of woollen cloth than before.

(The said report from the committee laid £8 per tun on French wines more than before, 20 per cent on all French goods except salt, and 6*d*. a bushel on salt.)

And the petition was received and read and referred to the committee the report was.

Then, according to order, the bill for preservation of Their Majesties' sacred persons and government was read a second time.[1]

Sir Robert Davers: I think this bill does not agree with the title. The body of the bill is to make words treason, which will in effect make all gentlemen slaves to their servants, and therefore I am against committing it.

Mr. Bromley (of Warwickshire) to the same, and the rather because of the new oath imposed by it, which would only prove a snare to catch good, conscientious men and will not hold the bad.

Mr. Hungerford to the same, for that he thought there was not one good thing in the bill save the title, but that he believed it was more Their Majesties' service to throw it out. For my part, I look upon it as a very pernicious bill. By the act of frauds and perjuries, a man by word of mouth can't make a bargain for above £10, and yet here by words a man shall talk himself out of his life and estate and ruin him and all his posterity. Then to the oath in the bill, I do not remember in history that ever an oath was imposed in assertion of the right of one against the right of another but it ended in the ruin of them for whose end it was or else brought in them again against whom it was

---

[1] The debate on the abjuration bill that follows lasted from 11 a.m. to 6 p.m.; Bodleian Carte MS. 130, f. 343.

intended. I look upon this bill to be a means of dividing us more and that I think we need not be; our divisions are great enough already. And I am so far from thinking this any defence or security to the government that I believe it will be one good step to destroy it, and therefore I am against committing the bill.

Sir John Lowther (of Lowther): Though there may be some things in this bill which I do not like, yet I cannot be against committing it but on the contrary am for it for that reason to amend it. I think there are some good things in it and which may be serviceable to this government, and there are others wanting to make it more useful. In King Charles II's time you had such an act as this to make words criminal; there was one good clause in that which is omitted in this— viz. to limit the prosecution in the case of words that information should be made of the words upon oath before a magistrate within 48 hours after they are spoken, whereby a man may easily recollect himself and know whether he spoke them or not. Then I would not have women obliged to take the oath here imposed as they must if it stands as it is. Then there are some words in the oath which I would have altered; I would not have it obligatory during my life. These are some things I think fit to be rectified and no doubt of it there are others, and therefore I desire the bill may be committed for that end.

Paul Foley: I am sorry to see we are making a law to catch little troublesome fellows and yet the great ones will escape, and that this must be by putting honest men in danger. It is very unsafe to make words treason and put it in the power of your servants to ruin you. I am against committing this bill because I do not think it will help you. Your disease lies in another place. If you had good ministers, you have good laws enough already and would have no need of this bill.

Mr. Comptroller Wharton: I am as much against some parts of this bill as any but I think that it may be amended. I would have it committed, for if you should throw it out it would look very ill abroad.

Lord Falkland: No man will deny but that there is absolute need to settle this government, which I take to be the end of this bill. And if there be anything in it not liked of, it may be amended at the committee, and therefore I am against rejecting it.

Lord Norris: I observe those gentlemen that have spoke for the bill urge nothing that is good in it but the title, and therefore I am against committing it.

Mr. Hutchinson: I am for committing this bill; it is no new thing but has been done in former reigns.

Col. Granville: I am against this bill; it tends so much to the prejudice of the subject that it cannot be for the service of the government. I have often wondered why criminals have been no better prosecuted; I am afraid it was to bring in such a bill.

Lord Falkland: I am for this bill because of the ill consequences it would have abroad if you should reject it—nay, it would be a great encouragement to the enemies of this government.

Goodwin Wharton: I think this may be made a good bill, and therefore I am for committing it. What is the reason of making new laws but the exigency of affairs requires it, and that I think now is very necessary. It is said you have enemies to your government at the helm; I hope this will find them out and turn them out, and therefore as the bill may be made it may be of service to you.

Sir Henry Gough: For the reason told you by the gentleman that spoke last (since the end of this bill is getting of places), I am entirely against this bill.

Mr. Bathurst: I am against this bill because this is not a time to encourage treasons when perjuries and subornations thereof are so frequent.

Sir John Morton: I do not wholly like this bill, and therefore would have it committed.

Sir John Guise for committing it because the bill might be altered.

Mr. Harley: I believe the multiplying of oaths will neither be for the service nor security of this government. In the late times, how many oaths were there taken? Yet when King Charles II returned, they took them again to him—nay, when the oath of abjuration of the royal family was taken some of those very men were at that time contriving to restore him. So that I think multitudes of oaths no great security; they serve but as a snare to some men and will not hold such as are your enemies. Then to make words treason I look on to be a very dangerous thing; it puts us in the power of our enemies. I remember once you had such a bill as this with a very specious title—'for preservation of the Protestant Religion'[1]—but, notwithstanding, you threw it out with a brand because the body of the bill did not answer the title, just as this, and therefore I move you to throw this out.

Lord Norris: For my part, I think the persons likely to take this oath to be the persons that will soonest betray it.

Mr. Neale was for committing it.

---

[1] A reference to the bill of autumn, 1678?

So the *Lord Coningsby*: This bill consists of three parts—to make words more punishable, to enjoin a new oath, and enforce taking the old ones.

Mr. Scobell was against committing it for that there were laws sufficient to punish offenders if they were executed.

Mr. Charles Montagu: The question now before you is only for the committing of this bill. The title of it is 'for preservation of Their Majesties' persons and government'; now if it be thought proper to throw this out, I submit to you. Some gentlemen have taken exceptions to some parts of the bill. I will not say it is irregular, but it is a little improper. But then consider, if you throw this out—though you should think something of this kind necessary—you can do nothing therein this sessions, and therefore I am for committing this.

Sir Charles Sedley was for committing it.

And so was *Sir Robert Howard*, because there are some things in the bill fit to be altered and some things omitted fitting to be added to it.

Mr. Francis Robartes and *Mr. Thomas Wyndham* were against committing it.

Mr. Attorney General Somers: The bill is pursuant to the order of the House, but whether the body of the bill agrees with the title I submit to you. The bill is of three parts—to make words punishable, a test upon persons, and to enforce taking the old oaths. As to the last part, it is no other than was before—to make it a *praemunire* to refuse the oaths a second time. As to the test herein imposed, it differs but little from the other oaths. Then for the first part of the bill to make words treason, I submit that to you to limit as you think fit either as to the time, prosecution, witnesses, etc., which is fit for a committee to regulate.

Nor is this matter any novelty. It was done in Edward VI's time—that words were a *praemunire* the first time and treason the second. So in Queen Elizabeth's reign, which is a reign so much magnified, yet even then words were treason the first time. The like was done in King Charles II's time. And if you have less zeal for this government than they had for theirs, I submit it to you. There are several gentlemen have spoke very learnedly against all oaths; as to that, if you please you may put in a clause now to repeal all oaths. Others against some parts of the bill; these are things fit for a committee, and therefore I desire the bill may be committed.

Sir John Trenchard was for committing the bill.

Mr. Harcourt: I hear of strange things and contrivances carrying on against this government, for which I am very sorry that they are so well known and yet no care is taken for their prosecution. You are going now to pass a bill to make words treason, which I can by no means agree to for I look upon it as very dangerous. Words are often spoken hastily and rashly, not with any design, and I would not presently hang a man for a rash word. Words are liable to be misconstrued, so your life is in danger that way. Then for the oath, I remember what a worthy gentleman said—that oaths were but cobwebs. I think so, too, with some men, and therefore I approve not of this. It is urged for this bill that it is for the service of this government. For my part I think clearly otherwise and that it will most effectually undermine it, and therefore I am against it.

Mr. Solicitor: I confess I brought in this bill and as near as I thought pursuant to your order. I own my infirmities are great, but therefore I hope so good a thing for the preservation of Their Majesties shall not suffer through my weakness, but I desire it may be committed that the House would please to rectify it as they think fit.

Sir John Darell was for committing it.

Sir Francis Winnington: This bill came in in a very extraordinary manner. It took its rise from a clause tendered you late in the evening to be tacked to a bill not very proper to it at a time when there were not above 100 in the House, which being irregular that clause was laid on the Table for the present and this bill you now have was ordered to be brought in. Now to the bill itself, you will hardly find that words were ever made treason but in the most sanguinary times. The statutes made to that effect in Queen Elizabeth's time were made on special and particular reasons, but after they were once made the times became more troublesome. For such laws tend to disquiet and disturb men's minds and render them uneasy, and much rather so now at this time when you are loading them with such heavy taxes, and therefore I am for throwing out this bill.

Mr. John Smith: The law is not made for a snare but as a caution directing men what they may do and what they must avoid. Some gentlemen have taken exceptions to some parts of the bill, and for that reason I am for committing it.

Mr. Peregrine Bertie junior was against committing this bill.

Marquess of Winchester, Mr. Hampden, and *Sir Henry Ashurst* were for committing this bill because it would look very strange to throw out a bill that is for preservation of Their Majesties' persons and which was brought in by your order.

Mr. Mordaunt was for committing the bill, the national time of the day requiring it to obviate the designs of our enemies.

Mr. Heneage Finch: The more I consider of the reasons urged for the commitment of this bill, the more I am against it. In all times when words have been made treason, parliaments have found mischiefs thereby and repealed them in some short time and reduced them to the standard of 25 E. III c. 1. It is said some men prevaricate with your former oath; perhaps so, but consider if the oaths you have already will not hold them, you will hardly make any oath that can or which they will not easily take. The security of this government lies not in oaths but in the good laws and the regular administration of justice and the love of the people. For my part, I think the oaths you have already are sufficient, and that thereby a man is bound to assist and to do all they can for the security of this government—the oath you have is the old oath of allegiance which was before 3 Jac. [I]. I did observe one gentleman did in effect tell us the commitment of this bill was not to mend it but to make an oath that some men shall not take, which I am not for but would not make more enemies to this government—we have too many already. Then for making words treason, I think it at all times very dangerous for words are liable to be mistaken and misunderstood, and it is not in such cases sufficient to prove by standers-by that they heard no such words spoken because one might hear what another did not. These are some of the reasons I cannot be for committing this bill.

It being late and dark, candles were ordered to be brought in upon the question.

Serj. Blencowe, Mr. Clarke, and *Sir Walter Yonge* were for committing it. So *Mr. Boscawen.*

But the *Lord Digby* was against it, being multiplying of treasons, which he thought not safe at this time.

So after a long debate, the question was put that this bill be committed. House divided—Yeas went out.

		Sir Walter Yonge	
	Yeas		175
		Mr. Clarke	
Tellers for the			
		Sir Robert Davers	
	Noes		200
		Mr. Bickerstaffe	

So carried in the negative.

Sir Christopher Musgrave: Since it hath been carried against committing this bill, the next question is for rejecting it, which he desired might be put.

So others to the same.

But some gentlemen opposed it for that it would look very strange on the *Votes* that we should reject a bill that was for preservation of Their Majesties' person and government, and therefore desired it might lie on the Table and leave might be given to bring in another more agreeable to the general sense of the House.

But this was refused. And the question of rejecting it being insisted on as the proper question, it was put that this bill be rejected, and carried in the affirmative.

And when this question of rejection was first spoke of, *Mr. Brownlow* stood up and desired instead of that they would put the question for rejecting King William and Queen Mary.

Speaker informed the House that though this bill was rejected, yet the clause to the bill of treasons was not, though to the same effect.

All committees adjourned.

So adjourned till 9 tomorrow morning.[1]

Thursday, 15 December

Mr. Onslow presented the petition from the merchants against the bill for bringing in Italian thrown silk overland.

Col. Pery presented the petition from the Buttonmakers.

The engrossed bill from the Lords for preventing the abuses committed by the searchers and weighers of butter and cheese was read the first time.

Mr. Papillon and *Mr. Bowyer* spoke against it.

Sir Thomas Clarges took exception to it for that here is one clause which establishes an office for the trying of butter and appoints a warehouse for keeping it and gives him the fee of 2*s*. 6*d*. for his pains from the maker of it—which being a penalty in nature of a tax and raising money upon the subject which the Lords have not power to do. And this House did but once admit the Lords to set the penalty of 2*s*. 6*d*. on a churchwarden and now in all your disputes with them about money you hear of that precedent, and therefore I am against this. *Mr. Hampden, Sir John Trenchard*, and *Sir Christopher Musgrave* all to the same, very largely.

[1] 8 a.m. in *CJ*, x. 744.

Which seeming to be the sense of the House, some friends to the bill moved that it might lie on the Table and leave be given to bring in another to the like effect. But this was thought not so very regular because the proper question was for reading the bill a second time. Then it was proposed that the debate upon this bill might be adjourned (not with an intent to take it up again) and leave might be given to bring in another bill to the same effect. And leave was given accordingly.

Several members were added to the committee about the bill of hawkers and pedlars.

The bill to make perjury and subornation of perjury to be felony ordered to be read on Monday.[1]

Then the House went into a Committee of the Whole House to consider of ways and means for raising the supply for Their Majesties. Speaker left the Chair; Mr. Attorney took the Chair of the committee.

Mr. Paul Foley moved to consider further of the land tax on which the committee was the last meeting, and that you will add some heads to it. The last time you laid 4*s.* in the pound on real estates; I desire the same may be charged on personal estates and all offices other than in the army and navy.

So the question was stated and resolved: That towards the supply to be granted to Their Majesties there be a charge of 4*s.* in the pound for one year upon all personal estates (other than household goods and stock upon all land) and upon all offices and employments of profit (other than military offices in the army and navy) according to the true yearly profit thereof.

Mr. Neale: There is a way to raise money without paying so much interest as you do on all your taxes—by settling a perpetual fund of £120,000 to pay the interest of £2,000,000. This will tend to strengthen your government by interesting so many persons to wish well to it and to endeavour to preserve it. I shall propose the fund to be on the hereditary excise and to lay 1*s.* a bushel on all salt made at the pan and 2*s.* a bushel on all foreign salt, and you may for further security give a clause of credit as you did on the poll act.

Mr. Paul Foley: I cannot agree to anything of a perpetual fund, for you can have no fruit of that unless you will force tallies or paper to go for ready money. But I will propose you a thing for a certain fund of £70,000 per annum. You shall have persons raise you a million of money, they to have £6 per annum for every £100, and if anyone die

---

[1] No such order is entered in the *Journal*.

his share to be divided amongst the survivors. This fund to be upon the hereditary excise. He that lives longest will have a mighty return for his money. It is a good provision for children and no burden on your land. Herein also I would give a clause of credit.

Mr. Harley: I approve of this very well, and though some may say it will not come to that sum, yet you will reap this advantage by it that you will have one year more to consider how to raise the sum.

Sir Thomas Clarges: Of all the new ways to raise money I think this the best, and therefore I am for it. But there must be great care taken in the penning of the act.

Sir Christopher Musgrave: I think this a very good thing and a careful provision for children, and therefore I am for it.

Sir Edward Seymour for the same, it being but trying an experiment which hath the appearance of reason. And though it has not been tried in this nation, yet it has elsewhere and taken very well.

Sir Robert Rich: I can by no means approve of this project for I look upon it no otherwise, and a very uncertain thing. Then I observe it is pawning the very flower of the revenue of the Crown, and I am afraid what you did yesterday will not much encourage persons to bring in.

Sir Peter Colleton and Sir Francis Blake were for it.

Sir Edward Seymour: I think an uncertainty is better than nothing at all. But I am of opinion this is a good thing to ease your land and to shut the door against a home excise. I have seven sons and I like this proposal so well that I will venture all mine. However, it is not regular for any gentleman to reflect upon what the House hath once passed.

Paul Foley: The fund of credit proposed for raising this money I desire may be but for three or four years when one 9*d.* on the excise will be out, and then you may transfer it to that.

Mr. Hampden: I am absolutely against this proposal because it is a new project to load the King's revenue.

Sir Edward Seymour: I am against rendering this government precarious as much as any, and therefore though the hereditary excise be a security for four years yet with the same breath I would settle the revenue of one 9*d.* at the four years' end in lieu of it for ever, which is the greater revenue.

Sir Richard Temple: I think this a very good method and what your enemies practise in France with success.

So the question was stated by the Chair, put and resolved: That towards the supply to be granted to Their Majesties there be a fund of £70,000 per annum set apart for the payment of the interest of a million of money to be raised by persons voluntarily paying in that sum; the principal paid in to be sunk and the persons paying in the same to receive during their lives their respective proportions of the said £70,000 according to the sums paid in by them, with the advantage of survivorship till all the lives be determined.

Then another question was stated, put, and resolved: That the said fund be out of the hereditary excise until the 17th day of May 1697 and afterwards by an additional excise upon beer, ale, and other liquors according to the proportions in an act of the first year of Their Majesties' reign entitled 'an act for an additional duty of excise upon beer, ale, and other liquors'.

Then another matter was proposed, to have a clause of credit therein. So a question to that effect was stated and resolved: That in case a million shall not be paid in upon the said fund before the 24th of June 1693, the remainder is to be taken up at interest not exceeding seven per cent per annum and to be paid to the lenders out of the next aids to be granted to Their Majesties by parliament.

So these resolutions were ordered to be reported, and that leave be desired to sit again. All which were done. The resolutions were reported and agreed to, and ordered to sit again on Saturday next. It was referred to Mr. Attorney General, Mr. Solicitor, Sir Christopher Musgrave, Sir Thomas Clarges, and Paul Foley to bring in a bill pursuant to the said resolutions and also a bill for the land tax of 4s. in the pound.

So adjourned till 8 tomorrow morning.

Friday, 16 December

Upon reading Mr. Hawley's private bill, *Sir Edward Seymour* inveighed much against private bills and the many mischiefs arising therefrom, and said the business of the Lords was upon appeals and this House was taken up with private bills to destroy the settlement of estates in England.

Col. Godfrey presented the petition from the Company of Pinmakers of London.

Sir Robert Davers reported specially from the committee to whom the aulnage bill was referred, praying the direction of the House therein. They find they cannot make a recompense to the Crown without laying an additional duty upon some manufactures.

Sir Edward Seymour: I am absolutely against the House's giving power to a private committee to lay any duty upon the subject or upon any commodity more than was before, for the rules of the House will not admit its being done but in a Committee of the Whole House.

But then it was debated how it could be done now, since a bill being committed to a private committee the House cannot take notice of it till it come reported from the committee, when the House may refer it to a Committee of the Whole House. So at last the committee to whom that bill was referred was revived in order to report what they had done with the same that the House might refer it back to a Committee of the Whole House.

Mr. Holt presented the petition of the Linendrapers of London against the hawkers and pedlars bill.

Then the House went into a Committee of the Whole House upon the advice to His Majesty. Speaker left the Chair; Sir Francis Winnington took the Chair of the committee.

Mr. Hoby complained to the House of the violent abuses and insolencies of soldiers about him, and instanced in several particulars. I shall, therefore, move you to advise His Majesty that there be a stricter discipline among the soldiers and that the officers commanding them may be ordered to their respective posts.

Sir Charles Sedley was for advising the King to constitute and declare another Secretary for that the business is too great for one man.

Sir Thomas Clarges: I think that matter about the soldiers not proper to be a head of advice, but I hope that worthy gentleman will take care to bring in a bill, as was the last sessions, to prevent false musters and to regulate the disorders of the soldiers; and this I hope will be sufficient.

Several other gentlemen spoke of many disorders committed by the soldiers, but this matter was thought not to come so proper now and therefore it was let fall.

Col. Cornewall: I think it a proper head for you to advise His Majesty upon that no foreigner, but only natives of England, be employed in your Tower of London or any other of your garrisons nor in the Office of Ordnance, stores, etc. For I think it dangerous that the Dutch should be acquainted so well therewith with whom you have had wars and may again.[1]

---

[1] The debate on this issue lasted over two hours; B.M. Add. MS. 34096, f. 240.

Sir John Lowther: I think this not very proper at this time. It seems to reflect a little on the King as if he had a greater kindness for foreigners than the English; I assure you not. I am well informed the King has as good an esteem of the English and as great a kindness for them as any men in the world. But the true reason is this nation has been long in peace and not versed in these matters, so the King is forced for the present to make use of them.

Sir Thomas Clarges, Col. Granville, and others thought it very dangerous and against the true interest of this nation to employ foreigners in our garrisons and stores, and therefore were for making this a head of advice.

Then a question was stated: That it is the opinion of this committee that the House be moved that His Majesty be humbly advised that he employ no foreigners in the Tower of London, in the Office of Ordnance or Storekeeper there.

But against this it was urged by some that there were but two persons employed in them, Sir Martin Beckman and Mr. Meesters. That the first was naturalized and had served this nation very well in Ireland and done them good service. And as to the other, he had been very useful in several new fire inventions. And thought it not worth the House's while to concern themselves therein.

So that question was let fall.

So he was ordered to report the proceedings of the committee with their resolutions thereon. So he left the Chair.

Speaker resumed the Chair. So *Sir Francis Winnington* reported the committee had considered of the matter referred to them and had agreed upon several resolutions which they had commanded him to report, which was ordered to be made on Tuesday morning next.

So adjourned till 8 tomorrow morning.

Saturday, 17 December

The bill for settling and ascertaining the salaries and fees to be paid to the judges and officers in Their Majesties' courts was read the second time. And a debate arising thereon by *Sir Joseph Tredenham, Sir William Wogan,* and several others who spoke against the bill, as that it did entrench upon the King's prerogative and would render judges independent upon the Crown. So the question being put that the bill be committed, it passed in the negative. Then the question was put that it should be rejected and resolved in the affirmative.

Sir Thomas Clarges presented the petition of William Goodwin and others, relating to the orphans' business.

Then the House went into a Committee of the Whole House upon the ways and means to raise the supply for Their Majesties; Mr. Attorney General took the Chair of the committee.

Sir Thomas Clarges proposed to lay an additional duty upon several commodities imported which would raise a considerable sum. That he had examined the whole book of rates and considered thereof with some merchants and others who understood them very well; and then proposed the several particulars with the duty which they thought proper to lay on them.

Mr. Papillon opposed this because it was the opinion of but one person; that it was a great thing and worthy consideration, being loading of trade which was against the interest of the nation.

Sir John Lowther thought this a very great thing and fit to be considered of in reference to our trade, which may be prejudiced if overloaded. Therefore, I think the proper way is to refer it to a private committee to consider of. Mr. Smith to the same.

Sir Edward Seymour: I think it very proper to consider of this matter now when you are in a Committee of the Whole House where you may examine it as well as in any private committee. You have merchants and others in the House that understand these matters very well, and I suppose you will not vote these in a lump but go head by head.

Sir Christopher Musgrave: I am against referring this to a private committee for I think that will be fruitless. For what can that committee do? It cannot bring in any sum—that must be done in a Committee of the Whole House. Then I must tell you it is a new thing to refer such matters to a private committee, but you have always dispatched this of laying duties on merchandises in a Committee of the Whole House. Therefore, I desire we may go upon them now.

So the several heads were read over. And after they were read over singly and put severally and resolved: That all amber beads that come from Prussia should pay £20 for every £100 worth more than they did before, after the 25th of December instant; all amber rough to pay 10 per cent more than before, after that time; oil of amber imported to pay 20 per cent more than before, etc.; anchovies, every little barrel to pay £5 more than before, etc.

Argol, white and red, imported; proposed to pay 10 per cent more than before. But this was opposed because it was a thing used only in dyeing cloth, and to lay this duty was laying a tax on the woollen manufacture, which was against the interest of the nation who have always avoided this that our merchants might be able to sell our English cloth the cheaper so to undersell all others our rivals in this manufacture at foreign markets. So this was laid aside.

[Resolved]: ashes of woad, weed, or soap imported to pay 6s. a last more than before, etc.; barbers' aprons and checks imported to pay 8d. a piece more than before, etc.; battery (that is, brass to make kettles) to pay 5s. for every hundred-pound weight (of 112 lbs.) more than before, etc.; so for metal for battery proportionable; books unbound to pay 4s. for every 112 lb. weight more than before, etc.; black and lampblack to pay £20 for every £100 value more than before, etc.; [boltering]¹ (that is, to make fine sieves) imported to pay £10 for every £100 value more than before; bracelets or necklaces of glass (these come from Venice) to pay 2s. 6d. on every gross more than before, etc.; brass wrought to pay £5 for every £100 value more, etc.; buckrams (this comes from Hamburg and is used to put up clothes, serges, etc. sent abroad to keep them from moths) to pay £5 for every £100 value more, etc.; buttons of hair to pay £10 for every £100 value more than before, etc.; bristles to pay £5 for every £100 value more than before, etc.; bacon, foreign, to pay 4d. per pound more than before.

Speaker took the Chair. So *Mr. Attorney* reported, according to order, that the committee had sat and made some progress and desired leave to sit again. So resolved to sit again on Tuesday next upon the ways and means to raise the supply for Their Majesties, etc.

So adjourned till Monday morning 8 of the clock.

Monday, 19 December

Mr. Goldwell presented the petition from the Company of Spectacle-makers against the bill for the convex lights.

Mr. Arnold presented the petition from the poor prisoners in the King's Bench.

Leave was moved from Mr. Brownlow to go into the country, but denied.

Mr. Boscawen moved for leave to bring in a bill to repeal the statute that prohibits the exportation of copper, and it was referred to a committee to consider of.

The bill for preserving, regulating, and establishing the East India

¹ In MS. 'bountel rains'.

trade was read the second time. Several spoke to diverse particulars and some things fit to be inserted in the bill which were omitted, as when the new company shall commence, when the old one shall determine, how to preserve the concerns of the old Company, etc. (*Mr. Papillon, Mr. Boscawen, Mr. Hutchinson, Sir Edward Seymour*, and others.) So the bill was committed to a Committee of the Whole House upon the debate of the House.

Sir Samuel Dashwood informed the House that the Sheriffs and Recorder of London were at the door with a petition from the Lord Mayor, Aldermen, and Common Council of London to present to the House.

But their calling in to present it was opposed by *Sir Joseph William-son* and others because not regular. The petition ought to be delivered by some members in the House and the nature of the petition opened by him, for it may be inconvenient and sometimes dangerous for the House to receive they know not what and many things are not fit to be presented to the House.

And the *Chair* informed the House they could not be called in for the reason aforesaid.

Then *Sir John Parsons*, a member of the House that serves for Reigate in Surrey, went out and fetched in the petition and presented it to the House, opening of it. And it was received and ordered to lie on the Table till the bill about the convex lights, to which it related, be reported.

Then the House, according to order, went into a Committee of the Whole House upon the bill touching free and impartial proceedings in parliament. Speaker left the Chair. Sir Edward Hussey took the Chair of the committee.

So the bill was read over by the Clerk of the committee. Then the preamble was read over and postponed. So the Chairman read over the several clauses in order; and the committee proceeded to fill up the blanks and made some amendments till they went through the bill; then finished the preamble and the bill was passed; and he commanded to report it and to leave the Chair.

So Speaker resumed the Chair. *Sir Edward Hussey* reported from the committee that they had sat and gone through the bill and made some amendments to it, which they had commanded him to report. And he being called upon to report, *he* went on with the same. And the House agreed to all the amendments and the bill was ordered to be engrossed.

Mr. Serj. Trenchard reported from the committee the bill about the convex lights and the petitions against it, and that the committee had come to a resolution thereon—that the passing the said bill would be no prejudice to the rights and liberties of the City of London.

Then the petition from the City against the said bill was read, praying leave to be heard at the Bar against the same. Several spoke for it that they might. But it was opposed by others as very irregular. After they had once petitioned the House and their petition had been referred to a committee and there examined, to come and petition again was a high reflection upon the committee as if they had not done right, and that this ought not to be endured for then there would be an end of all committees.

So the question was put for their being heard against passing the said bill at the Bar, and carried in the negative. Then the House ordered the bill to be engrossed. Then moved that the said bill should not be read a third time till after 11 of the clock.

So House adjourned till 8 tomorrow morning.

Tuesday, 20 December

Mr. Justice Eyre and Mr. Baron Powell came from the Lords with the message to desire a conference with this House to communicate the papers relating to the last summer's expedition. And being withdrawn, they were called in again and acquainted that the House had agreed to the same.

Sir Miles Cook and Sir James Astry brought the second message from the Lords with Sir George Parker's bill and also another private bill.

Some members were added to the committee appointed to consider of the privileges of the House.

Mr. Bathurst presented to the House the petition of Anthony Danby esq. and his wife, for leave to bring in a private bill.

Mr. [Thomas][1] Coulson merchant, being newly chosen a burgess for the borough of Totnes in Devon (in the room of Sir John Fowell, deceased), came into the House and took the oaths at the Table and subscribed his name.

Then the House named managers for the conference with the Lords and their names were after read over. And the time of the conference being come, the managers went up to the conference.

[1] In MS. 'John'.

The managers returned and *Col. Granville* reported from the con-ference: That the Lords had communicated to them several papers which were laid before their House from the King relating to the last summer's expedition at sea, which mentioning some members of this House their Lordships thought fit to transmit to this House. Which papers he delivered in at the Table, where they were read. And they contained a narrative by the Lord Nottingham concerning the descent and an abstract of several letters made by a committee of Lords under several heads—of things before the fight at sea last summer, touching the fight and after it, about the land forces, and other general matters.[1]

Mr. Russell: You have some papers brought before you with what intention I know not except to cast a reflection upon me. Then he proceeded and observed upon several particulars therein mentioned and answered some things which seemed to reflect upon him, and offered that he was very ready and willing to satisfy any gentleman if they had any questions to ask of him.

Col. Churchill justified him in several particulars he had mentioned and assured the House he knew them himself to be true, he being near Mr. Russell in the time of action.

Mr. Comptroller Wharton: Your honourable member appears to me to lie under the displeasure of a great lord, but I think it is not fit for the safety of this government that all things should depend on one man who is not of an opinion for the title of this King and Queen. As to the papers before you, I believe they were designed to displace your member from his post in the fleet. For my part I cannot act, nor I think any honest man, as long as he is at the helm, and therefore I move you for an address to His Majesty to remove this lord from his presence and councils. *Sir John Morton* seconded the same.

Mr. Smith: For my part I am very well satisfied with the answer your Admiral has given you to the papers now before you, and there-fore I think you can do no less than declare an entire satisfaction in his whole conduct and return him thanks for the same.

Mr. Goodwin Wharton: The gentleman that spoke last has not spoke to the question that was before you.

Mr. Palmes seconded the motion for thanks to the Admiral.

Sir Robert Howard proposed that on consideration of all matters the House would declare their entire satisfaction in the courage and conduct of your Admiral.

[1] Grey, x. 291–3 has a parallel account of the debate that follows.

Sir John Lowther (of Lowther): There is no doubt but your noble Admiral has behaved himself very well and is also faithful to your government. But on the other side, give me leave to offer something on behalf of that noble lord which I know to be true. He has deserved well of you and done all that is possible for man for your service, and I doubt not is very faithful to your government. I am afraid the designs of our enemies are now at work to endeavour to divide us more than we are. And whence arises all this noise—for want of success. I must say success does not always attend a good government. For my part I cannot say where the blame lies. Your Admiral has done well and so has this noble lord, whom I must say is not quiet one day but issuing out orders and giving instructions in matters touching the government. There is no want of zeal for this government in him, and therefore I think the better way is to let these papers lie on the Table for gentlemen to consider of.

Peregrine Bertie junior: Since it is plain there are men in employ in direct opposition to one another, I am for advising His Majesty to consult only with men of one principle and interest.

Mr. Hutchinson was for returning thanks to the Admiral for his great services.

Mr. Solicitor Trevor: I do take these papers to be designed to reflect upon your Admiral, and I am further confirmed in it by the timing of it. And though they do not directly charge him with anything, yet there are sly insinuations that show what they aim at. I think it, therefore, absolutely necessary to vote him thanks.

Sir Christopher Musgrave: I think it very proper to have these papers referred to a Committee of the Whole House and there examine them, and then assign the crime with which you will charge this noble lord. For my part, as yet I cannot give opinion of them. Then as to thanks to your Admiral, I must declare my opinion to be as it always has been—to give no thanks to any but the King. Therefore, I move you to refer these papers to a Committee of the Whole House.

Mr. Hampden: I desire you will state a question to this effect: that this House having perused the papers of the transactions of the fleet relating to the last summer's expedition, they are well satisfied with the fidelity, courage, and conduct of your Admiral.

Mr. Montagu to the same and proposed this vote: that it is the opinion of this House that Admiral Russell has behaved himself with fidelity, courage, and conduct during the whole summer's expedition.

Mr. Heneage Finch: I cannot sit still any longer and hear that said of a noble lord to whom I have some relation. Some gentlemen are pleased to say these papers were sent you down to reflect upon your Admiral and slyly to insinuate a misbehaviour in him, which to me seems very strange that any should make that construction of what comes down to you from the Lords and to them from His Majesty on their address to have the transactions of the fleet the last summer laid before them. And what is there related is collected out of letters and papers that come to the Secretary's office and to and from your Admiral. And for this noble lord I will be bold to say none was ever more diligent in your service, and he never goes to bed before all orders and dispatches are executed and leaves them not till the next morning. But then some gentlemen say he is not of right principles for this government. I do not well understand what they mean by that, but I think the way to judge of a man's principles is by his actions and let them speak for him. So that upon the whole matter I think these papers fit to lie on the Table for gentlemen to look into, and you may appoint another day to consider thereof.

Mr. Dolben thought the House was not ripe yet for either question but that these papers ought first to be considered, and that what he had heard of them he saw nothing reflected on the Admiral, and therefore thought it most proper to refer these papers to a Committee of the Whole House.

Mr. Chadwick and *Mr. Attorney General* for the question to return thanks to the Admiral.

So the question was stated and resolved: That Admiral Russell, in the command of the fleet during the last summer's expedition, has behaved himself with fidelity, courage, and conduct.

Col. Granville: You have now passed a very just vote. I desire we may send to the Lords and communicate this resolution to them at a conference.

And accordingly it was resolved that a conference be desired with the Lords upon the subject-matter of the last, and Sir John Morton was ordered to go up and desire it.

Mr. Russell thanked the House for the great honour they had done him in their vote, and that as he had done his best for the service of this government hitherto so he should continue the same in what lay in his power. But as to this noble lord, he had always appeared against him so that often he lay under great difficulties, and that though he had in some measure been able to bear up under him through the interest of some friends he had yet he questioned whether those who should succeed him in his place would be able to do it.

So adjourned till 8 tomorrow morning.

Wednesday, 21 December

Sir John Kay presented the petition from the clothiers and others of Leeds in Yorkshire. *Mr. Waller* presented another from those of York and town of Kingston upon Hull. Both which were read being on behalf of the Hamburg Company, praying an establishment thereof, and were referred to the committee to whom the bill for better preventing the exportation of wool and encouraging the woollen manufacture was referred.

Mr. Fenwick moved for leave to bring in a bill for taking special bail in the country, and ordered accordingly.

The Speaker left the Chair and the House went into a Committee of the Whole House upon the matter of supplies, and Mr. Attorney General took the Chair of the committee. Then the committee proceeded upon the heads of the other commodities on which a duty was to be laid.

Sir Thomas Clarges thought it necessary to lay a higher duty on French commodities and that the House would give encouragement to privateers. But one thing was to be taken great care of—to prevent a collusion between the privateer and the merchant so to hinder a trade from being carried on underhand with France. Some such ways as these: by giving the King a third part of the prize; that all shall be sold at the Customhouse by inch of candle publicly; and to lay a duty of at least 20 per cent more on French goods than before, and the surplus to be divided amongst the owners. He proposed also to lay a duty upon brandies and spirits of 2s. 6d. a gallon; this will raise itself about £80,000 per annum.

Some were for laying 4s. a gallon upon it, and it would encourage our own manufacture of spirits made of corn in making of which there is at the least 300,000 quarters of malt spent, besides the great encouragement it is to the plantations.

So put and passed for 2s. 6d. a gallon upon all single brandies, because if it should have been 4s. a gallon it would in a manner have been an absolute prohibition of all Spanish brandies and those from Portugal, too, which the House is inclinable to let come in though they are now all prohibited—as well Spanish and Portugal brandies as French.

But it is the intention of the House that the Spanish and Portugal brandies should come in, paying that duty, but not to let in the French or repeal the act of prohibition as to them. Then there is another advantage by laying a great duty on French goods in a time of war—that when a time of peace comes you will be better able to reduce the trade with France to a more equal balance, which otherwise you will never be able to do unless the duty be laid on their commodities in a time of war.

Then the time of the conference being come, the Attorney General was ordered to leave the Chair and desire the leave of the House to sit again. So the Speaker resumed the Chair and the *Attorney* desired that the committee might sit again, which was ordered as soon as the conference was over.

So the managers' names were read over and they were ordered to return the papers brought from the Lords and to acquaint them with the vote of the House as to Admiral Russell and not to debate anything at the conference. So the managers went up, and being returned *Col. Granville* acquainted the House that they had according to order communicated the resolution of this House to the Lords and delivered back the papers transmitted from their Lordships.

So the House went into a committee again upon the supply to Their Majesties. Attorney General took the Chair of the committee and they proceeded to the remaining heads. [Resolved]: calves' skins imported to pay £5 more for every £100 value, etc.; carpets of all sorts imported to pay £5 for every £100 value more than before, etc.

Cochineal; proposed to pay 12*d.* per pound more than before. But opposed because used in dyeing fine cloths. And if this commodity be dearer, you lay so much on your woollen manufacture and will throw the trade of dyeing into the hands of the Dutch. So this was let fall.

[Resolved]: catlings and fiddling things to pay 1*s.* 6*d.* on every gross more than before, etc.; coal (Scotch) to pay £5 for every £100 value more than before, etc.; copper unwrought imported to pay 7*s.* 6*d.* for every hundred-pound weight more than before, etc.; copper part wrought in plate, bars, rods, or razelled to pay 12*s.* 6*d.* for every 112 pound weight more than before, etc.; copper fully wrought to pay 17*s.* 6*d.* on every 112 pound weight more than before, etc.; coral beads or coral polished to pay £20 on every £100 value more than before, etc.; cowries (which is a shell from the East Indies) to pay £10 on every £100 value more than before, etc.; elephants' teeth to pay £10 on every £100 value more than before, etc.; flax rough to pay

£7 for every £100 value more than before, etc.; flax wrought to pay £15 for every £100 value more than before, etc.; tow to pay £5 for every £100 value more than before, etc.; flannel to pay 2*d.* a yard more than before, etc.; frieze to pay 3½*d.* a yard more than before, etc.; furs to pay £5 on every £100 value more than before, etc.; (galls was excused because used for dyeing); gold and silver thread and wire counterfeit to pay £5 in every £100 value more than before, etc.; goats' hair called Carmenia wool (which comes from India) to pay 4*d.* for every pound more than before, etc.; goats' hair of all sorts to pay 2*d.* per pound more than before.

So he was ordered to report further progress and desire leave to sit again. So he left the Chair.

Speaker resumed the Chair. So *Attorney General* reported further progress and moved for leave for the committee to sit again. So ordered again on Friday next.

So adjourned till 8 tomorrow morning.

Thursday, 22 December

Sir Robert Davers reported from the committee the bill for the aulnage with amendments and with some blanks to be filled up with sums or a duty to be imposed on the subject (which the private committee could not do). So the amendments were read over and agreed to and resolved that the bill should be committed to a Committee of the Whole House to fill up the blanks with the sums and that the House would go into a committee for that purpose on Wednesday next.

The bill touching free and impartial proceedings in parliament was read the third time.

Dr. Barbone spoke against this bill as a very dangerous one for that it excludes this House (who are a part of the legislative power) from having any administration of affairs of government. *Lord Falkland* spoke also against it.

Sir John Lowther (of Lowther) against it for that it puts all the power into the Lords and renders this House very low. Then besides, when this House hath once passed such a bill the Lords will not easily give it up again.

Sir Edward Seymour was against this bill for that in the preamble it reflects upon a former parliament, which I must say made some of your best laws which are the foundation of the English liberties, and by reflecting on them at such a rate you seem to reflect upon their laws and, in some measure, weaken the same. Then I believe this bill will not answer your intention for you will but put men upon more close contrivances, and besides this enjoins no more than the House may do without it.

Paul Foley: I think you have a very good bill before you—the only way to prevent corruption in this House. It is no new thing to see a man incline one way and when he is once got into a place to go another way.

Mr. Christie and others spoke for the bill, that this would settle the government on the English foundation and preserve the fountain in this House clear.

Mr. Boscawen tendered a rider to be added to the bill. That since this was a new law it was not so convenient to have it perpetual, and therefore he was for having it temporary—but for some years. *Sir Ralph Dutton* and *Sir Charles Sedley* were for it.

But upon the question to be read a second time, carried clearly in the negative. So the bill was read the third time and upon the question passed and the title thereof passed also. And Sir Edward Hussey [was] ordered to carry it up to the Lords for their concurrence.

Capt. Pitt complained to the House of an abuse done to him and some other members—that they had gone and printed a paper of the governor, deputy governor, and 24 committees for a new East India Company, which reflected upon him and others, and had made them members thereof when he knew nothing of the matter.

But the House looking on it as a simple thing and only a trick of some persons who were against the old Company, they let it fall.

So the Speaker left the Chair and the House, according to order, went into a Committee of the Whole House upon the bill touching the East India Company. But a dispute arising about naming the Chairman, the Speaker was forced to resume the Chair to determine it.[1] Which as soon as he [had] done, a friend to the old East India Company stood up and took notice of the time of day, that it was late and not fit to go on this bill, and therefore moved to adjourn. He was seconded.

Sir Christopher Musgrave: This is a way of proceeding I never saw in my life and is very irregular and not fair with the House.

---

[1] The confusion was apparently generated by 'Mr. Smith, who used to be their Chairman, going out of the House to avoid it now'; B.M. Add. MS. 34096, f. 246.

However, it being after 1 of the clock, though the thing was not fair, after the House had appointed another day to go into a committee upon the East India bill, the question of adjournment was put and carried.

So the House adjourned till 8 tomorrow morning.

Friday, 23 December

Mr. Attorney General reported from the committee the several laws that were expired and near expiring, and which were fit to be continued. To all which several resolutions the House agreed but one, and that was the bill for raising the militia for the year 1693 though the month's pay formerly advanced be not paid. To this exception was taken for that it being to charge the subject and raising money on them it could not come from a private committee, for then by this side wind any tax act might be continued or revived. Therefore this was laid aside. But when the report was over, the House was moved for leave to bring in such a bill, and ordered accordingly.

The land tax bill for 4*s.* in the pound was read a second time and committed to a Committee of the Whole House. Then a debate arose about the day. It was moved first for Friday next. Others were for Wednesday. After some time the question was stated for Friday, but the *Speaker*—irregularly of his own head without its being moved—put the previous question: whether that question for Friday should be now put. House divided and the *Speaker* (contrary to order) ordered the Yeas to go out (whereas the Noes ought, who were against dispatch of business in this question).

	Col. Granville	
Yeas		119
	Paul Foley	
Tellers for the		
	Sir John Guise	
Noes		200
	Mr. Freke junior[1]	

Sir Thomas Clarges (when the House was settled again) took notice publicly how irregular the Speaker was in starting the previous question himself and then afterwards in ordering the Yeas to go forth.

So the House resolved to go into a committee on Wednesday next upon the said bill.

[1] Mr. Clarke in *CJ*, x. 762.

The message from the Lords with Ralph Macclesfield's bill was brought by Sir Miles Cook and Sir James Astry.

Mr. John Howe reported from the committee the resolutions agreed upon touching the privilege of members in relation to suits in law and equity, all which were read.

Sir Robert Howard and *Sir Richard Temple* desired they might lie on the Table for some time that every member might see them, for that it was a very great matter and fit for the House to consider very well of before they pass such resolutions. *Sir Edward Seymour* to the same.

Sir Thomas Clarges was for going upon it. That it was for the honour and credit of the House and the good of our fellow subjects. That as we pretended to remedy grievances, we should hereby prevent ourselves from being the greatest grievance by hindering our fellow subjects from their just rights.

Mr. Howe for it very earnestly.

However, put off on the question till Friday next.

Leave was given to bring in a bill to prevent selling in false measures.[1]

So adjourned till Wednesday morning next 9 of the clock.

Wednesday, 28 December

Mr. Gwyn was ordered to carry up Mr. Popham's bill to the Lords for their concurrence.

So the House, according to order, went into a committee upon the bill of 4*s.* in the pound; Mr. Attorney General to the Chair. So the Clerk read over the bill. Then the Attorney began and read over the preamble of the bill, which was postponed. Then he read over the clauses severally in order, and the committee filled up the blanks and proceeded so far as to the names of the commissioners.

Sir Richard Temple: The good execution of laws is the life of them, and therefore anciently in subsidies the King had the naming of the commissioners. For this House to name them is but a late way. I am for the King's naming them out of such gentlemen as live in the country.

Lord Eland, Mr. Greenfield, and Mr. Harley were all zealously against that.

Mr. Goldwell was for the King's appointing them out of the last land tax.

But the committee did not settle this, so thought fit to postpone it, and proceeded on with other part[s] of the bill till they had gone

---

[1] No such order is entered in the *Journal.*

a good way through it. So he was ordered to report the committee had made some progress in the matter to them referred and to desire leave to sit again. So he left the Chair.

Speaker took the Chair. *Mr. Attorney General* reported accordingly, and the House resolved on Friday next to go into a committee again on the bill.

So House adjourned till 8 tomorrow morning.

Thursday, 29 December

Sir Edward Hussey was ordered to carry up a private bill for the sale of the estate of Anthony Eyre esq. and to acquaint their Lordships that this House had agreed to the same without any amendments.

Sir Edward Seymour and *Mr. Clarke* opposed the petition of the Earl of Sandwich, etc., for making the river to Bridgwater navigable, for that it would be very prejudicial to the county of Somerset and would only benefit some part of Wales.

However, the petition was referred to a committee to consider of.

Mr. Travers presented the petition of the Cheesemongers of London against the bill for packing and weighing of butter.

Mr. Papillon, Sir Samuel Dashwood, etc. spoke against that bill as designed only to carry on a particular interest of the county of Suffolk against all the Cheesemongers of London; that it was to repeal a very good law made to prevent abuses in making of butter and cheese, etc.

Mr. Clarke presented Mr. Thomas Greenhill's petition.

Then the House, according to order, went into a committee upon the bill for the East [India] Company. Speaker left the Chair; Sir John Guise was called to the Chair of the committee. So the Clerk read the bill over. Then the Chairman postponed the preamble. So they proceeded on the clauses of the bill in order, filling up the blanks, and made some alterations in them.

When they came to that for a company to be carried on by new subscriptions, several spoke against it on behalf of the old Company: that this was invading of men's properties, that the stock here proposed was too great, and that it would ruin the other trade of the nation. This was long debated. Some at last would have this blank postponed, but opposed by those for a new company. So that was put and carried in the negative. Then the question was put to fill up the blank with 'new subscriptions' and carried in the affirmative.

So they made some progress in the bill, which he was ordered to report and to desire leave to sit again. So he left the Chair. Speaker resumed the Chair. *Sir John Guise* reported the committee had made some progress in the matter to them referred and desired leave to sit again, which was resolved upon Wednesday next accordingly.

So the House adjourned till 8 tomorrow morning.

Friday, 30 December

Sir Christopher Musgrave was ordered to carry up to the Lords the engrossed bill that the inhabitants of the province of York may dispose of their personal estates by their will (notwithstanding the custom of that province) for their Lordships' concurrence.

The engrossed bill for granting a longer time to the persons concerned in the convex lights was read the third time.

Sir [Henry][1] *Ashurst* offered a rider on behalf of the City of London to save their right, that they may set up what lights they please in the City.

It was read twice and an amendment made to it. So read the third time and made part of the bill.

Then *Mr. Boscawen, Sir John Darell*, and *Sir William Wogan* spoke against the bill and urged that it was a pernicious bill hindering the consumption of the manufacture of the nation—tallow. That it was a direct monopoly and had been adjudged so at law. That it was no new invention, so not within the statute of 21 Jac. [I] to encourage such a patent. That it was not a good light but glares directly in your face and takes away your sight. And that to enlarge the patentees' term for seven years longer, as this bill does, is directly against the interest of the public.

Several others spoke against it as *Sir Christopher Musgrave, Sir John Guise, Sir Francis Blake, Sir Samuel Dashwood, Mr. Goodwin Wharton, Sir Robert Rich, Mr. Jeffrey Jeffreys*, etc.

So upon the question for passing the bill, it was carried in the negative.

House, according to order, went into a committee to consider farther of the bill for 4s. in the pound, and proceeded from where they left off last and came to that about imposing an oath on the assessors to make true presentments.

Several spoke against this—as that it signified little, that it was but a snare to some, and that others did not value their oath as they

[1] In MS. 'William'.

ought. And in the stead, it was proposed by some to inflict a penalty on the tenant or owner of any land that shall give in the value to be less than it is. Others proposed to make this an equal tax and that they might come up to the full 4*s.* in the pound that no tenant shall be obliged to pay his landlord any more rent during his term than such landlord shall give in the value of his land to be and that every landlord should give in or send the value of his estate. Others proposed that instead of the oath on the assessors the commissioners might take an oath to that effect, who were generally gentlemen who understood better what an oath was. Others proposed a reward to the assessors of so much in the pound out of what they should bring in more than the last monthly assessment was. But none of these was readily embraced. But the oath on the assessors was upon the question left out and no other of the former proposals would be received— the north-country gentlemen and those who were the easiest rated still finding some fault therein and taking exceptions to anything that was proposed to have an equal tax throughout England and rejected some clauses to that effect, as one of Mr. Freke that no tenant should pay more rent than according to the value of the estate the landlord gave in.

So they proceeded on the bill and passed several clauses. So Mr. Attorney was ordered to report further progress and to desire leave to sit again. Mr. Attorney General left the Chair of the committee. The Speaker resumed the Chair. *Mr. Attorney* reported accordingly, and the House resolved to go into a committee again tomorrow to consider of the said bill.

A message from the Lords by Sir Miles Cook and [Mr. Meredith],[1] Masters in Chancery, that the Lords desire a free conference tomorrow morning at 11 of the clock in the Painted Chamber on the subject-matter of the last conference.

The messengers being withdrawn, notice was taken in the House by some members that it was not mentioned with whom this conference was desired—the words 'with this House' being omitted.

Sir Christopher Musgrave thought it proper for the House to call in the messengers and to acquaint them that this House will send an answer by messengers of their own.

Sir Edward Seymour thought it best to return an answer that you are ready to meet the Lords at a conference when they desire it with this House.

---

[1] Blank in MS.; from *CJ*, x. 765.

But it being a mistake in the messenger, he was called in and acquainted by the *Speaker* that the House supposed there was some mistake in the message and therefore had sent for him to rectify it, if any. Which the messenger did, saying it was his mistake by omitting the words 'with this House'. So they withdrew again, and the *Speaker* reported the message again.

Some cried out to agree.

But *Mr. Smith* and *Mr. Greenfield* were against agreeing for that this conference was desired about a matter of moment and thought it too soon for a free conference, and desired as the Lords had taken a long time to consider of the last conference so they might of the free conference. *Paul Foley* to the same.

And *Mr. Hampden* thought it too soon to have a free conference after two conferences, and that about papers. Therefore, I think it best to consider of and to return an answer that you will send an answer by messengers of your own.

Sir Thomas Clarges and *Sir Edward Seymour* thought the House might turn this free conference into only a conference by hearing what the Lords say and for your managers to tell them they will report it to the House, and you may take time to consider thereof.

Sir Thomas Littleton was against a free conference for that it puts a great hardship upon the managers, who have not time to prepare themselves. But for your turning this free conference to a conference, I doubt you cannot. *Attorney General, Mr. Clarke, Mr. Montagu,* and others to the same.

But *Sir Christopher Musgrave* was against it.

So the question was stated to agree with the Lords in a free conference. But some gentlemen not liking the question, *Sir Thomas Clarges* proposed, lest that should be carried in the negative whereby all good correspondence between the two Houses would be destroyed, that the previous question should be put first. Which was. Upon which the House divided—the Yeas go forth.

		Mr. Gwyn	
Yeas			61
		Mr. Harcourt	
Tellers for the			
		Marquess of Winchester	
Noes			78
		Mr. Goodwin Wharton	

So the other question—that the House would send an answer by messengers of their own—was put and carried.

Then the messengers from the Lords were called in and acquainted therewith by *Mr. Speaker.*

So the House adjourned till 8 tomorrow morning.

Saturday, 31 December

The bill to prevent the exportation of gold and silver and melting down the coin of this realm was read a second time.

And upon the question for committing it, several spoke against it as *Mr. Harley* for that it did debase our coin and take so much out of everyone's pocket that shall be paid any money for the future. Then this will do no manner of good to foreign parts for nobody will take your money abroad for more than its intrinsic value.

Mr. Hutchinson was for it because it would be a means to keep your money in the nation, which was wanted here, for if of less value abroad than here at home you will keep it here. It is as good as your clipped money, besides which there is little other money now left in the nation. And this I do not take to be debasing your coin but only lessening it in weight, and why it should not go as well then as now clipped money does? No one at market, etc. scruples a clipped piece —why should they when your money is reduced? As for your milled and your heavy money, there is hardly any to be seen—it being melted down and sent beyond sea, it being really worth more in bullion than when coined. Therefore, you may be sure few persons will coin any bullion now. I must agree your merchant will be against this because it thwarts his interest—bullion being now become a manufacture which is exported to the best market and traded with where it yields most.

Mr. Boscawen was against it for that it lessened so much of every man's estate as you lessened your money.

Sir Richard Temple, Sir John Darell, Major Pery, and *Dr. Barbone* were for it to commit it.

Sir Robert Cotton, Paul Foley, and *Mr. Clarke* were against it for that it would be of no advantage to this nation, because as much as we lessened our coin so much would the exchange abroad rise against us, so the matter would be the same. And it would do no good but put people and things in confusion.

Sir John Lowther (of Lowther): It is objected against this bill that it debases your coin. I say not; it only makes it more equal to the value of bullion. Then it is said money is a commodity and that it is the balance of trade will govern it, and if that be against you money must go out to supply your occasions abroad if they be greater than your commodities exported, for so much as they fall short so much money must go out to make up. This I cannot deny, but then there is a trade of carrying out of money which will always be if it be more worth there than it is here; they will carry that by which they can gain most, and not your manufacture. Then you will never have any money coined here; though such vast quantities of bullion come hither yearly from Spain, there is none coined but all sent abroad again. Then for your own heavy money here, it is melted down by the goldsmiths—it being worth 2d. more in an ounce when uncoined than it is when it is coined. I think this a matter very well worth your consideration.

Sir Robert Howard was for committing the bill and that the committee might consider of a way to bring in all the clipped money and have it new coined.

Mr. Holt against this bill because it would not do what was aimed at. It is true bullion before it is coined is worth more than it is after, but the true cause thereof is the great want of money in Germany whither most of your bullion is sent and coined into a baser sort of money to pay their armies, which when that nation comes to be in peace they will find the load of. Bullion is a commodity and will go to such places where there is the best market. The best remedy I know of is to prohibit the exporting your home bullion, which you may by making the exporter take an oath that it is foreign coin or bullion, and hereby you will not want money here.

Sir Edward Hussey, *Jeffrey Jeffreys*, *Mr. Papillon*, and *Mr. Heneage Finch* were all against the bill for that it lessened every man's estate the 20th part. That the want of money would be remedied by increasing of trade, which is the thing will bring in money; and the lessening your money will signify nothing as to foreign parts, for as much as you lessen it so much more will the exchange rise against you and the foreign[er] ask so much the more for his commodity. And your home merchant will come to this too when he feels it from abroad; he must either sell less commodity for the like money or ask more money for the same quantity of commodity.

So upon the question for committing it, House divided—Yeas went out.

Sir Charles Blois

Yeas   137

Mr. Montagu

Tellers for the

Mr. Clarke

Noes   126

Mr. Colt

So the bill was committed to a Committee of the Whole House.

House went into a committee on the bill for the land tax; Mr. Attorney General to the Chair. So the committee proceeded where left off last and made an end of several clauses and ordered him to report further progress and to desire leave to sit again. So he left the Chair.

And the Speaker resumed the Chair. *Mr. Attorney General* reported accordingly, and the House resolved to go into a committee again upon this bill on Monday next.

So the House adjourned till Monday morning 8 of the clock.

Monday, 2 January 1692/3

The bill to prevent malicious informations in the Court of King's Bench was read the third time.

Mr. Waller (of York) presented a rider which would make the bill go the easier down in the House of Lords, which was by way of proviso that nothing in this act should extend to informations exhibited by the Attorney General.

Which proviso was read thrice and made part of the bill.

So the whole bill was passed with the title, and Mr. Waller ordered to carry it up to the Lords for their concurrence.

Mr. Palmes presented Mrs. Osbaston's petition touching a private bill.

The bill for raising the militia for the year 1693 though the former month's pay be not paid was read the second time.

Mr. Hutchinson moved that the committee might take care therein to provide that militia men when they lie out at quarters might not be exacted upon.

Sir Thomas Clarges proposed that the militia should not be called together but by order from the King and Council, because the muster-masters do often for their profit prevail upon the officers to call them out when there is no need.

So the bill was committed to a private committee upon the debate of the House though it was in a manner charging the subject in case of money, because it had in former sessions been committed to a private committee, and all that come were to have voices.

But *Sir Christopher Musgrave* objected that this bill ought not to be committed to a private committee because it is laying a charge on the subject, but it ought to be to a Committee of the Whole House.

(Which seemed to be the sense of the House. But it being passed, it could not be retracted. So that was added before to help it—that all that come should have voices—to make the committee larger.)

Col. Granville put the House in mind of the free conference desired by the Lords.

Paul Foley: After a conference on each side I agree in case of a bill it is usual to have a free conference; there it is known what is the matter in difference between the two Houses. But in this case it is not so; here is nothing appears wherein the Houses differ, and therefore I am for searching of precedents to see how it hath been in like cases. There are two, I think, in August 1660 which come somewhat to this case: one was where the Lords sent for a free conference at the first step; the other where the Lords desired a free conference on one conference had by you. But I look upon both those [as] very irregular. And therefore since we know not what to say or what the Lords would have, I desire you will appoint a committee to search precedents and to consider how we shall behave ourselves at the conference, if you think fit to agree to it.

Sir Christopher Musgrave: For my part I never knew any case after a conference had on each side where a free conference was ever denied, and therefore I am for agreeing to the free conference. For otherwise you will break the good correspondence between the two Houses. And I am sure a free conference is the lesser evil, if any.

Mr. Palmes and *Mr. Smith* were for a committee.

Sir Thomas Clarges was for a free conference, and yet he would not have the managers debate any matter but hear what the Lords will say and then acquaint them you will report it to the House. And upon that you may do as you think fit, and this the House hath done in many like cases.

So the question was put and resolved: That this House doth agree to a free conference with the Lords on the subject-matter of the last conference. Ordered that Col. Granville do go up to the Lords and acquaint them therewith. Then they resolved to have the same managers as they had before, and they are to meet this afternoon and to consider of what they think fit to offer. So the managers' names were read over and several others were added to them.

Then the Order of the Day for the call of the House was read, and it was proposed to put it off. So the question for adjournment of it to another day was put. House divided—Yeas went out.[1]

		Lord Falkland	
	Yeas		138
		Sir Joseph Tredenham	
Tellers for the			
		Col. Granville	
	Noes		194
		Lord William Powlett	

So it was called over. And each man in order according to the alphabet by their counties was called, and those present when their names were called stood up with their hats off and answered 'here', and the defaulters were noted down by the Clerk. When gone through the list, the defaulters in order were called over again, and divers members made excuses for several that were allowed and others not, of which there were six in number—viz. Sir Mark Milbank, Mr. Dawney, Sir Thomas Miller, Mr. John Bence, Mr. Henry Pelham, and Mr. James Butler. And there being a general order before for sending in custody for all that went out of town without leave, these were all ordered to be sent for in custody of the Serjeant at Arms, without putting a particular question upon every member as it must otherwise have been.

Ordered that the House be called over this day fortnight and that no member go out of town without leave on pain of being sent for in custody of the Serjeant at Arms.

Then the House went into a committee upon the land tax bill and made some further progress and ordered him to move to sit again (and ordered tomorrow). All which *he* [the Attorney General] did and the House did it accordingly, and ordered Mr. Attorney to prepare a borrowing clause to be added to the bill.

All committees were adjourned with a consent that the committee of the managers for the conference might sit this afternoon.

So adjourned till 8 tomorrow morning.

---

[1] Cf. *CJ*, x. 767, where the motion is worded to go on to the Order of the Day.

Tuesday, 3 January

Mr. Attorney General and *Mr. Serj. Wogan* spoke against the bill to regulate proceedings in the Crown Office of the King's Bench at Westminster—that it entrenched upon the rights of the Crown.

However, the bill was committed and the committee had power to send for persons, papers, and records. The petition from the Clerks of the Crown Office, relating to the said bill, was referred to the said committee.

Col. Granville reported from the committee of managers for the free conference: That they had considered the thing and were of opinion they could return no other answer to the Lords than that this free conference being desired on the subject-matter of the last conference —wherein there was no difference stated between the two Houses as is usual before a free conference—the Commons can only receive from their Lordships what they have to offer and will communicate the same to their House and receive their further directions therein.[1]

Mr. Montagu and the *Lord Coningsby* took some exceptions to it as to the words stating a difference, whereas there is no difference at all.

Speaker then proposed to put it in this frame: that the managers should appoint one to speak, and to hear first what the Lords will say, and then your manager may offer to this effect—that the Commons have agreed to this free conference to preserve the good correspondence between the two Houses and would acquaint their House with what their Lordships had offered and receive their further directions.

And the managers were ordered to do it in such general words.

Sir Miles Cook and Sir John Hoskins brought the message from the Lords.

Then the House, according to order, went into a committee upon the land tax bill. So they proceeded upon the same.

They came to the clause about empty houses whereon was a long debate. Some were for their paying; and others not and thought it punishment enough for the owners to have them empty, and therefore unreasonable to pay taxes for them too when as they made nothing of them as they do of land when untenanted, but houses are the worse for being empty. However, it was upon the question resolved they should pay; otherwise a great part of the tax would be lost.

Then to the clause of double taxing, Mr. Hutchinson, Sir John Guise, Mr. Howe, and Sir Richard Temple moved that if the papists

[1] No such report is recorded in the *Journal*.

would take the oath of allegiance, as they were informed, many would it might excuse them without taking that of supremacy wherein they are forced to renounce the Church of Rome.

Mr. Goldwell and Sir William Strickland were against that.

But the clause, on the question, stood as formerly.

So the committee went through the bill.

Mr. Paul Foley presented a clause that no land should pay less than double what they did to the 2*s.* act.

But Sir Christopher Musgrave opposed it because not regular to receive new clauses to a bill till the postponed clauses were determined.

But the House received it and read it once.

Several spoke against it as a hard and unequal clause for that those persons who were unequally taxed by that act would continue still so by this, for the double of that act will be the standard for this. Though you say no one shall be rated less, which implies they may more, but they that were underrated to that will continue so in this and they that were well affected and rated themselves to the full they shall be kept up by this double, which will be as hard as before.

However, it was put and added to the bill, thinking it to be a means to keep up the act, which perhaps would otherwise come to little.

Mr. Goldwell tendered a clause to make those that were underrated before to come up to the full on this act.

But it was opposed as irregular until all the postponed clauses were disposed of and the blanks for the commissioners' names were filled up.

Then the committee went upon the commissioners' names. Some proposed to name new commissioners. Others proposed to have the same as on the last land tax that were living, which would save much time. And others were for new ones as thinking that more expeditious, which seemed the general sense of the committee.

So Mr. Attorney was ordered to report further progress and to move the House that the commissioners' names should be prepared by the members and presented to the House. Then he left the Chair.

Speaker resumed the Chair, and *Mr. Attorney* reported accordingly and made that motion. And ordered that the members of this House do by Thursday morning next prepare and present the names of commissioners for the several counties, cities, and places (as usual) to be inserted into the said bill. And the House resolved to go into a committee on that day upon the said bill and to proceed upon no other matter that day.

So adjourned till 8 tomorrow morning.

Wednesday, 4 January

Mr. Neale was ordered to carry up Sir Anthony Brown's private bill to the Lords for their concurrence.

The bill for prohibiting the importation of foreign hair buttons and all other foreign buttons was read the second time.

Several spoke against it as that this was not the right method to keep them out (by a total prohibition of them), for that being small goods it would encourage the people but to smuggle them which might easily be done by putting them in the water, which does not hurt them at all. But the better way to prevent them is to lay a high duty upon them, and this will be the best prohibition and the Crown will get something thereby. But urged for the bill that it was desired by a numerous sort of poor people of our own nation who made this commodity; that the materials were all of our own growth which were carried beyond sea and then sent back hither made up, which would be more for the nation's benefit to manufacture them here.

So the question was put for committing the bill. House divided—Yeas went out.

		Mr. Pery	
	Yeas		97
		Mr. Goldwell	
Tellers for the			
		Sir Walter Yonge	
	Noes		76
		Mr. Harley[1]	

So it was committed.

The time of the conference being come, the managers' names were read over and some more added, and they went up to the same. And being returned, *Col. Granville* reported from the said free conference: That they had been there; and that the Lord Rochester opened it to be on the subject-matter of the last and to preserve a good correspondence between the two Houses; that when they sent down the papers to this House they did it with expectation this House would have given them some satisfaction in several particulars therein; and that as to the vote sent up by this House, it was altogether unusual without sending the reasons which moved you to it; and that your managers acquainted their Lordships that they had heard

---

[1] Henry Herbert in *CJ*, x. 769.

what their Lordships offered and had nothing further to say but would acquaint this House therewith to receive your farther directions.

Mr. Harley and *Sir Christopher Musgrave* complained of a scandalous practice, or at least a report that was spread about that there were some persons who solicited business in this House or had bills depending here that keep constant tables and committee dinners for members where they were treated.

Several others spoke to it too as a matter wherein was truth, and inveighed against it as a base thing.

Whereupon it was resolved: That no member of this House do presume to accept of any entertainment at any public house for the carrying on any matter under the consideration of the House upon pain of incurring the censure of the House.

After which arose a debate about the chairmen of committees and other members receiving of bribes and gratuities and of collections made without doors to carry on some bills within the House, which seemed to reflect on some particular members. The House censured this practice and condemned it but came to no resolution thereon, so it was let fall.

Then the House, according to order, went into a committee upon the East India bill. Sir John Guise was called to the Chair. But he, thinking himself reflected on in the former debate, would not take the Chair of the committee. So the Speaker resumed the Chair, and upon the question Sir John Guise was ordered to take the Chair of the said committee, which he did, and the committee proceeded in the bill.

They debated upon the time for the books to be provided—proposed to fill the blank up with 'ten days'. Committee divided thereon —Yeas to the right hand and Noes to the left.

	Yeas	Mr. Johnson	76
Tellers for the			
	Noes	Lord William Powlett	67

So they proceeded on, and after a little while the friends of the old Company proposed for the Chairman to leave the Chair, which was seconded. On which the committee divided again, but it was carried that he should not but to go on. So the committee did and made some further progress, which he was ordered to report and to desire leave to sit again. So he left the Chair.

Speaker resumed the Chair, and *Sir John Guise* reported accordingly and moved to sit again. And ordered on Monday next to go into a committee upon that bill.

So the House adjourned till 8 tomorrow morning.

Thursday, 5 January

Several members, according to order, delivered in at the Table lists of names of commissioners to be inserted into the land tax bill. They were not read once, as they ought in the House, but referred to the committee, and the residue of the lists were ordered to be presented to the committee.

So the House went into a Committee of the Whole House upon the land tax bill. And the lists of the commissioners' names were read twice over. Then the question was put upon all of a county or place to be commissioners for such county, etc.[1] Then another question was put for filling up the blank with these names.

So the Attorney was ordered to report the committee had made some further progress and to move for leave to sit again. Which *he* did, and ordered tomorrow morning and nothing to intervene.

All committees were adjourned but the Lord Villiers'.[2]

So adjourned till 8 tomorrow morning.

Friday, 6 January

Richard Leveson esq., being chosen a member for Newport in the Isle of Wight (in the room of Sir Robert Holmes, deceased), came into the House, took the oaths at the Table and subscribed the declaration, and after took his place in the House.

The committee to whom Mr. Bayntun's bill was referred was revived.[3]

Sir John Darell presented a petition from the Dyers, etc. of London, praying that no woollen manufacture might be exported white that the dyeing thereof might not be lost to this nation. It was read and referred to the Grand Committee of Trade.

---

[1] For a report of a division on one of these questions see *HMC Seventh Report*, p. 213.

[2] No such exception is recorded in the *Journal*.

[3] No such order is entered in the *Journal*.

Mr. Waller (of Bucks.) presented the petition of several masters and owners of ships and vessels against the bill for preventing the abuses in packing and weighing of butter. [It] was received, read, and referred to the committee to whom that was committed.

Then the House, according to order, went into a Committee of the Whole House upon the bill for the land tax; Mr. Attorney General to the Chair. And he presented the committee with a clause for the £750,000 borrowed on the poll act to this act as also another clause of credit for the King upon this act—both which were read twice and the blanks filled up and some amendments made to them, and so they were ordered to be made part of the bill.

Mr. Clarke tendered a clause for imposing the penalty of £500 on any commissioner that shall act without taking the oaths.

It was declared as the sense of the House that if a person be commissioner in several counties and he act in them, taking the oaths in one will not excuse for the other.

Mr. Clarke also offered that since commissioners were so very numerous, there might be some clause that no person should have power to act as a commissioner upon this act that did not pay as a gentleman upon the poll act.

Mr. Goldwell thought it might be hard to put it so generally—to exclude all that had not paid as gentlemen—for in corporations and some cities there would not be commissioners to put this act in execution. But if you please that no one that did not pay as a gentleman in a county shall be a commissioner I think it will do very well, and in a corporation unless he had paid 10s. as a trader worth £300.

Sir Thomas Clarges: It has been a practice not to admit the commissioners of the county at large to act within the borough, etc. Therefore if you think it fit, you may empower the adjacent commissioners within a county to act within corporations if there shall be a want of commissioners therein.

So Mr. Clarke's clause for imposing a penalty on the commissioners, etc. as before was made part of the bill, as also another framed to the effect above to disable such commissioners from acting.

Then it was taken notice that in some counties (particularly Merioneth and Caernarvon) there was but one person paid as a gentleman in each upon the late poll act, though there were in each a sheriff, two parliament men, and eight justices of peace, besides others. This was debated, and proposed to remedy this defect either by letting in the commissioners of [the] next county to act (but this thought not proper) or else by letting the King name commissioners for those counties. This was also not approved of because the committee have already agreed that such and such persons shall be commissioners. So it was let fall to rectify it in the House.

Mr. Smith presented a clause that no tenant should deduct more than 4*s.* in the pound out of what rent he pays, annuity, or rent charge, according to such proportion only as he is charged for the estate to the King.

But it was objected to it that it went on an ill supposition that the tax was not well executed, and perhaps it might have ill consequences and occasion a juggle between landlord and tenant to undervalue the estate and so defraud the King.

So it was withdrawn.

Sir Francis Blake presented a clause to empower mortgagees to deduct 4*s.* in the pound out of the interest money they pay.

Sir Charles Sedley for it and thought it very reasonable for them to bear their share, who escaped all manner of taxes, and to ease the land a little—which, to be sure, would pay the whole tax.

Mr. Brewer against it, and Sir Christopher Musgrave, for that it is not proper in this act, this being a tax on real and personal estates, too. Then it is unreasonable, for this would tax men that have money double or twice for the same. And if you would allow them to deduct what is stopped from them out of what they are charged to the King, this will lessen the tax to the King and no one be the better but the extravagant person who hath run himself in debt.

So it was withdrawn.

Henry Herbert offered a clause to raise this act to the full 4*s.* in the pound by giving the assessors so much in the pound as they shall raise more than double the 2*s.* in the pound, to be received by them from the Receiver.

Several liked hereof, and the blank in the clause was filled up with 1*s.* in the pound.

Sir Christopher Musgrave was against it for that it would have little effect, only tend to multiplying of appeals, be very vexatious to the people, and give a great deal of trouble to the commissioners.

The question for reading it a second time was put and carried in the negative.

Sir Charles Sedley presented a clause ordering the Navy to pay in course.

But thought not proper at present, so it was withdrawn.

Having done with their clauses, they went through the preamble. So finished the bill and ordered him to report it.

So the Speaker resumed the Chair. *Mr. Attorney General* reported that the committee had gone through the bill and made several amendments and commanded him to report it, which the House ordered tomorrow.

So adjourned till 8 tomorrow morning.

Saturday, 7 January

I was not well, so not at the House this day.

Monday, 9 January

Mr. Walcott's bill to make salt water fresh was read the first time.

Mr. Neale and some others spoke against it and said it was a monopoly and no new invention, it being done only by stilling without mixing anything therewith.

However, ordered a second reading.

Sir Robert Cotton (of Chester) ordered to carry up the Lord Villiers' bill to the Lords and acquaint them this House hath agreed to the same without any amendments.

Sir Miles Cook and Sir Adam Oatley, Masters in Chancery, brought the message from the Lords.

Then the House, according to order, proceeded in the further consideration of the report of the bill for the land tax. Several of the amendments the House agreed to.

The clause to excuse the University lands, etc. was long debated on both sides. And the question being put to agree with the committee in leaving it in, House divided—Noes went out.

	Noes	Mr. Henry Herbert[1]	132
		Mr. Freke junior	
Tellers for the			
	Yeas	Mr. Bromley	115
		Mr. Goldwell	

So the clause being to be left out, they would be charged.

[1] Mr. Howe in *CJ*, x. 772.

So the House went through the act and the several clauses.

Mr. Paul Foley proposed there might be an exception made in this act of all companies and joint stocks that shall be taxed by any act of this sessions to the end they might be taxed higher than 4*s.* the pound, if thought necessary in any other act this sessions.

So such an exception was inserted in this act as an amendment.

Then the *Attorney General* put the House in mind of the clauses about the commissioners of Merioneth and Caernarvon shires.

After debate, the House passed a general clause to supply the defect of commissioners that paid not on the poll act—empowering the King, where there shall be a want of them, to name them out of such persons as reside in those two counties, under his Great Seal.

Col. Granville tendered a clause to require an account to be given to parliament of this act.

But it being read on the question, it was to enlarge the Commission of Accounts unto the 25th of April 1693.

Sir John Lowther was against this clause because it was an irregular thing to tack such things together when it is more proper for a bill of itself, and this is a dangerous method for that one time or other it may be turned upon you. *Mr. Smith* was also against it. So others.

But *Col. Granville*, *Mr. Bathurst*, and *Sir Christopher Musgrave* spoke for it as highly necessary when so much money is given to have an account of it; it would be a satisfaction to the nation.

So the clause was read a second time and the question put for making it part of the bill. House divided—Yeas went out.

		Col. Granville	
	Yeas		106
		Mr. Harcourt	
Tellers for the			
		Mr. Montagu	
	Noes		128
		Sir Jonathan Jennings	

So rejected.

Then a clause of appropriation was tendered by *Mr. Hungerford* of part of this tax to such and such uses. It was received and read once.

Some spoke against it as comprehending not one clause but several, some of which were in the bill before; that it rendered the application of any of the money to any other service than the Navy very difficult; that it was differing from all other former clauses of appropriation.

But it being not well approved of, the debate thereof was adjourned till tomorrow, and Mr. Attorney General, Sir Christopher Musgrave, Mr. Paul Foley, and Mr. Smith were ordered to prepare another clause of appropriation against tomorrow.

Col. Granville moved for leave to bring in a bill to continue the Commissioners of Accounts for some time longer.

But it was opposed being very late in the day, and a new motion which ought not to be after such an hour. So let fall.

So adjourned till 8 tomorrow morning.

Tuesday, 10 January

Bill to prevent the profanation of the Lord's Day was read the first time and ordered a second reading.

Sir Edward Seymour desired that it might be provided in this act that no one should have the benefit of that act for the better observation of the Lord's Day which provides no writ, process, etc. shall be executed on a Sunday, whereby debtors make that day a sanctuary to go abroad in and commit disorders. But I would have a clause in this bill to that effect—that no one should be free from arrests, etc. on that day but he that did resort to some church or chapel or other place for divine service.

This was approved of but it was thought more proper to be stirred at the second reading of the bill.

The bill about fishing in the river Severn and repealing part of an act in 30 Car. II read the first time.

Sir Edward Seymour excepted against it; being a bill to repeal a former law, leave ought to be first asked for bringing in such a bill. Then it ought not to be presented the same day the leave was asked.

Therefore upon the question for a second reading, it was refused because irregular.

The bill about exchange of the living of Petworth, etc. concerned the King, the Duke of Somerset, and the College of Eton. The House was informed it was by agreement, the King also consenting.

Mr. Arnold moved for the bill against the lotteries.

Mr. Hungerford presented the petition of Sir William Scawen and others in relation to the Greenland trade, praying a revival of that law in 25 Car. II c. [7] and that they would endeavour to regain this trade, which hath been lost to this nation this 10 years and now wholly in the hands of the Dutch. But they desired some further encouragement—as a suspension of the act of navigation as to one part that they might sail with two-thirds foreign seamen, they having most occasion for Dutch seamen which they call 'harpineers' (who are they that take the whales) without which the trade is not to be carried on.

Sir Samuel Barnardiston and *Col. Pery* said this was a very beneficial trade but lost to this nation, being engrossed by the Dutch and the Hamburgers of whom we are forced to have the commodity at excessive rates. And that the only way to regain this trade was to incorporate them in a company with a joint stock exclusive to others.

Which was not liked of by some.

However, the petition was referred to a committee and to bring in a bill thereon if they thought fit.

Then the House, according to order, took up the adjourned debate of the clause of appropriation, and the same was by leave withdrawn. And *Mr. Smith* presented a new clause of appropriation, which was received [and] read once. It consisted of several parts: first, transferring about £735,000 (being what was borrowed on the quarterly poll) upon the credit of this act; and another part appropriating so much to the Navy (proposed £600,000); and another part for the land army. But the blank was filled up with £700,000 for the Navy. So the clause being long and intricate, it was put paragraph by paragraph and passed, and the clause made part of the bill.

Mr. Goodwin Wharton tendered a clause to enforce the Navy and the Victualling Office to pay in course. It was received [and] read twice.

And by some thought very necessary as what will support the credit of those offices and make persons the willinger to trust them when they know they shall be paid in course. And it would take it out of the power of the officers to play the knave and prefer one before another. *Sir Christopher Musgrave, Sir John Darell, Sir Robert Rich* for it.

But *Mr. Papillon, Mr. Mayne, Sir Edward Seymour*, etc. were against it. Though they approved of the thing if the Victualling Office were not in debt, but since the office is now £200,000 in debt if that must first be paid off you will have no persons will supply you with victuals, etc. for the fleet for this summer, so will have no fleet to go to sea.

So they proposed to make an exception in the clause as to the Victualling Office that they should not pay in course. The House divided thereon—Yeas went out.

Mr. Henry Herbert
Yeas   115
Mr. Mayne
Tellers for the
Mr. Bickerstaffe
Noes   74
Major Pery

So then the clause was made of the bill with that exception.

Sir Walter Yonge tendered a clause to empower the commissioners to summon any persons that shall come newly into any place and to tax them for their personal estates. Which was read twice and made part of the bill.

Sir William Strickland tendered a clause to suspend all pensions—whether for years, life, or inheritance—during the war but such as shall be allowed by the Barons of the Exchequer to be upon good and valuable consideration.

Sir Robert Davers spoke against it as unjust to put it in the power of the Barons to determine as they please.

Sir Richard Temple against it for that many persons have nothing else to depend upon and some of them have been granted upon very good considerations, and he thought it fitter for a bill by itself.

On the question to read it a second time, the House divided—the Yeas go out.

Sir Edward Hussey
Yeas   107
Sir William Strickland
Tellers for the
Sir Richard Temple
Noes   70
Sir Robert Davers

So it was read a second time.

Mr. Goodwin Wharton was for the clause, but thought it best to except all pensions that are under £50 per annum for they are generally charities, etc. which I would not take away.

Mr. Bickerstaffe was against it for that he doubted it would hinder and stop the bill.

Col. Pery: There is a pension granted to the Duchess of Cleveland which is confirmed by act of parliament, on which I have lent a considerable sum of money. This is my right, and before it be taken away

I desire I may be heard at the Bar by my counsel. *Sir Samuel Dashwood* to the same.

Sir Joseph Tredenham against this clause.

So *Sir Stephen Fox* for that this was an effectual course to stop the bill, for all the Lords concerned in the grant of pensions will be heard against it by their counsel which, though the bill should pass, the delay would [be] a sufficient prejudice. Then upon these pensions there is very little paid, but just enough to keep body and soul together. And for many of them I know they were granted upon good considerations. So that upon the whole matter, if this bill be delayed (as it certainly will if this clause be added) your service will be neglected and all things stand still. Your weekly payments to the Army will cease, which amount to a great sum and there is already hardly any money in the Exchequer to carry on this service now. Therefore, I desire you will lay it aside. *Mr. Smith* against the clause.

So was *Mr. Harley* because left to the judges to continue what you take away.

Mr. Heneage Finch against it for the same reason and because it is foreign to the bill.

But *Sir Walter Yonge* and *Mr. Palmes* for it because not a time to continue such large payments out of the revenue at this time, which should go towards carrying on the war.

So the clause was given leave to be withdrawn, and he might tender it to any other bill.

Mr. Arnold tendered a clause for the taxing the King's Bench prison in Southwark. Received, read twice, and made part of the bill.

Sir Edward Hussey tendered a clause to hinder the King from granting away any of his hereditary revenue or a pension out of the same—making such grant void.

Mr. Hampden opposed the receiving it.

So upon the question for bringing it up, House divided—Yeas went out.

	Mr. Harley	
Yeas		85
	Mr. Waller	
Tellers for the		
	Sir Jonathan Jennings	
Noes		81
	[Mr. Travers][1]	

[1] Blank in MS.; from *CJ*, x. 774.

So it was brought up to the Table, received, and read the first time.

Several spoke against it for that it tied up the hands of the Crown so that it could never grant any pension, though never so small and for never so good a piece of service.

So upon the question for a second reading, carried in the negative.

Mr. Hutchinson tendered a clause to reduce Sir Robert Howard's fees[1] to the ancient legal fees to be settled by the Barons.

It was read the first time. And on the question for a second reading carried in the negative.

So the bill with the amendments was ordered to be engrossed.

So the House adjourned till 8 tomorrow morning.

Wednesday, 11 January

Mr. Chadwick presented a petition from several Italian merchants that trade to Naples and Sicily. Which was received and read.

But exception to it was taken that it was irregular because it prayed the House to pass such a bill and to take [up] the report touching the bill for importation of fine Italian, Sicilian, and Naples thrown silk overland, which is altogether against the proceedings in this House to direct you and when you shall proceed.

So the petition was ordered to lie on the Table.

Upon the report of the bill for the importation of fine Italian, Sicilian, and Naples thrown silk overland, several spoke against the bill because it would bring in so much silk it would destroy the woollen manufacture and consequently ruin the Turkey trade, and under pretence of bringing in fine silk would bring in even the Turkey silk. *Mr. Onslow, Sir Thomas Vernon, Sir Samuel Dashwood,* and other Turkey merchants opposed it.

But *Goldwell* urged for it that on the contrary it would much encourage the woollen manufacture for with this fine silk and our wool they make very good stuffs, as good as before we did with Spanish wool. This bill if it be thrown out will ruin several thousand poor workmen who depend on this trade and will drive them out of the nation.

Upon the question of engrossing this bill, House divide[d]—Yeas go out.

---

[1] As Auditor of the Exchequer.

Col. Lee

Yeas   85

Mr. Goldwell

Tellers for the

Sir Samuel Barnardiston

Noes   89

Mr. Foot Onslow

So it passed in the negative.

(It was further urged for this bill, before the question was put, that this manufacture of silk was but newly brought into this kingdom but they had already brought it to great perfection; that if this bill should pass it would keep out foreign silks and thereby save this nation some £100,000 a year and destroy the great trade thereof at Lyons in France; that it will rather increase the Turkey trade by consuming so much of that silk more than formerly for this fine Italian silk is used but for particular purposes which the Turkey silk will not serve for, this fine silk makes one part of the wrought silk and the Turkey silk the other part and one cannot be used for the other but wrought both together they do best; then there is no possibility of bringing Turkey silk in overland instead of this fine silk because they are easily to be known asunder.)

Sir Francis Winnington reported from the committee the several heads agreed upon therein in relation to the advice to be given to His Majesty. Some of the questions were positive resolutions of the opinion of the committee for such and such things; others were that it is the opinion of this committee that the House be moved so and so.

The *Speaker* said as to the positive resolutions the question must be to agree with the committee or not, and thereon they that are against agreeing on a division must go out. But in case of the motions to the House, that is as a new matter in which on a division they that are for the motion must go out.

(All this was but the blunder of Winnington, the Chairman, which was apparent in his management of the matter.)

Sir Thomas Clarges thought these were resolutions of the committee and therefore that the question ought to be for agreeing or not agreeing. *Mr. Harley* to the same.

Sir Joseph Williamson thought otherwise and that they ought to come by so many several motions to the House as things *de novo*, for the committee have left it to the House to order therein as they think fit and it is not a positive resolution of the committee.

Sir Christopher Musgrave: I look upon these as positive resolutions of the committee for which the question must be agreeing or not, and you lay too much stress on the word 'moving the House'.

Sir Edward Seymour: I take these not to be resolutions of your committee but only directions for so many motions to be made by your Chairman to the House. It is every day's practice; your Chairman moves from the Committee of the Whole House by their direction for leave to sit again. This is the opinion of your committee, but the Chairman moves it not to agree therewith but as a new motion. So here in this case it ought to come by way of motion, and not for agreeing or not. *Mr. Hampden* to the same.

But *Paul Foley* thought it proper enough to put them as resolutions of the committee.

(So undoubtedly was the intention of the committee who took them to be resolutions or else the business need not have gone to a committee. But it was occasioned by the ignorance of the Chairman, who was topped upon by some in the committee to add those words 'that the House be moved', thereby to puzzle the matter.)

The *Chairman* then proposed the first matter and made it by way of motion to the House. Then the *Speaker* stated the question: That His Majesty be humbly advised to constitute a Commission of the Admiralty of such persons as are of known experience in maritime affairs.

Sir John Lowther (of Lowther) was against this question for that it reflected very highly on the present Commission of Admiralty, who are gentlemen very faithful to this government and, I believe, of understanding in their business. And as to the great clamour against them of so many merchants' ships being taken, it is not to be avoided unless you can hinder them from running away without their convoys. *Mr. Hutchinson, Sir Robert Cotton* (of Post Office), *Mr. John Howe, Sir Thomas Littleton*, and *Sir Orlando Gee* were against the question.

But *Sir John Knight, Col. Granville*, and *Sir Christopher Musgrave* were for it and did not think it any reflection upon them. For if they be gentlemen of experience they are not injured but no doubt of it will be continued; if they be not, it is fit, I am sure, we should have those that are, especially since our fleet is our chief security.

Sir John Guise and *Sir John Darell* were against the question.

Col. Churchill was very zealous for it and reflected much on the understanding of the Commissioners of the Admiralty and their want of experience, and plainly said they did not understand their business and instanced in several particulars, and therefore thought they ought to be turned out.

Lord Falkland answered some of the particular charges of Col. Churchill and said it was generally the fault of the merchants themselves in letting their ships go without convoys. And as to the reason of your trading ships being not gone, the true reason is the merchants are not ready themselves. The convoy for the Straits fleet is ready but they are not, your West India fleet is gone, and your grand fleet will be ready in February.

Sir Robert Rich and *Mr. Boscawen* were against the question. So was *Sir Joseph Williamson.*

But *Sir Charles Sedley, Mr. Harley, Mr. Peregrine Bertie* (the younger), and *Mr. Goodwin Wharton* were for it.

So at last the aforesaid question was put. House divided—Yeas went out.

	Col. Granville	
Yeas		112
	Col. Churchill	
Tellers for the		
	Mr. Goldwell	
Noes		135
	Mr. Hutchinson	

(All the persons in office, and generally the Whig party, were against this question, which was much wondered at.)

Then the *Chairman* made another motion and the *Speaker* stated the question: That His Majesty be humbly advised that for the future all orders for the management of the fleet do pass through the hands of the Lords Commissioners for the executing the office of Lord High Admiral of England.

Several spoke against this question. Some of those who were for the first question were against this and urged it might be very inconvenient to have all these orders be communicated to the Board of Admiralty. Then it might sometimes cause a delay in matters when it must pass through several places before the orders can be executed. But besides it hath been always customary for the Crown and the Privy Council to send orders to the fleet as they thought fit and to have a controlling power over the Admiralty, and if it should be otherwise sometimes it might be dangerous. Said on the other side that it was apparent there had been great miscarriages and things had been carried so underhand that they could not tell where to lay the blame, but by this way it was hoped it might be found out who were faulty.

So the question was put and carried.

So adjourned till 8 tomorrow morning.

Thursday, 12 January

Mr. Gwyn was ordered to carry a private bill of Mr. Popham up to the Lords and to acquaint them this House hath agreed to their Lordships' amendments to the said bill.

The message from the Lords was brought by Sir Miles Cook and Sir John Franklin, two Masters in Chancery.

The engrossed bill for an aid of 4*s.* in the pound for one year to Their Majesties was read the third time.

Mr. Boscawen offered a rider, which was received and read. It was to disable any person to act as a commissioner in the country in the parish wherein he lives.

Mr. Palmes and *Mr. Bickerstaffe* spoke against it for that they believed it would hinder the execution of the act.

So upon the question for a second reading, it was carried in the negative.

Mr. Chadwick tendered a rider, providing that where any estate was taxed double for the owner's being a papist, etc. and not taking the oaths, the double penalty should not lie on the tenant (though he be bound to pay all taxes) because it was occasioned by his landlord's own fault and not his.

So it was received and read thrice.

And the bill was passed unanimously, then the title of it, and Mr. Attorney General was ordered to carry it up to the Lords for their concurrence.

So adjourned till 8 tomorrow morning.

Friday, 13 January

Richard Norton, being chosen a member for the county of Southampton (in the room of Sir Robert Henley, deceased), came into the House and took the oaths at the Table and subscribed the test and after took his seat in the House.

The bill for making the rivers Wye and Lugg navigable was read a second time.

Several spoke against it, as the members for Gloucestershire, the Somersetshire, and some Welsh men, and urged that it was brought in now very untimely when there are so great taxes on the subject to support the government to lay more for the making of a river. Then it is unjust because more people will be prejudiced by this bill than will be benefited by it.

So House divided on the question to commit it—Yeas went out.

		Lord Coningsby	
	Yeas		107
		Sir Rowland Gwynne	
Tellers for the			
		Sir John Guise	
	Noes		118
		Mr. Arnold	

So it passed in the negative.

So adjourned till 8 tomorrow morning.

Saturday, 14 January

Mr. Campion was ordered to carry up to the Lords the private bill of Sir George Parker and to acquaint them this House hath agreed to the same without any amendments.

So Mr. Christie was ordered to carry up the private bill of Dr. William Wake with the same message.

Mr. Greenfield was ordered to carry up to the Lords the private bill of Mr. Molineux and to acquaint them this House hath agreed to the same with some amendments to which they desire their Lordships' concurrence.

Mr. Waller (of York) was ordered to carry up to the Lords the engrossed bill for preventing frauds by clandestine mortgages for their concurrence.

Then the House, according to order, went into a committee upon the million or fund bill; Mr. Attorney General to the Chair of the committee. So they proceeded in the bill and passed some paragraphs thereof, filling up the blanks.

But the House of Lords wanting Mr. Attorney General to attend them in a matter wherein the King was concerned (in the case of the

Lord Banbury)—the Lords claiming it as a privilege of their House
that the Attorney General ought to attend them, which the Commons
did deny in King James I his time when the Attorney General was
a member of their House. So to prevent a difference between the two
Houses, the Court Party moved that the Attorney might leave the
Chair, there being something extraordinary happened, and to desire
leave to sit again. But his leaving the Chair was opposed by several
members who would have gone on with the bill.

However, he put the question and then left the Chair very abruptly,
contrary to the general sense of the House. So *he* reported some progress and moved for the committee to sit again, which was ordered
upon Monday.

So adjourned till Monday morning 8 of the clock.

Monday, 16 January

Sir Thomas Mompesson presented the petition of the Cheesemongers,
etc. of London against the bill for packing and weighing of butter.

Upon the report of the bill touching royal mines and the agreement
to the amendments thereof, *Mr. Attorney General* and *Mr. Montagu*
desired that since the King's prerogative was so highly concerned
therein that the King might be heard by his Counsel at the Bar against
the same before it passed.

Sir Edward Seymour: The usual way in former times when the King
was concerned in a bill was to ask his leave first. But since that is not
done in this case, and no man will deny but the King hath such a prerogative, it is no great matter to hear the King by his Counsel. I think
you are obliged to it though it be but for form sake; otherwise a stop
may justly be put to the bill.

The House seemed inclined to hear the King's Counsel. Then debated whether they should be heard before the engrossing of it. And
it was thought the better way, for if the House should see cause to
amend it upon any objection they make against it, it cannot so well
be amended after engrossing as before, and thereby may the bill
be lost. So the King's Counsel were ordered to be heard on Friday
next.

Then the *Speaker* took notice of a very irregular thing in this bill.
The bill brought into the House had been transcribed over again
since it went to the committee and endorsed on the back of it '*lect. 1ª
vice*: *lect. 2ᵈᵃ vice*'—which ought by no means to be endured. And

though the old bill be here too and the new one is writ as the original bill was, yet it ought not to be passed over without some censure.

This took up a long debate. Some were for putting a mark upon this method of proceedings.

Mr. Montagu informed the House of a like case; Mr. Prynne was called to the Bar of the House for altering a bill brought into the House.

Sir Christopher Musgrave and others said he took the bill home with him and made amendments to it in material parts and after reported, and he was kindly used, too, that he was not expelled.

Speaker informed the House that the old bill and the new bill were the same—word for word, line for line—and that he believed it was not done with any design, but only the old bill being worn out this was transcribed that it might be easier read.

However, the House resented it very much. Some were for making a declaratory order of the House; others that this new bill might lie on the Table for some time as a punishment. But, however, at last after a long debate the matter was let fall, the House thinking this debate a sufficient censure of the matter.

Order of the Day for going into a Committee of the Whole House upon the fund bill was read.

Sir John Lowther moved for an instruction to the committee that if the whole million come not in on the survivorship, the committee might have power to increase the interest to 14 per cent without benefit of survivorship.

Mr. Foley and *Mr. Montagu* moved that the committee might have power to change the fund from the hereditary excise as it now was on. And that since the double excise was out, they might grant a new 9*d.* thereof which would be of itself a sufficient security (coming to about £140,000 per annum), and you need not stay so long as you must till 1697 if kept on the hereditary excise.

Sir Christopher Musgrave: I like the thing proposed very well but doubt it cannot regularly be done; the committee having already agreed it should be on the hereditary excise, they cannot alter it. But when it comes reported to the House, it may then.

So this was let fall.

Then the House went into a committee. The Attorney General took the Chair of the committee. So they proceeded in the bill for some time. After which he was ordered to report further progress and to leave the Chair, which he did upon the question.

Speaker resumed the Chair. So *he* reported accordingly, and the House resolved to go into a committee again tomorrow upon the bill.

All committees were adjourned.

So adjourned till 8 tomorrow morning.

Tuesday, 17 January

The bill for encouraging the art of pinmaking was read the first time.

Sir Christopher Musgrave spoke against it because it was to confirm several patents.

However, it was ordered a second reading.

Mr. Bathurst was ordered to carry up to the Lords Mr. Danby's private bill for their concurrence.

Mr. Fenwick was ordered to carry up to the Lords an engrossed bill for taking special bails in the country for their concurrence.

John Lemot Honeywood esq., being newly a member for the county of Essex (in the room of Col. Mildmay, deceased), came into the House and took the oaths and subscribed the test at the Table and after took his place in the House.

So the House, according to order, went into a committee upon the million bill and proceeded therein.

Mr. Goldwell tendered a clause to exempt the money put in hereon from paying taxes. It was received, read twice, and made part of the bill.

So the committee finished the bill and he was ordered to report the same. Speaker resumed the Chair and *Mr. Attorney* reported the committee had gone through the bill and made several amendments, which they had directed him to report. Ordered it to be reported tomorrow.

Mr. Gwyn presented Sir Eliab Harvey's petition against Mr. Honeywood's election. Received, read, and referred to the Committee of Elections.

Sir Miles Cook, etc., Masters in Chancery, brought the message from the Lords: That they had passed the bill of the aid of 4*s*. in the pound with an amendment to which they desire the concurrence of this House.

The amendment was after read, and it was a clause to appoint the Lords to be rated for their offices and personal estates by so many lords (named therein by them), that their persons should not be imprisoned for non-payment, and giving them power to appoint a collector for themselves.

Mr. Attorney General spoke much against it as a mere novelty, and by no means for this House to suffer the Lords to meddle with money bills. This is a clause they never had in any act where lands were charged. It is true they have the like clause in one poll act but never in any pound rate tax either in this reign or that of King Charles II, and therefore I hope you will very well consider of it before you pass it.

Mr. Arnold was against it for that the Lords by this means would pay very little to the tax.

Mr. Harley: I can not agree to this clause for I look upon it as unquestionable that the Lords have nothing to do with money bills but only to give their assent. Here in this clause the Lords have appointed commissioners; they have also appointed days of payment of their tax different from yours and have also appointed a collector to receive it, which is not to be suffered. I have known this House even refuse a conference with the Lords upon a money bill. This is the only thing the Commons have solely to themselves upon which they are valuable, and which I would by no means have them part with. *Mr. Hampden* and *Sir Richard Temple* were against this clause.

Sir Christopher Musgrave: This is a new clause not at all consisting with the privileges of this House whose sole right it is to dispose of money. But here the Lords have by this clause quite destroyed the same; they have hereby altered the whole frame of your bill—giving the Lords power to tax themselves for their personal estates and offices, too, and it appoints a collector to receive their taxes (even their land tax, too), which will occasion such confusion as not to be suffered. And if you allow of this clause the Lords at next step will give away your money.

Then the question was put (after the amendment had been but once read) to agree with the Lords in the same, and it passed in the negative *nemine contradicente.*

Mr. Montagu: I think the clause you have thrown out is of the last consequence, and therefore you have done very well to disagree therewith. If you had passed it there had been an end of this House.

Sir Edward Seymour: I think you have done yourselves right in rejecting this clause. I see by this and some other things I have lately took notice of the Lords are going to set up for themselves, and therefore I would not give the least countenance to this matter. Now as to what you have to do next, the Lords have sent you down an amendment to this bill by messengers of their own and you have disagreed thereto. Now you must communicate your disagreement thereto at a conference, with your reasons for the same.

So the House appointed a committee to prepare reasons to offer at a conference with the Lords, and the committee immediately withdrew into the Speaker's Chamber for that end. And being returned after a little time, *Sir Thomas Clarges* reported the reasons—which was one only, of the sole right of the Commons to grant supplies to the Crown and that the limitation of them as to matter, measure, manner, and time was in them, etc.—which were read and the House agreed thereto. And Sir Thomas Clarges was ordered to go up to the Lords and desire a conference with them upon the amendment sent down by their Lordships to a bill entitled etc.

The House divided upon a question for the report touching the privileges of members, etc. to come on upon Friday next—Yeas went out.

		Sir Samuel Barnardiston	
	Yeas		78
		Mr. Arnold	
Tellers for the			
		Sir William Strickland	
	Noes		28
		Sir William Forester	

Col. Pery moved for the bill for a court of conscience within Holborn and Finsbury divisions, and ordered accordingly.

Sir Thomas Clarges and others went up to the Lords to desire a conference. And staying very long, the *Speaker* took notice thereof and said it was not usual for the Lords to make your members to stay long. Yours are not like their messengers whose only business it is to come and go; yours have votes in all your debates. I am informed the Lords are upon a long debate of the Lord Banbury's case; therefore, I think you had best send for your messengers back.

Sir Joseph Williamson, Sir Christopher Musgrave, and *Col. Titus* were for sending for them back, and you may send them again tomorrow.

So the Clerk was ordered to go up to the messengers and acquaint them the House was going to adjourn and would have them come back.

And being returned, *Sir Thomas Clarges* acquainted the House that they had been up with the message and had attended in the Lords' Lobby two hours and had sent in their message, but the Lords thought not fit to admit us.

Speaker told them the message was not discharged but they might go up with it tomorrow.

So House adjourned till 8 tomorrow morning.

Wednesday, 18 January

Mr. Smith was ordered to carry up to the Lords Mr. Bayntun's private bill for their concurrence.

And Mr. Goldwell was ordered to carry up Sir William Mannock's private bill and to acquaint the Lords this House had agreed to the same without any amendments.

A petition of several whose husbands had been killed in the East India Company's war against the Mogul was tendered by *Sir Francis Blake*, but rejected because it was not signed. Which being afterwards signed, he tendered it again. And it was received, read, and referred to a particular committee.

Sir Thomas Clarges reported from the message to the Lords (after a stay of two hours) that he had been to desire a conference, etc., and the Lords did agree to the same and had appointed it at 4 of the clock this afternoon in the Painted Chamber.

Then the House went into a committee, according to order, upon the bill for an East India company. Sir John Guise took the Chair. And the committee made some progress, though not much because the members that were for the old Company were very troublesome and would not suffer the Chair hardly to put any question, but spun out the time by long and frequent speeches until the time for the conference being come. The Chairman was ordered to report further progress and to leave the Chair.

Speaker resumed the Chair. *Sir John Guise* reported further progress and desired leave to sit again. And it was moved for tomorrow.

House divided thereon—Yeas went out.

		Mr. Smith	
	Yeas		63
		[Mr. Arnold]¹	
Tellers for the			
		Col. Pery	
	Noes		66
		Mr. Harcourt	

¹ Blank in MS.; from *CJ*, x. 782.

Then proposed for Friday next. House divided again—Yeas went out.

Tellers for the
	Sir John Guise	
Yeas		81
	Goodwin Wharton	
	Col. Pery	
Noes		52
	Mr. Harcourt	

Then the House appointed the committee that drew up the reasons to be offered at the conference as managers for the same. So their names were read over and they went to the conference. And being returned, *Sir Thomas Clarges* reported that they had attended the conference and given their reasons for disagreeing with the Lords and had left the bill and the amendments with them.

So adjourned till 8 tomorrow morning.

Thursday, 19 January

Mr. Goldwell and others complained of the abuse offered to Col. Deane, a member, by one Holt (a solicitor). Ordered that he be taken into custody of the Serjeant.

But it was said he was a prisoner in execution in the King's Bench.

The *Speaker* said the Serjeant could not take him out of the Marshal's custody nor would the Marshal deliver him. But then you may send for the Marshal to give an account if he be in execution, and thereon you may take further order.

Sir Edward Seymour moved for the keeping of the 30th of January as a day of solemn humiliation for the murder of King Charles I, pursuant to the act of parliament, and that Mr. Binns (chaplain to the Duke of Somerset) might be desired to preach before the House that day. *Sir Orlando Gee* to the same.

And it was ordered accordingly, and Sir Orlando Gee to acquaint him therewith.

Then the House went into a committee upon the aulnage bill; Sir Robert Davers to the Chair of the committee. And the committee proceeded to fill up the blanks with the several sums imposed on divers sorts of woollen manufactures (which the private committee could not do) till they had finished the same. Which he was ordered to report.

Speaker resumed the Chair. *Sir Robert Davers* reported that the committee had gone through the matter to them referred, which he was ready to report. So ordered to be made on Saturday morning next.

The bill for encouragement of the woollen manufactures of this kingdom was read a second time.

Several spoke against it as *Mr. Richard Howe, Mr. John Howe, Sir Samuel Barnardiston, Sir John Somers, Sir John Darell*, etc. as that it was a project drove on by the factors of Blackwell Hall for their own interest.

Others spoke for it as *Sir John Guise, Sir Richard Temple, Col. Cooke*, etc.

However, upon the question for committing it it passed in the negative.

The bill for continuing part of the act made for the better preventing the exportation of wool, with the amendments thereto, was reported from the committee by *Sir Walter Yonge*. Which were read and agreed to.

Mr. Waller (of York) presented a clause on behalf the Hamburg Company, saving their right and giving them power only to export cloth to the rivers of Elbe, Weser, and Eider.

Several spoke against this clause as *Mr. Bowyer, Mr. Goldwell, Mr. Boscawen, Sir Edward Seymour*, etc. for that this would destroy the whole bill, and if it passed it would much hinder the exportation of your manufacture.

Others spoke for it as *Mr. Papillon, Sir Ralph Carr, Mr. Blofield, Col. Pery*, and *Sir John Guise*, etc.: Said that the Hamburg Company was very ancient and were beneficial to this nation; that they support and keep up the credit of your manufacture abroad; that the profit of the return of your woollen manufacture would (if this clause were passed) redound to this nation, but otherwise it goes all into the hands of foreigners who run away beyond sea with it, and the nation is never the better for it. And though it hath been said your exportations have been greater since there has been a free trade, there are other reasons for it as Ireland hath sent none abroad this three years nor France furnished Germany as it used before this war.

Sir Christopher Musgrave: The free exportation of your manufacture, generally speaking, seems most for your advantage. But then if the profit thereof be given to foreigners, you lose so much to the nation so that the nation will only gain the profit of the clothier, and that of the merchant (which is much greater) goes away to foreigners. If you will restrain the free exportation thereof to natives it will be something.

Sir Richard Temple to the same and thought though the exportation now is greater, yet in a little while the market would be overstocked and then it will not be so great.

Sir Robert Rich and *Col. Austen* were against the clause for that it seemed strange the more buyers there were it should ruin the trade.

Upon the question to read the clause a second time, House divided —Yeas went out.

		Henry Herbert	
	Yeas		65
		Mr. Papillon	
Tellers for the			
		Sir Walter Yonge	
	Noes		118
		Mr. Goldwell	

So the bill was ordered to be engrossed.

Some members were added to committees.

So adjourned till 8 tomorrow morning.

Friday, 20 January

Mr. England was ordered to carry up to the Lords Ralph Macclesfield's private bill and acquaint them this House hath agreed to the same with an amendment to which this House desires their Lordships' concurrence.

Serj. Blencowe presented the petition of the Goodwins.

Sir Orlando Gee reported he had, according to order, been to attend Mr. Binns and acquainted him with the request of the House to preach before them on the 30th of January. And he was pleased to return the House thanks for the great honour they had done him, and that he would prepare himself accordingly.

Simon Smith esq., a new member chosen for East Grinstead in Sussex (in the room of old Col. Sackville, deceased), came into the House and took the oaths at the Table and subscribed the declaration and after took his seat in the House.

Then the Counsel for the King were called in, who were Mr. Serj. Thompson, Sir William Williams, and Mr. Cowper. And being at the Bar on the left hand, [they] spoke against the bill touching royal mines. And after they withdrew.

Mr. Neale and *Sir Ralph Dutton* spoke against the bill.

Sir Thomas Clarges was for it and said it was not of right to hear the King's Counsel in this matter though the King may be concerned. For the Commons are his council, are trustees for him, and matters have been determined wherein the Crown has been concerned much more than here, as when the Court of Wards and Liveries was taken away. So in 21 Jac. I several prerogatives of the Crown were then cramped, and yet no entry in the Journal of hearing counsel. But in the case before you, it is of a prerogative that is no way useful to the Crown but very grievous to the people and prejudicial to the kingdom in general.

Mr. Attorney General thought it strange doctrine that the King should not be heard where he was concerned in interest—a privilege that is allowed to any private person to be heard by his counsel if desired.

Sir John Lowther (of Lowther) spoke against the bill.

However, the question for engrossing the bill with the amendments was put and carried clearly.

Col. Granville complained to the House of a most dangerous pamphlet that was lately published entitled *King William and Queen Mary Conquerors*, which undermines all your laws and liberties and renders you all slaves.[1] So he brought up one of the books to the Table.

Sir Thomas Clarges inveighed much against the same and moved to appoint a committee to examine into it—who was the author and printer of it—and that the most dangerous passages should be extracted out of it.

Mr. John Howe to the same and urged also the Bishop of Salisbury's [*A*] *Pastoral Letter* to be another such.[2]

Mr. John Smith to the same and he instanced in the Bishop of St. Asaph's book entitled [*A Discourse of*] *God's Ways of Dispos[ing] of Kingdoms*.[3] And as to the book before you, he was for sending for the Licenser of it and the printer whose names are apparent to you in the title of the book.

Sir Francis Winnington, Sir William Strickland, Mr. Goldwell, Col.

---

[1] [Charles Blount], London, 1693.   [2] Gilbert Burnet, London, 1689.
[3] William Lloyd, London, 1691.

Titus, Goodwin Wharton, Sir John Morton, Paul Foley, and *Mr. Palmes* were all for sending for the Licenser and printer.

At last the matter was stated: That complaint being made to the House of a printed pamphlet entitled *King William and Queen Mary Conquerors,* etc., wherein are several matters asserted of dangerous consequence to Their Majesties, to the liberty of the subject and peace of the kingdom, resolved that Edmund Bohun, the Licenser, be sent for in custody of the Serjeant at Arms. Ordered that Richard Baldwin (the person for whom it was printed) be summoned immediately to attend this House.

Mr. John Howe, Mr. Peregrine Bertie junior, and *Col. Granville* took notice also of the Bishop of Salisbury's [*A*] *Pastoral Letter* wherein were many dangerous positions, and desired a committee might be appointed to examine into those books.

But the *Speaker* and *Sir Thomas Clarges* said it was not regular unless the book be in the House and exception taken to the passages therein.

Sir John Hoskins and Sir Robert Legard, Masters in Chancery, came with the message to desire a present conference with this House on the subject-matter of the last conference. To which the House agreed, and appointed the same managers as managed the last conference. Their names were then read over and they went up to the conference.

And being returned, *Mr. Attorney General* reported from the same that the Lord Privy Seal managed it, who was the only person that spoke, and told them the Lords did apprehend they had a right to name commissioners as to their own personal estates, and thereof they had some precedents and one very lately. However, considering the present circumstances they did not think fit to insist upon their proviso.

A message from His Majesty by Sir Thomas Duppa, Usher of the Black Rod: Mr. Speaker; the King commands this honourable House to attend His Majesty in the House of Peers immediately. So Mr. Speaker went up with the House to attend His Majesty accordingly. And being returned, *Mr. Speaker* reported His Majesty had been pleased to give his assent to the several bills following: viz., the land tax bill, that to take away the custom in the province of York, to Anthony Eyre's private bill, to Mr. Hawley's, Lord Villiers', Sir John Wentworth's, Sir Anthony Brown's, Mr. Popham's, Sir George Parker's, Dr. Wake's, William Molineux's, Sir William Mannock's, and Barnham Powell's.

The bill for raising a million upon a fund for a certain number of years was read the third time. Some literal amendments were made at the Table.

Mr. *Dryden* tendered an engrossed clause to make void any grant of moneys arising by this act upon the death of any nominee. It was received and read thrice and made part of the bill.

Col. Pery tendered another for appropriating a part of the money coming in upon this act to pay the [? Navy].[1]

The clause was read twice and the blank was filled up with £500,000. But then it was doubted by some whether this act would raise so much, it being a new project; at least it was very uncertain. So this clause was laid aside.

Then the bill was passed and after the title, and Mr. Attorney General was ordered to carry it up to the Lords for their concurrence.

The House being informed that Richard Baldwin, the bookseller, attended according to order, the Speaker was directed what to ask him. So he was called in. And being asked, he answered to this effect: that he ordered the book to be printed, having the licence of Mr. Bohun for the same; that he could not tell the author of it but that he had the manuscript copy of it from Mr. Bentley, who gave it him to get printed after it was licensed; and I was to have a share with him.

So Baldwin was dismissed. And after, Mr. Bentley was ordered to be summoned to attend the House tomorrow morning.

Committees adjourned.

So adjourned till 8 tomorrow morning.

Saturday, 21 January

Sir Edward Phelips presented a petition of one George Searle and *Col. Pery* presented another of one William Searle, against the bill to enable Isaac Savery to take on him the name of Searle. [They] were received, read, and referred to the committee to whom that bill was committed.

Mr. *Colt* presented the petition of Mr. James Hamilton against the royal mine bill, so far as it relates to Ireland. [It] was received, read. Ordered he be heard at the Bar by his counsel on Wednesday next.

Mr. Balch had leave to go into the country for recovery of his health.[2]

The House being informed that Mr. Bentley was at the Bar, he was called in. Mr. *Speaker* examined him. And he gave an account that

---

[1] 'money' in MS.   [2] No such order is entered in the *Journal*.

he had the book brought him by the carrier of Stamford nor did he know the author of it. But I have had letters some years since from a gentleman whose hand was much like that of this book, which was Mr. Charles Blount.

Then Mr. Bohun, the Licenser, was called in and examined touching the book. And said he knew not the author, and thought there was no hurt in the book nor did he mean any hurt by licensing it, but only took it as a well-meaning book writ for this government to bring over even the disaffected by offering the title of conquest to their consideration.

Col. Granville, Mr. Arnold, and *Sir Walter Yonge* moved that the Licenser might be sent to the Gatehouse as a punishment for him.

Sir Thomas Clarges was for appointing a committee to examine into it and to extract out of it all the dangerous passages, and then you may pass your censure on it and I suppose will think fit to order it to be burnt by the hands of the common hangman.

Paul Foley was against sending the Licenser to the Gatehouse for then he would quickly get out upon a habeas corpus. I am for burning the book and to address to His Majesty to turn him out of his place of Licenser of the Press and that he may be turned out of the commission of the peace.

Speaker acquainted the House he never knew any precedent in his time of this House's ordering a book to be burnt, but you may appoint a committee to search precedents.

Sir Christopher Musgrave: You have a precedent in this matter in the case of one Withers. In the 12th of King Charles II, you ordered his book to be burnt; and as I remember, this House sent to the Lords for their concurrence and they told you you had meddled with matters of judicature which did not belong to you. However, you ordered the book to be burnt. *Sir Joseph Williamson* to the same purpose.

So the question was stated and resolved *nemine contradicente*: That a printed pamphlet entitled *King William and Queen Mary Conquerors*, etc., wherein are several matters asserted of dangerous consequence to Their Majesties, to the liberties of the subject and peace of the kingdom, be burnt by the hand of the common hangman. Ordered that the members of this House that are of His Majesty's Privy Council do humbly move His Majesty that Edmund Bohun, the Licenser of the Press, be removed from his employment.

Mr. Justice Dolben and Mr. Justice Rokesby came with the message from the Lords and the two bills.

Mr. John Howe then fell upon the pamphlet entitled *A Pastoral Letter* writ by the Bishop of Salisbury and inveighed much against it and the author with some severe reflections on him—that all knew he was no fool, and therefore left it to them [to][1] judge what he was to write such things as to set up a title by conquest to this crown.

Mr. Bromley (of Warwickshire) reflected very smartly on the book and instanced in several of the most dangerous passages in the book, and as it runs upon the same argument he desired it might suffer the same fate and be burnt by the hands of the common hangman. *Lord Norris* to the same.

Sir John Lowther (of Lowther) was against that for he did not know but it might tend to a breach between the two Houses.

Several spoke in behalf of the Bishop: how zealous he was for this government; what good service he had done for it and how instrumental he had been in this revolution; that the book was writ with no ill design but lays down the several grounds on which this government may be said to be laid for the satisfaction of all persons, and amongst the rest mentions that by conquest. Then besides, if it had been criminal to write this book there had been an act of oblivion since which pardoned the crime.

Others spoke against him and his book as zealously, and said though there had been an act of oblivion which pardoned the offence and the person yet it does not license the book or hinder you from condemning it, and that this could no way be construed a breach of privilege.

This held a long debate pro and con and several questions were stirred in it—some for burning the book, others for referring it to a committee, others to adjourn the debate, and others to adjourn the House. It was long debated which question ought to be put. Some said adjournment ought to be first put; others not, but the question that is first stated, and though it be not stated it was the duty of the Chair to state a question after so long a debate.

Paul Foley: I have searched your Journals and do find in the case of one Phillips for writing a pamphlet entitled *The Long Parliament Revived*, you did refer it to a committee to examine into and so I think you ought here. *Mr. Smith* and *Mr. Goodwin Wharton* to the same.

However, at last a question was stated: A complaint being made to the House of a printed book entitled *A Pastoral Letter* and a debate arising thereupon, resolved that the debate be adjourned.

So adjourned till 8 on Monday morning.

[1] 'he' in MS.

Monday, 23 January

The bill for repair of highways in the county of Hertford was read the second time. And upon the question of committing it, it was debated whether to a private committee or a Committee of the Whole House. Said it ought to be to the latter, being to raise money on the subject. But it was answered, though it was in some measure so yet it is but to revive an old law, and though it be to a private committee all that come may have voices as was done in the bill about the militia. But this was condemned as wholly irregular by the *Speaker, Mr. Hampden, Sir Christopher Musgrave,* and others, who all said such sort of bills ought always to be to Committees of the Whole House. So this was referred to a Committee of the Whole House and that upon Wednesday morning next.

So it was ordered that the book entitled *King William and Queen Mary Conquerors* should be burnt by the common hangman on Wednesday morning next at 10 of the clock in the Palace Yard, Westminster, and that the Serjeant at Arms attending this House do see the same performed and that the sheriffs of London and Middlesex do assist the Serjeant at Arms therein. (And thus it was done in the case of the Solemn League and Covenant.)

Then the adjourned debate of the *Pastoral Letter* was called for, as by the rules it ought when a debate is adjourned generally without any time it ought to be taken up when called for (so said *Sir Christopher Musgrave, Sir Edward Seymour,* and others). So the House proceeded upon that debate.

Some were for ordering it to be burnt as *Mr. John Howe, Mr. Bathurst, Mr. Bertie junior,* and *Mr. Mordaunt.*

Others were for referring it to a committee to inquire into it before you pass a censure upon it as *Mr. Hampden, Mr. Foley, Sir Thomas Clarges,* etc., and said it might be easy to find a dangerous passage in any book if you might pick it out where you would.

Mr. Bromley and *Sir Christopher Musgrave* were for doing the same justice upon this book, though in the case of a peer, as was done upon the other.

Mr. Montagu: For his part [he] saw no ill in the book nor did he believe there was any bad design.

Mr. Bromley took the book in his hand and desired any gentleman's opinion of some passages in it, particularly pp. 20, 21, 22, which he read—which if they did not set up an absolute title by conquest he understood nothing.

Mr. Heneage Finch spoke much in vindication of the Bishop and his book, and that he could not perceive it set up any such title in the Crown as conquest.

So after much debate, at last the question was stated: That the printed book entitled *A Pastoral Letter* be burnt by the hand of the common hangman. Then the previous question was proposed and after put. House divided thereon—Noes went forth.

		Mr. Montagu	
	Noes		136
		Mr. Palmes	
Tellers for the			
		Sir Edward Hussey	
	Yeas		160
		Mr. John Howe	

Then the main question was put, on which the House divided again —Yeas went forth.

		Mr. Colemore	
	Yeas		162
		Mr. Bromley (Warwick)	
Tellers for the			
		Mr. Hutchinson	
	Noes		155
		Mr. Goldwell	

So it was ordered to be burnt on Wednesday morning at time and place as the former, and the Serjeant at Arms was to see it performed and the sheriffs of London to assist the Serjeant therein.

Mr. Goodwin Wharton then moved against the Bishop of St. Asaph's book entitled [*A Discourse of*] *God's Ways of Disposing of Kingdoms*; that it went upon the same doctrine as the former and desired it might partake of the same fate, and he would have brought it up to the Table.

But it was thought the House had proceeded far enough already. So the bringing it up was opposed by several. And the question being put for bringing it up, it was clearly carried in the negative.

Committees were revived.

So House adjourned till 8 tomorrow morning.

Tuesday, 24 January

Mr. Boyle was ordered to carry up to the Lords the bill for exchange of livings between the King, Duke of Somerset, and Eton College, and desire their concurrence.

Mr. Christie was ordered to carry up to the Lords Mary Osbaston's private bill for their concurrence.

Sir Miles Cook and [Sir Adam Oatley],[1] Masters in Chancery, came with the message from the Lords.

Mr. Bentley, the bookseller, was ordered to have the manuscript of the book the House passed their censure on returned to him for that he is summoned to attend the House of Lords about the same matter.

Mr. Hampden reported the King's answer to the address of the House against Mr. Bohun: That he should be removed from being Licenser of the Press as was desired.

Then the House, according to order, went into a Committee of the Whole House upon the ways and means for raising the supply for Their Majesties; Mr. Attorney General to the Chair.

Dr. Barbone proposed to raise a million by way of a bank to make a note or paper go for money, which will be of as good value if you establish it by act of parliament. This is practised in Venice and Amsterdam; in Venice £100 in bank is worth £105 and at Amsterdam £102. This will answer the great want there is of money and will do your business as well.

But no one spoke to it.

Then the committee proceeded upon the heads for laying a duty upon several commodities, and began where left off. [Resolved]: hides, all sorts except buff and lasch, to pay £5 for every £100 value above all other duties, imported after 25 of December next; buff hides to pay 2s. for every hide more than before imported after 25 December; lasch hides to pay 1s. for every hide; hemp rough to pay £5 for every £100 value.

Indigo of foreign plantations to pay 4d. per pound more, and that of our own plantations 2d. per pound. But this was opposed and said it was to charge our own manufacture and it is what is used in dyeing, and by making that dearer, you will throw it into the hands of the Dutch. However, it was put and carried in the committee, upon a division, to charge it.

[Resolved]: Irish iron to pay £1. 13s. for every ton; latten shaven

---

[1] Blank in MS.; from *CJ*, x. 787.

black and round bottom to pay £10 for every hundred-pound weight; leather of all sorts to pay £5 for every £100 value; lime and lemon juice to pay £20 for every £100 value; litmarsh (which is a dross of indigo) to pay £5; madder to pay £5 for every £100 value (but it was opposed because used for dyeing); orchil (used in painting) to pay £5 for every hundred-pound weight; pintados (which are calico cubber-cloths) not from India or China to pay £10 for every £100 value; pitch other than of the growth of Scotland or our own plantations, to pay one moiety more than before; plate of silver, gilt or ungilt, to pay £5 on every £100 value; rice to pay £5 for every £100 value; rosin, except that from France and our own plantations, to pay £10 for every £100 value; salt, every wey to pay 5*s*. more than before; cottons, all manufactures thereof except dimities other than from China and East Indies to pay £5 for £100 value.

Silks raw, proposed to lay one moiety more than before. But opposed because this was the return of our cloth and it is manufactured here, which employs many poor. Then it is so dear already that you will ruin the new manufacture set up here. So it was let fall.

[Resolved]: silk thrown in the gum to pay £5 for every £100 value; silk ferret or floret to pay one moiety more than now; silk wrought of India to pay 2*s*. for every pound more than now by any law; skins of all sorts to pay £5 more for every £100 value; tar, except that from Scotland and the plantations, to pay one moiety more than before; ticks and ticking, except Scotch, to pay £5 for every £100 value; thread outnal to pay 4*s*. for every twelve-pound weight more; tapestry and Dorneck hangings, except those from France, to pay £10 for every £100 value; tapes and inkle to pay one moiety more than before; tiles, Dutch pan, to pay 8*s*. for every 1,000 more than before; wood dyeing, except drugs and logwood, to pay £5 for £100 value; wax, bees', to pay £5 for £100 value more; all other goods not rated by name in the book of rates nor in the additional act since in this reign paying duty and value shall pay £5 for every £100 value more than before; French wines to pay £8 per tun over all other duties; all other French commodities and merchandises (except wine, brandy, and vinegar) to pay £25 for every £100 value in lieu of all other duties; lutestrings and alamodes to pay the same duty as if from France.

Wool of all sorts, except cotton wool from our plantations, proposed to pay 5*s*. for every hundred-pound weight. But it was opposed because this would make our cloth dearer by laying a duty on Spanish wool, which is worked up with our own fine wool, without which we cannot make our fine cloths. So it was laid aside for all, they being free in the book of rates.

[Resolved]: pearls, diamonds, emeralds, jewels, and precious stones to pay 20*s.* more for every £100 value.

Currants and raisins; the duty on them before was now lessened, it being too high, they being now very dear of themselves, and when there was a less duty there were more spent, so no advantage by the high duty. Therefore, it was reduced to half what it was before. Coffee; the duty being very high was reduced to half what before, for the same reason. Chocolate for same reason reduced from 5*s.* per pound to 1*s.* per pound. Cacao nuts for same reason reduced from 1*s.* 6*d.* per pound to 6*d.* per pound. Tea for same reason reduced from 5*s.* per pound to 1*s.* per pound.

[Resolved]: double brandies or spirits above proof to pay 5*s.* per gallon above all other duties; latten brass or copper wire to pay for every hundred-pound weight 7*s.* 6*d.* above all other duties; walking canes to pay 25*s.* for every 1,000 more than before; rattans (that is, cane for chairs) to pay 5*s.* for every 1,000 more than before.

(These were all duties to be paid upon the importation of those several commodities.)

[Resolved]: lapis calaminaris (which is used for making brassware) to pay 20*s.* for every ton exported; coney wool (chiefly used in making hats) to pay 3*s.* for every pound that is exported more than before.

So having gone through the several heads, he was ordered to report these resolutions and to desire leave to sit again. Then he left the Chair.

Speaker resumed the Chair. *Mr. Attorney* reported the committee had made some progress in the matter referred and had come to several resolutions which they had commanded him to report (so report ordered to be made tomorrow) and that the committee desired leave to sit again (and ordered tomorrow after the report was over).

All committees adjourned.

So House adjourned till 8 tomorrow morning.

Wednesday, 25 January

The House, according to order, went into a committee upon the bill for reviving two laws for repair of the highways in Hertfordshire; Col. Titus to the Chair of the committee. So the Clerk read the bill over. The Chairman passed the preamble after he had read it over and the two acts it recites also. (The preamble was first passed as being the foundation of the bill.) So they passed the clauses and filled up the blanks until they had finished the bill, which he was ordered to report.

Speaker resumed the Chair. *Col. Titus* reported the committee had gone through the bill and made some amendments which they had commanded him to report, which *he* did presently. And the House agreed to the same and the bill with the amendments was ordered to be engrossed.

(Note: this was the first business this morning, and though in a case of raising money on the subject, yet reported the same day the committee went through it.)

Ordered no private bill be proceeded on till Saturday next.

Sir Miles Cook and Mr. Keck came with the message from the Lords for a conference.

The Serjeant had the leave of the House to go and see the Order of the House executed for burning the two books.

The bill for punishing mutineers and deserters was read the second time.

Mr. P. Foley desired that great care might be taken to prevent false musters.

Sir Thomas Clarges spoke against having of regiments, they being a new sort of officer who give great sums of money for their places and after cheat the poor soldier to make up their gains.

Others spoke to some other parts of it.

So it was committed to a Committee of the Whole House upon the debate of the House, upon Saturday next.

Another message from the Lords by Sir Miles Cook and Mr. Keck, Masters in Chancery.

The time for the conference being come, the managers' names were read over and they went up to the same. And being returned, *Mr. Boyle* reported from the conference that the Lord Mulgrave managed the same and communicated to them the resolution they had come to upon occasion of a libel entitled *King William and Queen Mary Conquerors*, which they had ordered to be burnt by the hand of the common hangman. So he delivered in the vote at the Table, where it was read.

And it was observed by some members that the Lords did not herein desire our concurrence nor had they left a blank to insert 'the Commons' as usual after 'Lords Spiritual and Temporal'. Then it was thought necessary by several members for this House to make such a declaratory vote (as *Col. Granville, Mr. Bertie, Sir Thomas Clarges,*

Goodwin Wharton, and *Sir Christopher Musgrave*) and that this House ought to communicate the same to the Lords at another conference.

So the vote of the Lords was passed here, the same in words, only with an amendment under which the line is drawn, which was put and resolved *nemine contradicente*: That the assertion of King William and Queen Mary's being King and Queen by conquest is highly injurious to Their Majesties' *rightful title to the Crown of this realm,* inconsistent with the principles on which this government is founded, and tending to the subversion of the rights of the people.

And it was ordered that this resolution be communicated to the Lords at a conference, and Mr. Boyle to go up and desire it. Which *he* did, and reported the Lords had agreed to a conference and had appointed it presently in the Painted Chamber.

Some managers' names were read over and they went up to the conference. And being returned, *Sir Edward Seymour* reported they had communicated the resolution of the House to the Lords at a conference.

Mr. Boscawen presented the petition of the orphans of London, relating to their business.

Mr. Attorney General reported the resolutions from the Committee of the Whole House in reference to the duty upon several merchandises, which he read and delivered in at the Table. Where the same were also read, and the further consideration thereof adjourned till tomorrow (when it will come on like an adjourned debate).

Committees revived.

So adjourned till 8 tomorrow morning.

Thursday, 26 January

Sir Miles Cook and [Mr. Meredith],[1] Masters in Chancery, brought the message from the Lords.

Then the House resumed the farther consideration of the report about the duties on merchandises and put them head by head. Several of them were agreed to, others laid aside, and in others some alterations made.

Brandy: the duty laid on all single spirits in the committee was 2*s.* 6*d.* a gallon. Proposed now to lessen it to 2*s.* for that it would bring in more money so than at 2*s.* 6*d.*, which would amount to a prohibition. But answered that if you lay so low a duty as 2*s.* there will such

[1] Blank in MS.; from *CJ*, x. 793.

a vast quantity come in that they will undersell your English spirits, so quite destroy that manufacture whereby the price of your corn (of which it is made) will fall very considerably. Then if the duty be so low, French brandies will come in, do what you can, so will furnish your enemies with money to carry on the war. But replied on the other side, the dearness of corn arises from the scarcity of it now and not from what is used for drawing of the spirits but also from the great exportations of it abroad. Then you proposed to raise money hereby, and if so you must give some encouragement that it may be brought in or you will deceive yourselves. And for keeping out French brandies, you may have the certificate of the consul in Spain or Portugal that they are the growth of those countries, and you need not fear for their own sakes they will not colour French brandies.

So at last the question was put for leaving out the 2*s*. 6*d*. House divided thereon—Yeas went out.[1]

		Mr. Hutchinson	
	Yeas		108
Tellers for the		Mr. England	
		Mr. Goldwell	
	Noes		90
		Mr. Freke junior	

Then on another question the word '2*s*.' was inserted in the room of it.

Flax was in the committee £7 for £100 value. Proposed to reduce it to but £5 per £100 for otherwise that high duty would be a prohibition of it which would destroy our linen manufacture, for unless they can have flax from abroad there is not enough grows here to employ them—it being here but just in its infancy.

So the question was put to agree with the committee. House divided—Noes went out.

		Sir John Darell	
	Yeas		47
Tellers for the		Mr. Clarke	
		Sir Robert Cotton	
	Noes		48
		Sir Thomas Vernon	

So carried against £7, and on another question it was reduced to £5.

[1] Cf. *CJ*, x. 793.

So the House proceeded as far as the letter 'S' with the report, and agreed therewith except as before, and the farther consideration of the said report was adjourned till tomorrow morning.

A message from His Majesty by Sir Thomas Duppa, Usher of the Black Rod, for this House to attend His Majesty immediately in the House of Peers.

And Mr. Speaker with the House went up. And being returned, the *Speaker* reported His Majesty had passed these bills: the bill for raising a million of money, the bill for taking special bails in the country, and Ralph Macclesfield's private bill.

So adjourned till 8 tomorrow morning.

Friday, 27 January

Mr. Goldwell presented Mr. Bohun's petition.

Engrossed bill touching royal mines read the third time.

And exception was taken by *Mr. Clarke, Sir Christopher Musgrave,* and *Mr. Harley,* etc. to the word 'Ireland' in the bill, for that the committee had made it to extend as well to Ireland as to England, which they ought not to have done without particular order.

So it was left out upon a question.

Mr. Granville tendered a rider to make void all grants, contracts, or promises made by Sir Carbery Price of any parts or shares in his lead mine to any persons whatsoever (he having parted with one-half of it to preserve the other against some great men who would have made a royal mine of it because of its greatness, being a prodigious rich lead mine said to be worth £20,000 per annum)—it being said to be perfect maintenance in them.

The clause was received, read once, and long debated. But upon the question it was denied a second reading.

So the bill was put and passed, and also the title, and Mr. Shakerley to carry it up to the Lords for their concurrence.

Then the House resumed the further consideration of the report from the committee [about the duties on merchandises] and proceeded on the same and read over the several heads that remained. [It] agreed to some and made amendments to others and finished the whole. (Coney wool exported to pay 3*s.* per pound was in the House disagreed to upon the division and stood not charged at all.)

So adjourned till 8 tomorrow morning.

Saturday, 28 January

Sir Francis Mollineux, newly chosen a member for the borough of Newark in Nottinghamshire (in the room of Mr. Sanderson, deceased), came into the House and took the oaths at the Table and subscribed the declaration and after took his seat in the House.

A motion was made for leave to bring in a bill to make the river Salwerp in Worcestershire navigable. House divided thereon—Yeas went out.

	Mr. Goldwell	
Yeas		65
	Mr. Hopkins	
Tellers for the		
	Sir Edward Hussey	
Noes		48
	Mr. Thomas Foley	

Then the House went upon the Order of the Day. And the Serjeant, with his mace, was sent into the several courts of justice in Westminster Hall to summon the gentlemen of the long robe that are members of this House to come and attend the service of the House. So the bill for frequent calling and meeting of parliaments was read the first time.[1]

Mr. Goldwell spoke against it that he thought it calculated for some particular ends rather than Their Majesties' service, and that how ripe soever this House might think themselves for a dissolution yet he hoped they never would suffer the Lords to be them that should cut them down. If this bill pass, the Lords will have great advantages over the Commons and be able to top upon you. And for the last clause in this bill, it strikes at your constitution. I look upon it as an ill-timed bill because it will help to divide us.

Sir Charles Sedley: I am against this bill for I am apt to suspect something when I see the Lords daily encroaching upon you; they are permanent themselves. For my part, I see no reason for this bill but that, I believe, the Lords do not like you; you are well versed in the methods of parliaments and the privileges of this House; the Lords are jealous of you and hope by a new choice to compass their ends. New elections will put the country in heats and animosities, and then our enemies may take advantage of them. Then this bill takes away the

---

[1] This bill originated in the Lords.

King's prerogative, and why he should not have the same prerogative as former kings I know not—he deserves it better since he came hither to save you. The Lords have already got the judicial power in their hands over all your estates, and therefore I am not for giving them more than they have, and therefore I am against this bill.

Mr. Thomas Pelham: I think this a very good bill notwithstanding what has been said, and that it is for the security of this government, a great service to our country, and to prevent pensionary and officered parliaments, and therefore I am for a second reading.

Sir Joseph Tredenham was against it for that it came from the Lords who are no ways concerned in it, for let a parliament be never so often dissolved they are still the same. Therefore, I think this a pernicious bill and to strike at your very constitution.

Mr. Hutchinson was for the bill.

Henry Herbert was for it for that he had rather have a standing army than a standing parliament.

Mr. Bowyer was for it because he thought long parliaments very pernicious, and it was one of the articles of your bill of rights to have frequent parliaments when this government was first settled. I have heard this present House said to be very well-officered, which I desire to prevent.

Mr. Bathurst was against this bill.

Sir John Morton was for it.

Sir Edward Seymour: Though frequent parliaments are very good for this nation, yet I do not take this bill to be contrived for those ends. This law has nothing in it but what is provided for already, but the main end it drives at is the dissolution of this present parliament, which I believe is a thing was never offered at before. It takes away the King's prerogative in a very material branch. Then I would not admit of the Lords to meddle with your constitution, who only represent themselves and have nothing to do with you. The Lords have some other end in it than is good. They strike at your foundation, the rights of the Crown, and what they may set up for next I cannot tell, so I am against this bill.

Mr. Harley thought the bill was for the honour of the King. He has engaged to do what is for the good, the peace, and safety of this nation, and that I think this bill is. Parliaments ought by the law to be held annually—so two statutes in Edward III's time. And for the bill in King Charles II's time for a triennial parliament, it was intended that a new parliament should be called every three years, though it is construed only that there must be session every three years—how that comes I know not. The bill before you I think a very good one, and therefore I hope it will never be said of this House they threw it out.

Sir John Lowther (of Lowther): I look on this bill [as] designed to throw dirt upon it who have been so steady and firm to this government. It casts a reflection upon those good laws you have passed for the service of this Crown. It is worth considering what may be the consequences hereof—perhaps public confusions and trouble. If there were anything in this bill that concerned the Lords to be chosen as you are, it would be something.

Sir Thomas Clarges: I think I am not worthy to sit here if I should be against this bill. For my part I think it is the best act that ever came into this House since Edward III's time. The worst of parliaments—even that which is so much run out against, that long pensionary parliament (as it was called) in King Charles II's time— took care to regulate their privileges and keep out officers, the two scandals of parliament. And if we must do nothing of that matter and have long parliaments, we shall become 500 grievances. And as to the objection that the bill came from the Lords I think it none at all for they may send you down any bill but one for money, nor do I think it any entrenching upon the prerogative, and therefore I am for it.

Paul Foley thought it a very good bill as it was, but he was also for adding something further to it to prevent corruption, if possible, in this House.

Sir Richard Temple was against the bill for that it was against the constitution of this government. It usurps on the very being and essence of this House, undermines the King's prerogative in a high degree, and is a precedent—the first in the kind but may not be the last, whenever the Lords do not like the face of this House.

Mr. Freke (the younger) was for the bill for the many good reasons that had been urged for it, with this further—that the Lords have as much to do to send you down this bill, though it does not immediately concern them, as this House had to send the Lords to purge their House of popish recusants and such as would not take the test which you did in King Charles II's time.

Sir Thomas Littleton was for reading the bill a second time in order to its commitment that it may be made a good bill.

Mr. Heneage Finch spoke very largely against the bill. The Lords have now sent you down a bill whereby they judge it fit that this parliament should be dissolved, which is what I hope this House will not endure. You have formerly denied the Lords to have any power to regulate elections; how much more then to regulate and direct the very being of this House? Then the bill now sent down is nothing but what is law already, only here is the addition of your dissolution. And though there have been those two laws in Edward III's time, observe but ever since that how the usage has been and you will find there have been two, three years, or more very often that parliaments have been intermitted. And I cannot but wonder any man should say this is not against the prerogative; there is nothing can be more, this being a prerogative vested in the Crown, exercised upon all occasions, and necessary for the very support of the government. I think this bill gives us but a melancholy prospect; it shows in the people a distrust of this King in particular and of kingly government in general. We had a bill to the like effect in King Charles I's time and we all know what followed soon after. Therefore, I leave it to you whether you think this bill for the service of this government.

Sir Francis Winnington: I think frequent parliaments to be the right of the people, and the fatal consequences of the long intermission of parliaments you have seen in some of the late reigns wherein popery and arbitrary power grew to so great a height. Then is the time for such illegal acts to be done, for such noxious weeds to spring up— it was even come to raising of money without parliaments. Whereas if they had been in being, they would have suppressed those mischiefs. And now you have a bill brought in to cut off these ill things at the root—will you throw it out at the first reading? What will people say without doors but that this House is well-officered within that they may perpetuate themselves?

Mr. Granville: I am for this bill and look upon it one of the best we ever had and the only good thing the Lords have done this sessions, and therefore I am for it as the only thing that will settle this government on a lasting foundation.

Lord Coningsby was against the bill for that it came from the Lords and yet it only concerns you, and was not like the test act for that concerned both Houses, and though it began here, as it turned out several lords so it did several members out of this House.

Sir Christopher Musgrave: I am for this bill and cannot imagine why gentlemen should be willing to be continued here unless it be for some private ends. It is said by some this bill is unseasonable whilst we are in such heats and in a time of war. That is in plain English to establish this parliament as long as this war lasts and how long that may be I know not—I see no end of it. I think this bill may be for the service of the nation. Therefore, I am for it. *Mr. Mordaunt* was for the bill.

So the question was put for reading it a second time. House divided —Yeas went out.

		Mr. Harley	
	Yeas		210
		Mr. Thomas Pelham	
Tellers for the			
		Mr. Goldwell	
	Noes		132
		Mr. Dyott	

So ordered to be read a second time on Thursday next.
So adjourned till Wednesday next at 8 in the morning.

Wednesday, 1 February

The committee to whom the bill of lotteries was referred had power to send for persons, papers, and records. And upon the instruction to them to prepare a clause to prevent wagering, it was said to be a pernicious practice now in use to lay wagers upon all sieges and other matters of state, which was very destructive to the men themselves and to the trade of the City and prejudicial to the government.

Col. Titus presented the Duchess of Richmond's petition against the aulnage bill. The House divided upon receiving it—Yeas went out.

		Sir Joseph Tredenham[1]	
	Yeas		52
		Mr. Gwyn	
Tellers for the			
		Mr. Clarke	
	Noes		75
		Mr. Thornhaugh	

The *Marquess of Winchester* presented a petition from Henry Killigrew esq. against the lottery bill, desiring either that the House would be pleased to except out of that bill his grant of £400 or, if all should be taken away, that he might have some recompense for it. It was received, read, but upon the question for a second reading denied.

---

[1] Mr. Tredenham in *CJ*, x. 800.

Sir Edward Seymour and *Mr. Hungerford* moved that since the House had been entertained on the 30th of January and, as they thought, with a very good discourse, they desired the gentleman might have the thanks of the House and be desired to print the same. And ordered accordingly, and that Mr. Boyle and Sir Orlando Gee do acquaint him therewith.

Sir Robert Cotton complained of a great abuse put upon the King and the several members of the House, there being several news-writers about town who have counterfeited the hands of divers members and franked letters to be sent by the post in their names, whereby also the King suffered in his revenue.

And mention being made of one Joshua Butler in particular that he had done it, he was ordered to be taken into custody. And also ordered that no letter from any member of this House shall go frank by the post but what shall be signed by the proper hand of such member.

Some gentlemen as *Mr. Hopkins* would have drove it further and had it that no one should send any letters frank unless the letter was sealed with his proper seal and all writ with his own hand.

Mr. Frankland (of the Post Office) said that anciently there was a book lay open in the Speaker's Chamber where every member set his name and put his seal to prevent any tricks.

But these proposals were looked on to go too far.

So House adjourned till 8 tomorrow morning.

Thursday, 2 February

Mr. Waller was ordered to carry up to the Lords the bill for naturalizing Henry Sheibel and others for their concurrence.

Sir Henry Gough moved for the bill for preservation of game against poachers.

Upon the report of the bill against hawkers and pedlars, *Sir John Darell* spoke against it for that it was to take away the living of several thousand people, which consequently would tend to dispeople the nation which he thought not our interest. Then this bill puts it into the inhabitants of corporations to exact upon the country gentlemen as they please. And it tends to spoil and ruin your servants whom you must [send] to a town if you want never so small a thing, whereas before they were brought home to your door. *Mr. Hampden* was also against the bill.

Mr. Neale against it for that it takes away a conveniency gentlemen have by buying things at home and will have this inconvenience—to hinder the expense of several commodities.

Mr. Boscawen thought it a very good bill because it would encourage the corporations who send you hither and make them better able to bear their share of taxes for support of this government.

Sir Edward Seymour was against it and not for passing it now which had been travelling in this House ever since he sat here. That he was sorry to see we were always taking care to sell cheap and buy dear, which would effectually be provided for in this bill by putting it in shopkeepers' hands to put their own prices upon you.

Sir Ralph Carr, Lord Castleton, and *Mr. Goldwell* were for it, being a sort of people that pay no taxes to the government nor contribute to any parish charges, that carry about libels against the government, and tend to corrupt your children and others by carrying letters and helping on other intrigues. Besides it is but a temporary law for five years, and if it be not found good the law will not be continued.

Mr. Blofield was for it. He computed these pedlars, who are generally Scotchmen, go away with a third part of the trade of the nation. *Sir John Morton* was also for the bill.

But *Sir Joseph Tredenham* was against it.

Mr. Freke (the younger) tendered a clause to give leave to any person who is an inhabitant or has a dwelling in any town or corporation to send goods abroad to sell by himself or his servant.

They who were for the bill were against this clause and said it would elude the whole bill.

It was received and read twice, and upon the question to be made part of the bill House divided—Yeas went out.

	Mr. Arnold	
Yeas		138
	Mr. Freke	
Tellers for the		
	Mr. Goldwell	
Noes		199
	Mr. Fenwick	

Mr. Harley was against the bill being engrossed and to enter it as the reason thereof—for that great sums of money had been collected for the carrying it on.

Sir Thomas Clarges against it also for that reason and also for that this would establish monopolies by act of parliament. *Mr. Arnold* against it. So *Mr. Jeffreys* and *Dr. Barbone* and *Col. Titus* also.

Sir Walter Yonge was for the bill.

So at last the question for engrossing the bill with the amendments was put. House divided—Yeas go forth.

	Sir Walter Yonge	
Yeas		230
	Sir Ralph Carr	
Tellers for the		
	Sir Samuel Barnardiston	
Noes		130
	Sir Robert Cotton	

Sir Christopher Musgrave complained of a breach of privilege in some persons who had pressed Thomas Gwyllim, servant to Mr. Mansell (a member of this House), being in his master's livery.

Mr. Mansell himself affirmed the same and that he was informed by a letter sent him by an unknown hand that he was carried to Harwich and would be sent thence for Flanders.

Sir Thomas Clarges, Lord Castleton, and others spoke to it that this trade of pressing for land service was become very common and a great oppression to the subject—who under colour of pressing seamen for sea service, which has been allowed of, they press others that never were at sea and then run them away to such places which they keep on purpose for this thing and there sell them to the officers of the army for land service at two and three guineas apiece (as they can make their markets) and send them to Flanders, and this is the way of raising soldiers.

Order was taken in the particular case complained of that the Mayor of Harwich and the Commissioners of Transports to search all vessels and ships in the harbour of Harwich, and take him thereout and send him to his master, and examine into the matter and return the House an account thereof.

Sir Thomas Clarges moved that the House would pass a declaratory vote that the pressing of landmen to the sea or land service was against the rights and liberties of the subject. *Mr. Bertie junior* to the same.

But it was let fall till the particular case was examined into.

The engrossed bill for frequent calling and meeting of parliaments was, according to order, read the second time.

Mr. Hopkins desired the bill might be read a third time since no gentleman took any exceptions to any part of it.

Sir Orlando Gee was against the bill but would rather address to His Majesty to dissolve this parliament when he thought it for his service.

Sir John Morton and *Lord Castleton* were for the bill.

Sir Edward Seymour: I am no more for setting up prerogative above the law than any man within this House, but I would support the prerogative that it may be able to preserve us and the law. This matter of calling and dissolving parliaments I look upon to be necessary thereunto. Such a prerogative I take this to be, not an ordinary one but an ancient right inherent in the Crown without which he cannot support himself or you. But then for the timing of this bill, this nation is now in a state of war and you have given great sums of money to carry on the same, a great part of which depends upon credit which you have engaged yourselves to make good, but whether a new parliament will think themselves obliged thereto is worthy your consideration.

Mr. Howe, Mr. Bertie (the younger) and *Mr. Brockman* were for the bill.

Sir John Lowther was against it because he knew no reason to be jealous more of this government than of the former, but he did not doubt as long as the nation had a good King and a good parliament they would be contented.

Sir Charles Sedley thought it a pernicious bill.

Mr. Dolben was against it for he was always jealous of the Lords in anything, finding them against doing what was for the interest and service of this House. You could never in any bill yet get them to regulate elections or do anything to make them more easy to you, and but lately they threw out the bill to keep out officers and courtiers out of your House.

Sir William Strickland was for it, as also *Mr. Goodwin Wharton* and *Mr. P. Foley*. And the last was, because if this House would not punish ill ministers it was fit the people should send those that would.

Mr. Neale for committing the bill.

Sir John Guise was against the bill.

Mr. Hungerford was for it though he thought the law already to be that we ought to have a new parliament every three years. But doubt having been made thereof, though it is none to me, I think this new bill necessary to confirm the former.

So at last the question for committing it was put and carried in the affirmative clearly. And it was committed to a Committee of the Whole House and [they] are to sit thereon on Monday next.

It being suggested the House would be very thin tomorrow because of the trial that was to be before the Lords in Parliament of the Lord Mohun for murder of Mr. Montfort, ordered that all the members of the House attend in their places tomorrow. (And it was said by some that this House might send their Serjeant tomorrow into that court to require the attendance of their members.)

So adjourned till 8 tomorrow morning.

Friday, 3 February

Sir John Guise presented the petition of Henry Atwood against the bill of Abel Atwood.

Mr. Waller presented the petition of Richard Holt.

Col. Deane (the member whom he had abused), being in the House, acquainted them he had received a letter from him begging his pardon, and said if the House were pleased to pardon him he was satisfied.

So he was ordered to be brought up tomorrow in order to his discharge.

The engrossed bill for repairing the highways of Hertfordshire was read the last time, passed with the title, and Col. Titus ordered to carry it up to the Lords for their concurrence.

Mr. Paul Foley made the complaint to the House that a privateer of ours having taken a French flyboat out of a fleet of 50 sail more that were going to Dunkirk and that he gave notice thereof to the commander of a squadron of 10 men-of-war that lay then in the Downs, but he replied he had no orders to stir.

Several others spoke to it as *Sir Christopher Musgrave*, etc., and it appeared to be a mismanagement in the Admiralty.

A committee was appointed to inquire into the same.

Mr. Goldwell presented the petition of the hackney coachmen, praying they may be established and a regulation made amongst them.

So the House, according to order, went into a committee upon the ways and means for raising the supply. Sir John Trenchard took the Chair of the committee, Mr. Attorney not being in the House.

Mr. Neale: I compute you have yet about £1,000,000 to raise. You have voted about £2,000,000 for the Navy, as much for the land forces, £750,000 the last quarterly poll falls short, there is about £600,000 for the charge of the civil list—in all about £5,300,000. Now towards this you have raised £2,000,000 upon the land tax, £1,000,000 on the fund bill, and about £1,000,000 the revenue will furnish you with, and about £300,000 or £400,000 on the new customs on several commodities. Now to raise the remaining £1,000,000, I shall propose it to be raised by a tax upon tradesmen, who have borne but little of the war. I would lay a tax upon all they bought the last year—about the two hundredth penny, which will be very easy to them and so much ready money to you. I compute it will raise about £1,000,000.

Paul Foley: You have by a clause in your land tax excused joint stocks with an intention to charge them higher in a particular act. I shall, therefore, begin with the East India Company and propose the laying on it a tax of 10 per cent—their stock, they say, is £740,000.

This was earnestly opposed by some that were members and friends to the old Company, and said it would ruin the Company.

It was debated some time but at last resolved: That towards the supply to be granted to Their Majesties, it is the opinion of this committee a charge of five per cent be laid on the joint stock of the East India Company.

Then the African Company came next on and it was proposed to lay five per cent on the same. But it was opposed by merchants and others that were friends to it that the original stock of that Company was but £110,000. It is true afterwards by a trick they thought fit to quadruple the same, yet a share there was worth but £45 and they were much in debt.

However, resolved that towards the raising the supply, etc., a charge of 20s. be laid on every share in the African Company.

Then it was proposed to lay £5 on every share in the Hudson's Bay Company. And said their original stock was but £11,000, but they have trebled it now. So put and resolved that towards the supply, etc., a charge of £5 be laid on every share in the Hudson's Bay Company.

Then it was proposed to lay a tax on these other companies—that of copper miners, of glass, of linen, and of paper.

On the first, proposed to lay £5 on every share. But answered, a share now is but £50, though in truth it be not worth above £15. But then it is a new manufacture of your own, which you are now setting up and endeavouring to gain from Sweden, and will be very beneficial if you can gain it.

So there was nothing further done in those Companies, being much upon the same reasons.

So the Chairman was ordered to report some progress and to desire leave to sit again. All which *he* did, and ordered to sit again tomorrow in a committee, etc.

All committees adjourned.

So adjourned till 8 tomorrow morning.

Saturday, 4 February

Col. Titus presented the petition of Mary Price, Ann Price, etc. against the bill of Roger Price.

The petition of Robert Fitzgerald esq. against Mr. Walcott's bill for making salt water fresh was presented by the *Lord Coningsby*.

Then the Order of the Day was called for to go upon the ways and means for raising a supply. House divided upon it whether to put it off till Monday next—Yeas went out.

	Mr. Pery	
Yeas		91
	Mr. Neale	
Tellers[1] for the		
	Sir William Forester	
Noes		103
	Sir Thomas Vernon	

So the House went into a committee presently. Serj. Trenchard took the Chair of the committee.

Mr. Neale proposed for raising part of the supply to lay a tax on all parchment, paper, etc. used for deeds, bonds, mortgages, recognisances, etc.

The House sat still for a considerable time.

Mr. Neale then proposed to lay an imposition upon all persons that marry, according to their several qualities, as also upon all who shall have legacies given them unless it be of what would have come to them by descent, as also upon all burials.

Sir Thomas Clarges: I cannot approve of that. I would rather lay a duty upon such as do not marry, for marriage of itself is already too much out of fashion. But if you will that everyone that is not married

---

[1] On this division, the *Journal* (which seems more likely to be correct) has Pery and Neale as tellers for the Noes, Forester and Vernon for the Yeas; *CJ*, x. 804.

shall pay according to their ages and respective qualities, with all my heart.

Sir Ralph Dutton proposed to lay an half year's tax on all new buildings.

But the committee were not minded to do anything.

So the Chairman left the Chair upon the question, and reported from the committee that they had directed him to move for leave to sit again.

Ordered no private bill to be proceeded on after 10 o'clock.

Ordered that the private bills now depending be dispatched before any new bill be proceeded in.

Then the House immediately resolved itself into a committee upon the bill for punishing mutineers and deserters, etc.; Sir Richard Temple to the Chair. Then the Clerk read the bill over and the Chairman read the preamble, and it was postponed. So the committee proceeded in the bill clause after clause, filling up the blanks, and passed them, and added some new clauses. So finished the bill, which he was ordered to report.

Speaker resumed the Chair. *Sir Richard Temple* reported the committee had gone through the bill and had made several amendments which they had directed him to report, and it was ordered to be made on Wednesday morning next.

So adjourned till Monday morning 8 of the clock.

Monday, 6 February

Sir John Brownlow presented the petition of the inhabitants of the town of Newark in the county of Nottingham and *Sir Edward Hussey* presented another from Sir Richard Earl, complaining of the undue election of Sir Francis Mollineux for that borough. They were received, read, and referred to the Committee of Elections and Privileges.

The bill for prohibiting the importation of foreign buttons was reported.

Sir John Darell, Mr. Clarke, and *Mr. Harley* spoke against it that it would only encourage a monopoly of the trade and make the workmen idle and exact more upon the people, and only put the importers of them to bring them in by stealth.

Sir Robert Cotton, Mr. Colt, and *Mr. Pery* spoke for the bill that it was to encourage our own manufacture—buttons being entirely so. The wood is our own and so is the horse hair, which is exported hence and returned you home manufactured, whereby you lose the employment of many of your poor and consequently they must lie upon your hands.

However, the bill with the amendments was ordered to be engrossed.

The engrossed bill for the aulnage was read the third time and passed, with the title, and Sir Robert Davers to carry it up to the Lords for their concurrence.

Then the House resolved itself immediately into a committee upon the ways and means for raising the supply for Their Majesties; Mr. Attorney to the Chair.

Mr. Neale proposed for raising the remainder of the taxes to lay a duty upon all paper and parchment used for public matters and all such to be made on this sealed paper and parchment.

Sir Thomas Clarges desired before the House went upon considering how to raise any more money, the House would compute what they had already given. The land tax I reckon at £2,200,000, the project bill at £1,000,000, the revenue £1,000,000, the continued impositions besides sugar £500,000, joint stocks £57,000. And for the duties I have offered to you I will present you with a computation thereof, and when that is done I do not think there will be above £200,000 to raise.

Sir Edward Seymour: As to your land tax, I believe it will not come to above £2,000,000 as the acts for this sort of tax have been executed. The project must be reckoned £1,000,000; I wish it may come to it. £400,000 clear out of the revenue after £600,000 is allowed for the civil list. The joint stock perhaps may come to £50,000. And as to the duties proposed by that worthy member I believe little will arise thence, these being the refuse of such commodities you thought not fit to charge in your last act. Then for the continued impositions, they are high already, and if you lay a further duty it will be very hard. Then you must give it for three years, and, though you do, the money must be taken up upon it on credit, and I think there is enough already on credit. So that on the whole I compute you have not raised above £3,400,000 and have yet about £1,300,000 to raise.

Sir Thomas Clarges: As to the commodities I have offered, they are better than those I offered in a former sessions which consisted but of 50 particulars, and here is now near 380 particulars. Those formerly I brought in I am sure have fully answered what I valued them at, which was but £80,000 per annum, and they do not make less than £140,000. These commodities I now propose but at £90,000 per annum and brandy alone at £80,000 per annum which is £170,000 per annum, which given but for three years will amount to £510,000, though I believe they will come to near £1,000,000 in that time.

You have voted £1,926,516. 10*s.* for the Navy, £2,090,563. 19*s.* 6*d.* for the Army, and the arrears on the quarterly poll bill £750,000; in all, about £4,700,000. Now you have given towards it £2,000,000 on the land tax, project bill £1,000,000, upon the revenue £400,000 clear besides bearing the civil list. Thus far is clearly estimated, and with what you have voted besides I reckon there will not be above £300,000 to raise.

Sir John Lowther (of Lowther): Your charge is right computed, but for the ways you propose the money to be raised they are so much upon credit that I am afraid your government may receive prejudice thereby. For if any ill news should come or unfortunate accident happen whereby people should not lend their money freely, a stop may be put to some of your services for the want of money.

Sir Thomas Clarges: I desire we may go on the remaining heads particularly and estimate them, and not in the general for then we shall have no end, and therefore I am for beginning with that of continued impositions.

Mr. Godolphin: The continued impositions is said to be £500,000. I am afraid they are much overvalued. They consist only of wine, vinegar, and tobacco. There is a debt already upon them which will not be paid till Christmas next two years, and whether you will anticipate that fund so long beforehand I submit to you; the interest of it will come to £200,000 if you borrow £500,000 thereon. There is now a debt of £380,000 on it which at Michaelmas next may be lessened to £300,000. But if you now add a further debt of £500,000 it makes £800,000, which with the interest will come to £1,000,000, which will not be paid under five years—the duty coming to but £200,000 per annum at a medium for several years computed together.

Sir Christopher Musgrave: I am afraid we must do as men in debt do and be contented to pay interest for what we raise since we can't raise it without, unless the gentlemen will give us leave to raise £1,000,000 on the forfeited Irish estates which we were once promised should be applied towards carrying on the war. But I hear they have got a new practice in that kingdom of granting custodians of those estates, but I hope there will a time come when we shall take those matters into consideration.

But after a long debate pro and con it was resolved: That towards the supply to be granted, etc., the sum of £500,000 be raised upon the duties of wine, vinegar, and tobacco mentioned in an act made in the second year of Their Majesties' reign entitled etc., and that in order thereto the said duties be continued for two years longer than the same are already granted.

So the Chairman was ordered to report further progress and to desire leave to sit again. All which *he* did, and the House resolved to go into a committee again upon Wednesday next.

So adjourned till 8 tomorrow morning.

Tuesday, 7 February

Mr. Harley presented the petition of Joshua Butler, the news-writer. Received and read.

Sir Miles Cook and [Mr. Meredith],[1] Masters in Chancery, came with the message from the Lords.

Sir Thomas Clarges complained that a servant of mine (a member of the House) going about my business was lately pressed and kept in custody in breach of the privileges of the House. Which *I* after justified and gave an account thereof at large to the House. So a committee was appointed to examine the said complaint as also into the abuses daily committed by pressmasters.

Lord Falkland presented the petition of Henry Acourt and others against the bill of lotteries. It was received, but on the question denied to be read.

Then the House, according to order, went into a committee upon the triennial bill or bill for frequent calling and meeting of parliaments; Col. Granville to the Chair. So the bill was read over and the preamble postponed. Then the first clause was read.

Sir John Lowther desired that the words for a parliament to be holden every year might be explained, for if by 'holding' it should be intended to make a sessions of parliament every year—that is, they must do some business or the sessions must continue till they do— consider what advantage the Lords have over you. Suppose they should pass a bill to confirm their judicature or that all great officers

---

[1] Blank in MS.; from *CJ*, x. 806.

should be chosen by them, etc. Though you in this House may be against it and the King too, yet you shall pass that or they will do nothing else, and they will continue sitting till you do. I take this to be a great alteration of the established government, and therefore I am against it.

Sir Robert Cotton (of the Post Office) was against it for that it would establish the Lords never to be tried but in parliament.

Mr. G. Wharton was for it because it did but confirm what was the law already.

Sir Christopher Musgrave was against this clause for that he thought it a great hardship upon country gentlemen to come up hither every year; if there was an annual sitting of parliament it would be burdensome and oppressive to them. He thought once in two years was enough; and I hope there will a time come when [there][1] will not be such need of an annual sessions as there is now.

Mr. Harley: Parliaments by the law of the land ought to be annually held: so a letter of King Edward I to Pope Gregory; and there are acts of parliament to that effect as 4 E. III c. [14], 36 E. III c. [10], 5 E. II [c. 29] at London, 50 E. III [blank], R. II [blank][2]—whereby it appears this was the ancient law of the land. And this stands now as law, and what is this bill now before you but enforcing those good laws?

Lord Coningsby was for leaving this clause out, for that it is unnecessary being the law already. But if it were so, how comes it that the law has been always otherwise construed both in good and bad kings' reigns?

Lord Castleton was for the clause; so Mr. John Howe. Mr. Foley and Mr. Hopkins thought it a very good one.

Charles Montagu: I do agree parliaments anciently were held annually—nay, at fixed, stated times. But parliaments then determined other sort of affairs than now; they heard then civil causes between party and party, but now your business is properly redress of grievances and to enact new laws; then it was necessary for doing right and justice to sit annually but not now.

Sir Richard Temple was against it, for that it was necessary heretofore because acts of parliament then did reserve a power to determine such and such matters in parliament, separate from the judges, and therefore they ought to sit frequently; there is not the same reason now. Mr. Neale and Sir Charles Sedley were against the clause.

[1] 'where' in MS.
[2] These two citations cannot be located in *Statutes of the Realm.*

Mr. Goodwin Wharton was for it.

Mr. Attorney General: As to the precedents cited of having annual parliaments, it was at a time when parliaments were in nature of courts of justice, but since courts of justice are settled parliaments are much altered to what they were then. I am afraid now the annual meeting of parliaments, unless there be occasion for it, will be thought a great grievance to the people. I am well assured this bill will tend to the exalting of the power of the House of Lords which they have now arbitrarily taken to themselves, for they declare openly they are not tied to any rules, so that I am afraid annual sessions will make the people and the Crown, too, weary of parliaments.

Mr. Robartes was against the clause for he thought an annual sessions would be an annual tax upon the people.

Mr. Mordaunt was for the clause, and Sir Edward Hussey, too.

Mr. Heneage Finch was against it, for though there were ancient laws to have annual parliaments yet the practice has been always otherwise since those laws made, and practice is the best expositor of old, obsolete laws and lets us know the true meaning of them. Nay, the very act of 16 Car. II c. [1] though it recites those old laws of Edward III yet it provides but for a triennial sessions, and the act 27 Eliz. c. 8 recites that parliaments have not been so frequently held as they ought but does not say annually. Parliaments ought to be frequently held, but whether to be annually held would not in these times be a punishment is worthy consideration. If this bill pass, the Lords will not want business to determine of all your rights and properties by their writs of error and appeals there, and when once it is passed you will find they will not part with it again.

Mr. Bowyer, Mr. Palmes, Mr. Smith, and Sir Robert Howard were for it.

Dr. Barbone against it, and Sir John Guise.

So upon the question for this clause to stand part of the bill, the committee divided—Yeas on the right hand and the Noes on the left.

	Yeas	Mr. Goodwin Wharton	179
Tellers for the			
	Noes	Sir Matthew Andrews	168

Mr. Hampden acquainted the committee that there was just now a matter happened which was fit to acquaint the House with, and therefore he desired the Chairman might leave the Chair and report some progress.

Which he did. Speaker to it. And reported accordingly.

Mr. Hampden acquainted the House that there was a matter happened at the committee which was fit to acquaint the House with—of a quarrel that had happened between the Lord Brandon and Sir Edward Seymour, occasioned by some words between them as they crossed the House on a division in the committee touching the bill, on which they were going out. Therefore, I think you can do no less than lay your commands on them both to prosecute this quarrel no further.

Mr. Thomas Howard acquainted the House therewith to the same effect.

So they were both ordered to prosecute this matter no further. And *both* stood up in their places, and said they would prosecute it no further but obey the commands of the House.

Then the *Speaker* took notice of the great reflections some gentlemen had in their speeches made upon others, which was wholly irregular and might be of very ill consequence.

So the House went again into a committee and proceeded on the bill till they had gone through it and made some amendments.

Mr. Paul Foley presented a clause that no one that was a member of parliament should have a place.

But this was laid aside by the friends to the bill because thought it would hinder its passing.

Sir John Lowther (of Lowther) tendered a clause to the effect that nothing in the act should extend to take away the King's prerogative to dissolve any parliament sooner than three years.

This occasioned a long debate. Said by the friends to the bill that this would destroy the bill itself. And by those on the other side, that if this clause was not admitted the King's prerogative would be so cramped that he could not dissolve a parliament within the three years let them do what they please, which may be of dangerous consequence and would take away the King's negative voice, because parliaments must be held every year and it cannot be held without there be a sessions and something must be done to make it a sessions (so [Sir Richard] Hutton, *Rep[orts]*, f. 61).

So after a long debate, this clause was put to be made part of the bill. Committee divided.

	Yeas Mr. Smith	143
Tellers for the		
	Noes Charles Boyle	150

Mr. Shakerley tendered another clause—to take away the privilege of parliament from the Lords and Commons but only when actually sitting and then only but for their persons.

But the friends to the bill rejected it for that it would clog the bill and hinder its passing.

Then the preamble of the bill was passed, and the Chairman was ordered to report it. So Speaker resumed the Chair. *Col. Granville* reported the committee had gone through the bill and had made some amendments which they had commanded him to report.

Then a debate arose. Some would have reported it immediately. But opposed because not usual to report such bills the same day the committee finished them unless the House be unanimously for it. So ordered it to be reported on Thursday.

All committees were adjourned.

So adjourned till 8 tomorrow morning.

Wednesday, 8 February

The bill for the increase and preservation of timber in the New Forest in Hampshire was read the second time.

Several spoke against it as the *Marquess of Winchester*, *Mr. Hoby*, *Mr. Smith*, *Mr. Burrard*, and other friends to the Duke of Bolton for that it would prejudice and waste the timber instead of preserving it, that it invades the right of commoners, and was designed only for private advantage.

Others spoke for it as *Sir Charles Sedley*, *Sir Joseph Tredenham*, *Col. Cooke*, etc. as being the only way to preserve the timber for building of ships, which was now so much wasted throughout the kingdom; that the commoner's right was preserved by the method taken in the bill; that it would prevent wasting and spoiling the King's timber.

Sir Edward Seymour: The only intention of this bill is to preserve 10,000 acres of this forest at a time by enclosing them for such a time that the trees may grow up big enough that the cattle hurt them not. Nor is there such prejudice to the commoners, the whole forest being very large and contains 90,000 acres out of which to enclose 10,000 acres is but a small number. And this is not without a precedent when in the Forest of Dean, which is but 24,000 acres, and yet you enclosed the same number as here, and now you enjoy the benefit thereof in having any timber fit for your service and will daily find the advantage thereof. And as to any private advantage which is suggested by some persons, there is no fear thereof; the law provides expressly against it and to make all such grants by the Crown to be void.

Sir *John Lowther* and *Mr. Hampden* were for it. So was *Sir William Wogan* and *Mr. Boscawen.*

But *Mr. Holt, Mr. Brydges,* and *Mr. Whithed* were against committing it.

So the question being put for committing it, House divided— Yeas went out.

		Mr. Bickerstaffe	
	Yeas		111
		Mr. Goldwell	
Tellers for the			
		Sir William Strickland	
	Noes		126
		Mr. Holt	

Then the House went into a Committee of the Whole House on the ways and means for raising the supply for Their Majesties; Attorney General to the Chair.

Sir Thomas Clarges: You have now about £890,000. 9*s.* 6*d.* to raise by my computation. The additional duties I offered I compute at £90,000 and the duty on brandies alone at £80,000—in all £170,000 per annum, which in three years' time comes to £510,000. But since you have encouraged privateers I am confident it will come to double. There are 80 merchandises charged particularly by name, besides 300 more which pay by the general clause of paying to value, which I doubt not will make up the sum I offer them at with good advantage.

Mr. Montagu: We are well informed that the duties without that of brandy will not come to above £50,000 per annum.

Sir Thomas Clarges: What that gentleman says perhaps may be true enough if the benefit of prizes be not considered.

Sir Edward Seymour: As to the Prize Office, it is so far from being a benefit to the Crown that the profit of it does not answer the charge thereof. Then for brandy, how it is possible for it to raise £80,000 per annum I do not understand when now though it is 4*s.* a gallon the duty there is nothing comes in upon it. Besides, this whole particular is carrying on the war upon credit, which if that fails your work must stand still.

Sir Thomas Clarges: The reason of laying so high a duty as 4*s.* in the gallon on brandy was that none at all might be brought in but that it should be a prohibition. As to the prizes, it is no wonder there was no benefit to be made of them because they were all to be staved or burned. But now they are to be sold you will find a great difference; in 1652 the prizes made about £700,000, and I doubt not after a little time money will come in weekly.

Charles Godolphin proposed to raise a considerable sum of money by advancing the stock of the East India Company to £500,000 and putting it up to dispose of it by inch of candle to him that will give most for it. And if it come to but £150 a share, if you apply to the public what is above £100 a share it will raise £250,000 for the public. And for these new duties, it is the opinion of Mr. Clarke and all the Customhouse officers that £50,000 is the utmost they will raise.

Paul Foley: I like the tax proposed the better because it is upon credit, for upon ready money there is going on the land tax of 4s. in the pound, the million act, and the revenue, on all which money comes in daily.

Lord Ranelagh: This of the duties ought to be £510,000 neat money, and therefore you must give it for longer than three years to make amends for the interest and the charge of collecting it.

Sir Edward Seymour and Mr. Montagu were both afraid that if the parliament depended on these duties for £510,000 and the continued impositions for £500,000, as they are proposed, they will find their service very much neglected and when it will be most wanted towards the end of the year to pay off the fleet they will be most disappointed in it. However, if the House are resolved in it, I desire it may be for four years.

Resolved: That, etc., that towards the supply to be granted to Their Majesties the sum of £510,000 be raised by granting to Their Majesties the additional duties upon brandy and other merchandises agreed unto by the House for the term of four years.

So he was ordered to report further progress and to desire leave to sit again. Which *he* did, and the House resolved to go into a committee again on Friday next.

Sir Thomas Middleton communicated to the House a letter he had from the Mayor of Harwich, giving an account of the great abuses committed in pressing men, the oppressions and exactions they used, and their buying and selling them after for Flanders.

Sir Samuel Barnardiston, Mr. Hoby, and others gave an account of divers great abuses committed by pressmasters.

Sir Edward Seymour acquainted the House he was this afternoon to attend His Majesty, and he would take an opportunity to lay this matter before him, and he did not doubt His Majesty would take effectual care to remedy the same.

Lord Ranelagh said the practice was carried on by the pressmasters under colour of pressing men for the Navy, and when they have got them they carry them to the Tower and then the land officers come and buy them and give a guinea or two apiece, though the King allows them £3 for every soldier that goes into Flanders and 40*s*. for every one that stays here—so the subject is abused and the King cheated.

So adjourned till 8 tomorrow morning.

Thursday, 9 February

Sir Miles Cook and Sir Adam Oatley, Masters in Chancery, came with the message from the House of Lords.

Col. Granville reported the engrossed bill for the frequent calling and meeting of parliaments with amendments, several of which were agreed to.

To that about the dissolution of this present parliament, *Sir Richard Temple* spoke against it as a new and unheard-of thing for a parliament to pass an act to dissolve themselves, which seems to me to be a great reflection upon you.

However it was put and agreed to.

Col. Granville moved that since this was a bill so much desired by some gentlemen that it might now be read the third time.

Lord Castleton seconded it, as thinking it for the King's service and the nation's good.

Sir John Lowther (of Lowther): I am for this government, and therefore must be against this bill which I think gives the greatest blow imaginable to it. This bill takes away the King's power to prorogue and dissolve parliaments. Then the word 'holden' in this act is of a doubtful construction; at least in several books of law it is said that a parliament is not held unless there be a sessions, and a sessions is not unless some act pass the royal assent. So that if this House or the Lords have a mind to attempt anything against the Crown they will not do anything else till the King pass what they shall tender him, so they shall sit on till they please to dismiss themselves, wherefore I am against this bill.

Sir Anthony Keck: As to the holding of a parliament it is not necessary there be a sessions, and though it were it is not necessary to have an act pass to make a sessions—a judgement by the Lords in a writ of error makes a sessions, and so is my Lord Coke. As to the Lords growing restive, I hope there is no fear of that. Then I do not think this does in the least invade the King's prerogative, for I am of opinion nothing tends more to it than frequent parliaments and to settle this government on a lasting foundation, which was also the opinion of King James I in several of his speeches. And you will find all your grievances and the mismanagements in government have been committed in the intervals of parliaments, so that I am entirely for this bill.

Sir Edward Seymour: I must always be against this bill for that it abridges, if not takes away, the King's prerogative of proroguing and dissolving of parliaments. There is something in this bill which carries a plausible face with it—the confirmation and revival of good old laws for a session to be held every year and a new parliament every third year. But the design that is carried on under this fair face is the dissolution of this parliament, which how convenient it is at this time I leave to you. The learned gentleman that spoke last grants there is no sessions unless an act pass or there be a judgement in the House of Lords, both which are equally in the power of the Lords to do or not to do as they will, and if so you are liable to the mischiefs suggested by the gentleman that spoke last but one. And it is strange it should be said this does not hurt the King's prerogative; I would fain see anything can do it in a higher point, which if the King please to part with he may by giving the royal assent to this bill (as he may to one to dethrone him if he please) and then because he assents to it you will say it is not against his prerogative. Wherefore I am against reading this bill a third time.

Mr. Harley: I think you have a useful bill before you, and therefore I am for giving it the last reading now. It is urged by many gentlemen that it is against the King's prerogative. I think not, for if saying so will do it may be as well said against the best of laws to take away the worst of grievances, and that in this case I take a standing parliament to be and therefore fit for you to remedy. Frequent parliaments are for the safety and security of any government; they are sure to be the true representatives of the people and will maintain the honour of this House.

Sir Charles Sedley: You have an extraordinary bill before you which comes to you in an extraordinary way—from the Lords, to dissolve your very being. I have a jealousy of the Lords since I see they are daily encroaching upon this House: they would name commissioners to take an account of that money you give; they would appoint persons to tax themselves because they will pay nothing. So that for my part I believe they do not like you and therefore would change you. I hear one gentleman say he would not cast reflections on the Lords; no more would I upon ourselves or upon the King whom I think you do herein too much suspect. Then I think this parliament cannot be called a long parliament, being yet not three years standing. Then you are engaged in a war and that with a powerful enemy, and if this be a convenient time to put things in a confusion I leave to you. For my part I am not concerned but this I will say: I converse sometimes with papists and Jacobites, the enemies of your government, and nothing pleases them better than this bill. For which reasons I am against it.

Lord Coningsby was also against it for that he thought it tended to the alteration of the ancient government, and the next step to that is anarchy and confusion. There was a bill of this nature in King Charles I's time, and when that was passed the next step was to sit as long as they pleased. I will not say this will be, but what has been may be, and therefore I am against this bill.

Col. Titus was for the bill.

Mr. Heneage Finch was against reading this bill a third time for notwithstanding all has been said it is highly injurious to the prerogative. It is true if the King will pass a law to take away his prerogative he may, but we ought to consider how fit it is to offer him such a bill. This bill, I think, takes away that inherent power the King hath to preserve his government and his people, and why we should take that away under which the people have lived so happily thus long I see no reason. I am for frequent parliaments as much as any and against long parliaments, but a parliament every year may perhaps be as grievous to the people, which when once established you cannot remedy without the consent of the Lords. Because long parliaments may be prejudicial, will you have none to last longer than three years let what will be the occasion? I am not ignorant the parliament that passed that law in 16 Car. I c. [1], whereby they showed a distrust of the Crown, never left till they would trust none but themselves and had thrust the King out, and therefore I am suspicious of this bill and would not read it again.

Sir Francis Winnington: I think this bill does not entrench upon the King's lawful prerogative but only to restrain the abuse of it. We are by the law to have frequent parliaments, which is all this law provides for. They are what will secure him and for his service, who has his title from the people, and they I doubt not will support him.

Lord Falkland: I am against this bill because I think the mischiefs it will do are much greater than the good that will come by it. You are very truly told it will entrench upon the King's prerogative; I think nothing more. For my part I must declare I am afraid something more is intended in this bill than we are aware of, because of the clause which was refused at the committee reserving a power in the Crown to dissolve a parliament within the three years if he saw it convenient and necessary. Then I observe your enemies without doors and such as refuse the oaths to this government are best pleased with this bill—nay, I am told some of them are making interests to be chosen in your new parliament. For which reasons I am against this bill.

Sir William Strickland was for it because it was the only way to secure frequent parliaments and to prevent long ones and to remedy the mischiefs arising from evil ministers. *Sir Edward Hussey* was for the bill, and *Sir John Brownlow*.

Sir George Hutchins was against it for that it takes away the inherent right in the King to preserve himself and his people. That the dissolution of parliaments by act of parliament was of the last consequence especially at this time when the nation is involved in such a war as it is, even for the very being thereof.

Sir Richard Temple: The question is not now for frequent parliaments nor the long interval of parliaments—that being provided for by former laws as much as is by this—but only whether we shall have an annual sessions and whether this shall be dissolved, which I think very mischievous at this time whatever it may be in a time of peace.

Paul Foley: I have looked over all the books cited relating to the holding of a parliament and cannot find any that it must be a sessions. It is true they say to make a sessions there must an act pass, but do not say that it is not holding a parliament unless an act pass. If you will preserve this government, you must pass this act.

Sir Christopher Musgrave: I cannot be of an opinion that this bill restrains the King's prerogative for I observe those laws about parliaments passed in the best of times when such kings governed who stood very highly on their prerogative. It is agreed by all that long parliaments are grievous; if so, who more proper to represent such grievances to the Crown than the two Houses? This bill is in nature of a petition to His Majesty for those ends, which if he please to pass into a law I doubt not will be for the good of the whole nation. *Mr. Mordaunt* was for the bill.

Question put to read it a third time. House divided upon it—Yeas went out.

		Col. Granville	
	Yeas		200
		Mr. Goodwin Wharton	
Tellers for the			
		Lord Falkland	
	Noes		161
		Lord Coningsby	

So the bill was read the third time.

Mr. Neale tendered a rider to explain what meant by the words 'holding a parliament'. But it was refused.

So the bill was put and passed, and Col. Granville was ordered to carry it up to the Lords for their concurrence to the said amendments.

All committees adjourned.

So adjourned till 8 tomorrow morning.

Friday, 10 February

An engrossed bill for better discovery of judgements in the King's Bench, Common Pleas, and Exchequer was read the third time and passed with the title, and Mr. Waller was ordered to carry it to the Lords for their concurrence.

Sir Joseph Tredenham was also ordered to carry to the Lords the engrossed bill for preventing the delay of proceedings at the quarter sessions for their concurrence.

Leave was asked for Mr. Pigott to go into the country. House divided upon it—Yeas went out.

		Sir Edward Hussey	
	Yeas		60
		Sir John Darell	
Tellers for the			
		Sir Thomas Barnardiston[1]	
	Noes		35
		Mr. Dyott	

[1] Sir Samuel Barnardiston in *CJ*, x. 809.

Divers members, on motions, were added to several committees.

Mr. Justice Gregory and Mr. Baron Turton brought the message from the Lords of their agreement to the amendments made by this House to the bill for the frequent calling and meeting of parliaments.

The bill for reviving and continuing of former laws was read the second time and committed.

Mr. Clarke, *Mr. Balch*, and others desired that the committee might have leave to add the port of Bridgwater to that about the bill for exportation of wool to make it lawful to import wool from [blank] Ireland thither.

But upon the question it was denied.

It was an instruction to the committee to consider of the penalty for exportation of wool; it was now death, and whether not better to lessen it by making it punishable by fine, forfeiture, imprisonment, etc.

Then the House, according to order, went into a committee to consider of ways and means for raising the supplies. Serj. Trenchard to the Chair.

Mr. John Howe proposed the raising a tax upon the hackney coaches either by an annual rent or else they will raise you a considerable sum—I am informed £100,000.

Sir Thomas Clarges thought this would raise a good sum of money but would rather preserve this to be settled for ever on an hospital to be erected for maintenance of poor, disabled seamen, their widows and children, which will be a noble foundation for this kingdom which is an island and should give some encouragement to seamen on whom they so much depend.

Sir Robert Davers proposed a single poll.

Mr. Fagg proposed that half the charge of the civil list might be struck off, that officers might have but half salaries, which was but reasonable that gentlemen who were forced to live on half their estates that officers also should live on half their salaries, and this would raise the sum that was wanting. Mr. Howe to the same.

Mr. Arnold and others were for a review of the poll bill.

Mr. Paul Foley proposed to lay a tax on all shipping according to their tonnage—1*s.* 6*d.* a ton on all shipping bound to Holland, etc.; 3*s.* a ton on those to Spain and Barbados; 4*s.* to Italy; 5*s.* to Turkey; 6*s.* to India; and 10*s.* a ton on all foreign bottoms. This, I am told, will raise £100,000.

Mr. Bickerstaffe was against it because there was enough upon shipping and trade already. Seamen's wages were very high.

E e

Sir Edward Seymour was for a review of the poll. And if you will but add a single poll of 12*d*. a head it will raise the sum that is wanting.

This was debated some time, and the House generally seemed to be against that of the single poll, and denied on the question. So after some time it was resolved that towards raising the supply to be granted to Their Majesties there be a review of the act for a quarterly poll.

So the Chairman was ordered to report some farther progress and to desire leave to sit again. All which *he* did, and the House resolved to go into committee tomorrow.

All committees were revived.

So adjourned till 8 tomorrow morning.

Saturday, 11 February

Mr. John Brewer was ordered to carry up to the Lords the bill for the encouraging the taking of highwaymen for their concurrence.

Sir Miles Cook and Mr. Keck, Masters in Chancery, came with the message from the Lords.

The bill against mutineers and deserters was reported by *Sir Richard Temple* with amendments. Some of which were agreed unto and others not.

And other amendments were made in the House, as *Sir Christopher Musgrave* tendered a clause for the muster rolls to be brought to the Paymaster, according to which he was to pay. Received, read twice, and made part of the bill.

Mr. Gwyn tendered a clause to prevent this irregular method of pressing. It was received, read once, but on the question denied a second reading.

Mr. Boyle tendered a clause against soldiers carrying their wives and children with them and quartering them upon the people. This was made part of the bill.

Mr. Holt tendered a clause to regulate the pressing of carriages and waggons, etc. Received and made part of the bill.

And a committee was appointed to prepare an engrossed clause upon a debate in the House and to tender it at the last reading of the bill.

So the bill with the amendments was ordered to be engrossed.

All committees adjourned.

House to be in a committee on Monday upon the ways and means for raising the supply.

So adjourned till 8 on Monday morning.

Monday, 13 February

Mr. Goldwell was ordered to carry up to the Lords the engrossed bill for delivering declarations to prisoners for their concurrence.

Sir Samuel Barnardiston was ordered to carry up to the Lords the engrossed bill to prevent the abuses committed by the traders in butter and cheese for their concurrence.

Sir Miles Cook and [Mr. Meredith],[1] Masters in Chancery, came with the message from the Lords.

Then the House, according to order, went into a committee on the ways and means for raising the supply to Their Majesties; Mr. Attorney to the Chair.

Mr. Hampden: The land tax is valued at £2,000,000, but since you have left out the assessor's oath I am confident it will fall short of it. If you had put the oath on the commissioners I believe it would have been more effectual. I think now you want about £300,000 to complete your sum, and you are at a loss to make it up. If you will give a clause of credit for £2,300,000 on the land tax your sum is made up.

Mr. P. Foley was for giving a clause of credit for that sum in case the land tax and review of the poll should fall short thereof.

Mr. Boscawen was for depending upon the review of the poll only for £300,000 without a clause of credit, for if that be added it will come to nothing.

Sir Thomas Clarges was for putting the clause of credit on the review of the poll only.

Others were for putting the clause of credit on the land tax only and others on that of the poll also.

But at last the question was put and resolved: That etc., that towards the supply etc. (in case the money upon the review of the poll shall not arise to the sum of £300,000), there be a clause of credit for making good that sum.

Sir John Lowther (of Lowther): Now you have made up your sum, but a good part of the taxes you have given are imaginary and depend upon credit, and it is very doubtful whether they may come in

---

[1] Blank in MS.; from *CJ*, x. 812.

or no, especially if any cross accident should happen—as that upon the fund bill, the £500,000 on continued impositions (which is very remote and may be much doubted whether any money will come in thereon). Therefore, I shall propose to add two years more to the duties upon East India goods and make them a collateral security to the continued impositions for raising £500,000 and no more.

Sir Stephen Fox, Mr. Montagu, Sir Robert Howard, Sir Thomas Littleton, Sir Edward Seymour all to the same, it being only to make good what you intend.

Sir Christopher Musgrave, Mr. Waller (of Bucks.), Sir Thomas Clarges, and Mr. Smith were against it, for that it is irregular; after you have settled your sums and the way you will raise them you cannot add anything thereto.

So the Attorney was commanded to report the several resolutions and left the Chair. And *he* reported the committee had come to several resolutions which they had commanded him to report. Ordered that the report be made on Wednesday next.

All committees were revived.

Some members were added to divers committees.

So adjourned till 8 tomorrow morning.

Tuesday, 14 February

Mr. Travers was ordered to carry up to the Lords the engrossed bill for making leases of the Duchy of Cornwall for their concurrence.

Sir John Knight presented the petition of the Pinmakers of Bristol against the bill for encouraging the art of pinmaking. Read and referred to the committee that bill is.

The bill for examining, taking, and stating the public accounts of the kingdom was read the second time.

Sir Christopher Musgrave and *Mr. Hutchinson* were for committing it.

Mr. Price was against committing till they had brought in their observations on the accounts, that they may be of some use to the House.

Sir Edward Seymour was against it for that he did not see any good was done by it answerable to what it costs you, which is about £10,000 per annum. At least if you are resolved to have such a commission, I desire other gentlemen may take their turn as well as these.

Mr. Harley (one of the Commissioners) spoke at large in vindication of themselves, setting forth the great difficulties they had met with from some offices; that the business was very troublesome and took up all their time; that they had complied with the orders and commands of the House, and if you will not make use of them they could not help it.

Sir Robert Howard said there was nothing in them but what any clerk of their office should be bound to present you with, but there are several mistakes in them which he would justify at any time.

Mr. Palmes: They are certainly of some use to you if it be but to let you know what your aids you give do raise, the value of the revenue, and how your money is disposed of.

Sir Thomas Clarges: The charge of this commission is but five thousand and odd pounds a year, but I find it is a sore place and I do not wonder some gentlemen are angry at it. As to the observations we brought you in upon the first book there are many useful things therein, and so you thought when you took them into consideration; and for the second, if you command us, we can give you some observations thereon perhaps not less useful. But for the mystery of the Exchequer which we have found out we may present you in time with some things that may be very fit for you to rectify—nay, there is absolute necessity for it. Then for your Commissioners of the Treasury, when they first came in about 14th year of King James I, they gave in their accounts upon oath, which are very great, and if it were so now it would be for your service.

Mr. P. Foley spoke largely in behalf of the same.

Mr. Boyle and *Sir Robert Cotton* (of the Post Office) was for it because it gives satisfaction to the nation.

Mr. John Howe was against it.

However, the bill—upon the question—was committed to a Committee of the Whole House.

Mr. Goodwin Wharton and *Sir John Morton* desired that the Commissioners might have further power given them in the act since they complain for want thereof.

Mr. Colt and others moved that the accounts of the army in Ireland might be brought before them.

Mr. P. Foley acquainted the House they had made some progress therein, but as yet they have not all the accounts relating thereto brought before them. But as far as they have gone, they find there is £700,000 or £800,000 paid to the army there more than their due according to the establishment, if there were no men run away, dead, etc.

So resolved thereon to take the state of Ireland into consideration on Saturday next.

Mr. Serj. Trenchard reported from the committee the election of a knight for the county of Essex with the resolutions of the committee in behalf of Sir Eliab Harvey against Mr. Honeywood.

Sir Robert Cotton (of the Post Office), *Mr. Clarke, Mr. Charles Montagu, Sir Robert Howard*, etc. spoke at large on behalf of Mr. Honeywood, against agreeing with the committee therein.

Sir Edward Seymour, Mr. Finch, etc. spoke in behalf of Sir Eliab Harvey and for agreeing with the committee in their resolutions.

So the first question was put for agreeing with the committee that Mr. Honeywood was not duly chosen. House divided thereon—Noes went out.

	Sir Robert Davers	
Yeas		149
	Mr. Gwyn	
Tellers for the		
	Sir Walter Yonge	
Noes		152
	Mr. Clarke	

Then a dispute arose that the House having disagreed with the committee in the first question, whether the other questions ought to be put. And it seemed not, for that the question being in the committee on Mr. Honeywood (the sitting member), whether he was duly chosen, and it being carried there in the negative it was necessary to have the other question put there upon the petitioner. But it being now in the House carried for disagreeing with the resolution of the committee upon the sitting member, it is in effect as if you had resolved he was duly chosen; so no need of putting the other questions. So they were not put.

Sir John Knight presented the petition of several merchants against the saltpetre bill.

It was stirred in the House that the bill for encouraging privateers had been referred to a private committee who had never yet proceeded in it because they thought it too weighty a matter for them, and therefore it was proposed to refer it to a Committee of the Whole House. But this was not thought regular, but that the committee should meet and they might order it to come by way of motion from the committee, and then the House would order in it accordingly. So let fall.

So adjourned till 8 tomorrow morning.

Wednesday, 15 February

The amendments made by the Lords to Mr. Bayntun's private bill were read and agreed to, and Sir Joseph Tredenham was ordered to carry the bill to the Lords and acquaint them this House hath agreed to the said amendments.

The private bill of Isaac Savery to enable him to take the name of Searle was reported without any amendments. Several spoke against it that it was an unjust bill to enable a stranger to take a name upon him that he might be capacitated to marry a woman who had an estate given her on condition she married one whose name was Searle and thereby to put by the next man in remainder whose name was Searle. So upon the question for engrossing the bill it was carried in the negative.

Engrossed bill to prevent the decay of trade in cities and corporations was read the third time. Several spoke against it that it would be found very mischievous and set up monopolies in the corporations.

Sir John Kay offered a clause to license persons to carry cloth about and other of our manufactures to sell to the shopkeepers only.

Several spoke against it that it would destroy the bill itself. But answered it was to carry the goods to the shopkeepers only, and then it is to carry about the woollen cloth; and if the bill be against that, they said it was an ill bill.

The clause was read twice, and an amendment was proposed to it to leave out the words 'or other manufactures', which was long debated. But at last the question was put for those words to stand in the question. House divided thereon—Noes went out.[1]

	Mr. Clarke	
Yeas		109
	Mr. Shakerley	
Tellers for the		
	Sir Robert Cotton	
Noes		69
	Mr. Colt	

So the clause was read the third time.

[1] *CJ*, x. 815 has Clarke and Shakerley as tellers for the Noes, Cotton and Colt for the Yeas, and also has 105 as the figure for the Yeas' total.

Then the question was put to make this clause part of the bill. House divided thereon—Yeas went out.

Tellers for the	Yeas	Sir Joseph Tredenham	101
		Sir Charles Raleigh	
	Noes	Sir Edward Phelips	86
		Sir John Knight	

Then the question was put for passing the bill. House divided—Yeas went out.

Tellers for the	Yeas	Mr. Onslow	146[1]
		Mr. Fenwick	
	Noes	Mr. Dyott	77
		[Sir John Darell][2]	

Then the title was passed and Mr. Fenwick was ordered to carry it up to the Lords for their concurrence.

Sir Miles Cook and Sir James Astry, Masters in Chancery, came with the message from the Lords.

Mr. Attorney General reported the bill for encouraging privateers: that it was a matter of great import, so the private committee did not think fit to proceed, but ordered him to lay it before the House. So the House discharged the private committee and referred it to a Committee of the whole House.

Mr. Attorney General reported from the Committee of the Whole House about the ways and means for raising the supply to Their Majesties the several resolutions, which were read. Those of the five per cent on the East India Company, 20*s*. on a share in the African Company, £5 on every share in the Hudson's Bay Company were all agreed to.

To that of £500,000 on the continued impositions, *Sir John Lowther*, *Mr. Montagu*, *Mr. Herbert*, etc. were for disagreeing with the committee therein for that £500,000 was too much on this fund, and therefore desired it might be but £250,000 on this or £300,000 at

---

[1] *CJ*, x. 815 has 143.   [2] Blank in MS.; from *CJ*, x. 815.

most, and transfer the remainder to another fund—to that of the duties upon East India goods.

Mr. Foley agreed that this should be but for £300,000.

So it was put and carried.

The resolutions of £510,000 on the new duties and the review of the poll with a clause of credit thereon for £300,000 were all read and agreed to. And a bill was ordered to be brought in upon these resolutions.

But here wanting £200,000 of the money (so much being struck off from the continued impositions), it was moved by some to go into a committee immediately for raising the same, which would not be half an hour. But opposed because irregular. So put off till tomorrow.

Mr. Dolben presented a petition of several merchants in relation to the duties you are now going to raise on the merchandises offered to you.

But opposed as wholly irregular, for if you will receive petitions against the taxes you raise you will never have done. Their representatives are here and their consent is sufficient.

So the petition was rejected.

Then the House went into a committee, according to order, upon the bill for granting the additional duties on merchandises; Mr. Attorney General to the Chair. So the bill was read over and the preamble postponed. So they proceeded in the bill, filled up the blanks and made amendments, and went through the same. So he was ordered to report the same.

Speaker resumed the Chair. *Mr. Attorney General* reported the committee had gone through the bill and made several amendments which they had commanded him to report. Ordered to be reported tomorrow.

So adjourned till 8 tomorrow morning.

Thursday, 16 February

The House went into a committee upon the business of the orphans of the City of London; Mr. Harcourt was called to the Chair of the committee. Then the petitions of the City and of the orphans were read, and also the state of the revenue of the City of London was read.

Sir Thomas Clarges proposed for the relief of the orphans the City out of their revenue should have such a portion thereof allotted them and the surplus to be applied towards payment of the orphans, and the whole put into the hands of trustees for the common benefit of both. That £3,500 per annum be allowed the Mayor for the government of the City, besides his benevolence money upon days of feasting. That £500 per annum be allowed to each sheriff, besides the fines and forfeitures of felons' goods. And I would allow £5,000 per annum for to bear the common and ordinary charges of the City— all which makes but £9,500 per annum. And so much would I allow the City and appropriate the remainder to the payment of the orphans' debts.

This was debated some time. At last a question was stated and resolved: That it is the opinion of this committee that there be in the first place charged on and allowed out of the whole revenues of the City of London the sum of £10,000 per annum to support the necessary charge of the government of the said City and the magistracy thereof.

Then it was debated, out of which a question was stated and resolved: That etc. that over and above the said sum of £10,000 per annum the whole revenues of the City of London in possession and reversion, with all improvements thereof and other contingencies in lands, disposition of offices, or otherwise, be applied towards raising a fund of perpetual interest of four per cent to satisfy the debts due to the orphans of the City of London.

Sir John Parsons: This surplus of the City revenue is computed at £12,000 per annum, which will not be sufficient. But as an addition I propose that every Alderman shall pay £4 per annum, every Common Councilman 40s. per annum, every liveryman 20s. per annum. This, by computation, may raise about £8,000 per annum more.

Which was debated and at last resolved: That etc. that towards raising a fund of perpetual interest for satisfying the debts due to the orphans of the City of London, there be yearly paid by every Alderman £5, by every Common Councilman 40s., and by every liveryman 20s.; That etc. that towards etc., there be yearly paid during their lives by all such who have or shall fine for the said offices the same respective sums with such persons who yearly serve in those places; That etc. that towards raising etc., there be paid by every person to be bound an apprentice in the City of London 2s. 6d. and by every person to be made free of the said City 5s., over and above what is now paid; That etc. that towards etc., there be yearly paid £4 by every unfree or foreign merchant trading beyond the seas from the said City who do inhabit within the said city or 10 miles thereof. (This last was much opposed by some rich merchants not free of the City in the House, but it was carried upon a division.)

Then the Chairman was ordered to report these resolutions and to leave the Chair, which he did. Then *he* reported the committee had met and come to several resolutions which they had directed him to report.

Some would have had them reported now. But opposed, being irregular to report resolutions from a Committee of the Whole House for raising money the same day the committee passed them.

The report ordered to be made tomorrow.

Committees adjourned.

So House adjourned till 8 tomorrow morning.

Friday, 17 February

Mr. Travers reported Mr. Bulkeley's bill with amendments, but withal desired it might be recommitted to rectify one mistake therein, which was for the satisfaction of all parties. So it was recommitted to the same committee.[1]

Mr. Hopkins presented the Booksellers' and the Printers' petition against continuing the act to regulate the press.

Sir Miles Cook and Sir James Astry brought the message from the Lords.

Mr. Harcourt reported the resolutions about the orphans of London, which were read and agreed to all as before. Ordered that a bill be brought in upon the said resolutions, and it was referred to some particular members. And it was ordered that consideration should be had of those that had bought any orphans' shares for little; that they should be repaid only what they had actually paid for the same with interest for it at six per cent and the overplus to the orphans that sold, and that a clause should be added to set aside Mr. Reading's composition he had made with the orphans.

Sir John Brownlow had leave to go into the country.[2]

The engrossed bill for reviving a part of the act for preventing the exportation of wool and encouraging the woollen manufactures was read the third time.

Sir John Guise offered a rider to raise the same duties for payment of

---

[1] This order is not entered in the *Journal*.
[2] No such order is entered in the *Journal*.

the Hamburg Company's debts as they paid before. But rejected because to raise money, which ought not to be but in a Committee of the Whole House.

Mr. Sandford: I am against this bill because it is to give our woollen trade to foreigners. Then it will ruin and destroy your trade at last, though at present it seems to be greater. And it sets aside the Hamburg Company who first brought this trade into the nation and have hitherto preserved it, and will if this bill do not pass.

Sir Walter Yonge was for it because it seemed highly reasonable to encourage the free exportation of any manufacture, for the more hands our cloth is carried out by the better—it raises your wool and is for the benefit of the country.

Sir John Knight was against the bill and urged that the price of wool, though it was somewhat better at present, did not arise from this bill. The true reason is Ireland, which used to send over a great deal of wool, has afforded you none lately. They made serges there formerly, so that a want there must occasion a greater consumption of it here. Besides, can any imagine if there be a vent for the commodity abroad that the Company will not export cloth enough for their own advantage? But this trade as it is now managed is carried on by foreigners who will not be very forward to maintain the credit of your manufacture, for all they mind is their own profit and the advantage that arises to them thereby is carried out of the nation, who are so much the poorer for it, whereas if this trade be carried on in the regular channel by the Hamburg Company the benefit will redound to the nation. This Company consists of your own native[s], have great privileges granted them at Hamburg, and have a bank there for carrying on this trade, which if you break your bullion must be exported to carry on the trade. Therefore, I am against the bill.

Sir John Darell was for the bill for that he thought it against the interest of the nation to limit and confine trade to companies, who will set the dice upon others and sell at their own price.

Mr. Smith was against the bill for that this [? was only true of] a joint [stock] in a company. Those, I agree, are mischievous and circumscribe trade, but when it is a well-regulated company it is otherwise—they will sell for a reasonable profit. Then here is no mischief, for any native of this kingdom may be free of it for £13. 6s. 8d., and if you will reduce the price thereof the Company are very willing.

Sir Edward Hussey was for the bill, because the more exporters of a manufacture the better.

Sir Samuel Dashwood was against the bill. The only argument for it is there has been more exported for three years past. I agree it in some measure to be true, but he did not think it arose from the exportation thereof that had been for the three years last past but from other causes.

Mr. Boscawen was for it because the more exporters the cheaper it would go out, and the cheaper it is the more you will send abroad and the better able to undersell your neighbours.

Sir Edward Seymour: The woollen manufacture is a specious thing, but I am afraid we are in this matter contending only for the name. If the bill were really for the benefit thereof, I doubt not but I should have heard from my corporation in the matter. But I take the bill before you to be a door to let in foreigners, and when they have got the trade into their hands they will beat you out of it or make their own terms with you and set their own prices. The true reason of exporting more of the woollen trade to Hamburg and Holland is because of the war. The sea in some measure to Italy is now shut up, and therefore you export it to Hamburg and Holland in greater quantities, and thence it is carried by land, etc. to those places. So that I do not think this bill for the interest of the nation.

Mr. Clarke: It is very strange that an open trade and a free exportation of any commodity should not be for the interest of this nation— the truth of which appears in comparing the Customhouse books of the port of London for the three last years with the three preceding. In the last, there has been £160,000 worth in the woollen manufacture exported more than before.

Sir Christopher Musgrave: The reasons of your greater exportations now than formerly are such as these: that Ireland has made no woollen cloths for three years past; the prohibition of trade with France by the German princes, who used to supply them with great quantities; then there have been several ships exported with this manufacture who being taken by French privateers the merchant has been forced to send the like quantity to supply the loss thereof, whereby double quantities have gone out. These are some of the reasons of the present greater exportation of it. Then they are foreigners who run away with this trade, and not the English, to encourage whom is against the policy of this nation before our English merchants who are not concerned in it—only one at Exeter, Mr. Elwill, who is the factor for the foreigners—so though there be many exporters of it yet there is in a manner but one buyer. But in the

Hamburg Company it is otherwise; every man buys for himself so the Company is not confined. For these reasons, he was against the bill. *Mr. Papillon* and *Mr. Pery* were against the bill.

Mr. Blofield also, and affirmed that though there had been more exported for the three years past (viz. 1689, 1690, 1691) than for the years before (viz. 1686, 1687, 1688) in the port of London, yet out of England in general from the several ports there had been less exported in the three last years than before—as has been undeniably made appear to him by the farmers of the aulnage duty. And it stands with reason that more should be exported from the port of London during the war because of the danger of the seas from privateers, etc., whom to avoid they send up their goods to London and export them hence because of the conveniency of convoys which go from hence.

Mr. Bowyer and *Sir Charles Sedley* were against the bill for that it would prejudice our navigation, for as it is always the policy of this nation to lay high duties on commodities brought in foreign bottoms to encourage your own shipping, so by this foreigners' goods will be excused by going in English bottoms.

Dr. Barbone was for the bill.

So the question was put that the bill do pass. House divided—Yeas go out.

		Sir Walter Yonge	
	Yeas		88
		Mr. Clarke	
Tellers for the			
		Sir John Guise	
	Noes		155
		Mr. Smith	

Then the House, according to order, went into a committee upon the bill of accounts; Col. Granville to the Chair. So they proceeded on the bill and went through it.

Mr. Clarke, Attorney General, Sir Edward Seymour, Mr. Montagu, and others desired a clause might be prepared to empower the Commissioners to state the debt due to the bankers—they pretending a great debt to be due to them when there really is not half so much as they have got letters patent for—and that this was the more necessary to be done because they are proceeding at law for the recovery of those debts they pretend and have a judgement for them.

Sir Thomas Clarges and others were against it for that the Court of Exchequer was the proper place to settle that matter, where it had been determined and they had got a legal judgement for their right. That this was but a contrivance to get you to put a stop to justice. Then it is a very unreasonable thing to ravel into this matter after people have stated their accounts and passed them and delivered up their vouchers for their debts, and will you go and set aside just and honest debts after so many years? But besides, if you find these debts just and honest I hope you will take care to pay them, but I think it not proper at this time to enter into the same.

So upon the question the clause was refused.[1]

Some also proposed to have a clause to make Lords Lieutenant and Deputy Lieutenants accountable for the trophy money.[2] The matter was approved of but thought more proper for a militia bill, so let fall.

So the preamble of the bill was passed, and the Chairman was ordered to report it. Speaker resumed the Chair, and *Col. Granville* reported the committee had gone through the bill and had made several amendments. Ordered it be reported on Monday.

Mr. Clarke presented the petition of the Company for making and refining of saltpetre against the bill touching the importation thereof. [It] was referred to the committee that bill was.

All committees were revived.

So adjourned till 8 tomorrow morning.

Saturday, 18 February

Sir Gilbert Clarke desired leave to go out of town. House divided thereon—Yeas went out.

		Sir Robert Cotton (of Cheshire)	
	Yeas		113
		Mr. Clarke	
Tellers for the			
		Mr. Boil[3]	
	Noes		72
		Mr. Forster	

---

[1] The debate on this proposal took up two hours; B.M. Add. MS. 34096, f. 281.

[2] A local levy to pay militia costs.

[3] Lutterell here seems to mean one of the two Boyles, but *CJ*, x. 819 has this teller as 'Mr. Baile'—? Christopher Bale who sat for Exeter.

Sir John Guise offered a petition of several merchants relating to the bill of impositions upon merchandises, that it might not have a retrospect to a time past—viz. the 25th of Dec. last. But it would not be received, being irregular to offer it before the bill was reported (which was just ready for it) because the House perhaps might not agree to the amendment from the committee.

Mr. Attorney General reported the said bill with the amendments, some of which were agreed to and others not.

Sir Thomas Clarges proposed to lay a duty on another commodity which was omitted. But opposed as irregular because in the House, which have no power to raise money—ought to come from a Committee of the Whole House.

Then it was proposed to leave out the duty imposed upon hair buttons because a bill was depending in the House to prohibit them absolutely. But thought better not because a duty may be consistent with an absolute prohibition, because if these goods be at any time brought in and discovered the practice of the Customhouse is to compound with the parties for them, so that by this duty standing the Crown will get something.

Sir Samuel Dashwood and *Mr. Goldwell* offered a clause to import Italian silks in foreign bottoms, which being to repeal the act of navigation was thrown by as irregular.

Mr. Clarke tendered a clause to revive a clause that was added to a former act, forbidding Excise men to meddle with elections of members to parliament. It was received and read twice.

Sir Thomas Clarges took exception to it; that was not full enough, being it did not recite the clauses at large.

So after some debate thereof, the House not liking the same, some proposed to have a rider prepared and offered to the bill at last reading thereof, others that the bill might lie on the Table till such a clause was drawn. But others thought it the better way. And so it was ordered at this time that two or three members should withdraw into the Speaker's Chamber and prepare the clause immediately. Which they did, and the clause was read twice and made part of the bill.

Sir Thomas Clarges tendered a clause of appropriation of £1,200,000 to the use of the Navy of all the money given.

But exception was taken to it as irregular because such clauses ought not to be brought in without leave, and that with a blank and not ready filled up as here.

Sir Thomas Clarges said it was regular to bring in any clause without leave, unless it were to repeal a law.

But the *Chair* and others thought such a clause as this ought not.

So Sir Thomas Clarges and others were ordered to prepare a clause of appropriation and of loan, too, and the bill to lie on the Table till done, and the further debate thereof adjourned till Monday.

So adjourned till 8 on Monday morning.

Monday, 20 February

Serj. Blencowe ordered to carry up the private engrossed bill of Thomas Goodwin unto the Lords for their concurrence.

Sir Edward Harley, a new member for the county of Hereford (in the room of Sir John Morgan, deceased), came into the House and took the oaths and subscribed the test at the Table and took his place in the House.

A message from the Lords by Sir Miles Cook and [Mr. Meredith],[1] Masters in Chancery, that the Lords had agreed to the bill entitled 'an act to prevent the abuses in packing and weighing of butter and cheese' with some amendments to which they desire the concurrence of this House.

Mr. Attorney reported the bill for continuing, reviving, and explaining several laws expired and expiring with amendments, some of which were agreed to.

As to that for making the towns of Plymouth and Bridgwater free whither wool might be imported from Ireland, the House divided on agreeing with the committee—Noes went out.

		Sir Joseph Tredenham	
	Noes		110
		Mr. Bale	
Tellers for the			
		Sir Walter Yonge	
	Yeas		82[2]
		Mr. Thomas Foley junior	

Then to the clause for reviving the act against unlicensed printing, the House divided on agreeing with the committee therein—Noes went out.

---

[1] Blank in MS.; from *CJ*, x. 819.   [2] 81 in *CJ*, x. 820.

Sir Samuel Barnardiston

Noes   80

Mr. Bowyer

Tellers for the

Mr. Goldwell

Yeas   99

Mr. Harcourt

So the amendments being finished, *Mr. John Howe* desired to know if he might not speak against any one clause in the bill—that for reviving the printing act.

Which was debated and seemed by the best opinion that it could not now because the House having but just agreed to the amendment they could not debate it over again, but the question is next for engrossing. But when the bill comes to be read the third time, any member may speak against the whole bill or any clause of it or to leave out a part of it though in the midst of the bill. The case now under debate was a clause that was in the bill when first brought in, which was read twice in the House and referred with the bill, and now it comes from the committee with an amendment in that clause to which the House have also agreed. It seems that this clause could not be now spoke against. (So said *Sir Christopher Musgrave.*) But if the committee had made no amendment to the clause or if the clause had been added by the committee or it had been offered in the House at the reporting of the bill, though it had been received by the House and amendments made to it, yet on the question for it to be made part of the bill you might speak against the clause in any of these cases and throw it out.

So after a long debate, the question was put for engrossing the bill (as being more regular at present) and ordered accordingly.

Then the House proceeded on the bill for the additional duties, and *Mr. Attorney General* presented two clauses to the House, one of appropriation and the other of loan. That of loan was read twice and the blanks filled up for this bill to be a fund for raising £510,000 at eight per cent. Then the clause of appropriation was read twice and the blank filled up.

Sir Thomas Clarges: I do not think it irregular to offer a clause of appropriation to a money bill without leave, though said otherwise when you were last on this bill, and that when the blank is filled up. I have known it done several times. It was done 19 Car. II by Sir

Thomas Osborne, by Mr. Sacheverell another time, and I myself did it in the second year of this reign to an act about the excise. And I take it [to be] very regular, especially when the sum is named to you for filling it up before I presented you with the clause.

Sir Edward Seymour: I cannot agree that clauses of appropriation may be brought in without leave. It is true when leave hath been given, in some cases the sum has been mentioned in the House and then the blank in the clause of appropriation hath been filled up with that sum.

Mr. Montagu: That precedent cited in *secundo* of this reign was a rider brought in for appropriation with a blank, for I have here the very Journal.

Mr. Smith offered a clause to hinder the officers and collectors of the Customs to intermeddle in elections of parliament. Received, read twice, and being thought too large it was denied to be made part of the bill.

Mr. Pery tendered a clause to excuse foreign stores for the use of the Navy that were already contracted for from paying this duty.

Sir John Darell offered a clause that the hoys and barges of Kent and Essex might come to London without taking of cockets, only with *transires* or 'let passes' (as they call them) paying 6d.

But this was rejected because vessels bound to foreign parts are they which only take cockets and give bond to the [Customhouse][1] to go to such port accordingly. But there is no bond given on *transires*, and this is a trick to smuggle prohibited goods, whereas if there be any goods on board a ship not in the cocket they are forfeited.

So the bill was ordered to be engrossed.

Sir Thomas Mompesson presented a petition from the Company of Shipwrights against the bill for building good and defensible ships. It was received, but being said it was to confirm a private patent which might be very mischievous, the petition was withdrawn on leave.

Committees adjourned.

So adjourned till 8 tomorrow morning.

Tuesday, 21 February

Sir John Guise was ordered to carry up to the Lords the bill for raising the militia for the year 1693 for their concurrence.

[1] Inserted in the margin by Luttrell in place of 'Admiralty'.

Sir John Guise presented the petition of Mr. Norwood against the bill for sale of the Fleet [Prison].

The bill for satisfying the debts due to the orphans was ordered to be read in a full House.

Sir Robert Howard, Sir John Guise, Mr. Smith, and others moved that since there was no probability to pass a bill this sessions to establish an East India Company by reason the sessions was pretty near an end and the friends to the old Company give such delays to the bill now in the House, that the House would come to a resolution to address to His Majesty to dissolve the present East India Company, pursuant to the power reserved by a clause in the charter at three years' end after notice. *Sir Christopher Musgrave* to the same.

But, however, it was thought better to adjourn the debate till Friday next.

Then the House, according to order, went into a committee upon the bill for encouragement of privateers, and Mr. Attorney General took the Chair. And the committee proceeded in the bill and made an end of it, only to receive clauses, and he was ordered to report it and desire leave to sit again.

Speaker resumed the Chair, and *Mr. Attorney* reported they had made a considerable progress and after desired leave to sit again, which was ordered on Thursday next.

All committees adjourned.

So adjourned till 8 tomorrow morning.

Wednesday, 22 February

Sir John Mainwaring was ordered to carry up to the Lords Mr. Richard Walthal's private bill and acquaint them this House hath agreed to the same without any amendments.

Col. Titus took notice of the multitude of private bills, and to save a great deal of trouble desired that leave might be given to bring in a bill to make all settlements valid and effectual but until the next sessions of parliament. It would save much time.

Mr. Goldwell was ordered to carry up to the Lords the engrossed bill for preventing abuses committed by traders in butter and cheese and to acquaint them this House hath agreed to the amendments made by their Lordships.

Then the House went upon the amendments made by the Lords to the bill to prevent malicious informations in the Court of King's

Bench. They were read and exceptions were taken to it that it confirms the unjust proceedings in a *quominus* in the Exchequer, for though it provides the *quominus* shall have an *ac etiam* or cause of action therein yet the party must give £40 bail therein, which in a manner confirms this oppressive practice. Besides, it was said to be wholly foreign to this bill and only with a design in the judges to break the neck of it. So the House disagreed with the same and appointed a committee to prepare reasons to be offered at a conference with the Lords for disagreeing to the said amendments.

The engrossed bill for prohibiting the importation of foreign buttons was read the last time.

Mr. Lloyd offered a rider in behalf of one Mr. Simpson to give him leave to import £4,000 worth of hair buttons which he had really contracted for before this bill was brought in.

Sir Edward Seymour and others spoke for it that it was just and reasonable and would be very hard to restrain which was lawful before, and in prohibitions you usually give some time for consuming what is in the nation.

Mr. Smith and others were against it for that this bill had been depending in the House for three months and you have heard nothing of this gentleman before, but now the bill is like to pass this clause is brought in to obstruct it. And if you pass this clause it will give a colour for much greater quantities to be brought in, and the fruits of such clauses have been found to be only to the advantage of the particular persons, of which you had a fresh example in the act about prohibition of brandies.

House divided on the question to receive it—Yeas went out.

		Mr. Colt	
	Yeas		60
		Mr. Clarke	
Tellers for the			
		Mr. Pery	
	Noes		87
		Mr. Fenwick	

So the bill was put and passed, with the title, and Sir Robert Cotton ordered to carry it up to the Lords.

Col. Granville was ordered to carry up the bill for taking the accounts of the kingdom to the Lords for their concurrence.

The engrossed bill against mutineers and deserters was read the last time.

Mr. Herbert tendered an engrossed clause for having an account made up between the officer and the Paymaster General. Which was received, read thrice and made part of the bill.

Mr. P. Foley tendered a rider to prevent false musters and to regulate the pay according to the true musters, requiring them to be countersigned by the Lords of the Treasury. Received, read thrice, and made part of the bill.

So the bill was passed, with the title, and the Lord Colchester was ordered to carry it up to the Lords for their concurrence.

Then the House, according to order, went upon the consideration of the state of Ireland.

Mr. Goodwin Wharton: There have been great abuses committed in that kingdom: the free quartering of soldiers whereby great debts are due to the country and yet deductions have been made from the soldiers as if they were really paid; the Irish have been required to bring in their arms, which has only served to make them hide them, and when search has been made after them it has been too late. There are a great many other things of which you may have an account if you will hear some gentlemen who, I am informed, attend at your door.

Sir Ralph Dutton: I hope the Commissioners of Accounts will give you some account of these matters.

Mr. Harley: We have made some inquiry into the Irish affairs, and particularly that of the forfeited estates there. We have seen the accounts what has been made both of the real and personal estate there, which we are ready to lay before you but not so fully as we could wish.

Sir Thomas Clarges: We have an account of £32,000 made in one year of the forfeited lands in Ireland and about £135,000 in goods, but cannot find that ever above £4,000 came to the Crown. What is become of the residue we know not; the Lords of the Treasury can best tell. I think the interest of the King and his people ought in that nation to be one entirely, and they that sow or make a difference between them are worthy your taking notice of. I have heard of a parliament being broke up there very abruptly, which has much dissatisfied the people there, and a Protestant House of Commons too it was, which that nation never had before. Then for the security of that kingdom there are but 7,000 men left in it—too small a number to defend it, for if the French but once get footing there again and regain but Kinsale it may cost you some millions before you beat them out of it. And for the forfeited estates in Ireland, the Lords of the Treasury can or ought to give you the best account thereof.

Mr. Smith: I think it worth your inquiry as to the forfeited estates in Ireland. You were resolved once, and the King has given his word for it, that those should go towards carrying on the war, which I think very necessary that after we have been at so vast a charge to regain that kingdom we should have some fruit thereof, and that is my motion.

Mr. Waller (of Bucks.) was for calling in those gentlemen at the door and hear what account they could give of matters there.

Mr. John Howe: You have two matters now before you—Ireland as it is in itself and as it relates to this nation. For the first, in general I hear the papists speak very well of the government there but no Protestant I can meet with does, which is very strange to me. I hear there are some gentlemen at the door that can give an account of these matters; I desire they may be called in to inform you how things are.

Mr. Palmes: If reports be true that I hear that kingdom is to be conquered again. For the forfeitures, I am told in two provinces they came to £30,000 per annum but when an account was brought in of all the four it sank to £10,000 per annum. So well things have been managed there.

Mr. Henry Boyle: If there have been miscarriages in Ireland (which I think few doubt of), now you are upon inquiring about them unless you do something to prevent them you will but confirm them. I have spoke with some gentlemen, and if what they tell me be true you will need neither an invasion nor a rebellion but the people will leave that kingdom—they are used so ill. There are some at your door will give you a larger account if you will but order them to attend the House— particularly one Sir Francis Brewster, a member of the House of Commons there.

Mr. Colt: The Commissioners of Accounts tell you there was £135,000 worth of forfeited goods seized in that kingdom but never above £4,000 accounted for, so that there is yet coming about £130,000—a sum worth your inquiry as to that particular.

Lord Coningsby: I do not think things are so bad in Ireland as some gentlemen have represented them or that there are so many miscarriages as you are told. As to the army's free quarter, I cannot excuse all their actions but they were not so well paid as they ought—

the charge of the army there came to about £1,600,000 and I never received in all above £700,000, whence arises that debt to the army. As to the disarming of the papists, it is a difficult matter to do it for they as soon as they hear of it take their guns and tallow them all over very well on the outside and stop the touch holes and the bore and so throw them into the loughs and rivers and take them up after and they are as good as ever. As to the forfeitures, I never was concerned in them, and for the decrease of the forfeited lands from £31,000 to £10,000 that arises from the Articles of Limerick, into which the Council there are inquiring to know the true value of the forfeitures. This is what I know of these matters.

Mr. Boscawen: Ireland is under a general discontent but why I cannot tell. The unseasonable prorogation of the parliament there may be one occasion. I think it fit to inquire into. *Sir Ralph Dutton* and *Sir Walter Yonge* to the same.

Mr. Clarke named another gentleman to be at the door, one Sir John Magill, who could give you also some account.

Mr. Brydges named one Lieut. Stafford and Sir William Gore.

Mr. Mordaunt named Mr. Sloane, the lawyer, another, and desired they might all be called in.

So they were all six called in by order and gave an account what they knew of matters there to the effect following.

Sir William Gore: My affairs lie chiefly in the country and what I have to say is touching the complaints about quarters: the soldiers lived at discretion and the country is yet unpaid for their quarters.

Sir Francis Brewster: What I know is touching the forfeited estates in Ireland. I know the rent roll thereof but of two provinces came to about £31,000, but when the other two provinces came to be reckoned too they fell to £10,000. We found leases were let of land at a great underrate to men that could not manage them; a hackney coachman, I remember, had a great lease. We suppose they were for some great men in trust. When lands were offered to be let, if they found any of the country were like to bid for them they were postponed, and others put up for the advantage of particular persons. We found it very grievous in the papists being protected against the Protestants' just debts.

Sir John Magill: The taking free quarters did very much discourage the Protestants, so much that if effectual care be not taken therein the Protestants will leave that kingdom.

Lieut. Stafford knew nothing material of the state of that kingdom.

Mr. Sloane: The grievances of the kingdom of Ireland are the quartering of soldiers, which continues to this time; then the embezzling of the revenue, which has been the occasion of the first; then the greatest of all is the encouragement that is given to papists and the Protestants are discouraged.

The manner of quartering was both upon the poor and the rich; the poor's cattle were taken away and made to provide shoes and other necessaries, and of the rich they levied money as if they had an act of parliament. The commissioners there were discountenanced and forbid not to give certificates of what due to the army.

The standing revenue there, consisting of the customs, excise, Hearth money, and quit rents, is computed at £200,000 per annum, which, with what came from hence, we judge sufficient to have paid all. The accounts they brought of the forfeitures to the Parliament of Ireland were so general we could make nothing of it. Mr. Culliford, a member of this House, was concerned in the revenue there and found very faulty, and when we were going on to inquire into it, he stood upon his privilege as a member of this House. And though we did not meddle with him, we examined several witnesses and found very great abuses in letting out the revenue more for his own private advantage than the King's—of which he instanced in several cases.

Then for the encouragement given to papists, many of them have been restored to their estates which we thought ought not. Then there are several papists licensed to bear arms. Then the papists have protections against the suits of the Protestants, and this the judges have order for; there were 300 protections to them entered in the Sheriff of Dublin's office.

But the greatest of all was the sudden breaking up of the parliament, which we took to be a very good one, when we were upon public business and about giving a supply suitable to our abilities for the support of the government there. We had a bill there before us for raising £70,000 per annum on land, and while we were finding other ways to raise more they sent us two bills—one for an excise on beer, etc., another for laying 1s. 3d. on every acre of corn. This we thought hard that the Commons must give money and yet not order on what it shall be raised, contrary to our ancient right to propose the heads of money bills to be sent to the Council in Ireland and they are to transmit it to the Council here in England who are to return it to the parliament in Ireland, and this according to Poynings' Law. But this proceeding of ours gave great offence and occasioned some hard expressions of us by the Lord Lieutenant, as if we had behaved ourselves undutifully and ungratefully, and thereon we were prorogued. Upon this, several gentlemen did make application to the Lord Lieutenant for leave to send over some gentlemen to represent us fairly to His Majesty, but that could not be obtained and we were told if we would send some to beg His Majesty's pardon we should. After we were gone we had all the discouragements and affronts put upon us. Several were turned out as Sir Arthur Rawdon was turned out of his government of Down, which was after tendered to the Lord Donegall, then to the Lord Mount-Alexander, but both refused it and to this day they cannot get one to take it. Then besides, there were several bills sent to the parliament which the papists had the privilege to see but no Protestants were admitted to that favour. There is one Mr. Kerne at the door who gives an account of some discourse of the Lord Lieutenant: that he would have no more parliaments there.

These are the things that render the prospect of affairs in Ireland very melancholy.

Then they withdrew.

Sir Ralph Dutton desired that Mr. Culliford might be sent to to attend the House to answer this charge against him, for if it be true he is not fit to sit here.

Mr. Smith moved that to remedy the mischiefs there and to set all things right that the House would address to His Majesty to call a parliament there to sit in some short time.

Ordered that Mr. Culliford, a member of this House, attend his service in the House on Friday next, and the Serjeant is to give him notice thereof.

Mr. Brydges renewed the motion of an address for the parliament to sit there.

Mr. Henry Boyle was against it for that he heard it was intended the parliament should sit very shortly, and was for adjourning the further debate of this matter till Friday.

Sir Edward Seymour: Since words are very apt to be mistaken and discourses liable to misconstruction, I desire these gentlemen may give in their several narratives in writing, and you may proceed thereon as you see fit and have something before you.

Others to the same for that you will more easily be able to distinguish what they say on their own knowledge and what upon hearsay, which last they hoped would not be admitted here.

So they were called in again and ordered that each of them should put in writing their several narratives of matters upon their own knowledge and what they can prove by witnesses, and each of them to sign their own papers and present them to the House on Friday next.

Mr. Kerne, being called in to give an account of the discourse between him and the Lord Lieutenant, did say he did not expect to be called to give an account of what had passed in private conversation, but did confess he was at dinner at the Lord Lieutenant's, where was some discourse of the next meeting of the parliament and of what temper and disposition they might be and it was said they believed they would insist on what they did at last meeting, on which his Lordship said something to this effect—that they were not like to have any more parliaments then. There were several gentlemen by at the same time, as the Lord Massereene, Col. Smith, etc.

So the further debate of this matter was adjourned to Friday next.

So House adjourned till 8 tomorrow morning.

Thursday, 23 February

Mr. Fenwick presented the petition from the officers, innkeepers, and clothiers that served, quartered, and clothed the army in 1677. Moved to refer it to a committee, but opposed because not a time for such things at the close of a sessions. But it being only to keep a claim on foot because they would not lose their right when a fit time should come, the debate thereof was adjourned *sine die*.

Sir Miles Cook and [Mr. Meredith],[1] two Masters in Chancery, brought the message from the Lords that they had passed a bill entitled 'an act to repeal the statute 10 E. III c. [10] for finding of sureties for the good abearing of him that hath a pardon for felony'.

The bill was read the first time.

Mr. Boscawen and *Mr. Palmes* were for rejecting it.

Sir Christopher Musgrave was against it for that he was afraid the not requiring sureties of felons when pardoned had been the great occasion so many felonies were committed.

Mr. Dolben was for it, being to repeal a statute that was never executed, being impracticable and impossible now for a criminal pardoned to find sureties for his life (which he must do by this act),

---

[1] Blank in MS.; from *CJ*, x. 824.

so that the King's pardon for never so small a felony is not available unless the party finds sureties for his good behaviour during life, which is very difficult for them to do. And to help this, before this revolution the pardons used to have a *non obstante* to this statute, but you have taken them away in all cases by your bill of rights.

So the bill was rejected upon the question.

The engrossed bill for preservation of the game was read the last time.

Mr. Brewer presented a rider to restrain apprentices and tradesmen from hunting, fishing, etc. It was read thrice, and after an amendment in it was made part of the bill.

Mr. Norris tendered another to enable every Protestant to keep a musket in his House for his defence.

Sir Christopher Musgrave was against it because irregular to bring in a clause to repeal a law without leave first had. Then it is a clause that quite destroys your bill and the intent of it. *Sir Joseph Tredenham* to the same.

Mr. Bowyer, Mr. Howe, Mr. Clarke, and *Mr. Goodwin Wharton* were for it and thought it a good clause and for the security of the government that all Protestants should be armed sufficiently to defend themselves.

Sir John Lowther was against it because not proper for this bill, which is for preservation of the game. And you would add a clause to it that savours of the politics to arm the mob, which I think is not very safe for any government.

So question put for reading it a second time. House divided thereon—Yeas went out.

	Sir Robert Cotton (of Cheshire)	
Yeas		65
	Mr. Clarke	
Tellers for the		
	Sir Joseph Tredenham	
Noes		169
	Mr. Goldwell	

So the bill was passed, then the title, and the Lord Digby was ordered to carry it up to the Lords for their concurrence.

The orphans' bill was read a second time.

Mr. Papillon spoke largely against it, and *Sir Thomas Clarges* for it.

Sir Edward Seymour: You have resolved to raise £400,000 on the revenue towards this year's charges. Now the customs being the chief of the revenue and has already a debt upon it of £300,000 and the customs continue no longer than till Christmas next a twelvemonth, I desire you will go tomorrow into a Committee of the Whole House to enlarge the same for some time longer. *Sir John Lowther* and *Mr. Hampden* to the same.

Mr. Paul Foley and *Sir Walter Yonge* were against it, for that this was giving more money, which you cannot now do.

Mr. Montagu and *Sir Stephen Fox* were for it, but *Mr. Harley* was against it.

Mr. Godolphin was for it and thought it not giving more money but only making that security good upon which you have resolved to raise so great a sum towards carrying on the war.

Sir Christopher Musgrave inveighed much against this motion as very unfair to stir such a thing as this at the close of a sessions, when many of your members are gone into the country. Then the House is very thin at this time and it is late in day, being 3 of the clock, which make this motion very irregular.

However, the *Speaker* framed the question: That a motion being made to enlarge the time for continuing the customs of tunnage and poundage to enable the better borrowing money for carrying on a vigorous war against France (and the question being put), that the House will resolve itself into a Committee of the Whole House tomorrow (which the *Speaker* added himself and for which *Sir Christopher Musgrave* checked him very severely, as being contrary to the duty of the Chair) to consider of the said motion. It was carried in the negative—Sir Edward Seymour only assenting.

The engrossed bill for the additional duties was read the third time. And there being some mistakes in it, the further consideration was put off till tomorrow.

Mr. Clarke presented the petition of Col. Leighton and *Mr. Arnold* presented that from the poor prisoners in the Fleet, both relating to the bill for sale of Thomas Bromhall's interest in the Fleet. They were read and referred to the same committee the bill is.

All committees adjourned.[1]

So House adjourned till 8 tomorrow morning.

---

[1] 'revived' in *CJ*, x. 824.

Friday, 24 February

Mr. Arnold[1] was ordered to carry up to the Lords the engrossed private bill of Edward Seymour esq. and to acquaint them this House hath agreed to the same without any amendments.

Mr. Colt presented the petition of Anthony Smith against the bill about the Fleet. And it was read and referred to that committee.

Sir Matthew Andrews was ordered to carry up to the Lords the bill for encouraging the Greenland trade for their concurrence.

Sir John Bolles moved to put off the election that was to be heard at the committee for the borough of Newark in Nottinghamshire, the petitioner and the sitting member being both agreed.

But it was doubted whether it could regularly be done, the matter being depending before the Committee of Elections who, it was agreed, might put it off. But, however, others thought it might be done now in the House.

So it was put off till the last Friday in March.

Sir Miles Cook and Sir Adam Oatley, two Masters in Chancery, brought the message from the Lords.

Then the House went upon the farther consideration of the bill for the additional duties, and some amendments were made to it.

Lapis calaminaris was charged 20*s.* for hundredweight on the exportation of it. It was proposed by some to alter it and make it but 5*s.* But this was doubted, being to alter it in a material part and dangerous, too, being in the case of money bills after they were engrossed. So it was let fall.

Sir John Darell presented a rider requiring the officers of the Customs to take an oath for the due and true execution of their places without taking any reward but the salary from Their Majesties. It was read thrice and made part of the bill.

So the bill was passed, then the title, and Mr. Attorney General was ordered to carry it up to the Lords for their concurrence.

Then the House resumed the debate touching the state of Ireland. And the gentlemen attending were called in—to wit, Sir Francis Brewster, Sir William Gore, Sir John Magill, Lieut. Stafford, Mr. Sloane, and Mr. Kerne—and delivered in their several narratives in writing, signed by them, and owned the same. So they withdrew.

Then the Serjeant gave an account that he had been to find out Mr. Culliford and had found where he lodged last and was informed

---

[1] Col. Granville in *CJ*, x. 825.

he had been out of England ever since September last but was expected home in a short time.

Then the several narratives of the Irish gentlemen were read over, which reflected much upon the Lord Coningsby and Mr. Culliford.

Lord Coningsby spoke very largely in vindication of himself, and very much to the satisfaction of the House.

Sir Robert Howard desired that these papers might be referred to a Committee of the Whole House who might inquire into the value of the forfeited estates, what was taken off by the Articles of Limerick, and what had been given away.

Mr. Bertie and *Mr. John Howe* expressed their satisfaction the noble lord that spoke last but one had given them, but as to the other member, Mr. Culliford, having insisted upon his privilege against right, they desired he might be expelled the House. *Mr. Mordaunt* to the same.

Sir John Morton was against that for he was not willing to condemn a man unheard.

Mr. Goodwin Wharton, Mr. Harley, Mr. Henry Boyle, and others were for an address to His Majesty that he will be pleased to call the parliament together in that kingdom and give them leave to sit to pass some bills absolutely necessary for the preservation of that kingdom, which otherwise might be of fatal consequence to this nation.

Sir Robert Cotton (of Post Office) was against that, for it might be fatal to let them pass what bills they please; they may make that kingdom independent of this.

Col. Granville was for an address to His Majesty to put a stop to the further granting away any of the forfeited Irish estates and that the residue might be taken care of and let out to the best advantage, and I doubt not they will yield you a good sum of money the next year for carrying on the war. *Mr. Boyle* to the same. And *Mr. Smith*, and further that the Commissioners of the Revenue might be ordered to take a particular account of the forfeited estates, both real and personal—what they were, how disposed of, and where the residue is.

Mr. Waller (of Bucks.): I think your address ought to consist of several parts, one of which that the Protestants there ought to have agents here to attend His Majesty in their behalf.

Sir Christopher Musgrave: I am informed there was a subsequent article made after the surrender of Limerick which did much mischief to the Protestant interest in that kingdom and restored many considerable Irish estates which would otherwise have been forfeited.

This I think fit to take notice of in your address. I should be glad to know how that article came to be made when there was no necessity or obligation for it. Then to desire that an account may be taken of the Irish forfeitures of all sorts and be prepared against the next meeting of the parliament.

Mr. Palmes was for making some previous votes beforehand whereon to ground your address and in order to it to pass this first: that upon the informations this House has received, they are satisfied there has been great abuses and miscarriages committed in Ireland. *Col. Granville, Sir Francis Winnington, Mr. Mordaunt, Mr. Goodwin Wharton* to the same, and *Mr. Clarke*.

So the question was stated and resolved: That upon the informations given to this House it doth appear that there have been great abuses and mismanagements in the affairs of Ireland.

Then another question was stated and resolved: That an humble address be presented to His Majesty setting forth the abuses and mismanagements of affairs in Ireland. And a committee was appointed to prepare and bring in the same upon the debate of the House.

Committees adjourned.

So adjourned till tomorrow morning 8 of the clock.[1]

Saturday, 25 February

Mr. Hoby was ordered to carry up to the Lords Mr. Pitt's private bill and acquaint them this House had agreed to the same with an amendment to which they desire their Lordships' concurrence.

Sir Miles Cook and Sir John Hoskins, two Masters in Chancery, brought the message from the Lords.

Mr. Arnold complained to the House that there had been an offer made to him by a gentleman of £100 per annum to bribe him from prosecuting the bill for prohibiting the use of lotteries.

On which the House cried out, 'name him, name him'. Which *he* did, and said it was one Mr. Radford of the Temple and one Mr. Clifton.

Some would have had them summoned to attend the House to give an account of it. Others were for referring it to the committee the bill was. And it was ordered accordingly.

Then the House immediately resolved itself into a committee to consider of ways and means for raising the supply; Mr. Charles Montagu took the Chair of the committee. And they agreed upon

---

[1] The House had sat till about 7 p.m.; Bodleian Carte MS. 130, f. 345.

a resolution for raising the remaining £200,000 (which was taken off from the continued impositions) by adding two years more to the time for the duties on East India goods and continuing that bill to the 10th of November 1697.

So *he* left the Chair and reported the said resolution, to which the House agreed.

It was moved to be an instruction to the committee upon the second reading of the bill for the review of the poll that the King might name commissioners, as also that the former poll bill might be explained in several particulars which was somewhat doubtful, and it would thereby make the bill come to something which otherwise would come to little. As to commissioners, it was agreed the committee might name what they would, but could not bring [in] an explanatory clause without order. So ordered accordingly.

Then the House resumed the adjourned debate about the East India Company.

Sir Ralph Dutton, Sir John Morton, Sir Charles Sedley, and *Mr. Hutchinson* were all for the address to His Majesty to dissolve the present Company. *Sir John Lowther* and *Sir John Guise* were for it, too.

Sir Richard Temple was against it.

Sir Thomas Clarges desired the former address and the King's answer to it might be read, and they were accordingly.

Sir Joseph Tredenham, Serj. Blencowe, Sir Samuel Dashwood, Col. Pery, Sir Joseph Herne, Sir Thomas Littleton, Mr. Goldwell, and *Mr. Godolphin* were all against the address.

But *Mr. Smith, Sir Robert Howard, Sir Christopher Musgrave, Mr. Harley, Mr. Finch,* and *Sir Edward Seymour* were for it.

However, after some debate, the question was put and resolved: That an humble address be presented to His Majesty that he will please to dissolve the East India Company upon three years' warning to the said Company, according to the power reserved in their charter.

Resolved that the whole House would go up with the address. And it was ordered that such members of this House as are of the Privy Council do wait on His Majesty to know his pleasure when he will be attended with the address.

Mr. Clarke presented the petition of one Bradbury, etc., relating to the orphans' bill. Ordered to lie on the Table till that bill comes on.

All committees were revived.

Several members were added to divers committees.

So adjourned till 8 on Monday morning.

Monday, 27 February

Mr. Luttrell was ordered to carry up to the Lords the engrossed bill of the Bishop of Bangor and acquaint them this House hath agreed to the same without any amendments.

Mr. Waller (of York) was ordered to carry up Mr. Towers' private bill with the same message.

Mr. Boyle was also ordered to carry up to the Lords the Lord Shannon's bill with the same message.

Sir Miles Cook and Sir John Hoskins brought the message from the Lords.

The engrossed bill from the Lords to indemnify such as had acted for Their Majesties' service in defence of the kingdom was read the first time.

Sir Edward Seymour desired it might have a second reading.

Sir Christopher Musgrave was against this bill, it being in his opinion a very dangerous one, having a clause in it that sets aside the habeas corpus act.

Sir John Guise: This bill is only to indemnify such as acted in defence of your government and not to make them liable to suits if they have done anything in time of danger that was not by law so strictly justifiable. Otherwise you will have few persons that will appear in defence of it.

Mr. Smith, Sir John Lowther, Mr. Ettrick, Sir Walter Yonge, and *Mr. Goldwell* were for a second reading that it might be amended if anything amiss in it.

Mr. Norris, Mr. Hopkins, Mr. P. Foley, and *Sir John Bolles* were against it.

Mr. Henry Boyle was for throwing it out.

So the question was put that this bill be read a second time. House divided thereon—Yeas went out.

		Mr. Montagu	
	Yeas		124
		Mr. Herbert	
Tellers for the			
		Sir John Bolles	
	Noes		76
		Mr. H. Boyle	

Engrossed bill from the Lords for the reversal of a fine and re-coveries touching an estate in Wales in contest between the Lord Jeffreys and the Earl of Pembroke was read the first time. Several persons spoke against it as a matter of great concern, touching the inheritances and settlements of the subject. It was ordered a second reading.

Sir Christopher Musgrave desired that a day might be appointed for it, and that it might not be read but in a full house, and that all the members of the long robe might then attend, and that counsel might be heard upon the same.

Mr. P. Foley: This is a bill to shake the common assurances of the nation, which I hope you will be very cautious in. There are two cases like this since 1660—one Powell's case, and another. In the first, the bill was read the first time and ordered a second reading the next sessions, which I desire may be so in this.

Mr. Smith: This is not to shake the assurances of the nation but to set aside some errors that were made in the levying a fine and suffering two recoveries, which were illegally amended, and only putting the party in the same condition he was as if those amendments had not been made. As to hearing of counsel, that I suppose you will do on the second reading of it.

Sir Edward Seymour: You are not only now in your legislative capacity but in your judicial capacity, and as such I think you ought to hear counsel and to hear the witnesses so that you may do that which is just and equal.

Sir Thomas Clarges was against appointing counsel to be heard unless desired by the parties themselves.

So it was ordered to be read a second time on Thursday next, and that the members of the long robe do then attend the service of the House, and that the counsel and witnesses of the parties on both sides (for the Lord Pembroke and for the Lord Jeffreys) do then attend to be heard at the Bar of the House to the merits of the cause upon the said bill if they think fit.

Mr. P. Foley complained of the strange method now used in pressing men, which is grown worse than ever. They press shopkeepers, apprentices, seamen for land service, and keep them in custody till they can send them away and handcuff them as if they were criminals. That one Thomas Anderton, a seaman, was served so, and he is now at the door with another to give you an account thereof.

So one Thomas Anderton and Joseph Streater were called in and gave an account of this matter at large: that they were pressed and kept at the King's Head in Parker's Lane, and that he was forced to send to the captain he served on board of, who with much ado got him off; that there are 30 or 40 more kept prisoners there, one of which paid £20 taxes to the King; and that one Capt. Winter pressed him—he lives at the Ship & Greyhound in Whitefriars.

So they withdrew, and the House debated what to do thereon. At last it was resolved that Winter should be sent for into custody of the Serjeant at Arms. And that the Serjeant should go to the houses of Bright and Davis where the men [were][1] kept and bring them with them to the House. And that the Speaker send his warrant for the same, directing the Sheriffs of London to be assisting.

Sir Thomas Vernon presented a petition from the Lord Mayor, Aldermen, and Common Council of London, praying to be heard by their counsel what they have to offer against the bill for satisfying the debts due to the orphans.

Sir Thomas Clarges opposed the receiving of it.

But, however, upon the question it was brought up and read, and a long debate whether they should be heard by their counsel. House divided thereon—Yeas went out.

		Sir Robert Cotton	
	Yeas		99
		Sir Robert Clayton	
Tellers for the			
		Sir William Pritchard	
	Noes		84
		Mr. Goldwell	

So they were ordered to be heard by their counsel on Wednesday next before the House go into a committee upon the said bill.

The bill for reviving and continuing laws expired and now expiring was read the last time.

Sir Edward Seymour offered a rider to exclude the City of Exeter from being a port to which wool may be imported from Ireland, being no advantage to the city and was but a pretence of which the nation is prejudiced by carrying wool into France. So it was received, read thrice, and made part of the bill.[2]

---

[1] 'where' in MS.
[2] The proposal and approval of this rider is omitted in the *Journal*.

Mr. Arnold tendered a rider to revive the act of poor prisoners for one year. But it was refused to be received, being a very dangerous precedent.

So the bill was passed, and the title, and Mr. Attorney ordered to carry it to the Lords for their concurrence.

The Serjeant returned from the houses he went to about the pressed men, and they were all called in. One Robert Davis, a marshal to the Provost Marshal General, who had them in custody, and was examined touching the matter, as also eight or 10 of the pressed men that were in his house were examined touching the same. And it appeared to be a most cruel and barbarous piece of practice; some of the men appeared to be kidnapped and sold for soldiers, one or two of them were deserters.

So being all withdrawn, *Mr. Harley* moved that these poor men might be discharged and that Davis, the marshal, might be made an example of. *Mr. Harcourt*, *Mr. Smith*, and others to the same.

So they were all called in again to the Bar and were discharged, and Davis, the marshal, there made to unhandcuff them. There were nine of them in all.

All committees were adjourned.

So the House adjourned till 8 tomorrow morning.

Tuesday, 28 February

Mr. Arnold was ordered to carry up to the Lords Sir John Williams' private bill and to acquaint them this House hath agreed to the same with some amendments to which they desire their Lordships' concurrence.

Mr. Travers was ordered to carry up Mr. Price's private bill with the same message. And Mr. Travers was ordered to put their Lordships in mind of a bill passed by this House and sent up to their Lordships entitled 'a bill to prevent delays at the quarter sessions'.

Mr. Chadwick was ordered to carry up to the Lords Mr. Walcott's private bill to make salt water fresh for their concurrence.

Then the House went upon the amendments made by the Lords to the bill for delivering declarations to prisoners and agreed to them with an amendment. And Mr. Goldwell was ordered to carry it up to the Lords and acquaint them this House hath agreed to the amendments made by their Lordships with an amendment, to which amendment this House desires their Lordships' concurrence.

Sir John Darell presented the petition of Henry Acourt and others, and *Sir Joseph Tredenham* presented the petition of Mr. Vaughan, against the bill for taking away lotteries. [They] were received and read and to lie on the Table till that bill is reported.

Mr. Serj. Trenchard reported he had been with the Lords to desire a conference, and they had agreed to the same and appointed to-morrow at 1 of the clock in the Painted Chamber.

Capt. Winter, being at the door, was called in. And being examined touching the complaint against him for pressing, he disowned that he ever did it, having no commission or power to do any such thing.

So the Serjeant at Arms was ordered to carry him before the Chief Justice to be examined, and that Thomas Anderton do attend his Lordship also to give his information, in order to the prosecution of the said Capt. Winter.

Lieut. Scott and Ensign Penny were called in, and giving a fair account of themselves were dismissed any further attendance.

But Davis, the deputy marshal, was ordered to be taken into custody of the Serjeant at Arms.

Mr. Clarke was ordered to carry up to the Lords the engrossed bill to prevent false and double returns of members to parliament for their concurrence.

The House, according to order, went into a committee on the bill for encouragement of privateers; Mr. Attorney General to the Chair. The committee having done the bill last sitting but only now to receive clauses, the Chairman offered a clause he had prepared by order of the committee touching prizes taken in the Straits, West Indies, etc., which was read twice and made part of the bill.

Mr. P. Foley offered a clause for the privateers to have all the goods taken in French prizes that were not of the growth of France. Read twice and made part of the bill.

Sir Walter Yonge offered a clause to prevent the abuses committed by privateers in taking prizes here in our ports. Read twice and made part of the bill.

Mr. Clarke offered a clause to give privateers a full moiety of all such ships as they shall take carrying wool into France. Read twice and made part of the bill.

Mr. Pery offered a clause to ascertain what each captain, etc. shall have for salvage of any ship—in some cases an eighth part, in some a third, and in some a moiety. Read twice, and amendments made to it, and made part of the bill.

So the committee finished the bill and ordered the Chairman to report it. Speaker resumed the Chair, and *Mr. Attorney* reported they had gone through the bill and made several amendments which they had directed him to report. Ordered to be made on Thursday next.

So adjourned till 8 tomorrow morning.

Wednesday, 1 March

An engrossed bill of William Stephens read the third time.

Col. Pery spoke against it as an unjust bill.

Question put for passing it. House divided thereon—Yeas went out.

	Mr. Bickerstaffe	
Yeas		32
	Mr. Goldwell	
Tellers for the		
	Sir John Parsons[1]	
Noes		33
	Mr. Pery	

So it passed in the negative.

Col. Titus presented a petition from Ann Wright and *Mr. Goldwell* presented another from John Chappel, praying that they might be considered as orphans of the City. Received and read and ordered to be considered of when that bill comes on.

The engrossed bill from the Lords to indemnify those that have acted for Their Majesties' service was read the second time.

Sir Walter Yonge and *Mr. P. Foley* thought it a dangerous bill.

Sir Edward Seymour and *Mr. Hampden* were for it, being only to indemnify those who act for the defence of the government in dangerous times. *Sir John Lowther* (of Lowther) to the same.

Mr. Price was against the whole bill for that it remits all the extravagant actions done by great men, and puts it in the power oʟ six Privy Councillors to imprison whom they please, and renders the English liberties thereby very precarious.

Sir John Bolles thought it a pernicious bill because it pardons all illegal actions already done by our ministers and licenses them to do the like for the time to come.

Mr. Boscawen was for it.

---

[1] Mr. Parsons in *CJ*, x. 838.

Mr. John Howe was for committing the bill for the sake of the first part of the bill.

Mr. P. Foley would consent to the committing it on condition it should extend to indemnify only such as had acted in the country and not our Privy Councillors here.

Sir Joseph Tredenham thought the former part of the bill might be necessary but was against the latter part.

Mr. Machell was against the whole bill.

Sir Christopher Musgrave liked no part of the bill, but if any of it only the first part with this declaration—that it shall not be brought into precedent for the future. *Mr. Harley* and *Mr. Goodwin Wharton* to the same.

So it was referred to a Committee of the Whole House upon the debate of the House.

The time of the conference being come, the names of the managers (which drew up the reasons) were read over and they were appointed managers and went up to the conference. And after a little time *Mr. Serj. Trenchard* returned and reported that they had been at the place appointed for the conference but had noticed that the Lords were not sitting.

Speaker said this was in the nature of refusing a conference with the House and a breach of the good correspondence between the two Houses.

Col. Titus: I know no precedent of this matter but I think you may lawfully demand a conference upon some matters relating to the last conference.

Sir Edward Seymour: This is an accident I have never met with but I think your regular way is to desire a conference to preserve the good correspondence between the two Houses. *Sir Richard Temple* and *Mr. Hampden* to the same.

So it was resolved that a conference be desired with the Lords upon the method of proceedings between the two Houses. Several ancient members were added to the former managers, and they are to prepare reasons to be offered at the same and are to meet tomorrow morning at 9 of the clock in the Speaker's Chamber.

So the House, according to order, went upon the orphans' business, and the counsel for the Lord Mayor, Aldermen, and Common Council of London (viz., Mr. Serj. Lovell, Mr. Ward, Sir Bartholomew Shower, and Mr. Crisp) [and] the orphans had counsel there. The counsel for the City were heard to the matter in the bill at large.

Then there was a dispute whether the orphans' counsel should be heard, there being no order for their having any counsel. So they were all ordered to withdraw and the matter was much debated. Those that were against the bill were for hearing their counsel to delay the matter; those that were favourable to the orphans were against it. House divided thereon—Yeas went out.

	Sir Walter Yonge	
Yeas		101
	Sir John Guise	
Tellers for the		
	Sir Joseph Tredenham	
Noes		96
	Mr. Gwyn	

So the parties were called in again and the counsel for the orphans heard, who said very little because they would not obstruct the House's going into a committee on the bill.

Then they all withdrew. And upon that the Whig party (who were no friends to the orphans) moved to adjourn. This was debated, and said to be irregular to move to adjourn in the midst of a debate. However, the question of adjournment was put. House divided thereon —Yeas went forth.

	Sir William Strickland	
Yeas		55
	Mr. Randyll	
Tellers for the		
	Sir Joseph Tredenham	
Noes		136
	Mr. Fenwick	

When they came in again, *Mr. Attorney General, Mr. Smith, Mr. Montagu* (who being of those that went out) took notice of the Speaker's irregularity in sending the Yeas out—which ought not in this case, being it was a question of adjournment and after 1 of the clock; otherwise if it had been before 1.

But the *Speaker* said he thought it very regular, being there was an Order of the Day to go into a committee upon the orphans' bill and this question of adjournment was against that, for if it be carried to adjourn no other question can be put after. (And this seemed the best opinion. Besides, it was proposed, too, in the midst of a debate.)

Several petitions of persons praying to have equal consideration with the orphans were referred to the committee that bill is.

Sir Miles Cook and [Sir Robert Legard],[1] two Masters in Chancery, came with a message from the Lords to excuse their not meeting the Commons at a conference: that their Speaker lived two miles out of town and the badness of the road at present was the only occasion of their Lordships' not coming to the conference at the time appointed.

Then the House, according to order, went into a committee upon the orphans' bill; Mr. Harcourt took the Chair of the committee. The Clerk read the bill over; then the several petitions referred to them he read over. Chairman read over the preamble and postponed it. So they proceeded on the bill upon the clauses in order by filling up the blanks, etc. But the Whig party opposed it all they could by debating everything and making long speeches, even upon frivolous pretences, and putting the committee to the trouble of dividing several times and three or four times upon the only question of the Chairman's leaving the Chair (and all to excuse the Whigs in the City, who had got the government thereof chiefly into their hands and might thereby pay towards the orphans' charge). However, it was still carried against the Whigs and the committee sat till 9 and made some progress, which he was ordered to report and to desire leave to sit again.

So Speaker resumed the Chair, and the *Chairman* reported. And it was ordered to go into a committee again on Saturday next.

All committees were adjourned.

So adjourned till 8 tomorrow morning.

Thursday, 2 March

Upon the report of the bill against lotteries from the committee, exception was taken to it that the committee had not prepared a clause against wagering according to the debate of the House. However, the bill was ordered with the amendments to be engrossed.

Sir Miles Cook and Sir Adam Oatley, two Masters in Chancery, brought the message from the Lords.

Mr. Attorney General reported the bill to encourage privateers from the committee with the amendments, and the same were agreed unto.

Col. Pery offered a clause to prevent the embezzling the goods of a prize. It was received, read twice, and made part of the bill.

[1] Blank in MS.; from *CJ*, x. 839.

Attorney General offered a clause to require the officers of the Admiralty to give this act in charge and in their instructions to all men-of-war and privateers that they may not pretend ignorance. Received, read twice, and made part of the bill.

Mr. *Goodwin Wharton* offered a clause to give privateers that go into the Mediterranean leave to carry half their tonnage in goods, so also those that go to the East Indies, being it would encourage them to send privateers to those parts, which otherwise they would not, being long voyages and must go unladen.

Mr. *Attorney* and others spoke against it because it would ruin all the merchants and forestall their markets or make all merchants turn privateering or else run away without their convoy for the advantage of a market.

Others would have merchants empowered in their commissions to take prizes, which will increase the customs and make the merchants go with ships of greater force.

Said for this clause that it would increase the consumption of our manufactures by going half-laden with goods, and so while others are preparing at the port they go to the ships may go out a privateering, whereby they will lose no time. This the Dutch and French do, and there is nothing that makes this practice unlawful now but only the Admiralty require bonds from the men-of-war and privateers that they shall not carry out any goods. Then this clause will encourage men to set out large privateers, thereby to annoy your enemies the most in the Mediterranean and other distant places where their trade lies most, and by the profit of the half-freight of goods they will be better able to bear the charge of the voyage.

The clause was read twice. And on the question to make it part of the bill, the House divided—Yeas went out.

		Sir Samuel Barnardiston	
	Yeas		101
		Sir John Darell	
Tellers for the			
		Mr. Colt	
	Noes		77
		Mr. Goldwell	

So the bill with the amendments was ordered to be engrossed.

The House went upon the amendments to the bill for punishing mutineers and deserters. Which being read were severally put and agreed to, and the Lord Cornbury ordered to carry up the bill to the Lords and acquaint them this House hath agreed to the same.

Then they went on those made to the bill for settling etc. the Greenland trade and agreed to the same, and Sir Samuel Barnardiston ordered to carry it up with the like message.

The House did the like to those made unto the bill for preservation of the game, and the Lord Eland was ordered to carry that up also with the like message, but afterwards Mr. Waller was ordered to carry it up.

Mr. Waller was ordered to go up with the message to the Lords to put them in mind of the bill to prevent frauds by clandestine mortgages and also of the bill for better discovery of judgements. He was also ordered to desire a conference with the Lords upon the subject-matter of the amendments to the bill entitled 'an act to prevent malicious informations in the Court of King's Bench', etc.

All committees revived.

So adjourned till 8 tomorrow morning.

Friday, 3 March

Mr. Waller reported the bill for making the river Salwerp navigable with some amendments. Exception was taken to the management of this bill at the committee—that it was carried on with less than eight members, etc. Therefore, the bill was recommitted.

Then the House, according to order, went into a committee upon the bill for the review of the quarterly poll; Mr. Attorney General to the Chair of the committee. And they proceeded upon the bill to the clause about the commissioners.

The Court party were for having the King name them out of the act of 4s. in the pound, whereby the tax would rise to more and prevent a dispute between the Lords and you about naming the commissioners, which the Lords pretend to name commissioners for themselves in poll bills. But this was opposed, and said it had not been found so beneficial and the King's naming some more than others would cause heats and divisions in the country. And for the other reason of the Lords naming commissioners, they have generally done it in poll bills for their personal estates, but here having the same commissioners generally as upon the 4s. act, the Lords will not break in upon that nor is it proper in this case because the Lords did not name any commissioners in the original poll act.

Therefore agreed they should be the same as on the land tax.

The time of the conference being come, the Attorney General left the Chair of the committee. And it was agreed to go into a committee again as soon as the conference was over.

So the managers' names were read over and they went to the conference. The managers returned and *Mr. Serj. Trenchard* reported from the conference: That they had been at the conference with the Lords upon the subject-matter of the amendments to the bill entitled 'an act to prevent malicious informations in the Court of King's Bench' etc. and that they had delivered in their reasons and left the bill with the Lords.

Then the House went into committee again on the poll bill, and Mr. Attorney to the Chair, and the committee proceeded in the bill.

It was proposed to tax yeomen as gentlemen. But opposed because the committee have not power to raise a new tax by any instruction to them, as this would be if admitted. So let fall.

Mr. Clarke offered a clause to make cracked money current. Received and read twice and made part of the bill.

So they proceeded in the bill and made an end of it, which he was ordered to report. Speaker resumed the Chair, and *Mr. Attorney* reported the committee had finished the bill and made some amendments which they had directed him to report. Ordered to be made tomorrow.

Several members were added to divers committees.

So adjourned till 8 tomorrow morning.

Saturday, 4 March

Mr. Waller was ordered to carry up the private bill for sale of Thomas Bromhall's interest in the office of Warden of the Fleet and to acquaint the Lords that this House hath agreed to the same with some amendments. Mr. Waller was also to carry up the bill for naturalization of several persons and to acquaint the Lords that this House hath agreed to the amendments made by their Lordships unto the same. He was also ordered to put them in mind of the bill touching the collection of the duty of aulnage and transferring it to the Customhouse.

Mr. Clarke was ordered to carry up to the Lords the engrossed bill for the exchange of lands between the Bishop of London and the Earl of Monmouth and to acquaint them this House hath agreed to the same with some amendments to which their Lordships' concurrence is desired.

The message from the Lords was brought by Sir Miles Cook and [Mr. Meredith],[1] two Masters in Chancery.

Mr. Goodwin Wharton reported the address from the committee concerning the state of Ireland setting forth the abuses and mismanagement of affairs in that kingdom by the miseries of free quarter and licentiousness of the soldiers, by recruiting His Majesty's troops with Irish papists, by granting protections to Irish papists, by reversing the outlawries of several for high treason not within the Articles of Limerick, by letting the forfeited estates at underrates, by embezzlement of His Majesty's stores, and the additional article made to the Articles of Limerick, offering expedient for the redress thereof.

It was received, read over; and no exception being taken to any part of it, it was not passed paragraph by paragraph as usual but agreed to on one single question. It was also resolved to be presented by the whole House and that the members of this House as are of His Majesty's Privy Council do humbly know his pleasure when he will be attended by this House.

Mr. Clarke offered it to the consideration of the House whether not best for the greater solemnity of the matter to have the Lords' concurrence thereto.

But it was thought upon consideration not to be so convenient because perhaps disputes and differences might thereby happen between the Lords and us which might obstruct the thing if not lose it quite—the sessions being so near an end. And there are some things in it which you offer as a remedy—viz. the laying of accounts before you—which you will not allow the Lords to meddle with. So it was waived.

Mr. Attorney General reported the bill for the review of the poll with the amendments, which were read and agreed unto.

Mr. Hutchinson offered a clause to restrain the officers of the Exchequer or others to take any fees of the Receivers of the Taxes other than such ancient fees as shall be allowed by the Barons of the Exchequer. Received, read twice, and made part of the bill.

Mr. Harley offered a clause for laying a penalty on Receivers if they do not return duplicates of the taxes into the Exchequer. Received, read twice, and made part of the bill.

[1] Blank in MS.; from *CJ*, x. 842.

So the bill with the amendments was ordered to be engrossed.

Mr. Montagu moved that it might be an instruction to the Committee of the Whole House in the orphans' business to consider of further or other ways for satisfying the debts due to the orphans for that the way the bill goes is absolutely destructive of the government of the City.

But the *Speaker* said the committee could not bring in a new tax but must proceed in this case as usual in others.

So Speaker left the Chair and House went into a committee upon the bill for satisfying the orphans; Mr. Harcourt to the Chair of the committee.

So the committee proceeded in the bill. But the fanatic and Whig party gave it all the obstruction possible as before.

So after some hours, he was ordered to report further progress and to desire leave to sit again, all which *he* did. And it was ordered again to go into a committee on Tuesday next.

Mr. Harcourt, the Chairman, moved the House that having extraordinary business which called him into the country, they would be pleased to dispense with his attendance in the House and dismiss him the Chair of this committee. And he had leave accordingly.[1]

So adjourned till 8 on Monday morning.[2]

Monday, 6 March

Mr. Hungerford was ordered to carry up to the Lords Sir Robert Smith's private bill and to acquaint them this House hath agreed to the same with some amendments to which their Lordships' concurrence is desired.

Sir Jonathan Jennings presented the petition of Robert Davis, deputy to the Provost Marshal.

The engrossed bill for prohibiting the use of lotteries was read the third time.

Mr. Arnold presented a rider on behalf of Col. Vaughan to preserve a debt of his for payment of which he hath so much by letters patent out of the farm of this lottery and to transfer the same debt upon the excise.

But said it was irregular to charge the revenue by way of a rider; it ought to come from a Committee of the Whole House.

---

[1] There is no entry of this in the *Journal*.
[2] 9 o'clock in *CJ*, x. 843.

However, it was received. And upon the question to read it, the House divided—Yeas went out.

		Sir John Knight	
	Yeas		30
		Mr. Shakerley	
Tellers for the			
		Sir Samuel Barnardiston	
	Noes		72
		Mr. Waller (of Bucks.)	

Col. Pery offered a rider to prevent wagering on the events of war, etc.

Received and read once. But exception was taken to it that it was too general and might be construed to restrain the insurance of merchant ships. So it was on the question denied a second reading.

So bill passed, then the title, and Col. Pery ordered to carry it up to the Lords for their concurrence.

Sir John Fleet, Lord Mayor of London, being newly elected a member for the City of London (in the room of Sir William Turner, deceased), came into the House and took the oaths and the test at the Table and after sat in the House.

The engrossed bill to encourage privateers was read the third time.

Mr. Montagu moved to leave out the last clause in the bill though it was an engrossed bill, which was that licensing privateers to carry out goods, because it would be destructive absolutely of the Turkey trade and others that are settled by charters, for these sorts of ships will always go before and forestall the market and thereby ruin all your regulated trade. *Sir Samuel Dashwood, Sir Thomas Vernon, Mr. Nicholas* (of the Customhouse), and *Sir Charles Sedley* to the same.

Sir Edward Seymour said this would elude the whole act and carry on a trade with France, and it is no new thing to take a whole clause even out of an engrossed bill.

So upon the question for this clause to stand part of the bill, it was carried in the negative. So that clause was rased out.

Attorney General tendered a rider for the privateer to have his share of the prizes within three days after on the penalty of double the sum detained. Received, read thrice, and made part of the bill.

So the bill was passed, then the title, and Mr. Attorney was ordered to carry it to the Lords for their concurrence.

Sir [John] Frankl[in] and Sir John Hoskins, two Masters in Chancery, brought the message from the Lords.

Then the House went upon the Order of the Day and the engrossed bill from the Lords for setting aside amendments and alterations made in the records and writs and fine and two recoveries in Wales was read the second time. Then the counsel and witnesses for the Earl of Pembroke and those for the Lord Jeffreys and his lady were called in. The counsel for the Lord Pembroke in behalf of the bill were Sir William Williams, Mr. Serj. Levinz, and Mr. Filmer. Those for the Lord Jeffreys were Sir Thomas Powis, Mr. Ward, and Mr. Hollis. So the counsel for the Lord Pembroke to make good the bill began.

Sir William Williams urged that these amendments were made 13 years after both the recoveries suffered without which they are very naught. They were amended by one that was a *bene placito* judge. The writ of covenant upon the record was teste'd 1 April 27 Car. II and there is a new writ of covenant made teste before—viz. 1 November 26 Car. II. No one can deny this to be vicious and this they have amended. But to warrant it there is no writing nor any other thing to show it was only the mistake of the clerk. This amendment was not made only 13 years after the fault committed but also after the death of the party that suffered the recovery. Now by this the Earl of Pembroke hath a manifest injury. He is remainderman in tail to this estate which the fine would not cut off but the recovery only wherein the mistake is. The fine was to make a good tenant to the freehold which being teste'd the same time with the writ of entry or *quid ei deforceat* it was not good because there was no good tenant to the freehold, wherefore necessary to alter the date of the writ of covenant and make it prior to the writ of entry. There is also another error, being a mistake of the commissioners' names between the *dedimus* and the commission.

Serj. Levinz: This bill is not to destroy the fine and recovery nor give the Lord Pembroke the estate but only to set his Lordship in the same condition he was before those amendments made, which this bill only sets aside, so that if these amendments can be made by law they may still notwithstanding this bill, if they are but mistakes of the clerk. They may be amended by the statute 8 H. VI c. 12 which provides no judgement shall be reversed for such errors, so then the Lord Jeffreys is safe. But on the other side, if the errors are such as the law does not warrant to be amended the Lord Pembroke, I hope, shall not be without remedy, but that this bill shall set the amendments aside that he may come at the errors, which he cannot otherwise without the help of this bill. Now the errors are many: (1) the writ of covenant and the writ of entry have one date; (2) then there is one that took the fine as a commissioner, one Herbert Saladine, that was not in the *dedimus* for taking it; (3) then it is a writ of entry *sur le seisen* in the post, which is never in Wales; (4) then the *quid ei deforceat* is teste the 2nd and returnable the 17th so there wants a day of 15 days between the teste and the return, which ought to be in all original writs exclusive of the teste day. As to the case of Gage, which I know will be insisted on, it is misreported in [Sir Edward Coke, *The Fifth Part of the Reports*, f. 45*b*];[1] it is otherwise in [Sir Francis] Moore's *Report*, f. [571], and the pleadings therein are at large in the Lord Coke's [*A Book of*] *Entries*, f. 252. It will be objected that recoveries are the common assurances, so will receive a favourable construction and which the judges may amend. As to that, at common law they were strict; they could not amend anything after a judgement. Then came the statute 14 E. III c. [1] which gives power to amend the mistakes of a letter; then 8 H. VI c. [12] gives power to amend the mistakes of the clerk (that is, such mistakes as he hath instructions to have made right), and so is Blackamore's case. But matters of law are not amendable. The mistakes in the present case are substantial ones and such as none of the statutes warrant the amendment of. And then as to the merits of the case, the old Lord Pembroke had a power to give away the estate in fee, before and after this recovery; then there is no limitation over to the issue. And for the jointure, that is out upon the estate; that is not touched and there is a proviso in the bill for the daughter to have the mother's portion, so that she will be no loser.

Mr. Filmer: It is a very dangerous thing to leave it in the power of judges to make alterations in records. Then for the thing itself, it is no new thing for parliaments to meddle in these matters, for in Sir Peter Vanlore's and Powell's case you set aside several fines and recoveries.

Sir Thomas Powis (for the Lord Jeffreys and against the bill): The contest before you is between the heir general of the late Lord Pembroke, the Lady Charlotte his daughter (married to the Lord Jeffreys), and the special heir in tail, the now Lord Pembroke. It is in a matter that concerns all England, and Wales particularly. In September 1675 there was a deed of settlement of the late Lord Pembroke of his estate

---

[1] Blank in MS.

upon his marriage with the Lady Charlotte's mother. In that deed was a limitation of the uses of the fines and recoveries that were to be levied to his right heirs. Thus all things rested several years, being thought very safe. But about the year 1687 the now Earl of Pembroke brought writs of error to reverse those fines and recoveries, at which they were alarmed and it was time then to look after that matter. And these mistakes being found out, it was moved below in the Great Sessions to amend the same; and rules were given to show cause why they should not, and after cause not being shown they were amended by the court below by Mr. Justice Geeres with the consent of the other judge, Mr. Justice Wynne. The bill does not say there was any corruption in the judge so that at best it was but an error in judgement. But now as to the mistakes, they are—with submission— amendable in law. As to the case of Gage, it is true that case is in Moore and in my Lord Coke, too, and the judgement reversed, but not for what they say but for want of proclamations on the fine; and so is the Lord Coke, so the Lord Hales (Commonplace book, lit. amendment num. 67).[1] There is also the case of Goswell and Brown, Trin. [blank], and several other cases where mistakes in writs of entry, covenant, etc. have been amended. Then as to the other, the supplying the want of a *dedimus*, no lawyer will say but if there was once one the court may supply it if it be after lost. But suppose these were such mistakes as were not amendable, the question is whether you will by your legislative power set aside amendments that are actually made when there is hardly anything more encouraged than amendments. It appears plainly here was the intent of the party who had the ownership and the right in the estate and power to do this, to settle the estate thus, which by a slip shall now be avoided. There have been attempts to do the like things in parliament, as in the manuscript of the Lord Dyer's[2] *Reports*, the case of the Lord Powis and Vernon, the case of the Lord Derby the last sessions—the bills were thrown out. If this bill should pass, mighty mischiefs may ensue. No man is certain or safe in his estate if all mistakes in fines and recoveries amended shall be set aside. The judges here cannot amend original writs because they come out of another court, the Chancery, where they amend them frequently. But in Wales the judges have a power not only in matters of law but in equity also, so frequently amend original writs there and even judicial writs, too.

---

[1] ? The MS. 'Great Commonplace Book of Reports or Cases in the Law' left among Sir Matthew Hale's MSS.   [2] Sir James Dyer.

Mr. Ward: It is most certain the intent of the old Earl of Pembroke was to do what he has done, and he had full power to do it. But by the persons employed in it arises the mistakes which are amended, and now this bill is to make them bad again—which I hope you will not. Nothing is more common motion in Chancery, or rather petition, to make new original writs to supply the defect of those lost, to amend mistakes in old ones; of this there are several precedents—one in Moore's *Report*, f. 125, Norris and Braybrook.

Mr. Hollis: This, I believe, is the first precedent wherever complaint was made against judges for amending. It has been a common saying: blessed is the mending hand. There is nothing more common where an original is lost to file a new one to amend errors in them.

Then several witnesses were examined for the Lord Jefferys—as Edwards an attorney, one David Thomas an attorney—who proved it to be the common practice in Wales to make out *dedimus*'s with blanks for the commissioners' names which are inserted after, sometimes after the writs are sealed. And the witness Thomas owned he inserted the name of Herbert Saladine into the *dedimus* after he had it from the Cursitor. Two precedents were produced in the Lord North's time where amendments had been made in a case just like this.

Then witnesses were examined on behalf of the Lord Pembroke. Mr. Philpot testified the *dedimus* for the recovery was 'Roberto' with a blank, and 'Herbert Saladine' was not in; and I was offered 100 guineas to say I had seen the *dedimus* with Herbert Saladine's name in it. One Gibbs testified the judge did not amend the mistake but ordered a new writ, which was made out and the record on the roll remained as it was.

So the counsel and witnesses having done, they all withdrew.

Paul Foley: This is a great case before you—several books cited and many matters of fact stated. I shall, therefore, that the matter may be well considered of, move you to adjourn it. I can never find but one case in parliament to this purpose, that of Powell; it was three days hearing in this House and four days after considering.

Sir John Lowther (of Lowther) desired this bill might go on as other bills use to do and not be postponed.

Sir Robert Howard informed the House that the intention of the late Lord Pembroke was that his estate should go to the heir male and not the heir general, and that the only reason of levying the fine, etc. was to enable him to make a jointure.

Mr. Harcourt spoke very largely against the bill as being to disinherit the heir at law, who is always favoured at a time when he is under age and so not in a condition to appear for himself. It tends also to the undoing of all settlements and breaking of all families and goes against the intent of the parties.

Mr. Herbert was zealously for the bill.

Sir George Hutchins strongly against it, and *Mr. Brewer*.

Mr. Ettrick was strongly for the bill and urged several cases like ours, as Gobert and [? Wright] in [Sir George] Cro[ke], [*The First Part of the Reports . . . during the reign of*] *Eliz*[*abeth*]; so in Herbert and Binion's case.

Sir Christopher Musgrave was against the bill, and the rather for that he observed the conjuror of the fine lived eight years after the fine levied and might have limited it otherwise if he would.

Sir Richard Temple, Mr. Boscawen, the *Lord Falkland, Mr. Serj. Trenchard, Mr. Bockland, Mr. Smith*, Serj. Blencowe, etc. spoke for the bill.

Mr. Waller (of Bucks.), *Mr. Hungerford, Sir Edward Seymour*, and *Mr. Robert Price* were all against it, and the last cited the case of Wynne and Lloyd in 1 [Thomas] Siderfin, [*Les Reports*], f. [214].

So at last the question was put for committing the bill. House divided—Yeas went out.

		Mr. Smith	
	Yeas		81
		Mr. Herbert	
Tellers for the			
		Mr. Harcourt	
	Noes		107
		Mr. Brereton	

Then it being an engrossed bill and carried in the negative for not committing it, the question was put (as it ought) for reading it a third time. And it was put accordingly and carried in the negative.

All committees adjourned.

So adjourned till 9 tomorrow morning.

Tuesday, 7 March

Sir William Cowper ordered to carry up Abraham Hinde's private bill unto the Lords and to acquaint them this House hath agreed to the same without any amendments.

The engrossed bill to regulate proceedings in the Crown Office was read the third time and passed, with the title, and Mr. Price was ordered to carry it to the Lords for their concurrence.

House went into a committee on the bill for the continued impositions and joint stocks, and Mr. Attorney took the Chair of the committee. And they proceeded in the bill and finished the same. So it was ordered to be reported tomorrow.

Committees were revived.

So House [adjourned] till 9 tomorrow morning.

Wednesday, 8 March

Sir Miles Cook and [Sir John Franklin],[1] two Masters in Chancery, brought the message from the Lords.

Mr. Attorney General was ordered to carry up to the Lords the engrossed bill for the review of the quarterly poll for their concurrence.

Some members were added to the committee to whom the bill for uniting the churches of etc. was referred.

Then the House went upon the amendments made by the Lords unto the bill for enabling His Majesty to make leases of the Duchy of Cornwall. They were read over and some of them were agreed to. But one wherein the Lords had altered the fee for making such leases, the Commons having made it but £10 to the officers, the Lords had made it £20 fee where the fine was above £40.

Several spoke against agreeing to this as *Sir Edward Seymour*, *Mr. Boscawen*, etc. because it was laying a charge upon the subject in matters of money, which the Lords cannot do.

Wherefore the House disagreed with the same and appointed a committee to prepare reasons to offer at a conference with the Lords for disagreeing to the said amendment.

Several members were added to the committee for the bill of saltpetre.

Mr. Palmes reported from the committee to inquire of precedents touching absent members or such as have been employed in foreign services, which was read. And there was a case of some members of the House employed as ambassadors abroad and of some in places in Ireland in the parliament in Nov. 1606 (4 Jac. I) wherein the House

---

[1] Blank in MS.; from *CJ*, x. 845.

held in the first case the ambassadors having only their places at will no new writs should go, but in the other they having offices for life it was ordered then new writs should go and accordingly then writs did go for the election of new members in their room. And the report of the committee now was without any opinion in the matter.

Mr. Goodwin Wharton desired that Mr. Culliford having absented himself from the service of the House and being accused of divers misdemeanours that he might not have the privilege of the House to protect him from them or being called to an account for the same. *Mr. Hutchinson* to the same.

But *Mr. Bowyer* thought that was not enough but desired he might be expelled.

Sir Edward Seymour: I must agree your Journals before Queen Elizabeth are very imperfect; to King James I's time they are embezzled; but from his time they are in some order. The matter now before you is such wherein you have not many precedents. It is a matter wherein you ought to be very tender—that of expelling members—because the people that send them hither have a right to their service and the King and this House have a right to their advice and assistance. So that since it hath slept unto this time from King James I his time, I desire it may not now be revived.

Mr. John Howe seconded the motion for expelling Mr. Culliford.

Sir Christopher Musgrave: I cannot agree to that motion. I do not think it enough to accuse a man and punish him presently without inquiring whether he be guilty or not. As to his being absent, you might have sent for him in custody; but being you did not, you have tacitly allowed his absence. However, I cannot but take notice of this report being made now after it hath slept so long, as if it were timed for this particular case. But I think it doth [not] come up at all to the precedent that has been presented to you, and therefore I am against any such question has been offered.

Sir William Strickland and *Mr. Bertie junior* were for it.

Mr. Waller (of Bucks.) was for a general vote that no member should accept of any place or office whatever.

Mr. P. Foley: There are some precedents where members have been turned out of the House for sickness but you are not now inclined to come up so high. And I believe gentlemen are not yet ripe for the question, and therefore I am for adjourning the debate. *Sir Joseph Tredenham* to the same.

But *Mr. Mordaunt* was for expelling him.

Mr. Herbert desired Mr. Culliford might not have the privilege of this House in Ireland. *Sir Robert Howard* to the same.

Sir Thomas Clarges desired that this report might be referred to the Committee of Elections, as was done in the case in King James I's time, before you come to any resolution thereon.

Mr. Harley: I think you ought to do something in the matter. But as to Mr. Culliford I think it a perplexed business and not so fit to subject a member of your House to the examination of an Irish parliament, which I confess I am against for I would always keep Ireland in subordination to England. Therefore as to Mr. Culliford, I think you had better order him yourselves to be taken into custody. And as to members taking places and employments whilst they are attending here, I am against it. For as you have some taken off thereby, so you may more. So you will lose their service here in the House and the several places that choose them want their representatives, for members when chosen ought to attend, and anciently they found manucaptors that they would attend. You have precedents of members turned out for non-attendance and writs gone out to choose new ones. So that on the whole matter it is very necessary for you to do something in it.

Mr. Clarke proposed this question: that if any person shall accept of any place or employment that requires his attendance from the service of this House new writs shall go to choose other persons in their places.

Mr. Palmes thought it absolutely necessary by some vote or resolution to have something appear in your Journal to that effect.

The *Speaker* observed on this report of the precedent in King James I's time that it was a very high assertion of the privileges of this House; that the Lord Chancellor had submitted to you to do what you please with ambassadors and others put into places. But I must also acquaint you that Sir Richard Reynell, Chief Justice in Ireland, and Sir Richard Levinge, Solicitor General there, had writ over to me that if this House did require their attendance here they would quit that service and attend you.

Mr. Hampden moved that the House would suspend Mr. Culliford from the privilege of the House till he attended the service of the House.

Mr. Speaker took notice in the report of the case in King James I his time, the question was there put upon each particular member and not a general one.

So the question was stated: That Mr. Culliford, a member of this House, having been accused of several misdemeanours and being ordered to attend in his place and having neglected the same, resolved that Mr. Culliford shall be suspended the benefit of the privilege of this House until he shall attend in his place.

Sir Christopher Musgrave: You have a report of great weight before you, and therefore I think it not fit to go off so but desire as was done in the former precedent you will do also in this—refer it to the Committee of Elections and let them report their opinions therein to the House. *Col. Titus* to the same.

So the farther consideration of the said report was referred to the Committee of Privileges and Elections and that they do report their opinions therein to the House.

All committees adjourned.

So House adjourned till 8 tomorrow morning.

Thursday, 9 March

Mr. Waller was ordered to carry up to the Lords the engrossed bill for making the river Salwerp navigable for their concurrence.

Ordered that Davis, the deputy marshal, have his book and papers delivered him.

Sir [John] Franklin and Sir John Hoskins, two Masters in Chancery, brought the message from the Lords.

Mr. Attorney General was ordered to carry up to the Lords the engrossed bill for charging the joint stocks and continuing the acts for the continued impositions for their concurrence.

Sir John Bolles presented a petition from several tradesmen to desire this House to address to His Majesty to issue his proclamation for putting the laws in execution against hawkers and pedlars. But upon the question for receiving it, it was carried in the negative—the House not thinking it proper, and nothing but what the Justices of Peace might do if they pleased.

Then the House went into a committee upon the engrossed bill from the Lords to prevent suits against such as have acted for Their Majesties' service in the defence of the kingdom; Mr. John Howe was called to the Chair of the committee. And they proceeded upon the bill, and generally by consent left out the latter part of the bill (being the greatest part), and finished the same. And he was ordered to report it.

So the Speaker resumed the Chair, and *Mr. Howe* reported the bill with the amendments. Which were read and agreed to, and the bill ordered to be read the third time tomorrow morning.

Mr. Waller reported from the committee the reasons prepared to be offered at a conference with the Lords for disagreeing to the amendments made to the bill for enabling Their Majesties to make leases of their Duchy of Cornwall.

Which were read, and exceptions were taken by some members to the three first reasons (which related more particularly to the amendment in the bill) because they were a weakening of the last reason, which was the inherent right of the Commons to dispose of matters of money. And giving other reasons than this last might give the Lords room to debate this matter, which must not be allowed by the Commons.

So the question was put upon the three first reasons severally—to agree with the committee that this be one of the reasons to be offered at a conference to be desired with the Lords for disagreeing to the amendments made by their Lordships to the bill entitled, etc.—and disagreed with the three first reasons, and agreed only to the last. And it was ordered that a conference should be desired with the Lords upon the subject-matter of the amendments made by the Lords to the said bill, and Mr. Scobell was to go up and desire it.

So the House adjourned till 4 in the afternoon.

Post Meridiem

The House met and walked in a body orderly, two and two, with the Speaker at the head of them unto Whitehall up into the Banqueting House, where the Speaker presented His Majesty with their address touching the state of the kingdom of Ireland.

But before the House went up, they adjourned all committees. And then the House adjourned till 8 tomorrow morning.[1]

Friday, 10 March

Mr. Speaker reported that yesterday he did present the address of this House to His Majesty touching the state of Ireland, and that His Majesty was pleased to answer to this effect: Gentlemen, I shall always have great consideration of what comes from the House of

---

[1] 9 o'clock in *CJ*, x. 847.

Commons and I shall take great care that what is amiss shall be remedied.

Message from the Lords brought by Sir [John] Franklin and Sir John Hoskins, two Masters in Chancery.

Mr. Scobell was ordered to put the Lords in mind of the bill for transferring the duty of aulnage to the Customhouse.

Mr. Arnold reported from the committee to whom the petition of the poor prisoners in the King's Bench was referred: That the number of the poor prisoners now there was 3,705,[1] and gave in a list of their names in order to be ready against the next meeting of the parliament that some way may be considered of for their relief.

Mr. John Howe was ordered to carry up to the Lords the engrossed bill entitled 'an act to prevent suits against such as have acted for Their Majesties' service in defence of this government' and to acquaint them this House hath agreed to the same with some amendments, to which amendments they desire their Lordships' concurrence.

Mr. Scobell reported that, according to their order, he had been with the Lords to desire a conference upon the subject-matter of the amendments made by the Lords to etc. The Lords had agreed to the same and appointed it immediately in the Painted Chamber.

So the same managers were appointed as prepared the reasons and ordered to be the managers for this conference, and their names were read over. So they went up to the conference. And being returned, *Sir Joseph Tredenham* [reported] from the said conference: That the managers had attended the same and given the Lords the reasons for disagreeing to the amendments made by their Lordships to the said bill and had left the bill and amendments with the Lords.

Mr. Hopkins moved that since the House had little to do we might go upon the report touching the privilege of the House, as a thing which would be very grateful to the people at this time and which would prevent this House from being a grievance to their fellow subjects. *Sir Joseph Tredenham, Mr. John Howe,* and *Sir John Guise* to the same.

Col. Granville was for going upon the report of the advice as being most necessary now for that part of the money which you have even given this sessions, I hear, is granted away (meaning to the Lord Carmarthen). *Mr. Palmes, Mr. Bertie junior,* and *Mr. Goodwin Wharton* were all for going on upon the advice.

[1] 3,737 in *CJ*, x. 848.

But *Sir Christopher Musgrave* and others thought it not so proper to go now upon such matters at the close of a sessions that had lain so long upon the Table and nothing said of them and when so many members are gone out of town. Therefore moved to adjourn.

All committees revived.

So House adjourned till 10 tomorrow morning.

Saturday, 11 March

Sir Miles Cook and Sir John Hoskins, two Masters in Chancery, brought the message from the Lords.

The Lord William Powlett was ordered to carry up to the Lords the engrossed bill to make parishioners of the church united contributors to the repairs and ornaments of the church to whom the union was made and to acquaint them this House hath agreed to the same without any amendments.

The bill to explain the former law for ascertaining the tithes of hemp and flax was read the first time.

(This bill was brought in on the desire of the Bishop of Lincoln, on behalf of several ministers in Lincolnshire, the chief profits of whose livings consisted in the tithe of hemp and flax, and that anciently, not sowed lately, thereby declaring the former act not to extend to make such ministers to take 4s. an acre for their tithe, which would ruin those ministers whose tithes before that act were very great, and the intention of the act was only for flax and hemp newly sowed.)

However, *Mr. Clarke* and *Mr. Palmes* were against the bill for that it would discourage the sowing hemp and flax and the passing this bill would in a manner repeal the former.

So upon the question for a second reading, it was carried in the negative.

So adjourned till 10 on Monday morning.

Monday, 13 March

Sir Miles Cook and Sir [John] Franklin brought the message from the Lords.

Mr. Waller (of York) was ordered to carry up to the Lords the bill entitled 'an act for regulating the proceedings in the Crown Office of the Court of King's Bench' and to acquaint them this House hath agreed to the amendments made by their Lordships to the said bill.

He was also ordered to carry up the bill for better discovery of judgements in the Courts of King's Bench, Common Pleas, and Exchequer and acquaint the Lords that this House hath agreed to the amendments made by their Lordships to this bill with some amendments, to which they desire their Lordships' concurrence.

Then the House took into consideration the amendments made by the Lords to the bill for encouraging privateers, which were read and severally put, and some were agreed to with amendments by this House. But one of them, which was for appointing £10 to be paid to the privateer for every gun taken in a prize, etc., which the Commons had appointed to be paid by the Commissioners of Prizes out of their Majesties' share of prizes, the Lords had altered this and made it payable by the Collector of the Customs in any port, etc.

Mr. Godolphin was against agreeing with this amendment for that the consequence thereof will be the turning the bill against itself and will often interfere with the other uses for which the customs are given.

Sir Christopher Musgrave: I cannot but say this amendment is better than it was for the privateer, but it is worth your consideration whether this be not the disposition of money. The manner of it I am sure it is, and the Lords—if you give it them—will make this a precedent against you.

Mr. Attorney was not willing to give the Lords such a power. But I think by way of expedient you may make it payable by the officers of the Excise.

Mr. Harley would not in the least countenance the Lords' power to give money.

Mr. Clarke was against agreeing to it for it was allowing the Lords a power to order the manner of disposing of money.

Col. Austen was entirely for disagreeing with the Lords for the reasons aforesaid.

Mr. Montagu: Though this is not directly raising of money yet it nearly relates to it, and therefore I am against agreeing with it and would insert the Commissioners of Excise to pay it. *Sir Richard Temple* to the same.

Mr. Hampden was against agreeing to the Lords' amendment or making any amendment to it; that was a tacit allowance of their amendment.

Sir Christopher Musgrave: I see no great hurt in it if you do agree to it and make it payable by the officer of the Excise. I am the more inclinable to it because if you differ with them now in this bill it may endanger the same, and then the trade with France will be open which this law also prohibits. And but the last sessions to the bill to prohibit deer stealing the Lords added a penalty, what did you—not agree to it but turned the penalty into an imprisonment of the party.

Sir Edward Seymour: It is a nice point that is now in question. I see on all occasions the Lords are aiming at money matters, which if you will preserve entire you must guard the frontiers. And though it be but an amendment, yet if you make an amendment to it it is allowing their amendment. But now you are going to transfer it to be paid by the officers of the Excise, which I think is in a manner giving up the point. But if you will, you may add some such amendment as this— that it shall be paid by the Commissioners of Prizes before their own salaries.

So the question was put to agree with the amendment made by the Lords and it was carried in the negative *nemine contradicente*.

So several members were named as a committee and they were ordered to withdraw immediately into the Speaker's Chamber and to prepare reasons to be offered at a conference with the Lords for disagreeing to their amendment. And after some time the members returned, and *Mr. Attorney General* reported the reasons, which are as follows: (1) that the reward mentioned in the clause, etc. being for prizes taken, it is most proper that it should be paid out of prizes; (2) that by a clause sent up by the Commons and agreed to by your Lordships the customs of all prize goods are appropriated to other uses; (3) that the other branches of the customs are already appropriated or charged; (4) that by the amendments proposed by the Commons to clause 'A' there is sufficient care taken that the persons interested in private men-of-war should receive the reward intended. (These reasons the committee thought most proper at this time to offer rather than that known one of money.)

The reasons were read and agreed to and ordered to be offered at the conference with the Lords. Ordered that a conference be desired with the Lords on the subject-matter of the said amendments made by the Lords to the said bill, and Mr. Attorney General was ordered to go up and desire it.

Sir John Hoskins and Sir Robert Legard, two Masters in Chancery, brought the message from the Lords.

Sir Ralph Dutton took notice that he saw Mr. Culliford, a member of this House, in his place, upon whom such reflections had been lately cast. He desired he would stand up and vindicate himself.

So *Mr. Culliford* stood up and justified himself and protested his innocency, and assured the House his accusation came only from such persons whom he had hindered from cheating His Majesty.

After a silence some time in the House, *Mr. Mordaunt* stood up and desired the order of suspension of him from his privilege might be continued upon him.

Mr. Culliford said he was willing it should, if the House so pleased.

Mr. Speaker said to him if it is your request to waive your privilege? On which *he* said it was.

So the question was put and resolved: That Mr. Culliford, a member of this House, have leave to waive his privilege.

So adjourned till 10 tomorrow morning.

Tuesday, 14 March

The time of the conference being come, the managers' names were read over. So they went up to the conference. And being returned, *Mr. Attorney General* reported from the conference: That the managers had attended the same, and that the Lord President managed it for the Lords, and acquainted their Lordships that this House had agreed to some amendments made by their Lordships with amendments and had disagreed to one other amendment, and delivered the reasons for disagreeing to the same and had left the bill with the amendments with the Lords.

A message from the Lords by Sir Miles Cook and Sir Robert Legard that the Lords had agreed to the amendments made by this House and offered at the conference to the amendments made by the Lords to the bill for encouraging privateers.

Sir Thomas Duppa, Usher of the Black Rod, came with a message from His Majesty to command this honourable House to attend him in the House of Peers immediately. So the Speaker and the House went up.

And His Majesty was pleased to give the royal assent unto several public and private bills, to wit:

21 public bills: the bill for the additional impositions; that of the review of the quarterly poll; the duty on joint stocks and continued impositions, bill of indemnity, etc.; Hertfordshire highways; bill against highwaymen; that about butter and cheese in Suffolk, etc.; the militia bill; the bill of accounts; that to prohibit foreign buttons; that for delivering declarations to prisoners; the bill against poachers

and destroyers of the game; that to establish the Greenland Company; that against mutineers and deserters; that to prevent malicious informations in the King's Bench Court; that against frauds by clandestine mortgages; that for revival of laws expired and expiring; that for uniting of churches; that to regulate proceedings in the Crown Office in King's Bench; that for discovery of judgements; and that for encouragement of privateers.

And to two public bills His Majesty etc. '*Le Roy et la Reyne s'aviseront*' were refused—that for frequent parliaments and the bill of royal mines.

As also to 22 private bills the royal assent was given, viz.: that for exchange of livings (the Duke of Somerset's bill); that for exchange of lands between the Bishop of London and the Earl of Monmouth; Lord Shannon's bill; Mr. Bayntun's bill; Francis Osbaston's; Sir Robert Smith's; Bishop of Bangor's; Sir John Williams's bill; Mr. Seymour's bill for woodlands; Anthony Eyre's bill; Matthew Pitt's; Richard Walthal's; Mr. Tower's; Abraham Hinde's bill; Mr. Hamilton's bill; Roger Price's bill; Sir Thomas Wroth's; Isaac Woolaston's; naturalization bill; Thomas Goodwin's bill; Thomas Bromhall's about the Fleet; and Abel Atwood's bill.

And then the King made a short speech to the effect following: to thank them for the large supplies they had given him, and assured them they should be applied to the uses given; and then recommended to them the preserving the peace in their several counties; that he would leave a number of troops in this kingdom, he hoped sufficient to suppress all the attempts of their enemies; that the time now required his presence abroad; and that as he had ventured his life on all occasions for the safety of this nation, so he should still be ready to do all things possible to make this a glorious and a happy nation.

After which the Lord Chief Baron (as Speaker of the House of Lords) by His Majesty's command prorogued this present parliament unto the 2nd day of May next.

Prorogued to the 2nd of May next.

Tuesday, 2 May

This day the Parliament met pursuant to their former prorogation. And such members of the Commons that were in town met in their own House. And just before the Black Rod came, the Speaker took the Chair.

Then he came in: Mr. Speaker, the Lords authorized by virtue of Their Majesties' commission desire the immediate attendance of this honourable House in the House of Peers to hear the said commission read.

So the Speaker, with the House, went up, where the Clerk of the House read the commission—the Lords so authorized, or some of them, sitting in their robes on a seat before the Throne. Then the Lord Keeper moved his hat, and putting it on again addressed himself in a short speech to both Houses to the effect following: My Lords and Gentlemen, by virtue of Their Majesties' commission unto us directed and now read we do in Their Majesties' name prorogue this present parliament unto the 19th day of September next, and this parliament is prorogued unto Tuesday, the 19th day of September next accordingly.

From 2 May 1693 to 19 September 1693.

Tuesday, 19 September

This day the parliament met pursuant to their last prorogation and were by commission, as formerly, prorogued by the Lord Keeper, etc. to Tuesday, 3rd day of Oct. next.

From 19 September 1693 to 3rd of October 1693.

Tuesday, 3 October

This day the parliament met pursuant to their last prorogation and were by commission, as formerly, prorogued by the Lord Keeper, etc. unto Thursday, the 26th of this instant October.

From Tuesday, 3 October 1693, to Thursday, 26th of October 1693.

Thursday, 26 October

This day the parliament met pursuant to their last prorogation, and were to have sat for dispatch of business according to a proclamation for that purpose. But the King not being come from Holland, being hindered by the contrary winds, they were by commission, as formerly, prorogued by the Lord Keeper, etc. unto Tuesday, the 7th day of November next.

From Thursday, 26 October 1693, to Tuesday, 7 November 1693.

BIOGRAPHICAL APPENDIX OF SPEAKERS AND TELLERS

THIS appendix contains an entry for every member recorded as speaking or serving as a teller by Luttrell. The entries comprise the following types of information.

I. *Name and life dates.* (When Luttrell fails to distinguish among members with the same surnames, his designation is given in quotations followed by biographical information on the most probable of the possible individuals, whose full name is given in brackets. In three cases where the speaker's identity is not clear, the names of the possible individuals and their life dates are listed.)

II. *Seats held.* (When a member was returned for more than one seat for a given parliament, only the seat that he elected is indicated. For members who sat for the entire life of a parliament, only a single date is given—e.g. 1685 for the parliament of 1685–7. For members returned after the date of a general election, the month and year of the date when the writ was returned is given. For members who were obliged to give up their seats before the end of a parliament, the month and year of their retirement is given.)

III. *Relationship to other speakers.* (Only close relationships by blood and marriage are given.)

IV. *Profession and/or social status.* (Elevations in formal rank are noted as is profession. Members for whom no professional information is given are known or presumed to be landed gentry. Information on wealth is noted only when a member was extremely wealthy or in serious financial difficulties. The only educational datum included is that of members known to have been called to the bar for whom no evidence of legal practice has been found. Membership in the Royal Society is also noted.)

V. *Offices.* ('Salaried' posts in the royal administration are given, as are municipal positions such as mayor, alderman, recorder, and steward. Dates of tenure are also given when known; a single date in parentheses indicates that the position was held at that time, but that full information on tenure is lacking. In addition, posts in the major commercial companies are listed, as are positions in the Inns of Court for those lawyers who did not attain legal office under the Crown. Not entered are unsalaried local positions such as Deputy-Lieutenant or Justice of the Peace.)

VI. *Religious views.* (Such information is given only for Nonconformists. Data on this point and also the categories used are derived mainly from D. Lacey,

Dissent and Parliamentary Politics in England 1661–1689, Rutgers University Press, New Brunswick, 1969.)

VII. *Political views.* Five separate sub-categories have been used here:

1. Attitude towards Exclusion (for members sitting between 1679 and 1681). Data have been drawn from A. Browning and D. Milne, 'An Exclusion Bill Division List', *Bulletin of the Institute of Historical Research,* xxiii, 205–24; J. R. Jones, 'Shaftesbury's "Worthy Men": A Whig View of the Parliament of 1679', ibid., xxx, 232–41; Grey, vii. 240–60, 313–14, 396–413, 418–21, 425–30.

2. Activity during 1687–8: i.e. either collaboration with James during the latter phases of his reign or activity on behalf of William before he reached London in mid-December 1688.

3. Behaviour during the Convention Parliament: i.e. either voting or speaking against the 'Abdication' resolution in the opening days of the Convention and/or voting or speaking for the Sacheverell clause in January 1690. Data have been drawn from Browning, iii. 164–72; Grey, ix, 7–25, 46–9, 50, 53–65, 510–20.

4. Position during the parliament of 1690–5: members have been designated either as 'Court Supporters', 'Listed Court Opponents', or 'Probable Court Opponents' on the basis of a list in Bodleian MS. D846, f. 5, drawn up by Samuel Grascombe in 1693. For a discussion of this list see I. Burton *et al., Political Parties in the reigns of William III and Anne: The Evidence of Division Lists (Bulletin of the Institute of Historical Research,* Special Supplement no. 7, November 1968), pp. 40–1. It should be noted that members sitting for a few Yorkshire constituencies, all the Cinque Ports, and all Welsh seats are not included on the Grascombe list.

5. Voting behaviour between 1695 and 1715 (for members who sat subsequently to the 1690–5 parliament). On the basis principally of the lists employed in I. Burton, *Political Parties,* pp. 40–1 and 53–4, such members have been designated as 'Whigs', 'Tories', or 'Mixed'.

VIII. *Committee and teller activity.* Members particularly active during the 1691–2 and/or 1692–3 sessions in terms of nominations to committees dealing with public business and/or as tellers on divisions involving public business are indicated. For an explanation of these ratings, see T. Moore and H. Horwitz, 'Who Runs the House? Aspects of Parliamentary Organization n the later Seventeenth Century', *Journal of Modern History,* xliii. 205–27.

In compiling this appendix, the editor has been much indebted to Professor B. D. Henning of Yale University and his staff preparing the 1660–90 section of the *History of Parliament* and to Mr. E. Mullins, Executive Secretary to the Editorial Board of the *History of Parliament,* for making available to him a large number of *preliminary* drafts of biographies of members of the 1690–5 parliament who had sat before 1690.

The following abbreviations have been used throughout the Appendix:

*	entry in *Dictionary of National Biography*	Gen.	(as Solicitor General or as military rank)
Bt.	created Baronet	Gent.	Gentleman (of the Privy Chamber, etc.)
c.	*circa*		
Capt.	Captain	Gov.	Governor
CJ	Chief Justice (of Common Pleas, etc.)	[I]	Irish (post or peerage)
		J	Justice (of Common Pleas, etc.)
Co.	Company	KC	King's Counsel
Col.	Colonel	Kt.	Knighted
Comm.	Commissioner (of the Treasury, etc.)	LJ	Lord Justice (of the realm)
		Lieut.	Lieutenant
CP	Court of Common Pleas	PC	Privy Councillor or Privy Council
CPA	Commissioner of Public Accounts		
		RAC	Royal African Co.
cr.	created	[S]	Scottish
d.	death	Sec.	Secretary
EIC	East India Co.	Serj.	Serjeant-at-law
Ex.	Exchequer	succ.	succeeded (to peerage)
FRS	Fellow of the Royal Society	Treas.	Treasurer
		[W]	Welsh

SIR EDWARD ABNEY (*c.* 1634–1728): Leicester; also 1695. Civilian; Kt. 1673; one of Six Clerks of Chancery 1670–82; CPA 1694–5. (4) Court Supporter; (5) Whig.

SIR MATTHEWS ANDREWS (*c.* 1630–1711): Shaftesbury; also 1680, 1681, 1689, 1695. EIC servant in 1650s and early nabob; later shipbuilder; Kt. 1675; Gent. of Privy Chamber 1689–1702; CPA 1691–4; Treas. Hon. Artillery Co. 1681–1703. (1) Anti-Exclusionist sympathies; (3) Sacheverell clause; (4) Probable Court Opponent; (5) Whig. Active on committees.

JOHN ARNOLD (*c.* 1635–1703): Southwark; also 1689; also Monmouth November 1680, 1681, 1695. (1) Exclusionist; (3) Sacheverell clause; (4) Court Supporter; (5) Whig. Active on committees and as teller.

WILLIAM ASHE (1647–1713): Heytesbury; also 1668, 1679, 1680, 1681, 1685, 1695, 1698, 1700; also Wiltshire 1701. (1) Exclusionist; (2) ? Collaborator; (4) Court Supporter; (5) Whig.

SIR HENRY ASHURST BT. (1645–1711): Truro; also 1681, 1689; also Wilton 1698, 1701. Wealthy Turkey merchant; Bt. 1668; London Alderman; Comm. of Excise 1680–91; agent for Massachusetts and Connecticut; Nonconformist. (1) Exclusionist sympathies; (2) ? Collaborator; (3) Sacheverell clause; (4) Listed Court Opponent; (5) ? Whig.

ROBERT AUSTEN (*c.* 1646–96): Winchelsea; also 1666, 1679, 1680, 1689, 1695–August 1696. Uncle of Thomas Freke (*infra*); CPA 1691–4; Comm. of Admiralty 1691–d. (1) Exclusionist sympathies; (3) Sacheverell clause; (5) Whig.

JOHN BACKWELL (1654–1708): Wendover; also 1685, 1690, 1695, 1698, 1700. Called to bar; joint Comptroller of Customs (London) 1671–d. (2) ? Collaborator; (4) Probable Court Opponent; (5) Tory.

ROBERT BALCH (c. 1652–1705): Bridgwater February 1692. (4) Court Supporter.

CHRISTOPHER BALE (c. 1635–c. 1708): Exeter; also June 1689. Local merchant; Mayor of Exeter 1688–9, 1696–7; Receiver of Aids (Exeter and Devon 1691–4); 'Tory, creature of S[ir] E[dward] S[eymour]'. (4) Probable Court Opponent. Active on committees.

SIR JOHN BANKS BT. (1627–99): Queenborough; also Maidstone 1654, 1656, 1659, 1695; also Winchelsea February–March 1678; also Rochester 1679, 1680, 1681, 1685, 1689. Wealthy merchant and government creditor; Bt. 1661; Gov. EIC 1672–3; Sub-Gov. RAC 1674–5; FRS. (1) Anti-Exclusionist; (3) Against 'Abdication'; (4) Probable Court Opponent; (5) Tory.

*DR. NICHOLAS BARBON (1641–98): Bramber; also 1695. Economic writer, speculative builder, projector, originator of fire insurance; died in debt. (4) Court Supporter; (5) Mixed.

*SIR SAMUEL BARNARDISTON BT. of Brightwell (1620–1707): Suffolk; also 1674, 1679, 1680, 1681, 1695, 1698, 1700, 1701. Retired merchant; Bt. 1663; Deputy-Gov. EIC 1668–70; CPA 1691–4; Nonconformist; described as a 'stiff Republicarian' as late as 1693 by Humphrey Prideaux. (1) Exclusionist; (2) ? Collaborator; (4) 'Query'; (5) Tory. Active on committees and as teller.

SIR THOMAS BARNARDISTON 2ND BT. of Kedington (c. 1646–98): Sudbury; also 1695 and elected 1698; also Great Grimsby 1685, 1689. Nephew of Sir Samuel (supra); Recorder of Grimsby 1686–8. (2) ? Collaborator; (4) Court Supporter; (5) Whig. Active on committees.

THEODORE BATHURST (c. 1647–97): Richmond. Called to bar.

*HON. JOHN BEAUMONT (c. 1636–1701): Hastings; also August 1689; also Nottingham 1685. FRS; Gent. of Privy Chamber 1660–c. 1682; Col. Princess Anne's Foot 1688, 1689–95; Lieut.-Gov. Dover Castle 1681–8, 1689–93; chief organizer of Court interests in the Cinque Ports in 1690 election. (2) Active in Revolution.

JOHN BENNETT (?–1723): Newton (Lancs.) December 1691; also Morpeth 1708. Barrister; Kt. 1706; legal posts in Duchy of Lancaster 1685 until after 1702; Master in Chancery. (4) Probable Court Opponent; (5) Whig.

THOMAS BERE (1652–1725): Tiverton; also 1695, 1698, 1700, 1701, 1702, 1705, 1708, October–December 1710, 1715, 1722–June 1725. Comm. for Victualling 1706–d. (4) Court Supporter; (5) Whig.

JOHN (BERKELEY) 4TH VISCOUNT FITZHARDING [I] (1650–1712): Hindon April 1691; also Windsor 1695, 1698, 1700, 1701, 1702, 1705, 1708. Col. Princess Anne's Dragoons 1685–8; 1689–d.; Teller of Ex. 1694–d.; Treas. of Chamber 1702–d. (4) Court Supporter; (5) Whig. Active on committees.

'MR. BERTIE' [HON. CHARLES BERTIE] (c. 1635–1711): Stamford; also February 1678, 1685, 1689, 1695, 1698, 1700, 1701, 1702, 1705, 1708, 1710–March 1711. Sec. to Treasury 1673–9; Treas. of Ordnance 1681–99, 1702–5. (2) Remained loyal to James until his flight; (3) Against 'Abdication'; (4) Court Supporter; (5) Tory.

HON. PEREGRINE BERTIE JUNIOR (c. 1663–1711): Boston May 1690; also 1685, 1695, 1701, 1702, 1708, 1710–July 1711; also Truro November 1705. Nephew of Charles Bertie (supra) and Thomas Wharton (infra); PC 1695; Vice-Chamberlain 1694–1701, 1702–6; Teller of Ex. 1706–d. (2) Active in Revolution; (4) Court Supporter; (5) Mixed. Active on committees.

PHILIP BICKERSTAFFE (before 1648 to after 1710): Northumberland; also 1689, 1695; also Berwick 1685. Army capt. (1679), then retired; supernumerary Household clerk in 1690s; in debtors' prison (1710). (2) Active in Revolution; (3) Against 'Abdication'; (4) Court Supporter; (5) Tory. Active on committees and as teller.

MICHAEL BIDDULPH (1661–97): Tamworth. Elected on the 'Church interest'. (4) Court Supporter. Active on committees.

SIR FRANCIS BLAKE (1639–1718): Berwick; also 1689, 1698; also Northumberland 1701, 1702. Kt. 1689; minor offices in CP 1679–87; Register of Fines in CP (1691). (3) Sacheverell clause; (4) Court Supporter; (5) Whig.

SIR JOHN BLAND 4TH BT. (1663–1715): Pontefract; also 1698, 1700, 1701, 1702, 1705, 1708, 1710; also Appleby 1681. Comm. of Revenue [I] 1704–6. (4) Probable Court Opponent; (5) Tory.

*JOHN BLENCOWE (1642–1726): Brackley. Serj. 1689; Kt. 1697; Baron of Ex. 1696–7; J of CP 1697–1722. (4) Court Supporter.

THOMAS BLOFIELD (c. 1634–1708): Norwich; also 1689, 1695, 1698, 1700, 1702. Receiver-Gen. of Poll Tax (Norwich, 1692); Mayor of Norwich 1691–2. (4) Probable Court Opponent; (5) Tory. Active on committees.

SIR CHARLES BLOIS BT. (1657–1738): Ipswich; also May 1689; also Dunwich January 1700, 1700, 1701, 1702, 1705, 1708–February 1709. Son-in-law of Ralph Hawtrey (infra); Bt. 1686. (4) Probable Court Opponent; (5) Tory. Active on committees.

MAURICE BOCKLAND (c. 1647–98): Downton; also Oct. 1678, 1679, 1680, 1681, 1685, 1689, February 1698. (1) Exclusionist; (3) Sacheverell clause; (4) Court Supporter.

SIR JOHN BOLLES 4TH BT. (1669–1714): Lincoln; also 1695, 1698, 1700, 1701. Reputed mad by latter part of reign. (4) Probable Court Opponent; (5) Tory. Active on committees.

HUGH BOSCAWEN (1625–1701): Cornwall; also 1646–8; 1659, July 1660, 1689, 1695, 1698, 1700; also Grampound April–July 1660; also Tregony 1661, 1679, 1680, 1681. PC 1689–d.; Comm. of Prize Appeals 1694–? 8; Gov. of St. Mawes Castle 1696–1701; Nonconformist. (1) Exclusionist; (3) Sacheverell clause; (4) Listed Court Opponent; (5) Whig. Active on committees.

ANTHONY BOWYER (1633–1709): Southwark; also 1685, 1695. Barrister; Treas. Inner Temple 1698. (4) Court Supporter; (5) Whig. Active on committees.

HON. CHARLES BOYLE (before 1658–1704): Appleby to October 1694. Elder brother of Hon. Henry Boyle (*infra*); called to Lords in 1694 as Baron Clifford; succ. as 2nd Earl of Burlington 1697; Gent. of Bedchamber 1697–1702. (4) Court Supporter.

*HON. HENRY BOYLE (1658–1725): Cambridge University November 1692; also 1695, 1698, 1700, 1701, 1702; also Tamworth May 1689; also Westminster 1705–February 1708, February 1708, 1708. Cr. Baron Carleton 1714; CPA 1695–7; PC 1701–d.; Comm. of Treasury 1699–1702; Chancellor of Ex.1701–8; Sec. of State 1708–10. (2) Active in Revolution; (3) Sacheverell clause; (4) Probable Court Opponent; (5) Mixed. Active on committees.

LORD BRANDON—*see* Charles Gerard.

EDWARD BRERETON (1642–1725): Denbigh; also 1689, 1695, 1698, 1700, 1701, 1702. Comm. of Prizes 1703–6; Comm. of Salt Office 1705–14; Mayor of Holt. (3) Against 'Abdication'; (5) Tory.

JOHN BREWER (*c.* 1654–1724): New Romney; also 1689, 1695, 1698, 1700, 1701, 1702, 1705, 1708. Barrister; Surveyor of Customs (Hythe 1680–5); Treas. of Prizes 1702–7; Recorder of Romney 1687–?; Recorder of Deal 1699–?; Register of Cinque Ports 1691–d. (5) Mixed. Active on committees.

WILLIAM BROCKMAN (1658–1741): Hythe. Described in 1695 as a man of 'the 48 size and cut'. Active on committees.

*WILLIAM BROMLEY (1664–1732): Warwickshire; also 1695; also Oxford University March 1701, 1701, 1702, 1705, 1708, 1710, 1713, 1715, 1727–February 1732. CPA 1696–7, 1702–4; Tory candidate for Speaker 1705; Speaker 1710–13; Sec. of State 1713–14. (4) Probable Court Opponent; (5) Tory.

SIR JOHN BROWNLOW 3RD BT. (1659–97): Grantham; also 1689, 1695–July 1697. (3) Against 'Abdication' and for Sacheverell clause; (4) Probable Court Opponent.

WILLIAM BROWNLOW (1665–1701): Peterborough; also December 1689, 1695; also Bishop's Castle 1698–February 1700. Succ. his brother Sir John (*supra*) as 4th Bt.; died in debt. (4) Court Supporter; (5) Whig.

GEORGE RODNEY BRYDGES (*c.* 1642–1714): Haslemere; also 1695; also Winchester 1700, 1701, 1702, 1705, 1708, 1710, 1713–February 1714. Pension of £600 (1701). (4) Court Supporter; (5) Whig. Active on committees.

JOHN BURRARD (*c.* 1646–98): New Lymington; also May 1679, 1680, 1681, 1685, 1689, 1695–May 1698. Mayor of Lymington 1672, 1692–4; Ranger, New Forest 1689–d. (1) Exclusionist sympathies; (4) Court Supporter; (5) Whig.

*SIR HENRY CAPEL (1638–96): Tewkesbury to May 1692; also 1660, 1661, 1679, 1680, 1681; also Cockermouth 1689. Kt. of the Bath 1661; cr. Baron Capel 1692; PC 1679–80, 1689–d.; First Comm. of Admiralty 1679–80; Comm. of Treasury 1689–90; LJ [I] 1693–5; Lord Deputy [I] 1695–6. (1) Exclusionist; (3) Sacheverell clause.

SIR RALPH CARR (1634–1709): Newcastle upon Tyne; also 1680, 1681, 1689. Merchant; Kt. 1676; Mayor of Newcastle 1677, 1693, 1705. (3) Against 'Abdication'; (4) Court Supporter. Active on committees.

ANTHONY (CARY) 4TH VISCOUNT FALKLAND [S] (1656–94): Great Bedwin to May 1694; also Great Marlow 1689; also Oxfordshire 1685. Treas. of Navy 1681–8; Comm. of Admiralty 1691–d.; PC 1692; died in debt. (3) Spoke against Sacheverell clause; (4) Probable Court Opponent. Active on committees.

'MR. CARY' [EDWARD CARY] (*c.* 1656–92): Colchester to August 1692. High Bailiff of Westminster. Active on committees and as teller.

LORD CASTLETON—*see* George Saunderson.

JAMES CHADWICK (*c.* 1660–97): Dover; also 1695–May 1697; also New Romney 1689. Comm. of Customs 1694–d. (3) Sacheverell clause; (5) Whig. Active on committees.

THOMAS CHRISTIE (*c.* 1622–96): Bedford; also 1685, 1689. Attorney. (4) Probable Court Opponent. Active on committees.

*GEORGE CHURCHILL (1654–1710): St. Albans; also 1685, 1689, 1695, 1698, 1700, 1701, 1702, 1705; also Portsmouth 1708–May 1710. Brother-in-law of Charles Godfrey (*infra*); naval captain but resigned command in 1693; Comm. of Admiralty 1701–2; member of Prince George's Admiralty Council 1702–8; Groom of Bedchamber 1709–d. (2) Active in Revolution; (4) Listed Court Opponent; (5) Mixed.

*SIR THOMAS CLARGES (*c.* 1618–95): Oxford University; also 1689; also Ross and Cromarty 1656; also Aberdeen 1659; also Westminster 1660; also Southwark 1666; also Christchurch 1679, 1680, 1681, 1685. Kt. 1660; Commissary-Gen. of Musters 1660–7; CPA 1691–d. (1) Anti-Exclusionist; (3) Against 'Abdication'; (4) Probable Court Opponent. Active on committees.

SIR WALTER CLARGES BT. (*c.* 1654–1706): Westminster; also 1702; also Colchester 1679, 1680, 1685. Son of Sir Thomas (*supra*); Bt. 1674; Army officer before 1688. (1) Anti-Exclusionist; (4) Probable Court Opponent; (5) Tory.

EDWARD CLARKE (*c.* 1651–1710): Taunton; also 1695, 1698, 1700, 1701, 1702, 1705, 1708. Auditor to Queen (1692); Comm. of Excise 1694–1700; one of Locke's 'College'. (4) Court Supporter; (5) Whig. Active on committees and as teller.

SIR GILBERT CLARKE (*c.* 1645–1701): Derbyshire; also 1685, 1689, 1695. Kt. 1671. (4) Probable Court Opponent; (5) Tory.

*SIR ROBERT CLAYTON (1629–1707); Bletchingly; also 1698, December 1702; also London 1679, 1680, 1681, 1689, 1695, 1700, 1701, 1705–July 1707. Wealthy scrivener; Kt. 1671; Treas. Hudson's Bay Co. 1678; Assistant RAC; Director of Bank; Mayor of London 1679–80; President Hon. Artillery Co. 1690–1703; Comm. of Customs 1689–97; FRS. (1) Exclusionist; (2) Active in Revolution; (3) Sacheverell clause; (4) Court Supporter; (5) Whig. Active on committees.

VISCOUNT COLCHESTER—*see* Richard Savage.

WILLIAM COLEMORE (1649–1723): Warwick; also 1689. (3) Against 'Abdication'; (4) Probable Court Opponent.

SIR PETER COLLETON 2ND BT. (? 1635–94): Bossiney to March 1694; also 1681, 1689. CPA 1691–d.; a Proprietor of the Carolinas and Bahamas; Assistant RAC; FRS. (3) Sacheverell clause; (4) Probable Court Opponent. Active on committees.

JOHN DUTTON COLT (1643–1722): Leominster; also 1679, 1680, 1681, 1689, 1695, January–April 1701. Collector of Customs (Bristol 1689–1700). (1) Exclusionist; (3) Sacheverell clause; (4) Court Supporter; (5) Whig. Active on committees and as teller.

*THOMAS BARON CONINGSBY [I] (*c.* 1656–1729): Leominster; also 1680, 1681, 1685, 1689, 1695, 1698, 1700, 1701, 1702, 1705, 1708, 1715–June 1716. Cr. Baron [I] 1692; cr. Baron Coningsby 1716; cr. Earl of Coningsby 1719; LJ [I] 1690–2; joint Paymaster Gen. [I] 1690–8; Vice-Treas. [I] 1692–1710; PC

1693–1724; High Steward of Hereford 1695–d. (1) Exclusionist sympathies; (2) Active in Revolution; (4) Probable Court Opponent; (5) Whig.

WILLIAM COOKE (1621–95): Gloucester; also 1679, 1689. Mayor of Gloucester 1673, 1688. (1) 'Base'; (3) Against 'Abdication'; (4) Probable Court Opponent. Active on committees.

VISCOUNT CORNBURY—*see* Edward Hyde.

HENRY CORNEWALL (*c.* 1654–1717): Hereford; also June 1689; also Weobley 1685, 1700, 1702, 1705, 1710; also Herefordshire 1698. Page to Duke of York (1669); Col. 1685–8. (4) Probable Court Opponent; (5) Mixed. Active as teller.

SIR ROBERT COTTON (1642–1709): Cambridgeshire; also 1680, 1681, 1685, 1689; also Newport (Hants) 1695, 1698; also Truro February 1702. Kt. 1663; joint Postmaster-Gen. 1691–1708. (3) Against 'Abdication'; (4) Listed Court Opponent; (5) Whig. Active on committees and as teller.

SIR ROBERT COTTON KT. AND BT. (*c.* 1635–1712): Cheshire; also 1680, 1681, 1689, 1695, 1698, 1700, 1701. Kt. 1660; Bt. 1677; Steward of lordship of Denbigh 1689–d. (1) Exclusionist sympathies; (3) Sacheverell clause; (4) Probable Court Opponent; (5) Tory. Active on committees and as teller.

SIR WILLIAM COWPER 2ND BT. (1639–1706): Hertford; also 1680, 1681, 1689, 1695, 1698. (1) Exclusionist; (3) Sacheverell clause; (4) Listed Court Opponent; (5) Whig.

WILLIAM CULLIFORD (?–1723): Corfe Castle; also 1695, 1698–April 1699. Customs post since 1670s; Surveyor-Gen. of Customs 1696–?; Comm. of Customs 1701–12; Comm. of Revenue [I] 1690–2. (4) Court Supporter.

SIR THOMAS DARCY BT. (1632–93): Maldon to November 1693; also 1680, 1681, 1685, 1689. Bt. 1660. (4) Probable Court Opponent. Active on committees.

SIR JOHN DARELL (*c.* 1645–94): Rye to January 1694; also 1680, 1681, 1689; also Maidstone 1679. Kt. 1670; Recorder of Canterbury 1687–8. (1) Exclusionist; (2) ? Collaborator. Active on committees and as teller.

SIR SAMUEL DASHWOOD (*c.* 1643–1705): London; also 1685. Brother-in-law of John Smith (*infra*); merchant; Kt. 1684; Mayor of London 1702–3; Assistant RAC and Levant Co.; Deputy-Gov. EIC 1700–2; Comm. of Excise 1683–98. Elected in 1690 on Church interest. (4) Probable Court Opponent.

SIR ROBERT DAVERS 2ND BT. (1653–1722): Bury St. Edmunds; also 1689, 1695, 1698, 1701, November 1703; also Suffolk 1705, 1708, 1710,

1713, 1715, elected 1722. Returned Barbados planter. (3) Against 'Abdication'; (4) Probable Court Opponent; (5) Tory. Active on committees and as teller.

JOHN DEANE (*c.* 1635–95): Ludgershall to January 1695; also 1689; also Great Bedwin 1679. Lieut. (1662); received £470 as royal bounty 1694. (1) Anti-Exclusionist; (2) Active in Revolution; (3) Against 'Abdication'; (4) Probable Court Opponent.

★WILLIAM 5TH BARON DIGBY [I] (1660–1752): Warwick; also 1689, 1695. (3) Against 'Abdication'; (4) Probable Court Opponent; (5) Tory. Active on committees.

★GILBERT DOLBEN (1658–1722): Peterborough; also 1689, 1695, 1700, 1701, 1702, 1705, 1708; also Ripon 1685; also Yarmouth (Hants) 1713, 1715. Bt. 1704; CJ of CP [I] 1701–20; Tory candidate for chairmanship of Committee of Elections 1705. (4) Court Supporter; (5) Tory. Active on committees.

THOMAS DONE (*c.* 1651–1703): Newtown (Hants); also 1685, 1689, 1695. Called to bar; Auditor of Imprests 1677–d. (3) Against 'Abdication'; (4) Probable Court Opponent; (5) Tory.

SIR FRANCIS DRAKE 3RD BT. (*c.* 1647–1718): Tavistock; also 1673, 1679, 1680, 1681, 1689, November 1696, 1698. Nephew of John Pollexfen (*infra*); Recorder of Plymouth 1696–? d. (1) Exclusionist; (2) Active in Revolution; (3) Sacheverell clause; (4) Court Supporter.

JOHN DRYDEN (*c.* 1635–1708): Huntingdonshire; also April 1699, 1700, 1701, 1702, 1705–January 1708. (4) Court Supporter; (5) ? Whig.

SIR RALPH DUTTON BT. (?–1721): Gloucestershire; also 1689, 1695; also Gloucester 1679, 1680. Bt. 1678. (1) Exclusionist; (3) Sacheverell clause; (4) Court Supporter; (5) Whig. Active on committees.

RICHARD DYOTT (1667–1719): Lichfield; also 1698, 1700, 1701, 1702, 1705, 1710, 1713. Comm. of Stamp Office 1702–10. (4) Court Supporter; (5) Tory. Active on committees.

SIR ROBERT EDEN BT. (*c.* 1644–1720): Durham County; also 1679, 1698, 1702, 1705, 1708, 1710. Bt. 1672; called to bar; Surveyor of Customs (1678). (1) Anti-Exclusionist; (4) Probable Court Opponent; (5) Tory. Active on committees.

LORD ELAND—*see* William Savile.

SIR GERVASE ELWES BT. (1628–1706): Suffolk; also 1679, 1695; also Sudbury 1677, 1680, 1681, February 1700, 1700, 1701, 1702, 1705–April 1706. Bt. 1660; Clerk of CP, Duchy of Lancaster 1660–d.; Receiver-Gen. of Excise, Duchy of Lancaster (1693). (1) Exclusionist; (2) ? Collaborator; (4) Court Supporter; (5) Whig. Active on committees.

GEORGE ENGLAND (1643–1702): Great Yarmouth; also 1680, 1681, 1689, 1695, 1698, 1700. Called to bar; Recorder of Great Yarmouth 1691–d.; Nonconformist sympathies. (1) Exclusionist sympathies; (3) Sacheverell clause; (4) Court Supporter; (5) Mixed. Active on committees.

*THOMAS ERLE (c. 1650–1720): Wareham; also 1679, 1680, 1681, 1685, 1689, 1695, 1701, 1702, 1705, 1708, 1710, 1713, 1715–March 1718; also Portsmouth 1698, 1700. Col. 1689; Brigadier 1693; Gov. of Portsmouth 1694–1712, 1714–18; Major-Gen. 1696; Commander-in-Chief [I] 1701–5; Lieut.-Gen. 1703; Lieut.-Gen. of Ordnance 1705–12, 1714–18; Gen. of Foot 1711. (1) Exclusionist; (2) Active in Revolution; (4) Court Supporter; (5) Whig.

WILLIAM ETTRICK (1651–1716): Christchurch; also 1689, 1695, 1698, 1700, 1701, 1702, 1705, 1708, 1710, 1713, 1715–December 1716; also Poole 1685. Barrister; Attorney to Prince George? 1692–1708; Counsel to Admiralty 1711. (3) Against 'Abdication'; (4) Probable Court Opponent; (5) Tory.

*SIR JOHN FAGG BT. (1627–1701): Steyning; also 1660, 1661, 1679, 1680, 1685, 1689, 1695, 1698, elected 1700; also Rye 1645; also Sussex 1654, 1656, 1659, 1681. Bt. 1660; Council of State 1659–60; Nonconformist. (1) 'Worthy'; (2) ? Collaborator; (3) Sacheverell clause; (4) Court Supporter; (5) Whig.

ROBERT FAGG (c. 1649–1715): Steyning; also March–April 1700, 1701; also New Shoreham 1679, 1681. Called to bar; succ. his father Sir John (supra) as 2nd Bt.; Nonconformist sympathies. (1) Exclusionist; (2) ? Collaborator; (4) Court Supporter; (5) Tory.

VISCOUNT FALKLAND—see Anthony Cary.

ROGER FENWICK (c. 1662–c. 1701): Morpeth; also 1689. Called to bar. (3) Against 'Abdication'; (4) Probable Court Opponent. Active on committees and as teller.

*HON. HENEAGE FINCH (c. 1649–1719): Oxford University; also 1679, 1689, 1695, 1700, 1701, 1702–March 1703; also Guildford 1685. Son-in-law of Sir J. Banks (supra); cr. Baron Guernsey 1703 and Earl of Aylesford 1714; Solicitor-Gen. 1679–86; PC 1703–8, 1712–16; Chancellor of Duchy of Lancaster 1714–16. (1) Anti-Exclusionist; (3) Spoke against 'Abdication' and Sacheverell clause; (4) Probable Court Opponent; (5) Tory.

VISCOUNT FITZHARDING—see John Berkeley.

*PAUL FOLEY (c. 1645–99): Hereford; also 1679, 1680, 1681, 1689, 1695, 1698–November 1699. Barrister; Bencher Middle Temple 1683; CPA 1691–7; Speaker March 1695–98; Nonconformist sympathies. (1) Exclusionist; (3) Sacheverell clause; (4) Probable Court Opponent. Active on committees.

THOMAS FOLEY SENIOR (*c.* 1641–1701): Worcestershire; also 1679, 1680, 1681, 1689, 1695; also Droitwich January 1699, elected 1700. Elder brother of Paul (*supra*); father-in-law of R. Harley (*infra*); probable Nonconformist. (1) Exclusionist; (3) Sacheverell clause; (4) Probable Court Opponent; (5) Whig. Active on committees.

THOMAS FOLEY JUNIOR (*c.* 1670–1737): Weobley June 1691; also 1695, 1698; also Hereford 1700, 1701, 1702, 1705, 1708, 1710, 1713, 1715; also Stafford 1722, 1727, 1734–December 1737. Son of Paul (*supra*); Prothonotary of CP 1702–12; Comm. of Trade 1712–13; joint Auditor of Imprests 1713–d. (4) Probable Court Opponent; (5) Tory.

SIR WILLIAM FORESTER (1655–1718): Much Wenlock; also 1679, 1680, 1681, 1689, 1690, 1695, 1698, 1700, 1701, 1702, 1705, 1708, 1710, 1713. Kt. 1689; a Clerk of Green Cloth ? 1689–d. (4) Court Supporter; (5) Whig.

WILLIAM FORSTER (1667–1700): Northumberland; also 1689, 1695, 1698–September 1700. (3) Against 'Abdication'; (4) Listed Court Opponent; (5) Tory.

CHARLES FOX (1659–1713): Cricklade; also 1685, 1689, 1695; also Eye 1680; also New Sarum 1698, July 1701, 1701, 1702, 1705, 1708, 1710, elected 1713. Son of Sir Stephen (*infra*); joint Paymaster-Gen. 1680–2 and sole 1682–5; acting (for father) joint Paymaster [I] 1690–8; acting (for father) Paymaster of Forces Abroad 1702–5. (3) Against 'Abdication'; (4) Court Supporter; (5) Tory.

*SIR STEPHEN FOX (1627–1716): Westminster November 1691; also 1679, 1695; also New Sarum November 1661, 1685, March 1714; also Cricklade January 1699, 1700, 1701. Kt. 1665; first Clerk of Board of Green Cloth 1660–79; Paymaster-Gen. 1661–76; Comm. of Treasury 1679–85, 1687–8, 1690–1702. (1) 'Vile'; (4) Court Supporter; (5) Whig. Active on committees.

THOMAS FRANKLAND (1665–1726): Thirsk; also 1685, 1689, 1698, 1700, 1701, 1702, 1705, 1708, 1710–May 1711; also Hedon December 1695. Succ. father as 2nd Bt. 1697; Comm. of Excise 1689–90; joint Postmaster-Gen. 1690–1715; Comm. of Customs 1715–18. (4) Court Supporter; (5) Whig.

THOMAS FREKE (1660–1721): Weymouth and Melcombe Regis May 1691; also 1695, 1698; also Cricklade March–June 1685, April 1689; also Lyme Regis 1705, 1708. (3) Sacheverell clause; (4) Court Supporter; (5) Whig.

SAMUEL FULLER (*c.* 1647–1721): Great Yarmouth; also 1689, 1695, 1700. Mayor of Great Yarmouth 1707–8. (4) Court Supporter; (5) Mixed. Active on committees.

SIR ORLANDO GEE (1619–1709): Cockermouth; also 1679, 1680, 1681, 1685. Kt. 1682; factor for 4th and 5th Earls of Northumberland; Registrar of Court of Admiralty 1660–d. (1) Anti-Exclusionist; (4) Probable Court Opponent.

*CHARLES GERARD styled Viscount Brandon (*c.* 1659–1701): Lancashire to January 1694; also 1679, 1680, 1681, 1689. Succ. as 2nd Earl of Macclesfield 1694; Col. (1679); Major-Gen. 1694–d.; envoy to Hanover 1701. (1) Exclusionist; (2) Collaborator; (3) Sacheverell clause; (4) Court Supporter. Active on committees.

CHARLES GODFREY (*c.* 1648–1715): Chipping Wycombe October 1691; also 1695, 1698, 1700, 1701, 1702, 1705, 1708, 1710; also Malmesbury 1689. Capt. 1688; later Col.; Master of Jewel House ? 1698–1704; Clerk Comptroller of Green Cloth ? 1704–12. (2) Active in Revolution; (3) Sacheverell clause; (4) Court Supporter; (5) Whig.

CHARLES GODOLPHIN (1650–1720): Helston; also 1681, 1685, 1689, 1695, 1698, 1700. Called to bar; Assistant RAC; Assay Master of Stannaries 1681–d.; Comm. of Customs 1691–1715. (3) Against 'Abdication'; (4) Court Supporter; (5) Mixed.

SIDNEY GODOLPHIN (1652–1732): Penryn April, 1690; also Helston 1685, 1698, 1700, 1701, 1702, 1705, 1708, 1710, 1715; also St. Mawes 1722; also St. Germans 1727–September 1732. Cousin of Charles (*supra*); Capt. 1685; Lieut.-Col. 1694; Lieut.-Gov. Scilly Islands (1690), and Gov. 1700–d.; Auditor of Crown Lands [W] 1702–d. (4) Court Supporter; (5) Mixed.

HENRY GOLDWELL (*c.* 1653–94): Bury St. Edmunds to March 1694. (4) Probable Court Opponent. Active on committees and as teller.

*SIR HENRY GOODRICKE 2ND BT. (1642–1705): Boroughbridge; also 1673, 1679, 1685, 1689, 1695, 1698, 1700, 1701, 1702–March 1705. Col. (1678); Envoy Extraordinary to Madrid 1678–82; Lieut.-Gen. of Ordnance 1689–1702; PC 1690. (1) Anti-Exclusionist; (2) Active in Revolution; (3) Spoke against Sacheverell clause; (4) Listed Court Opponent; (5) Mixed.

SIR HENRY GOUGH (1649–1724): Tamworth; also 1685, 1689, 1695, March 1699, 1700; also Lichfield 1705. Kt. 1678. (3) Against 'Abdication'; (4) Probable Court Opponent; (5) Tory.

BERNARD GRANVILLE (1631–1701): Launceston; also 1679; also Liskeard May 1661; also Saltash 1681, 1689; also Plymouth 1685; also Lostwithiel 1695. Groom of Bedchamber 1672–85; Comptroller-Gen. of Wine Licences (1685); Crown pension (1692); Recorder of Doncaster (1685). (1) Anti-Exclusionist; (4) Listed Court Opponent; (5) Tory.

HON. JOHN GRANVILLE (1665–1707): Plymouth; also July 1689, 1695; also Launceston 1685; also Newport (Corn.) 1698; also Fowey 1700; also Cornwall 1701, 1702–March 1703. Cr. Baron Granville 1703; Col. to 1690; Gov. of Deal Castle 1689–90; CPA 1696–7; Lord Warden of Stannaries 1702–5; Lieut.-Gen. of Ordnance 1702–5; Ranger, St. James's Park 1703–7; a Proprietor of Carolina. (4) 'Query'; (5) Tory. Active on committees and as teller.

CHRISTOPHER GREENFIELD (?–1706): Preston. Kt. 1693; Chamberlain of Chester, attorney for Earl of Derby. (4) Court Supporter. Active on committees.

'MR. GREY' [*HON. ANCHITELL GREY] (c. 1624–1702): Derby; also 1665, 1679, 1680, 1681, 1689. The parliamentary diarist. (1) Exclusionist; (3) Sacheverell clause: (4) Court Supporter.

SIR JOHN GUISE 2ND BT. (1654–95): Gloucestershire; also 1679, 1680, 1681, 1689, elected 1695. Col. 1689 and resigned; grant of £1,000 yearly for six years (1693); Mayor of Gloucester 1690. (1) Anti-Exclusionist; (2) Active in Revolution; (3) Sacheverell clause; (4) Court Supporter. Active on committees and as teller.

*FRANCIS GWYN (c. 1648–1734): Christchurch; also 1689, 1701, 1702, 1705, 1708, March 1717; also Chippenham 1673; also Cardiff 1685; also Callington 1695; also Totnes January 1699, 1700, 1710, 1713; also Wells 1722. Comm. of Revenue [I] 1676–81; a clerk of PC 1679–85; joint Sec. to Treasury 1685–7; CPA 1696–7; Comm. of Trade 1711–13; Sec. at War 1713–14; Prothonotary for south Wales for life; Steward of Brecknock; Recorder of Totnes. (3) Against 'Abdication'; (4) Listed Court Opponent; (5) Tory. Active on committees and as teller.

SIR ROWLAND GWYNNE (1659–1726): Breconshire; also 1698, 1700, 1701; also Radnorshire 1679, 1680, 1681, 1699; also Beeralston December 1695. Kt. 1680; Treas. of Chamber 1689–92; FRS. (1) Exclusionist; (2) Active in Revolution; (3) Sacheverell clause; (5) Whig.

*RICHARD HAMPDEN (1631–95): Buckinghamshire; also 1656, 1681; also Wendover 1660, 1661, 1679, 1680, 1689. Uncle of Sir Thomas Trevor (infra); one of Cromwell's 'Other House'; Comm. of Treasury 1689–94; Chancellor of Ex. 1690–4; PC 1689; Nonconformist. (1) Exclusionist; (3) Sacheverell clause; (4) Court Supporter. Active on committees.

WILLIAM HARBORD (1635–92): Launceston to July 1692; also 1689; also Dartmouth 1661; also Thetford 1679, 1680, 1681. Auditor of Duchy of Cornwall 1661–d.; Surveyor-Gen. of Land Revenues 1679–d.; Paymaster-Gen. [I] 1689–90; PC 1689; died while going on embassy to Turkey. (1) Anti-Exclusionist (1679) and Exclusionist (1680); (2) Active in Revolution; (3) Sacheverell clause.

*SIMON HARCOURT (? 1661–1727): Abingdon; also 1695, 1698, 1700, 1701, 1702, 1708–January 1709, October–December 1710; also Bossiney 1705; also Cardigan February 1710. Kt. 1702; cr. Baron Harcourt 1710; cr. Viscount Harcourt 1721; Solicitor-Gen. 1702–7; Attorney-Gen. 1707–8; Lord Keeper 1710–13; Lord Chancellor 1713–14; LJ 1723, 1725, 1727; Recorder of

Abingdon. (4) Probable Court Opponent; (5) Tory. Active on committees and as teller.

*ROBERT HARLEY (1661–1724): New Radnor November 1690; also 1695, 1698, 1700, 1701, 1702, 1705, 1708, 1710–May 1711; also Tregony April 1689. Cr. Earl of Oxford 1711; CPA 1691–7; Speaker February 1701–5; Sec. of State 1704–8; Chancellor of Ex. 1710–11; Lord Treas. 1711–14; Nonconformist sympathies. (2) Active in Revolution; (3) Sacheverell clause; (4) Probable Court Opponent; (5) Tory. Active on committees.

SIR RICHARD HART (?–1701): Bristol; also 1681, November 1685, 1689. Kt. 1680; Mayor of Bristol 1680. (3) Against 'Abdication'; (4) Probable Court Opponent. Active on committees.

RALPH HAWTREY (1626–1725): Middlesex; also 1685, 1689. (3) Against 'Abdication'; (4) Probable Court Opponent. Active on committees.

SIR ROBERT HENLEY (c. 1642–92): Hampshire November 1691–December 1692; also Andover 1680. Barrister; Kt. 1663; Chief Prothonotary of King's Bench 1660–d.; Master of King's Bench ? 1671–d. (1) Exclusionist. Active on committees.

*HENRY HERBERT (1654–1709): Bewdley to April 1694; also 1677, 1689; also Worcester 1681. Cr. Baron Herbert 1694; Crown pensioner (1693); Deputy Privy Seal (1697); Comm. of Trade 1707–d. (2) Active in Revolution; (3) Sacheverell clause; (4) Court Supporter. Active as teller.

SIR JOSEPH HERNE (1639–99): Dartmouth; also November 1689, 1695, 1698–February 1699. Merchant; Kt. 1690; Gov. EIC 1690–2; London Alderman. (4) Probable Court Opponent.

SIR THOMAS HESILRIGE 4TH BT. (c. 1664–1700): Leicestershire. (4) Probable Court Opponent. Active on committees.

THOMAS HOBY (1642–1707): New Sarum; also 1689, 1695; also Great Marlow 1681. (1) Exclusionist sympathies; (4) Court Supporter; (5) Whig.

RICHARD HOLT (c. 1639–1710): Petersfield; also 1695; also New Lymington 1685, 1689. Capt. (1667). (4) Court Supporter.

SIR WILLIAM HONEYWOOD 2ND BT. (c. 1654–1748): Canterbury; also 1685, 1689, 1695. Comm. of Excise Appeals 1689–1710; Mayor of Canterbury 1685–6. (3) Sacheverell clause; (4) Court Supporter; (5) Whig.

RICHARD HOPKINS (1639–1708): Coventry; also 1670, 1679, 1680, 1681, 1698. Called to bar. (1) Exclusionist; (4) Court Supporter. Active on committees.

*SIR ROBERT HOWARD (1626–98): Castle Rising; also 1679, 1680, 1681, 1689, 1695; also Stockbridge 1661. Dramatist; Kt. 1644; Col. (1667); Auditor of Ex. 1673-d.; PC 1689. (1) Exclusionist; (2) Active in Revolution; (3) Sacheverell clause; (4) Court Supporter; (5) Whig.

THOMAS HOWARD (1651–1701): Bletchingly; also 1689, 1695; also Castle Rising 1685, 1698, 1700–April 1701. Son of Sir Robert (*supra*); Teller of Ex. 1689-d. (3) Sacheverell Clause; (4) Court Supporter; (5) Whig.

'MR. HOWE' [JOHN HOWE] (1657–1722): Cirencester November 1690; also 1689, 1695; also Gloucestershire 1698, 1700, 1702. Vice-Chamberlain to Queen 1689–92; PC 1702–14; joint Paymaster of Guards and Garrisons 1703–14. (2) Active in Revolution; (3) Sacheverell clause; (4) Probable Court Opponent; (5) Tory. Active on committees.

RICHARD HOWE (*c.* 1651–1730): Cirencester; also 1695; also Hindon 1679, 1680; also Tamworth 1685; also Wiltshire 1700, 1702, 1705, 1708, 1710, 1713, 1715, 1722. Cousin of John (*supra*); succ. as 3rd Bt. 1703. (1) Exclusionist; (4) Probable Court Opponent; (5) Tory.

SIR SCROPE HOWE (1648–1713): Nottinghamshire; also 1673, 1679, 1680, 1681, 1689, 1695, 1710–January 1713. Elder brother of John (*supra*); Kt. 1663; cr. Viscount Howe [I] 1701; Groom of Bedchamber 1689–1702; Comptroller of Excise 1693–1710. (1) 'Worthy'; (2) Active in Revolution; (3) Sacheverell clause; (4) Court Supporter; (5)? Whig.

*JOHN HUNGERFORD (?–1729): Scarborough April 1692–March 1695; also 1702, November 1707, 1708, 1710, 1713, 1715, 1722, 1727–June 1729. Standing counsel to EIC; Cursitor of Chancery ? 1687-d.; expelled for bribery 1695; Comm. of Alienations 1711–14. (4) Court Supporter; (5) ? Tory. Active on committees.

SIR EDWARD HUSSEY 3RD BT. of Caythorpe (*c.* 1662–1725): Lincoln; also May 1689, 1698, 1701, 1702. (3) Sacheverell clause; (4) Probable Court Opponent. Active on committees and as teller.

SIR THOMAS HUSSEY 2ND BT. of Honington (1639–1706): Lincolnshire; also 1685, 1689, 1695; also Lincoln 1681. Cousin of Sir Edward (*supra*). (4) Court Opponent; (5) Tory.

*SIR GEORGE HUTCHINS (?–1705): Barnstaple. Barrister; Serj. 1686; Kt. 1690; Comm. of Great Seal 1690–3. (4) Probable Court Opponent.

CHARLES HUTCHINSON (*c.* 1638–95): Nottingham; also elected 1695. CPA 1694–5. (4) Court Supporter. Active on committees.

EDWARD HYDE styled Viscount Cornbury (1661–1723): Wiltshire; also 1685, 1689; also Christchurch 1695, 1698, 1700. Succ. as 3rd Earl of Clarendon 1709; Col. 1685–9; Master of Horse to Prince George 1685–90; Gov. of New York and New Jersey 1701–8; PC 1711–14; Envoy-Extraordinary to Hanover

1714. (2) Active in Revolution; (3) Against 'Abdication'; (4) Court Supporter; (5) Whig.

'MR. JEFFREYS' [GEOFFREY JEFFREYS] (?-1709): Brecon; also 1695, 1700, 1701, 1702, 1705, 1708–November 1709. Merchant; Kt. 1699; London Alderman; Vice-President Hon. Artillery Co. 1707–8. (5) Tory.

JOHN JEFFREYS (c. 1658–1715): Radnorshire November 1692; also 1695; also Marlborough 1700, 1701, 1705; also Breconshire 1702. Partner of his elder brother Geoffrey (supra); London Alderman. (5) Tory.

SIR JONATHAN JENNINGS (c. 1633–1707): Ripon; also 1659, 1689. Kt. 1678; Mayor of Ripon 1664–5; Comm. of Prizes (1692). (3) Against 'Abdication'; (4) Probable Court Opponent. Active on committees and as teller.

SIR HENRY JOHNSON (c. 1661–1719): Aldeburgh; also 1689, 1695, 1698, 1700, 1701, 1702, 1705, 1708, 1710, 1713, 1715–September 1719. Kt. 1685; wealthy shipbuilder. (3) Against 'Abdication'; (4) Probable Court Opponent; (5) Tory. Active on committees.

WILLIAM JOHNSON (c. 1662–1718): Aldeburgh; also 1689, 1695, 1698, 1700, 1701, 1702, 1705, 1708, 1710, 1713, 1715–November 1718. Younger brother of Sir Henry (supra); merchant; Assistant RAC; Committee EIC. (3) Against 'Abdication'; (4) Probable Court Opponent; (5) Tory.

*RICHARD (JONES) EARL OF RANELAGH [I] (1641–1712): Newtown (Hants); also 1689; also Plymouth 1685; also Chichester 1695; also Marlborough 1698, 1700; also W. Looe 1701, 1702–February 1703. 3rd Viscount [I] and cr. Earl 1677; Lord of Bedchamber 1679–85; Paymaster Gen. 1685–8, 1691–1702; PC 1692; expelled 1703 after investigation of his accounts; FRS. (3) Against 'Abdication'; (4) Court Supporter; (5) Whig. Active on committees.

SIR JOHN KAY 2ND BT. (1641–1706): Yorkshire; also 1685, 1689, 1695, 1700, 1702, 1705–August 1706. (4) Probable Court Opponent; (5) ? Tory. Active on committees.

*SIR ANTHONY KECK (1630–95): Tiverton April 1691. Chancery barrister; Kt. 1689; Comm. of Great Seal 1689–90. (4) Court Supporter.

SIR JOHN KNATCHBULL 2ND BT. (1636–96): Kent; also 1685, 1689; also New Romney 1660. Comm. of Privy Seal 1690–2. (3) Sacheverell clause; (4) Court Supporter.

*SIR JOHN KNIGHT (?-1718): Bristol; also 1689. Kt. 1682; merchant; Mayor of Bristol 1690. (3) Against 'Abdication'; (4) Probable Court Opponent. Active on committees.

EDWARD KYNASTON (?–1699): Shropshire; also 1685, 1689, 1695, 1698–May 1699; also Shrewsbury 1679, 1680, 1681. (3) Against 'Abdication'; (4) Probable Court Opponent; (5) Tory.

HENRY LEE (1657-1734): Canterbury; also 1685, 1689, 1698, 1700, 1071, 1702, 1705, 1710–November 1711, December 1711, 1713; also Hindon December 1697. Comm. for Sick and Wounded 1702–4; Comm. of Victualling 1704–6, 1711–14; Mayor of Canterbury 1687–8. (3) Sacheverell clause; (4) Probable Court Opponent; (5) Tory.

SIR WILLIAM LEVESON-GOWER 4TH BT. (c. 1640–91): Newcastle under Lyme to December 1691; also 1675, 1679, 1680, 1689; also Shropshire 1681. Brother-in-law of John Granville (supra). (1) Exclusionist; (2) ? Collaborator.

*RICHARD LEVINGE (c. 1656–1724): Chester; also Derby 1710–December 1711. Kt. 1692; Bt. 1704; Solicitor-Gen. [I] 1690–4, 1704–11; Attorney-Gen. [I] 1711 20; CJ of CP [I] 1720 d.; Comm. of Forfeited Lands [I] 1699–1700; Speaker of Commons [I] 1692–5; Recorder of Chester (1686). (4) Listed Court Opponent. Active on committees.

*SIR THOMAS LITTLETON 3RD BT. (1647–1710): Woodstock; also 1689, 1695, 1698, 1700, 1701; also Castle Rising 1702; also Chichester 1705; also Portsmouth December 1708–January 1710. Called to bar; Comm. of Prizes 1689–90; Clerk of Ordnance 1690–6; Comm. of Treasury 1696–9; Treas. of Navy 1699–d.; Speaker 1698–1700 and Court candidate in March 1695 and December 1701; Recorder of Woodstock 1695–1710. (3) Sacheverell clause; (4) Court Supporter; (5) Whig. Active on committees.

FRANCIS LLOYD (1655–1704): Ludlow January 1691. Attorney-Gen. south Wales 1689–95; judge [W] 1695–1702; Recorder of Ludlow 1692–d. (4) Court Supporter. Active on committees.

*SIR JOHN LOWTHER 2ND BT. of Lowther (1655–1700): Westmorland; also 1677, 1679, 1681, 1685, 1695–May 1696. Cr. Viscount Lonsdale 1696; called to bar; Vice-Chamberlain 1689–90; Comm. of Treasury 1690–2; Lord Privy Seal 1699–d.; LJ 1699; FRS. (1) 'Worthy'; (2) Active in Revolution; (4) Court Supporter; (5) Whig.

JOHN MACHELL (1637–1704): Horsham; also 1681, 1685, 1689, 1695, 1698. Called to bar. (3) Sacheverell clause; (4) Court Supporter; (5) Whig.

SIR JOHN MAINWARING 2ND BT. (1656–1702): Cheshire; also 1689, 1695, 1698, 1700, 1701. Brother-in-law of Thomas Whitley (infra): Chester Alderman 1688–d.; died in debt. (2) Active in Revolution; (3) Sacheverell clause; (4) Court Supporter; (5) Whig.

'MR. MANSELL'—either Bussey Mansell (1623–99) or Thomas Mansell (1667–1723).

SIR FRANCIS MASHAM 3RD BT. (*c.* 1646–1723): Essex; also 1695, 1698, 1700, 1701, 1702, 1705, 1708. Locke's host at Oates. (4) Court Supporter; (5) Whig. Active on committees.

SIMON MAYNE (1644–1725): Aylesbury April 1691; also 1705, 1708. Mercer; Comm. of Victualling 1689–1702. (4) Court Supporter; (5) Whig.

*JOHN METHUEN (*c.* 1650–1706): Devizes December 1690; also 1695, 1698, 1701, 1702, 1705–July 1706. Master in Chancery 1685–d.; Lord Chancellor [I] 1697–1703; Minister to Portugal 1691–6 and Ambassador 1702–6; Comm. of Trade 1696–1703. (4) Court Supporter; (5) Whig.

SIR THOMAS MIDDLETON (1654–1702): Harwich; also 1680, 1681, 1689, 1695, February 1699. Kt. 1675. (3) Sacheverell clause; (4) Court Supporter; (5) Whig.

HENRY MILDMAY (1616–92): Essex to December 1692; also 1654, 1656, 1679, 1680, 1681, 1689; also Maldon 1659, April–May 1660. Called to bar; member of high court of justice 1649; Nonconformist sympathies. (1) Exclusionist; (3) Sacheverell clause.

SIR THOMAS MOMPESSON (?–1701): Old Sarum; also 1681, 1685; also Wilton 1661; also New Sarum 1679, 1680, 1695, 1700–June 1701; also Wiltshire 1689. Kt. 1661; called to bar; Comm. of Privy Seal 1697–9. (1) Exclusionist; (3) Sacheverell clause; (4) Court Supporter; (5) Whig.

*CHARLES MONTAGU (1661–1715): Maldon; also 1689; also Westminster 1695, 1698. Cr. Baron Halifax 1700 and Earl of Halifax 1714; Clerk of PC 1689–92; Chancellor of Ex. 1694–9; Comm. of Treasury 1692–7 and first Comm. 1697–9, 1714–d.; Auditor of the Receipt 1699–1714; Envoy to Hanover 1706 and to The Hague 1709–10; LJ 1698, 1699, 1714; President Royal Society 1695–8. (2) Active in Revolution; (4) Court Supporter; (5) Whig. Active on committees and as teller.

*HON. WILLIAM MONTAGU (*c.* 1618–1706): Amersham October 1690; also Huntingdon April 1640; also Cambridge University June 1660; also Stamford 1661–April 1676. Attorney-Gen. to Queen 1662–76; Baron of Ex. 1676–86, then returned to the bar. (4) Probable Court Opponent.

HENRY MORDAUNT (*c.* 1663–1720): Brackley January 1692; also 1695, 1700, 1701, November 1705; also Richmond 1708, 1710, 1713, 1715–January 1720. Capt. (1692); Col. 1694; Brigadier 1705; Lieut.-Gen. 1709; Treas. of Ordnance 1699–1702, 1705–d. (4) Court Supporter; (5) Whig.

SIR JOHN MORTON 2ND BT. (*c.* 1628–99): Weymouth and Melcombe Regis; also 1680, 1681, 1685, 1689; also Poole May 1661. Gent. of Privy

Chamber ? 1663–85, 1689–d. (1) Exclusionist sympathies; (2) Active in Revolution; (3) Sacheverell clause; (4) Court Supporter. Active on committees.

*SIR CHRISTOPHER MUSGRAVE KT. AND 4TH BT. (c. 1631–1704): Westmorland; also 1700, 1702–July 1704; also Carlisle 1661, 1679, 1680, 1681, 1685, 1689; also Appleby 1695; also Oxford University 1698; also Totnes 1701. Kt. 1671; Lieut.-Gen. of Ordnance 1681–87; Teller of Ex. 1702–d.; Chairman of the Committee of Elections 1685; Mayor of Carlisle 1672–3; Mayor of Appleby 1701. (1) Anti-Exclusionist; (2) Active in Revolution; (3) Against 'Abdication'; (4) Probable Court Opponent; (5) Tory. Active on committees.

CHRISTOPHER MUSGRAVE (c. 1663–1718): Carlisle; also 1702. 2nd son of Sir Christopher (supra); Clerk of Deliveries in Ordance ? 1689–96; Clerk of Ordance 1696–1714; Comm. of Privy Seal 1701–2; Extraordinary Clerk of PC 1695–1704 and Clerk 1704–? 10. (4) Probable Court Opponent; (5) Tory.

*THOMAS NEALE (c. 1642–99): Ludgershall; also 1679, 1680, 1681, 1685, 1695, 1698–February 1699; also Petersfield 1668; also Stockbridge December 1689. Deviser of the loan lottery on the salt duty; Groom Porter 1678–d.; Master of Mint 1686–d.; FRS. (1) Anti-Exclusionist; (4) Court Supporter; (5) Whig.

SIR BENJAMIN NEWLAND (c. 1633–99): Southampton; also November 1678, 1679, 1680, 1681, 1685, 1689, 1695, 1698–December 1699. Kt. 1679; Southampton merchant active in London; Sub-Gov. RAC 1680–1; London Alderman; CPA 1691–4. (1) 'Vile'; (3) Against 'Abdication'; (4) Probable Court Opponent; (5) Tory.

EDWARD NICHOLAS (1662–1726): Shaftesbury; also 1689, 1695, 1698, 1700, 1701, 1702, 1705, 1708, 1710, 1713, January–May 1715, May 1715, 1722–April 1726. Treas. to Queen 1693–4; Paymaster of Queen Anne's pensions 1702–7, 1713–14; Comm. of Privy Seal 1711–13. (3) Against 'Abdication'; (4) Court Supporter; (5) Mixed.

GEORGE NICHOLAS (c. 1633–1707): Morpeth November 1692; also 1695. Surveyor-Gen. of Customhouse 166?–d. (4) Court Supporter; (5) ? Whig.

THOMAS NORRIS (1653–1700): Liverpool; also 1689. (4) Court Supporter.

LORD NORRIS—see Montagu Venables-Bertie.

FOOT ONSLOW (1655–1710): Guildford; also 1689, 1695, 1698. Merchant; Comm. of Excise 1694–d. (3) Sacheverell clause; (4) Court Supporter; (5) Whig. Active on committees and as teller.

*SIR RICHARD ONSLOW 2ND BT. (1654–1717): Surrey; also 1689, 1695, 1698, 1700, 1701, 1702, 1705, 1708, 1713, January–November 1715; also Guildford 1679, 1680, 1681, 1685; also St. Mawes 1710. Elder brother of Foot (*supra*); cr. Baron Onslow 1716; Comm. of Admiralty 1690–3; Speaker 1708–10; Comm. of Treasury and Chancellor of Ex. 1714–15; Teller of Ex. 1715–d.; Gov. Levant Co. 1710–d. (1) 'Honest'; (3) Sacheverell clause; (4) Court Supporter; (5) Whig. Active on committees.

WILLIAM PALMES (*c.* 1638–?): Malton; also 1668, 1679, 1680, 1681, 1689, 1695, 1698, 1700, 1701, 1702, 1705, December 1708, 1710. Given pension in 1702 after his son Guy lost Tellership of Ex. he had held since 1694. (1) 'Worthy'; (3) Sacheverell clause; (4) Court Supporter; (5) Whig. Active on committees.

*THOMAS PAPILLON (1623–1702): Dover; also 1674, 1679, 1680, 1681, 1689; also London 1695, 1698. Merchant; four times Master London Mercers Co.; Deputy-Gov. EIC 1680–2; member Council of Trade 1668–72; Comm. for Victualling 1689–99; Nonconformist sympathies. (1) Exclusionist; (3) Sacheverell clause; (5) Whig. Active on committees.

SIR JOHN PARSONS (?–1717): Reigate; also 1685, January–March 1689, 1695, 1700, 1701, 1702, 1705, 1708, 1710, 1713, 1715–January 1717. Brewer; Kt. 1687; farmer of the Excise 1670s; Comm. for Victualling 1683–9; Mayor of London 1703–4. (4) Probable Court Opponent; (5) Tory.

*THOMAS PELHAM (*c.* 1653–1712): Lewes; also 1680, 1681, 1685, 1689, 1695, 1698, 1700, 1701; also East Grinstead October 1678, 1679; also Sussex 1702. Succ. as 4th Bt. 1703; cr. Baron Pelham 1706; Comm. of Customs 1689–91; Comm. of Treasury 1690–2, 1697–9, 1701–2. (1) 'Honest'; (4) Court Supporter; (5) Whig. Active on committees.

JOHN PERY (*c.* 1640–1732): New Shoreham; also 1695, 1698, 1702. Committee EIC; Assistant RAC and Sec. 1699–? (4) Probable Court Opponent; (5) Tory. Active on committees and as teller.

SIR EDWARD PHELIPS (1638–99): Somerset; also 1698–April 1699; also Ilchester 1661, 1685. Kt. *c.* 1679. (4) Probable Court Opponent.

GRANADO PIGOTT (?–1724): Cambridge; also Cambridgeshire 1702. Called to bar. (4) Probable Court Opponent; (5) Tory. Active on committees.

*THOMAS PITT (1653–1726): New Sarum; also May 1689; also Old Sarum January–March 1689, 1695, 1710, 1713, 1715–August 1716, 1722–April 1726; also Thirsk July 1717. Wealthy East India interloper and later Co. servant; Gov. Jamaica 1716–17. (3) Sacheverell clause; (4) Court Supporter; (5) ? Whig.

*JOHN POLLEXFEN (*c.* 1636–1714): Plympton April 1690; also 1680, 1681, 1689. Devonshire merchant and economic writer; Gent. of Privy Chamber 1690–?; Comm. of Trade 1696–1707. (1) Exclusionist sympathies; (4) Court Supporter.

CHARLES (POWLETT) styled Marquess of Winchester (1661–1722): Hampshire; also 1681, 1685, 1689, 1695. Succ. as 2nd Duke of Bolton 1699; Col. (1692); Lord Chamberlain to Queen 1689–94; LJ [I] 1697–1700; Gov. Isle of Wight 1707–9; LJ 1714, 1720; Lord Chamberlain 1715–17; Lord Deputy [I] 1717–19. (1) Exclusionist sympathies; (2) Active in Revolution; (3) Sacheverell clause; (4) Court Supporter; (5) Whig.

WILLIAM POWLETT styled Lord Powlett (c. 1667–1729): Winchester; also 1689, 1695, 1698, 1700, 1701, 1702, 1705, 1708, 1715, 1722, 1727–September 1729; also New Lymington 1710, 1713. Younger brother of Charles (supra); Crown grant 1690 for 41 years; Teller of Ex. 1715–d.; Mayor of Lymington 1701, 1702–3, 1724, 1728. (3) Sacheverell clause; (4) Court Supporter; (5) Whig. Active on committees.

*ROBERT PRICE (1655–1733): Weobley; also 1685, 1695, 1698, 1701. Attorney-Gen. south Wales 1682–8; judge [W] 1700–2; Baron of Ex. 1702–6; J of CP 1726–d.; Recorder of Radnor 1683–? (4) Probable Court Opponent; (5) Tory. Active on committees.

*SIR WILLIAM PRITCHARD (c. 1632–1705): London; also 1685, also 1702–February 1705. Merchant; Kt. 1672; Mayor of London 1682–3; President Hon. Artillery Co. 1681–7, 1703–d.; Committee EIC; Assistant RAC. (4) Probable Court Opponent.

SIR CHARLES RALEIGH (1653–98): Downton; also 1685, 1689, 1695–April 1698. Kt. 1681; Gent. of Privy Chamber ? 1689–d.; Comm. of Prizes (1692). (3) Sacheverell clause; (4) Court Supporter; (5) Whig.

JOHN RAMSDEN (c. 1657–1718): Kingston-upon-Hull; also 1685, 1689. (4) Probable Court Opponent.

MORGAN RANDYLL (1649–after 1738): Guildford; also 1680, 1681, 1695, 1698, 1700, 1701, 1702, 1708, February 1711, 1713, 1715. Called to bar; died in debt. (4) Probable Court Opponent; (5) Tory.

SIR RICHARD REYNELL KT. AND BT. (?–1699): Ashburton. Kt. 1673; Bt. 1678; judge [I] 1674–86; PC [I] 1682–6; CJ King's Bench [I] 1690–5. (4) Court Supporter.

SIR ROBERT RICH KT. AND 2ND BT. (1648–99): Dunwich; also 1689, 1695, 1698–October 1699. Kt. 1676; Comm. of Admiralty 1691–d.; CPA 1691–4; Nonconformist. (2) ? Collaborator; (3) Sacheverell clause; (4) Court Supporter; (5) Whig. Active on committees.

*HON. FRANCIS ROBARTES (1650–1718): Cornwall; also 1679, 1680, 1681, August 1685; also Bossiney 1673; also Lostwithiel 1689, December 1709; also Tregony 1695, 1698, 1700, 1701; also Bodmin December 1702, 1705, 1710, 1713, 1715–March 1718. Comm. of Revenue [I] 1692–1704,

1710–14; Teller of Ex. 1704–10; FRS. (1) 'Worthy'; (3) Against 'Abdication'; (4) Listed Court Opponent; (5) Mixed.

SIR THOMAS ROBERTS 4TH BT. (1658–1706): Kent November 1691; also 1695, 1702–November 1704. (4) Court Supporter; (5) Whig.

*EDWARD RUSSELL (1652–1727): Portsmouth; also Launceston 1689; also Cambridgeshire 1695–December 1697. Brother-in-law of William Harbord (*supra*); cr. Earl of Orford 1697; Commander of the Fleet 1691–2, 1693–7; Comm. of Admiralty 1690–1 and first Comm. 1694–9, 1709–10, 1714–17; Treas. of Navy 1689–99; LJ 1697, 1698, 1714. (2) Active in Revolution; (3) Sacheverell clause; (4) Court Supporter; (5) Whig.

THOMAS SACKVILLE (1622–93): East Grinstead to January 1693; also 1689. Royalist col.; Yeoman of Removing Wardrobe 1690–d. (2) ? Collaborator. Active on committees.

SIR THOMAS SAMWELL BT. (c. 1645–94): Northampton to February 1694; also Northamptonshire June 1689. Bt. 1675. (3) Sacheverell clause; (4) Probable Court Opponent.

JOHN SANFORD (c. 1639–1711): Minehead September 1690; also 1695; also Taunton 1685, 1689. Merchant; Treas. Hamburg Co. 1676; Remembrancer of London 1697–8. (3) Against 'Abdication'; (4) Probable Court Opponent; (5) Tory. Active on committees.

GEORGE (SAUNDERSON) 5TH VISCOUNT CASTLETON [I] (1631–1714): Lincolnshire; also 1660, 1661, 1679, 1680, 1681, 1685, 1689, 1695. Col. 1689–94. (1) 'Worthy'; (4) Probable Court Opponent; (5) Tory. Active on committees.

*RICHARD SAVAGE styled Viscount Colchester (c. 1654–1712): Liverpool to Sept. 1694; also 1689; also Wigan 1681. Succ. as 4th Earl Rivers 1694; Col. 1688; Major-Gen. 1693 and served also under Anne; Envoy to Hanover 1710; Constable of Tower 1710-11; Master of Ordnance 1712. (1) Exclusionist sympathies; (2) Active in Revolution; (3) Sacheverell clause; (4) Court Supporter.

WILLIAM SAVILE styled Lord Eland (c. 1665–1700): Newark to April 1695; also 1689. Succ. as 2nd Marquess of Halifax 1695. (3) Against 'Abdication'; (4) Probable Court Opponent.

*SIR ROBERT SAWYER (1633–92): Cambridge University to July 1692; also 1689–January 1690; also Chipping Wycombe 1673. Kt. 1677; Speaker April–May 1678; Attorney-Gen. 1681–7; expelled 1690 for part in prosecution of Sir Thomas Armstrong. (3) Against 'Abdication'.

FRANCIS SCOBELL (?–?): Michael; also Grampound January 1699, 1700, 1701, 1702, 1705; also St. Germans 1708; also Launceston 1710; also St.

Mawes 1713. Son-in-law of Sir Joseph Tredenham (*infra*); called to bar; CPA 1702–4; Receiver-Gen. of Stannaries 1712–? (4) Probable Court Opponent; (5) Tory. Active on committees.

*SIR CHARLES SEDLEY 5TH BT. (1639–1701): New Romney; also 1668, 1679, 1680, 1681, November 1696, 1698, 1700–September 1701. Court wit and poet. (1) 'Worthy'. Active on committees.

*SIR EDWARD SEYMOUR 4TH BT. (1633–1708): Exeter, also 1685, 1689, 1698, 1700, 1701, 1702, 1705–April 1708; also Hindon 1661; also Devonshire 1679; also Totnes 1680, 1695. Clerk of Hanaper 1667–d.; Treas. of Navy 1673–81; Speaker 1673–8; Comm. of Treasury 1692–4; Comptroller of Household 1702–4. (1) Anti-Exclusionist; (2) Active in Revolution; (3) Against 'Abdication'; (4) 'Query'; (5) Tory. Active on committees.

PETER SHAKERLEY (*c.* 1650–1726): Wigan; also 1695; also Chester 1698, 1700, 1701, 1702, 1705, 1708, 1710, 1713. Brother-in-law of Sir John Mainwaring (*supra*); Gov. of Chester in James's reign and 1702–5. (4) Probable Court Opponent; (5) Tory. Active on committees.

*JOHN SMITH (*c.* 1655–1723): Beeralston December 1691; also Ludgershall 1679, 1681, 1689; also Andover 1695, 1698, 1700, 1701, 1702, 1705, 1708, 1710; also E. Looe 1715, 1722–October 1723. Comm. of Treasury 1694–1701; Chancellor of Ex. 1699–1701, 1708–10; Speaker 1705–8; Teller of Ex. 1710–12, 1715–d. (1) Exclusionist; (4) Court Supporter; (5) Whig. Active on committees and as teller.

*SIR JOHN SOMERS (1651–1716): Worcester to March 1693; also 1689. Kt. 1689; cr. Baron Somers 1697; Solicitor-Gen. 1689–92; Attorney-Gen. 1692–3; Lord Keeper 1693–7; Lord Chancellor 1697–1700; LJ 1695–9; Lord President 1708–10; President Royal Society 1698–1703. (3) Sacheverell clause. Active on committees.

SIR WILLIAM STRICKLAND 3RD BT. (1665–1724): Malton; also 1689, 1695, 1700, 1701, 1702, 1705, 1722–May 1724; also Yorkshire 1708; also Old Sarum 1716. Son-in-law of William Palmes and brother-in-law of John Smith (*supra*). Muster-Master Gen. 1720–d. (3) Sacheverell clause; (4) Court Supporter; (5) Whig. Active on committees and as teller.

CHRISTOPHER TANCRED (1659–1705): Aldborough; also 1689, 1695. Son-in-law of Sir Walter Clarges (*supra*); Master of King's Harriers 1690–1701. (2) Active in Revolution; (3) Against 'Abdication'; (4) Probable Court Opponent.

WILLIAM TEMPEST (1654–1700): Durham; also 1679, 1681. Capt. 1673–88; Mayor of Hartlepool 1681, 1687, 1693; Receiver of Hearth Money (Newcastle and northern counties 1686–8); Prothonotary of CP 1691–d. (1) Anti-Exclusionist; (2) Opposed Revolution; (4) Probable Court Opponent.

*SIR RICHARD TEMPLE 3RD BT. (1634–97): Buckingham; also 1659, 1660, 1661, 1680, 1681, 1685, 1689, 1695–May 1697; also Warwickshire 1654. Kt. of the Bath 1661; Comm. of Customs 1672–85, 1689–94. (1) Anti-Exclusionist; (4) Listed Court Opponent; (5) Tory.

*SIR JOHN THOMPSON BT. (c. 1648–1710): Gatton, also 1685, 1689, 1695–November 1696. Bt. 1673; cr. Baron Haversham 1696; CPA 1695–6; Comm. of Admiralty 1699–1701; Nonconformist. (2) Active in Revolution; (3) Sacheverell clause; (4) Probable Court Opponent; (5) Whig (but became Tory in Anne's reign).

'MR. THOMPSON'—either Francis Thompson (1656–93), Henry Thompson (1657–1700), or William Thompson (1629–92).

JOHN THORNHAUGH (1648–1723): East Retford; also 1689, 1695, 1698, 1700, 1701; also Nottinghamshire March 1704, 1705, 1708. (2) Collaborator; (4) Court Supporter; (5) Whig. Active on committees.

*SILIUS TITUS (c. 1623–1704): Ludlow January 1691; also Ludgershall July 1660; also Lostwithiel 1670; also Hertfordshire 1679; also Huntingdonshire 1680, 1681. Parliamentary capt.; Groom of Bedchamber 1661–75; PC 1688, 1701–d.; FRS. (1) Exclusionist; (2) ? Collaborator; (4) Court Supporter. Active on committees.

SAMUEL TRAVERS (c. 1655–1725): Bossiney; also 1708; also Lostwithiel 1695, 1698; also New Windsor April 1715; also St. Mawes 1722–September 1725. Barrister; Surveyor-Gen. of Land Revenue 1693–1710; Auditor to Prince of Wales 1715–d.; Deputy-Gov. Royal Fishery Co. (1694). (2) Active in Revolution; (4) Court Supporter; (5) Whig. Active on committees.

SIR THOMAS TRAWELL (c. 1657–1724): Milborne; also 1695, 1698, 1700, 1701, 1702, 1705, 1708, 1710, 1713. Kt. 1684; Capt. (1694); Major (1706). (4) Court Supporter; (5) Whig.

*SIR GEORGE TREBY (1643–1700): Plympton April 1690 to May 1692; also 1677, 1679, 1680, 1681, 1689. Kt. 1681; Recorder of London 1680–3, 1688–92; Solicitor-Gen. 1689; Attorney-Gen. 1689–92; CJ of CP 1692–d.; Recorder of Plympton. (1) Exclusionist; (3) Sacheverell clause.

*JOHN TREDENHAM (c. 1668–1710): St. Mawes April 1690; also 1695, 1698, 1700, 1701, 1702, November 1707, 1708, September–December 1710. Son of Sir Joseph (infra); died in debt. (4) Probable Court Opponent; (5) Tory.

SIR JOSEPH TREDENHAM (?–1707): St. Mawes; also 1666, 1680, 1681, 1689, 1698, 1700, 1701, 1702, 1705–October 1707; also Grampound 1679, 1685. Brother-in-law of Sir E. Seymour (supra); Kt. 167?; Vice-Warden of

Stannaries 1682-?d.; Gov. of St. Mawes Castle 1678–96; Comptroller of Army Accounts 1703–d. (1) Anti-Exclusionist; (3) Against 'Abdication'; (4) Listed Court Opponent; (5) Tory. Active on committees and as teller.

*SIR JOHN TREMAINE (?–1694): Tregony to February 1694. Serj. and Kt. 1689. (4) Probable Court Opponent.

*SIR JOHN TRENCHARD (1649–95): Poole to April 1695; also Taunton 1679, 1680, 1681; also Thetford June 1689. Kt. 1689; CJ of Chester 1689–d.; Sec. of State 1693–d. (1) Exclusionist; (2) Active in Revolution; (3) Sacheverell clause; (4) Court Supporter. Active on committees.

*SIR JOHN TREVOR (1637–1717): Yarmouth (Hants) to March 1695; also Castle Rising 1673; also Beeralston March 1679, 1680, May 1689; also Denbighshire 1681; also Denbigh 1685. Kt. 1671; KC 1683; Master of Rolls 1685–8, 1693–d.; Speaker 1685, 1690–March 1695 (when compelled to resign); first Comm. of Great Seal 1690–3; PC 1688, 1691–5, 1702–14. (1) Anti-Exclusionist; (2) Collaborator; (4) Court Supporter.

*SIR THOMAS TREVOR (1658–1730): Plympton November 1692; also 1695; also Lewes 1700–June 1701. Kt. 1692; cr. Baron Trevor 1712; Solicitor-Gen. 1692–5; Attorney-Gen. 1695–1701; CJ of CP 1701–26; Lord Privy Seal 1726–30; FRS. (4) Court Supporter; (5) Whig.

SIR WILLIAM TURNER (1615–93): London to February 1693. Merchant; Kt. 1662; Mayor of London 1668–9; Committee EIC; Assistant RAC. Elected as Tory in 1690.

'MR. VAUGHAN'—either Edward Vaughan (?–1718) or Richard Vaughan (?1655–1724).

MONTAGU VENABLES-BERTIE styled Lord Norris (1673–1743): Oxfordshire; also 1695, 1698–May 1699; also Berkshire 1689. Succ. as 2nd Earl of Abingdon 1699; CJ in Eyre south of Trent 1702–6, 1711–15; Constable of Tower 1702–5; LJ 1714. (3) Against 'Abdication'; (4) Probable Court Opponent; (5) Tory.

SIR THOMAS VERNON (?–1711): London. Merchant; Kt. 1685; Director New EIC; Assistant RAC. (4) Probable Court Opponent. Active on committees.

SHADRACK VINCENT (c. 1651–1700): Fowey; also 1689. Major (1689); Surveyor of Customs (Cornwall, 1682); Collector of Customs (Fowey, 1684–7). (4) Court Supporter. Active on committees.

EDMUND WALLER (1652–1700): Amersham; also 1689, 1695. Called to bar; Recorder of Wycombe 1689–95; converted to Quakerism 1698. (4) Probable Court Opponent; (5) Tory.

ROBERT WALLER (*c.* 1632–98): York. Attorney; Mayor 1684, 1688; elected with Carmarthen's backing. (4) Court Supporter. Active on committees.

HON. GOODWIN WHARTON (1653–1704): Malmesbury; also East Grinstead 1680; also Westmorland December 1689; also Cockermouth 1695; also Buckinghamshire 1698, 1700, 1701, 1702–November 1704. Resigned Lieut.-Colonelship 1703; Comm. of Admiralty 1697–9. (1) Exclusionist; (4) Court Supporter; (5) Whig. Active on committees and as teller.

*HON. THOMAS WHARTON (1648–1716): Buckinghamshire; also 1679, 1680, 1681, 1685, 1689, 1695–February 1696; also Wendover 1673. Succ. as 5th Baron Wharton 1696; cr. 1st Marquess 1705; elder brother of Goodwin (*supra*); Comptroller of Household 1689–1702; CJ in Eyre south of Trent 1697–9, 1706–10; Lord Deputy [I] 1708–10; Lord Privy Seal 1714–d. (1) Exclusionist; (2) Active in Revolution; (3) Sacheverell clause; (4) Court Supporter; (5) Whig.

RICHARD WHITHED (*c.* 1660–93): Stockbridge to March 1693; also 1689. Son-in-law of Sir Anthony Keck and nephew of Richard Holt (*supra*).

THOMAS WHITLEY (1651–96): Flint; also 1681. Receiver of Crown Revenues (north Wales and Chester ? 1670–86); Comptroller of Fines (north Wales and Chester 1689–d.). (1) Exclusionist sympathies.

SIR WILLIAM WHITLOCK (*c.* 1636–1717): Great Marlow; also December 1689; also West Looe 1659; also Oxford University November 1703, 1705, 1708, 1710, 1713, 1715–November 1717. Kt. and KC 1689. (4) Probable Court Opponent; (5) Tory.

*SIR JOSEPH WILLIAMSON (1633–1701): Rochester; also 1695, 1698, 1700–October 1701; also Thetford 1669, 1679, 1680, 1681, June 1685. Kt. 1672; Sec. of State 1674–9; Ambassador to the Hague 1696–8; PC 1674–9, 1696–d.; President Royal Society 1677–80; Recorder of Thetford 1682–8; Assistant RAC. (1) Anti-Exclusionist; (4) Probable Court Opponent; (5) Whig. Active on committees.

*SIR FRANCIS WINNINGTON (1634–1700): Tewkesbury November 1692; also 1695; also New Windsor 1677; also Worcester 1679, 1680, 1681. Kt. 1672; Solicitor-Gen. 1674–9. (1) Exclusionist; (2) Collaborator; (4) Probable Court Opponent; (5) Tory.

SIR WILLIAM WOGAN (?–1708): Haverfordwest; also 1679, 1685, 1689, 1695, 1698; also Pembrokeshire 1681. Serj. and Kt. 1689; judge [W] 1689–1701. (1) Anti-Exclusionist; (3) Against 'Abdication'; (5) Tory. Active on committees.

SIR CHARLES WYNDHAM (before 1640–1707): Southampton; also 1680, 1681, 1685, December 1689, 1695; also St. Ives 1698. Kt. *c.* 1668; Sewer to

Queen ? 1669–85. (1) Anti-Exclusionist; (2) ? Collaborator; (4) Court Supporter.

THOMAS WYNDHAM (*c.* 1664–98): Wilton; also 1689; also Yarmouth (Hants) 1685. Called to bar. (4) Probable Court Opponent.

SIR WALTER YONGE 3RD BT. (1653–1731): Honiton; also 1679, 1680, 1681, 1695, 1698, 1700, 1701, 1702, 1705, 1708; also Ashburton 1689. Comm. of Customs 1694–1701, 1714–d.; Nonconformist. (1) Exclusionist; (2) ? Collaborator; (3) Sacheverell clause; (4) Court Supporter; (5) Whig. Active on committees and as teller.

INDEX

(Asterisk indicates the individual appears in the Biographical Appendix)